1992

PRENTICE HALL OPERATIONS MANAGEMENT

ABCNEWS

Moving Images
Lasting Impressions

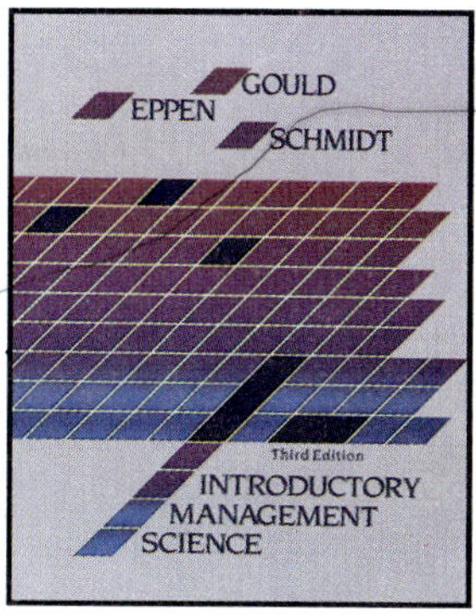

The New York Times
CONTEMPORARY VIEW

One habit
worth forming

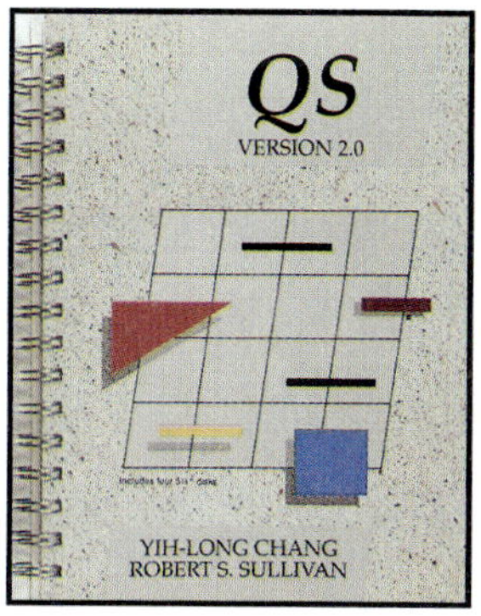

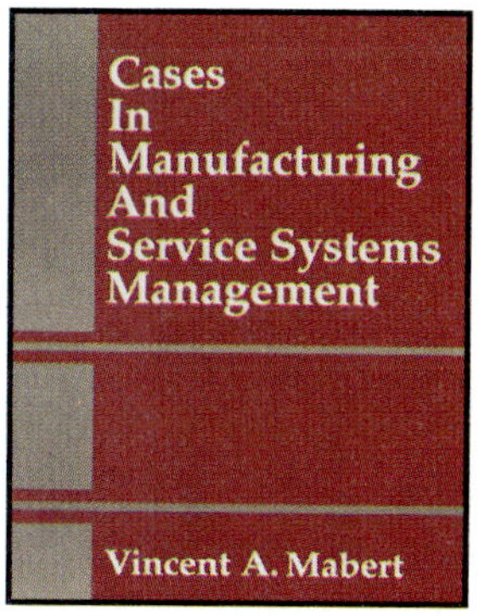

SHOW US QUALITY AND WE'LL

PRENTICE HALL

Simon & Schuster Education Group
113 Sylvan Avenue, Route 9W
Englewood Cliffs, NJ 07632
201-592-2000

Dear Customer,

This year Prentice Hall is pleased to present an outstanding list of titles and software for your management science and operations management courses. Beginning with the publication of David Garvin's ***Operations Strategy: Text and Cases*** in September, we think you will agree that in quality and selection of titles we are unmatched in the industry.

We would also like to take this opportunity to announce that we are now offering the Personal STORM software products in addition to our extremely successful Chang packages. The descriptions of these products, including the new Macintosh versions of Chang's QSB, QSOM and QS, are included in this brochure. The real benefit lies in your ability to make these tools accessible to the student in conjunction with the book. For that reason, these software products are available shrinkwrapped to many of our titles at a discounted price.

Quality texts and software packages for the classroom are the foundation. We also feel that supplements which highlight important text concepts or bring new perspectives to the classroom can make learning more interesting for the student and teaching more rewarding for you. Therefore, we are offering two exclusive promotions in these markets: the ABC/Prentice Hall Video Library in Operations Management and The New York Times Contemporary View Program.

We hope you enjoy the brochure which provides a detailed "preview" of the fifth edition of Adam and Ebert, ***Production and Operations Management: Concepts, Models and Behavior*** as well as listings and ISBN numbers for our entire list. We are always open to suggestions and customer needs—it is the only way we know to make things better—and hope you will feel free to call us with reactions to our 1992 offerings!

Thanks in advance for your anticipated time and attention.

Valerie A. Ashton
Executive Editor

Sandra M. Steiner
Sr Marketing Manager

SHOW YOU ITS MAKER.

ADAM/EBERT
Production and Operations Management: Concepts, Models, and Behavior, 5/e
title code (71800-7); ISBN 0-13-718008X

ASSAD
Excellence in Management Science Practice: A Readings Book
title code (29710-1); ISBN 0-13-297102-X

CHANG
QSB+ Version 2.0, Quantitative Systems for Business (1991)
3 1/2″ TC 74717-0, 0-13-747171-8
5 1/4″ TC 74718-8, 0-13-747189-0
MacQSB+, Quantitative Systems for Business (1992)
title code (55360-2); ISBN 0-13-553603-0

CHANG
QSOM Version 2.0, Quantitative Systems for Operations Management (1991)
3 1/2″ 74719-6, 0-13-747197-1
5 1/4″ 74716-2, 0-13-747163-7
MacQSOM, Quantitative Systems for Operations Management (1992)
title code (55362-8); ISBN 0-13-553629-4

CHANG
QS Version 2.0, Quantitative Systems (1991)
3 1/2″ 74721-2, 0-13-747213-7
5 1/4″ 74720-4, 0-13-747205-6
Mac QS, Quantitative Systems (1992)
title code (55361-0); ISBN 0-13-553611-1

EPPEN/GOULD/SCHMIDT
Introductory Management Science, 3/e
title code (50028-0); ISBN 0-13-500281-8

GARVIN
Operations Strategy: Text and Cases
title code (63892-4); ISBN 0-13-638925-2

MABERT
Cases in Manufacturing and Service Systems Management
title code (11627-7); ISBN 0-13-116278-0

MCCLAIN/THOMAS/MAZZOLA
Operations Management: Production of Goods and Services, 3/e
title code (63613-4); ISBN 0-13-636135-8

PERSONAL STORM 2.0 (1989)
3 1/2″ title code (84742-6); ISBN 0-13-847427-3
5 1/4″ title code (84738-4); ISBN 0-13-847385-4

PERSONAL STORM 2.0 Manual Only
84739-2 0-13-847393-5

PERSONAL STORM 3.0 (1992)
3 1/2″ title code (84745-9); ISBN 0-13-847450-8
5 1/4″ title code (84744-2); ISBN 0-13-847443-5

PRODUCTION & OPERATIONS MANAGEMENT

Fifth Edition

EVERETT E. ADAM, JR. ▪ RONALD J. EBERT

NEW FEATURES AND CHANGES OF THE FIFTH EDITION:

NEW

- Features a new chapter that closely examines Japanese contributions to manufacturing management (*"Japanese Contributions to World Class Manufacturing"*, Ch. 15).

NEW

- Increases its focus on globalization and international operations and management, as well as its service operations management coverage.

NEW

- Four-color presentation and special pedagogical photo "blueprints" help the students visualize a factory layout or machine design.

NEW

- Incorporates insightful and informative Operations Management Highlight boxes throughout.

NEW

- To complete the visual orientation of the text, Prentice Hall offers a unique series of *plant tour* and *ABC News Video Libraries.*

The authors integrative framework of planning, organizing, and controlling provides for a text with a managerial emphasis while end of chapter supplements add more rigorous quantitative analysis.

PART VIII

PRODUCTION AND SERVICES

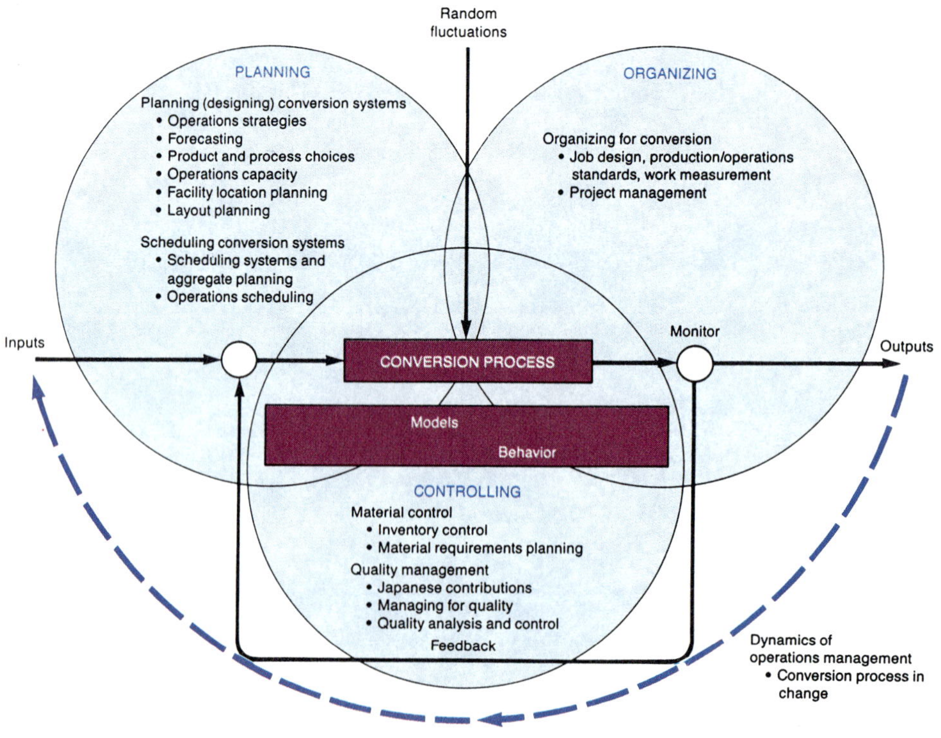

Does Quality Cost or Pay?

American manufacturers have embraced the concept of quality for over a decade now. Advertising campaigns promote superior quality. Experts such as Deming, Juran, and Crosby espouse quality techniques. Standards of excellence recognize outstanding quality achievements. Yet, what effect has attention to quality had on financial performance? Most managers admit that quantifying the costs and benefits of quality programs is difficult. Employee training and the price of not shipping defective products are usually regarded as two of the most important costs. The price of nonconformance—the cost of not doing things right the first time—and the return on investment are usually regarded as two of the most important benefits.

Examined below are the quality programs of four U.S. manufacturers, each of which has received the Malcolm Baldrige National Quality Award, to be discussed later in this chapter (See page 235). Of particular interest is how each of these companies defines the costs and benefits of its quality programs.

Milliken & Company. This textile manufacturer, headquartered in Spartanburg, South Carolina, produces over 48,000 textile and chemical products. In 1981, Milliken initiated its Pursuit of Excellence program to create an overall commitment to customer satisfaction at all levels of the organization. As part of the program, Milliken reduced the number of management levels and dispersed authority throughout the company. Some 14,300 associates (employees) were reorganized into self-managed teams. The teams were formed to address business challenges and to respond to customer needs. Milliken's investment in training is substantial: approximately $1300 per associate in 1988. The company believes that the investment was worthwhile. The percentage of on-time deliveries increased from 75 percent in 1984 to an industry-leading 99 percent in 1988. The price of nonconformance has been reduced by 60 percent. Because of these improvements, Milliken has made significant inroads into the Japanese and Korean auto-manufacturing markets.

Motorola, Inc. This electronics manufacturer, headquartered in Schaumburg, Illinois, initiated its quality improvement program because of fierce competition from the Japanese. In 1981, Motorola set a goal to improve the quality of its products and services tenfold within five years. In 1987, after having achieved its initial goal, Motorola set two additional goals. One was to improve its quality tenfold within two years; the second was to improve quality one-hundredfold within four years. To reach its goals, Motorola established a training center and invested $170 million in training between 1983 and 1987. Data from employees, customer surveys,

Courtesy Steuben

Sources: "A New Era for Auto Quality," *Business Week* (October 22, 1990), 84–96; Garrett DeYoung, "Does Quality Pay," *CFO*, (September 1990), 24–34; "Malcolm Baldridge National Quality Award: Globe Metallurgical, Inc. & Westinghouse Electric Corporation—Commercial Nuclear Fuel Division," *Business America*, (December 15, 1988), 6–7, 10–11; and Brad Stratton, "Xerox and Milliken Receive Malcolm Baldrige National Quality Awards," *Quality Progress* (December 1989), 17–20.

A Picture Paints a Thousand Words

That's why in ***Production and Operations Management: Concepts, Models, and Behavior, Fifth Edition*** you'll find "blueprints" accompanying several key photographs. Carefully labeled blueprints that will give your students a clearer picture of the floor plan of a factory, the machines in an assembly line. . . exactly how computers control operations functions. It's just another facet to the very visual orientation of Adam and Ebert's fifth edition.

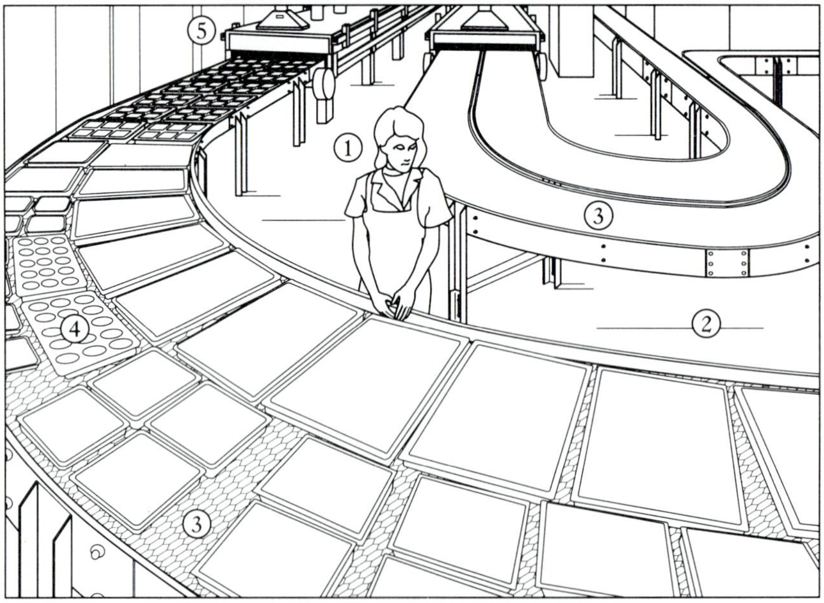

1. Line employee at work
2. Aisle
3. U-shaped conveyors
4. Food-work in process
5. Food drying oven

Retained in this edition:
Optional chapter supplements that cover techniques and methodology at a more rigorous, quantitative level

SUPPLEMENT TO CHAPTER 2

FINANCIAL AND ECONOMIC ANALYSES IN OPERATIONS

THE NEED FOR FINANCIAL AND ECONOMIC ANALYSES

Operations managers make strategic choices on the basis of both external and internal analyses. Externally, markets and environments are assessed. Internally, operating and financial capabilities are analyzed. To analyze internally, operations managers must have an understanding of financial analysis. Managers need to understand such concepts as the time value of money and cost flows, as well as appropriate analytic models. Operations managers face many facility and process choices—for both initial and replacement investments—that they must accurately assess. Let's examine some useful financial concepts and models.

TERMINOLOGY AND CONCEPTS

Although it is not always possible to do so, decision makers try to evaluate alternatives logically and comparably. Toward this end, economic analysis borrows some standard terminology from finance and accounting.

Cost and Revenues Managers are interested in the costs of owning and operating facilities and equipment. *The costs used in economic analysis are current, actual costs:* Let's examine a few costs that become important to us in analysis.

Opportunity costs are the returns that are lost or foregone as a result of selecting one alternative instead of another. The amount of the opportunity cost is determined by comparing the benefits or advantages of one alternative with those of another. *Sunk costs* are past expenditures that are irrelevant to current decisions. The salvage value of facilities and equipment may be an opportunity cost, since assets that are abandoned or replaced may be saleable. For example, the income from selling an asset is counted as salvage value. Salvage value is a market value, similar to the concepts of current, actual costs.

Depreciation is an accounting procedure to recover outlays (expenditures) for an asset over its lifetime. Depreciation does not reflect current market values. Since we are interested only in market values, of what value is depreciation to the economics of change (replacement)? Depreciation is important only in that it affects income taxes, and income taxes affect actual cash flows. The higher the value of the depreciation in any one period, the lower the taxes paid and the greater the cash flows (revenues less expenses). For our purposes here, we simplify matters by ignoring both depreciation and taxes.

MOVING IMAGES

ABC NEWS/PRENTICE HALL VIDEO LIBRARY

OPERATIONS MANAGEMENT

The power of the moving image. In class, students often ask, "How does this relate to the real world?" And they wonder, "How does this relate to me?" Sometimes you need the power of the image to shift their focus beyond classroom walls and into the world arena.

Prentice Hall and ABC News have brought together their talents in academic publishing and global reporting and are proud to present the most comprehensive video ancillaries available in the college market today.

Quality in broadcast journalism

No other network can match ABC News' award-winning program line-up. Prominent and respected anchors, such as David Brinkley, Ted Koppel, and Peter Jennings, bring together their insights in Operations Management into your classroom.

LASTING IMPRESSIONS

ABC and Prentice Hall offer your students a resource of these feature and documentary-style videos, which relate directly to the concepts and applications in Adam and Ebert's *Production and Operations Management: Concepts, Models, and Behavior, 5/e.*

The ABC News/PH Video Library pulls together critically acclaimed selections from *Nightline, Business World, This Week with David Brinkley,* and *World News Tonight.* The programs are of extremely high production quality, present substantial content, and are hosted by well-versed, well-known anchors. Carefully researched selections effectively complement and enhance the material in *Production and Operations Management: Concepts, Models, and Behavior, 5/e.*

Here's just a sample of some of the video topics we'll be offering:

- "Japanese Cars: Really Better?" (Nightline)
- "Japanese Economic Threat—U.S./Japanese Automakers" (Business World)
- "Delivery Services" (On Business)
- "Building Better Mousetraps" (20/20)

Bring the world's moving images into focus with the ABC News/Prentice Hall Video Libraries.

The New York Times

and

PRENTICE HALL

present

OPERATIONS MANAGEMENT

Selected Readings A Contemporary View

A CONTEMPORARY VIEW

The *New York Times* and Prentice Hall, two leading publishers in academia and world news, are proud to cosponsor **A CONTEMPORARY VIEW,** a program designed to enhance student access to current and relevant information in the world of Operations Management.

The New York Times
and
PRENTICE HALL
present
Operations Management
A Contemporary View
Selected Readings

U.S. Air Fleet in the Latin Drug War Is Hobbled by Management Problems

Your students will receive a 16-page dodger—a student version of the *New York Times* containing approximately 30 articles to be used in conjunction with Adam and Ebert's *Production and Operations Management: Concepts, Models, and Behavior, 5/E;* Garvin's *Operations Strategy: Text and Cases;* McClain/Thomas/Mazzola's *Operations Management: Production of Goods and Services, 3/E;* and Eppen/Gould/Schmidt's *Introductory Management Science, 3/E.* The stories in the dodger are actual articles that appeared in current issues of the *New York Times* and relate specifically to the world of operations management.

THE VALUE OF THE *NEW YORK TIMES*

Knowledge of world events is invaluable. Reading a premier news publication such as the *New York Times* establishes a practice of staying abreast of the events happening in today's society. Students who deepen their appreciation of print in the learning environment will remain devoted to the medium throughout their professional and personal lives.

SERVICE IS OUR CORNERSTONE

Prentice Hall continues to lead the way in classroom innovation. The key to the Contemporary View Program is relevance. Therefore, a new collection of articles will be available each year. As a professor using *Production and Operations Management: Concepts, Models, and Behavior, 5/E,* you are eligible to receive a complimentary one-semester subscription of the *New York Times** for classroom use. Your students may subscribe at a special reduced rate. To order the *New York Times* for your class, or for more information, call toll free: **1-800-631-1222**

Prentice Hall and the *New York Times.* Together, we will offer the most comprehensive and beneficial teaching package available.

*within a deliverable area

1992

STORM: PERSONAL VERSION 3.0

QUANTITATIVE MODELING FOR DECISION SUPPORT

A DECISION SUPPORT TOOL THAT COVERS THREE KEY AREAS OF BUSINESS IN ONE INTEGRATED SOFTWARE PACKAGE

Operations Research Management Science

Production Operations Management

Statistical Methods

As a new publisher and distributor of the popular management science and operations management software Personal STORM, we're pleased to be able to offer you one of the bestselling integrated software packages on the market. Menu driven for convenience and flexibility, Version 2.0 is a flexible and accessible program that puts the most frequently-used quantitative modeling techniques for business and engineering problems at your fingertips.

In addition to Version 2.0, we'll soon be making available a *new* version of the product—*Personal STORM 3.0*—for your Fall 1992 adoption.

Highlights of this new version include:

1) decision analysis and decision tree capabilities.
2) increased problem size in all modules.
3) ability to import and export data in ASCII forms.

CHANG'S BESTSELLING SOFTWARE NOW WRITTEN EXCLUSIVELY *FOR* AND DESIGNED EXCLUSIVELY *ON* THE MACINTOSH. . . .

You can now take advantage of Macintosh's impressive graphic abilities and powerful user interface with Chang's exciting MacQSB, MacQSOM, and MacQS software/manual packages.

MacQSB *(Quantitative Systems for Business, Mac Version)* consists of 16 modules; three 3.5″ disks:

- Linear Programming
- Integer Linear Programming
- Goal Programming
- Quadratic Programming
- Transportation and Transshipment Problem
- Assignment and Traveling Salesman
- Network Modeling
- Critical Path Method
- Program Evaluation and Review Technique
- Dynamic Programming
- Inventory Theory
- Queuing Theory
- Queuing System Simulation
- Decision/Probability Theory
- Markov Process
- Time Series Forecasting

MacQSOM *(Quantitative Systems for Operations Management, Mac Version)* includes three 3.5″ microdisks which contain the following modules:

- Aggregate Production Planning (APP)
- Critical Path Method (CPM)
- Facility Location (FACLOC)
- Flow Shop Scheduling (FLOWSHOP)
- Inventory Theory (INVT)
- Job Shop Scheduling (JOBSHOP)
- Facility Layout (LAYOUT)
- Learning Curves and Work Measurement (LCWM)
- Lot Sizing (LOT)
- Material Requirements Planning (MRP)
- Program Evaluation and Review Technique (PERT)
- Production Line Balancing (PLB)
- Linear Programming (LP)
- Quality Control (QC)
- Queuing Theory (QUEUE)
- Transshipment and Transportation Problem (TRP)
- Time Series Forecasting (TSFC)

MacQS *(Quantitative Systems, Mac Version)* offers a combination of these two powerful packages.

PRODUCTION AND OPERATIONS MANAGEMENT: CONCEPTS, MODELS, AND BEHAVIOR, 5/E

by Everett E. Adam, Jr. and Ronald J. Ebert

Please contact your local Prentice Hall representative for more information and/or a free examination copy(ies) of any of the outstanding texts or software packages featured in this preview.

© 1992, (71794-2); 0-13-717943-X

PART I. MANAGING OPERATIONS

1. **Operations Management.** The operations function in organization. Historical evolution of production and operations management. A systems view of operations: Defining the subsystem. A framework for managing operations. The strategic role of operations. Trends in operations management. Production and operations management careers. Contemporary operations management careers. Contemporary operations mangement topics. Supplement to Chapter 1: The role of models in operations management. Classifying problems. 2. **Operations Strategies for Competitive Advantage.** Strategic planning. Productivity and quality. Technology and mechanization. International operations management. Meeting the international challenges in production and operations management. Meeting the competitive challenge in operations management. Supplement to Chapter 2: Financial and economic analyses in operations.

PART II. PLANNING (DESIGNING) THE CONVERSION SYSTEM

3. **Forecasting.** Forecasting in operations. Useful forcasting models for operations. Selection of the forecasting model. Behavioral dimensions of forecasting. 4. **Designing Products, Services, and Processes.** New product design (product development). Manufacturing process technology. Design of services and service processes. Supplement to Chapter 4: Learning curves. 5. **Operations Capacity.** Capacity planning environment. Capacity planning modeling. Supplement to Chapter 5: Linear programming: The graphical and simplex methods. 6. **Locating Production and Service Facilities.** Need for facility location planning. General procedures for facility location planning. Facility location models. Behavioral impact in facility location. Supplement to Chapter 6: Linear programming: The transportation method. 7. **Layout Planning.** Layout concepts. Developing the process layout: Models and behavior. Developing the product layout: Models and behavior.

PART III. ORGANIZING THE CONVERSION SYSTEM

8. **Job Design, Production and Operations Standards, and Work Measurement.** Effective job design: Combining engineering and behavioral approaches. Production and operations standards. Work measurement. Compensation. 9. **Project Management.** Project planning. Project scheduling models. Managing the product.

PART IV. SCHEDULING PRODUCTION AND SERVICE SYSTEMS

10. **Scheduling Systems and Aggregate Planning.** Operations planning and scheduling systems. The aggregate planning process. Strategies for aggregate planning. Master scheduling and rough-cut capacity planning. Aggregate planning for service organizations. Implementing aggregate plans and master schedules. 11. **Operations Scheduling.** Intermittent systems. Intermittent scheduling concepts and processes. Loading. Priority sequencing. Detailed scheduling. Finite loading. Expediting. Input-output (short-term capacity) control. Optimized production technology (OPT). Behavioral elements in intermittent systems.

PART V. CONTROLLING THE CONVERSION SYSTEM

12. **Inventory Control Fundamentals.** Demand and control system characteristics. Inventory concepts. Inventory costs. Inventory modeling. Deterministic inventory models. Supplement to Chapter 12: Optimization and inventory control. 13. **Inventory Control Applications.** Deterministic inventory models. Stochastic inventory models. Inventory control in application. Behavioral pitfalls in inventory control. 14. **Material Requirement Planning.** Planning for material needs. Applying MRP as a scheduling and ordering system. Detailed capacity planning. Limitations and advantages of MRP. Manufacturing resources planning (MRPII). Purchasing.

PART VI. MANAGING FOR WORLD CLASS COMPETITION

15. **Japanese Contributions to World Class Manufacturing.** Japanese management overview. Just-in-time manufacturing. 16. **Managing for Quality.** Managerial responsibility in managing for quality. Product quality. Managing for quality products and services. Analysis for improvement, assurance, and control. Management-initiated approaches and actions to improve quality. Behavior and quality. 17. **Quality Analysis and Control.** Process variation. Statistical process control. Inspection. Acceptance sampling. 18. **The Conversion Process in Change.** Dynamics of production and operations management. Systems dynamics. Overview of production and operations management.

APPENDIX.

Appendix Table A: Areas of a standard normal distribution. Appendix Table B: 8% compound interest factors. Appendix Table C: 10% compound interest factors. Appendix Table D: Random digits.

INSTRUCTOR'S EDITION

FIFTH EDITION

PRODUCTION AND OPERATIONS MANAGEMENT

CONCEPTS, MODELS, AND BEHAVIOR

INSTRUCTOR'S EDITION

FIFTH EDITION

PRODUCTION AND OPERATIONS MANAGEMENT

CONCEPTS, MODELS, AND BEHAVIOR

EVERETT E. ADAM, JR.
RONALD J. EBERT

Prentice Hall Englewood Cliffs, NJ 07632

Acquisition Editor: *Valerie Ashton*
Development Editor: *Laurie Golson*
Editorial/Production Supervision: *York Production Services; Marilyn James*
In-house Production Liaison: *Lisa Kinne*
Marketing Manager: *Sandra Steiner*
Copy Editing: *York Production Services*
Designer: *York Production Services*
Cover Designer: *Jerry Votta*
Prepress Buyer: *Trudy Pisciotti*
Manufacturing Buyer: *Bob Anderson*
Supplements Editor: *David Scholder*
Editorial Assistant: *AnnMarie Dunn*
Production Assistant: *Renee Pelletier*
Photo Editor: *Lorinda Morris-Nantz*
Photo Research: *Fran Antmann, Teri Stratford, William Luggen*
Cover Art: Dallas Museum of Art, Foundation for the Arts
Collection, Gift of the Artist

a Simon & Schuster Company
Englewood Cliffs, New Jersey 07632

Printed in the United States of America
10 9 8 7 6 5 4 3 2 1

ISBN 0-13-718008-X

Prentice-Hall International (UK) Limited, *London*
Prentice-Hall of Australia Pty. Limited, *Sydney*
Prentice-Hall Canada Inc., *Toronto*
Prentice-Hall Hispanoamericana, S.A., *Mexico*
Prentice-Hall of India Private Limited, *New Delhi*
Prentice-Hall of Japan, Inc., *Tokyo*
Prentice-Hall of Southweast Asia Pte Ltd., *Singapore*
Editora Prentice-Hall do Brasil, Ltda., *Rio de Janeiro*

To Joy, Scott, and Kevin
Mary, Kristen, and Matt

BRIEF CONTENTS

CONTENTS

PART FIVE Controlling The Conversion System 449

PART SEVEN Dynamics of Operations Management 671

PREFACE

This fifth edition of *Production and Operations Management: Concepts, Models, and Behavior* was developed to retain the core concepts, models, and managerial orientation of previous editions and to reflect current production and operations management practices and research results. It emphasizes practice through new chapter Highlights and color photos and through an extensive supplemental package of computer software, videos, study guides, and practice problems—all to enhance student learning.

In the educational setting, students are often left with the feeling that operations is distinctly different and separate from management. In some instances, analysis and quantitative techniques are emphasized at the expense of a basic unifying framework for the overall role of operations management in organizations. We continue our efforts to fill this void with the unifying theme of the book: planning, organizing, and controlling—the classical process school of management. Within this framework are the actual issues practicing operations managers confront—the chapters of this book.

For students and teachers alike, our integrative framework serves admirably in lending coherence to the numerous revisions that appear in the fifth edition. We retain design features crucial to the success of previous editions: the book is readable (clarity, level, explanations of analyses, etc.), comprehensive, integrative, contemporary in content, and uses many examples and summary tables. We have grouped the Japanese management material from the previous edition and expanded it into a new chapter, Chapter 15, "Japanese Contributions to World Class Manufacturing." The new Operations Management Highlights and color photos throughout the text provide the student with lively, current illustrations of operations management practice. Margin definitions of key terms have been added as well. We are enthused over the integration of *QSOM, Version 2.0* into the problem set, adding linear programming and the transportation technique software to previous applications throughout the book, and over the new customized video package built around current ABC business program segments. Collectively, these changes reshape the book to provide the reader with a contemporary treatment of production and operations management.

Reflecting the desires of many practitioners, we continue to emphasize a balance between the quantitative aspects and important behavioral applications. When problems are behavioral (quality motivation, for example), we introduce such contemporary techniques as behavior modification, quality circles, and attitude change procedures to deal with them; when they are quantitative (quality assurance, for example) we stress appropriate techniques of quality analysis such as statistical process control.

Other important features that continue to be a major portion of this book are a use of supplements to present more rigorous quantitative analysis (yet a book that stands alone without the use of supplements); the continued use of service sector applications and examples that reinforce "operations" as a broad term encompassing manufacturing, agriculture, and services; and a book organized so readers understand the flow—moving from managing operations (Part I) through design (Parts II and III), and then operating the facility (Parts IV, V, VI, and VII).

Our intent, as in previous editions, is to provide a student-oriented presentation at an introductory level. The material is presented in a simple, straightforward fashion. To assist student understanding, we provide end-of-chapter materials designed to reinforce the essentials of each chapter: solved problems, revised review questions and problems, usually a case, and computer-assisted exercises. The computer exercises use the Quantitative Systems for Operations Management (*QSOM, Version 2.0*) microcomputer software package developed by Prentice Hall for this edition. It is user friendly and leaves the student with an appreciation of how the computer can be used in operations management to increase decision-making accuracy for moderately complex situations. The software is available through Prentice Hall.

To sum up, distinguishing features of this book are (1) an integrating framework, featuring management process, resource conversion, and concepts, models, and behavior; (2) behavioral applications within production/operations; (3) inclusion of the service sector via an operations orientation; and (4) a student emphasis. This last feature encompasses an introductory treatment, continuity among chapters, and learning enhancement within chapters with specially prepared executive comments, numerous examples, chapter summaries, cases, glossaries, review and discussion questions, problems, computer exercises, special videos, practice problems, and the student *Study Guide and Workbook*, featuring an independent study approach.

We wish to thank our many peers nationally who, after thoughtful use of the first four editions, provided constructive suggestions for this edition. We appreciate the time and effort expended by the operations managers and executives who prepared the chapter introductions. They have made a voluntary contribution; we hope students will enjoy and benefit from their comments. We are also indebted to those who reviewed this and previous editions. Valerie Ashton (Acquisition Editor), Laurie Golson (Development Editor), and Marilyn James (Editorial/Production Coordinator) have each contributed significantly to this edition. This edition has an extensive supplementary package, and we would like to express our thanks to the quality work contributed by: Yih Long Chang, Georgia Institute of Technology, the software supplement *QSOM;* Dave Denzler, San Jose State University, the video productions; T.S. Lee, University of Utah, the *Instructor's Manual, and Video Guide;* Bill Luggen, General Electric, photo selection and photo blueprints for the book; Jim Patterson, and Ron Satterfield, Indiana University-Bloomington, the *Practicing P/OM* problem set; and Larry Taube and Jim Weeks, University of North Carolina-Greensboro, the *Study Guide.* We appreciate the interaction with and support from our colleagues at the University of Missouri, especially Tom Foster and Paul Swamidass, and the contribution of Marilyn Kippley, our typist, who is professional in every aspect of her work. We also wish to acknowledge the resource support of the University of Missouri-Columbia.

Everett E. Adam, Jr.

Ronald J. Ebert

SUPPLEMENT AUTHORS

David Denzler, San Jose State University
T.S. Lee, University of Utah
James H. Patterson, Indiana University-Bloomington
Ron Satterfield, Indiana University-Bloomington
Larry Taube, University of North Carolina-Greensboro
James K. Weeks, University of North Carolina-Greensboro

Study Guide: (71985-6) Larry Taube and James K. Weeks, University of North Carolina-Greensboro. Contains Learning Objectives, key terms and concepts, chapter outlines, review questions, and problem sets.

Instructor's Manual and Video Guide: (71989-6) T.S. Lee, University of Utah. The Instructor's Manual contains Teaching Notes, Instructional Objectives, Case Analyses, Answers to Review and Discussion Questions, Solutions to Text Problems, and Test Questions.

ABC NEWS/PH Video Library for PRODUCTION & OPERATIONS MANAGEMENT 5/E: (71988-0) David Denzler, San Jose State University. Feature and documentary-style news clips that are tied directly to the book. Award-winning television news coverage features programming from Nightline, World News Tonight, 20/20, Business World, On Business, and This Week with David Brinkley.

Practicing POM: (71996-3) James Patterson and Ron Satterfield. Additional problems and solutions. Class tested by over 600 students at Indiana University, this supplement provides drill problems and additional quantitative material for class use.

NEW YORK TIMES dodger: A collection of articles from recent editions of the New York Times that are keyed to chapter coverage in the text. Upon adoption of the book, copies are available to adopting instructors in class quantities free of charge.

QSOM Version 2.0: (74716-2) Yih Long Chang. Interactive Operations Management Software which contains modules designed to support decision-making in operations management.

STORM 3.0, STORM Software Inc.: (84744-2) The new 1992 version of this interactive operations management software is now available through Prentice Hall.

Both software packages are available at discounted prices to adopters of this text.

PART I

MANAGING OPERATIONS

Management variables and the operations conversion system

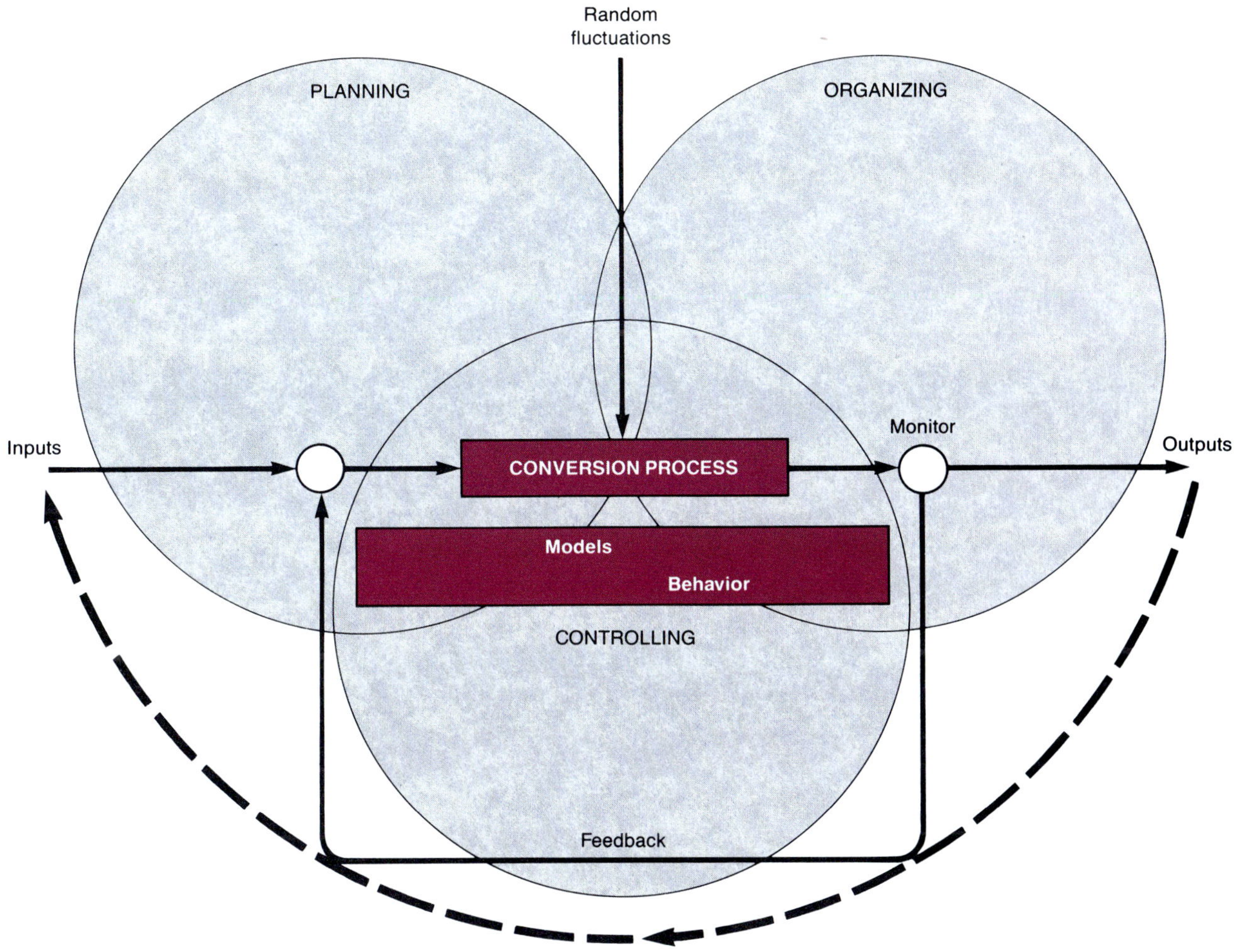

CHAPTER 1

OPERATIONS MANAGEMENT

While all managers are involved in planning, organizing, and controlling, operations managers have the direct responsibility of "getting the job done." They must provide the leadership that is needed to produce the product or service demanded by the customer.

In the air conditioning and refrigeration industries, the concepts of factory focus were implemented in the 1980s and many organizations achieved higher performance levels through the application of these principles. As we move into the 1990s, the missions of these focused factories must be modified. There will be a greater emphasis on excelling in the arena of time-based competition. Not only must parts and products flow through factories at accelerating rates, but the time between product development and production will need to be shortened by a factor of three or four. The quality concepts of the 1980s must be expanded to involve every employee in a significant way. The best organizations will empower their employees to identify and solve a vast array of problems quickly. Dealing with these new complexities, missions, and competitive arenas will demand operations managers with a depth and breadth not previously required.

With quality, productivity, and timeliness more competitively significant than ever before, operations management has added behavioral and modeling approaches to its historical use of the classical/scientific schools of management techniques.

All of these many elements come into play in the fascinating field of operations management.

Dean M. Ruwe
President
Chief Operating Officer
Copeland Corporation
Sidney, Ohio

Mr. Ruwe's comments exemplify the widely shared experience of managers in many organizations and industries. Operations management is a significant part of our lives; it is multifaceted, involving diverse activities and skills; and it is an interesting, action-oriented area. Looking beyond Mr. Ruwe's comments, however, across thousands of organizations nationwide, some serious concerns persist about the well-being of operations management and its role in our nation's economic future.

To produce this scroll air compressor, Copeland's operations management coordinates the conversion of inputs, such as metal, wiring, technical skills, and production workers to make compressors used in commercial refrigeration and commercial and home air conditioning.
***Source:* Copeland Corporation**

At the onset of the 1980s, while Japan's productivity continued its healthy surges, the leaders of business and government worldwide were alarmed that productivity was stagnating in the United States. What had happened to the giant of commerce and industry? What led to its lethargy? What have we learned in the ensuing years? What can be done to restore its stately posture? Answers to these questions reside in the ways we manage our organizations and their operations.

While U.S. productivity waned, Americans grew increasingly concerned about other related issues: maintaining adequate energy sources, protecting the environment, and meeting the demand for goods and services at home and abroad. These factors continue to impose complex demands on our organizations. Today management faces unparalleled challenges from a society more educated, affluent, demanding, and concerned than ever before, and from international competition keener than ever before. Never before have these challenges—and the costs of failure—been greater.

And never before have the techniques and knowledge to meet these challenges been more available to operating managers.

The complexities of our contemporary world have heightened our dependence on organizations and the people who manage them; yet often we fail to understand and appreciate the process of management. Moreover, as we've learned from foreign competitors, we have seriously neglected the operations of our organizations. We have taken for granted our preeminence as capable producers. No longer can we afford to do so. We need to reexamine the processes by which goods and services are created and to revitalize the ways that we manage the human and material resources for doing so. This book aims to meet these needs. It presents the concepts, terminology, problems, and opportunities that comprise operations management.

We begin this first chapter by describing what is meant by the "operations function" in organizations. Then, by tracing its history, we observe how operations management has evolved from simple beginnings to achieve its current stature as a major element of competitive strategy in contemporary organizations.

THE OPERATIONS FUNCTION IN ORGANIZATIONS

Operations system The part of an organization that produces the organization's physical goods or services.

Conversion process The process of changing **inputs** of labor, capital, land, and management into **outputs** of goods and services.

The *operations system (function) of an organization is the part that produces the organization's products.* In some organizations the product is a physical good (refrigerators, breakfast cereal), while in others it is a service (insurance, health care for the elderly). What do such diverse organizations as manufacturing companies, financial institutions, and health care facilities all have in common within their operations system? The basic elements they share are shown in Figure 1.1. They have a *conversion process,* some resource *inputs* into that process, the *outputs* resulting from the conversion of the inputs, and *information feedback* about the activities in the operations system.

FIGURE 1.1

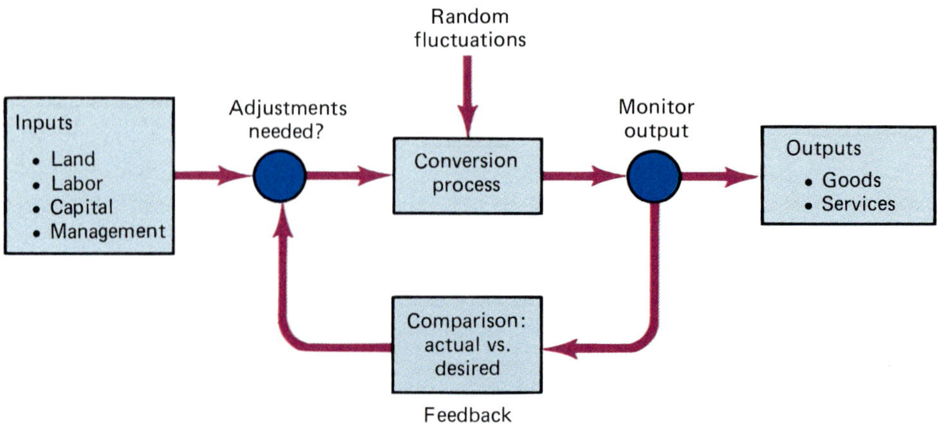

Once goods and services are produced, they are converted into cash (sold) to acquire more resources to keep the conversion process alive.

Try to recall examples of real organizations as you think about the conversion process shown in Figure 1.1. Perhaps you have worked in a department store, on a farm, for a construction company, or in an automobile assembly plant. What were the inputs? A department store's inputs include the land upon which the building is located; your labor as a stock clerk; capital in the form of the building, equipment, and merchandise; and the management skills of the store managers (see Figure 1.2).

On a farm the operations system is the transformation that occurs when the farmer's inputs (land, equipment, labor, etc.) are converted into such outputs as corn, wheat, or milk. The exact form of the conversion process varies from industry to industry, but it is an economic phenomenon that exists in every industry. Economists refer to this transformation of resources into goods and services as the *production*

FIGURE 1.2 **The operations systems for a department store and a farm**

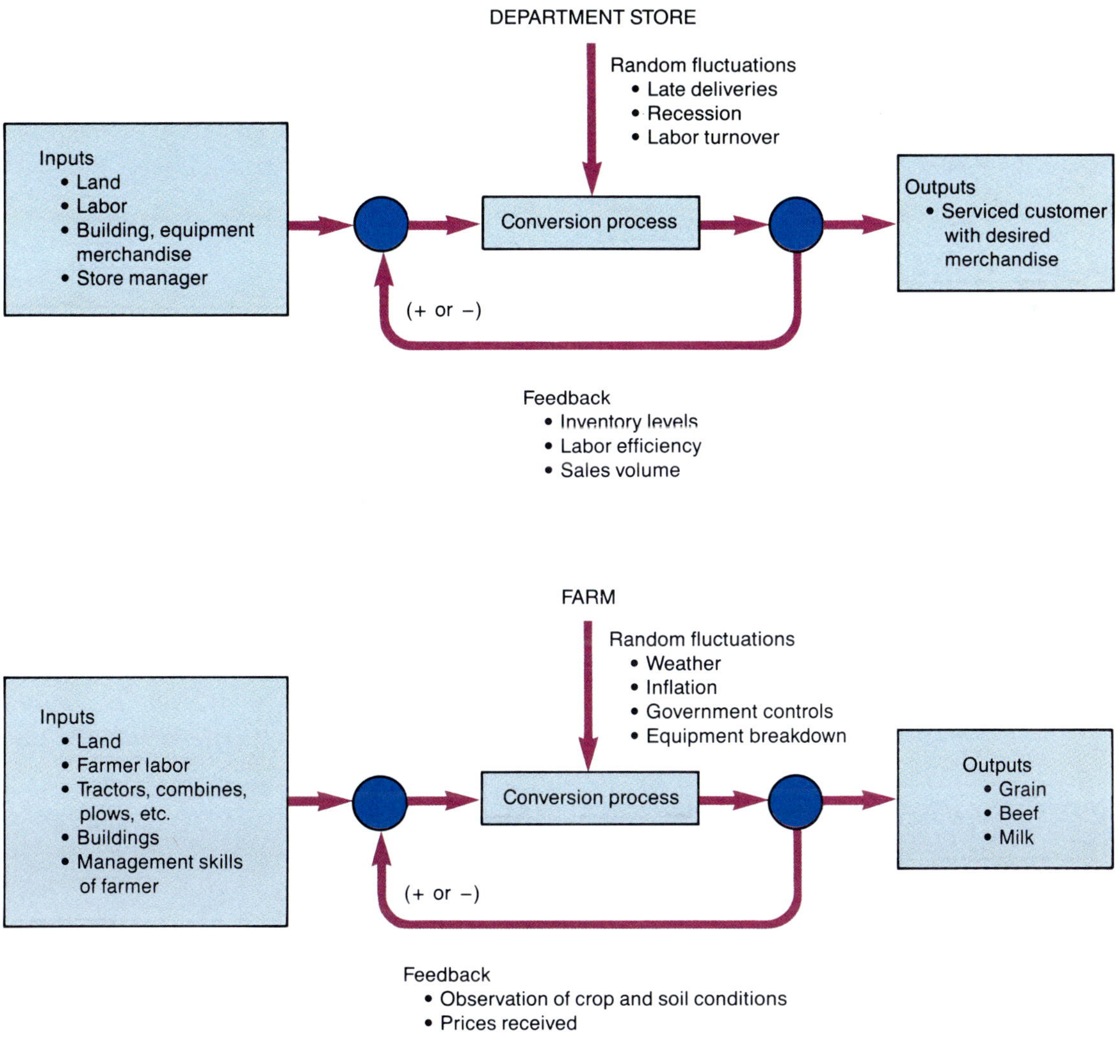

Value-added When blending inputs into a product or service, the increased value of outputs compared to the sum of the values of inputs.

Random fluctuations Unplanned or uncontrollable environmental influences (strikes, floods, etc.) that cause planned and actual output to differ.

Feedback Information in the control process that allows management to decide whether organizational activities need adjustment.

Technology The level of scientific sophistication in plant, equipment, and skills in the conversion process.

function. For all operations systems the general goal is to create some kind of *value-added,* so that the outputs are worth more to consumers than just the sum of the individual inputs.

The *random fluctuations* listed in Figures 1.1 and 1.2 consist of unplanned or uncontrollable influences that cause the actual output to differ from the expected output. Random fluctuations can arise from external sources (fire, floods, or lightning, for example), or they can result from internal problems, such as imperfections in materials and equipment, or simple human error. In fact, fluctuations are the rule rather than the exception in production processes and reducing fluctuations (variations) is a major management task.

The feedback loop in Figure 1.1 provides key information to managers. Without feedback, managers cannot control operations because they do not know the results of their decisions.

TECHNOLOGIES OF CONVERSION

The conversion of inputs into outputs varies considerably with the technology used. By *technology,* we mean the level of scientific sophistication in plant, equipment, skills, and product (or service) in the conversion (transformation) process. A soft-drink bottling operation, for example, features a highly mechanized, capital-intensive conversion process. A scientific research laboratory utilizes highly trained, professional scientists and specialized equipment. Other industries use low-skilled labor, minimal equipment, and simple processes to provide products and services.

MANUFACTURING OPERATIONS VERSUS SERVICE OPERATIONS

A conversion process that includes manufacturing (or production) yields a *tangible* output: a product. In contrast, a conversion process that includes service yields an *intangible* output: a deed, a performance, an effort. Consider McDonnell Douglas Corporation (MDC), an aerospace firm and the United States' largest defense contractor. Subsidiary Douglas Aircraft Company produces airplanes, clearly a product. Yet, other MDC components, such as the Information Systems Group (ISG), provide services. ISG, for example, delivers computer services to hospitals, architects, and other businesses—services such as programming, data analysis, and data storage using ISG's computers. Other MDC components launch spacecraft, provide contract research services, assemble missiles, and design and manufacture fighter aircraft. This mixture of service and manufacturing is typical of most aerospace firms.

Distinguishing Between Manufacturing and Service Operations Distinguishing between manufacturing and service operations can be difficult. Generally, we consider characteristics such as:

- Tangible/intangible nature of output
- Consumption of output
- Nature of work (jobs)
- Degree of customer contact
- Customer participation in conversion
- Measurement of performance.

Service-oriented businesses such as this dental health clinic utilize custom-tailored conversion of the unique combination of tools, chemicals, customer situations, and professional skills that provide the output of quality dental care for this patient.

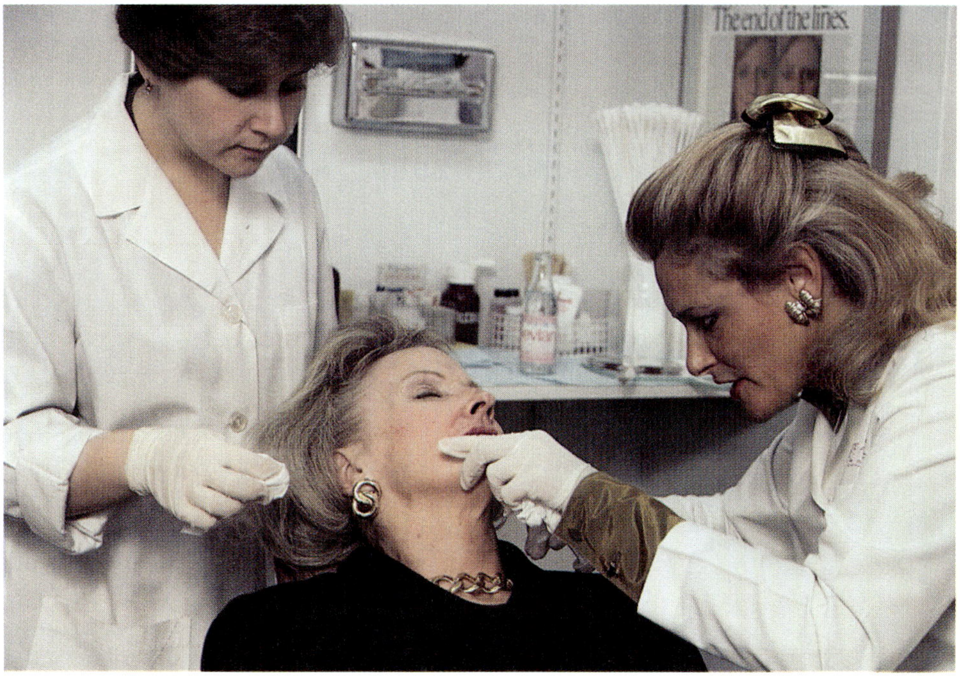

Source: Nina Barnett

To oversimplify, manufacturing is characterized by tangible outputs (products), outputs that customers consume over time, jobs that use less labor and more equipment, little customer contact, no customer participation in the conversion process (in production), and sophisticated methods for measuring production activities and resource consumption as products are made. Service, on the other hand, is characterized by intangible outputs, outputs that customers consume immediately, jobs that use more labor and less equipment, direct customer contact, frequent customer participation in the conversion process, and elementary methods for measuring conversion activities and resource consumption. Some service is equipment-based—computer programming services, railroad services, and telephone services—whereas other service is people-based—tax accounting services, hair styling, and golf instruction.

Throughputs Items going through the conversion process, contrasted with outputs coming out of the conversion process.

Let's look a little closer at the extent to which customers participate in the conversion process. In service operations, managers sometimes find it useful to distinguish between *output* and *throughput* types of customer participation. Output is a generated service, throughput is an item going through the process. In a pediatrics clinic the output is the medical service to the child who, by going through the conversion process, is also the throughput. At a fast-food restaurant, in contrast, the customer does not go through the conversion process. The outputs are hamburgers and french fries served in a hurry (both goods and services), while the throughputs are the food items as they are prepared and converted. The customer is neither a throughput nor an output. Both the clinic and the restaurant provide services, even though the outputs and throughputs differ considerably.

In this book we seek a balance between manufacturing and service. As much as possible we will use the term *operations* to include both manufacturing and service. Examples, too, will be drawn from both manufacturing and service industries.

HISTORICAL EVOLUTION OF PRODUCTION AND OPERATIONS MANAGEMENT

For over two centuries operations management has been recognized as an important factor in a country's economic well-being.

Progressing through a series of names—*manufacturing management, production management,* and *operations management*—all of which describe the same general discipline, the evolution of the term reflects the evolution of modern operations management. The traditional view of *manufacturing management* began in the eighteenth century when Adam Smith recognized the economic benefits of specialization of labor. He recommended breaking jobs down into subtasks and reassigning workers to specialized tasks in which they would become highly skilled and efficient. In the early twentieth century, Frederick W. Taylor implemented Smith's theories and crusaded for scientific management throughout the vast manufacturing complex of his day. From then until about 1930, the traditional view prevailed, and many techniques we still use today were developed. A brief sketch of these and other contributions to manufacturing management is highlighted in Table 1.1.

Production management became the more widely accepted term from the 1930s through the 1950s. As Frederick Taylor's work became more widely known, managers developed techniques that focused on economic efficiency in manufacturing. Workers were "put under a microscope" and studied in great detail to eliminate wasteful efforts and achieve greater efficiency. At this same time, however, management also began discovering that workers have multiple needs, not just economic needs. Psychologists, sociologists, and other social scientists began to study people and human behavior in the work environment. In addition, economists, mathematicians, and computer scientists contributed newer, more sophisticated analytical approaches.

With the 1970s emerges two distinct changes in our views. The most obvious of these, reflected in the new name—*operations management*—was a shift in the service and manufacturing sectors of the economy. As the service sector became more prominent, the change from "production" to "operations" emphasized the broadening of our field to service organizations. The second, more subtle change was the beginning of an emphasis on synthesis, rather than just analysis, in management practices. Spearheaded most notably by Wickham Skinner, American industry was awakened to its ignorance of the operations function as a vital weapon in the organization's overall competitive strategy. Previously preoccupied with an intensive analytical orientation and an emphasis on marketing and finance, managers had failed to integrate operations activities coherently into the highest levels of strategy and policy. Today, the operations function is experiencing a renewed role as a vital strategic element. Consequently, organizational goals are better focused to meet consumers' needs throughout the world.

TABLE 1.1 Historical summary of operations management

Date (approximate)	Contribution	Contributor
1776	Specialization of labor in manufacturing	Adam Smith
1799	Interchangeable parts, cost accounting	Eli Whitney and others
1832	Division of labor by skill; assignment of jobs by skill; basics of time study	Charles Babbage
1900	Scientific management; time study and work study developed; dividing planning and doing of work	Frederick W. Taylor
1900	Motion study of jobs	Frank B. Gilbreth
1901	Scheduling techniques for employees, machines, jobs in manufacturing	Henry L. Gantt
1915	Economic lot sizes for inventory control	F. W. Harris
1927	Human relations; the Hawthorne studies	Elton Mayo
1931	Statistical inference applied to product quality; quality control charts	Walter A. Shewhart
1935	Statistical sampling applied to quality control; inspection sampling plans	H. F. Dodge and H. G. Romig
1940	Operations research applications in World War II	P. M. S. Blacket and others
1946	Digital computer	John Mauchly and J. P. Eckert
1947	Linear programming	George B. Dantzig, William Orchard-Hays, and others
1950	Mathematical programming, nonlinear and stochastic processes	A. Charnes, W. W. Cooper, H. Raiffa, and others
1951	Commercial digital computer; large-scale computations available	Sperry Univac
1960	Organizational behavior; continued study of people at work	L. Cummings, L. Porter, and others
1970	Integrating operations into overall strategy and policy	W. Skinner
	Computer applications to manufacturing, scheduling, and control, material requirements planning (MRP)	J. Orlicky and O. Wright
1980	Quality and productivity applications from Japan; robotics, computer-aided design and manufacturing (CAD/CAM)	W. E. Deming and J. Juran

A SYSTEMS VIEW OF OPERATIONS: DEFINING THE SUBSYSTEM

ORGANIZATIONS VIEWED AS SYSTEMS

System A collection of objects related by regular interaction and interdependence.

What is a system? In a very general sense, a *system* is a collection of objects related by regular interaction and interdependence. Systems can vary from the large—nationwide communications networks, for example—to the small—a system for processing paperwork in an office, for example. To help people communicate about a system, models are often developed that represent a system or some aspect of it. The systems model, as applied to organizations, can help develop your understanding of operations.

A systems model of the organization identifies the subsystems, or subcomponents, that make up the organization. As Figure 1.3 shows, a business firm might well have finance, marketing, accounting, personnel, engineering, purchasing, and physical distribution systems in addition to the operations system. These systems are not independent but are interrelated to one another in many vital ways. We have chosen to show production/operations with major interactions between finance and marketing and lesser interaction with other functions. Decisions made in the production/operations subsystem often affect the behavior and performance of other subsystems. Finally, we should understand that the boundaries separating the various subsystems are not clear and distinct. Where do the responsibilities of production/operations end and those of physical distribution begin? The answers to such questions are often unclear and sometimes never resolved.

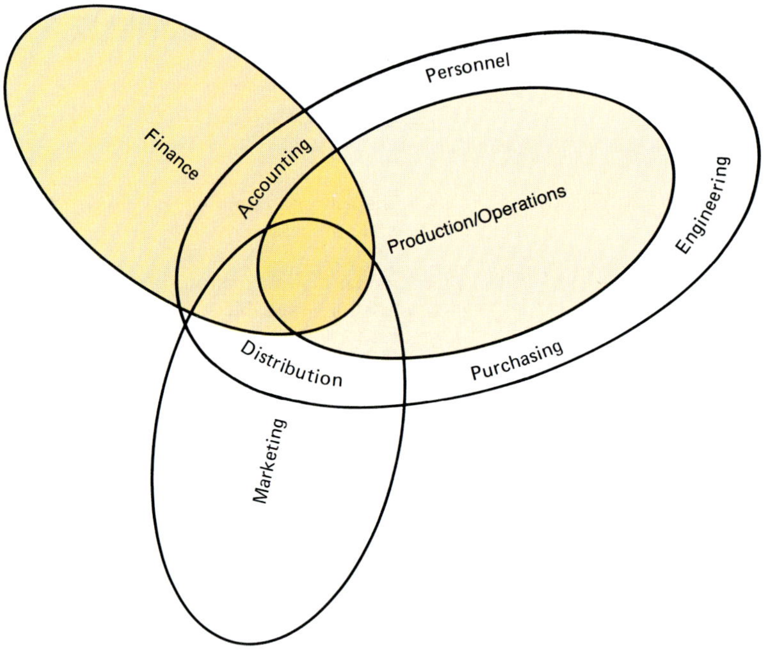

FIGURE 1.3 **The business firm: A systems view**

MANAGING THE OPERATIONS SUBSYSTEM

We have described the operations subsystem; the real challenge, however, is not to identify it but to operate it effectively. The conversion process must be managed by someone, and that someone is the operations manager.

OPERATIONS MANAGEMENT DEFINED

Operations management Management of the conversion process, which converts land, labor, capital, and management inputs into desired outputs of goods and services.

The operations manager's job is to manage the process of converting inputs into desired outputs. Our definition of operations management is, then, the management of the conversion process, which converts land, labor, capital, and management inputs into desired outputs of goods and services. In doing so, the manager uses various approaches from the *classical, behavioral,* and *modeling* views of management. As summarized in Table 1.2,

TABLE 1.2 Operations management elements from various schools of management thought

School	Some Important Assumptions	Primary Focus	General Contributions to Management
Classical			
Scientific management	People motivated by economics alone Managerial rationality Organization a closed system (certainty)	Economic efficiency Physical aspects of work environment Scientific analysis of work tasks Applications of techniques to work tasks	Demonstration of benefits from specialization of labor, division of labor, job analysis, separation of planning and doing
Process orientation	Management activities separable	Management processes	Identification of principles and functions of management
Behavioral			
Human relations	People complex; possess multiple needs	Behavior of individual in work environment	Awareness of individuals
Behavioral science	Human beings social creatures	Interpersonal and social aspects of work environment	Identification of behavioral variables that relate to organizational behavior
Social systems	Organization an open system	Interactive relationships of organization with its environment	Development of theories relating organizational behavior to human characteristics and organizational variables
Modeling			
Decision making	Decision-making processes are the primary managerial behaviors	Information acquisition, utilization, and choice processes	Development of guides for improving decision making
Systems theory	Organization—an open system Organization—a complex of interrelated subcomponents	Identification of organization boundaries, interrelationships among subsystems, and relationships between organization and larger environment	Development of approaches for predicting and explaining system behavior
Mathematical modeling	Main elements of organizations can be abstracted, interrelated, and expressed mathematically	Quantification of decision problems and systems Optimization of small set of situations	Development of explicit rules for management decisions Development of methods for analyzing organization systems or subsystems

Classical management One of three primary theories of management, emphasizing efficiency at the production core, the separation of planning and doing work, and management principles and functions.

Scientific management One of several theories of classical management, emphasizing economic efficiency at the production core through management rationality, the economic motivation of workers, and the separation of planning and doing work.

our perceptions of management responsibilities and concepts have evolved through the years, and we have gained insights from a variety of sources with different orientations.

CLASSICAL MANAGEMENT

Classical management has contributed the *scientific management* and *process orientation* theories to the operations manager's knowledge. The basis of *scientific management* is a focus on economic efficiency at the production core of the organization. Of central importance is the belief that rationality on the part of management will yield economic efficiency. *Economic efficiency,* a term that many organizations still use today, refers to a ratio of outputs to inputs. *Organization efficiency* refers to a ratio of outputs to land, capital, or labor inputs.

$$\text{Efficiency (\%)} = \frac{\text{Output}}{\text{Input}} \times 100\% \tag{1.1}$$

Restricted to an input of labor, the ratio is termed *labor efficiency.*

EXAMPLE

Management is concerned with labor efficiency, especially when labor is costly. To determine how efficient labor is in a given situation, management sets an *individual standard,* a goal reflecting an average worker's output per unit of time under normal working conditions. Say that the standard in a cafeteria is the preparation of 200 salads per hour. If labor input produces 150 salads per hour, how efficient is the salad operation?

$$\text{Labor efficiency} = \frac{\text{Labor output}}{\text{Labor input}} \times 100\% = \frac{150 \text{ salads}}{200 \text{ salads}} \times 100\%$$
$$= 75\%$$

Compared with the standard, this operation is 75 percent efficient in the preparation of salads.

Process management One of several theories of classical management, emphasizing management as a continuous process of planning, organizing, and controlling to influence the others' actions.

The school of *process management,* also referred to as the *administrative or functional approach* to management, was developed in the early 1900s. Management is viewed as a continuous process of planning, organizing, and controlling.

1. *Planning* includes all activities that establish a course of action. These activities guide future decision making.
2. *Organizing* includes all activities that establish a structure of tasks and authority.
3. *Controlling* includes all activities that ensure that actual performance is in accordance with planned performance.

These activities overlap in practice, as shown in Figure 1.4.

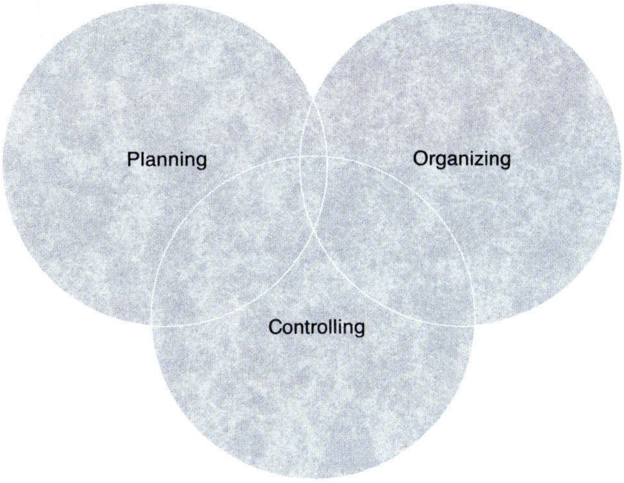

FIGURE 1.4 **The management process**

Behavioral management One of the primary theories of management, emphasizing human relations and the behavioral sciences.

Human relations Phenomenon recognized by behavioral scientists that people are complex and have multiple needs and that the subordinate-supervisor relationship directly affects productivity.

Behavioral science A science that explores how human behavior is affected by leadership, motivation, communication, interpersonal relationships, and attitude change.

Modeling management One of the primary theories of management, emphasizing decision-making, systems, and mathematical modeling.

BEHAVIORAL MANAGEMENT

The school of *behavioral management* began in the 1920s with a *human relations* movement that emerged quite unexpectedly from a typical scientific management research study. The study intended to measure how changes in the work environment affected output. Some social scientists on the research team, however, observed that changes in output were often due to factors other than physical changes in the work environment. Workers seemed to respond favorably to the attention and interest the experimenters had shown toward the workers, and productivity increased. This research spawned a new attitude that seriously undermined the scientific management man-as-machine concept.

Behavioral management theories espouse that people in their work environment, as elsewhere, are extremely complex. Applied psychologists have developed *behavioral science* theories of the individual; social psychologists, sociologists, and cultural anthropologists have developed *social systems* theories of groups of people at work. Operations Management Highlight 1.1 explores how employee behavior is of critical concern to the operations manager.

MODELING AS MANAGEMENT

The school of *modeling management* is concerned with decision making and systems theory, and mathematical modeling of these theories. The *decision-making* orientation considers making decisions to be the central purpose of management. Advocates of *systems theory* stress the importance of studying organizations from a "total systems" point of view. According to this school, identifying subsystem relationships, predicting effects of changes in the system, and properly implementing system change are all part of managing the total organization. With its foundations in operations research and management science, *mathematical modeling* focuses on creating mathematical representations of management problems and organizations. For a particular problem, the variables are expressed mathematically, and the model is used to demonstrate different

OPERATIONS MANAGEMENT HIGHLIGHT 1.1

Source: Janeart Ltd./The Image Bank

Operations Managers Seek Employee Participation

As industrial societies move into the 1990s, the shortage of skilled workers continues, especially in manufacturing. The shortage exists in spite of the fact that 16 million people in the European Community and over 5 million people in the United States are unemployed. Could managers use what they have

Mathematical modeling Creating and using mathematical representations of management problems and organizations to predict outcomes of proposed courses of action.

outcomes that would result from various possible managerial choices. The supplement to this chapter expands upon modeling and management by presenting the role of models in operations management.

A FRAMEWORK FOR MANAGING OPERATIONS

In this book, we create from these three approaches a framework for our study of operations management. This framework is depicted in Figure 1.5.

learned about behavior in the workplace to make jobs more rewarding, thus developing more skilled workers and alleviating the shortage?

One partial solution, for example, may be to ***increase participation*** in the workplace. According to the National Association of Suggestion Systems (NASS), employee participation programs in the United States made jobs more satisfying and in the process saved organizations $2.2 billion in 1988 alone. NASS distinguishes eight types of suggestion systems: suggestion boxes, improvement teams, organization surveys, work redesign, quality of work life, participative goal setting, gain sharing, and wellness programs. We will look more closely at work redesign in Chapter 8, examining popular approaches such as job enrichment, a job-characteristics approach, quality of work life, and the Japanese-style management focusing on Hito No Wa (harmony and teamwork among all people).

Are these work redesign efforts effective and are they being used? An abundant number of studies support the conclusion that employees perform better and are more satisfied in their jobs when work redesign is implemented. Yet it is not clear whether work redesign is the cause for improvement or other simultaneous changes are the causes—for example, a change to group work, new layouts, different equipment, or new pay systems and pay levels. Canadian companies particularly are benefiting from a wide variety of innovative ways of organizing, rewarding, and managing workers. A nationwide survey conducted from 1985 to 1986 provided ample evidence that the use of innovative pay systems (pay for knowledge, gain sharing, profit sharing), job sharing, job enrichment, semi-autonomous work groups, and other programs to improve employee participation and satisfaction are sharply increasing. There is no evidence that this increase is only part of a "cycle of participation" that will taper off, as some experts have suggested.

Sources: Jill Kanin-Lovers, "Meeting the Challenge of Workforce 2000," *Journal of Compensation and Benefits* 5, no. 4, (January/February 1990), 233–36; Don Nichols, "Bottom-Up Strategies: Asking Employees for Advice," *Management Review* 78, no. 12 (December 1989), 44–49; Richard J. Long, "Patterns of Workplace Innovation in Canada," *Industrial Relations*, (Canada) 44, no. 4 (Autumn 1989), 805–24; Marcelo Malentacchi, "Improving the Work Environment: Developments in the European Community," *ILR Report* 27, no. 1 (fall 1989), 30–34; and Barbara Mandell, "Does a Better Worklife Boost Productivity?" *Personnel* 66, no. 10 (October 1989), pp. 48–52.

Planning Activities that establish a course of action and guide future decision making.

Planning The operations manager defines the objectives for the operations subsystem of the organization, and the policies, programs, and procedures for achieving the objectives. This stage includes clarifying the role and focus of operations in the organization's overall strategy. It also involves product planning, facilities designing, and using the conversion process.

Organizing Activities that establish a structure of tasks and authority.

Organizing Operations managers establish a structure of roles and the flow of information within the operations subsystem. They determine the activities required to achieve the operations subsystem's goals and assign authority and responsibility for carrying them out.

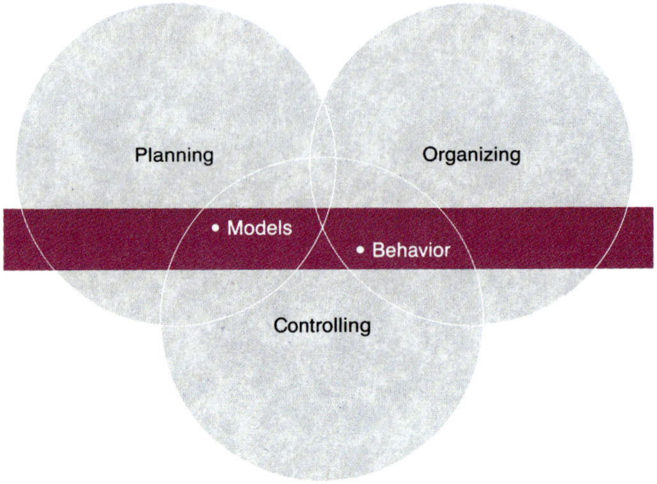

FIGURE 1.5 Management themes in operations

Controlling Activities that assure that actual performance is in accordance with planned performance.

Controlling To ensure that the plans for the operations subsystem are accomplished, the operations manager must also exercise control by measuring actual outputs and comparing them to planned outputs. Controlling costs, quality, and schedules is at the very heart of operations management.

Behavior Operations managers are concerned with how their efforts to plan, organize, and control affect human behavior. They also want to know how the behavior of subordinates can affect management's planning, organizing, and controlling actions. In operations we are interested in the behavior of managers as well, especially their decision-making behavior.

Models As operations managers plan, organize, and control the conversion process, they encounter many problems and must make many decisions. They can frequently simplify these difficulties by using models. Types of models and examples of their uses are illustrated in some detail as we cover functional problems of operations management throughout the text.

PROBLEMS OF THE OPERATIONS MANAGER

Operating managers are concerned with many different problem areas: cost control in brokerage houses, quality of services in hospitals, and rates of production output in furniture factories. Although operations managers occupy positions at several levels of their organizations, and although they work in different kinds of organizations, they all share certain kinds of problems. *The Manufacturing Futures Project,* a study conducted at Boston University, reveals the kinds of activities 160 executives are concerned with in U.S. and Canadian firms. The respondents—managers or directors of operations, plant managers, divisional general managers, vice presidents, and others with related duties—showed that many of their firms' most prominent activities for improving operations had to do with planning, organizing, and controlling the operations system and its conversion process (Table 1.3). Production planning, defining manufacturing

TABLE 1.3 Activities emphasized by organizations to improve operations

%[a]	Activity	%[a]	Activity
90.6	Production planning, scheduling/inventory control systems	44.4	Developing new processes for new products
76.9	Supervisor training	43.1	Vendor relations, procurement procedures
66.3	Capacity expansion	42.5	Focusing factories
63.1	Worker safety programs	41.3	Narrowing product line; standardizing
58.8	Defining a manufacturing strategy	39.4	Making existing systems work better
57.5	Motivating direct labor employees	35.0	Giving workers a broader range of tasks to perform
55.0	Value analysis-product redesign	33.1	CAD (computer-aided design)
54.4	Improved maintenance practices	31.9	Giving workers more responsibility for planning and organizing work
53.1	Changing the manufacturing organization	29.4	CAM (computer-aided manufacture)
51.3	Changing labor/management relationships	26.9	Plant relocation
50.0	Developing integrated information systems	25.0	Group technology
48.1	Lead-time reduction	21.3	Office automation
47.5	Quality circles	20.0	Zero defects programs
46.9	Developing new processes for old products	20.6	Reducing size of manufacturing units
46.3	Automating jobs		

[a]Percentage of respondents whose business unit has placed an emphasis on this activity in the last five years with the objective of improving operations.
Source: The Manufacturing Futures Project: Summary of Survey Responses (Boston University School of Management, 1982), 20–21.

strategy, and product redesign, for example, are *planning* activities. Changing the organization, labor/management relations, and developing integrated information systems are *organizing* activities. Inventory control, maintenance improvement, and lead-time reduction are *controlling* activities. The more recent manufacturing surveys do not collect these data. We doubt there have been major changes in the activities, only in their relative rankings. This is explained somewhat in the next chapter when a more recent survey is reviewed.

THE STRATEGIC ROLE OF OPERATIONS

As you study and practice operations management, it is easy to become preoccupied with the detailed economic and engineering aspects of the conversion process and lose sight of its fundamental purpose. This, in fact, has occurred in many U.S. companies, and the results have been costly from an overall organizational viewpoint. Economy and efficiency of conversion operations are secondary goals, not primary goals, of the overall organization. Primary goals are related to market opportunities.

A STRATEGIC PERSPECTIVE

In Figure 1.6 you should come to understand the basic downward flow of strategy influence leading to managing conversion operations and results. The general thrust of the process is guided by competitive and market conditions in the industry, which provide the basis for determining the organization's strategy. Where is the industry now, and where will it be in the future? What are the existing and potential markets? What market gaps exist, and what competencies do we have for filling them? A careful analysis of market segments and the ability of our competitors and ourselves to meet

FIGURE 1.6 **Operations as a strategic element in accomplishing organizational goals**

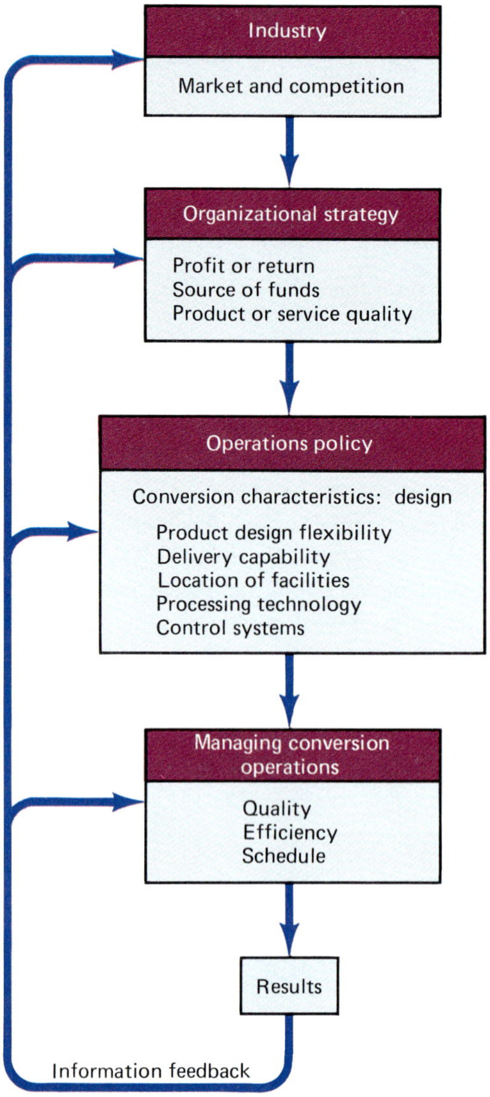

the needs of these segments will determine the best direction for focusing an organization's efforts.

After assessing the potential within an industry, an overall organizational strategy must be developed, including some basic choices of the primary basis for competing. In doing so, priorities are established among the following four characteristics:

- Quality (product performance)
- Cost efficiency (low product price)
- Dependability (reliable, timely delivery of orders to customers)
- Flexibility (responding rapidly with new products or changes in output volume)

In recent years, we have learned that most organizations cannot be best on all these dimensions and, by trying to do so, they end up doing nothing well. Furthermore, when a competency exists in one of these areas, an attempt to switch to a different one can lead to a downfall in *effectiveness* (meeting the primary objectives).

Time is emerging as a critical dimension of competition in both manufacturing and service industries. In any industry the firm with the fastest response to customer demands has the potential to achieve an overwhelming market advantage. Mr. Ruwe, in this chapter introduction, alluded to this trend and its importance to Copeland Corporation.

In an era of time-based competition, a firm's competitive advantage is defined not by cost but by the *total time* required to produce a product or service. Firms able to respond quickly have reported growth rates over three times the industry average and double the profitability. Thus the payoff for quick response is market dominance.[1]

These basic strategic choices, then, set the tone for the shape and content of the operations function and what it accomplishes. A conversion process designed for one type of focus is often ill-suited for success in another, alternative, focus.

OPERATIONS OBJECTIVES

The overall objective of the operations subsystem is to provide conversion capabilities for meeting the organization's goals and strategy. The subgoals of the operations subsystem, then, must specify the following:

1. Product/service characteristics
2. Process characteristics
3. Product/service quality
4. Efficiency
   (a) Effective employee relations and cost control of labor
   (b) Cost control of material
   (c) Cost control in facility utilization
5. Customer service (schedule)
   (a) Producing quantities to meet expected demand
   (b) Meeting the required delivery date for goods or services
6. Adaptability for future survival

[1]Joseph D. Blackburn, *Time-Based Competition: The Next Battleground in American Manufacturing,* Business One (Homewood, Ill.; Irwin 1990).

The priorities among these operations subgoals and their relative emphases should be direct reflections of the organization's mission. Relating these six operations subgoals to the broader strategic choices above, it is clear that quality, efficiency, and dependability (customer service) are reflected in the subgoals. Flexibility encompasses adaptability but also relates to product/service and process characteristics. As we'll see in Chapter 4, once choices about product and process are made, boundaries for meeting the other operations objectives are set.

Manufacturing in this textile mill produces large volumes of tangible products - a standard line of cloth and fabrics - by converting raw materials on high-speed machinery.
Source: **SuperStock**

Operations Alternatives and Tradeoffs

The operations subgoals—that is, the objectives—can be attained through the decisions that are made in the various operations areas. Each decision involves important tradeoffs between choices about product and process versus choices about quality, efficiency, schedule, and adaptability.

Consider the late-1980s and early-1990s popularity of frozen yogurt desserts as an alternative to ice cream. Once a decision is made to sell yogurt in ice cream–type parlors, many choices must be made. Where should facilities be located? How large should they be? What degree of automation should be used? How skilled must labor be to operate the automated equipment? Will the frozen yogurt be produced on site? How do these decisions impact quality, efficiency, schedule (customer service), and adaptability? Are we prepared for changes in product or service, or do these decisions lock in our operations? These are examples of the tough, crucial tradeoffs that are at the heart of understanding the choices that must be made when planning strategically and tactically.

TRENDS IN OPERATIONS MANAGEMENT

What new demands are being made of operations managers today? How will their jobs change in the future? Answers to such questions are speculative, but we can find some clues by observing recent trends in overall economic activities.

Shifts in Economic Activity

Are people doing the same kinds of work today that they have done in the past? The question is important because operations management can usually be found where economic activity is increasing. Table 1.4 provides us with some answers. We can see that there has been an employment shift from agriculture and other extractive (mining and contract construction) industries to the service sector: agriculture decreased from 38 percent of the employed workers in 1900 to 3 percent in 1989 and service workers increased from 28 percent in 1900 to 70 percent in 1989. The percentage of workers employed in industry has dwindled steadily. Will this trend continue? It is quite possible that the percentage of workers in the service sector will gradually continue to grow, but this growth most likely will be relatively slow. The most recent data predict workers shifting from industry to the service sector, while the percentage of agricultural workers will remain around 3 percent.

One point is clear. The largest sector of the U.S. economy today is in services. Of the 47.6 million people employed in the United States in 1929, 18.1 million were employed in services. In 1989, 117.3 million people were employed, 82.1 million in services. The fastest growing service sector has been government, with repair services a

TABLE 1.4 **Distribution of employed workers by major sectors of the economy, 1900–1985**

Year	Agriculture and Other Extractive Industries	Industry	Services	Total
1900	38%	34%	28%	100%
1910	34	37	29	100
1920	30	39	31	100
1930	27	35	38	100
1940	25	34	41	100
1950	15	40	45	100
1960	11	39	50	100
1970	5	34	61	100
1980	4	28	68	100
1989	3	27	70	100

Source: Victor Fuchs, *The Service Economy* (New York: Columbia University Press, 1968), p. 207, with permission of the NBER; *Statistical Abstract of the United States 1972,* pp. 227–30; U.S. Department of Labor, Bureau of Labor Statistics, 1975, 1979, 1984, 1990.

close second. The total labor force has increased some 69 million workers—64.0 million of whom work in the service sector.[2] Consumer expenditures have also shifted toward services.

Increasing economic activity in the service sector suggests that many of you may find yourselves employed in service industries. In this book we take the position that operations management concepts, skills, and techniques are transferable *across* the industry/service sectors and *within* industries and services. Our examples and explanations therefore apply to both kinds of operations, even if only one is mentioned.[3]

A Global Perspective

Not all nations are shifting from industrialization to a manufacturing/service balance as described above for the U.S. economy—many are not yet industrialized. There are three major industrialized world economic regions with reasonable balances between production and consumption: the Pacific Rim, North America, and Western Europe. Outside these regions production often lags behind demand. Supply is limited. Many nations are simply poor and are unable to produce effectively and therefore cannot compete in a world economy.

One region under transition is Eastern Europe. In fact, *all* socialist cultures throughout the world seem to be in transition. Operations Management Highlight 1.2 explores operations management in socialist cultures. As you can see, managing in capitalist democracies such as Canada or the United States is very different.

PRODUCTION AND OPERATIONS MANAGEMENT CAREERS

In 1989, 117.3 million workers comprised the U.S. labor force. Some 7 million of these, we estimate, filled supervisory positions in finance, operations, and marketing. The characteristically high labor intensity in operations means a disproportionately high share of managerial jobs in this area. In production and operations, many future managers can find careers.

Entry Positions in Production/Operations Management

If your career objectives are to advance to a top management position, operations is a reasonable avenue to travel. One *Fortune* survey of the 500 largest U.S. individual

[2]U.S. Department of Labor, Bureau of Labor Statistics, 1972, 1975, 1979, 1984, 1986, and 1990.

[3]The development of operations problem solutions and their transfer to service sector organizations is discussed in V. A. Mabert, "Service Operations Management: Research and Application," *Journal of Operations Management* 2, no. 4 (August 1982), 203–9.

companies found that chief executive officers had a production/operations career emphasis 18.6 percent of the time.[4] Besides the top position in the organization, generally a vice president or similar officer is responsible for production/operations. How might you gain such a position? What entry positions allow you to gain experience for promotion within operations?

Two entry tracks are available: line and staff. Line positions are directly related to achievement of the organization's financial, marketing, and operating objectives while staff positions are supportive of line throughout the organization. Typical operations line positions include first-line supervisors, management trainees, and foremen. Operations staff positions include computer analysts, project analysts, inventory and material planning and control, production planning, logistics, and quality control. Opportunities abound in all these areas, especially in first-line supervision and computer-related and materials management positions. In any of these jobs you will likely obtain product or service knowledge about the firm for which you work—a necessity for most top management positions.

EXAMPLE

Recently, two guests visited an undergraduate operations management class. Responding to student questions on careers, one guest, the personnel manager at a new Quaker Oats Company manufacturing facility, stressed an interest in management, operations management, and industrial engineering students for entry first-line foreman positions. As she explained, the jobs were in a clean, modern facility with good opportunity for line or staff advancement. The second guest, the operations vice president at Boatmen's Bank of Kansas City, stressed an interest in operations management majors for entry positions in operations analysis, a staff function directly supporting bank operations. After six months to two years, operations analysts typically move to line supervisory positions. In both cases, promotion was available within operations and to other functions (marketing, finance, etc.) as well.

Career Choice in Production/Operations Management

Your choice of career deserves reasoned thought and direction. We suggest that in making career choices in production/operations management you consider (1) opportunity for advancement, professional development, and visibility in the organization; (2) job satisfaction; (3) monetary rewards; (4) quality of life (climate, entertainment, etc.); (5) work group characteristics; and (6) individual needs and desires (location, health considerations, etc.). Operations management career decisions are amenable to change. Although you might have to learn new technology in a major job change, operations management skills are generally transferable across services and manufacturing and within each sector. Professional organizations and journals occasionally summarize career opportunities in their operations management areas, thus providing a good source of information.

[4]Charles G. Burch, "A Group Profile of the *Fortune* 500 Chief Executives," *Fortune* (May 1976), pp. 173–77, 308–12.

OPERATIONS MANAGEMENT HIGHLIGHT 1.2

Source: **Jay Freis/The Image Bank**

Managing Operations in Socialist Cultures

In their dramatic and massive political and economic liberalization, Eastern European countries are seeking a framework for management that will work in their cultures. The Soviet Union and, to some extent, China are freeing their economies as well. However, production and consumption in these nations drastically lag behind Western nations. How will manufacturing and operations managers cope in these changing socialist systems? Will they be able to copy North American, Asian, and Western European management styles and practices? How have managers been behaving under the more repressive and controlled political and economic structure of these countries?

Experts tend to agree that Eastern European countries, Soviet states, and the provinces of the People's Republic of China must deal with a paradox. How can they acquire skills and expertise for managing in a free market system yet not simply copy what works for other free market cultures? Similarly, it is rather clear that Japanese management practices are not directly transferable to the United States, just as U.S. practices do not always work well in many other cultures (including Western Europe and Japan). This principle will most likely hold for Eastern Europe as well.

Within a specific area of the world, there are great variations in how people work. In Asia, for example, the differences between the hierarchical Koreans and the harmonistic Indonesians are even greater than the differences between Americans and Japanese. Likewise, in Eastern Europe, Romanians are highly individualistic and adversarial, while the Poles are more cooperative. There are some people in Eastern Europe who worked under free market systems about 40 years ago. In Russia, however, hardly anyone would remember life as it was before the 70-year socialist regime began. For the most part, managers in these regions will have to learn new ways to do their jobs.

Professor Magoroh Maruyama, an international management expert at Auyoma Gakuin University in Tokyo, suggests that when the free market system is introduced into Eastern Europe, there will be much resistance from workers who would rather not work hard, from administrators and managers who have become used to living on bribes, and from grantsmen who did not have to account for profit or loss. Maruyama recommends that these countries send management trainees to many other parts of the world and examine carefully their own cultures at the same time. In 1990, 5,000 Soviets studied business abroad, which suggests that Maruyama's views hold merit with at least one nation.

How do the Chinese lead their subordinates? Professor James A. Wall, Jr., of the University of Missouri, interviewed 50 workers and 120 managers in the Jiangsu province of the People's Republic of China during 1989, and found some interesting results. Wall discovered that Deng Xiaoping's "reform" program and inflation have had the strongest impacts upon managers. These, along with the Communist Party, 40 years of socialism, feudalistic values, ***guanxi*** (influence peddling), and the labor-intensive economy mold the management at this time. As a consequence, China's managers develop warm relationships with workers, offer favors, and at times even shame workers in order to obtain favors in return.

Common traits of the systems in China, Eastern Europe, and the Soviet Union are the bribery of managers and laziness of workers. The prevalence of these traits leads to questions concerning ethics and challenges to the concept of the "goodness of work," a commonly accepted work ethic of North America, Western Europe, and Japan.

As the globalization of business continues, management techniques in a foreign country will be a major problem for international firms. Operations management requires that superior-subordinate relationships be developed at the lowest levels in the firm, which suggests that a wide variety of leadership styles will have to emerge.

Sources: "Crash Courses in Capitalism for Ivan the Globe-Trotter," _Business Week_ (May 28, 1990), 42–44; "Eastern Europe: A New Frontier," _National Business_ (April 1, 1990), 45–49; M. Maruyama, "Some Management Considerations in the Economic Reorganization of Eastern Europe," _Academy of Management Executive_ 2, no. 4 (1990), 90–91; J. A. Wall, Jr., "Managers in the People's Republic of China," _Academy of Management Executive_ 2, no. 4 (1990), 19–32.

CONTEMPORARY OPERATIONS MANAGEMENT TOPICS

This book is organized around the management subfunctions of planning, organizing, and controlling, striving for an integrated perspective (see Figure 1.7). By relating each operations problem area to a common theme, we hope to suggest a continuity of thought to illustrate the fundamentals of operations management. Within this framework, we have found it useful to approach the planning subfunction by dividing it into two major parts: *planning* and *scheduling* the conversion system. Planning the conversion system revolves around its design; scheduling focuses on operating it once it exists.

One major topic, for example, is controlling the conversion system. In control we deal with inventory control, materials management, and quality management—all

FIGURE 1.7 General model for managing operations

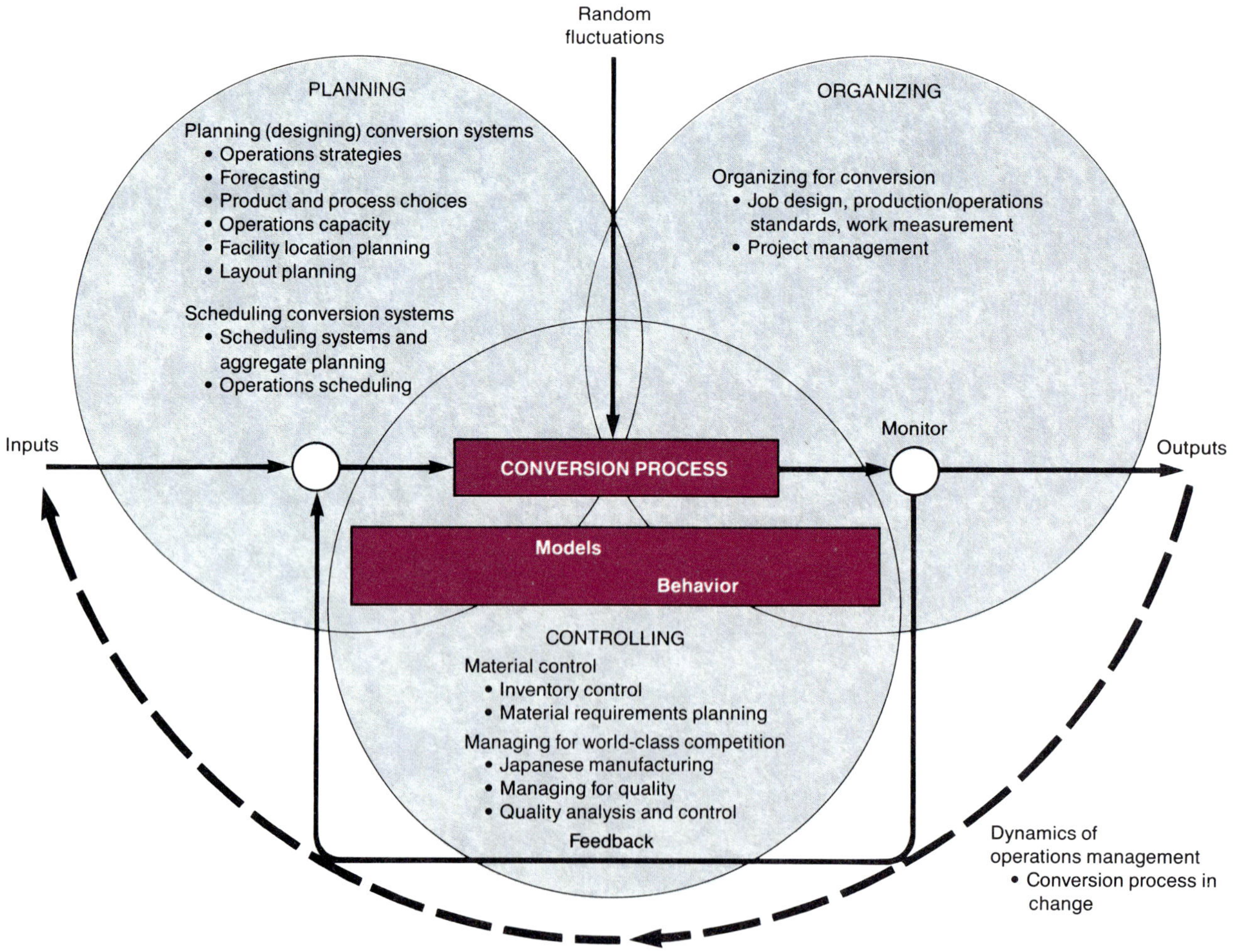

necessary activities of operating managers. Industry today, whether service or product related, is complex. Operations management is charged with unraveling the complexity, identifying problems, and creating solutions. When problems are behavioral (e.g., quality motivation), we introduce contemporary techniques like quality circles and attitude change procedures to deal with them. When problems are process-oriented (e.g., quality analysis control), we show why models and such methods as sampling theory and statistical process control procedures are appropriate.

Before considering specific solutions to operations problems, however, we must first explore the major problems, issues, and challenges that are facing operations managers. These include questions on productivity, technology, competition, and strategies, all of which create the challenges for effective performance today. It is this set of questions that we consider next.

SUMMARY

This chapter has highlighted the role of the operations function in organizations and the importance of managing it effectively. *Operations* was defined in terms of the mission it serves for the organization, the technology it employs, and the human and managerial processes it involves. Using this approach, we were able to see the breadth of issues the operations manager faces, as well as the kinds of problems and decisions that arise in operations management.

To understand and solve operations problems we adopted a framework that draws upon the concepts from three schools of management thought—classical, behavioral, and modeling. Systems concepts can be useful for understanding organizations and the role of the operations function within them. Operations management makes use of these systems, models, and various techniques in directing the conversion process, which converts inputs into desired outputs. Operations managers must become involved in planning, organizing, and controlling operations. As they decide among alternatives, they must consider the organization's goals and overall strategy.

Historical shifts in economic activity and predicted changes in the growth of major industries indicate the increasing importance of the service sector. These changes present some new challenges to operations management, and transferring our knowledge of production management into the service sector is chief among them.

CASE

Kare-Full Katering

Harrison T. Wenk III is 43, married, and has two children, ages 10 and 14. He has a master's degree in education and teaches junior high school music in a small town in Ohio. Harrison's father passed away two months ago, leaving his only child an unusual business opportunity. According to his father's will, Harrison has 12 months to become active in the family food-catering business, Kare-Full Katering, Inc., or it will be sold to two key employees for a reasonable and fair price. If Harrison becomes involved, the two employees have the option to purchase a significant, but less than majority, interest in the firm.

Harrison's only involvement with this business, which his grandfather established, was as an hourly employee during high school and college summers. He is confident that he could learn and perhaps enjoy the marketing side of the business, and that he could retain the long-time head of accounting/finance. But he would never really enjoy day-to-day operations. In fact, he doesn't understand what operations management really involves.

In 1991 Kare-Full Katering, Inc., had $3.75 million in sales in central Ohio. Net profit after taxes was $105,000, the eleventh consecutive year of profitable operations and the seventeenth in the last 20 years. There are 210 employees in this labor-intense business. Institutional contracts account for over 70 percent of sales and include partial food services for three colleges, six commercial establishments (primarily manufacturing plants and banks), two long-term care facilities, and five grade schools. Some customer locations employ a permanent operations manager; others are served from the main kitchens of Kare-Full Katering. Harrison believes that if he becomes active in the business, one of the two key employees, the vice president of operations, will leave the firm.

Harrison has decided to complete the final two months of this school year and then spend the summer around Kare-Full Katering—as well as institutions with their own food services—to assess whether he wants to become involved in the business. He is particularly interested in finding out as much as possible about operations. Harrison believes he owes it to his wife and children to fairly evaluate this opportunity.

Case Questions

1. Prepare a worksheet of operations activities that Harrison should inquire about this summer.
2. To manage the firm, how much does Harrison need to know about operations? Why?
3. What problems do you expect Harrison to encounter this summer—both at Kare-Full and at other institutions?
4. If you were Harrison, what would you do? Why?

CASE

Operations Management in a Veterinary Clinic

See if you can identify the inputs, outputs, and conversion processes in a veterinary clinic consisting of three veterinarians, a clerical staff, and two animal control assistants. Identify the primary operations management activities (use Table 1.3 as a guide) in this setting. Lay them out in a framework similar to the one in Figure 1.1. You should consider how the addition of an operations manager to the clinic staff would affect the cost and effectiveness of medical services. Normally in a situation like this, the operations manager would be one of the veterinarians. Could you explain to them why they should hire you to manage the operations of the clinic?

REVIEW AND DISCUSSION QUESTIONS

1. Organizations may be viewed as systems. The systems view is important to operations managers since (a) the production/operations system is a part of the firm or organization and (b) within the production/operations function there are subsystems. Explain.
2. Using Figure 1.1, explain the conversion process in a fast-food outlet (McDonald's, for example) and a public swimming pool.
3. (a) What are operations subgoals?
   (b) What is the overall objective of the operations subsystem?
   (c) How do they relate to each other?
4. Energy conservation is an individual, firm, and national concern. If you were a manager of a large department store employing 200 people and spending over $10,000 a month on utilities, which approach to (or school of) management might assist you best in reducing energy costs? Why?
5. How does production/operations policy relate to accounting and financial policy and marketing policy? What does this relationship accomplish?
6. Accomplishing an organization's goals requires that operations management account for the organization's industry, strategy, operations policy, and conversion process. How do these elements relate to one another? How do they relate to accomplishing organization goals?
7. Relate the conversion diagram in Figure 1.1 to the first 15 activity areas listed by operations managers in Table 1.3.
8. Compare and contrast the three broad categories of management theory: classical, behavioral, and modeling schools.
9. As an industrialized nation becomes more affluent, people have more leisure time and demand more services. Many workers enter the labor force at an older age and leave it at a younger age. How do these changes affect the role of the traditional production/operations manager?
10. A problem with modern assembly line techniques seems to be that workers are apathetic. How could scientific management be used as a basis for solving this problem? How could a human relations philosophy help solve it?
11. Why is there a need for a behavioral theory of management? From your own experience or observation, provide a supervisor-subordinate situation that supports your answer.
12. Relate the general model for managing operations (Figure 1.7) to each theory of management.
13. How do inflation, energy shortages, and a shorter work week each present new challenges to production/operations managers?

PROBLEMS

1. The manager of a cola bottling plant came to work early on Friday, having been out of town on business throughout the week. Before others arrived, he checked the daily labor efficiency report for the bottling plant. Daily efficiency was 102 percent Monday, 94 percent Tuesday, and 87 percent Wednesday. Going to the assistant manager's desk, he found that on Thursday employees worked 96 hours and

bottled 1,025 cases. The standard for labor output is 12.5 cases per hour. What, if any, questions should the manager ask when employees arrive Friday?

2. The labor output standard for an insurance claims office is 150 claims processed per day. So far this week, 160, 125, 140, and 100 claims have been processed daily. The claims backlog is building. Prepare a graph of daily efficiency. What does the graph indicate?

KEY TERMS

Behavioral management 13
Behavioral science 13
Classical management 12
Controlling 16
Conversion process 4
Feedback 6
Human relations 13
Inputs 4
Mathematical modeling 14
Modeling management 13
Operations management 8
Operations system 4
Organizing 15
Outputs 4
Planning 15
Process management 12
Random fluctuations 6
Scientific management 12
System 8
Technology 6
Throughputs 7
Value-added 6

SELECTED READINGS

Andrew, C. G., and G. A. Johnson, "The Crucial Importance of Production and Operations Management," *Academy of Management Review* 7, no. 1 (January 1982), 143–47.

Collins, Robert W., Roger W. Schmenner, and D. Clay Whybark, "Pan-European Manufacturing: The Yellow Brick Road to 1992," *Business Horizons* 33, no. 3 (1990), 15–22.

Ettlie, John E., Michael C. Burnstein, Avi Fiegenbaum, eds., *Manufacturing Strategy*, Boston: Kluwer Academic Publishers, 1990.

Mabert, V. A., "Service Operations Management: Research and Application," *Journal of Operations Management* 2, no. 4 (August 1982), 203–9.

Skinner, Wickham, "Manufacturing—Missing Link in Corporate Strategy," *Harvard Business Review* 47, no. 3 (May–June 1969).

———, *Manufacturing in the Corporate Strategy*. New York: John Wiley, 1978.

Sullivan, R. S., "The Service Sector: Challenges and Imperatives for Research in Operations," *Journal of Operations Management* 2, no. 4 (August 1982), 211–14.

SUPPLEMENT TO CHAPTER 1

THE ROLE OF MODELS IN OPERATIONS MANAGEMENT

The context in which we use the term *mathematical modeling* refers to the creation of mathematical representations of management problems and organizations in order to determine outcomes of proposed courses of action. In spite of their utility, we must recognize models for what they are—artificial representations of things that are real. As such, they fall short of fully duplicating their real world counterparts. This incompleteness of models should not be interpreted as a strictly negative feature. In fact, it can be desirable, because it clears away extraneous elements and concentrates on the heart of the problem. The modeling process can give us a simplified version of the situation, a representation in which all the minor considerations have been stripped away so the major factors are clearly visible.

Types of Models in Production and Operations Management (P/OM)

In operations management, we use several types of models of varying levels of sophistication.

Verbal Models *Verbal* or *written models express in words the relationships among variables.* Verbal models are descriptive. Suppose a passing motorist asks you to give directions to the nearest gas station. If you tell him the way, you are giving a verbal model. If you write the directions in words (not pictures), you are giving a descriptive model.

Schematic Models *Schematic models show a pictorial relationship among variables.* If you give the passing motorist a map showing the way to the nearest gas station, you would be giving a schematic model. Charts and diagrams are also schematic; they are very useful for showing relationships among variables, as long as all the legends, symbols, and scales are explained.

Iconic Models *Iconic models are scaled physical replicas of objects or processes.* Architectural models of new buildings and highway engineering replicas of a proposed overpass system are iconic models.

Mathematical Models *Mathematical models show functional relationships among variables by using mathematical symbols and equations.* In any equation, x, y, and similar symbols are used to express precise functional relationships among the variables.

Mathematical Models in Production and Operations Management

Optimization Operations managers often use models to help analyze problems and suggest solutions. To assist, they often find it helpful to use an *algorithm*, a prescribed set of steps (a procedure) that attains a goal. In *optimization* models, for example, we want to find the *best* solution (the goal), and an *optimization algorithm* identifies the steps for doing so. In operations management we strive for optimization algorithms as aids in problem solving.

Heuristics In other cases, a *heuristic* approach is used. A heuristic is a way (a strategy) of using rules of thumb or defined decision procedures to attack a problem. In general, when we use heuristics we do not expect to attain the best possible solution to a problem; instead, we hope for a *satisfactory* solution *quickly*. Formally developed heuristic procedures are called *heuristic algorithms*. They are useful for problems for which optimization algorithms have not yet been developed.

Modeling Benefits

The extensive use of models, especially schematic and mathematical models, is sometimes questioned by students and practitioners of P/OM. Using models often requires making questionable assumptions, applying hard-to-get cost and other data, and figuring in future events that are not easily predicted. Even so, the knowledge gained from working with models and attempting to apply them can yield valuable insights about a particular problem and what types of decisions are required. Simply recognizing the decision points can be a major step forward in many situations. Moreover, by using models, managers can recognize

1. variables that can be controlled to affect performance of the system
2. relevant costs and their magnitudes, and
3. the relationship of costs to variables, including important tradeoffs among costs.

CLASSIFYING PROBLEMS

Since the operations analyst encounters many different kinds of problems, it is a good idea to have a convenient starting point, or frame of reference, for initiating the analysis. Classifying problems into different types makes it easier to select models and criteria to use in the analysis. We'll consider two ways of classifying problems: by the degree to which the outcome is uncertain, and by the degree to which the decisions are interdependent.

Uncertainty of Outcomes

When we know for sure what the outcome of each decision will be, we are dealing with a problem under conditions of *certainty*. When a decision has more than one possible outcome and we know the likelihood of each outcome, we are dealing with a problem under conditions of *risk*. Finally, when a decision has more than one possible outcome and we do not know the likelihood of each outcome, we are dealing with a problem under conditions of *uncertainty*. Some examples may clarify these conditions of certainty, risk, and uncertainty.

EXAMPLE CERTAINTY

A chain of supermarkets is going to open a new store at one of four possible locations. Management wishes to select the location that will maximize profitability over the next ten years. An extensive analysis was performed to determine the costs, revenues, and profits for each alternative. The results are shown below.

Location	Ten-year Annual Profit ($ millions)
1	.70
2	.95
3	.60
4	.84

Management has a high degree of confidence in these figures. The decision criterion (profit) has been explicitly identified and accurately calculated for each alternative. Management's strategy is to select the alternative with the highest criterion value, in this case, location 2.

EXAMPLE RISK

Further analysis of the supermarket chain's problem reveals that the profit associated with each location is not known for sure. Management is convinced that the ten-year profitability of each location will depend upon regional population growth. Therefore management cannot predict the outcome with certainty. Three possible rates of population growth were identified: low, medium, and high. The profitability ($ millions) associated with each location and each rate of population growth was calculated, as shown below.

	Rate of Population Growth		
Location	Low (5% or less)	Medium (above 5% but below 10%)	High (10% or more)
1	$.3	$.8	$ .9
2	.2	.6	1.1
3	.4	.5	.6
4	.6	.7	.8
Probability (p)	.2	.3	.5

The figures at the bottom of the table give the probability (likelihood) of each rate of population growth. Decision strategy in this situation is more difficult than it is under conditions of certainty.

EXAMPLE
UNCERTAINTY

Even further analysis has cast doubt on the probability of the rates of population growth. New management doesn't know the probabilities of low, medium, or high growth, and is faced with a problem under conditions of uncertainty. Obviously, strategy is much harder to come by in this case.

Under conditions of certainty, the best location is easily identified. Location 2 clearly yields the highest profit. Under conditions of risk, however, the choice is not so easy. We do not know which location will be best because the rate of future population growth is not known for certain. In analyzing this situation, we have to arrange the data differently than we did under conditions of certainty. Look at the table in the risk example. (A table arranged like this is called a *matrix.*) The profit for low, medium, and high population growth is listed separately for each location. Which alternative is best? If population growth turns out to be low, location 4 is best ($.6 million). If growth is medium, location 1 is best ($.8 million), and if it is high, location 2 is best ($1.1 million). In the analyst's language, the three rates of population growth are called *states of nature.*

A procedure called calculating the *expected value* has been applied to our example (see Table S1.1). Expected value is explained by following the table headings. For each alternative location, we calculate the product of each outcome and its probability. The sum of these products is the expected value of the alternative location. The expected value is highest for alternative 2: $.77 million. If management faced this situation many times and always chose alternative 2, its average profit would be higher than for any other alternative.[5]

Problems under conditions of uncertainty can also be structured in matrix form. Since the probabilities are not known, however, rational strategies for decision making are not well defined or straightforward. We discuss three approaches from among several that analysts use. The first, *maximax,* is an optimistic approach; the analyst considers only the best outcome for each alternative regardless of probability. Looking at the table for the risk example and ignoring the probability row, the outcomes that would be considered are $.9 million for alternative 1, $1.1 million for alternative 2, $.6 million for alternative 3, and $.8 million for alternative 4. Among these, alternative 2 yields the maximum profit, and that is the one that would be chosen.

The second approach is *maximin,* a pessimistic approach; the analyst considers only the worst outcome for each alternative and chooses the "best of the worst." In the table in the risk example, the outcomes that would be considered are $.3 million for alternative 1, $.2 million for alternative 2, $.4 million for alternative 3, and $.6 million for alternative 4. The best of these is alternative 4.

The third approach, the *principle of insufficient reason,* assumes that since we know

[5]You may have noticed something important about location 3. For every population rate (state of nature), location 4 has a better outcome than location 3. When one alternative is equal to or better than another for every possible state of nature, analysts say that it *dominates* that alternative. In this case, 4 dominates 3. Therefore 3 could be eliminated immediately.

TABLE S1.1 **Calculation of expected value ($ million)**

Alternative	Outcomes × Probabilities			Summation	Expected Value (profit)
1	$.3 × .2 = .06	$.8 × .3 = .24	$ .9 × .5 = .45	.06 + .24 + .45	= $.75
2	.2 × .2 = .04	.6 × .3 = .18	1.1 × .5 = .55	.04 + .18 + .55	= .77
3	.4 × .2 = .08	.5 × .3 = .15	.6 × .5 = .30	.08 + .15 + .30	= .53
4	.6 × .2 = .12	.7 × .3 = .21	.8 × .5 = .40	.12 + .21 + .40	= .73

absolutely nothing about the probabilities of any state of nature, we should treat each with equal probability, calculate the expected values accordingly, and choose the alternative whose expected value is highest. Using this approach, we would choose alternative 4.

Interdependence Among Decisions

A second way to classify problems relates to the number of decision stages that must be considered. At one extreme are single-stage, or static, problems; at the other are multistage, or sequential, problems. Static problems entail essentially "one-time-only" decisions. Decisions concerning inventory, "make versus buy," product mix, and location of new facility are often treated as static problems. Our supermarket chain example was treated this way. To simplify the situation, the decision is treated as if it were independent of other decisions.

Multistage problems, on the other hand, entail several sequential decisions related to one another. The outcome of the first decision affects the attractiveness of the choices at the next decision stage, and so on down the line at each decision point. With multistage problems, the concern is not how to get the best outcome at any single stage but how to make a *series* of choices that will finally result in the best overall set of outcomes from beginning to end. Sequential problems are commonly encountered by the operations manager in project management, capacity planning, and aggregate scheduling.

CASE

Safety Sight Company

Safety Sight Company owns two plants that manufacture bicycle headlights. The Edgewater plant is fully operational; the Garland facility has been shut down for the past two years. Management anticipates a large increase in demand for bicycle lights, and is now developing plans for future production. Revenue from the sale of headlights is expected to average $8 per unit over the foreseeable future.

The Edgewater plant has been using a single shift of workers with fixed costs of $2.5 million and a production capacity of 500,000 units annually. Unit variable costs have been $1.60 for this range of output. Greater output could be achieved by starting up a second shift. It is estimated that unit variable costs on the new shift would be either $6.3, $5.7, or $5.1 with probabilities of .09, .33, and .58, respectively. Production capacity on the second shift would be 500,000 units annually.

Alternatively, greater output could be achieved by reopening the Garland facility. The exact annual fixed cost of operating this facility is unknown. Three recent estimates were: $1.8, $1.65, and $1.55 million with probabilities of .4, .5, and .1, respectively. Unit variable cost for first shift operations is expected to be $1.60, the same as for the Edgewater plant. The first shift capacity of the Garland plant is expected to be 500,000 headlights per year.

Management is considering two alternatives: operate the Edgewater plant on two shifts, keeping the Garland plant shut down; or operate both plants on a single shift. Management is sure either alternative would provide capacity to meet the new expected demand. What should they do?

REVIEW AND DISCUSSION QUESTIONS

1. Discuss the advantages and disadvantages of these models in operations management:
   (a) Verbal
   (b) Schematic
   (c) Iconic
   (d) Mathematical
2. By definition, models are incomplete representations of the things being modeled. Discuss the reasons for this fact and its implications from a managerial point of view.
3. Develop a model of the operations function of a large apartment complex or a dormitory. Discuss the ways in which your model is useful and the ways it is limited.

PROBLEMS

1. A delivery company is considering the purchase of a used truck. Its useful service life is estimated to be 3 years with a probability of .1; 4 years with a probability of .4; 5 years with a probability of .3; and 6 years with probability of .2. What is the expected useful life of the used truck?
2. A cab company is considering three makes of autos—A, B, or C—to add to its taxi fleet. The daily operating cost of each make depends on the daily usage rate (demand) as shown here:

Cost per Day of Operation

	Daily Usage Rate		
Make	Low	Moderate	High
A	$100	$200	$300
B	190	200	220
C	150	190	230

Which make is best according to the maximin approach? According to the principles of insufficient reason? If the probabilities of low, moderate, and high usage are .5, .2, and .3, respectively, which make has the highest expected value?

3. Four alternative manufacturing methods are being considered for a new product. Profitability, which depends on method of manufacture and level of consumer acceptance, is anticipated as shown here.

Profits ($ thousands) from New Product

	Projected Consumer Acceptance			
Manufacturing Method	Low	Moderate	High	Very High
I	$100	$200	$300	$600
II	175	300	400	500
III	250	300	350	425
IV	100	300	400	450
Probability	.25	.35	.20	.20

(a) What is the best manufacturing method according to each of these approaches?
  (1) Expected value
  (2) Maximin
  (3) Maximax
  (4) Insufficient reason

(b) Which manufacturing method should be selected? Why?

CHAPTER 2

OPERATIONS STRATEGIES FOR COMPETITIVE ADVANTAGE

Arkansas Freightways is a regional, scheduled, for hire, common and contract motor carrier that transports primarily less-than-truckload (LTL) shipments of general commodities. We opened for business in October 1982 during the early stages of deregulation and at the peak of a recession. Initially, we operated 20 terminals and offered service to all points in Arkansas, as well as to Memphis, Tennessee; Dallas, Texas; and Kansas City, St. Louis, and Springfield, Missouri.

People in the industry—mainly our competitors—said I had lost my mind; we wouldn't last a month. From our inception, we targeted our resources to the service-sensitive segment rather than the price-sensitive segment of the market. Our strategy has been to emphasize pricing relative to the value of service to our customers; least price is not necessarily least cost.

AF's philosophy is to support its marketing efforts with quality performance to ensure a high rate of customer retention. We operate in a highly compressed time frame since our service standards call for the majority of freight to be delivered overnight or second day. So we place strong emphasis on achieving a consistently high level of performance. One of our biggest challenges has been developing managers that get the job done right the first time, yet at a very fast pace.

While our equipment may be the most visible aspect of our operations, we recognize that it is our people who set us apart from competitors. When we formed AF, we established five basic principles to guide us:

1. Take care of our customers
2. Take care of our people

3. Honor our commitments
4. Work hard, work smart, and work together
5. Have fun

They're very simple but they work for us. Since 1982 we have added 92 terminals. Today AF employs over 2,600 people and operates a fleet of over 1,300 tractors and 3,100 trailers. We now serve every point in Alabama, Arkansas, Kansas, Louisiana, Mississippi, Missouri, Oklahoma, Tennessee, Texas, and the metropolitan areas of Atlanta and Chicago.

F.S. Garrison
President & CEO
Arkansas Freightways, Inc.
Harrison, Arkansas

The best way to determine an organization's strategy is to observe what the organization actually accomplishes over time. Arkansas Freightways, Inc., it would appear, has followed a growth strategy, staying in the service business and market area it knows best. We know, however, that this successful business has emphasized profitable growth; growth with quality customer service, productive operations, and orderly development of capable operations managers and employees.

Arkansas Freightways' clean and modern fleet of tractors and trailers is the most visible proof of how the company represents the customer and cares for its freight.
Source: **Arkansas Freightways**

In this chapter we introduce strategic planning for production and operations and then identify several competitive pressures that successful managers, like Mr. Garrison, can turn into operating advantages for their firms.

STRATEGIC PLANNING

Strategic planning A process of thinking through the organization's current mission and environment and then setting forth a guide for tomorrow's decisions and results.

Strategic planning is the process of thinking through the current mission of the organization and *the current environmental conditions facing it, then setting forth a guide for tomorrow's decisions and results.* Strategic planning is built on fundamental concepts: that current decisions are based on *future* conditions and results, that strategic planning is a *process,* that it embodies a *philosophy,* and that it provides a *linkage* or structure within the organization.

STRATEGIC PLANNING FOR PRODUCTION AND OPERATIONS

Planning for operations Establishing a program of action for converting resources into goods or services.

Planning the conversion system Establishing a program of action for acquiring the necessary physical facilities to be used in the conversion process.

In the production or operations function, strategic planning is the broad, overall planning that precedes the more detailed operational planning. Executives who head the production and operations function are actively involved in strategic planning, developing plans that are consistent with the firm's overall strategies as well as such functions as marketing, finance accounting, and engineering.[1] Once developed, production and operations strategic plans are the basis for (1) operational planning of *facilities* (design) and (2) operational planning for the *use* of these facilities. In this book we emphasize these last two planning efforts, but we must also stress that such operational planning should not be done in a vacuum. It must come under the umbrella of effective strategic planning.

Strategic Planning Approaches for Production/Operations One specialist on strategic planning suggests three contrasting modes of strategic planning: the entrepreneurial, the adaptive, and the planning modes.[2] In the entrepreneurial mode, one strong, bold leader takes planning action on behalf of the production/operations function. In the adaptive mode, a manager's plan is formulated in a series of small, disjointed steps in reaction to a disjointed environment. The planning model uses planning essentials combined with the logical analysis of management science.

There are many approaches to strategic planning. The key point we want to make is that operations strategies must be consistent with the overall strategies of the firm. Our observations lead us to the conclusion that operations typically utilize the overall corporate approach to strategic planning, with special modifications and, of course, a focus upon operations issues and opportunities. For that reason we want to introduce one general approach to strategic planning—a forced choice model—and one specific approach especially developed for operations.

A Strategic Planning Forced Choice Model One of many planning models that has been used in strategic planning is a *forced choice model,* shown in Figure 2.1. In group sessions or individually, analysts assess environmental considerations together with the organization's current production/operations position, thus forcing management to

[1]Skinner makes this point when he argues that manufacturing and corporate strategy must be linked through an integrating mechanism—manufacturing strategy. See Wickham Skinner, *Manufacturing in the Corporate Strategy* (New York: John Wiley & Sons, 1978), 27–29.

[2]Henry Mintzberg, "Strategy-Making in Three Modes," *California Management Review* 16, no. 2 (Winter 1973), 44–53.

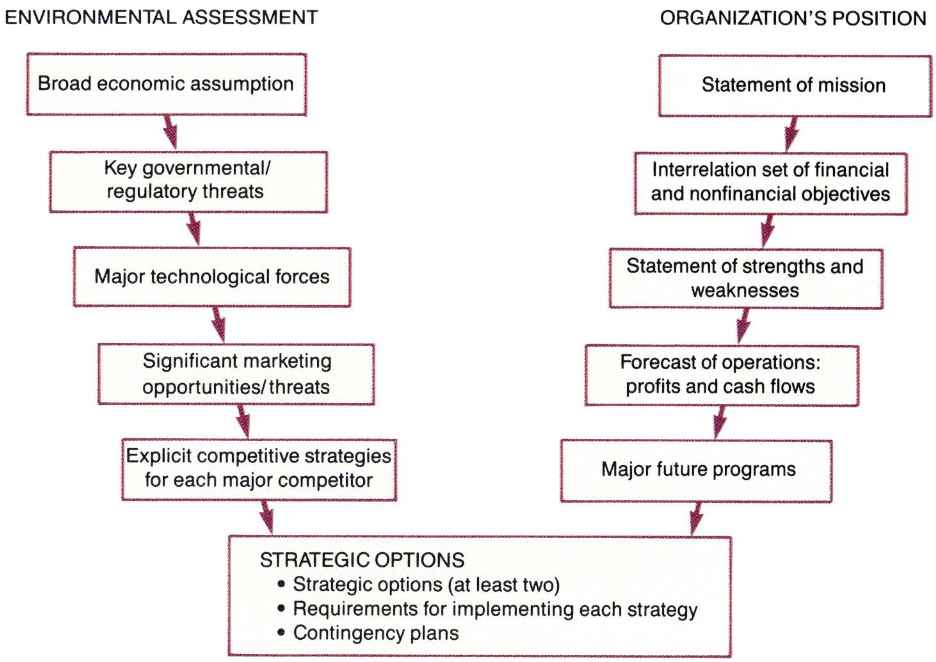

FIGURE 2.1 **A forced choice model of strategic planning for operations**
Source: Charles N. Greene, Everett E. Adam, Jr., and Ronald J. Ebert, *Management for Effective Performance* (Englewood Cliffs, N.J.: Prentice Hall, 1985), 544.

develop strategic options for operations. This model is explained in considerable detail, including how to apply it using structured group techniques, elsewhere.[3]

A Strategic Planning Operations Model Professor Chris A. Voss of the London Business School, England, has set forth a framework for strategy and policy development in manufacturing, which we have modified for services as well.[4] His concept is that manufacturing strategy tries to link the policy decisions associated with operations to the marketplace, the environment, and the company's overall goals. A simplified framework for examining operations strategy is shown in Figure 2.2. Note the relationship between the top of Figure 2.2 and Figure 2.1.

One feature of Professor Voss's approach that is crucial to competitiveness (and well understood by the Japanese) is his market-based view of strategic planning. He suggests that any strategic business unit of a company operates in the context of its corporate resources, the general and competitive industry environment, and the specific corporate goals of the company. In any area in which the company chooses to compete is a set of specific *market-based criteria for success,* as shown in Figure 2.3.

Efficiency makes low price possible, a prime criterion for success. A low-cost, high productivity operation makes efficiency possible. Minimum use of scarce resources—

[3]See Charles N. Greene, Everett E. Adam, Jr., and Ronald J. Ebert, *Management for Effective Performance* (Englewood Cliffs, N.J.: Prentice Hall, 1985), Ch. 17.

[4]Chris A. Voss, *Managing New Manufacturing Technologies,* Operations Management Association, Monograph No. 1 (1986), Appendix 2, pp. 65–68.

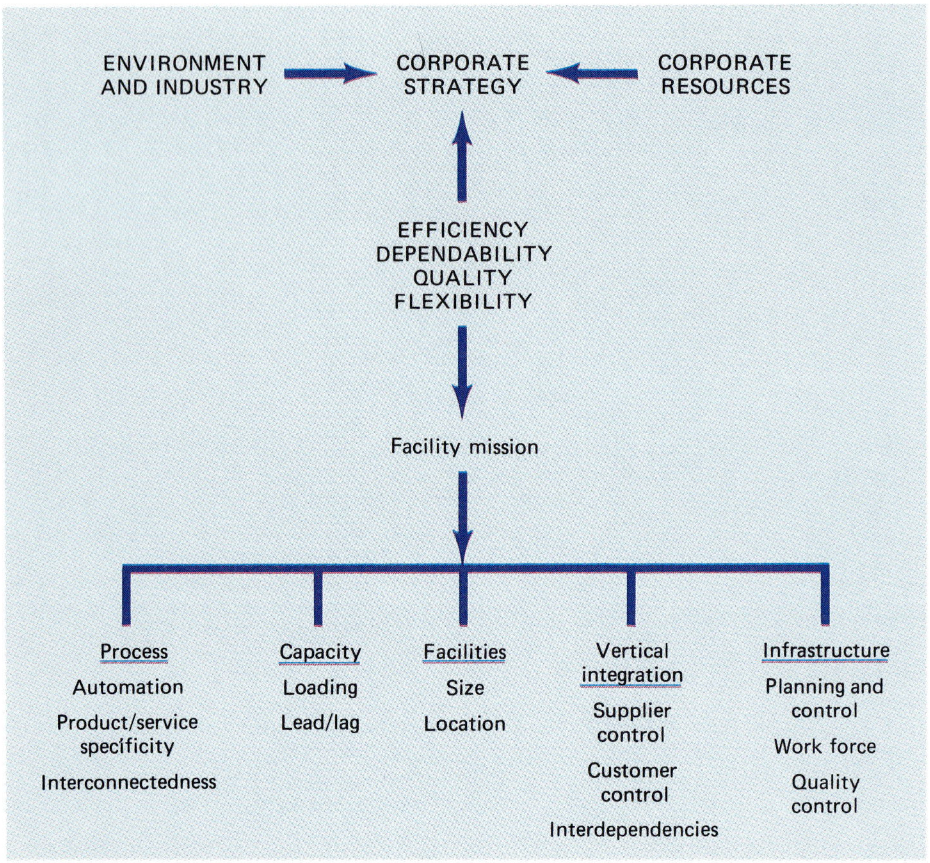

FIGURE 2.2 **Operations strategy framework**

labor, management, materials, equipment/facilities, and energy—while sustaining high outputs is the key to productivity. *Effectiveness* is how well a company is able to meet specific criteria such as delivery schedules and technical capability. *Quality* is the degree to which the product or service meets customer and organization expectations. Quality reflects the "goodness" of the product or service to the consumer. *Flexibility* is adaptability, the capability to change as business conditions change.

How does the planning model of Figure 2.2 work? Given a specific operations mission *established from market-based criteria for success*, operations managers must make choices. The main areas of choices, upon which we elaborate in Chapter 4, are

- *Facilities*—for example, the scale, location, and focus of the facilities
- *Aggregate capacity*—the policies governing the management of the sum capability of all business units; the maximum production available
- *Choice of process*—the type, technology, and product/service produced
- *Vertical integration*—the degree and nature of dependence from resources purchased through production to the consumer
- *Operations integration*—the labor policies, payment methods, systems of production and inventory control, which are key elements for management control

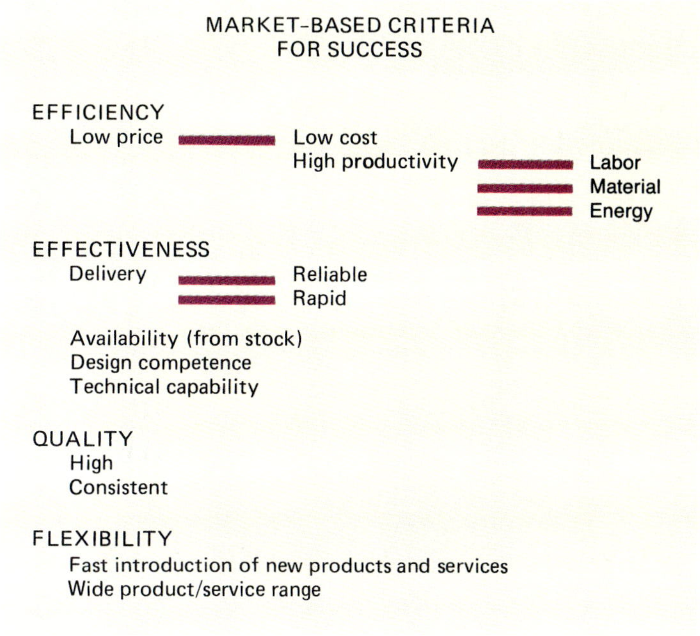

FIGURE 2.3 **Market-based criteria for success**

- *Operations interface with other functions*—the mechanisms for communicating with other functions

The combinations of choices made in all of the areas listed above represent the operations strategy of a particular firm.

Interestingly, Professor Voss explains failure in terms of market-based criteria as well. How does an organization fail? If a company is doing the following, it is liable to fail:

- Focusing on manufacturing performance criteria that do not match the market criteria for success
- Trying to meet incompatible criteria for success within a single market
- Trying to produce goods in a single factory for markets with very different criteria for success

Although there are many approaches to successful operations strategic planning, the question remains: What is the fundamental relationship between operations and markets?[5] We agree with Professor Voss in that either *the operations strategy must be changed and adapted to maximize the market criteria for success, or the chosen markets should*

[5]For other guides to successful manufacturing strategic planning and case implementation, see Skinner, *Manufacturing in the Corporate Strategy;* Roger W. Schmenner, "Multiplant Manufacturing Strategies Among the *Fortune* 500," *Journal of Operations Management* 2, no. 2 (February 1982), 77–86; Terry Hill, *Manufacturing Strategy* (London: Macmillan, 1985); and Roger G. Schroeder and T. N. Lahr, "Development of Manufacturing Strategy: A Proven Process," in *Manufacturing Strategy,* edited by John E. Ettlie et al. (Boston: Kluwer Academic Publishers, 1990), 3–14.

be changed to match more closely operations capability in terms of market criteria for success. Operations Management Highlight 2.1 further explores the process and content of operations strategies.

OPERATIONS MANAGEMENT HIGHLIGHT 2.1

Source: Stephen Marks/Stockphotos

The *Process* and *Content* of Operations Strategies

As firms sharpen their corporate strategies, a process develops that requires functional strategies in areas such as finance, marketing, and manufacturing or operations. The production and operations management discipline is actively addressing both the ***process*** and the ***content*** of manufacturing/operations

There are three competitive challenges to a firm's operations capability, and to these challenges we now turn: productivity and quality, technology and mechanization, and international operations management.

strategies in academics and practice alike. Business (corporate) strategic planners provided the example for the ***process*** and ***content*** approach. This dual approach to planning is beneficial for students and managers alike. Production management in the classroom can use strategic planning as an umbrella for covering operations decisions, thus providing structure for many detailed concepts and techniques. In firms everywhere production and operations managers are finding that their roles in strategic planning make them more proactive rather than simply reactive. In short, they can now help shape the firm and the directions the firm will take.

To illustrate, consider two major academic/industry conferences held in 1990 to share research and practice accomplishments—one in the United States at the University of Michigan and the other in England at the London Business School. They were co-sponsored by the Operations Management Association (OMA) and OMA-UK, respectively. Professor John Ettlie spearheaded the first conference while Professor Chris Voss, whose market-based criteria for success is presented here, headed the second. It was clear from presentations concerning the ***process*** of strategic planning that academics and industry can work together to develop guidelines for manufacturing strategy. (For example, a professor from the University of Minnesota has worked with the 3M company to develop a ten-step planning process that helps 3M operations managers, responsible for over 50,000 products manufactured world-wide, develop and carry out operations strategies. In England, professors from the Engineering College at Cambridge have developed a similar manufacturing planning process for a number of firms. The process is important, but what about the ***content*** of a good manufacturing (operations) strategy?

Wickham Skinner, a professor at the Harvard Business School and a pioneer in contemporary approaches to strategic planning, addresses content, suggesting that throughout the 1980s there was a great deal of research and experimentation concerning major "core" variables in manufacturing: productivity, cost, quality, delivery, and flexibility. He suggests that quality is the only variable that has significantly improved in the past ten years, and, even so, in the United States this improvement has ranked only four or five on a scale of ten. A great deal remains to be accomplished in academics and practice to improve manufacturing performance, not only for each "core" dimension but for the combinations of core dimensions.

Sources: John E. Ettlie, Michael C. Burstein, Avi Fiegenbaum, eds. _Manufacturing Strategy_ (Boston: Kluwer Academic Publishers, 1990); Chris A. Voss, ed. _"Manufacturing Strategy_—Theory and Practice," Proceedings of the 5th International Conference of the Operations Management Association—U.K., vols. I and II, June 1990; K. W. Platts and M. J. Gregory, "A Manufacturing Audit Approach to Strategy Formulation," in Voss, _Manufacturing Strategy_—Theory and Practice, 636–54; and Wickham Skinner, _"Manufacturing Strategy:_ On the S-Curve," Keynote address, Industry-University Conference on Manufacturing Strategy, University of Michigan, Ann Arbor, January 8, 1990. Everett E. Adam, Jr. and Paul M. Swamidass, "Assessing Operations Management from a Strategic Perspective," _Journal of Management_, 13, no. 2 (1989) 181–203; Roger G. Schroeder and T.N. Lahr, "Development of Manufacturing Strategy: A Proven Process," in Ettlie, _Manufacturing Strategy_, 3–4; Peter T. Ward, G. Keong Leong, and David L. Snyder, _"Manufacturing Strategy:_ An Overview of Current Process and Content Models," in Ettlie, _Manufacturing Strategy_, 189–99.

PRODUCTIVITY AND QUALITY

Efficiency, productivity, performance—these are terms we tend to use interchangeably in discussing behavior and achievement. Efficiency and productivity refer to a ratio of outputs to inputs; performance actually is a broader term incorporating efficiency and productivity in overall achievement.

Productivity Efficiency; a ratio of outputs to inputs. **Total factor productivity** is the ratio of outputs to the total inputs of labor, capital, materials, and energy; **partial factor productivity** is the ratio of outputs to one, two, or three of these inputs.

Productivity can be expressed on a *total factor* basis or on a *partial factor* basis. Total factor productivity is the ratio of outputs to all inputs:

$$\text{Productivity} = \frac{\text{Outputs}}{\text{Labor} + \text{Capital} + \text{Materials} + \text{Energy}} \tag{2.1}$$

Outputs relative to one, two, or three of these inputs labor, capital, materials, or energy—are *partial* measures of productivity. Output per labor hour, often called *labor efficiency,* is perhaps the most common partial measure of productivity.

EXAMPLE

Over the past year, a small restaurant has averaged 224 customers served each day. Hours are 6:00 A.M. to 2:00 P.M., and three employees make-up the total staff. Average labor productivity could be expressed as

$$\begin{aligned}\text{Labor productivity} &= \frac{\text{Output}}{\text{Labor input}}\\ &= \frac{\text{224 Customers served}}{\text{3 employees} \times \text{8 hours/employee}} = \frac{\text{224 customers}}{\text{24 hours}}\\ &= \text{8.1 customers served/hour}\end{aligned}$$

On Tuesday of this week, 264 customers were served by a full staff. On Wednesday, 232 customers were served, with two employees working full days and one working but two hours. We can find labor productivity for each day as

$$\text{Labor productivity (Tuesday)} = \frac{264}{3 \times 8} = \text{11.0 customers served/hour}$$

$$\text{Labor productivity (Wednesday)} = \frac{232}{(2 \times 8) + 2} = \text{12.9 customers served/hour}$$

For each day, labor productivity was well above the year's average, a level of labor performance that should please the owner (unless it caused customers to wait excessively for service).

Labor efficiency The ratio of outputs to labor input, the labor actually worked to achieve that output; A partial factor productivity measure.

LEVELS OF PRODUCTIVITY

Productivity can be viewed at two extremes. We can look at the level of an entire nation or at the level of an individual employee. In between these two extremes are industry, organization (firm), division (business unit), and work group levels. Figure 2.4 illustrates multifactor productivity—as well as the partial factors, capital and labor—for the U.S. business economy over a 20-year span. The data in the figure represent percent growth, calculated by finding the ratio of productivity for one year to the productivity for the next year. We can see that although it has been relatively stable, growth in labor productivity declined in the late 1970s before a recent increase.

	Annual Percent Growth Private, Non-Farm		
Period	Labor Productivity	Capital Productivity	Multifactor Productivity
1968-78	1.3%	(0.9)%	0.5%
1978-82	(0.4)	(4.4)	(1.8)
1982-86	2.1	1.6	2.0
1987	1.1	0.7	1.0
1988	2.1	N/A	N/A

FIGURE 2.4 **Multifactor Productivity Growth in the United States**
Source: Perspectives 1990 (Houston, Tex.: American Productivity and Quality Center, 1990), 3.

PRODUCTIVITY TRENDS

In Figure 2.4, we see a portion of stagnant U.S. productivity for the past decade. From 1960 to 1988, labor productivity growth never exceeded 4 percent in any one year. What about the contribution of capital? This is important to operations managers, as the tradeoff between investment and labor is always under scrutiny. Figure 2.4 illustrates that capital productivity is always less than multifactor productivity. Even though capital productivity has been increasing since 1982, it is still a drag on multifactor productivity.[6]

What does this mean? It means that capital has not contributed positively, overall, to productivity growth during the last few years in the U.S. economy. Prudent operations managers should be aware of this and should seek investments that clearly enhance productivity in their operations.

QUALITY AND PRODUCTIVITY

Quality The degree to which the design specifications for a product or service are appropriate to its function and use, and the degree to which a product or service conforms to its design specifications.

One reason that the competitive position of a firm can falter is that the quality of goods and services produced does not meet the customer's expectations. When *quality*—the appropriateness of design specifications to function and use as well as the degree to which outputs conform to the design specifications—is poor, demand for products and services can diminish quickly. But what does this have to do with productivity?

There is a clear relationship between quality and productivity. Generally, when quality increases, so will productivity. Why? Because waste is eliminated. The amount of inputs (the denominator of the productivity ratio) required to produce outputs (the numerator) is reduced. Productivity increases.

If this is so simple, why haven't all U.S. firms figured this out? Many have. Even if one accepts this view, however, achieving high quality is not all that simple. There are also other views of the quality-productivity relationship.

One such view is that quality and productivity move in opposite directions. Think

[6] *Productivity Perspectives 90* (Houston, Tex.: American Productivity and Quality Center, 1990), 3.

Productivity and quality go hand-in-hand on this computer assembly line. Productivity increases when quality is improved because waste and rework are reduced.
Source: **Jay Brousseau / The Image Bank**

about such processes as typing or data entry at a computer keyboard. As your speed increases, what tends to happen? You tend to make more errors, especially when you go very fast. Logically, it follows that if you type slowly and carefully, you will make fewer errors. There is a tradeoff between accuracy and speed. As accuracy (quality) increases, speed (and productivity) decrease.

How can these two contrasting positions concerning quality-productivity relationships be resolved? We believe the answer is in the concept of *capability*. We suggest that as long as there is unused capability in the individual (such as the typist) or the operations system (such as a manufacturing facility), increases in speed (and productivity) can be achieved without declines in quality. Or, alternatively, quality can be improved without changing speed. If we focus on improving quality while holding speed constant, quality should increase, waste should be eliminated, and productivity should increase. This can happen as long as the individual, or group of individuals, is willing to exert effort and has the capability to achieve the quality-productivity levels desired. It is the operations manager's task to provide the facilities, tools, and desire (motivation) to do so. This is a very difficult task.

A Quality-Productivity Strategy Improving quality is one important way to maintain a competitive position in today's markets. Quality can be promoted to customers and employees. Consumers want quality products and services, and employees at all levels in the organization like to be associated with a winner. Most people associate high quality with a winning competitive position. Although employees may balk when they are encouraged to work more productively (because they feel they are being told to work faster), very few, if any, will argue with quality as a goal.

From an economic perspective, when quality is emphasized and subsequently improved, waste is decreased or eliminated. Hours are not wasted reworking products.

Material is not thrown away. Operations costs are reduced. At the same time, the customer receives products and services that are "fit" for use. Moreover, prices can be lowered to share this productivity gain with customers, thereby stimulating an increase in the firm's market share. Or, alternatively, the higher-quality product (as compared with competitors' product offerings) can command a premium price and temporarily secure a market niche. Market niche is often temporary since high price invites competitors. To employees, these results mean increased job security because of a sound competitive position. Stockholders can benefit through higher overall profits and improved asset utilization. In short, high quality can make everyone a winner—a message some firms and managers seem to understand better than others.

Understanding and accepting this quality-productivity strategy is a first step toward its achievement. We encourage you to think seriously about this line of reasoning as you read on.

QUALITY AND PRODUCTIVITY IMPROVEMENT EFFORTS

Let's look at a few examples of firms that are seeking to improve productivity and quality and, thus, their competitive positions.

EXAMPLE

Westinghouse Electric Company, as a worldwide competitor in a variety of consumer, industrial, defense, and aerospace sectors, has a vital interest in improving quality and productivity. Thomas J. Murrin, president of the Public Systems Company, a division of Westinghouse, remarked at a conference in Washington a few years ago:

"At Westinghouse, we are putting top-priority emphasis on productivity and quality improvement, not only because it is necessary for the well-being of our corporation, but because we believe it is vital for the economic survival of our nation and for our national security.

About three and one-half years ago, we started this corporatewide top-priority emphasis on productivity improvement for two basic reasons. First was our need to further improve our corporate performance, and the second was our concern over increasing international competition. We didn't want this to be a one-shot effort, but rather we wanted productivity improvement to become a way of life throughout the corporation.

In early 1979 we formed a Corporate Committee on Productivity, and I was assigned to chair it. Initially, our committee spent many months studying the situation—first in the United States, then in Europe, and then in the Pacific Basin, particularly in Japan. Significantly, we didn't anticipate, at the outset, that most of our studies would find the Japanese to be so formidable. In my case, I've been visiting Japan for almost 20 years. But for the first 17 years, as a teacher—and only the past three years, as a student. This "role change" makes an immense difference.

Significantly also, we didn't realize, at the outset, that quality is as important to productivity as are people and technology."[7]

As Mr. Murrin's remarks illustrate, members of Westinghouse management were profoundly impressed with Japanese manufacturing technology. They were particularly

[7]Thomas J. Murrin, "Productivity and Quality Improvement," Remarks to Defense Logistics Agency, Bottom Line Conference (Washington, D.C., May 13, 1982).

affected by the devotion to quality among their Japanese counterparts. Since then, Westinghouse has undertaken initiatives to adopt quality circles, new technology, and a quality improvement emphasis by concurrently designing both the product and the manufacturing process. What has Westinghouse achieved? Setting a goal of 6 percent a year in value added (by Westinghouse) per employee, the Westinghouse Public Systems Company achieved a 7-percent-a-year gain over three years (1979–1982). The Public Systems Company is now seeking a 10 percent improvement per year.

In addition to individual company examples, a new service industry is organizing improvement efforts into productivity centers and institutes, with more than 300 known centers worldwide.[8] These centers typically have any of four thrusts—training and education, information distribution and promotion, sociotechnical approaches, and

[8]Robert R. Britney, *1984–85 International Directory of Productivity Centers* (University of Western Ontario, 1985); Robert R. Britney, Randolph P. Kudar, David A. Johnston, and John Walsh, "A Comparison of International Productivity Centers," *National Productivity Review*

OPERATIONS MANAGEMENT HIGHLIGHT 2.2

Source: John Zoiner

TRW Translates People into Productivity Improvement

TRW is a multinational, highly diversified corporation with over $7 billion in sales, $3 billion in assets, and 73,000 employees operating in 27 different countries. Products range from car parts to satellite industrial engineering and managerial economic emphasis—reflecting the interests of the firms (consumers of center services) they are serving. Perhaps the best known North American facility is the American Productivity and Quality Center located in Houston, Texas.

Services, Quality, and Productivity It should be emphasized that the changes in our thinking about productivity and quality apply not just to factories and blue-collar workers but to service industries and offices as well. What promise is there for productivity and quality improvement in services, particularly in white-collar services? Operations Management Highlight 2.2 provides some insight into the quest for improved white-collar productivity.

(Winter 1986–1987) 71–76; and Robert R. Britney, David A. Johnston, J. M. Legentil, and John Walsh, "Planning for Productivity Gains Within the Firm," Working Paper 82–38 (London, Canada: School of Business Administration, University of Western Ontario, October 1982).

systems; about one-half of sales comes from aerospace and defense and about one-half from the automotive business.

TRW is the second largest computer software producer in the nation, behind only IBM. While 40 percent of TRW's workers are now involved in manufacturing, that number will fall to 5 percent by the year 2000, according to Henry P. Conn, TRW's former vice president for productivity.

TRW has one fundamental objective: to achieve superior performance, with special emphasis on high-quality products and services. This translates into seven goals: high quality at competitive prices, market strength, diversification, management and technological innovation, maximum productivity, and effective use of outside-the-company resources (consultants, training, etc.).

TRW achieves their objectives by focusing on people. Managers are doing what they should be doing—planning, guiding, communicating, and supporting employees at all levels. Employees are working with a new sense of involvement. TRW utilizes a variety of involvement techniques, including a "pay for knowledge" approach at the Romeo, Michigan, automotive air bag supply plant. At Romeo, production workers can achieve one of five levels based on knowledge, ascending to master technician or master leader. A strategic approach that integrates human relations into functional strategies is paying off for the firm.

For example, TRW has improved efficiency in computer software–writer jobs. Writers spend less time talking on the telephone, filing, attending meetings, or staring out windows. Instead, they spend as much time as possible actually writing the lines of code that guide missiles or track satellites. They now have individual rather than grouped terminals, computerized mail, and teleconferencing—all with the intent of working more at line activities that add value to the service the company is producing and selling. In yet another example, TRW saves $1.3 million per year in electricity by using occupancy sensors in 8,000 offices, laboratories, and rooms to turn off the lights. If no motion is detected in a room for 8 to 12 minutes, the lights go off. This investment paid for itself in just over one year. White-collar employees—engineers in this example—came up with a bright idea indeed!

Sources: *Moody's Industrial Manual,* 1989; Jon Martin, "Let People Deal with the Issues," *Manufacturing Engineering* 103, 2, (August 1989), 75–76; "Automatic Lighting Controls," *Plant Engineering* 43, no. 11 (June 1989), 88–90; and Martha I. Finnely, "From Suits to Satellites," *Personnel Administrator* 34, no. 6 (June 1989), 54–58; "Faced with a Changing Work Force, TRW Pushes to Raise White Collar Productivity," *Wall Street Journal,* August 22, 1983; William A. Ruch, "the Measurement of White-Collar Productivity," *National Productivity Review* (Autumn 1982), pp. 416–26; and William A. Ruch and William B. Werther, Jr., "Productivity Strategies at TRW," *National Productivity Review* (Spring 1983), pp. 109–26.

TECHNOLOGY AND MECHANIZATION

In Chapter 1 we referred to the *conversion process* as the central element of the production and operations function. The work of operations management revolves around conversion, where resource inputs are converted or transformed into useful products and services. This conversion process is present in most organizations, but it is distinctly different for a bank, an aerospace firm, or a public utility. The basic technologies of operations differ among industries as well as within various organizations in any one industry. In the public utility, for example, the firm requires engineering skills to design facilities, maintenance skills for various mechanical and electrical applications, and operating skills for larger pieces of equipment used in operations. *The blending of labor, land, capital, and management—and the scientific expertise needed for this task—are at the very heart of technology* in operations.

Strategic planning is important to service as well as manufacturing operations.
Source: **Oscar Palmquist / Lightwave**

Mechanization The process of bringing about the use of equipment and machinery in production and operations.

In some instances, machinery is substituted for hand labor. *Mechanization is the process of bringing about the use of equipment and machinery* in production and operations. In a bank, for example, some jobs—such as reconciling checking accounts and preparing statements—are mechanized. Other tasks, such as the interview in which information is gathered by a loan officer to start the loan process, are not mechanized.

Organizations today face decisions about which technology to use and the degree of mechanization. Many of the challenges for improved productivity and quality are answered by managers and owners as they adopt more sophisticated technologies and increased mechanization. Competitors who effectively substitute capital and equipment for labor to lower operating costs may increase market share very quickly. For example, highly mechanized companies in Japan and Korea caused the U.S. steel industry to lose market shares. On the other hand, mechanization, when it is unnecessary or inappropriate, may be quite costly. A firm may be saddled with high fixed costs relative to other companies in the industry. Management may be unable to reduce variable costs of manufacturing sufficiently to recover the costs of mechanization.

What degree of technological change, mechanization, and automation is strategically best for any one organization? Responding correctly to this question is often critical to the survival of the business. It takes experience and wisdom to make such a decision; these qualities cannot be learned in a book. However, we can introduce you to some of the mechanization alternatives that businesses face today. Through our discussion of these choices—such as computers, robotics, and computer-aided design—in Chapter 4, you may gain some insights into the complexity of these decisions and the cost/benefit tradeoffs that are involved.

INTERNATIONAL OPERATIONS MANAGEMENT

The world is shrinking, and worldwide economic competition is intensifying. Improvements in transportation and communication makes nations seem closer together. As one nation becomes aware of the products and services available in the world at large, demand for those items and services tends to increase. And how is that demand met? In some cases it is not met, especially among poor nations. In other cases, products and services are produced by a given country for internal consumption. In still other situations, goods are imported while services are still produced locally (since most services cannot be stored). Yet another alternative is for the producing nation to transfer its conversion know-how to the consuming nation. This approach is currently being used by companies that provide services; it is also increasingly prevalent among firms that manufacture products (through licensing arrangements). As a result, there is heightened interest in the *international dimension of production and operations.* Although our interest is managerial, that is, an interest in the similarities and differences of operations management within different nations, we cannot fully understand the management issues without some understanding of the economics involved.

THE INTERNATIONAL PRODUCTIVITY CHALLENGE IN PRODUCTION AND OPERATIONS

How does the growth in productivity in the United States compare with that in other industrialized countries? Between 1979 and 1988, the average annual increase in labor productivity was 1.0 percent in the United States, 1.2 percent in Canada, 1.8 percent in the United Kingdom, 2.0 percent in France, 3.0 percent in Japan, and 5.5 percent in Korea. Korea is at the forefront and the United States and Canada bring up the rear.

Rate of growth is important over the long term, but what are the relative bases of each nation? That is, now that we see who is running the fastest (Korea), who is at the head of the pack? As Figure 2.5 illustrates, Switzerland and the United States are first, with most other industrial nations ahead of Korea in terms of gross domestic product (GDP, an output measure) per employee. The nations most likely to surpass the United States are Japan, West Germany, and France, as they have both high productivity and high productivity growth rates.

$000/Capita	Western Hemisphere	Europe	Pacific Basin	Africa & Near East
18.6 +		Switzerland		
18.5	United States			
12.8–18.4	Canada	Norway Sweden Denmark West Germany Finland France	Japan	United Arab Emirates Kuwait
10.3–12.7		Austria Netherlands Belgium United Kingdom Italy	Australia	
4.0–10.2	Trinidad	Ireland Spain Greece	Hong Kong New Zealand Singapore	Saudi Arabia Israel Oman Libya
1.8–3.9	Venezuela Argentina Surinam Panama Uruguay Brazil Mexico	Portugal Yugoslavia Hungary Poland	Korea Malaysia	Gabon Algeria South Africa

FIGURE 2.5 Level of GNP per Capita for the Top 45 Reporting Countries, 1987
Source: Perspectives 1990 (Houston, Tex.: American Productivity and Quality Center, 1990), 3.

MAJOR MANUFACTURING DIFFERENCES AMONG JAPAN, EUROPE, AND NORTH AMERICA

Further insights into differences among nations are revealed in a major study by Professors Arnaud DeMeyer and Kasra Ferdows (INSEAD, France), Jinchiro Nakane (Science Institute, Japan), and Jeffrey G. Miller (Boston University, U.S.A.), who conduct an annual survey of future directions in manufacturing. Their report for 1987 contrasted the opinions of 186 U.S., 174 European, and 214 Japanese executives.[9] In 1986, these high-level executives had average sales of $918 million in their business unit.

Competitive Priorities One way to compare manufacturing among industrial centers in the world is to examine the varying competitive priorities listed in Table 2.1.[10] In this table, priorities are presented in decreasing order of importance. The North American executives reflect an emphasis on quality, performance, and service. The Japanese are more concerned with price, speed, and new products. European executives are more like their North American counterparts; they list quality, performance, and service as being most important.

TABLE 2.1 Competitive priorities*

Europe	North America	Japan
1. Consistent quality (1) (1) (1)	1. Consistent quality (1) (1) (1)	1. Low prices (1) (1) (1)
2. High-performance products (3) (2) (2)	2. High-performance products (2) (2) (3)	2. Rapid design changes (2) (2) (2)
3. Dependable deliveries (2) (3) (3)	3. Dependable deliveries (3) (3) (2)	2. Consistent quality (3) (3) (2)
4. Fast delivery (6) (6) (5)	4. Low prices (6) (5) (5)	4. Dependable deliveries (4) (4) (5)
5. Low prices (5) (5) (6)	5. Fast deliveries (4) (4) (4)	5. Rapid volume changes (6) (6) (6)
6. Rapid design changes (5) (5) (6)	6. Rapid design changes (7) (5) (7)	6. High-performance products (4) (4) (4)
7. After-sales service (8) (8) (7)	7. After-sales service (5) (7) (6)	7. Fast delivery (8) (7) (7)
8. Rapid volume changes (7) (7) (8)	8. Rapid volume changes (8) (8) (8)	8. After-sales service (7) (8) (8)

*The priorities are listed according to their importance as ranked in the 1986 survey. Numbers within brackets indicate the ranking of the competitive priorities in 1983, 1984, and 1985, respectively.
Source: DeMeyer, et al., 1987, "Flexibility."

What are the groups doing about these competitive practices? Here we see fewer similarities between North America and Europe (Table 2.2). North American executives are clearly focused on quality improvement, with their top three action items and four of their top six items. The top three action items for European executives are direct labor motivation, production and inventory control systems, and automating jobs. Japanese executives have action plans focused on flexible manufacturing systems,

[9]Arnaud DeMeyer, Jinchiro Nakane, Jeffrey G. Miller, and Kasra Ferdows, "Flexibility: The Next Competitive Battle," *Manufacturing Roundtable Research Report Series* (Boston University School of Management, February 1987). The authors express their gratitude for a willingness on the part of these scholars to share their study results.

[10]*Ibid.*, p. 9.

quality circles, and production and inventory control systems. Reacting to this North American concern for quality, treatment of quality improvement comprises two chapters in this book (Chapters 16 and 17).

TABLE 2.2 The ten most important action plans*

Europe	North America	Japan
Direct labor motivation (3)	Statistical process control (7)	Flexible manufacturing systems (1)
Production and inventory control systems (4)	Zero defects ( )	Quality circles (3)
Automating jobs (2)	Vendor quality (2)	Production and inventory control systems (4)
Integrating information systems in manufacturing (1)	Improving new product introduction capability ( )	Automating jobs (2)
Supervisor training (6)	Production and inventory control systems (1)	Lead-time reduction (9)
Manufacturing reorganization (10)	Statistical product control ( )	Introduction of new processes for new products (2)
Integrating information systems across functions (7)	Integration of information systems in manufacturing (1)	Reducing set-up time (10)
Defining a manufacturing strategy (11)	Developing new process for new products (10)	Direct labor motivation (8)
Lead-time reduction (12)	Direct labor motivation (8)	Worker safety (6)
Vendor quality (5)	Lead-time reduction ( )	Giving workers a broader range of tasks ( )

*Numbers between brackets indicate rank order in 1985. If no rank order is indicated, in 1985 the rank order was higher than 12. For previous years, these data were collected somewhat differently, and comparisons of rank orders are difficult to make.
Source: DeMeyer, et al., 1987, "Flexibility."

The 1990 manufacturing futures survey of 184 U.S. executives indicates significant changes in both their competitive priorities and their action plans.[11] The emphasis on quality remains dominant. Competing on price and developing products faster have become significantly more important. Action plans have changed as well. Statistical process control continues to be important but plans also emphasize job

[11]Jeffrey G. Miller and Jay S. Kim, "Beyond the Quality Revolution: U. S. Manufacturing Strategy in the 1990s," *Executive Summary of the 1990 Manufacturing Futures Survey* (Boston University School of Management, 1990).

enrichment, training, and work teams. All of the changes reflect the increasing role of U.S. manufacturers in the global market.

UNDERSTANDING THE JAPANESE CHALLENGE FOR PRODUCTION AND OPERATIONS

The Japanese post–World War II economic success has been phenomenal by any historical standard. Japan has experienced a higher growth rate in productivity (6.2 percent) than the United States (1.5 percent) over the last decade. Yet Japan's overall productivity, as measured by gross domestic production per employee, was but 75.5 percent of that of the United States in 1985. Japan is catching up with the United States, but it still needs to make a lot of progress. Still, North American managers and students are keenly interested in Japanese management style and in discovering what the Japanese do differently. We have chosen to defer our discussion of Japan to Chapter 15. By that point in the book, you can better assess Japanese contributions because you will be more familiar with the concepts, models, and behaviors within the operations function.

MEETING THE INTERNATIONAL CHALLENGES IN PRODUCTION AND OPERATIONS MANAGEMENT

Predictions about the critical international issues that will face operations managers in the mid-1990s and beyond are speculative indeed. Operations Management Highlight 2.3 introduces us to *maquiladora* traffic, an interesting development between the United States and Mexico. Clearly, however, as you begin your career in operations, you will encounter issues and problems at the grass-roots level within the organization. And, as you progress through your career, you will become more involved with deciding the overall strategies your firm must pursue in its operations. With this broader perspective in mind, the following operations issues are important to ensure success in international competition.

1. Productivity is increasing at a faster rate in other nations than it is in the United States. This progress must be monitored both in terms of nations and individual firms. Which countries are moving fastest to catch the leader in productivity, the United States?
2. Industry-by-industry productivity analyses within a national economy allow operations executives to focus broadly on their competition.
3. Firm-by-firm comparisons and case situations in other nations can be helpful. What are our strongest foreign competitors doing? How are they doing it? Why?
4. Quality might well be the strategic variable to make a firm competitive internationally.
5. If developing nations have labor advantages, what should the operations strategy be? Replace high-cost U.S. workers with (1) mechanization, or (2) direct ownership of overseas (foreign) plants in developing countries with low labor costs? What are the economic tradeoffs among mechanization, worldwide labor costs, transportation, and other cost factors in our operations?

OPERATIONS MANAGEMENT HIGHLIGHT 2.3

Source: John Zoiner

Maquiladoras — an International Development with Far-Reaching Potential for U.S. Manufacturing

North Americans don't have to study Pacific Basin nations or Eastern Europe to examine the impact of lower labor costs on manufacturing and trade. While Japan utilizes satellite plants in South Korea and Taiwan, and Germany has become one nation with two distinct labor forces, U.S. businesses need only to look south to the Mexican border for manufacturing labor advantages.

During 1990 some $50 billion flowed across the Mexican–U.S. border in ***maquiladora*** traffic, up from about $30 billion during 1986. The center of the flow is El Paso, Texas, where over 400 facilities straddle the United States and Mexico. The effect of the ***maquiladora*** development is somewhat analogous to the way the railroad helped to settle the western United States over a century ago, though the economics are different. ***Maquiladora*** means "twin plant," which refers to production plants in two different places. In this situation, the twins are in the United States and Mexico.

The lure for U.S. industry is cheap Mexican labor. Foreign-owned Mexican manufacturing plants have demonstrated they can compete on labor costs not only with the United States, but, with Asia. Mexican workers are plentiful and are paid about one-seventh the U.S. wage. Chrysler, Ford, General Foods, General Electric, Miller Brewing . . . the list of major American firms operating on the U.S.–Mexican border grows: over 500,000 Mexican workers are employed in some 1,800 ***maquiladora*** plants.

Mexico is looking for European and Japanese investors as well. For the time being, however, it is primarily U.S. firms that bring parts to the border, where they are assembled by low-cost labor and then returned to U.S. markets. Transportation within the United States and Mexico is still controlled and operated by each country. Problems abound in the education and technology of the Mexican work force, as well as in the cultural attitudes about quality craftsmanship. Yet the economics, for now, seem to favor investment in plants, equipment, and the work force. Will a free trade zone emerge? Will North America resemble a Pacific Basin or European manufacturing region without national boundaries? If a free trade zone did emerge, a Canadian–United States–Mexican trading block would outstrip the Western Europe Economic Community 1992, some $6 trillion to $4.8 trillion in annual output. This certainly will not occur immediately, but the ***maquiladoras*** are an international development to monitor and understand.

Source: **"Inching Toward a North American Market"** ***Business Week*** **(June 25, 1990), 40–41; "Along the Border, Free Trade Is Becoming a Fact of Life,"** ***Business Week*** **(June 18, 1990), 41–42; William C. Gruben, "Mexican Maquiladora Growth: Does It Cost U.S. Jobs?"** ***Economic Review*** **(Federal Reserve Bank of Dallas, January 1990), 15–29; Philip Mirowski and Susan Helper, "Maquiladoras: Mexico's Tiger by the Tail?"** ***Challenge*** **2, no. 3 (May/June 1990), 24–30; and Mariah E. DeForest, "A Manager's Guide to a Successful Maquiladora,"** ***Manufacturing Systems*** **6, no. 6 (June 1988), 24–25.**

6. What can we learn from the Pacific Basin countries, especially Japan, about management style and manufacturing practices?[12]
7. As the political and economic climate changes—for example, as changes in Eastern Europe and the Soviet Union occur—what opportunities and threats exist for the operations function?

These issues seem critical to successful global operations. We hope that you share our excitement about this challenge.

MEETING THE COMPETITIVE CHALLENGE IN OPERATIONS MANAGEMENT

Our attention has been focused on strategic planning and three major competitive issues: productivity and quality, mechanization and technology, and international operations management. The challenges are before us. It should be exhilarating to manage operations in the remainder of this century. Businesses, government agencies, academics, and students are taking production and operations management seriously. The function is becoming increasingly significant in our society. In the remainder of this book, we will try to equip you with a knowledge of the concepts, models, and behavioral approaches you will need in order to meet the challenges ahead.

SUMMARY

This chapter illustrated how a firm's broad strategy is reflected in specific operations strategies so that managers can respond to market changes or, over time, find new markets for the firm's operations capacity.

Consumers, owners, citizens, and employees are increasingly aware of the competitive environment in which they live. Within individual organizations, operations challenges are substantial. In this chapter we focused on *productivity and quality, technology and mechanization,* and *international operations management.* We discovered that recent U.S. productivity has not increased as rapidly as during the post–World War II period. The quality-productivity connection was discussed as a strategic issue for the firm. Our presentation of the international challenge in operations built upon your growing knowledge of productivity; we also examined the accomplishments of Europe and Japan as compared with the United States.

The competitive challenges presented in this chapter abound in many organizations. The balance of the book focuses on meeting these challenges through a better understanding of operations concepts, models, and behavioral approaches.

[12]We have not touched on activities in China, both the Peoples Republic of China and Taiwan, which are emerging competitors with Korea and other nations. See, for example, Leon S. Lasdon, "Operations Research in China," *Interfaces* 10, no. 1 (February 1980), 23–27, and Paul Gray and Burton V. Dean, "The Chinese–U.S. Symposium on Systems Analysis," *Interfaces* 12, no. 1 (February 1982), 44–49.

CASE

Martha's Burger Queen

Martha Thompson, who has worked in restaurants for 20 years, opened her first short-order "Mom-and-Pop" café 12 years ago. She is regarded in her community as an excellent small-business person. In 1985 she sold her small café and went to work as a professional manager for a fast-food hamburger franchise. In 1987 she resigned and opened Martha's Original Burger Queen. Martha's salary is 25 percent higher than the one she earned as a professional manager. In 1987 her Burger Queen broke even; in 1988 it had a net profit after taxes of $10,000. Martha then opened two more restaurants in the same city. The results of all three restaurants are summarized in the accompanying comprehensive report.

Martha states her strategy: "My restaurant concept is to copy fast-food chains such as McDonald's, Burger King, and Jack-in-the-Box. I've tried parties, soybean burgers, breakfast, and larger sandwiches to increase dollar sales per customer. I believe that I should expand rapidly just as those chains seem to be doing, yet maintain a personable, local operations staff and a 'homey' atmosphere. But I seem to have less efficient operations than we did when I managed for a chain. I think my layout is good, as is my food quality. I can't buy in larger volumes, but I do try to turn over my inventory at least weekly. I believe in women employees, especially in management positions. I hire Caucasians, African-Americans, and Mexican-Americans, so no one can say I'm prejudiced."

Martha's response to net income difficulties at the second and third restaurants is, "I need to open more restaurants to spread out my fixed costs. Expansion of operations is my strategy, but I'm finding financing hard to come by now."

Martha's Burger Queen comprehensive report

	Martha's Original Restaurant: MBQ1		MBQ2		MBQ3	
	1989	1990	1989	1990	1989	1990
Sales summary						
Revenues	$330,000	$370,000	$210,000	$200,000	$170,000	$150,000
Number of customers	132,000	130,000	91,000	90,000	85,000	85,000
Revenues/customer	$2.50	$2.84	$2.30	$2.22	$2.00	$1.76
Expense summary						
Equipment depreciation	$16,500	$16,500	$10,500	$10,500	$8,500	$8,500
Building lease	33,000	33,000	21,000	21,000	17,000	17,000
Operations: Food	82,500	83,400	52,500	52,500	42,500	51,000
Labor	115,500	129,000	73,500	73,500	68,000	68,000
Supplies	16,000	18,000	10,000	10,000	8,500	8,500
Overhead	17,000	17,000	11,000	11,000	8,500	8,500
Gross margin selling and administrative costs						
Advertising	15,000	15,000	12,000	12,000	9,000	9,000
Administration	18,000	18,000	9,000	9,000	8,000	8,000
Net income (loss) before taxes						
	$16,500	$40,100	$10,500	$500	-0-	($28,500)

Case Questions

1. Of the various strategic planning modes, which do you believe most typifies Martha's Burger Queen? List characteristics of both the strategy mode and Martha's operations that support your choice.
2. Examining the comprehensive report, does the data support the idea that Martha needs a change in operations strategy? If so, which data?
3. Set forth what you believe is a good overall business strategy for Martha. Specify an operations strategy that is consistent with the overall strategy.

REVIEW AND DISCUSSION QUESTIONS

1. Explain total factor productivity. What is partial factor productivity? What partial factor productivity is likely to be measured most frequently in production/operations management?
2. Figure 2.1 provides a good *process* for strategic planning in operations, while Figure 2.2 provides more detail on the *content* of an operations strategy. Explain.
3. Explain the relationship between quality and productivity. Discuss the theory that says quality and productivity (a) move in the same direction or (b) move in opposing directions. Which do you accept? Why?
4. If a firm accepts quality as the strategic variable for improving operations, what results might the firm expect? How would the firm go about improving its competitive position in that manner?
5. Do operations strategies take into account changing market conditions by adapting capability to the market or by finding new markets to fit existing operations capability? Discuss.
6. Consider beginning a new venture—opening a wine and cheese shop in a shopping mall. Using Figure 2.2 as a guide, develope an operations strategy to guide the overall operations of your new venture.
7. Contrast the major manufacturing differences among Japan, Europe, and North America based on the executive survey conducted by DeMeyer, Nakane, Miller, and Ferdows (1987).
8. Near the end of this chapter is a speculative list of several operations issues important to success in international competition. Select any one of these aspects and explain why you think it is important.
9. Briefly explain how *productivity, technology and mechanization,* and *international business* interrelate as they collectively become a formidable challenge to production and operations managers during the remainder of this century.

PROBLEMS

REINFORCING FUNDAMENTALS

1. An insurance company has a group standard in the claims department to process 1,250 claims per day when fully staffed with 52 employees. Consider the following data and compute labor productivity for each of the last four weeks. What do your results suggest?

Week (5 days)	Average Employees	Claims Processed
35	50	6250
36	51	6200
37	51	5850
38	51	5950

2. In Problem 1, if the group productivity standard is maintained, the contribution to profit for each claim processed is $11. To achieve this contribution, $13.75/hour in total labor and fringe benefits is expended, as well as computer equipment and labor support of $12,000/employee/year. In the most recent month, computer costs average $1,200/employee in the claims department.

(a) Compute total standard costs per month for claims.

(b) Determine the total factor productivity (labor and computer) in claims last month.

(c) What is the net contribution to profit, after productivity gains (or losses), for the month?

KEY TERMS

Labor efficiency 46
Mechanization 52
Partial factor productivity 46
Planning for operations 40
Planning the conversion system 40
Productivity 46
Quality 47
Strategic planning 40
Total factor productivity 46

SELECTED READINGS

Adam, Everett E., Jr. and Paul M. Swamidass, "Assessing Operations Management from a Strategic Perspective," *Journal of Management* Vol 13, no. 2 (1989), 181–203.

American Productivity Center, *Productivity Perspectives.* Houston, Tex., 1987.

Cole, R. E., *Work, Mobility, and Participation: A Comparative Study of American and Japanese Industry.* Berkeley, Calif.: University of California Press, 1979.

Collins, Robert W., Roger W. Schmenner, and D. Clay Whybark, "Pan-European Manufacturing: The Yellow Brick Road to 1992," *Business Horizons* 3, no. 3 (May-June 1990), 15–22.

DeMeyer, Arnaud, Jinchiro Nakane, Jeffrey G. Miller, and Kasra Ferdows, "Flexibility: The Next Competitive Battle," *Manufacturing Roundtable Research Report Series,* Boston University School of Management, February 1987.

Ettlie, John E., Michael C. Burstein, and Avi Fiegenbaum, eds., *Manufacturing Strategy.* Boston: Kluwer Academic Publishers, 1990.

Hill, Terry, *Manufacturing Strategy.* London, England: Macmillan, 1985.

Schmenner, Roger W., "Multiplant Manufacturing Strategies Among the Fortune 500," *Journal of Operations Management* 2, no. 2 (February 1982), 77–86.

Schonberger, Richard J., *Japanese Manufacturing Techniques.* New York: Free Press, 1982.

Skinner, Wickham, *Manufacturing in the Corporate Strategy.* New York: John Wiley, 1978.

Voss, Chris A., *Managing New Manufacturing Technologies.* Operations Management Association, Monograph No. 1, 1986, Appendix 2, "The Manufacturing Strategy Concept," pp. 65–68.

Voss, Chris A., ed., "Manufacturing Strategy—Theory and Practice." *Proceedings of the 5th International Conference of the Operations Management Association—U.K.,* vols. I and II, June 1990.

SUPPLEMENT TO CHAPTER 2

FINANCIAL AND ECONOMIC ANALYSES IN OPERATIONS

THE NEED FOR FINANCIAL AND ECONOMIC ANALYSES

Operations managers make strategic choices on the basis of both external and internal analyses. Externally, markets and environments are assessed. Internally, operating and financial capabilities are analyzed. To analyze internally, operations managers must have an understanding of financial analysis. Managers need to understand such concepts as the time value of money and cost flows, as well as appropriate analytic models. Operations managers face many facility and process choices—for both initial and replacement investments—that they must accurately assess. Let's examine some useful financial concepts and models.

TERMINOLOGY AND CONCEPTS

Terminology and Concepts Although it is not always possible to do so, decision makers try to evaluate alternatives logically and comparably. Toward this end, economic analysis borrows some standard terminology from finance and accounting.

Cost and Revenues Managers are interested in the costs of owning and operating facilities and equipment. *The costs used in economic analysis are current, actual costs.* Let's examine a few costs that become important to us in analysis.

Opportunity costs Returns that are lost or forgone as a result of selecting one alternative over another.

Sunk costs Past expenditures that are irrelevant to current decision.

Salvage value Income from selling an asset.

Depreciation An accounting procedure to recover expenditures for an asset over its lifetime.

Opportunity costs are the returns that are lost or forgone as a result of selecting one alternative instead of another. The amount of the opportunity cost is determined by comparing the benefits or advantages of one alternative with those of another. *Sunk costs* are past expenditures that are irrelevant to current decisions. The salvage value of facilities and equipment may be an opportunity cost, since assets that are abandoned or replaced may be saleable. For example, the income from selling an asset is called its *salvage value.* Salvage value is a market value, similar to the concept of current, actual costs.

Depreciation is an accounting procedure to recover outlays (expenditures) for an asset over its lifetime. Depreciation does not reflect current market values. Since we are interested only in market values, of what value is depreciation to the economics of change (replacement)? Depreciation is important only in that it affects income taxes, and income taxes affect actual cash flows. The higher the value of the depreciation in any one period, the lower the taxes paid and the greater the cash flows (revenues less expenses). For our purposes here, we simplify matters by ignoring both depreciation and taxes.

Incremental Cash Flows When we evaluate and compare investment opportunities, we have to consider the alternatives' *incremental* cash flows. When we compare costs of two alternatives, we are interested only in the cost differences, or increments, between them; obviously, costs common to both alternatives are irrelevant. Cash flows are of central interest in evaluating any investment proposal. All inflows and outflows that result from adopting an alternative should enter into the analysis, including not only initial outlays but also ongoing outlays; anticipated costs of owning, operating, and maintaining the asset should therefore be considered. To determine incremental cash flows, we must also consider expected revenue from asset sales and possible salvage decisions. Also important are the *magnitude* (size) of cash flows, the *direction* (revenue or expense) of cash flows, and the *patterns* of cash flows (exactly when cash flows take place).

Accounting life Length of an asset's life determined for the purpose of a depreciation schedule.

LIFE OF THE ASSET

There are several ways of viewing the life of an asset. Consider the life of a piece of equipment. First, we can determine its *accounting life,* the duration of its depreciation schedule. Second, we can consider its *machine life,* the length of time the machine could actually function. At the end of the machine life, there might or might not be some salvage value. Machine life typically is of secondary interest to us in economic analysis. We are primarily interested in *economic life,* the length of time the asset performs a useful economic service. These three measurements—accounting, machine, and economic—may be widely divergent.

Machine life Length of time an asset is capable of functioning.

Economic life Length of time an asset is useful.

TIME VALUE OF MONEY

Time value of money The potential for money to generate revenue over time.

When analysts speak of the *time value of money,* they mean the revenues that may be received for money over time. Money may either depreciate or appreciate in value over time (*depending on inflation* or deflation), but it will not earn any *revenues* unless it is invested. Money invested over time has value over time. This idea of money having value over time is an important consideration in evaluating proposed changes. An example would be a birthday gift of \$100 invested to earn 8 percent interest compounded annually. The initial value is \$100, after one year \$108, and after two years \$116.64.

CASH FLOW PATTERNS AND ASSOCIATED COMPOUND INTEREST FACTORS

Cash Flow Patterns In operations investment or replacement situations, we observe six basic patterns of income and expense flows. Figure S2.1 shows three of these patterns, and since each pattern has a reverse flow as well, there are six possible cash flows. The three not shown (given P to find S, given P to find R, and given S to find R) would have the same graphical patterns as their counterparts, except that the cash flows would be reversed.

Compound Interest Factors Which income flow pattern applies to our birthday gift example? Given a present sum of money (P), find a future sum of money (S) after n periods. If we consider the time value of money at interest rate i over n years, we have the concept of a compound interest factor. Let's call this particular factor a single

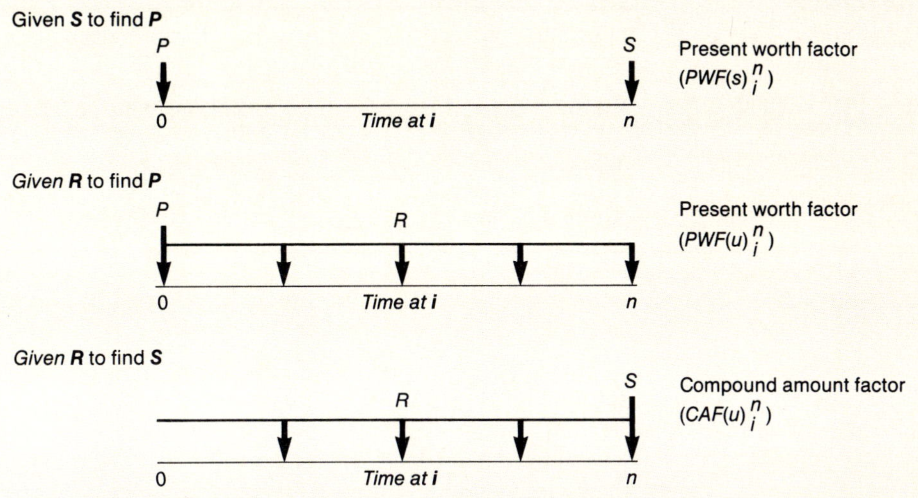

P	Present worth of a future series of payments or receipts
S	Future sum of money equivalent to P at the interest rate i for n periods
R	Uniform annual series; the year end annual payments or receipts in a uniform (equal) series continuing for n periods; the entire series is equivalent to P at the interest rate i for n periods
n	Number of interest periods, assuming an interest period to be one year
i	Rate of interest per year in percent

FIGURE S2.1 **Cash flow patterns and compound interest factors**

payment compound amount factor. It could be symbolized as $CAF(s)^n_i$ and illustrated:

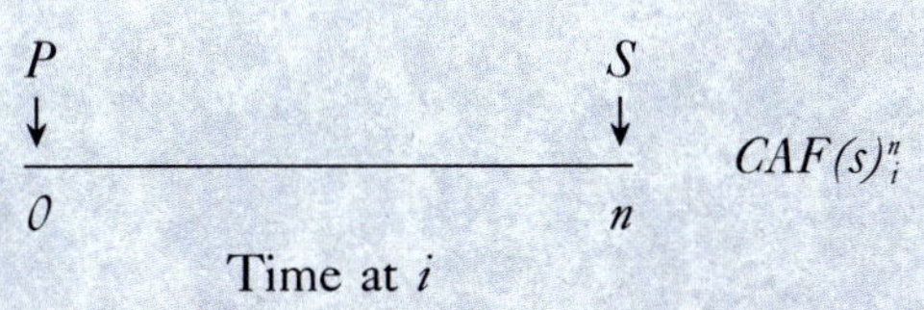

In terms of our example, the future sum of money, S, is found by looking up the factor in Appendix B (at the end of the text) and solving for S as follows:

$$S = P\,[CAF(s)^n_i] \qquad (S2.1)$$

$$= \$100\,[CAF(s)^{2}_{.08}]$$
$$= 100\,(1.1664)$$
$$= \$116.64$$

The compound interest factors associated with varying cash flows are listed in Table S2.1. You do not have to remember the name of the factor (the single payment compound amount factor) or the interest formula from which the factor was derived $[(1 + i)^n]$ to use the table. *You need to understand only the logic of the investment situation, the cash flow patterns given and sought.*

TABLE S2.1 **Compound interest factors**

Cash Flow	Factor Name	Factor Symbol
Given S to find P	Present worth factor	$PWF(s)_i^n$
Given P to find S	Compound amount factor	$CAF(s)_i^n$
Given R to find P	Present worth factor	$PWF(u)_i^n$
Given P to find R	Capital recovery factor	CRF_i^n
Given R to find S	Compound amount factor	$CAF(u)_i^n$
Given S to find R	Sinking fund factor	SFF_i^n

METHODS OF EVALUATION

Several formal financial methods are available to evaluate proposed operations changes. They vary in simplicity and the type of information they provide. We continue to focus on the facility and equipment investment or replacement problem. We will choose one method that is simple to calculate, the *payback* method, and one method that is not as simple to calculate but is often more informative, the *net present value* method.

Payback Method One of the most commonly used methods of evaluating investment proposals is to calculate the payback period of the investment as follows:

$$\text{Payback period} = \frac{\text{Net investment}}{\text{Net annual income from investment}}$$

Payback period Length of time required to recover one's investment; the ratio of net income to net annual income from investment.

Net investment for the asset includes its purchase and installation costs less its anticipated future salvage value. *Net annual income* is the annual financial benefit (income less expenses) expected from using the asset. The *payback period,* then, is the *length of time* required to recover one's investment.

For several reasons, the payback criterion should be used with caution. First, it does not consider the time value of funds. Second, uneven expense and revenue flow patterns cannot be considered. Finally, it ignores all inflows that occur after the payback period. On the other hand, the payback method has the advantages of simplicity and ease of communication. We recommend it not be used as the sole basis of decision but in conjunction with, or as a supplement to, other methods of analysis.

EXAMPLE

Two different orange pickers are being considered by Arizona Orchards, Inc. Alternative A requires a net investment of $10,000 and is expected to return $2,500/year in net annual income. Investment B is slightly more expensive, $12,000, but is expected to return $2,750/year in income. Calculating the payback period,

$$\text{Payback A} = \frac{\$10{,}000}{\$2{,}500/\text{year}} = 4 \text{ years}$$

$$\text{Payback B} = \frac{\$12{,}000}{\$2{,}750/\text{year}} = 4.36 \text{ years}$$

Alternative A has the shorter payback period.

Net present value The result of discounting all cash flows of an investment back to their present values and netting out the inflows against the outflows.

Net Present Value Method Net present value (present worth, discounted cash flow method) considers all cash flows associated with an investment, discounts each unique flow (revenue or expense) back through time to its current equivalent value by using the appropriate compound interest factor, and then sums the net value of all discounted flows at the present time. The result is a *net present value.*

$$\text{Net present value} = \sum\left(\left[\begin{pmatrix}\text{Periodic}\\\text{revenue}\end{pmatrix} - \begin{pmatrix}\text{Periodic}\\\text{expense}\end{pmatrix}\right]\begin{pmatrix}\text{Compound}\\\text{interest}\\\text{factor}\end{pmatrix}\right) - I \qquad \text{(S2.2)}$$

$$NPV = \sum_{t=1}^{n} (v_t - c_t)\ [PWF(s)_i^t]] - \mathrm{I} \qquad \text{(S2.3)}$$

where

i = rate of interest per year, in percent
I = initial investment made at present time, in dollars
n = life of investment, in years
v_t = income or receipts occuring in period t, in dollars
c_t = expenses or disbursements occurring in period t, in dollars

The procedure for using net present value is as follows:

1. Separate all data by alternatives. Repeat each of the following steps for each alternative.
2. Identify the cash flows. (A diagram of cash flow might be helpful.) On the diagram identify the interest rate and time periods.
3. Write a total net present value equation in words to reflect the situation, the cash flow patterns.
4. Substitute the appropriate dollars and compound amount factors for each flow in the equation.
5. Find the compound amount factors in the appendices and solve, finding the net present value for each alternative.
6. Choose the alternatives with the *greatest* net present value.

Once you have solved a few problems, you'll probably be able to shortcut this procedure considerably. To simplify NPV analysis, we assume that cash flows that occur throughout the year always occur at year-end. Let's take one example through the complete procedure.

EXAMPLE

Fireway Company must replace a piece of equipment and is considering models offered by two competing equipment manufacturers. Both models have a useful life expectancy of six years (no expected salvage value), and Fireway has a cost of capital of 10 percent for its investments. Each model provides an income of $4,000 annually. Alternative A requires an initial outlay of $10,000 and requires maintenance expenditures of $1,000 annually. Alternative B, a deluxe model, requires an initial outlay of $12,000 and annual maintenance costs of $500. Which alternative is less costly? The first step has been completed as the data are already organized according to investment alternative. The cash flows are as follows:

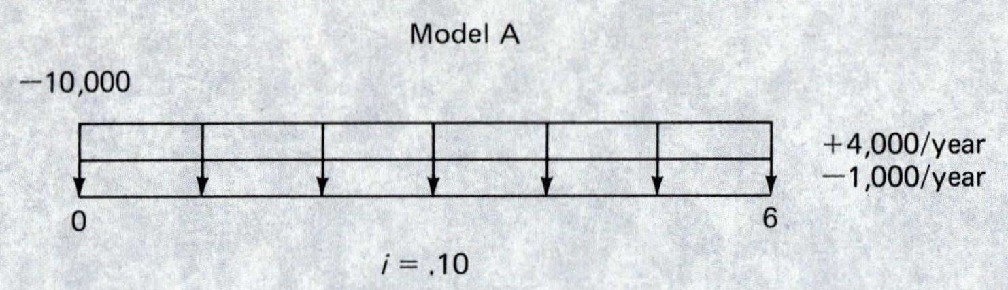

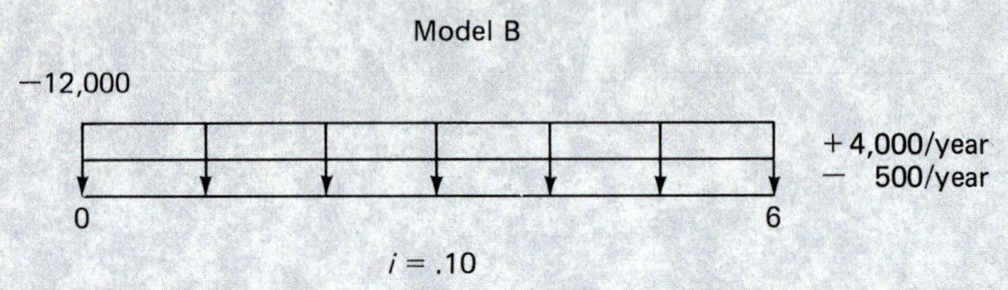

The net present value equation for A would be:

$$\begin{aligned} NPV(\text{A}) &= \text{Sum of (revenue} - \text{expense) (factor for each of six years), minus } I \\ &= (4{,}000 - 1{,}000)\,(\text{given } R \text{ to find } P) - I \\ &= (4{,}000 - 1{,}000)\,PWF(u)^{6}_{.10} - 10{,}000 \\ &= 3{,}000(4.355) - 10{,}000 \\ &= 13{,}065 - 10{,}000 \\ NPV(\text{A}) &= +\$3{,}065 \end{aligned}$$

Similarly, the net present value for B would be:

$$\begin{aligned} NPV(\text{B}) &= (4{,}000 - 500)\ (\text{given } R \text{ to find } P) - 12{,}000 \\ &= 3{,}500\ PWF(u)^{6}_{.10} - 12{,}000 \\ &= 3{,}500\ (4.355) - 12{,}000 \\ &= 15{,}242 - 12{,}000 \\ &= +\$3{,}242 \end{aligned}$$

Choose alternative B over A because $3,242 > $3,065.

As you might have figured out, another method of solution could also be used. With this method, use separate present worth factors for each of the six periods and sum the six amounts and the initial investment at the current time, time zero. The answers should be equivalent or nearly so using the rounded table factors with those we calculated above for alternatives *A* and *B*. Let's look at a more complex example.

EXAMPLE

Hopi Trucking has just paid $16,000 cash for a new truck. Hopi management estimates that the useful life of the truck is four years. At the end of four years, the estimated salvage value will be $2,500. Maintenance and other operating costs are expected to be $10,000/year for three years and $12,000 for the fourth year. Assuming we can replace the truck in four years for the same price, how much money must be generated each year from this investment to have at least enough to purchase another truck in four years? Money is worth 8 percent to Hopi, and revenues flow in uniformly to the firm.

First, we must recognize that we are being asked for a dollar amount four years hence, not at the present time. Second we should realize that the $16,000 truck we now have is a sunk cost. Since we are not considering depreciation and taxes, they will not influence our decision. Let X be the dollars of revenue required each year to cover expenses and provide \$16,000 at the end of four years. Our problem then is as follows:

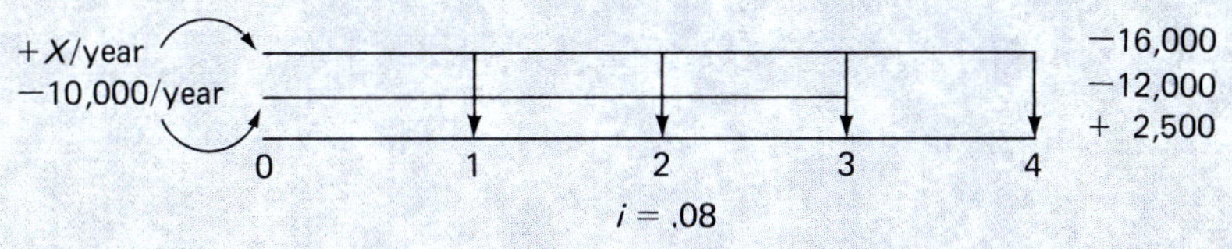

Because of operating costs, we have −\$10,000 per year occurring for three years and −\$12,000 for the fourth year. We also have −\$16,000, accounting for the purchase price, and +\$2,500, accounting for the salvage value. The cash inflow we are looking for is X per year for four years. This can be expressed *at year four:*

$$\begin{aligned}
NPV &= -10{,}000 \underset{\substack{n=3\\ i=.08}}{(\text{given } R \text{ to find } P)} \underset{\substack{n=4\\ i=.08}}{(\text{given } P \text{ to find } S)} \\
&\quad + X \underset{\substack{n=4\\ i=.08}}{(R \text{ to find } S)} - 16{,}000 - 12{,}000 \\
&\quad + 2{,}500 \\
&= -10{,}000\text{PWF}(u)^{3}_{.08}]\,[\text{CAF}(s)^{4}_{.08}] \\
&\quad + \text{X}[\text{CAF}(u)^{4}_{.08}] - 25{,}500 \\
&= -10{,}000\ (2.577)(1.360) + 4.506\ X - 25{,}500 \\
&= 4.506\ X - (35{,}047 + 25{,}500) \\
NPV &= 4.506\ \text{X} - 60{,}547
\end{aligned}$$

Setting $NPV = 0$ (the breakeven for sales and expenses at four years) and solving for X gives:

$$\begin{aligned}
0 &= 4.506X - 60{,}547 \\
X &= 60{,}547/4.506 \\
&= \$13{,}437
\end{aligned}$$

Annual sales revenue will have to be \$13,437 to cover expenses and provide \$16,000 cash at the end of four years.

What should we do if the investment alternatives have *unequal lives?* Clearly, we can't compare them directly. Let's assume that like-for-like replacement can occur at the end of the life of each asset and use the least common multiple of lives over which to compare the investment. If one alternative has a three-year life and one a two-year life, we would make the comparison over six years.

At times, organizations want investments to meet a minimum rate of return. If the net present value at that rate of return is positive, the investment provides greater returns than would the rate used in determining the present value. The investment is made. On the other hand, if the present value is negative, the return is less than that provided by the interest rate used, and the investment is unattractive.

Internal rate of return
Interest rate at which the present value of outflows equals the present value of inflows.

Internal Rate of Return Suppose you have identified the inflows and outflows of an alternative and wish to determine the rate of return it offers. *The internal rate of return is the interest rate i at which net cash flows for the alternative equal zero.* Finding the value of i for which the present value of outflows equals the present value of inflows is determined by process of trial and error.

REVIEW AND DISCUSSION QUESTIONS

1. Define the following:
   (a) Opportunity cost
   (b) Sunk cost
   (c) Salvage value
   (d) Depreciation
2. Define accounting life, machine life, and economic life of an asset.
3. Compare the major features of payback, net present value, and internal rate of return methods of evaluation.

PROBLEMS

REINFORCING FUNDAMENTALS

1. What is the present value of $1,000 to be invested for seven years at 8 percent interest? At 10 percent interest?
2. What is the present value of a 15-year series of $800 investments if the interest rate is 8 percent? 10 percent?
3. A company is considering two alternative relayout designs. Alternative 1 requires an initial investment of $100,000, will result in $20,000 annual cost savings for the next ten years, and is expected to have salvage value of $20,000 at the end of ten years. Alternative 2 requires an $80,000 initial investment, will result in $16,000 annual cost savings, and will have no salvage value after ten years. The interest rate is 10 percent.
   (a) Which alternative is best using the payback method?
   (b) Which alternative is best using the net present value method?
4. An investment alternative requires an initial outlay of $71,500, is expected to have a five-year useful life, and will have a salvage value of $10,600 after five years. Annual increment revenues will be $20,500, and annual increment operating expenses will be $7,200 during the useful life. What is the internal rate of return for this alternative?
5. A hospital is evaluating two machines for analyzing blood samples. One unit is more expensive than the other, but because of its high degree of automation it has a lower labor cost. Both machines meet the hospital's needs and are essentially worthless at the end of their economic life. Money is worth 10 percent.

	Unit 1	Unit 2
Purchase cost	$15,000	$22,000
Economic life	3 years	3 years
Labor costs per year	$14,000	$ 9,000
Installation cost	$ 4,000	$ 5,000
Maintenance costs		
First year	$ 500	$ 1,000
Increase per year	$ 100	$ 500
Book value		
End of first year	$15,000	$20,000
End of third year	$ 3,000	$ 3,000

(a) Using the *present worth* (net present value) method, which unit should the hospital purchase?

(b) Explain to the pathologist (an MD) in charge of the lab how the *present worth* method can provide useful data for capital budgeting purposes.

CHALLENGING EXERCISES

6. As purchasing agent for Kansas City Industries, you have the following two alternatives for replacing equipment:

	Alternative 1	Alternative 2
Machine life (years)	2	3
Economic life (years)	1	2
Initial investment	Negotiable	$20,000
Annual maintenance cost	-0-	$ 1,000
Salvage value end of machine life	$1,000	$ 2,000
Salvage value end of economic life	$4,000	$ 5,000
Value of money	10%	10%

Your problem is to find the upper bound (or maximum amount) of the initial investment you are willing to negotiate in alternative 1 (i.e., any amount greater than the upper bound would make alternative 2 the most economical). Use the present worth (net present value) method to determine the upper bound.

7. The vice president of operations for a telephone company has decided to replace a central dispatching office. In one of the design details, two alternatives are proposed. The more costly of the two alternatives will require an additional investment (over and above the other alternative) of $35,000 in construction costs. However, this alternative will make it easier to bring in additional cables, since service expansion is required later. The estimated savings are $6,000/year for the fifth to ninth year. What must the minimum savings be from the tenth to twentieth year in order to make the additional investment attractive, if the rate of interest is 10 percent and the estimated life of the office is 20 years? No savings are expected for the first 4 years.

KEY TERMS

Accounting life 66
Depreciation 65
Economic life 66
Internal rate of return 72
Machine life 66
Net present value 69
Opportunity costs 65
Payback period 68
Salvage value 65
Sunk costs 65
Time value of money 66

PART II

PLANNING (DESIGNING) THE CONVERSION SYSTEM

Production and operations management activities

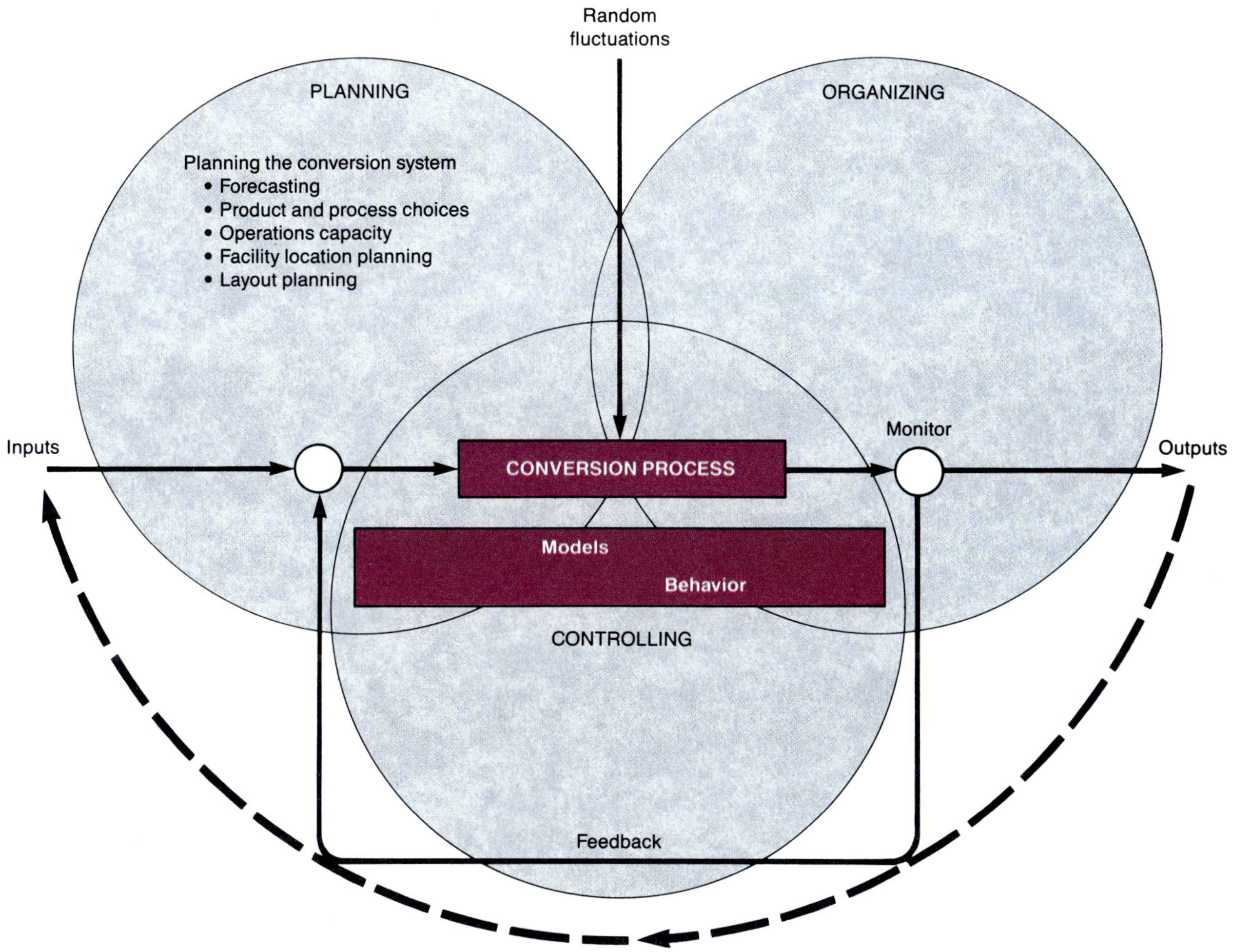

CHAPTER 3

FORECASTING

While all elements of operations management are important, I view forecasting as one of the key elements in the operations structure. This chapter is an excellent overview of forecasting techniques and models. It will help you recognize the different models and when to use them according to your needs.

At Donaldson Company, Inc., we serve a multitude of customers with a wide variety of products ranging from the size of a house to the size of a filter for 3½-inch disc drives. We serve our customers through our plants in the United States and throughout the world. The needs of the market are changing for us, and we have to respond more quickly than ever before with product delivery. To do so, we have placed a higher emphasis on forecasting, that is, using data from past events to determine future events. At Donaldson Company, forecasting is essential to improving our competitive edge.

Richard M. Negri
Vice President and General Manager
Manufacturing Division
Donaldson Company, Inc.
Minneapolis, Minnesota

As a key decision-maker, Mr. Negri knows that forecasting enables his company to respond more quickly and accurately to market changes than would otherwise be possible. How does forecasting relate to the management processes of planning, organizing, and controlling? These processes are not independent processes; they interrelate and overlap. If operations have been properly planned and organized, control is easier and smoother. This is where forecasting comes in. It can reduce the costs of adjusting operations in response to unexpected deviations by specifying future demand. Clearly, if future demand for goods and services is accurately estimated, operating efficiency increases. Let's see how successful firms such as Donaldson might use forecasting in operations.

Donaldson needs forecasts for each product line so it can reliably supply a wide range of products when customers need them throughout the world.

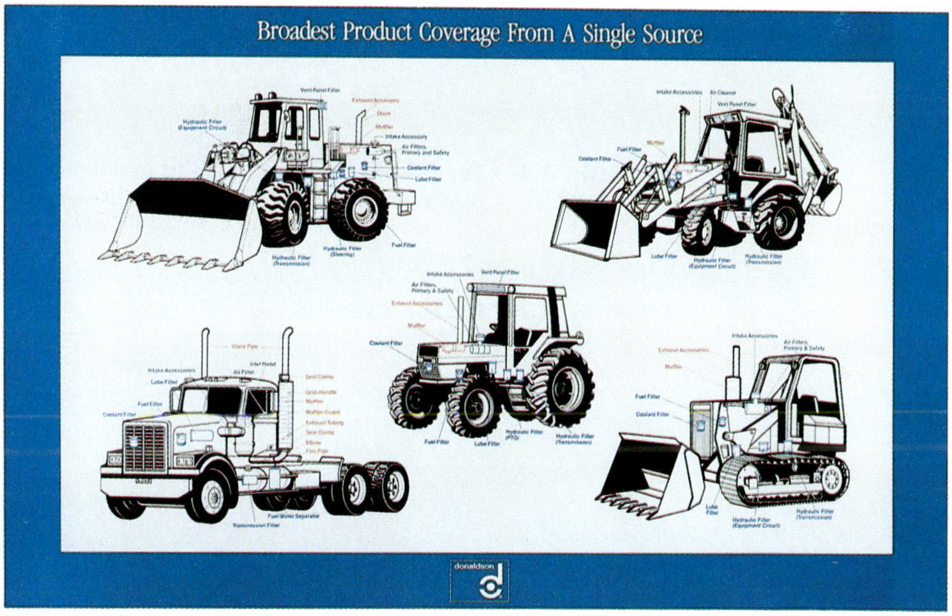

Source: **Donaldson Company, Inc.**

FORECASTING IN OPERATIONS

In general terms, forecasting presents an unresolved philosophical dilemma. "You can never plan the future by the past," said Edmund Burke. But Patrick Henry disagreed: "I know of no way of judging the future but by the past." Operations managers try to forecast a wide range of future events that potentially affect success. Most often the concern is forecasting customer demand for products or services. Managers may want long-run estimates of overall demand or short-run estimates of demand for each individual product. Even more detailed estimates are needed for specific items or subcomponents that go into each product.

We can distinguish among these different kinds of forecasting needs by considering how far into the future they focus. Detailed forecasts for individual items are used to plan the short-run use of the conversion system. At the other extreme, overall or *aggregate* product-demand forecasts are used to plan for capacity, location, and layout over a much longer time span. As Figure 3.1 shows, different types of planning decisions depend on different types of information, which in turn depend on what are called the *forecasting time horizons,* or the future times to which the forecasting points.

In business, economic, and political communities, *forecasting* has various meanings. In operations management, we adopt a rather specific definition of *forecast,* and we distinguish it from the broader concept of *prediction.*

Forecast Use of past data to determine future events; an objective computation.

Prediction Subjective estimates of the future.

A forecast is an estimate of a future event achieved by systematically combining and casting forward in a predetermined way data about the past.

A prediction is an estimate of a future event achieved through subjective considerations other than just past data; this subjective consideration need not occur in any predetermined way.[1]

As these definitions make clear, forecasts are possible only when a history of data exists. An established TV manufacturer, for example, can use past data to forecast the

FIGURE 3.1 **Forecasting requirements in production operations management**

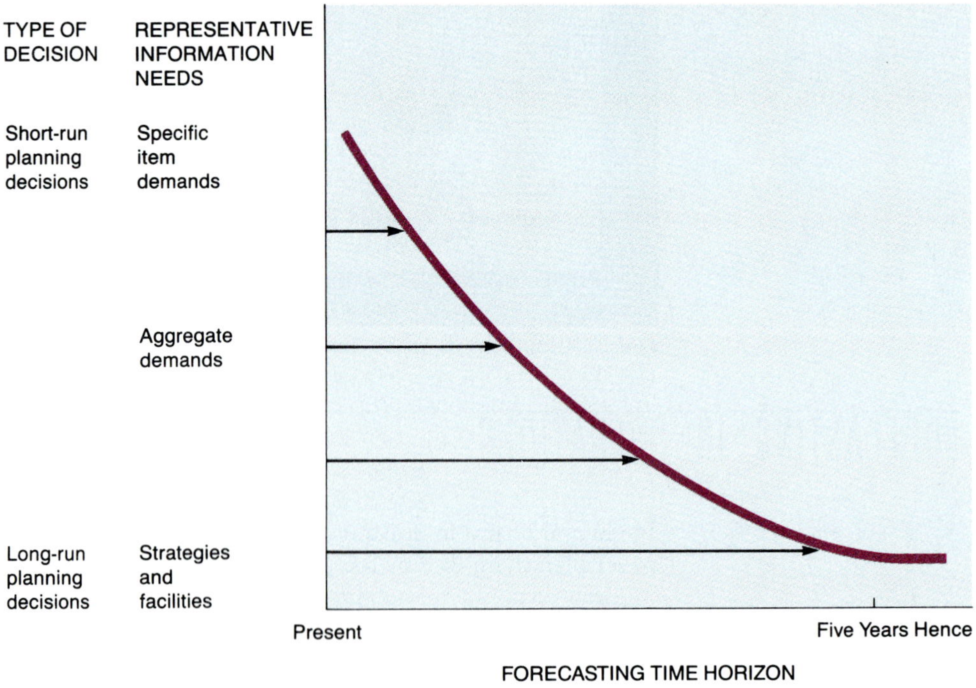

[1]R. G. Brown, *Smoothing Forecasting and Prediction of Discrete Time Series* (Englewood Cliffs, N.J.: Prentice Hall, 1963), p. 2.

number of picture screens required for next week's TV assembly schedule. A fast-food restaurant can use past data to forecast the number of hamburger buns required for this weekend's operations. But suppose the manufacturer offers a new TV model or the restaurant decides to offer a new item. Since no past data exist to estimate first year sales of the new products, prediction, not forecasting, is required. For predicting, good subjective estimates can be based on the manager's skill, experience, and judgment; but forecasting requires statistical and management science techniques.

In general, when business people speak of forecasts, they usually mean some combination of both forecasting and prediction. Commonly, forecasting is substituted freely for *economic forecasting,* and often implies some combination of objective calculations and subjective judgments. We caution students and operations managers to avoid misunderstandings by clarifying what they mean by "forecasting" when they are discussing problems, solutions, and actions based on forecasts.

FORECASTING AND OPERATIONS SUBSYSTEMS

The aggregate demand forecast is normally obtained by estimating expected volumes of sales, expressed in dollars, and then converting the sales dollars into homogeneous production units. Production units—such as the number of televisions in a plant, the number of patients fed in a hospital, the number of books circulated in a library, or the number of lots of common stock sold in a brokerage house—can then be subdivided into component parts and converted into labor or material requirements. These resource forecasts are used to plan and control operation subsystems, as shown in Figure 3.2.

In studying forecasting, we must be careful not to immerse ourselves in techniques and lose track of the reasons for forecasting. Forecasting is an important component of strategic and operational planning. It establishes the link between planning and controlling systems. Forecasts are necessary for planning, scheduling, and controlling the system to facilitate effective and efficient output of goods and services.

Planning (Designing) the System As Figure 3.2 shows, in planning the system, managers need to forecast aggregate demands so they can design or redesign processes necessary to meet demand. The degree of automation, for example, depends a great deal upon future product demand. Automated, continuous flows facilitate high production volumes; manual or semiautomated, intermittent flows (batching) are generally more economical for smaller production volumes. The demand forecast is critical to this design decision. Once process design, product design, and equipment investment decisions have been made for an anticipated volume, managers are locked into a facility of specified capacity. Thereafter wide variations between anticipated demand and actual demand can result in excessive production and operating costs.

Capacity planning that makes use of long-run forecasts is one of the areas in production/operations that is both critical and not well understood or developed. In the steel, power generation, and other basic industries, if capacity is not expanded fast enough, both individual firms and the national economy suffer. On the other hand, too much capacity is burdensome. For example, jet aircraft, at $20 million each, cannot be purchased and stocked for occasional demand, since the cost of excess capacity is considerable. Boeing, McDonnell Douglas, and Airbus—the world's largest commercial aircraft producers—try very hard to have manufacturing plants sized to meet exactly the number of aircraft demanded. If the plants are too large, unneeded airplanes are produced or facilities must be idled. Either is costly to the firm.

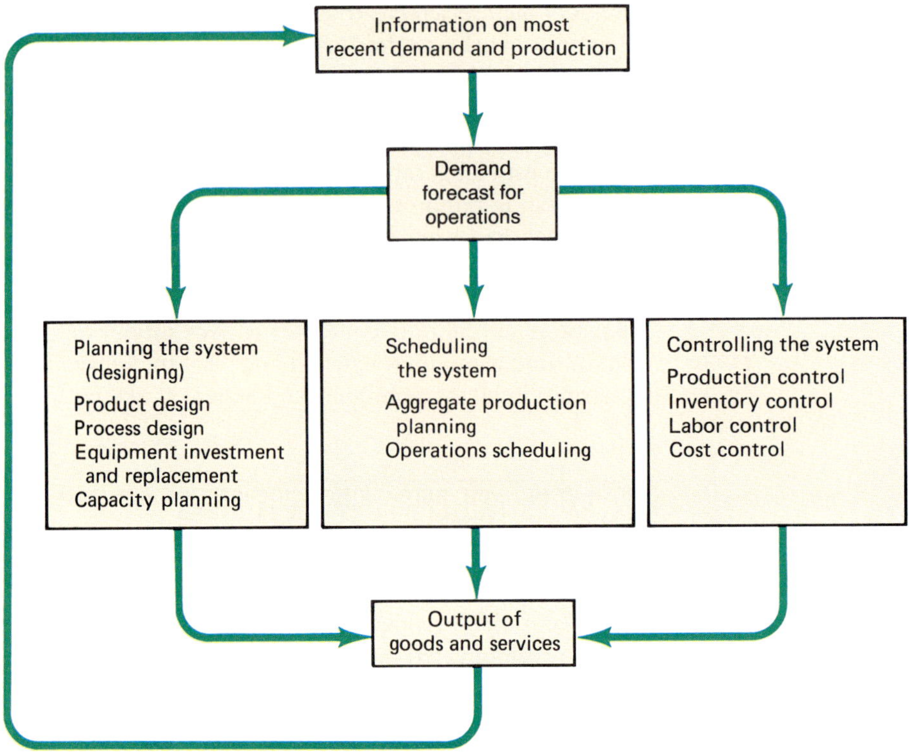

FIGURE 3.2 **Using demand forecasting and production/operations subsystems**

Scheduling the System When deciding how best to use the existing conversion system, accurate demand forecasts are very important. Managers need intermediate-run demand forecasts for three months, six months, and a year into the future. Both current and future work force levels and production rates must be established from these forecasts. Job scheduling in intermittent and continuous operations is more stable if demand forecasts are accurate.

Controlling the System Managers need forecasts of demand to make decisions about controlling inventory, production, labor, and overall costs. Accurate forecasts are needed for the immediate future—hours, days, and weeks ahead. No longer acceptable is an earlier generation's assumption that "any service that is offered will be purchased," or that "all that is produced can be sold."

A 1987 study of small businesses suggested the number one use of forecasting is production scheduling, and the number two use is inventory control. Lower-ranked uses are marketing and financial tasks. Interestingly, the majority of the 483 respondents were more dissatisfied than satisfied with their forecasts. One reason was a lack of understanding about forecasting, demonstrating that knowing when and how to use a forecast is as important as the forecast itself.[2]

---

[2]Robin T. Peterson, "The State of the Forecasting Art in Small Businesses," *Journal of Business Forecasting* 6, no. 2 (Summer 1987), 2–4, 13.

Time series analysis In forecasting problems, analysis of demand data plotted on a time scale to reveal patterns of demand.

Demand pattern General shape of a time series; usually constant, trend, seasonal, or some combination of these shapes.

CHARACTERISTICS OF DEMAND OVER TIME

To systematically analyze historical data for forecasting, managers commonly use a *time series analysis.* Analysts plot demand data on a time scale, study the plots, and look for consistent shapes or patterns. A time series of demand might have, for example, a constant, trend, or seasonal (cyclical) pattern (Figure 3.3) or some combination of these patterns (Figure 3.4). The pattern is the general shape of the time series. Although some individual data points do not fall on the pattern, they all tend to cluster around it. To describe the points clustered about a pattern, we use the term *noise.* Low noise means all or most of the points lie very close to the pattern. *High noise* means many of the points lie relatively far away from the pattern. Figure 3.4 shows both high and low noise levels. If you tried to envision the data in Figure 3.4 without the solid line showing the pattern, you might find it difficult to identify the pattern. Because noise in the demand patterns can disguise the pattern, forecasting, even with computers, can be very difficult; the result can be forecasting errors and, eventually, operations errors.

FIGURE 3.3 Demand patterns

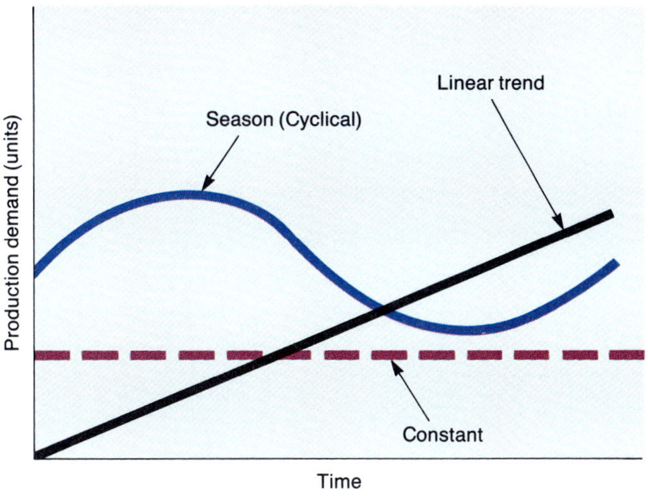

Analysts use the term *demand stability* to describe the tendency of a time series to

FIGURE 3.4 Noise in demand

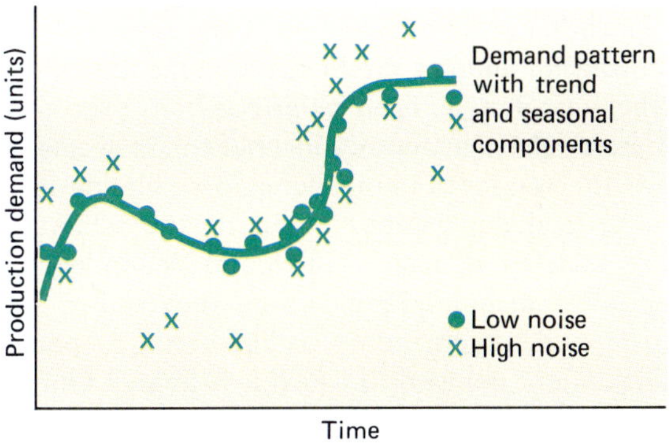

Demand stability Tendency of a time series to retain the same general pattern over time.

Noise Dispersion of demand about a demand pattern.

retain the same general pattern over time. The demand patterns for some products or services change over a period of time, and the patterns for others do not. Demands are easier to forecast when the pattern is *stationary* (stable) than when it is *dynamic* (unstable). Figure 3.5 is taken from a study of demand for frosted microscope slides in a large medical center, an example of a dynamic demand pattern. Notice that demand shifts upward beginning at about period (week) 150. Later, these shifts become more pronounced. In the study, two forecasting models—*simple exponential smoothing* and *adaptive exponential smoothing*—were used. These models are discussed later in this chapter; here we observe that the adaptive model responds more quickly to demand shifts than the exponential model.

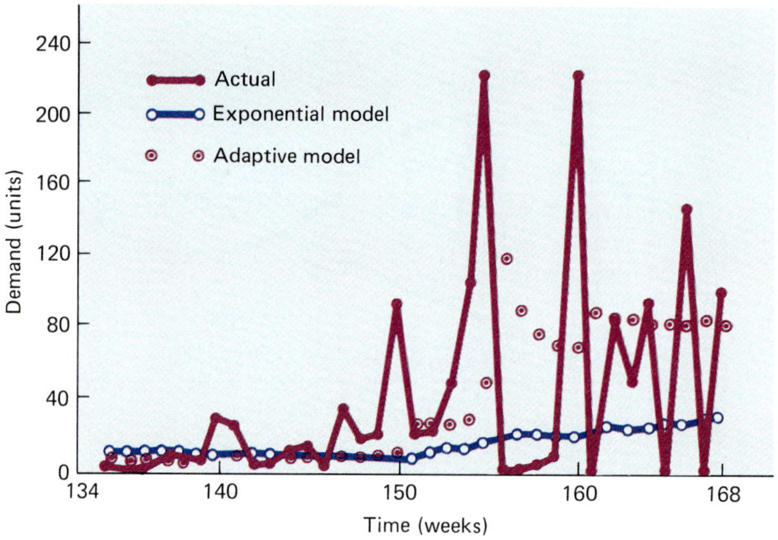

FIGURE 3.5 **Frosted microscope slide demand**
Source: Everett E. Adams, Jr., William L. Berry, and D. Clay Whybark, "The Hospital Administrator and Management Science," *Hospital & Health Services Administration* 19, no. 1 (Winter 1974), 38.

DEPENDENT VERSUS INDEPENDENT DEMAND

Independent demand Demand for an item that occurs separately of demand for any other item.

Dependent demand Demand for an item that can be linked to the demand for another item.

Demand for a product or service is termed *independent* when it occurs independently of demand for any other product or service. Conversely, when demand for one product is linked to demand for another product, the demand is termed *dependent.* Dependency may occur when one item demand is derived from a second item (vertical dependency) or when one item relates in another manner to the second item (horizontal dependency). In a movie theater, for example, demand for film postage is independent of demand for popcorn. Vertical dependency might be the relationship between popcorn and theater ticket (patron) demand. Horizontal dependency might be the relationship between popcorn demand and popcorn box demand.

Only independent demand needs forecasting; dependent demand can be derived from the independent demand to which it is linked. Our discussion in Chapter 14 on material requirements planning (MRP) will further develop this concept.

FORECAST ERROR

Forecast error The numeric difference of forecasted demand and actual demand.

Later, when we evaluate different forecasting methods, we'll need a measure of effectiveness. Forecast error is the scorekeeping mechanism most commonly used. *Forecast error is the numeric difference of forecasted demand and actual demand.* Obviously, a forecast method yielding large errors is less desirable than one yielding smaller errors.

Mean absolute deviation (MAD) A forecast error measure that is the average forecast error without regard to direction; calculated as the sum of the absolute value of forecast error for all periods divided by the total number of periods evaluated.

MAD Equation 3.1 defines a most important error measure, termed *mean absolute deviation* (MAD):

$$MAD = \frac{\text{sum of the absolute value of forecast error for all periods}}{\text{number of periods}} \tag{3.1}$$

$$= \frac{\sum_{i=1}^{n} |\text{forecast error}_i|}{n}$$

$$= \frac{\sum_{i=1}^{n} |\text{forecasted demand}_i \text{—actual demand}_i|}{n}$$

where n is the number of periods.

For each period (i), you find the difference between the forecasted demand and the actual demand. If your forecast was perfect, actual demand equals the forecasted demand, and the forecast error is zero. As forecasting continues, the forecast error is recorded and accumulated, period by period. After any number of periods (n) have elapsed, you use Equation 3.1 to calculate the average (mean) forecasting error to date. Notice that MAD is an average of the absolute value of forecast errors; errors are measured without regard to sign. MAD expresses the *magnitude* but not the *direction* of error. This measure of absolute values is called *absolute deviation.*

There is a relationship between mean absolute deviation and the classical measure of dispersion for forecast error, the standard deviation (σ_e). *If the forecast is working properly, forecast errors are normally distributed. When this is so, the smoothed mean absolute deviation* (SMAD) is used to estimate the standard deviation. The relationship is

$$\sigma_e \cong 1.25 \text{ SMAD}$$

Expontential smoothing will be explained later in this chapter; for now you may think of exponentially smoothed MAD as an average MAD over time.

Bias A forecast error measure that is the average of forecast error with regard to direction and shows any tendency consistently to over- or underforecast; calculated as the sum of the actual forecast error for all periods divided by the total number of periods evaluated.

Bias Equation 3.2 is a less commonly used error measure called *bias:*

$$Bias = \frac{\text{sum of forecast error for all periods}}{\text{number of periods}} \tag{3.2}$$

$$= \frac{\sum_{i=1}^{n} \text{forecasted error}}{n}$$

$$= \frac{\sum_{i=1}^{n} (\text{forecasted demand}_i \text{—actual demand}_i)}{n}$$

Unlike MAD, Bias indicates the *directional* tendency of forecast errors. If the forecast repeatedly overestimates actual demand, Bias will have a positive value; consistent underestimation will be indicated by a negative value.

EXAMPLE

An aluminum extruder forecasted the demand for a shower stall extrusion to be 500 per month for each of three months. The actual demands turned out to be 400, 560, and 700. His forecast errors, MAD and Bias, are calculated here.

$$\text{MAD} = \frac{|500 - 400| + |500 - 560| + |500 - 700|}{3}$$

$$= \frac{100 + 60 - 200}{3}$$

$$= 120 \text{ units}$$

$$Bias = \frac{(500 - 400) + (500 - 560) + (500 - 700)}{3}$$

$$= \frac{100 - 60 - 200}{3}$$

$$= -53 \text{ units}$$

As you can see, MAD is 120 units, and Bias is −53 units. Since MAD measures the overall accuracy of the forecasting method, we would conclude that this aluminum extruder does not have a very accurate model. He has a high average absolute error, 24 percent of the forecasted number of shower stall extrusions. Bias measures the *tendency consistently to over- or underforecast.* In this example, the extrusion forecaster has a tendency to underestimate by 53 units; since actual demand averages 553 units, Bias is, on the average, a 9.6 percent "underforecast."

An ideal forecast will have zero MAD and Bias. We find in practice, however, that there is usually a tradeoff between MAD and Bias; in some situations, one measure must be held low at the expense of the other. If you must stress one at the expense of the other, perhaps MAD should be the focus. Lowering MAD to near zero will automatically hold Bias low also.

Costs of Errors How important is forecast accuracy? When important decisions are based on forecasts, large errors can result in very costly mistakes. Some kinds of estimation errors are more costly than others. In some settings, the *direction* of error is critical; in other cases the *magnitude* of error is most important. Although the exact costs of errors are often difficult to determine, forecast errors can and should be converted into costs, even though such a conversion may have to be approximated intuitively. Recent studies are investigating the impact of forecast error on production-inventory cost. These studies illustrate how reducing forecast error can result in lower overall manufacturing costs.[3]

The computer is often utilized for scorekeeping in forecasting. Operations Management Highlight 3.1 illustrates the computer's overall use in forecasting for operations, both for product and service industries.

[3]Joseph R. Biggs and William M. Campion, "The Effect and Cost of Forecast Error Bias for Multi-Stage Production-Inventory Systems," *Decision Sciences* 13, no. 4 (October 1982), 570–84; T. S. Lee and Everett E. Adam, Jr., "Forecasting Error Evaluation in Material Requirements Planning (MRP) Production-Inventory Systems," *Management Science* 32, no. 9 (September 1986), 1186–1205.

Intuitive forecasts Forecasts that essentially are a manager's guesses and judgements concerning future events; qualitative forecasting methods.

Statistical forecasting models Casting forward past data in some systematic method; used in time series analysis and projection.

Demand-based forecasting models A statistical forecasting model based solely on historical demand data.

Causal forecasting models A statistical forecasting model based on historical demand data as well as on variables believed to influence demand.

INTUITIVE OR FORMAL APPROACHES?

In operations management today, two fundamental approaches to forecasting are dominant—intuitive estimates of the future and formal statistical modeling. The *intuitive approach,* which is based on experience, is essentially a summary of a manager's guesses, hunches, and judgments concerning future events. The *statistical modeling approach* systematically combines specific numerical data into a summary value that is then used as a forecast. Within the statistical approach are two basic types of models, which are distinguished by the type of data they use. *Demand-based* models rely solely on historical data about the item that is being forecasted. If a monthly demand forecast for a lounge chair is desired, for example, the demand-based model requires historic monthly demand data for lounge chairs. *Causal* models, on the other hand, may use additional types of data as well. These models might formally relate lounge chair demand to other variables believed to influence demand, such as the number of new houses being built.

Costs and Accuracy There is clearly a cost/accuracy tradeoff in selecting a forecasting approach. The more sophisticated approaches tend to have relatively high costs of implementation and maintanance, but they often provide more accurate forecasts, resulting in lower operating costs. Figure 3.6 illustrates one hypothetical cost situation. Note that for any forecasting situation there is an optimal region where reasonable accuracy and cost are obtained. Our goal in forecasting for operations is to operate somewhere in this optimal region.

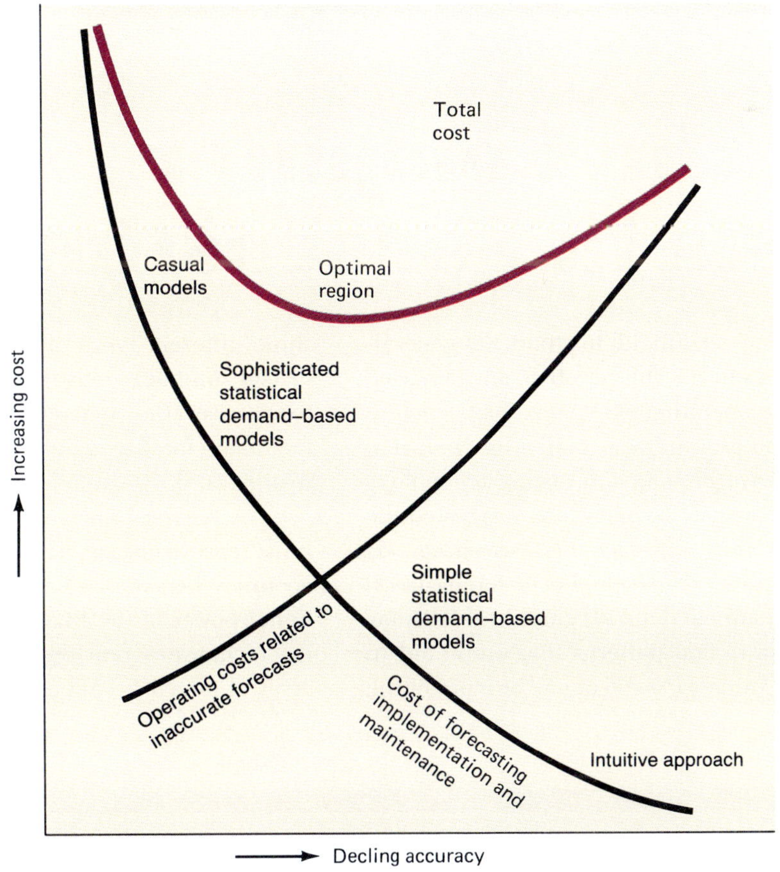

FIGURE 3.6 Cost/accuracy tradeoffs in forecasting

OPERATIONS MANAGEMENT HIGHLIGHT 3.1

Source: Walter Bibikow/The Image Bank

How the Computer Assists in Forecasting

Forecasting accuracy is difficult to attain, yet generally worth the extra effort. The payoff is an increased chance to improve operating efficiency. Tools such as the digital computer, and especially the personal computer (PC), have brought forecasting technology to almost every manager. Experts have suggested the following step-by-step approach to forecasting: (1) establish the purpose of developing a forecast; (2) collect relevant historical data; (3) graphically display the historical data to find patterns that would aid in predicting future values; (4) select one or more of the three different types of forecast models (time series, causal, and subjective); (5) test specific techniques; (6) assess the impact of relevant non-numerical factors on forecast value; (7) document processes and results; and (8) calculate the forecast error.

A barrier to accurate forecasting is data availability and accuracy, step 2 in the above list. Data accuracy becomes a major issue since the computational power of the PC and preprogrammed forecasting techniques provide the means to project a wide array of forecasts. Yet careful analysis of poor-quality data will provide spurious forecasts at best. More than one expert cites slow growth in data availability and a retrenchment in the quality and quantity of data in private industry as barriers to a wider use of forecasting.

Other key steps in this procedure—selecting and testing specific techniques—are no small chore. A recent ***Harvard Business Review*** article provides a chart that compares 20 common forecasting techniques according to 16 parameters, and lists 16 questions managers should ask when selecting a forecasting technique.

Business schools quite actively teach forecasting techniques, which reflects the needs of business management. The 570 member-schools of the American Assembly of Collegiate Schools of Business in Canada and the United States conduct curriculum surveys. Comparing the 1987 and 1983 surveys reveals a clear increase in teaching forecasting in basic courses. Furthermore, more professors are requiring computer forecasting packages in their coursework.

How are industries using this increased knowledge about forecasting? American Airlines, for one, uses a forecasting technique to determine computer software and hardware needs. Their approach is a two-step process: First they forecast the demand for computer services, and then they identify the hardware and software to meet that demand.

The Indianapolis Police Department evaluated six forecasting models and found that simple modeling approaches worked well for them. Similarly, Canada's Manitoba Telephone system used the simplest of forecasting models to predict telephone-center demand. Results allowed a 45 percent inventory reduction at telephone centers while maintaining a 95 percent service level.

Like service industries, manufacturing firms successfully couple accurate forecasts to a variety of operating decisions. Using computers, managers at Rubbermaid Home Products Division calculate 30-day, 60-day, 90-day, and annual demand forecasts for approximately 600 products. The computer then tells how to distribute products according to colors and raw material requirements among three different manufacturing plants. For the 30-, 60-, and 90-day forecasts, several statistical criteria are used to select the best forecast. For the longer term, more management judgment is introduced by having product managers actively involved in the annual forecast. If the forecast error is large, the result would be an inventory of the wrong colors and raw materials at the plants, resulting in missed shipments and dissatisfied customers. It is difficult to place a dollar cost on such errors, but they are considerable. If Rubbermaid purchasing and manufacturing employees executed perfectly the plans made on the basis of poor forecasts, the result would be poor performance and high costs to the firm. That's why firms like Rubbermaid Home Products take forecasting so seriously.

Sources: John Hanke, "Forecasting in Business Schools: A Follow-Up Survey," ***International Journal of Forecasting*** (Netherlands) 5, no. 2 (1989), 259–62; Robert R. Auray, "Revolution in Business Forecasting," ***Journal of Business Forecasting*** 8, no. 2 (Summer 1989), 12–14; Michael Barron and David Targett, "Managing Forecasts: User and Expert," ***Management Decision*** (UK) 26, no. 1 (1988) 41–44; Richard B. Barrett and David J. Kitska, "Forecasting System at Rubbermaid," ***Journal of Business Forecasting*** 6, no. 1, (Spring 1987), 7–9; Cohen Rochelle and Fraser Dunford, "Forecasting for Inventory Control: An Example of When 'Simple' Means 'Better,'" ***Interfaces*** 16, no. 6 (November/December 1986), 95–99; "Workload Demand Forecasting," ***EDP Performance Review*** 14, no. 8 (August 1986), 6–7; Richard A. Reid, "How to Set Up a Forecasting Process," ***Journal of Business Forecasting*** 4, no. 4 (Winter 1985–86), 9–10; David M. Georgoff and Robert G. Murdick, "Managers Guide to Forecasting," ***Harvard Business Review*** 64, no. 1 (January/February 1986), 110–120; and Vincent A. Mabert, "Short Interval Forecasting of Emergency Phone Call (911) Work Loads," ***Journal of Operations Management*** 5, no. 3 (May 1985), 259–71.

USEFUL FORECASTING MODELS FOR OPERATIONS

AN OVERVIEW OF SPECIFIC FORECASTING METHODS

We have emphasized that forecasting is a critical part of strategic and operational planning. Rather than get too deeply into specifying types of forecasts for varying situations, we summarize: The less analytical qualitative forecasting methods are frequently used for longer-range strategic planning and facilities decisions; the more analytical, time series analysis models are frequently used for operational planning, such as in production and inventory control. Causal forecasting techniques are used for a variety of planning situations but are especially helpful in intermediate-term planning.

Table 3.1 summarizes modern forecasting techniques. The techniques have been grouped into qualitative models, naive (time series) models, and causal models. The most frequently used techniques in operations management are the qualitative and naive (time series) models. The causal models are often more costly to implement and do not offer the increased accuracy for short-term forecasting typically needed by the production/operations manager. Even though qualitative techniques are very popular, they have definite accuracy limitations. We'll limit ourselves to a brief discussion of two qualitative methods and then proceed to some useful naive (time series) and causal models.

TABLE 3.1 **Summary of representative forecasting techniques**

Model Type	Description
Qualitative Models	
Delphi method	Questions panel of experts for opinions
Historical data	Makes analogies to the past in a judgmental manner
Nominal group technique	Group process allowing participation with forced voting
Naive (Time Series) Quantitative Models	
Simple average	Averages past data to predict the future based on that average
Exponential smoothing	Weights old forecasts and most recent demand
Causal Quantitative Models	
Regression analysis	Depicts a functional relationship among variables
Economic modeling	Provides an overall forecast for a variable such as gross national product (GNP)

QUALITATIVE MODELS

Delphi technique A qualitative forecasting technique in which a panel of experts working separately and not meeting, arrive at a consensus through the summarizing of ideas by a skilled coordinator.

Delphi The *Delphi technique* is a group process intended to achieve a consensus forecast. A panel of experts from either within or without the organization provides written comments on the point in question.

The procedure works as follows:

1. A coordinator poses a question, in writing, to each expert on a panel. Each expert writes a brief prediction.
2. The coordinator brings the written predictions together, edits them, and summarizes them.
3. On the basis of the summary, the coordinator writes a new set of questions and gives them to the experts. These are answered in writing.
4. Again, the coordinator edits and summarizes the answers, repeating the process until the coordinator is satisfied with the overall prediction synthesized from the experts.

The key to the Delphi technique lies in the coordinator and experts. The experts frequently have diverse backgrounds: Two physicists, a chemist, an electrical engineer, and an economist might make up a panel. The coordinator must be talented enough to synthesize diverse and wide-ranging statements and arrive at both a structured set of questions and a forecast.

An advantage of this method is that direct interpersonal relations are avoided. Hence personalities do not conflict, nor can one strong-willed member dominate the group. The Delphi method has worked successfully for technological forecasting: for example, to forecast market penetration of solar electric energy for the year 2000.[4]

EXAMPLE

American Hoist and Derrick Company management felt a need for incorporating its judgments into sales forecasting. Starting with an annual sales forecast, management wanted to increase forecasting accuracy to determine just how fast production capacity should be expanded. The Delphi technique was selected to temper historical data with informed judgment. Three rounds of questionnaires were necessary to synthesize judgments of 23 key corporate individuals. Previous forecast errors ranged between ± 20 percent. In the base year the Delphi forecast was $359.1 million, and actual sales $360.2 million, an error of +0.3 percent. The next year forecast was $410 million, and actual sales $397 million, an error of −3.3 percent. The previous forecasting errors were reduced significantly, from 20 percent to less than 4 percent.[5]

---

[4]Rakesh K. Sarin, "An Approach for Long-Term Forecasting with an Application to Solar Energy," *Management Science* 25, no. 6 (June 1979), 543–54.

[5]Shankar Basu and Roger G. Schroeder, "Incorporating Judgments in Sales Forecasts: Application of the Delphi Method at American Hoist and Derrick," *Interfaces* 7, no. 3 (May 1977), 18–27.

Nominal group technique A qualitative forecasting technique in which a panel of experts working together in a meeting, arrive at a consensus through discussion and ranking of ideas.

Nominal Group Technique Like the Delphi technique, the nominal group technique involves a panel of experts. Unlike the Delphi technique, the nominal group technique affords opportunity for discussion among the experts.

The process works like this. Seven to ten experts are asked to sit around a table in full view of one another, but they are asked not to speak to one another. A group facilitator hands out copies of the question needing a forecast. Each expert is asked to write down a list of ideas about the question. After a few minutes, the group facilitator asks each expert in turn to share one idea from his or her list. A recorder writes each idea on a flip chart so that everyone can see it. The experts continue to give their ideas in a round-robin manner until all the ideas have been written on the flip chart. No discussion takes place in this phase of the meeting.

Usually between 15 and 25 ideas result from the round-robin. During the next phase of the meeting, the experts discuss the ideas that have been presented. The facilitator makes sure that all the ideas are discussed. Often similar ideas are combined, reducing the total number of ideas. When all discussion has ended, the experts are asked to rank the ideas, in writing, according to priority. The group concensus is the mathematically derived outcome of the individual rankings.

The keys to the nominal group process are clearly identifying the question, allowing creativity, encouraging discussion, and ultimately, ruling for concensus.

NAIVE (TIME-SERIES) QUANTITATIVE MODELS

Many models use historical data to calculate an average of past demand. This average is then used as a forecast. There are several ways of calculating an average; here are a few.

Simple average Average of demands occurring in all previous periods; the demands of all periods are equally weighted.

Simple Average A *simple average* (SA) is the average of the demands occurring in all previous periods. The demands of all periods are equally weighted:

$$\text{SA} = \frac{\text{sum of demands for all periods}}{\text{number of periods}} \tag{3.3}$$

$$= \frac{\sum_{i=1}^{n} D_i}{n}$$

$$= \frac{D_1 + D_2 + \ldots D_n}{n}$$

where

n = the number of periods
D_i = the demand in the ith period

Before proceeding, perhaps we should consider why we are averaging at all. As you may remember from our earlier discussion of "noise" in the demand data, we are trying to detect the underlying general pattern or central tendency of demand. The demand for any one period will probably be above or below the underlying pattern, and the demands for several periods will be dispersed or scattered around the pattern. Therefore, if we average all past demands, high demands in some periods will tend to offset low demands in other periods. The result will be an average that is representative of the pattern, particularly as the number of periods used in the average increases. Averaging reduces the chances of being misled by gross fluctuations that may occur in any single period. However, if the underlying pattern changes over time, simple averaging will not detect this change.

EXAMPLE

At Welds Supplies, demand for a new welding rod was 50 dozen in the first quarter, 60 dozen in the second, and 40 dozen in the third. The average demand has been:

$$\text{SA} = \frac{D_1 + D_2 + D_3}{3} = \frac{50 + 60 + 40}{3} = 50$$

A forecast for all future quarters could be based on this simple average and would be 50 dozen welding rods per quarter.

Simple moving average Average of demands occuring in several of the most recent periods; most recent periods are added and oldes ones dropped to keep calculations current.

Simple Moving Average A *simple moving average* (MA) combines the demand data from several of the most recent periods, their average being the forecast for the next period. Once the number of past periods to be used in the calculations has been selected, it is held constant. We may use a 3-period moving average or a 20-period moving average, but once we decide, we must continue to use the same number of periods. The demands for all periods are equally weighted. The average "moves" over time, in that, after each period elapses, the demand for the oldest period is discarded and the demand for the newest period is added for the next calculation, overcoming the major shortcoming of the simple averaging model.

A simple moving average is calculated as follows:

$$MA = \frac{\text{sum of demands for periods}}{\text{chosen number of periods}} \tag{3.4}$$

$$MA = \frac{\sum_{t=1}^{n} D_i}{n} = \frac{1}{n} D_1 + \frac{1}{n} D_2 + \ \ldots \frac{1}{n} D_n$$

where

n = the chosen number of periods
t = 1 is the oldest period in the n-period average
t = n is the most recent period
D_i = the demand in the ith period

EXAMPLE

Frigerware has experienced the following demand for ice coolers during the past six months:

Month	Ice Coolers Demanded
January	200
February	300
March	200
April	400
May	500
June	600

The plant manager has requested that you prepare a forecast using a six-period moving average to forecast July sales. It is now July 2, and we are to begin our production of ice coolers on July 6.

$$MA = \frac{\sum_{t=1}^{6} D_i}{6} = \frac{200 + 300 + 200 + 400 + 500 + 600}{6}$$
$$= 367$$

Using a six-month moving average, the July forecast is 367. Now examine the data. A three-month moving average might be a more accurate forecast. If we use three months, the forecast for July is:

$$MA = \frac{\sum_{t=1}^{3} D_i}{3} = \frac{400 + 500 + 600}{3}$$
$$= 500$$

If we use a one-month moving average, the forecasted demand for July is the actual demand for June, so the July forecast is 600.

We must make some recommendation to the plant manager for Frigerware. For now, let's recommend using a three-month moving average of 500 ice coolers for July, since that number looks more representative of the time-series pattern than does the six-month moving average, and it is based on more data than is the one-month moving average.

Weighted moving average An averaging method that allows for varying weighting of old demands.

Weighted Moving Average Sometimes the forecaster wants to use a moving average but does not want all n periods equally weighted. A *weighted moving average (WMA)* allows for varying, not equal, weighting of old demands:

$$WMA = \text{Each period's demand times a weight, summed over all periods in the moving average} \quad (3.5)$$

$$\text{n} = \sum_{t=1}^{n} C_t D_t$$

where

$$0 \leq C_t \leq 1$$
$$\sum_{t=1}^{n} C_t = 1$$

This model allows uneven weighting of demand. If n is three, for example, we could weight the most recent period twice as heavily as the other periods by setting $C_1 = .25$, $C_2 = .25$, and $C_3 = .50$.

EXAMPLE

For Frigerware, a forecast of demand for July using a three-period model with the most recent period's demand weighted twice as heavily as each of the previous two periods' demand is:

$$\text{WMA} = \sum_{t=1}^{3} C_t D_t = .25(400) + .25(500) + .50(600)$$

$$\text{WMA} = 525$$

An advantage of this model is that it allows you to compensate for some trend or seasonality by carefully fitting the coefficients, C_t. If you want to, you can weight recent months most heavily and still dampen somewhat the effects of noise by placing small weightings on older demands. Of course, the modeler or manager still has to choose the coefficients, and this choice is critical to model success or failure.

EXPONENTIAL SMOOTHING

Exponential smoothing An averaging method that exponentially decreases the weighting of old demands.

Exponential smoothing models are well known and often used in operations management. The reasons for their popularity are two: They are readily available in standard computer software packages, and they require relatively little data storage and computation, an important consideration when forecasts are needed for each of many individual items. Many computer companies have spent considerable time developing and marketing forecasting software and educating managers in how to use it. In addition, some major professional and trade associations, among them the American Production and Inventory Control Society (APICS), have introduced their members to these techniques.

Exponential smoothing is distinguishable by the special way it weights each past demand. The pattern of weights is *exponential* in form. Demand for the most recent period is weighted most heavily; the weights placed on successively older periods decrease exponentially. In other words, the weights decrease in magnitude the further back in time the data are weighted; the decrease is nonlinear (exponential).

First-Order Exponential Smoothing To begin, let's examine the computational aspect of first-order exponential smoothing. The equation for creating a new or updated forecast uses two pieces of information: actual demand for the most recent period and the most recent demand forecast. As each time period expires, a new forecast is made:

$$\begin{array}{l}\text{Forecast of next}\\ \text{period's demand}\end{array} = \alpha \begin{pmatrix}\text{actual}\\ \text{demand}\\ \text{for most}\\ \text{recent}\\ \text{period}\end{pmatrix} + (1-\alpha)\begin{pmatrix}\text{demand}\\ \text{forecast}\\ \text{for most}\\ \text{recent}\\ \text{period}\end{pmatrix} \qquad (3.6)$$

$$F_t = \alpha D_{t-1} + (1-\alpha)F_{t-1}$$

where

$$0 \le \alpha \le 1, \text{ and } t \text{ is the period}$$

After period $t - 1$ ends, you know the actual demand D_{t-1} for period $t - 1$. At the *beginning* of period $t - 1$, you made a forecast F_{t-1} of the demand during period $t - 1$. Therefore, at the *end* of $t - 1$, you have both pieces of information needed for calculating a forecast of demand for the next period F_t.

Why is this model called *exponential smoothing?* An expansion of Equation 3.6 shows

Since

$$F_t = \alpha\, D_{t-1} + (1 - \alpha)F_{t-1} \tag{3.7}$$

then

$$F_{t-1} = \alpha\, D_{t-2} + (1 - \alpha)F_{t-2} \tag{3.8}$$

and similarly

$$F_{t-2} = \alpha\, D_{t-3} + (1 - \alpha)F_{t-3} \tag{3.9}$$

We begin expanding by replacing F_{t-1} in Equation 3.7 with its equivalent, the right side of Equation 3.8.

$$F_t = \alpha\, D_{t-1} + (1 - \alpha)\ [\alpha\, D_{t-2} + (1 - \alpha)F_{t-2}] \tag{3.10}$$

$$F_t = \alpha\, D_{t-1} + \alpha(1 - \alpha)D_{t-2} + (1 - \alpha)^2 F_{t-2}$$

We continue expanding by replacing F_{t-2} in Equation 3.10 with its equivalent, the right side of Equation 3.9:

$$F_t = \alpha\, D_{t-1} + \alpha(1 - \alpha)D_{t-2} + (1 - \alpha)^2\ [\alpha\, D_{t-3} + (1 - \alpha)F_{t+3}] \tag{3.11}$$

$$F_t = \alpha\, D_{t-1} + \alpha(1 - \alpha)D_{t-2} + \alpha(1 - \alpha)^2\, D_{t-3} + (1 - \alpha)^3\, F_{t-3}$$

Equation 3.11 can be rewritten as follows:

$$F_t = \alpha(1 - \alpha)^0\, D_{t-1} + \alpha(1 - \alpha)^1\, D_{t-2} + \alpha(1 - \alpha)^2\, D_{t-3} + (1 - \alpha)^3\, F_{t-3} \tag{3.12}$$

We have expanded Equation 3.7 to obtain Equation 3.12. The expansion could be continued further, but it is not necessary for illustrating our point; Equation 3.12 shows the relative weight that is placed on each past period's demand in arriving at a new forecast.

Since $0 \leq \alpha \leq 1$, the terms $\alpha(1 - \alpha)^0$, $\alpha(1 - \alpha)^1$, $\alpha(1 - \alpha)^2$, and so forth are successively smaller in Equation 3.12. More specifically, these weights decrease exponentially. The most recent demand, D_{t-1}, is given the most weight, while the older data are weighted less and less heavily. Suppose, for example, that we are using $\alpha = .2$. Then $\alpha(1 - \alpha)^0 = .2$, $\alpha(1 - \alpha)^1 = .16$, $\alpha(1 - \alpha)^2 = .128$, and so forth, and these are the relative weightings being placed on D_{t-1}, D_{t-2}, D_{t-3}, and so forth, respectively. Remember, all of this is being accomplished automatically when you use Equation 3.7, the simple forecasting equation.

EXAMPLE

Phoenix General Hospital has experienced irregular, and usually increasing, demand for disposable kits throughout the hospital. The demand for a disposable plastic tubing in pediatrics for September was 300 units and for October, 350 units. The old forecast procedure was to use last year's average monthly demand as the forecast for each month this year. Last year's average monthly demand was 200 units. Using 200 units as the September forecast and a smoothing coefficient of .7 to weight recent demand most heavily, the forecast for *this* month, October, would have been (t = October):

$$
\begin{aligned}
F_t &= \alpha\, D_{t-1} + (1 - \alpha)F_{t-1} \\
&= .7(300) + (1 - .7)200 \\
&= 210 + 60 \\
&= 270
\end{aligned}
$$

The forecast for November would be (t = November):

$$
\begin{aligned}
F_t &= \alpha\, D_{t-1} + (1 - \alpha)F_{t-1} \\
&= .7(350) + (1 - .7)270 \\
&= 245 + 81 \\
&= 326
\end{aligned}
$$

Instead of last year's monthly demand for 200 units, November's forecast is 326 units. The old forecasting method, based on a simple average, provided a considerably different forecast from the exponential smoothing model.

Smoothing coefficient A numerical parameter that determines the weighting of old demands in exponential smoothing.

Smoothing Coefficient Selection As with other statistical forecasting models, in exponential smoothing we have the problem of parameter selection; that is, we must fit the model to the data. To begin forecasting, some reasonable estimate for an old beginning forecast is necessary. Likewise, a *smoothing coefficient,* α, must be selected. This choice is critical. As Equation 3.6 shows, a high α places heavy weight on the most

Service companies, such as McDonalds, need forecasts so managers can make decisions about inventory, production, labor, and overall costs.

Source: **Charles Weckler**

recent demand, and a low α weights recent demand less heavily. A high smoothing coefficient could be more appropriate for new products or items for which the underlying demand is shifting about (dynamic or unstable). An α of .7, .8, or .9 might be best for these conditions, although we question the use of exponential smoothing at all if unstable conditions are known to exist. If demand is very stable and believed to be representative of the future, the forecaster wants to select a low α value to smooth out any sudden noise that might have occurred. The forecasting procedure, then, does not overreact to the most recent demand. Under these stable conditions, an appropriate smoothing coefficient might be .1, .2, or .3. When demand is slightly unstable, smoothing coefficients of .4, .5, or .6 might provide the most accurate forecasts.

Figure 3.7 illustrates forecasting performance for two different smoothing coefficients for an unstable demand pattern. The exponential smoothing model with the higher α value performs best; it adapts more quickly to the shift in demand in period 4 than did the lower α value.

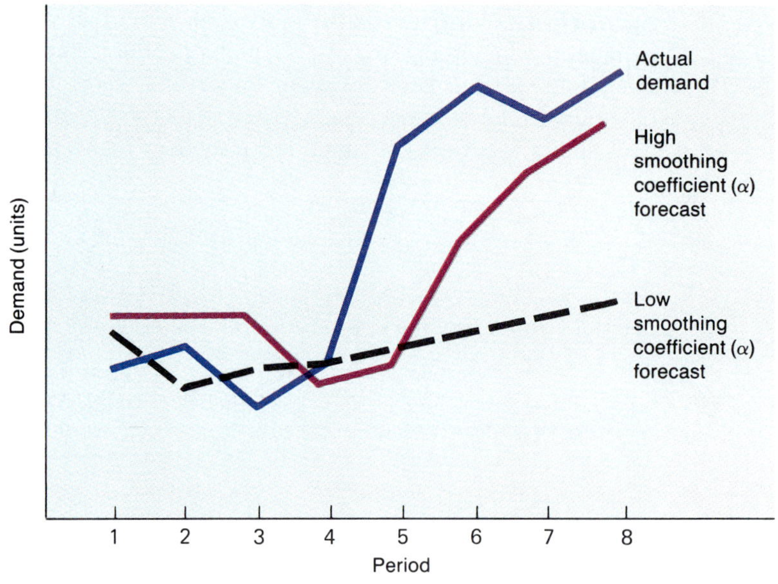

FIGURE 3.7 **Selection of smoothing coefficients**

Advantages Simple exponential smoothing and the other exponential smoothing models share the advantage of requiring that very few data points be stored. To update the forecast from period to period, you need only α, last period's demand, and last period's forecast. Remember, this model incorporates in the new forecast *all past demands.* The model is easy to understand and easily computerized for thousands of part numbers, supply items, or inventory items. The smoothing coefficient can be set for classes or families of items to minimize the cost of parameter selection. We have observed use of the model in both the manufacturing and service sectors. The model's operating simplicity and efficiency for economically obtaining "quick and easy" forecasts are its main advantages.

Selecting Forecasting Parameters and Comparing Models The procedure for selecting forecasting parameters is given in the first four steps that follow; the fifth step is used for comparing and selecting models:

1. Partition the available data into two subsets, one for fitting parameters (the "test" set) and the other for forecasting.
2. Select an error measure to evaluate forecast accuracy of the parameters to be tried. MAD and/or bias are useful error measures.
3. Select a range of α values. Using one of the α values, apply the forecasting model to the test set of data, recording the resulting forecast errors. Then, selecting a new value for α, repeat the process. Continue this process until representative α values in the selected range have been tested.
4. Select the α value that resulted in the lowest forecast error when applied to the test set. Your model is now fitted to the demand data.
5. Forecast using the balance of the data with the exponential (or moving average) model that you have fitted to the test set. Use the results to compare alternative models that have previously been fitted to representative demand data.

If you do not intend to compare models, there is no need to partition the data; *all* the data can be used in the test set in steps 1 through 4. Those familiar with computer programming can visualize how using computers can speed computations when this procedure is followed. Let's look at what a few companies are doing in Operations Management Highlight 3.2.

Adaptive exponential smoothing An average method in which a smoothing coefficient is not fixed but is set initially and then allowed to fluctuate over time based upon changes in the demand pattern.

Adaptive Exponential Smoothing If the modeler or manager is unsure about the stability or form of the demand pattern, *adaptive exponential smoothing* provides a good forecasting alternative. In adaptive exponential smoothing, the smoothing coefficient, α, is not fixed; it is set initially and then allowed to fluctuate over time based upon changes in the demand pattern.

Incorporating Trend and Seasonal Components Exponential smoothing models, as well as moving average models, can be modified to incorporate trend and seasonal components. So far, we have been forecasting the entire time series as though it had only a constant component (see Figure 3.3). If there is a trend, we could exponentially forecast the trend component. Similarly, we could exponentially forecast a seasonal component. Then we could build a composite forecast by putting the constant, trend, and seasonal together.

For example, a constant forecast of 1,050 units could be adjusted for a positive trend that was exponentially forecast to be 100 units, giving a total of 1,150 units. The forecast could be further adjusted by a multiplicative exponentially forecast seasonal factor. Assume that the seasonal factor is only 90 percent due to a natural downturn (seasonality). The resulting composite forecast is 1,035 units (90 percent of 1,150). Formulas are readily available for models such as this exponential smoothing model with additive trend and multiplicative seasonal factors.

OPERATIONS MANAGEMENT HIGHLIGHT 3.2

Source: Steve Niedorf/The Image Bank

Manufacturers Apply Forecasting in Operations

Wang Laboratories, Inc., has developed a monthly updated manufacturing plan that has analysts and management interacting as they forecast and schedule 98 percent of the corporation's hardware dollars. A 22-member manufacturing business planning group takes the view that manufacturing must control their forecasting destiny to validate marketing's sales goals and respond to finance's inventory and cost demands. Accurate, computerized forecasts allow Wang to generate each month a four-quarter plan. The procedure provides Wang a close look at the month ahead as they construct the corporate ship and build plans. The monthly master schedule covers 1,200 manufacturing end items. The forecasting software, Smart Forecasts II, is used to project product demand, shipments, and production assembly at both the aggregate and the manufacturing end-item levels.

Best Foods, a division of CPC International, ties nine plants and ten distribution centers together through a computerized forecasting-inventory system. Production, materials management, inventory control, and distribution are linked; the system is driven by forecasts. A forecasting software package that takes into account customer orders, lead times, and inventory safety stocks, firms up the production plan for the next two weeks. Within production the manufacturing planners and logistic schedulers can perform their jobs against firm plans. As a result, inventory was reduced by more than 15 percent in three years.

Some forecasting applications are more focused, directed at a small part of a manufacturer's task. Grumman Electronics Systems Division in Great River, New York, realized the need for a floor-space forecasting system that could answer such specific questions as whether a certain job could be fit into a certain facility or whether a night shift might be required to get a job done. The procedure was straightforward: A forecasting algorithm was developed, the database required from each department was determined, output was structured so that management could and would use the information, and the system was tested and implemented. This forecasting method has been in use for over ten years, forecasting floor-space needs for production, administrative, and laboratory needs.

At Abbott Laboratories, a focused application was the use of a forecasting model to relate productivity goals to direct and indirect labor requirements. Forecasters gave special attention to indirect labor, downtime, and quality assurance elements. Standards were determined and, using regression analysis, related to total production costs. Mathematical expressions relating indirect and direct labor hours to production costs were used as a basis for the computer forecasting program.

How accurate are computerized forecasting routines? The answer depends upon the value management places on accuracy. The Mennen Company, a leading manufacturer of health and beauty products, uses a short-range forecasting system that has an error rate of 9.6 percent, as compared to the industry average of 25 percent. Mennen is in a highly competitive, promotion-driven market that demands rapid changes in plans in reaction to competitors' actions. Demand is forecast for families of products rather than individual products by focusing on a key family member according to overall volume. To forecast, a 12-month actual sales history is secured, as well as a 12-month history on each product's proportion of the family's volume. Next, a 3-month forecast is made for each family. The family forecast is then broken down, product-by-product, to project individual sales. Managers at Mennen seem to have found they can achieve greater accuracy by forecasting high-volume representative products rather than forecasting each individual product in their line.

What do these applications all have in common? First, the computer was utilized because of the large number of products. Second, the focus was short-term, usually 2 to 4 weeks ahead, with a period-by-period updating in the planning horizon. Third, the forecasts for actual short-term manufacturing were driven by past data, ***not*** by managers' opinions. The past was repeatedly projected forward for many products. Finally, the focus was ***not*** on highly sophisticated models. They are naive, simple averaging models similar to those in this chapter. It would be too expensive for Wang, Best Foods, Grumman, Abbott, and Mennen to develop sophisticated causal models for each of their individual products.

Sources: "Balancing Plans Through Forecasting," ***Manufacturing Systems*** 7, no. 8 (August 1989), 54–55; Charles W. Chase, Jr., "Short-Range Production Based Forecasting at the Mennen Company," ***Journal of Business Forecasting*** 7, no. 4 (Winter 1988/1989), 2–5; Arthur B. Davis, "Forecast Modelling: A Practical Approach to Productivity Improvement," ***Industrial Management*** 30, no. 3 (May/June 1988), pp. 14–17; Jan Gordon, "The Best Approach to Integrated Logistics," ***Distribution*** 87, no. 2 (February 1988), 46, 48; and Paul J. Andrisani, "Manufacturing Floor Space Forecasting," ***Computers and Industrial Engineering*** 13, nos. 1–4 (1987), 92–95.

Double Exponential Smoothing Double exponential smoothing tends to smooth out noise in a stable demand time series. One large pharmaceutical manufacturer uses this model to forecast demand for thousands of drugs produced.

The model is straightforward; it smooths the first order exponential smoothing forecast and the old double exponential smoothing forecast.

$$\text{Forecast of next period's demand} = \alpha \begin{pmatrix} \text{first order} \\ \text{exponential} \\ \text{smoothing} \\ \text{forecast} \\ \text{for next} \\ \text{period} \end{pmatrix} + (1 - \alpha) \begin{pmatrix} \text{double} \\ \text{exponential} \\ \text{smoothing} \\ \text{forcast} \\ \text{for most recent} \\ \text{period} \end{pmatrix} \tag{3.13}$$

$$FD_t = \alpha F_t + (1 - \alpha)\ FD_{t-1}$$

where

$$0 \leq \alpha \leq 1$$

Notice that F_t is the first order exponential smoothing model set forth as Equation 3.6 and must be calculated *before* FD_t can be found.

EXAMPLE

Milo, Inc., has a first order exponential smoothing model that has forecasted 103,500 bushels for #3 grade wheat in Boone County for July. Last year's June production of #3 grade wheat was 70,500 bushels. We will use that figure as an estimate of the most recent double exponential smoothing forecast. Given that $\alpha = .20$ appears to be a good smoothing coefficient for Milo, calculate a double exponential smoothed forecast for July.

Let t = July

Then,

$$\begin{aligned} FD_t &= \alpha F_t + (1 - \alpha) FD_{t-1} \\ &= .2\ (103{,}500) + (1 - .2)(70{,}500) \\ &= 20{,}700 + 56{,}400 \\ &= 77{,}100 \end{aligned}$$

Our forecast for July is 77,100 bushels.

REGRESSION

Regression analysis A causal forecasting model in which, from historical data, a functional relationship is established between variables and then used to forecast dependent variable values.

Linear Regression *Regression analysis* is a forecasting technique that establishes a relationship between variables. One variable is known or assumed, and used to forecast the value of an unknown variable. Past data establishes a functional relationship between the two variables. We consider the simplest regression situation here, for only two variables and their linear functional relationship.

Our forecast of the period's demand, F_t, is expressed by

$$F_t = a + bX_t \tag{3.14}$$

where F_t is the forecast for period t, given we know the value of the variable X in period t. The coefficients a and b are constants; a is the intercept value for the vertical (F) axis and b is the slope of the line. Often this equation is expressed in the more familiar form

$$Y = a + bX \tag{3.15}$$

We have substituted F for Y, to indicate F is the forecasted value. In Equation 3.14, forecasted demand, F_t, reflects the future. However, to actually find coefficients a and b, old demand is utilized rather than the old forecast. We use D_t to reflect old demand and to find coefficients a and b. Then, once we want to forecast new demand, we use F_t to represent forecasted demand. The coefficients a and b are computed by the following two equations:

$$b = \frac{n\,(\Sigma X_t D_t) - (\Sigma X_t)\,(\Sigma D_t)}{n\,(\Sigma X_t^2) - (\Sigma X_t)^2} \tag{3.16}$$

$$a = \frac{\Sigma D_t - b\Sigma X_t}{n} \tag{3.17}$$

where

$$D = a + bX \text{ and} \tag{3.18}$$

$$n = \text{number of periods}$$

EXAMPLE

A paper box company makes carryout pizza boxes. The operations planning department knows that the pizza sales of a major client are a function of the advertizing dollars the client spends, an account of which they can receive in advance of the expenditure. Operations planning is interested in determining this relationship between the client's advertising and sales. The amount of pizza boxes the client will order, in dollar volume, is known to be a fixed percent of sales.

Quarterly advertising and sales

Quarter	Advertising (\$100,000)	Sales (\$1,000,000)
1	4	1
2	10	4
3	15	5
4	12	4
5	8	3
6	16	4
7	5	2
8	7	1
9	9	4
10	10	2

Computing b and then a, where advertising is X_t for quarter t, sales are D_t for quarter t, and forecast is F_t for future period t.

Quarter (t)	X_t Advertising (in \$100,000)	D_t Sales (in \$1,000,000)	D_t^2	X_tD_t
1	4	1	16	4
2	10	4	100	40
3	15	5	225	75
4	12	4	144	48
5	8	3	64	24
6	16	4	256	64
7	5	2	25	10
8	7	1	49	7
9	9	4	81	36
10	10	2	100	20
Σ	96	30	1060	328

$$b = \frac{10(328) - (96)30}{10(1060) - (96)^2} = .29$$

$$a = \frac{30 - .29(96)}{10} = .22$$

Thus, the estimated regression line, the relationship between future sales F_t and advertising X_t is

$$F_t = .22 + .29\ X_t$$

The operations planner can now ask for planned advertising expenditures, and from that sales can be forecast. Say, for example, next quarter advertising is expected to be \$1,100,000, or 11 \$100,000s. Substituting 11 for X_t into the equation above gives

$$F_t = .22 + .29(11) = 3.41$$

Sales are forecast as \$3,410,000. If box orders are 5 percent of sales, the operations planner could expect the total dollar orders to be \$170,500 for the quarter (.05 × \$3,410,000). Such an estimate can be very helpful in overall operations planning.

Although linear regression is computationally more complex than the other models we've discussed, it has been found useful in some situations. It may be applied, for example, when a plot of the data suggests that the demand pattern is a straight line, or nearly so. It requires much data, however, which can be cumbersome and costly to store. It is also costly to perform the required calculations period by period, often weekly, for thousands of items.

SELECTION OF THE FORECASTING MODEL

We've discussed several statistical forecasting models for demand estimation in planning and control. As a manager, you now have the task of selecting the best model for your needs. Which one should you choose, and what criteria should you use to make the decision?

As we've said before, important criteria are *cost* and *accuracy*. Accuracy (forecast error), as measured by MAD and Bias, can be converted into cost (dollars). *Costs to be considered in model selection are implementation costs, systemic costs, and forecast error costs.* Of the three, forecast error costs are perhaps the most complex to evaluate. They depend upon the noise in the time series, the demand pattern, the length of forecast period, and the measure of forecast error. There is no substitute for careful analysis of typical item demands, including plots, when a model is being selected.

Several studies have evaluated and compared the performance of different models. In general, different models are best, depending on the demand pattern, noise level, and length of forecast period. It is typical to have a choice of several good models for any one demand pattern, when the choice is based only on forecast error. Double exponential smoothing is the best model in many studies.

COMBINING NAIVE FORECASTING MODELS

In comprehensive studies it has been found that simple average and weighted average of forecasts from different forecasting methods outperformed most or perhaps even all the individual methods.[6] From these studies we can conclude that forecasting accuracy improves, and that the variability of accuracy among different combinations decreases, as the number of methods in the average increases. Combining forecasting models holds considerable promise for operations. As Makridakis and Winkler state, "Combining forecasts seem to be a reasonable practical alternative when, as is often the case, a true model of the data-generating process or a single best-forecast method cannot or is not, for whatever reason, identified."[7]

BEHAVIORAL DIMENSIONS OF FORECASTING

To understand some of the dimensions of forecasting it is wise to consider human behaviors, because forecasts are not always made with statistical models. Individuals can and do forecast by intuitively casting forth past data, and they often intervene in other ways in the statistical forecasting procedure as well. A manager may feel that item forecasts generated by models must be checked for reasonableness by qualified operating decision makers. Forecasts generated by models should not be followed blindly; potential cost consequences must be carefully considered. Decision makers can take into account qualitative data that are not in the model. Decision makers should use the forecasting model as an *aid* in decision making; they should not rely totally on the forecasting model for all decisions.

Many, perhaps most, forecasts for production/operations management are indi-

[6]Spyros Makridakis, et al., "The Accuracy of Extrapolation (Time Series) Methods: Result of a Forecasting Competition," *Journal of Forecasting* 1 (1982), 111–53; Spyros Makridakis and Robert L. Winkler, "Averages of Forecasts: Some Empirical Results," *Management Science* 29, no. 9 (September 1983), 987–96; Spyros Makridakis, "The Art and Science of Forecasting: An Assessment and Future Directions," *International Journal of Forecasting* 2 (1986), 15–39; Michael J. Lawrence, et al., "The Accuracy of Combining Judgmental and Statistical Forecasts," *Management Science* 32 (1986), 1521–32; and Thomas D. Russell and Everett E. Adam, Jr., "An Empirical Evaluation of Alternative Forecasting Combinations," *Management Science* 33 (1987), 1267–76.

[7]Makridakis and Winkler, "Averages of Forecasts," p. 987.

vidual intuitive forecasts. We have observed intuitive forecasts, for example, in large firebrick manufacturing facilities and in hospitals. One of the problems for implementing item forecasting models is convincing the intuitive forecaster that he or she is not doing as good a job as could be done by a model.

INTUITIVE FORECASTING AS A JUDGMENTAL PROCESS

Currently, little is known about the effectiveness of intuitive forecasting. We can, however, analyze some of the mental processes involved. A forecast may be regarded as the culmination of a process consisting of several stages, including information search and information processing. It results in human inferences about the future that are based on particular patterns of historical data presented to the forecaster. We can speculate about a number of environmental factors that may affect these mental processes and thereby affect intuitive forecasting.

Meaningfulness Forecasting requires considering a restricted set of information about historical demand. When we discuss job enrichment and job design (Chapter 8), we will find that, if repetitious tasks can be made meaningful to the person performing them, positive effects usually result. Imparting meaningfulness to the task of forecasting, then, may be expected to affect the reliability of intuitive forecasting: the more meaningful the forecasting task, the more accurate the intuitive forecast.

Pattern Complexity *Pattern complexity,* the shape of the demand pattern, is a critical variable in intuitive forecasting, just as it is in model forecasting. Some behavioral studies suggest that intuitive forecasters may perform better on linear than on nonlinear demand patterns. In addition, people apparently try to use nonlinear data in a linear manner.

Degree of Noise Given sufficient historical data, the forecasting problems are trivial for most cases without noise. Introducing random variations, however, often brings about a condition called *cue uncertainty.* Very high noise levels obscure the basis for accurate forecasting, and often the result is lower forecast accuracy.

Individual Variability Another finding in intuitive forecasting studies is the wide variability of performance among the forecasters. When comparing forecasters with models, there are typically a few very good forecasters, but there are even more very poor forecasters. If planning and directing production and operations are based on poor intuitive forecasts, these variations in performance can be very expensive.

Individual Versus Model Performance How do individuals compare to naive forecasting models? In studies, exponential smoothing models, when fit to the historical demands given to intuitive forecasters, significantly outperformed group average performance. Only a very few good intuitive forecasters outperformed the models. The operations manager would be wise to consider models as an alternative to individuals. Models generally are more accurate, and if a large number of items must be forecast, the models are more economical.

Forecasting, Planning, and Behavior An excellent literature review and evaluation compares many modeling and psychological dimensions of forecasting, planning, and decision making.[8] Many information processing limitations and biases involving human judgment apply to forecasting and planning as well. Errors in forecasting procedures are caused by using redundant information, failing to seek possible disconfirming evidence, and being overconfident about judgments. In addition, numerous studies show that the predictive judgment of humans is frequently less reliable than that of simple quantitative models. Those interested in the behavioral aspects of forecasting will want to examine this literature review more closely.

SUMMARY

This chapter illustrated that in operations management, we deviate from the general business concept of business forecasting and define forecasting as the use of past data to determine future events. Prediction, on the other hand, refers to subjective estimates of the future. A manager's skill, experience, and sound judgment are required for good predictions; often statistical and management science techniques must be used to make reasonable forecasts.

We studied the tradeoffs between cost and accuracy in forecasting approaches. Generally, the less expensive the forecasting approach, the less accurate the results. We discussed three basic groupings of forecasting techniques: qualitative models, naive (time series) models, and causal models. The individual item forecasting situation most frequently encountered in production/operations management is best approached with naive (time series) models.

Research results illustrated that the best forecasting model to use depends upon the length of the forecast period; the level of noise; the measure of forecast error; and, most important, the demand pattern. We noted that there appears to be no one forecasting model that is best for all demand patterns, although double exponential smoothing does as well as any other.

Often, forecasts are not made with statistical models; individuals can and do intuitively use past data to forecast future events. Our discussion showed, however, that individual forecasting performance generally *decreases* with meaninglessness, pattern complexity, and cue uncertainty. Forecast models tend to outperform most intuitive forecasts, though a few individuals can consistently outperform the models.

CASE

Northwestern Hospital Supply

Suzi Trotter was hired by a hospital supply company, Northwestern Hospital Supply, Inc., as a salesperson two years ago. Having successfully developed sales in western Oregon, Suzi has been shifted to operations and is now an operations analyst. She knows that if she can perform well in this job, she will likely be a regional operations manager or an area sales manager in 12 to 36 months.

[8] Robin M. Hogarth and Spyros Makridakis, "Forecasting and Planning: An Evaluation," *Management Science* 27, no. 2 (February 1981), 115–38.

Suzi's first assignment is to recommend an item forecasting procedure for a family of parts that includes orthopedic supplies. The demand for one representative item, burn dressing rolls, is shown in the table below. The current forecasting procedure for this item is to rely on the intuitive forecast made by an experienced supply clerk. After reviewing class notes from an operations course she took three years ago at Oregon State, Suzi has decided to test a first-order exponential smoothing model. Her supervisor thinks the data are seasonal and would like a model that reflects seasonality. Suzi would like to use the company's computer to test differing values of the smoothing coefficient, but she is unsure of her programming skills.

After thinking about a forecasting model and selecting parameters (starting values and smoothing coefficients), Suzi has decided to use MAD as her primary evaluation mechanism. She has heard of Bias, but remembers nothing of significance that would suggest she should use it.

Burn dressing roll demand

Time Period (week)	Sales	Time Period (week)	Sales
1	1084	25	964
2	1056	26	936
3	1090	27	970
4	953	28	833
5	868	29	748
6	868	30	847
7	1034	31	905
8	1088	32	968
9	1069	33	861
10	856	34	736
11	876	35	757
12	796	36	752
13	1023	37	903
14	1003	38	883
15	1036	39	916
16	835	40	715
17	747	41	691
18	856	42	736
19	1008	43	888
20	1036	44	908
21	920	45	909
22	805	46	685
23	816	47	696
24	776	48	692

Case Questions

1. What patterns do you observe when you plot the data?
2. Design an analysis procedure for Suzi Trotter. Include forecasting model(s), evaluation measure(s), and the procedure for setting starting values and model parameters.

3. How could simple moving average and first order exponential models be modified to include adjustments for trend and seasonal data?
4. Implement the recommended analysis procedure. A computer with software such as the QSOM package or programmable calculator might be helpful, but neither is necessary.
5. Discuss the implementation problems Suzi might encounter once her analysis is complete.

CASE

Spradling Enterprises

Spradling Enterprises manufactures household cleaning products. One product, Stain-ReMover, product number SRM-10, has been difficult to produce in enough volume to sustain inventory between production batches. The table below illustrates monthly demand for the last 15 months, essentially the total life of SRM-10.

Monthly demand for Stain-ReMover

Month	Demand (in 24-case lots)	Month	Demand (in 24-case lots)
December 1990	22	August	57
January 1991	40	September	55
February	32	October	65
March	55	November	73
April	67	December	90
May	53	January 1992	81
June	90	February	93
July	62		

The production manager has asked production control to reexamine the item forecasting procedure for this product. For a new product, one that has been on the market less than 12 months, an initial 12-month forecast from marketing is typically used. In the absence of other instructions, marketing's forecast of 50 lots per month has been used to date for SRM-10.

Once a product has been on the market for 12 months, Spradling Enterprises uses first order exponential smoothing for forecasting demand. For each product, either a slow smoothing (smoothing coefficient of .2) or a fast smoothing (smoothing coefficient of .7) model is used. The choice of fast or slow smoothing is based primarily on mean absolute deviation (MAD) over the last six periods of data, with some consideration given secondarily to Bias. The initial forecast needed to evaluate fast or slow smoothing for a new product is always the marketing forecast.

The production control manager is concerned about changing the Stain-ReMover forecast to correspond with current procedures, and the more general problem of developing a checklist for reviewing the existing forecasting procedure.

REVIEW AND DISCUSSION QUESTIONS

1. Contrast forecasting and prediction and give an example of each.
2. Forecasting is important for operations subsystem decisions. Explain what might be forecast for a supermarket operation and relate that information to Figure 3.2.
3. Explain what demand noise, pattern, and stability are in time-series analyses.
4. Which would you use in evaluating a forecast, MAD or Bias? Why?
5. Present evidence that suggests forecasting is an important tool in the service sector.
6. Examine Table 3.1, which summarizes modern forecasting techniques. Is there any one best technique? What can be concluded from this table?
7. Describe the cost/accuracy tradeoffs associated with both sophisticated statistical models and intuitive forecasting.
8. Explain how the nominal group technique delivers a consensus forecast.
9. Explain how the Delphi technique delivers a consensus forecast.
10. What are some of the variables that affect the accuracy of intuitive forecasts?
11. Compare intuitive forecasting to naive statistical forecasting models. As an operations manager, how would you forecast—intuitive, or by model? Why?

PROBLEMS

SOLVED PROBLEMS

1. Demand for part number 2710 was 200 in April, 50 in May, and 150 in June. The forecast for April was 100 units. With a smoothing constant of .20 and using first order exponential smoothing, what is the July forecast? Is .20 a good choice as a smoothing constant?

SOLUTION

$$
\begin{aligned}
F_t &= \alpha D_{t-1} + (1 - \alpha)F_{t-1} \\
F_{\text{MAY}} &= .20(200) + (1 - .2)100 \\
&= 120 \\
F_{\text{JUNE}} &= .2(50) + (1 - .2)120 \\
&= 106 \\
F_{\text{JULY}} &= .2(150) + (1 - .2)106 \\
&= 114.8 \\
&\cong 115
\end{aligned}
$$

The July forecast is 115 units (fractional units should be rounded to be realistic). Given the .20 smoothing constant, recent demand is not weighted heavily. This seems appropriate for this data. If demand is unstable, a higher constant should be used. The forecast should react quickly to changes in demand. However, if demand smooths out over a long period, the .20 constant may be satisfactory, since it helps to remove noise. It is almost impossible to select a smoothing coefficient with only three periods of data.

2. An ice cream parlor experienced the following demand for ice cream last month. The current forecasting procedure is to use last year's corresponding weekly sales as this year's forecast.

Week	Forecasted Demand (in gallons)	Actual Demand (in gallons)
June 1	210	200
June 8	235	225
June 15	225	200
June 22	270	260

Calculate MAD and Bias and interpret each.

SOLUTION

$$\begin{aligned} \text{MAD} &= |210 - 200| + |235 - 225| + |225 - 200| + |270 - 260| \\ &= \frac{55}{4} \\ &= 13.75 \\ \text{Bias} &= (210 - 200) + (235 - 225) + (225 - 200) + (270 - 260) \\ &= \frac{55}{4} \\ &= +13.75 \end{aligned}$$

Since all monthly errors are positive, each error measure gives the same results: The forecasts are consistently high, an average of 13.75 gallons per week.

REINFORCING FUNDAMENTALS

3. A manufacturer of mole and gopher poison has experienced the following monthly demand for an environmentally sound pesticide poison.

Month	Actual Demand (in cases)
February	620
March	840
April	770
May	950
June	1000

(a) Using a simple average, what would the forecast have been for May and June?

(b) What would the three-month simple moving average have been for May and June?

(c) Which forecasting method would you recommend? Why?

4. The monthly cost of overstocking crates of bananas in a grocery chain is estimated to be $5.50 times the absolute value of average daily Bias for any one month.

(a) Express this relationship as a cost function.

(b) If daily Bias was a positive 137 crates last month, what was the total cost for that error?

(c) How much should management be willing to spend for a perfect forecast?

5. Max's hardware chain experienced the following demand for paint last month. The current forecasting procedure is to use last year's corresponding weekly sales as this year's forecast. Calculate MAD and Bias and interpret each.

Week	Forecasted Demand (in gallons)	Actual Demand (in gallons)
June 1	2,320	2,310
June 8	2,335	2,325
June 15	2,350	2,325
June 22	2,370	2,360

6. A department store analyst is interested in using the change in price of sugar in any given month to predict the change in price of candy the following month. She observes the following monthly sequence of sugar prices (not sugar price changes);

80, 82, 85, 81, 80, 80, 80, 84, 88, 89, 90, 88, 84.

Candy prices in the same months are:

105, 100, 105, 114, 107, 105, 104, 105, 110, 117, 120, 121, 118.

(a) Construct the appropriate scales for graphing and plot the data.

(b) Find the estimated regression line.

(c) What do you conclude about the relationship between the change in sugar price and the change in candy price? Might this knowledge lead to improved forecasts? How can that help store operations?

7. Blakeman's Supply stocks three-horsepower motors. Weekly demand for 12 typical weeks is:

Week	Demand for 3-hp Motor	Week	Demand for 3-hp Motor
42	20	48	9
43	17	49	4
44	12	50	6
45	14	51	5
46	8	52	4
47	10	53	3

(a) Calculate a weighted moving average forecast for weeks 54 and 55 using a three-period model with the most recent period's demand weighted three times as heavily as each of the previous two period's demands. After forecasting period 54, actual demand was 6 motors for the period.

(b) Examining the data visually, what would you suggest as a possible alternative to the weighted moving average model? Why?

8. A small electronics company produces pocket calculators and records the demand monthly. The following demand data are for a representative calculator: November, 45; December, 57; January, 60. Using 50 as the first order exponential smoothing forecast for November, forecast February sales.

9. New Cap is introducing a new line of men's hunting caps. New Cap wants to forecast component items for these hats with its existing simple exponential smoothing forecasting model. Management has no historical data for these hunting caps.

(a) What do you recommend to New Cap for the initial parameters and a smoothing coefficient for monthly forecasts for the next six months? Why?

(b) After four months you have the following data on actual demand. Would you agree with New Cap's choice of a smoothing coefficient of .3, or would you choose .9, the only other value New Cap will consider for now? Assume that the June forecast was 100.

Month	Caps Shipped (in dozen)
June	150
July	275
August	310
September	475

10. A company statistician is interested in the relationship between the length and the weight of extrusions. Extrusions come in all sizes, shapes, and thicknesses. A random sample of extrusions is taken, with the following results (X = length in inches, F = weight in pounds):

X: 70 75 64 67 71 70 68 76 68 69 70

F: 175 198 156 180 178 182 160 204 167 169 162

(a) Construct a plot of the data.

(b) Find a and b, and draw the estimated regression line, choosing F as the dependent variable.

(c) Does the use of a linear regression model improve our ability to predict F, given X?

(d) If an extrusion is chosen at random and is 70 inches long, use the estimated regression line to predict weight. Such a "prediction" is different from "demand forecasting" but is an important use of regression in operations.

11. A university central store experiences demand for staplers, which appears to follow this distribution:

Time Period	Staplers Demand	Time Period	Staplers Demanded
10	92	15	138
11	117	16	"182"
12	105	17	"187"
13	135	18	"185"
14	143	19	"210"

The forecast for period 16 was 150 units. The quotes (" ") mean actual demand is known at the end of that period. Using first order exponential smoothing with a moderately responsive smoothing coefficient of .3, forecast the demand for periods 17 through 20. Now plot the actual and forecasted demand for all periods for which you have data. Recommend to management an improved forecasting method and support your recommendation.

12. Smithton Corporation uses a first order exponential smoothing model. For one item, the model provided a demand forecast of 75,500 units. This forecast was used as November's production requirements. Although demand was actually 72,700 units during November, 75,500 units were produced. Calculate a double exponential smoothed forecast for December using 70,000 units as November's double exponential smoothed forecast. Use .3 for all smoothing coefficients.

CHALLENGING EXERCISES

13. For the last three years, Professor Gregopolus has been intuitively forecasting the number of students who will enroll in her classes. She really believes that no one knows as much about the value of her classes as she does. Therefore, how could others possibly forecast enrollments better than she? Her forecasts and actual enrollments are given below (rounded to multiples of ten).

Semester	Forecasted Enrollment	Actual Enrollment	Semester	Forecasted Enrollment	Actual Enrollment
Fall 1987	———	70	Fall 1989	80	120
Spring 1988	90	60	Spring 1990	120	80
Fall 1988	90	70	Fall 1990	150	60
Spring 1989	100	60			

(a) How accurate has Professor Gregopolus's been, based on MAD and Bias? Explain what this accuracy means to Professor Gregopolus.

(b) Use 60 students as the forecast for Spring 1988, a smoothing coefficient of .2, and MAD to evaluate the model forecast with first order exponential smoothing.

(c) What can you tell Professor Gregopolus about intuition versus modeling as approaches to forecasting?

(d) Based on all of the above, what do you recommend to Professor Gregopolus as a forecasting approach?

14. An operations manager is interested in forecasting how training will affect efficiency for production workers assigned to a new job. He gave five different amounts of training, varying from one-half a day to 4 days. Ten workers took each of the training levels, 50 workers in all. The table below shows each worker's labor efficiency for the first week's work, 100 being the standard or expected output.

	Training (in days)				
	0.50	1	2	3	4
Efficiency	117	106	76	125	85
	85	81	88	113	129
	112	74	115	93	90
	81	79	113	89	124
	105	118	108	117	117
	80	82	83	81	97
	73	86	81	86	93
	110	111	112	88	122
	78	113	120	120	92

(a) Find the linear regression equation for predicting efficiency, given training.
(b) Plot the linear regression equation, along with the data, on a scatter diagram. What does this result mean to the manager?
(c) Calculate the mean and variance for each training group. What can you conclude from comparing groups?

15. Recently, demand for a new carburetor filter stocked by a regional supply house has increased drastically (mechanics and the general public are becoming aware of the filter's fuel economy). Weekly demand is given below.

Week	Actual Demand	Week	Actual Demand	Week	Actual Demand
23	100	31	450	39	927
24	75	32	510	40	950
25	210	33	600	41	945
26	250	34	550	42	1,050
27	350	35	725	43	1,150
28	365	36	775	44	1,200
29	400	37	750	45	1,210
30	425	38	825	46	1,295

(a) Fit a first order exponential smoothing model that minimizes MAD to these data.

(b) Attempt to reduce the overall MAD (for the 24 periods of data) by using another model. Feel free to develop a model or to choose a model from a source other than this text. Explain *why* you proceeded as you did.

16. Barfy Burgers, Inc., is a northeastern generic hamburger chain that has just completed its fifth year of operation. Every month Barfy must purchase meat for the succeeding month. Due to historical demand fluctuations, Buster Barfy, vice president of operations, has difficulty knowing what future sales to expect. Shown below are the number of thousand pounds of meat demanded during each month of the firm's first five years of operation.

	Jan	Feb	Mar	Apr	May	June	July	Aug	Sept	Oct	Nov	Dec
1987	695	693	714	733	740	684	723	750	790	734	718	730
1988	768	772	765	722	719	777	753	762	732	780	750	705
1989	828	776	823	859	778	776	763	810	759	834	837	786
1990	814	790	841	817	849	769	904	808	809	828	885	849
1991	866	850	869	818	802	754	844	811	811	817	801	810

Based on Barfy's past demand, determine the monthly demand for January 1992.

17. Compare first order exponential smoothing and double exponential smoothing over March and April. Minimize the tracking signal (TS)

$$TS = \frac{\text{Bias}}{\text{MAD}}$$

for your recommendation of a model.

Month	Parts Demanded	First Order Exponential Smoothing (smoothing coefficient = .4)	Double Exponential Smoothing (all smoothing coefficients = .4)
January	100	120	110
February	"200"[a]		
March	"150"		
April	"120"		

18. E-Z Photocopying Service has experienced weekly demand for photocopying at the university copying center, as shown below. Currently, the forecasting procedure is to use the previous week's average daily demand as the next week's daily forecast. Staffing decisions for the next week are based on this forecast.

Week	Average Daily Demand (in thousands)	Week	Average Daily Demand (in thousands)
Feburary 7	27	March 6	32
Feburary 14	20	March 13	30
Feburary 21	22	March 21	38
Feburary 28	30	March 28	

(a) Forecast the demand for the week of March 28 using double exponential smoothing as the forecasting model. Use smoothing constants of .2, and February 28 actual demand as the estimate for March 6 forecasted demand required. Forecast for March 28 based on experience in March (i.e., do not forecast February at all).

(b) Using MAD as your criterion for evaluation, do you recommend double exponential smoothing or the current forecasting procedure?

(c) What might E-Z management do to further improve forecasting accuracy?

UTILIZING QSOM COMPUTER SOFTWARE[9]

19. Reconsider the data in Problem 15.

(a) Using the QSOM time series forecasting option, fit a first order experimental smoothing model that minimizes MAD to this data.

(b) Plot and print your results for the best fitting model.

20. Consider the quarterly houseboat demand, below, for URboat, a regional manufacturer.

Year	Quarter	Actual Demand	Year	Quarter	Actual Demand
1983	1	50	1986	1	62
	2	45		2	56
	3	52		3	65
	4	56		4	71
1984	1	53	1987	1	65
	2	48		2	60
	3	57		3	70
	4	62		4	77
1985	1	56	1988	1	73
	2	50		2	66
	3	60		3	75
	4	67		4	85

[9]QSOM is a software package developed by Prentice-Hall as an operations management text supplement. QSOM utilizes microcomputers. See the Preface, and contact Prentice-Hall regarding availability. Instructors should see the *Instructor's Manual.*

(a) Plot the data and examine for trends and seasonality. Read the data into QSOM.

(b) Using smoothing coefficients of .2, .4, .6, and .8, along with first order exponential smoothing, select the best coefficient (lowest MAD and bias values, equally weighted). Plot and print out results for your best-fitting model.

(c) If your examination of the data shows no trend and/or seasonality, use the double exponential smoothing model. If there is trend in the data, try exponential smoothing with linear trend utilizing a smoothing coefficient of .2. Record the MAD value.

(d) If there is trend and seasonality, try the Winter's model presented in QSOM. For this model, you must enter three coefficients for each run (coefficient 1 = constant component, coefficient 2 = trend component, coefficient 3 = seasonal component). All coefficients may be the same. Use a smoothing coefficient of .2 for all three components and record the MAD value.

(e) Select one of these three models in parts (c) and (d) and do an analysis similar to your first order exponential smoothing analysis in part (b) for the best-fitting model. Print results with lowest MAD value of best-fitting model. Note: If Winter's model is the best fitting, use all combinations of .3 and .7 for each of the three coefficients to determine lowest MAD and for printout.

KEY TERMS

Adaptive exponential smoothing 97
Bias 83
Causal forecasting models 85
Delphi technique 89
Demand stability 82
Demand pattern 81
Demand-based forecasting models 85
Dependent demand 82
Exponential smoothing 93
Forecast error 82
Forecast 78
Independent demand 82
Intuitive forecasts 85
Mean absolute deviation (MAD) 82
Noise 82
Nominal group technique 90
Prediction 78
Regression analysis 100
Simple average 90
Simple moving average 91
Smoothing coefficient 95
Statistical forecasting models 85
Time series analysis 81
Weighted moving average 92

SELECTED READINGS

Biggs, Joseph R., and William M. Campion, "The Effect and Cost of Forecast Error Bias for Multi-Stage Production-Inventory Systems," *Decision Sciences* 13, no. 4 (October 1982), 570–84.

Box, G. E. P., and G. M. Jenkins, *Time Series Analysis, Forecasting, and Control.* San Francisco: Holden-Day, 1970.

Brown, R. G., *Smoothing, Forecasting & Prediction of Discrete Time Series.* Englewood Cliffs, N.J.: Prentice Hall, 1963.

Delbecq, Andre, Andrew Van deVen, and David Gustafson, *Group Techniques for Program Planning.* Glenview, Ill.: Scott, Foresman, 1975.

Hanke, John, "Forecasting in Business Schools: A Follow-Up Survey," *International Journal of Forecasting* (Netherlands) 5, no. 2 (1989), 259–62.

Hogarth, Robin M., and Spyros Makridakis, "Forecasting and Planning: An Evaluation," *Management Science* 27, no. 2 (February 1981) 115–38.

Lawrence, Michael J., et al., "The Accuracy of Combining Judgmental and Statistical Forecasts," *Management Science* 32 (1986), 1521–32.

Lee, T.S., and Everett E. Adam, Jr., "Forecasting Error Evaluation in Material Requirements Planning (MRP) Production-Inventory Systems," *Management Science* 32, no. 9 (September 1986), 1186–1205.

Makridakis, Spyros, et al., "The Accuracy of Extrapolation (Time Series) Methods: Results of a Forecasting Competition," *Journal of Forecasting* 1 (1982), 111–153.

Makridakis, Spyros and S. C. Wheelwright, *Forecasting Methods and Applications.* New York: John Wiley, 1978.

Muth, J. F., "Optimal Properties of Exponentially Weighted Forecasts," *Journal of the American Statistical Association* 55, no. 290 (June 1960), 297–306.

CHAPTER 4

DESIGNING PRODUCTS, SERVICES, AND PROCESSES

Developing a turbofan engine to power a modern commercial passenger transport requires an investment of $1 billion and takes approximately four years of design and testing.

The investment must begin, along with the engineering effort, before the actual market is developed. As the market unfolds, the aircraft and the engine are modified to insure acceptability and profitability at the time of introduction.

During the initial design period, dialogue must be firmly established between the engineering teams and the manufacturing teams. This dialogue and the resultant team-building not only assures a "design to cost" philosophy but aids the development process when a component must be redesigned for cost, market, or reliability reasons.

Throughout the design and development phase, "real time" data allow the entire team to know the status of drawing releases, hardware promises, required dates, and problem areas. It is only with this knowledge that program management can make the decisions and implement the actions needed for an on-time, on-budget engine development program.

Because of their complexities, the core of engine development programs is team effort; specialists from manufacturing, engineering, test, and marketing join together using a common "real time" database to identify and provide solutions to the problems. This teamwork ensures the product will be accepted in the market and yield an acceptable return on investment.

James W. Tucker, General Manager
Evendale Product Engineering Operation
Aircraft Engine Engineering Division
General Electric Company
Cincinnati, Ohio

In planning the conversion system, major decisions are made concerning the design of the product or service as well as the design of conversion processes to produce the product or service. We address these decisions by first presenting the design of new products, followed by the design of manufacturing processes. After presenting each separately for manufacturing, we consider service product and process design choices together.

NEW PRODUCT DESIGN (PRODUCT DEVELOPMENT)

THE ORIGIN OF NEW PRODUCTS

Entrepreneurs frequently form new businesses on the basis of a unique product idea or needed service. As competitors infringe on the market, replicating products and services, or as the useful product life diminishes, firms ordinarily prepare to bring out new products or services. These new product and service ideas come from various sources, including customers, top management, and staff from marketing, research and development, production, and engineering. Once launched, even good products have limited lives and, to remain viable, the organization seeks a flow of new product possibilities. Let's examine the product's birth-to-mortality pattern.

PRODUCT LIFE CYCLE

Product life cycle Pattern of demand throughout the product's life; similar patterns and stages can be identified for the useful life of a process.

The demand for a product—its market acceptance—generally tends to follow a predictable pattern called the *product life cycle*.[1] Products go through a series of stages, beginning with low demand during market development, proceeding through growth, maturity, high-volume saturation, and finally decline. The time spans of the stages vary considerably across industries. For novelty products, the time from birth to death may be as short as a few weeks or months. For other products the life cycle may span many years or even decades. In any case the very nature of this pattern raises significant questions for operations management. When will the various stages occur, and how must operations accommodate them? What facilities, materials, labor, and management systems are optimal for meeting demand? What should be done with existing facilities and conversion processes as products proceed through their various stages? Let's look at some major operations issues arising from the product life cycle.

Operations Issues in the Product Life Cycle From an operations management viewpoint, the life cycle can be reconstructed into four stages, as shown in Figure 4.1, to reveal four important issue areas. As you can see, the operations strategy and conversion technology have to be adaptive throughout the life cycle because product variety, volume, industry structure, and form of competition all are changing. Consider,

[1]For an empirical approach to evaluating product life cycles, see Cornelis A. deKluyver, "Innovation and Industrial Product Life Cycles," *California Management Review* 20, no. 1 (Fall 1977), 21–3. Process and facility life cycles are discussed in Roger W. Schmenner, "Every Factory Has a Cycle," *Harvard Business Review* 61, no. 2 (March–April 1983), 121–29.

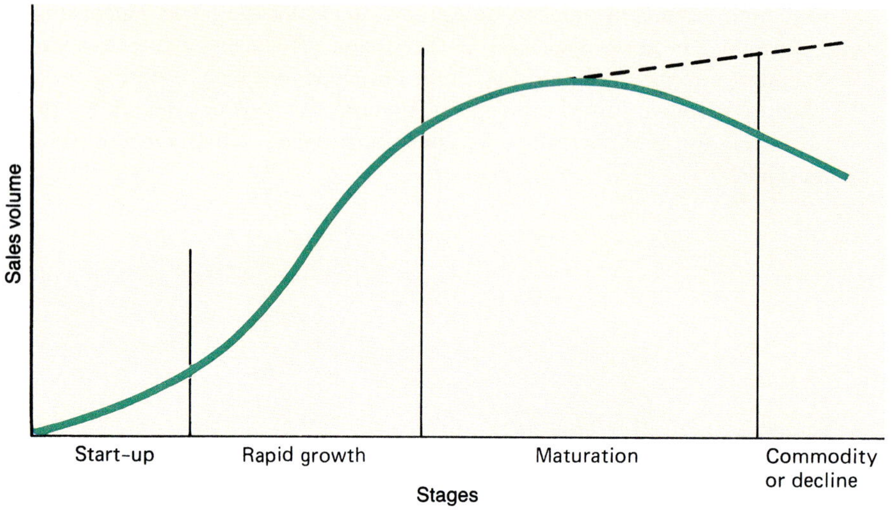

Product variety:	Great variety	Increasing standardization	Emergence of a "dominant design"	High standardization "commodity" characteristics
Product volume/model:	Low volume	Increasing volume	High volume	High volume
Industry structure:	Small competitors	Fallout and consolidation	Few large companies	"Survivors"
Form of competition:	Product characteristics	Product quality and availability	Price and dependability	Price

FIGURE 4.1 **Characteristics of the product life cycle important to manufacturing process technology**
Source: **R. H. Hayes and S. C. Wheelwright, *Restoring Our Competitive Edge* (New York: John Wiley, 1984), 203.**

for example, differences in the demands on product design and production in the start-up phase, where design changes are frequent, versus the final stage where the design of the product is stable and, consequently, so is the conversion process.

As fewer but larger competitors emerge, the form of competition shifts dramatically, requiring commensurate changes in the manufacturing competence. Whereas the early life-cycle stages emphasize the product's unique characteristics and quality, later life-cycle stages emphasize price competition and delivery capabilities. Survival in the market depends on producing a stable product with high volume in contrast to the earlier emphasis on a high product variety, low-volume conversion process. The conversion process has changed substantially, including new types of human skills and orientations, equipment and facility revisions, and planning and control systems. What can be done to prepare for and influence these adaptations? Part of the answer is to use research and development (R&D) to create new products and production processes.

Phasing Multiple Products A general strategy of phasing new products in and phasing old products out sustains existing processing technology: As existing products are demanded less during the later stages of their life cycles, new products are developed and produced so that output capacity can remain stable.

Of course, transitions are not always smooth; rarely does capacity remain constant. The technologies needed to produce different products are not identical, and changes are almost always necessary. Organizations do not always have a new product waiting for introduction at the precise moment that an existing product begins to decline. Furthermore, rates of growth and decline may not be predictable. Promotional efforts, however, can sometimes influence rates of growth and decline. IBM, an expert at planned change, has introduced new computer lines since the late 1950s. Phasing new computers in to and old ones out of its basic product line, IBM plans for the changes in its market.

Research and development (R&D) Organizational efforts directed toward product and process innovation; includes stages of basic research, applied research, development, and implementation.

Research and Development (R&D) Many organizations, especially larger ones, do not leave the development of new products and processes to chance. They devote their efforts toward creating new products, find new uses for existing products, and develop new processes that will reduce capital or manufacturing costs. These are the objectives of research and development.[2]

Developing a successful new product or process takes many steps and involves the talent and expertise of many people. As new-product ideas are created, they are evaluated for economic feasibility, market potential, functional testing, and so on. As shown in Figure 4.2, only a small percentage of new-product ideas become commercial

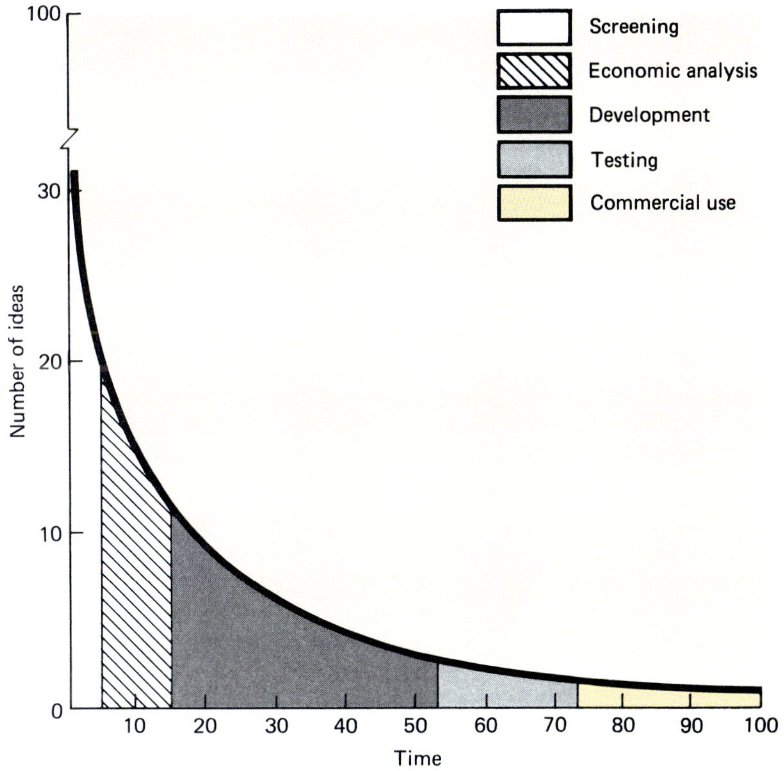

FIGURE 4.2 Decay curve of new product ideas
Source: **R. A. Johnson, W. T. Newell, and R. C. Vergin, *Production and Operations Management: A Systems Concept* (Boston: Houghton Mifflin Company, Copyright © 1974), 144. Used with permission.**

[2]The role of R&D in organizational change is discussed by Neil V. Hakala, "Administration of Industrial Technology," *Business Horizons* 20, no. 5 (October 1977), 4–10.

realities, illustrating why R&D is so expensive. Some new-product ideas survive several stages of costly development before dying because of technological infeasibility; their R&D costs are never recovered. These risks are offset, however, by those few successful products that generate sufficient revenues to make R&D a worthwhile long-term venture.

Consider, for example, a relatively new process for tagging salmon used in wildlife management. Historically the process meant physically catching the fish, tagging it, and releasing it. The new process is to "tag" by remote laser beam, thus eliminating the need for physically catching, tagging, and releasing. Now think of the research and development efforts that were required to bring about this new process. Many years ago the theories of physics underlying the laser were conceptualized. Later, developmental research in physics and electronics resulted in a working laser beam. Since then many scientists and engineers have developed applications of laser beams in space explorations, health, science, industry, and other settings.

Components of Innovation Four generic components of technological innovation are: basic research, applied research, development, and implementation.

Basic research Research for the advancement of scientific knowledge that is not intended for specific commercial uses.

Applied research Research for the advancement of scientific knowledge that has specific commercial uses.

Development Technical activities concerned with translating basic applied research results into products or processes.

Implementation Activities concerned with designing and building pilot models, equipment, and facilities for, and with initiating the marketing channels for, products or services emerging from research and development.

- *Basic research* is research for the advancement of scientific knowledge that has no specific commercial uses. Basic research may, however, be in the field of present or potential interest to the company.
- *Applied research* is research for the advancement of scientific knowledge that has specific potential commercial uses.
- *Development* is technical activity concerned with translating basic or applied research results into products or processes.
- *Implementation* is activity concerned with designing and building pilot models, equipment, and facilities, and initiating the marketing channels for products or services emerging from research and development.

Organization of R&D In most companies R&D is a staff function located at either the corporate or divisional level. Three examples of R&D organizational structure are shown in Figure 4.3. In part (a) R&D is centrally located. From this location, R&D can economically serve the needs of all divisions and avoid duplicated effort. A disadvantage is that the R&D unit may be geographically and organizationally remote from the immediate needs of the various divisions. This difficulty is overcome by decentralized R&D, as shown in part (b). This structure, however, can tend to raise the costs of R&D since efforts may be duplicated. Decentralization is well suited to companies in which applied research and development dominates, particularly when the products and processes are keenly differentiated along divisional lines. Here R&D is specialized, tailored to the technology and products of each division.

The combination structure, part (c), attempts to reap the best of the benefits offered by both centralization and decentralization. R&D units at divisional levels can be tailored to the special needs at that level, especially in the developmental and applied areas. Some of the applied research and perhaps all of the basic research may be centralized at the corporate level. The dotted lines between the R&D units reflect a sharing of information and responsibilities.

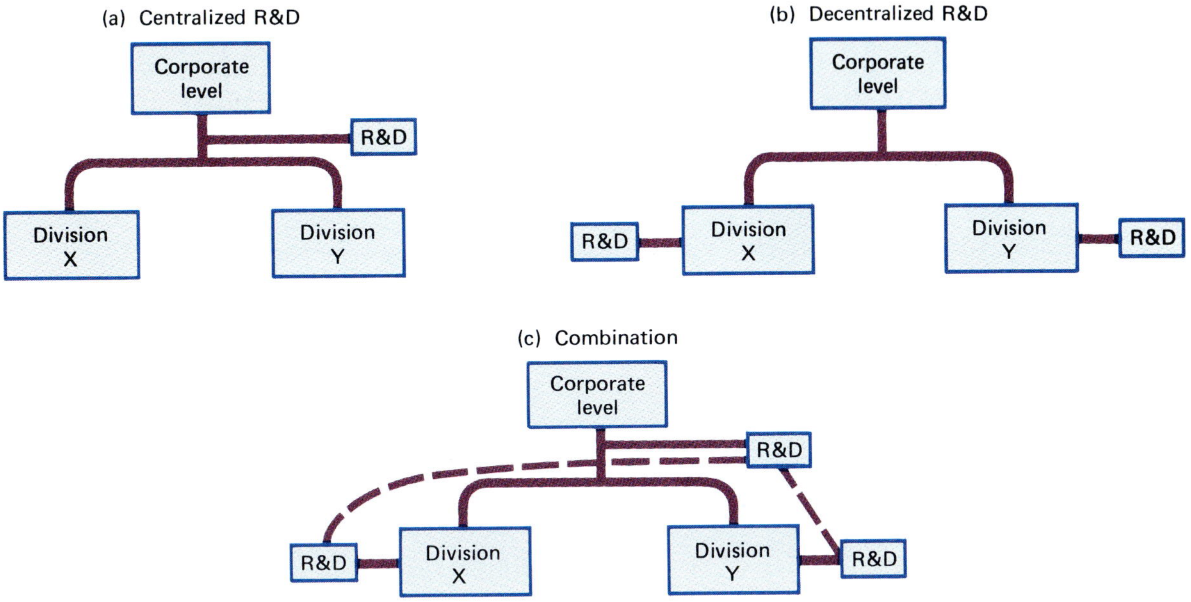

FIGURE 4.3 **R&D location in organization structure**

THE PRODUCT DEVELOPMENT PROCESS

Developing a new product is a major undertaking that has identifiable stages, as shown in Figure 4.4. As development progresses through each phase, its risks and potential are scrutinized, both technically and businesswise, so that any new-product proposal may die or be delayed at any stage in the process. Operations Management Highlight 4.1 explores the nature of this risk for a multibillion dollar product from General Electric.

FIGURE 4.4 **Product development process**

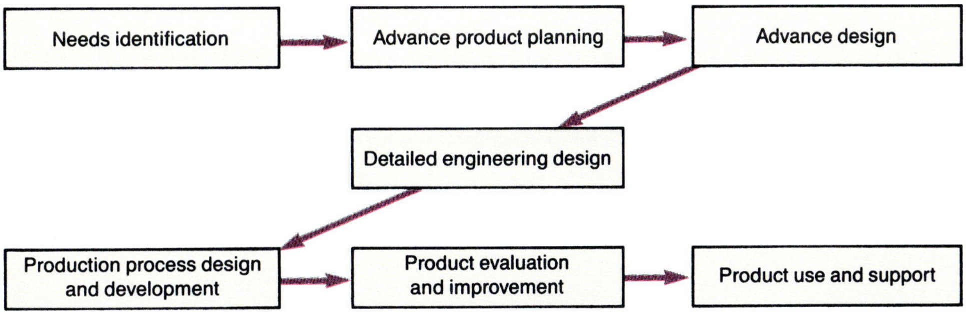

OPERATIONS MANAGEMENT HIGHLIGHT 4.1

Source: John Zoiner

Developing New Products and Processes Is a Risky Business

How comfortable would you feel if you were in charge of the following situation?

> You have the opportunity to invest $2 billion for your company to develop a new jet engine for commercial aircraft. Development will span five years. The final product, costing $10 million per unit, could reach a sales potential, eventually, of $50 billion. The new engine can be placed in service five years from now, but

only if it qualifies four years from now for certification for commercial use, and only if it meets Federal Aviation Administration's ever-tightening standards for noise reduction. Two other jet engine companies—Pratt & Whitney and Rolls Royce—are developing competing engines. If you decide to proceed with the project, you must also determine where the new engines will be produced and develop the manufacturing facilities. If you decline to proceed with this project, your company could invest its resources elsewhere and, based on its track record, get attractive returns. What would you do?

In January 1990 General Electric announced its plans to go ahead with its new GE90 long-range jet engine. Compared to existing engines it will reduce fuel consumption by 10 percent, reduce emissions by 30 percent, and be much quieter. The engines are expected to be produced in France and the United States, but detailed production plans have not been revealed and probably will not be settled for some time yet.

Is this a risky project? Yes, even for this large ($50 billion revenues and $110 billion assets in 1988), diversified (major appliances, locomotives, medical equipment systems, broadcasting) corporation. The development cost matches GE's entire cash position at year-end, 1988 ($2.1 billion).

Although the GE90 is designed for Boeing's planned 767X jet, GE needs other markets to make the new engine profitable. At this time there are but three major commercial aircraft manufacturers in the world: Airbus (a European consortium); Boeing (United States); and Douglas (United States). Though the commercial aircraft market is limited, it is well defined. If GE can hold to their plans, they hope the project will enable their jet engine products—which account for 13 percent of GE revenues and 17 percent of GE profits—to continue as a significant contributor to GE's success in 1995 and beyond.

Sources: "GE, Partners Plan Cleaner Jet Engine," *St. Louis Post-Dispatch* (January 17, 1990), 3B; Standard & Poor's Corp., *Standard NYSE Stock Reports* 56, no. 230, sec. 12 (December 1, 1989), 966; Standard & Poor's Corp., *Standard Corporation Descriptions* 50, no. 15 (August 1989), 1899–903.

Needs Identification Once a product idea surfaces, it must be demonstrated that the product fulfills some consumer need, and that existing products do not already fulfill the need.

Advance Product Planning (Feasibility Study) Following this demonstration is product planning. It includes preliminary market analyses; creating alternative concepts for the product; clarifying operational requirements; establishing design criteria and their priorities; and estimating logistics requirements for producing, distributing, and maintaining the product in the market.

An important result from this stage of development is the conceptual design of the product. The conceptual design for a new kind of fishing rod, for example, would articulate its weight, strength, shape, bending characteristics, retail price, and so on. These basic properties are also called the *product concept* or *design concept.* Many industries have learned that production and operations personnel should be involved in concept design. By doing so, new production processes can be designed and tested early in the development process.

Advance planning poses a point of friction between business and technical personnel when solid technical ideas are adjudged to have insufficient business merit and, hence, fall by the wayside. Preliminary market analysis including sales projections, and economic analysis including estimates of production operating costs, overhead, and profitability, may suggest abandoning a technically attractive new idea.

Advance Design Basic and applied researchers investigate technical feasibility and identify in greater detail the tradeoffs in product design. Promising design alternatives are evaluated according to critical parameters to determine whether design support such as analytical testing, experimentation, physical modeling, and prototype testing will be required.

Detailed Engineering Design This stage is a series of engineering activities to develop a detailed definition of the product, including its subsystems and components, materials, sizes, shapes, and so on. The engineering process typically involves analysis, experimentation, and data collection to find designs that meet several *design objectives:* (1) design for *function* so the product will perform as intended; (2) design for *reliability* so the product will perform consistently; (3) design for *maintainability* so the product can be economically maintenanced; (4) design for *safety* so the product will perform with minimal hazard to the user and the environment; and (5) design for *producibility* so the product can be produced at the intended cost and volumes. Computer analyses, simulations, and physical prototypes (mockups) allow for testing various design alternatives, and validate that the final design meets the design objectives. Since objectives can conflict with each other, tradeoffs are inevitably in the optimal design. Typically, the final design includes drawings and other documentation as well as a working *prototype* of the product.[3]

[3]For details of the engineering design activities, see B. S. Blanchard, *Engineering Organization and Management* (Englewood Cliffs, N.J.: Prentice Hall, 1976), chap. 5.

Production Process Design and Development Working with the detailed product design, engineers and manufacturing specialists prepare plans for materials acquisitions, production, warehousing, transportation, and distribution. Activities here, however, go beyond just hardware considerations: This stage involves planning, too, for production and control systems, computer information systems, and human resource systems.

Product Evaluation and Improvement Most products are continually reevaluated for improvement possibilities throughout their lives. Field performance and failure data, technical breakthroughs in materials and equipment, and formal research all are used to monitor, analyze, and redesign the product.

Product Use and Support An important stage of product development considers support for the consumer who uses the product. Support systems might (1) educate users on specific applications of the product; (2) provide warranty and repair service; (3) distribute replacement parts; or (4) upgrade the product with design improvements.

COMPETITIVE LOSSES FROM DISINTEGRATED DESIGN PROCESSES

U.S. industry is suffering extensive losses to its competitors, most notably the Japanese, by adopting a disintegrated and sequential approach to new product development. The Western approach subdivides the overall development effort into subtasks for technical specialists in diverse departments. Often isolated, these specialists tend to focus on their own specialty expertise without much concern for integrating their efforts with others. Consequently, the development process is executed sequentially in isolated stages. The result is slow, nonintegrated, and expensive development. In many companies, for example, process engineers are not brought into the development project until after the detailed product design is finished. Consequently, months or even years are lost in launching the design and development of the manufacturing equipment. U.S. competitors, however, have fewer organizational compartments for development, utilizing more technical generalists than specialists, and being willing to clarify design objectives at the outset of development.[4] The result is that these competitors get new products into the marketplace twice as fast—in two years rather than four.

PRODUCT RELIABILITY

A top executive for a major automotive manufacturer recently reviewed what North American consumers want most in cars. Of the five to ten top attributes, reliability was first, ahead of comfort, price, style, and many other important product features. We define *product reliability as the probability that the product will perform as intended for a prescribed lifetime under specified operating conditions.* Unreliability is reflected in the

Product reliability The probability that a product will perform as intended for a prescribed lifetime under specified operating conditions.

[4]See R. J. Ebert, E. A. Slusher, and K. M. Ragsdell, "Information Flows in Product Engineering Design Productivity," in *Engineering Management: Theory and Applications,* eds. D. J. Leech, J. Middleton, and G. N. Pande (Redruth, Cornwall, England: M. Jackson & Son Publishing Ltd., 1986), 329–36.

product's failure rate. When, during its intended life, does the product fail to meet its performance objectives? Figure 4.5 shows the shape of the failure rate for a typical product. The highest rates of failure occur (a) during initial use due to previously undetected faulty subcomponents or shipping damage, and (b) in the wear-out phase following its useful performance life. New product design is especially concerned with the failure rate during the useful performance life (the shallow portion of the "bathtub" curve). Reliability engineering determines the least height (failure rate) and the greatest length (useful performance life) for each new product, based on financial, technical, and consumer considerations. Products such as bandages, newspapers, and food are expected to have short lives or to be used only once. Other products, refrigerators, for instance, comprise many subcomponents expected to function in concert for extended time periods. Once engineers know the desired reliability, two design questions arise: What reliability is required of each subcomponent to achieve the overall product reliability? Which subcomponents should be used to most economically meet this required reliability?

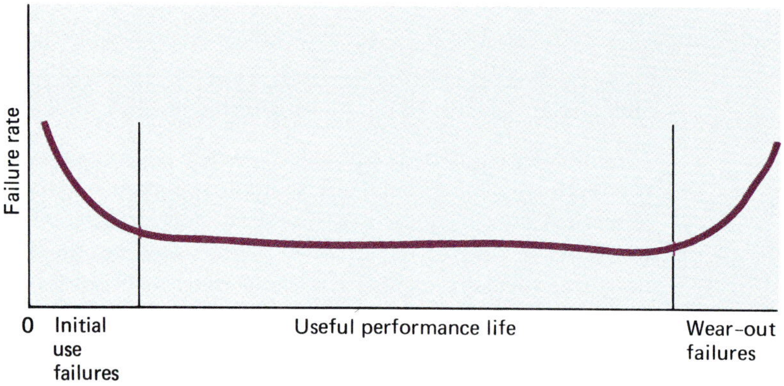

FIGURE 4.5 Product failure curve

Often a final product does not perform properly unless *all* of its subcomponents function correctly. In cases such as these the reliabilities of individual subcomponents must be greater than the reliability desired for the final product. This situation exists whenever the chances of failure for each subcomponent are independent of one another.

Product reliability is usually expressed in terms of a probability. The probability that the product will function successfully equals the mathematical product of the probabilities of all its subcomponents. Once reliability has been achieved, subcomponents can be selected on the basis of economic considerations.

EXAMPLE

Suppose we want to produce a product comprising two subcomponents. We want the product to have a useful life expectancy of one year with .90 probability. The product functions successfully only as long as *both* subcomponents function. How reliable must each subcomponent be? The table below shows the prices of the two subcomponents according to levels of reliability.

Subcomponent	Reliability		
	.90	.95	.98
A	$50	$90	$140
B	70	90	110

Since we want a product reliability of .90, we might select subcomponents each having .90 reliability. Our product will meet our reliability standard only if both subcomponents function successfully for one year; so the reliability of the final product is the mathematical product of the subcomponent reliabilities. If we choose subcomponent reliabilities of .90, then final product reliability P = .90 × .90 = .81. We see, then, that subcomponent reliability must be greater than the desired reliability of the final product.

Choosing subcomponents where reliabilities are .98 would yield final P = .98 × .98 = .9604.

Similarly, for A and B having .95 reliabilities, P = .9025. Both of these options would meet or exceed the desired product reliability.

Which versions of subcomponents A and B should be used in our product? We answer the question by first identifying all combinations of A and B that satisfy our final product reliability goal. Then we pick the combination of A and B that is least costly. Four combinations of A and B meet or exceed the product reliability goal; five combinations are unsatisfactory.

	A		B		Final Product	
Combination	Reliability	Cost	Reliability	Cost	Reliability	Cost
1	.90	50	.90	70	.90 × .90 = .8100	50 + 70 = 120
2	.90	50	.95	90	.90 × .95 = .8550	50 + 90 = 140
3	.90	50	.98	110	.90 × .98 = .8820	50 + 110 = 160
4	.95	90	.90	70	.95 × .90 = .8550	90 + 70 = 160
5	.95	90	.95	90	.95 × .95 = .9025	90 + 90 = 180
6	.95	90	.98	110	.95 × .98 = .9310	90 + 110 = 200
7	.98	140	.90	70	.98 × .90 = .8820	140 + 70 = 210
8	.98	140	.95	90	.98 × .95 = .9310	140 + 90 = 230
9	.98	140	.98	110	.98 × .98 = .9604	140 + 110 = 250

We would select combination 5 on the basis of economic criteria.

The data needed to determine probabilities of reliability, called *failure-rate data,* are obtained from test results and field use experience. Evaluating how subcomponent failures affect overall product reliability helps in evaluating alternative product designs.

MODULAR DESIGN AND STANDARDIZATION

Modular design and component standardization are two aspects of product design with special significance to operations management because they directly affect the complexity and cost of the conversion process.

Modular design The creation of products from some combination of basic, preexisting subsystems.

Modular Design *Modular design* is the creation of products from some combination of basic, preexisting subsystems. In selecting a personal computer system, for example, you may have your choice of three video monitors, two keyboards, two computers, and three printers, all of which are compatible. All possible combinations make a total of 36 ($3 \times 2 \times 2 \times 3$) different computer systems from which to choose. The modular design concept gives consumers a range of product options and, at the same time, offers considerable advantages in manufacturing and product design. Stabilizing the designs of the modules makes them easier to build. Problems are easier to diagnose, and the modules are easier to service. Production proficiency increases as personnel make refinements to and gain experience with the manufacturing processes for standardized sets of modules. Similarly, materials planning and inventory control can be simplified, especially in finished goods inventories. Now, rather than storing inventories of all 36 finished computer systems, only some of which will be needed, we instead store just the subsystems or modules. Then, when a particular computer system is demanded, the producer can focus on quickly retrieving and assembling the appropriate modules into the desired configurations and avoid the high costs of idle finished goods inventories.

Standardization Product standardization offers benefits to consumers and producers alike. Customers can count on simplicity and convenience in purchasing standardized products like household doors, screws and other fasteners, spark plugs, and so on. Similarly, uniform (standardized) pricing code labels has meant greater efficiency for the retailer. In designing new products, standardization can bolster productivity by (1) avoiding unnecessary engineering design when a suitable component already exists; (2) simplifying materials planning and control during production because fewer components are in the system; (3) reducing components production (if the components are produced in-house) or reducing purchasing requirements and limiting the number of vendors (if components are purchased). The risky side of standardization is that your competitor may upstage you with a new product feature that you cannot match because your design capabilities have become stagnant.

MANUFACTURING PROCESS TECHNOLOGY

Process technology Equipment, people, and systems used to produce a firm's products and services.

New products are not physical realities until they are manufactured. *Process technology* refers to the equipment, people, and systems used to produce a firm's products and services.[5] Key process technology decisions relate to organizing the process flows, choosing the appropriate product-process mix, adapting the process to meet strategic requirements, and evaluating automation and high-technology processes.

[5]Hayes and Wheelwright, *Restoring,* 165. See also Terry Hill, *Manufacturing Strategy: Text and Cases* (Homewood, Ill.: Richard D. Irwin, 1989).

WAYS TO ORGANIZE PROCESS FLOWS

Five types of process technologies are project, job shop, batch, assembly line, and continuous. Each is more or less suited to different product/market situations, and each has its unique operating characteristics, problems, and challenges. Selected characteristics of these five technologies are summarized in Table 4.1.

Project technology A process technology suitable for producing one-of-a-kind products.

Project *Project technology* deals with one-of-a-kind products that are tailored to the unique requirements of each customer. A general construction company, with its many kinds and sizes of projects, is an example. Since the products cannot be standardized, the conversion process must be flexible in its equipment capabilities, human skills, and procedures. The conversion process features problem solving, teamwork, and coordinated design and production of unique products.

TABLE 4.1 Characteristics of process technologies

Characteristic	Project	Job Shop	Batch	Assembly Line	Continuous
		Equipment and Physical Layout Characteristics			
Typical size of facility	Varies	Usually small	Moderate	Often large	Large
Process flow	No pattern	Several dominant patterns	A few dominant patterns	A rigid pattern	Inflexible, dictated by technology
Speed	Varies	Slow	Moderate	Fast	Very fast
Run lengths	Very short	Short	Moderate	Long	Very long
Rate of change	Slow	Slow	Moderate	Moderate to high	Moderate to high
		Direct Labor and Work Force Characteristics			
Labor intensiveness	High	Very high	Varies	Low	Very low
Worker skill level	High	High	Mixed	Low	Varies
Worker training requirements	Very high	High	Moderate	Low	Varies
		Material and Information Control Characteristics			
Material requirements	Varies	Difficult to predict	More predictable	Predictable	Very predictable
Production information requirements	Very high	High	Varies	Moderate	Low
Scheduling	Uncertain, frequent changes	Uncertain, frequent changes	Varies, frequent expediting	Fixed	Inflexible, dictated by technology
		Primary Operating Management Characteristics			
Challenges	Estimating, sequencing tasks, pacing	Estimating, labor utilization, fast response, debottlenecking	Designing procedures, balancing stages, responding to diverse needs	Productivity improvement, adjusting staffing levels, rebalancing when needed	Avoiding downtime, timing expansions, cost minimization

Source: Adapted from Hayes and Wheelwright, *Restoring,* 180–82.

Job shop technology A process technology suitable for a variety of custom-designed products in small volumes.

Job Shop *Job shop technology* is appropriate for manufacturers of small batches of many different products, each of which is custom designed and, consequently, requires its own unique set of processing steps, or routing, through the production process. Consider, for example, the jobs done by a printing shop. Each product uses only a small portion of the shop's human resources and general purpose equipment. With large numbers of diverse jobs, elaborate job-tracking and control systems are used. Much time is spent waiting for access to equipment; some equipment is overloaded while other equipment is idle, depending upon the mix of jobs at hand.

Batch technology A process technology suitable for a variety of products in varying volumes.

Batch *Batch technology* is a step up from job shop technology in terms of product standardization, but it is not as standardized as assembly line technology. Within the wide range of products in the batch facility, several are demanded repeatedly and in large volumes. These few dominant products differentiate batch facilities from job shops; however, no product is sufficiently dominant to warrant dedicated equipment and processes. Consequently, like job shops, batch facilities produce a wide variety of products in a wide variety of volumes. The system must be flexible for the low-volume/high-variety products, but the higher volume products can be processed differently—for example, by producing some batches for stocking rather than for customer order.

Assembly line technology A process technology suitable for a narrow range of standardized products in high volumes.

Assembly Line *Assembly line* (or simply line) *technology* is for facilities that produce a narrow range of standardized products. Laundry appliances are a representative example. Since the product designs are relatively stable, specialized equipment, human skills, and management systems can be developed and dedicated to the limited range of products and volumes. Beyond this range, the system is inflexible.

Continuous flow technology A process technology suitable for producing a continuous flow of products.

Continuous Users of *continuous flow technology* are exemplified by chemical plants and oil refineries. Materials and products are produced in continuous, endless flows, rather than in batches or discrete units. The product is highly standardized, as are all of the manufacturing procedures, the sequence of product buildup, materials, and equipment. Continuous flow technology affords high-volume, around-the-clock operation with capital-intensive, specialized automation.

PROCESS TECHNOLOGY LIFE CYCLE

Process technologies have life cycles related to product life cycles, as shown in Figure 4.6. Over time, unit manufacturing costs diminish for mature products. From product start-up to decline, manufacturing processes change in organization, throughput volume, rates of process innovation, and automation. To illustrate, the process technology is typically job shop at start-up and moves toward a continuous flow technology if the product survives to become a commodity. Throughput volumes and automation are low at start-up and high during maturation and decline. These changes require appropriately matching up the manufacturer's product and process structures, as we see in the next section.[6]

[6]For a discussion of product and process life-cycle relationships, see Hayes and Wheelwright, "Restoring." See also Hill, *Manufacturing Strategy*.

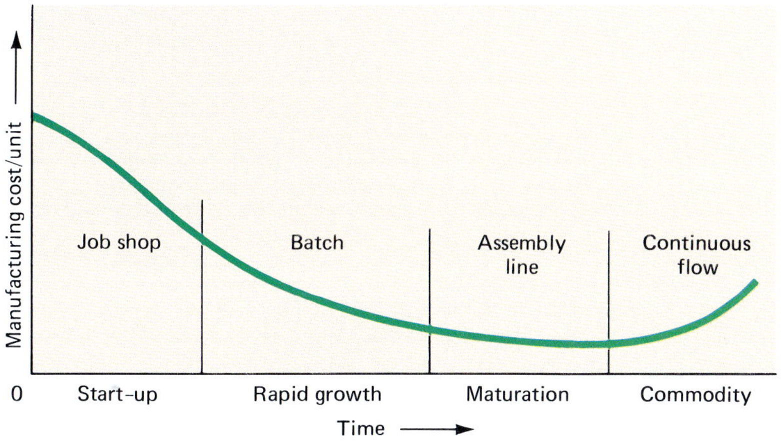

FIGURE 4.6 **The process life cycle**

PRODUCT-PROCESS MIX

Typical combinations of product-process structures are illustrated in Figure 4.7. Representative industries are listed on the diagonal of the matrix, and the two "voided" corners indicate product-process combinations that are incompatible and infeasible. Most companies, divisions, or plants can be located on the matrix, depending upon the current life-cycle stage of their dominant product line. As the product shifts to a different stage, the manufacturing process structure also shifts, and new manufacturing priorities emerge. Whereas manufacturing flexibility and quality are competitive priorities in earlier stages, priorities shift toward dependable delivery and competitive cost in later stages.

This product-process matrix helps us understand why and how companies change their production operations. As products, market requirements, and competition change, so must equipment, procedures, and human resources. If process changes are not made to accommodate product life cycles, product and process are incompatible: the result is competitive disadvantage.

FLEXIBLE MANUFACTURING SYSTEMS (FMS)

Some experts estimate that over 50 percent of all U.S. manufacturing uses batch technology, in units of 100, 50, or fewer.[7] Small batches of finished goods or components are expensive to make in traditional manufacturing facilities; rigid production systems designed for producing high-volume, low-variety products are simply uneconomical, unresponsive, and noncompetitive in the small-batch, higher-

[7]M. P. Groover, *Automation, Production Systems, and Computer-Integrated Manufacturing* (Englewood Cliffs, N.J.: Prentice Hall, 1987), 433.

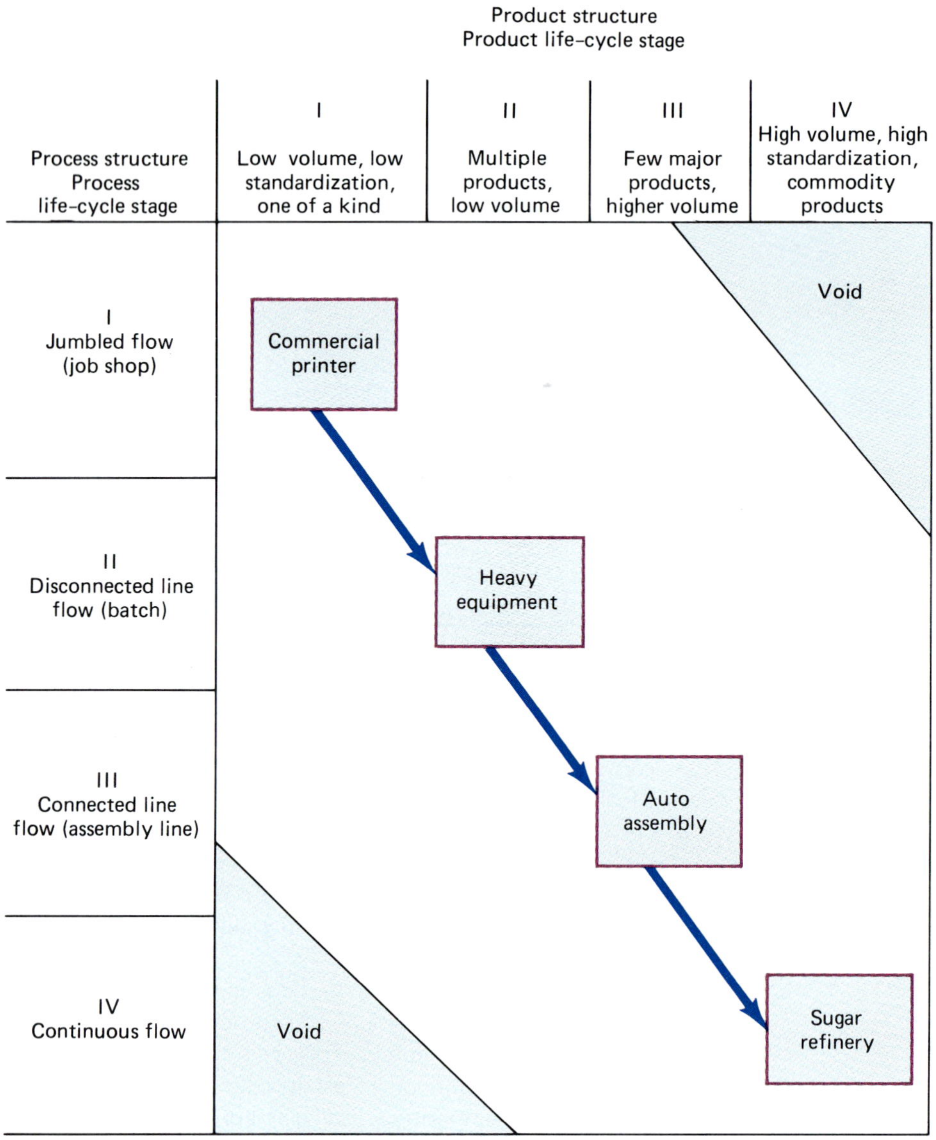

FIGURE 4.7 Matching major stages of product and process life cycles—the product-process matrix
Source: Hayes and Wheelwright, *Restoring*, p. 209.

variety marketplace. Increasingly, customers are demanding greater variety of products and shorter delivery times. Flexible manufacturing systems are appropriate for meeting these needs.

Flexible manufacturing system (FMS) A computer-controlled process technology suitable for producing a moderate variety of products in moderate volumes.

DEFINITION OF AN FMS

Although many definitions are available, key aspects of an *FMS* are generally agreed upon. First, FMS is a computer-controlled system. It contains several work stations, each geared to different operations. Work-station machines are automated and programmable. Automated materials-handling equipment move components to the appropriate work station, then onto the preprogrammed machines that select, position, and activate the specific tools for each job. Hundreds of tool options are available. Once the machine has finished one batch, the computer signals the next quantity or component, and the machine automatically repositions and retools accordingly. Meanwhile, the just-finished batch is automatically transferred to the next work station in its routing.

CHARACTERISTICS OF AN FMS

An FMS is a process technology that can produce a moderate variety of products in modest volumes, and can do so quickly and with high quality. Operating costs, too, can be reduced with an FMS; lower direct labor costs lead to lower manufacturing costs. These benefits, however, are not free; an FMS requires very large capital investments in equipment, planning and control systems, and human resources.

An FMS is generally appropriate when:

1. All products are variations of a stable basic design;
2. All products utilize the same family of components;
3. The number of components is only moderate (10 to 50);
4. The volume of each component is moderate (1,000 to 30,000 units annually), but in lot sizes as small as one unit.[8]

An FMS is most often used in manufacturing components that require several machining operations.[9] A work station consists of a machine or a robot that performs a particular class of tasks such as drilling holes, bending metal in various directions, and so on. Specialized tools are continuously available for one-at-a-time use, and changed automatically by computers according to the unique requirements for each component as it progresses through the system. Because the investment in machines and tools is great, one can easily understand why the product design must be stable and why products must use the same family of components. Otherwise, even greater investments would be needed for new equipment and computers. The costs would be prohibitive.

GOAL OF AN FMS

The goal is to produce a moderate variety of products in moderate, flexible quantities.[10] Clearly, an FMS is more flexible than conventional high-volume production systems (millions of units annually of one or a few products). It is less flexible than a job shop that specializes in one-of-a-kind products. An FMS is a "mid-range" system appropriate for moderate variety/moderate volume markets.

[8]Chris A. Voss, *Managing New Manufacturing Technologies* (East Lansing: Operations Management Association, Michigan State University, 1986), 12–13.

[9]P. M. Swamidass, *Manufacturing Flexibility* (Waco, Tex.: Operations Management Association, 1988), 19.

[10]P. M. Swamidass, *Manufacturing Flexibility*, 19.

THE GROWTH OF COMPUTER-INTEGRATED MANUFACTURING (CIM)

Computer-integrated manufacturing (CIM) Computer information systems utilizing a shared manufacturing database for engineering design, manufacturing engineering, factory production, and information management.

Although the technology of the FMS is an impressive advancement, it is merely the beginning of anticipated changes in technology and automation known as the "factory of the future." The driving force behind this factory will be a series of digital computers. Some manufacturing specialists refer to this futuristic manufacturing concept as *computer-integrated manufacturing* (CIM).[11] CIM centers around a shared database for four primary manufacturing functions: engineering design, manufacturing engineering, factory production, and information management, as shown in Figure 4.8. The shared database is the glue that synchronizes the four functions, thereby yielding gains in productivity. The database stores all product- and process-related information required to produce a component or product. It contains information about machines, tools, materials, manufacturing steps, quantities demanded, due dates, and vendors.

EXAMPLE

Certainly some of the most complex products being manufactured today are large airplanes such as the Boeing 727 and 747 and the Douglas DC10 and MD80. Over 200,000 parts must be assembled to produce a complete airplane. Members of engineering design, manufacturing engineering, factory production, and information management retrieve or reenter data from a centralized database. The production and support staffs are very large—typically 15,000 or more employees to design and manufacture one airplane model. Several airplanes a month may be produced, with approximate sales of $20 million each. The technological challenges of such production are great. At present, no nation in the world approaches the sophistication, reliability, and performance of U.S. commercial and military aerospace manufacturers.

Computer-integrated manufacturing is not yet a reality but a vision of things to come.[12] Some elements of CIM are operational in many companies today, and the impetus is toward a computer-based system that more fully integrates the entire product development process from concept to market. In a sense, then, the "manufacturing" in "computer-integrated manufacturing" is a misnomer, because the system involves engineering as well as production.

Computer-aided design (CAD) Computer software programs that allow a designer to carry out geometric transformations rapidly.

Computer-Aided Design (CAD) The design process for new products and components traditionally has been an iterative one in which product specifications are refined in successive stages based upon the designer's experience, computations,

[11]Basic reference material utilized in this section includes Thomas G. Gunn, "Computer Integrated Manufacturing," *Proceedings of the 1982 Academic-Practitioners Liaison Operations Management Workshop* (Michigan State University, July 1982), pp. 1–22; Thomas G. Gunn, "The Mechanization of Design and Manufacturing," *Scientific American* 247, no. 3 (September 1982), pp. 114–31; and promotional materials provided by McAuto, a subsidiary of McDonnell Douglas Corporation, St. Louis, Mo.

[12]See W. H. Slautterback and W. B. Werther, Jr., "The Third Revolution: Computer-Integrated Manufacturing," *National Productivity Review* 3, no. 4 (Autumn 1984), 367–74.

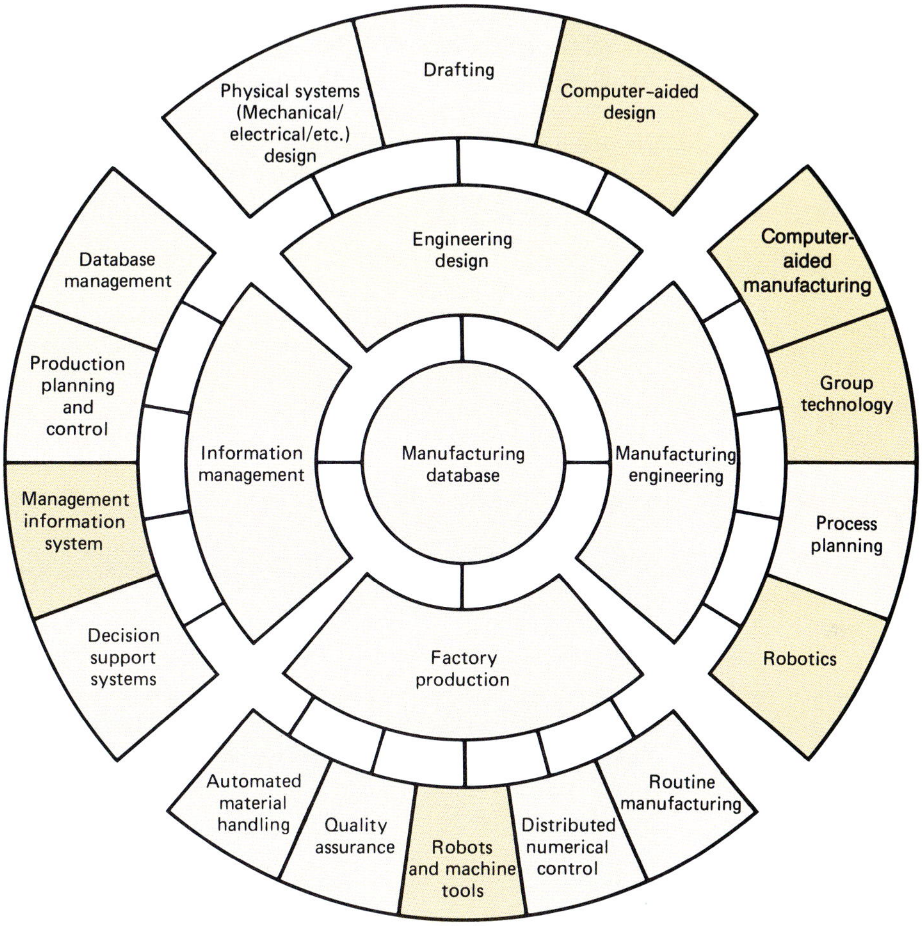

FIGURE 4.8 Computer-integrated manufacturing functions

sketches, and drawings. CAD uses computational and graphics software and has substantially enhanced design productivity. The geometry of the component can be graphically displayed and manipulated easily on video monitors. Alternative designs can be posed and evaluated more quickly, and some of the time and expense of physical mock-ups, models, and prototypes are eliminated. Furthermore, by accessing the database, an already-existing design may be found, thereby eliminating duplicated design efforts. Once a design is satisfactory it is stored in the database and can be transmitted electronically to manufacturing engineering, production, and purchasing.

What does CAD accomplish? Generally, drafting productivity improves by a factor of three or more, and engineering lead time shrinks. At General Motors, for example, the design time for a new automobile was reduced from 24 months to 14. A manufacturer of molds for plastic parts increased annual output from 30 molds to 140, solely because of the increased efficiency afforded by CAD.[13] Similar savings in time and gains in productivity are common in other manufacturing settings.

[13]Gunn, "Mechanization," 121.

Computer-aided manufacturing (CAM) Manufacturing systems utilizing computer software programs that control the actual machine on the shop floor.

Computer-Aided Manufacturing (CAM) *Computer-aided manufacturing* systems control the machine tools on the shop floor. The machines typically perform a variety of operations, not just one, and the machine receives instructions from a computer on the sequence and specifications of its operations. The computer programs can be stored in the manufacturing database; retrieved, updated, and revised as components are added or redesigned; and transmitted electronically in-house or externally by satellite to other divisions and facilities.

This engineer is using a computer-aided design system to explore new shapes for redesigning an instrument kit (the white container near the keyboard). Design productivity is increased because she can explore many different designs without having to build expensive physical mock-ups.

Source: **Abbott Laboratories/Robert C. Laemle**

CAM offers several production benefits: instructions from a computer are usually more reliable than those from a skilled operator; product quality is more consistent from unit to unit; closer tolerances can be obtained; and labor costs are lower because less operator time is needed. These benefits, of course, don't come cost-free. Engineers must create the equipment and software that govern machine operation.

Further, a major aerospace manufacturer advises that *too much* CAM can be costly. Errors in a computer program can result in a great many erroneous parts being produced, even though they are produced quite efficiently. Under the watchful eye of a machine operator, such mistakes can be minimized. Thus human involvement is not being eliminated by the CAD/CAM technology; rather, it is being deployed in new ways.

EXAMPLE

The Business Forms Division of Harris Corporation in Dayton, Ohio, uses McAuto's UNIGRAPHICS CAD/CAM to produce presses.[14] The first five-terminal network was installed in 1976 and paid for itself through increased productivity in just 2.6 years. A second five-terminal network was installed in 1978 with a payback in 1.9 years. Mike Kuntz, manager of the CAD/CAM group at Harris, reflected on the CAD/CAM installations: "In engineering work, our overall productivity increase due to UNIGRAPHICS is 3.5 to 1, although some applications show as much as 24-to-1 savings."

Robot A programmable machine capable of moving materials and performing routine, repetitive tasks.

Robotics The science of selecting robots for various applications.

Robotics and Robots A *robot* is a programmable machine, which means that a sequence of moves can be preset to be repeated time after time, then reset again to perform another set of moves. Robots replace humans for some very heavy, dirty, dangerous, unpleasant or monotonous tasks. The science of selecting robots for various uses—and knowing when *not* to use them—is called *robotics.*

Among the more common uses of robots in the United States are loading and unloading machine tools, painting, and spot welding—especially in the automotive and appliance industries. The primary advantage of robots over humans is that robot performance never varies. The robot shows for work each day and is just as consistent Monday morning and Friday evening as every other hour of the week. A robot does not get tired or become distracted. Robots can perform a variety of specialized tasks and sequences to precise specifications, and they require less plant space than do alternative production processes.

Economically, a robot in the United States costs from $50,000 to $100,000 installed. The following example shows how a robot can be economically justified.[15]

EXAMPLE

A robot, installed, will cost $76,500 to perform the monotonous job of stacking full cans of paint in a paint factory. The robot can be used 20 hours/day, on the average, seven days/week. The robot should last five to ten years, with but a few major repairs. An employee is paid $10/hour in wages and $7/hour in fringe benefits, including social security payments by the company. To recover only the initial investment, the robot need work:

$$\text{Hours to work} = \frac{\$76{,}500}{\$17/\text{hour}}$$
$$= 4{,}500 \text{ hours}$$

The plant operates only two shifts, a total of 16 hours/day, 5 days/week, 50 weeks/year. The total hours a robot would be used per year would be:

[14]"Harris Uses McAuto UNIGRAPHICS for Quality Presses," A McAuto Client Profile (St. Louis, Mo.: McAuto, A Division of McDonnell Douglas Corporation, 1984).

[15]In 1983 the average price of spot-welding robots was $78,000. In 1965 the average hourly cost of an autoworker was $5 per hour, as was the hourly cost of a robot. By 1980 costs were $16 and $5 per hour, respectively. From Emilia Askari, "The Robots of '1984'," *Miami Herald,* (March 19, 1984), 9. Also see Kenneth M. Jenkins and Alan R. Raedels, "The Robot Revolution: Strategic Considerations for Managers," *Operations Management Review* 7, no. 2 (Winter 1983), 41–44.

Robot moving paper products from one point to another.
Source: Courtesy of Cincinnati Milacron

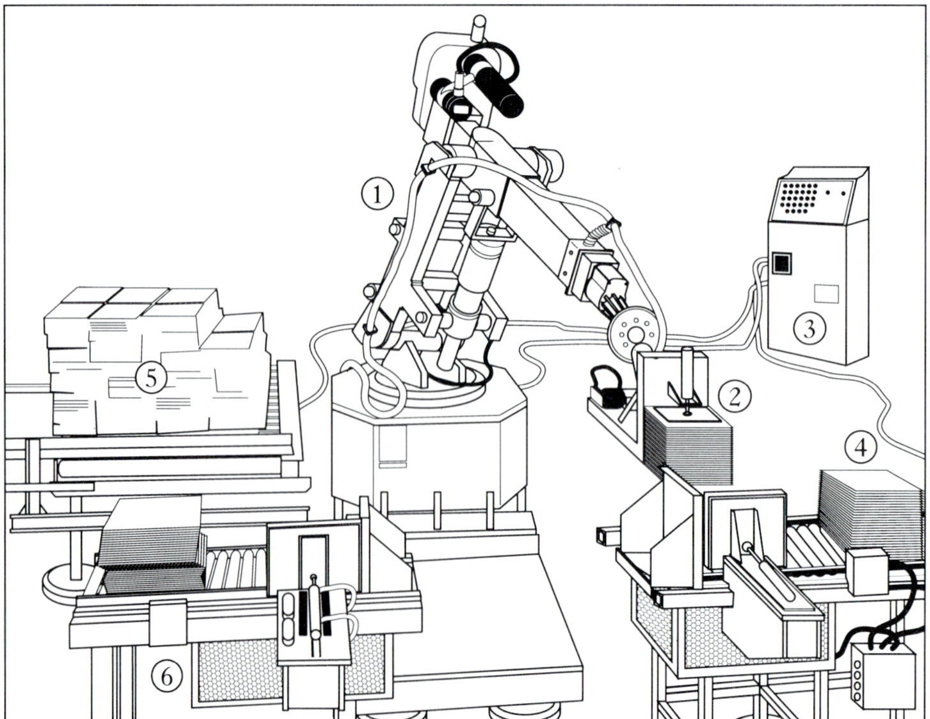

1. Robot; 2. Robot hand; 3. Control panel; 4. Incoming stacks of paper; 5. Outgoing stacks of paper; 6. Roller conveyors.

$$\text{Hours/year plant open} = 16 \text{ hours/day} \times 5 \text{ days/week} \times 50 \text{ weeks/year}$$
$$= 4{,}000 \text{ hours/year}$$

In a little over a year, the initial outlay for the robot would be recovered. The payback period would be:

$$\text{Years to payback} = \frac{4{,}500 \text{ hours}}{4{,}000 \text{ hours/year}}$$
$$= 1.125 \text{ years}$$

The rapid recovery of the initial investment is indeed very attractive.

Although the operating costs for the robot were ignored in the simplified example, we see that a robot can offer attractive financial returns to the firm.[16]

How many robots will we need by the year 2000? In 1979 fewer than ten U.S. companies turned out $28 million worth of robots. By early 1984, American industry was buying $169 million a year worth of robots from more than 60 manufacturers. Giants such as General Motors, Westinghouse, IBM, and General Electric had incorporated robots into their operations.[17]

To accommodate robots, engineers are rethinking their traditional overdesign practices. In spot-welding metal components, for example, engineers traditionally have overdesigned manufacturing specifications by calling for more welds than were really needed, anticipating that the human welder would miss one or two welds as he grew tired or distracted. Robots, in contrast, never miss a weld.

While the robot's computer programs and operational specifications do not reside in the manufacturing database of most organizations today, the CIM is aimed toward doing so in the future.

Group technology A way of organizing and using data for components that have similar properties and manufacturing requirements.

Group Technology *Group technology* is a way of organizing and using data for components that have similar properties and manufacturing requirements. Characteristics such as length, diameter, type of material, and density are recorded for each component in the manufacturing system. The computer can then sort for all similar components—for example, all titanium screws less than 1½ inches long and of ½ inch maximum diameter. A designer might well find an existing useful titanium screw and avoid the cost of designing a new one.[18]

EXAMPLE

At Otis Engineering, an engineering and manufacturing company, group technology was applied in an environment with over 200,000 drawings to search. Historically, Otis employees had found that it was usually faster to design a new component than to

[16]For insight into managing installations, see Fred K. Foulkes and Jeffrey L. Hirsch, "People Make Robots Work," *Harvard Business Review* (January–February 1984).

[17]Askari, "Robots," 1, 7–11.

[18]See a user survey in Nancy Lea Hyer, "Management's Guide to Group Technology," *Operations Management Review* 2, no. 2 (Winter 1984), 36–42.

search for one that already existed. In addition to savings in design, group technology helped save operations costs as well. After only ten months, approximately 580 hours of setup time was saved, averaging 12 minutes/component. Some work centers showed a 55 percent capacity savings. The program was expanded, resulting in approximately 8,500 machine hours saved, a 45 percent capacity savings, and a nine-month payback for training and coding. The scheduling department experienced similar positive results. Components that workers had previously produced in 80 days now cleared manufacturing in only 38 days.[19]

From the Otis Engineering experience we see that group technology can go beyond the design stage and carry over into production as well. Components in a family often have similar manufacturing requirements, so equipment and machines can be grouped together. These *machine groups* (or cells) facilitate work flow, making setups, run-times, and in-process inventory more efficient.

DESIGN OF SERVICES AND SERVICE PROCESSES

Services constitute a larger sector of the U.S. economy, in terms of both workers and gross national product than products do, but the demarcation between a "product" and a "service" is not clear. While many people think of IBM as a producer of computers, for example, others contend their primary business is service, helping customers, use, maintain, upgrade, and service computer systems. The fact is that in today's competitive world, most businesses offer a combination of product and service, as shown in Figure 4.9. The idea is that everything sold falls somewhere on the continuum of service/product dominance. A standard necktie is clearly product-dominant; in contrast, a tailored suit pertains to service as well as to product. To be competitive, organizations have to recognize differences in the product/service elements of their market offerings, and develop process technologies accordingly.

DESIGN OF SERVICES

The design of services involves the same stages as the design of products (Figure 4.4). It begins with identifying a consumer need and developing a service concept that fulfills the need. When Federal Express saw the need for fast, dependable shipping services, they developed a new delivery system that features private ownership, a limited range of services, and a complete pickup-process-delivery cycle that emphasizes convenience and nationwide accessibility. Identifying the concept led to detailed design of the

[19]Bob Alton, "Group Technology," *Proceedings of the 1982 Academic-Practitioners Liaison Operations Management Workshop* (Michigan State University, July 1982), 38–42.

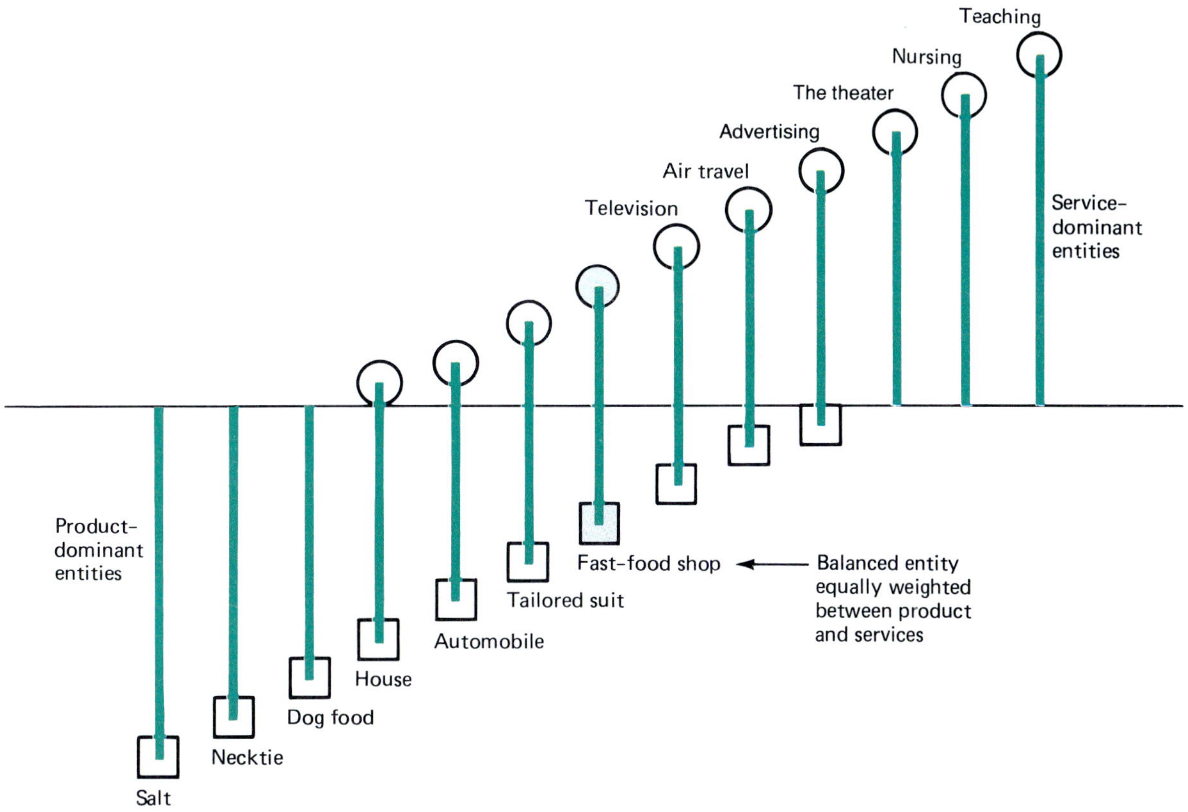

FIGURE 4.9 **Scale of service versus product dominance**
Source: G. Lynn Shostack, "How to Design a Service," *European Journal of Marketing* 16, no. 1 (1982), 52.

services and the unique processing technologies (including equipment, human resources, and procedures), and continues today with refinement and redesign of the services in the field.

Although the generic steps may be the same, there are some big differences between product and service design. Services that do not include a physical component do not require the engineering, testing, components analyses, and prototype building of product design. Further along in service design, the process technology involves different issues and considerations than those for products, primarily because clients or customers are present in the conversion process.

SERVICE PROCESS TECHNOLOGIES

Process technologies for services are at least as diverse, and perhaps more so, than product process technologies. Services vary in the amount of customer contact and in the intensiveness of labor versus capital. Service process technologies vary accordingly. These variations are examined for health fitness services in Operations Management Highlight 4.2.

OPERATIONS MANAGEMENT HIGHLIGHT 4.2

Source: Brownie Harris/The Stock Market

Fitness-Related Services Are a Growth Area for Operations

Power-walking, jogging, swimming, weight lifting, and dieting are just some of the many activities related to the growing market for fitness and health. America's elderly, along with millions of maturing baby boomers, want smaller waistlines and relief from sedentary lifestyles. To help them, communities offer public recreation facilities and fitness classes. Shopping malls have "walking trails" and posters for warm-up exercises. Health clubs and resorts are on the upswing. Among the diet centers, Weight Watchers alone has an average of a million people attending classes each week. Nutri/System and Diet Center, combined, have over 4,000 outlets in an industry that is expected to grow to $3 billion a year in the 1990s. For those who prefer at-home activity, the Richard Simmons television show entertains viewers with organized workouts and suggestions on nutrition. He provides video tapes and a variety of books as well. Thousands of hospitals promote complete fitness programs including personalized evaluations by nutritionists, physicians, psychologists, and physical therapists prescribing safe, supervised programs for each individual's fitness needs. Hundreds of companies, too, provide employees-only facilities and programs. AT&T, Levi Strauss, and Tenneco are just a few of the many companies with substantial investments in fitness services for employees.

In each of the diverse programs mentioned above, there are big differences among the services they offer and among the service processes they use. In full-service hospital programs, customers are involved in the ***design*** of custom-tailored services, much more so than when they watch television shows or use the community recreation facilities. Televised fitness shows (mass services) deliver to large audiences a limited range of standardized fitness activities (the telecommunications network is a capital-intensive technology and the standardized exercises are a rigid process technology). Individualized full-service hospital programs, in contrast, use more labor-intensive professional expertise (for example, medical diagnosis and supervision) and custom-shop services featuring unique dietary regimens and electronically monitored physical activities on a variety of expensive equipment.

Clearly, then, the differences in process technology among these fitness businesses are huge: facilities, equipment, human resources, and types of customer contact vary widely in this mega-billion dollar service industry.

Sources: Brian O'Reilly, "New Truths About Staying Healthy," *Fortune* (September 25, 1989), 57–66; Roger Thompson, "Curbing the High Cost of Health Care," *Nation's Business* (September 1989), 18–26; Brian O'Reilly, "Diet Centers Are Really in Fat City," *Fortune* (June 5, 1989), 137–40; Roger Thompson, "A Checkup on Health Benefits," *Nation's Business* (March 1989), 45.

Customer Contact *Customer contact* occurs in two ways. First is the customer's involvement in *designing or customizing* the service. In building a new home, for example, the customer can be intensively active in the design, working closely with an architect. Or the customer can opt for a standard design without any customizing.

A second way customer contact occurs is in *creating* the service. Hair styling, for example, is a high-contact process because the customer participates in creating the service. Wig and toupee repair is often a low-contact process.

We can use the degree of customer contact to classify and evaluate service organizations and to understand how they operate. By categorizing services on a continuum ranging from low- to high-contact, we can better appreciate the tradeoffs between flexibility and efficiency of operations.[20] Generally, high contact process technology is more flexible to accommodate the unique needs of diverse customers. When flexibility is high, however, efficiency is often low because the conversion process cannot be standardized. At the low-contact end of the continuum, the process technology can be less flexible because customers are absent during the conversion process and, consequently, the operations can be oriented more toward standardization and efficiency.

Labor Intensiveness Some services, such as nursing and teaching, are labor-intensive; whereas others, such as the 24-hour automatic teller machines, are capital-intensive. These different services obviously present contrasting operating problems. While employee scheduling and training are dominant concerns for a labor-intensive service company, technological advancements and capital investments are dominant concerns for a capital-intensive service company.

Quasi-manufacturing technology A process technology suitable for capital intensive, low customer contact services.

Mass service technology A process technology suitable for labor intensive, low customer contact services.

Custom-shop service technology A process technology suitable for capital intensive, high customer contact services.

Professional service technology A process technology suitable for labor intensive, high customer contact services.

Service Process Matrix Combining the two dimensions—customer contact and labor intensiveness—produces four distinctive types of service process technologies (Figure 4.10). Many service organizations fit clearly into each cell of the matrix, and they have differing operations challenges and problems.

Quasi-manufacturing (for example, Federal Express), with low labor intensity and low customer contact, offers rigidly standardized services, is very concerned with developing reliable delivery schedules, and makes major capital equipment decisions in a bureaucratized setting.

Mass services (for example, the city school system), while still a system offering standardized services, are much more involved with training, development, and scheduling of the human resources so critical for successful service delivery in this labor-intensive conversion process.

Custom-shop services (for example, a hospital) must be capable of providing customized patient services with a professional staff in a relatively capital-intensive conversion technology that emphasizes cost containment and large capital investment decisions.

The hallmark of *professional services* (for example, tutoring) is customized service through intensive interaction between the customer and professional personnel. Since

[20]See R. Chase, "Where Does the Customer Fit in a Service Operation?" *Harvard Business Review* 56, no. 6 (November-December 1978), 137–42.

	LOW CUSTOMER CONTACT	HIGH CUSTOMER CONTACT
CAPITAL INTENSIVE	**Quasi-manufacturing** Postal services, check processing, automated warehousing	**Custom-shop Services** Charter travel services, long-distance telephone services, medical treatment
LABOR INTENSIVE	**Mass Services** Teaching, live entertainment, cafeteria	**Professional Services** Legal counseling, medical diagnosis, tutoring
	Rigid process technology	Flexible process technology

FIGURE 4.10 **A matrix of service processes**

the professional is governed as much or more by professional norms than by organizational rules, superior-subordinate relationships are looser, and the professional's skills in relating to the customer are essential.

TRENDS IN SERVICE AUTOMATION

Technology issues are as important to services as they are to manufacturing. Consider your own experience with mechanized services such as automated banking, electronic grocery scanners, and the like. A less visible but equally inviting area for automation is the office operations of businesses, such as commercial banking and insurance.

Office automation (OA) Computer-based systems for managing information resources.

Office automation (OA) is a computer-based system for managing information resources. Word processing, generating reports, and handling data may all be part of OA. It seeks to maximize the productivity of office resources.[21]

OA's most distinctive feature is the emphasis on *integrated* automation:

> The goal of the integrated electronic office is to connect every piece of office equipment—mainframes, personal computers, photocopiers, and other devices—to every other, not only in one location but in company branches and in suppliers' and customers' offices throughout the world. . . .[22]

Highly integrated systems are feasible today because advanced telecommunications and electronics technologies are now abundant and affordable. OA has changed white-collar jobs dramatically, streamlining the flow of communication among work stations and people. Information is created and transmitted more rapidly and directly

[21]J. C. Crawford, "Successfully Evaluating and Implementing Office Automation," *CA Magazine* (August 1984), 106.

[22]M. Hart, "How the Office of the Future Is Shaping Up," *CA Magazine* (August 1984), 72.

than ever before. Desktop terminals allow messages, by voice or keyboard, to be transmitted directly to the recipient's terminal. Photocopies or facsimilies of the message can be produced quickly on equipment that is integrated with the sender's or receiver's terminal. Teleconferencing through terminals affords direct communication among executives in remote locations, thus avoiding mail delays or traveling costs. User-friendly word processing systems are faster and more accurate. Electronic spreadsheets, database software, and graphics software facilitate problem analysis, decision making, and reporting.

SUMMARY

In planning conversion systems, we discussed three major decision areas—the design of new products, the design of conversion processes, and the design of services to be offered. We illustrated how and why the conversion process changes according to stages in a product's life cycle. As products mature and decline, new products emerge from research and development. The product development process, beginning with identifying needs and continuing through customer support was shown to involve technical, organizational, and behavioral elements. Closely associated with product development is the design of production processes, which also have life cycles. Five different production technologies differ in their equipment, human resource requirements, procedures, and operating characteristics. In shifting from products to services, we found that the design of services entails the same basic steps as product design, but the details of those steps are quite different. The basis for the differences stems from service process technologies, which vary according to the degree of customer contact and labor intensiveness. The implications of these differences for operations management were summarized in a matrix of service processes.

CASE

Melanie's Dilemma

An established manufacturer supplies high-voltage transformers to utilities throughout the world. Located in southern Indiana, the firm averaged sales over the last three years of 60 percent in North America, 20 percent in South America, and 20 percent in the Pacific Basin. The table shows selected manufacturing data for the plant that manufactures all the transformers.

Chris, the plant manager, and his brother Nat, the director of engineering, are at odds about purchasing several state-of-the-art robots for welding continuous seams on the transformers. The company's transformers are designed to hang on telephone poles. Since the transformers are used outdoors, they must be totally airtight. Nat points out that accurate welding is critical to an airtight, high-quality transformer. He argues that using robots will improve the overall quality of the welding department and reduce manufacturing expenses and Nat claims another potential advantage is that the engineering group will develop robotics skills for future use. Chris insists that the costs of the robots are not justified; he also fears they will cause problems with the employees now doing the welding. Chris is concerned that using robots may jeopardize upcoming labor negotiations and that it will force manufacturing to use equipment they don't know how to operate.

Indiana plant data

Last year (1990) sales	$13,750,000
Cost of goods sold (1990)	$11,500,000
Labor	$ 4,750,000
Material	$ 6,000,000
Overhead	$ 750,000
Invested capital (1990)	$ 3,500,000
Number of employees	1,150
Direct labor	750
Direct labor, welding	121
Nondirect labor	400
Average direct labor wages and fringes	$18.75/hour
Welding labor productivity (current month)	93.7%
Welding material usage variance (positive usage is more than standard; current month)	+16%
Cost one robot, installed	$103,000
Robot characteristics	
Direct workers replaced (two shifts)	3
Total cost operation annually	$ 10,300
Estimated useful life	5 years
Plant operations	2 shifts, 50 weeks/year

Melanie works for the group vice president at corporate headquarters in Chicago. As the vice president's staff assistant, Melanie has been asked to gather facts about the Indiana plant's intended robotics application. She is to make a recommendation to Chris, Nat, and the group vice president at a meeting at the plant in three weeks. Melanie knows that the entire plant may be moved to the Philippine Islands in the next two years. Average labor rates and fringe benefits in the Philippines are expected to be $4.75/hour. The decision to move will be based in part on results of the upcoming union negotiation and on the willingness of the union to participate in the change. Melanie's assignment is to get all the economic and judgmental issues on the table, not to make a final choice for the company.

Case Questions

1. In the role of Melanie, prepare the best case to support Chris's position.
2. Prepare the best case to support Nat's position.
3. With three weeks remaining, what additional information would you gather? Why?
4. If you were asked for a recommendation without additional information, what would you suggest? Why?

REVIEW AND DISCUSSION QUESTIONS

1. Explain the relationships between technology, mechanization, and the work force by (a) defining each and (b) explaining how technology and mechanization are affecting the work force.

2. Explain computer-integrated manufacturing. Figure 4.8 should be useful in your discussion.
3. Robots, CAD, CAM, manufacturing database, and group technology are terms used in manufacturing that are difficult to grasp. After studying each, prepare a short essay that explains these terms in nontechnical language a high school senior could be expected to understand.
4. What are the significant issues about robots and robotics?
5. Identify and discuss difficulties and problems that can arise in implementing an integrated information system for new product development.
6. The concept of product and process life cycles has implications for technological changes, employee behavior, and organizational structure. Discuss these implications.
7. Select four products or services that can be brought into the classroom for demonstration. Analyze the characteristics of each of them and show where they are located on Figure 4.9.
8. Identify two services that clearly fit in the cells of Figure 4.10. Identify two other services that are not reasonably identifiable with any cell in the matrix.
9. Demonstrate how the growth of automation can affect the product/service development process. Use specific products and services for examples.
10. Identify examples of operations that fall on the major diagonal of the product-process matrix (Figure 4.7).
11. Select a simple product (e.g., dog house, barbecue grill, spoon) and describe what would be involved in a major redesign of the product. Address each stage of the product development process, including its major operations issues and problems.
12. Identify a consumer service need (keep it simple) and outline what would have to be done in each stage of the development process to create a service that fulfills the need.
13. As an operations manager, what steps would you take to improve your company's performance on lead time for new product development? Suppose your product is small photocopy machines and you want to reduce development lead time from three years down to 18 months.
14. If you were beginning a new venture—opening a wine and cheese shop in a shopping mall—what would your short-term production/operations objectives be?
15. Explain how a flexible manufacturing system differs from a job shop and from an assembly line system.

PROBLEMS

SOLVED PROBLEMS

1. A commercial airplane manufacturer is concerned about the reliability of the cockpit radar system used for automatic landings.

   Ten radar systems were tested in 500 simulated flights each. Flight landings averaged 20 minutes. Two radar systems failed, one after 121 flights and the second after 273 flights.

   Given the data, analyze the reliability of the radar system.

   First compute the percentage of radar systems failing:

$$\begin{aligned}\% \text{ failures} &= \frac{\text{number of failures}}{\text{number tested}} \times 100\% \\ &= 2/10 \times 100\% \\ &= 20\%\end{aligned}$$

Next compute the number of failures per operating hour:

$$\begin{aligned}\text{failures/hour} &= \frac{\text{number of failures}}{\text{operating hours}} \\ \text{operating hours} &= \text{total hours} - \text{nonoperating hours} \\ \text{total hours} &= 10 \times 500 \times .33 \\ &= 1650 \text{ hours} \\ \text{nonoperating hours} &= 1 \times 379 \times .33 + 1 \times 227 \times .33 \\ &= 200 \text{ hours} \\ \text{operating hours} &= 1650 - 200 \\ &= 1450 \text{ hours} \\ \text{failures/hour} &= \frac{2}{1450} \\ &= .000138\end{aligned}$$

The failure/hour rate of .000138 seems low. However, it is very likely this is too high for the airline to have but one radar system in the plane.

REINFORCING FUNDAMENTALS

2. A product has two subcomponents, A and B. Failure of either A or B results in failure of the product. The probabilities of A and B performing successfully for 1,500 times are .96 and .92, respectively, and are independent.
   (a) What is the probability that the product will operate properly 1,500 or more times?
   (b) What is your answer to part (a) if the probabilities for A and B are .85 and .75, respectively?
3. A product has three subcomponents, A, B, and C. Failure of A can cause the failure of the product. Failure of either only B or C would not cause the failure of the product. However, the product fails if both B and C fail simultaneously. The probabilities of A, B, and C performing successfully are .95, .85, .80, respectively.
   (a) Draw a system diagram for this reliability situation.
   (b) What is the probability that the product works successfully?
4. A robot, installed, is estimated to cost $68,000. This robotics application is directed at replacing one employee per shift on a routine, repetitive task that the employee and robot can do equally well. The plant works three shifts a day, five days a week, 47 weeks a year. Total labor wages and fringes average $9.25/hour in this facility. Absenteeism has averaged 11 percent the last year in this job. Every hour the equipment is idle from absenteeism, the company loses a $5 contribution to profit, which cannot be recovered. The robot is expected to be "down" (not available) 1 percent of the time and is expected to have a three-year useful life. Should the company make the investment based on this economic analysis?
5. Consider the impact of the robot installation on the three employees in Problem 4. If you could get absenteeism reduced to 1 percent by showing this analysis to employees, could they keep their jobs? If not, what alternatives typically exist for retaining the employees?
6. In Problem 4, what wage rate would be necessary for the employees to be economically equivalent to the robot, if all other factors remained constant? Would employees be likely to accept this rate? Why?

CHALLENGING EXERCISES

7. Relectro Corporation produces a miniature electric motor consisting of four components: coil, prime circuit, switch, and simo-wire. Relectro promises its customers a two-year motor life with a probability of .95. Failure of any of the basic components renders the motor useless. Consideration is being given to redesigning the product to reduce costs. Engineers have gathered the following reliability and cost data for components that could be purchased from new vendors. Prepare a reliability and cost analysis to support your recommendation that the motor be redesigned.

Data for existing components

Component	Unit Cost	Two-year Failure Probability
Coil	$17.00	.01
Prime circuit	8.50	.03
Switch	1.50	.05
Simo-wire	4.00	.01

Data for new vendors

	Unit Cost		Two-year Failure Probability	
Component	Vendor X	Vendor Y	Vendor X	Vendor Y
Coil	$16.25	$21.00	0.010	0.005
Prime circuit	12.00	15.00	0.020	0.001
Switch	2.50	4.00	0.030	0.025
Simo-wire	4.00	4.50	0.010	0.010

KEY TERMS

Applied research 122
Assembly line technology 132
Basic research 122
Batch technology 132
Computer-aided design (CAD) 136
Computer-aided manufacturing (CAM) 138
Computer-integrated manufacturing (CIM) 136
Continuous flow technology 132
Custom-shop service technology 146
Development 122
Flexible manufacturing system (FMS) 134
Group technology 141
Implementation 122
Job shop technology 132
Mass service technology 146
Modular design 130
Office automation (OA) 147
Process technology 130
Product life cycle 119
Product reliability 127
Professional service technology 146
Project technology 130
Quasi-manufacturing technology 146
Research and development 121
Robot 139
Robotics 139

SELECTED READINGS

Abernathy, W. J., "Production Process Structure and Technological Change," *Decision Sciences* 7, no. 4 (October 1976), 607–19.

Blanchard, B. S., *Logistics Engineering and Management,* 2nd ed. Englewood Cliffs, N.J.: Prentice Hall, 1981.

deKluyver, C. A., "Innovation and Industrial Product Life Cycles," *California Management Review* 20, no. 1 (Fall 1977), 21–33.

Grant, E. L., W. G. Ireson, and R. S. Leavenworth, *Principles of Engineering Economy,* 6th ed. New York: Ronald Press, 1976.

Gunn, Thomas G., "The Mechanization of Design and Manufacturing," *Scientific American* 247, no. 3 (September 1982), 116.

Hakala, N. V., "Administration of Industrial Technology," *Business Horizons* 20, no. 5 (October 1977), 4–10.

Hayes, R. H., and S. C. Wheelwright, "Link Manufacturing Process and Product Life Cycles," *Harvard Business Review* 57, no. 1 (January-February, 1979), 133–40.

———, *Restoring Our Competitive Edge: Competing Through Manufacturing.* New York: John Wiley, 1984.

Hetzner, William A., Louis G. Tornatzky, and Katherine J. Klein, "Manufacturing Technology in the 1980s: A Survey of Federal Programs and Practices," *Management Science* 29, no. 8 (August 1983), 951–61.

Hill, Terry, *Manufacturing Strategy: Text and Cases* (Homewood, Ill.: Richard D. Irwin, 1989).

Hyer, Nancy Lea, "Management's Guide to Group Technology," *Operations Management Review* 2, no. 2 (Winter 1984), 36–42.

Liao, W. M., "Effects of Learning on Resource Allocation Decisions," *Decision Sciences* 10, no. 1 (January 1979), 116–25.

Schmenner, Roger W., "Every Factory Has a Cycle," *Harvard Business Review* 61, no. 2 (March-April 1983), 121–29.

Shostack, G. Lynn, "How to Design a Service," *European Journal of Marketing* 16, no. 1 (1982), 49–63.

Stobaugh, Robert, and Piero Telesio, "Match Manufacturing Policies and Product Strategies," *Harvard Business Review* 61, no. 2 (March-April 1983), 113–20.

SUPPLEMENT TO CHAPTER 4

LEARNING CURVES

In our discussion of product and process design choices, we considered the future impact of the choice—that is, how operations managers have to live out the life of the product and process. We also discussed how the manufacturing or service process *changes* over time. *Learning curve* analysis is one way of evaluating the effects of changes in tasks; it is based on traditional industrial engineering techniques. The learning curve methodology is helpful for identifying and evaluating change alternatives, and it can play an important role in the scientific approach to problem solving.

LEARNING CURVE ANALYSIS

When a new model of an existing product is introduced, especially if the work content is similar, learning curve analysis can be helpful in its manufacture.[23] As an organization gains experience in manufacturing a product, the resource inputs required per unit of output diminish over the life of the product. The hours of labor that go into manufacturing the first unit of a new automobile are typically much higher than those needed for the one-hundredth unit, for example. As the cumulative output of the model grows, the labor inputs continue to decline. As you know, if you repeat a new task continually, your performance improves. The performance time drops off rather dramatically at first, and it continues to fall at some slower rate until a performance plateau, a leveling off, is reached. This learning pattern applies to groups and organizations as well as individuals. Furthermore, it is often regular and predictable. The general form of this pattern, called the *learning curve,* is shown in Figure S4.1. This exponential curve becomes a straight line when plotted on *logarithmic coordinates* as opposed to *arithmetic coordinates.* In this example, the initial unit requires 60 labor hours to manufacture. As output and experience continue, labor hours diminish to about 23 for the twentieth unit. The general equation for this curve is:

$$Y_i = k\, i^b \qquad \text{(S4.1)}$$

where

Y_i = labor hours required to produce the ith unit
k = labor hours required to produce the first unit (initial productivity)
b = index of learning
i = ordinal number of unit, that is, 1st, 2nd, 3rd, and so on

[23]For a review of learning curve development, see Louis E. Yelle, "The Learning Curve: Historical Review and Comprehensive Survey," *Decision Sciences* 10, no. 2 (April 1979), 302–28.

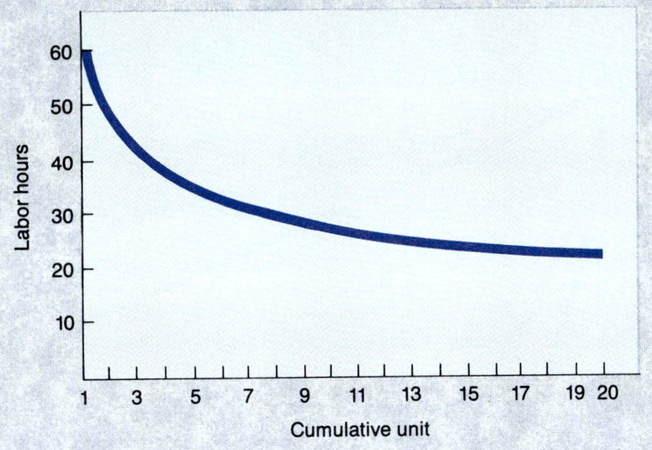

FIGURE S4.1 **An 80% learning curve plotted on arithmetic coordinates; the first unit requires 60 labor hours**

Rate of Learning The rate of learning is not the same in all manufacturing applications. Learning occurs at a higher rate in some applications than others and is reflected by a more rapid descent of the curve. By convention the learning rate is specified as a percentage. A 90 percent curve, for example, means that each time cumulative output doubles, the most recent unit of output requires 90 percent of the labor input of the reference unit: if unit 1 requires 100 labor hours, unit 2 requires 90 percent of 100, or 90 hours; unit 4 requires 90 percent of 90 hours, or 81 hours, and so on. Labor hours required for 70, 80, and 90 percent curves are shown here for various levels of cumulative output, assuming 100 labor hours are required for the first unit.

	Labor Hours Required for Cumulative Unit		
Cumulative Unit	70% Curve	80% Curve	90% Curve
1	100.0	100.0	100.0
2	70.0	80.0	90.0
4	49.0	64.0	81.0
8	34.3	51.2	72.9
16	24.0	41.0	65.6

In Figure S4.2 are plotted three curves on arithmetic and logarithmic coordinates for 16 cumulative units of output. The rate of learning is reflected by b, the index of learning. In Figure S4.1, the index of learning for the 90 percent learning curve is $-.1520$. Table S4.1 shows computed values of i^b for 80 and 90 percent curves. By using Equation S4.1, you can extend these calculations to cover any desired level of cumulative output beyond the 50 given in the table.

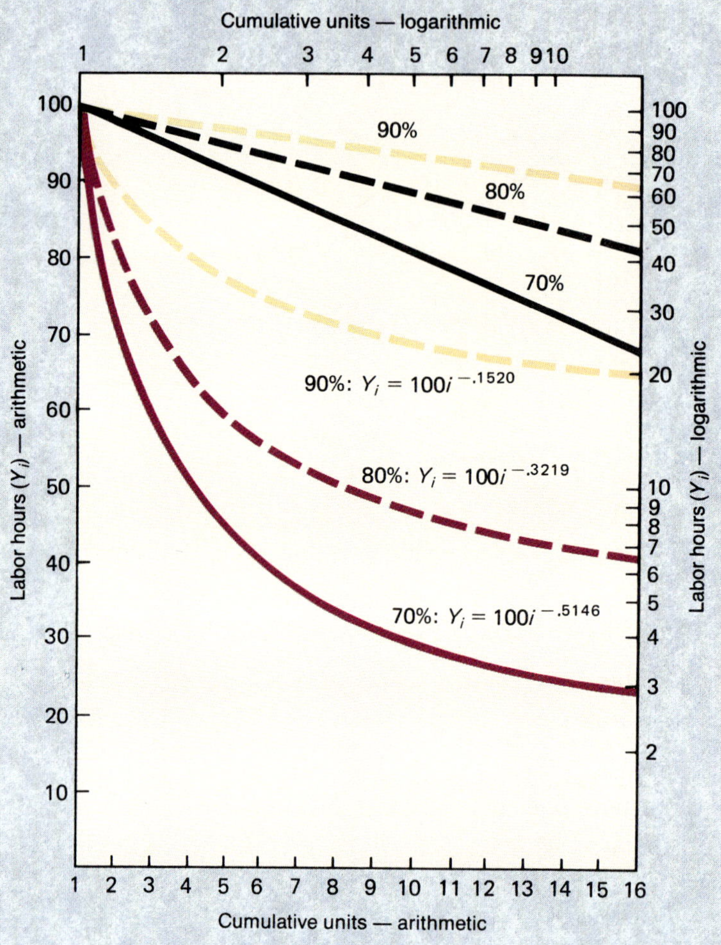

FIGURE S4.2 **Arithmetic and logarithmic coordinates for 70, 80, and 90 percent learning curves; first unit requires 100 labor hours**

EXAMPLE

Surefloat Boat Builders has been receiving customer orders for a new model yacht. Based on previous experience, Surefloat engineers estimate that an 80 percent improvement curve is applicable and that the first unit of the new model will require 500 hours of labor. Surefloat has received customer orders for delivery in the next five months as follows:

Month	Number of Yachts Ordered
1	2
2	6
3	10
4	10
5	15
Total	43

TABLE S4.1 Values of i^b for 80% and 90% curves

Cumulative Unit	80% Curve ($b = -.3219$)	90% Curve ($b = -.1520$)	Cumulative Unit	80% Curve ($b = -.3219$)	90% Curve ($b = -.1520$)
1	1.0000	1.0000	26	.3504	.6094
2	.7999	.9000	27	.3461	.6059
3	.7021	.8462	28	.3421	.6026
4	.6400	.8100	29	.3379	.5994
5	.5957	.7830	30	.3346	.5963
6	.5617	.7616	31	.3311	.5934
7	.5345	.7440	32	.3277	.5905
8	.5120	.7290	33	.3245	.5878
9	.4930	.7161	34	.3214	.5851
10	.4766	.7047	35	.3184	.5825
11	.4621	.6946	36	.3155	.5800
12	.4494	.6854	37	.3128	.5776
13	.4380	.6771	38	.3101	.5753
14	.4276	.6696	39	.3075	.5730
15	.4182	.6626	40	.3050	.5708
16	.4096	.6561	41	.3026	.5687
17	.4017	.6501	42	.3002	.5666
18	.3944	.6445	43	.2980	.5646
19	.3876	.6392	44	.2958	.5626
20	.3819	.6342	45	.2937	.5607
21	.3753	.6295	46	.2916	.5588
22	.3697	.6251	47	.2896	.5570
23	.3645	.6209	48	.2876	.5552
24	.3595	.6169	49	.2857	.5535
25	.3548	.6131	50	.2839	.5518

The manufacturing manager is concerned about the manpower requirements for meeting these commitments to customers. The manufacturing engineer was asked to provide some information that could be used for manpower planning.

Equation S4.1 applied to the Surefloat situation becomes

$$Y_i = (500)i^{-.3219} \qquad \text{(S4.2)}$$

Using equation S4.2 (or tabled values) for the 80 percent curve, the engineer generated the data in Table S4.2. Surefloat management can use these data to decide how many yachts to produce each month so that the manpower requirements are smoothed across months. The data also help determine work-force size. Notice the effects of learning in the data. Commitments to customers in month 2 are 200 percent greater than in month 1; yet the manpower to accomplish this increases by only 98 percent over the previous month. As the second column shows, labor hours are reduced rather dramatically initially and then taper off to relatively small increments as the effects of learning diminish with experience.

TABLE S4.2 **Surefloat engineering data for use in manpower planning**

Cumulative Unit	Labor Hours Required for Cummulative Unit (rounded)[a]	Month	Yachts Promised	Labor Hours Required for Monthly Commitments	Change in Labor Hours from Previous Month	Change in Output from Previous Month	Monthly Manpower Equivalents (number of people)[b]
1	500	1	2	900			5.62
2	400						
3	351	2	6	1,773	+98.1%	+200.0%	11.08
4	320						
5	298						
6	281						
7	267						
8	256						
9	246	3	10	2,185	+23.2	+67.7	13.65
10	238						
19	194	4	10	1,816	−16.8	—0—	11.35
28	171						
29	169	5	15	2,373	+31.0	+50.0	14.83
42	150						
43	149						
				Total labor hours = 9,047	Total yachts = 43		

[a]Obtained from Table S4.1 and Equation S4.1, labor hours for yacht one = Y_1 = (500)(1.000) = 500.
[b]A person is assumed to work 20 days/month, 8 hours/day. Thus a "manpower equivalent" is 20 × 8 = 160 labor hours/month. For each month the manpower equivalent is found by dividing the monthly labor hours by 160. Hence, for month 1,900 ÷ 160 = 5.62.

EXAMPLE

Surefloat management has decided on a selling price of $12,000 per yacht. It expects to receive payment the month following delivery. Each yacht will be produced and delivered during the month in which it was promised. Work force size will equal the monthly manpower equivalents shown in Table S4.2. Standard wages are $1,000/month/employee. Costs of direct materials, variable materials, overhead and fixed administrative and marketing overhead are shown in Table S4.3. All these costs are incurred during the month of production.

Uses of Learning Curves Just as learning curve analysis can be used for manpower planning, it can also be helpful in cash flow planning.[24] Cash flow planning involves the timing of cash outlays and inflows associated with a new product. Notice in the last example that monthly inflows are less than outlays for each of the first three months. Cumulative cash flows are negative through month 5, and Surefloat will have to borrow funds or divert them from other projects to finance operations on the new model yacht during these months.

[24]Use of the learning curve in decision making is discussed in Woody M. Liao, "Effects of Learning on Resource Allocation Decisions," *Decision Sciences* 10, no. 1 (January 1979), 116–25.

TABLE S4.3 Surefloat cash flow for six months

	Month					
	1	2	3	4	5	6
Units produced and delivered	2	6	10	10	15	15
Cash inflow from sales	—0—	$24,000	$72,000	$120,000	$120,000	$180,000
Outflows						
Wages	$ 5,620	$11,080	$13,650	$ 11,350	$ 14,830	$ 13,500
Direct materials ($6,000 per yacht)	12,000	36,000	60,000	60,000	90,000	90,000
Variable materials overhead (10% of direct materials)	1,200	3,600	6,000	6,000	9,000	9,000
Fixed administrative and marketing overhead	10,000	10,000	10,000	10,000	10,000	10,000
Monthly outflow	$28,820	$60,680	$89,650	$187,350	$123,830	$122,500
Net monthly cash flow (inflow-outflow)	(28,820)[a]	(36,680)	(17,650)	32,650	(3,830)	57,500
Cumulative cash flow position (month-end)	(28,820)	(65,500)	(83,150)	(50,500)	(54,330)	3,170

[a]Parentheses denote negative cash flow.

Parameter Estimation Two parameters, k and b, must be estimated for learning curve analysis. If these parameters are seriously in error, results can be very misleading. Estimates of labor hours for the initial unit are based primarily on staff experience and familiarity with the history of the conversion process. Estimation of the appropriate learning rate is typically based on regression analysis of data for similar products.

Reasons for Improvement While the learning curve depicts improvement in productivity over time, productivity does not improve solely because workers are learning. The reasons are numerous, including changes in work methods, product engineering, facilities layout, equipment redesign, employee training, and others. We intend the term *learning curve* to subsume the effects of all these reasons for changing productivity. Learning curve analysis is generally of greatest benefit in labor-intensive conversion processes.

CASE

Cleanair Corporation

Cleanair Corporation designs and manufactures small contaminant-filtration units. These units are used in various industrial facilities to reduce emissions contributing to air pollution. Cleanair's research and development department has developed and tested a new model, the Minigasp III, which it believes is now suitable for full-scale marketing. Minigasp I has been successfully marketed for eight years and Minigasp II for four. Cleanair management believes that Minigasp III faces even brighter marketing prospects. Although similar in many ways to its predecessors, Minigasp III contains an innovative chemical processing system that should give Cleanair a competitive edge in the industry. Management must now decide whether to add Minigasp III to its product line.

The marketing manager says that a $3,000/unit selling price would be very competitive and anticipates sales of one unit in each of months 1 and 2, two units in month 3, three units in month 4, and four units in each month thereafter. Payment is expected during the month of purchase. The operations manager believes he can meet these market demands if the changeover of facilities is started immediately. An initial outlay of $30,000 is necessary to renovate part of the plant and equipment. Costs have been estimated as follows:

Direct materials = $700/unit
Indirect materials = 10% of direct materials cost
Direct labor = $7/labor hour
Indirect labor = 20% of direct labor cost
Additional administrative and marketing costs = $3,000/month

In addition, maintenance expenses will be $1,000 in month 1; $750 in month 2; and $500 in each month thereafter. Production engineers estimate the initial unit of Minigasp III will require 200 hours of labor to manufacture. Thereafter they believe an 80 percent learning curve is applicable.

The finance manager questions the advisability of adopting the new product because of the risks involved. If new government regulations were to be created, always a major factor in this industry, the marketability of Minigasp III could be damaged. Consequently, he suggests the project not be undertaken unless the funds from sales can fully recover the initial $30,000 outlay during the first year of production. As operations manager you are expected to respond to the finance manager.

REVIEW AND DISCUSSION QUESTIONS

1. Under what circumstances is learning curve analysis most applicable?
2. What are the reasons for changes in productivity that cause the learning phenomenon?
3. For what kinds of operating decisions can learning curve analysis provide data?

PROBLEMS

1. In response to a consumer inquiry, a manufacturing company is estimating the costs of 25 units of a new product, which is similar to an existing one. Estimates indicate that 400 labor hours are required to produce the first unit. Draw graphs of labor requirements for units 1 through 25 for 80 percent and 90 percent learning curves.
2. Reconsider Problem 1 using the 80 percent learning curve. Direct labor and variable overhead are estimated at $9/labor hour. Direct materials will cost $600 for each unit produced. Initial tooling for the product costs $15,000. Monthly

overhead will cost $6,000/month during the life of the project. The available work force consists of 10 operators, each available for 160 hours/month. If a profit of 10 percent on selling price is desired, what should be the selling price?

UTILIZING QSOM COMPUTER SOFTWARE

3. A manufacturer of industrial transformers is introducing a new product line. The first of a series of similar new transformers was recently completed in 1,600 hours. Assuming a learning curve of 75 percent, use QSOM to develop the learning curve for this situation and the production times for the first 25 units. Now compare your solution to a learning curve of 85 percent. Compare production times for units 10, 20, and 25 for the 75 percent and 85 percent curves, and interpret the differences for management.

CHAPTER 5

OPERATIONS CAPACITY

On first thought, capacity planning may not seem relevant to a service business like trucking. Actually, it is very important. The key reason is that the volume of freight fluctuates significantly, not only from year to year but from day to day. And any freight not handled today is probably lost forever. You can't stockpile or back order freight; fast service is essential.

Our principal trucking subsidiary, Consolidated Freightways Motor Freight, has 550 freight terminals and has been adding more than one per week for the past five years. We expect this pace to continue for several years.

Some years ago it became obvious that we could not achieve our ultimate goal of serving the entire United States by simply adding terminals to our existing system, in which we moved freight directly from the origin to the destination. We concluded we would have to devise a system of connected "hubs" or distribution centers, each serving 20 or more "spokes" or satellite terminals. We determined that we would eventually need approximately 32 strategically located centers and 700 or more satellites. We began in 1975 and today most of that system is in place, operating even more efficiently than we had hoped.

Raymond F. O'Brien
Chairman and Chief Executive Officer
Consolidated Freightways, Inc.
Palo Alto, California

Strategic planning for operations helps managers define the operations function: It specifies what we want to accomplish in operations. Having specified this mission, planning guides our choices on operations capacity, location, and layout in the long term, and these choices, in turn, affect the ways we use our resources and facilities in the short term. According to Mr. O'Brien, Consolidated Freightways Motor Freight has been planning strategically for capacity and location since 1975, and the results have been very satisfactory.

In this chapter we investigate capacity planning. We consider how capacity planning affects operations costs and break-even relationships, service levels, required investment, and organizational risks.

CAPACITY PLANNING ENVIRONMENT

Capacity A facility's maximum productive capability, usually expressed as volume of output per period of time.

Capacity is the rate of productive capability of a facility. Capacity is usually expressed as volume of output per time period. Operations managers are concerned with capacity for several reasons. First, they want sufficient capacity to meet customer demand in a timely manner. Second, capacity affects the cost efficiency of operations, the ease or difficulty of scheduling output, and the costs of maintaining the facility. Finally, capacity requires an investment. Since managers seek a good return on investment, both the costs and revenues of a capacity planning decision must be carefully evaluated.

THE NEED FOR CAPACITY PLANNING

Capacity planning is the first step when an organization decides to produce more or a new product. Once capacity is evaluated and a need for new or expanded facilities is determined, facility location and process technology activities occur. Too much capacity would require exploring ways to reduce capacity, such as temporarily closing, selling, or consolidating facilities. Consolidation might involve relocation, a combining of technologies, or a rearrangement of equipment and processes.

RELATIONSHIP OF CAPACITY AND LOCATION DECISIONS

Often decisions about capacity are inseparable from decisions about location: Capacity depends upon demand and demand often depends on location. Commercial banks, for example, simultaneously expand capacity and demand by building branch banks. Decisions about the size and location of the branch are made according to projections about neighborhood population densities and growth, geographic locations of market segments, transportation (traffic) flows, and the locations of competitors. Adding a new branch offers greater convenience to some existing customers and, management hopes, attracts new customers as well. Obviously this decision affects the revenues, operating costs, and capital costs of the organization.

In the public sector, the capacity decision involves similar considerations. Municipalities face ever-increasing demands for public services, strong public sentiment for tightening budgets, and greater performance accountability. Consequently, officials have increased their efforts to rearrange public resources so that service capacity is increased but the cost of operation is not. Municipal emergency services, for example, are periodically expanded by adding new stations. First, the geographic dispersion of demand is analyzed to show population growth and shifts. Next, municipal officials plan where to locate new stations, taking into consideration both areas of greatest need and costs of operation and facilities. Although the capacity decision may not involve direct revenues, cost savings for citizens can be considered a form of indirect revenues. These cost savings can result in reduced tax burdens or lower insurance rates in areas with improved emergency services.

Modeling techniques, which we will illustrate later in this chapter, are playing a central role in these planning processes. One study, for example, explains how mathematical programming is used for greater ambulance effectiveness considering time-to-scene, time-to-hospital, and distance-to-hospital factors, thereby increasing effective service system capacity.[1] Another study shows how mathematical modeling can determine optimal fleet sizes and vehicle routes for a commercial common carrier.[2] Yet another study demonstrates the value of queuing models in a computer-based information system for the St. Louis County Police Department.[3] The system gives a way to allocate police patrols, thereby using existing capacity more efficiently or reducing the size of operations without diminishing existing service levels. All these examples show how systematic analysis and planning can lead to effective use and improvement of capacity.

CAPACITY PLANNING DECISIONS

Capacity planning normally involves the following activities:

1. Assessing existing capacity
2. Forecasting capacity needs
3. Identifying alternative ways to modify capacity
4. Evaluating financial, economical, and technological capacity alternatives
5. Selecting a capacity alternative most suited to achieving strategic mission

MEASURING CAPACITY

For some organizations capacity is simple to measure. Kraft, Inc., can use "tons of cheese per year." General Motors Corporation can use "number of automobiles per year." But what about organizations whose product lines are more diverse? For these firms, it is hard to find a common unit of output.

As a substitute, capacity can be expressed in terms of *input*. A legal office may express capacity in terms of the number of attorneys employed per year. A custom job shop or an auto repair shop may express capacity in terms of available labor hours and/or machine hours per week, month, or year.

---

[1]C. Saydam and M. McKnew, "A Separable Programming Approach to Expected Coverage: An Application to Ambulance Location," *Decision Sciences* 16, no. 4 (Fall 1985), 381–98.

[2]M. O. Ball, B. L. Golden, A. A. Assad, and L. D. Bodin, "Planning for Truck Fleet Size in the Presence of a Common-Carrier Option," *Decision Sciences*, 14, no. 1 (January 1983), 103–20.

[3]N. K. Kwak and M. B. Leavitt, "Police Patrol Beat Design: Allocation of Effort and Evaluation of Expected Performance," *Decision Sciences* 15, no. 3 (Summer 1984), 421–33.

Capacity, then, may be measured in terms of the inputs or the outputs of the conversion process. Some common examples of capacity measures are shown in Table 5.1.

TABLE 5.1 **Measures of operating capacity**

Organization	Measure
Output	
Automobile manufacturer	Number of autos
Brewery	Barrels of beer
Cannery	Tons of food
Steel producer	Tons of steel
Power company	Megawatts of electricity
Input	
Airline	Number of seats
Hospital	Number of beds
Job shop	Labor and/or machine hours
Merchandising	Square feet of display or sales area
Movie theater	Number of seats
Restaurant	Number of seats or tables
Tax office	Number of accountants
University	Number of students and/or faculty
Warehouse	Square or cubic feet of storage space

It's often difficult to measure capacity realistically because of day-to-day variations. Employees are absent or late, equipment breaks down, facility downtime is needed for maintenance and repair, machine setups are required for product changeovers, and vacations must be scheduled. Since all these variations occur from time to time, you can see that the capacity of a facility can rarely be measured in precise terms, so measurements must be interpreted cautiously. It's not unusual, for example, for a facility to operate at more than 100% capacity, as we illustrate in Operations Management Highlight 5.1.

ESTIMATING FUTURE CAPACITY NEEDS

Capacity requirements can be evaluated from two extreme perspectives—short-term and long-term.

Short-term Requirements Managers often use forecasts of product demand to estimate the short-term work load the facility must handle. By looking ahead up to 12 months, managers anticipate output requirements for different products or services. Then they compare requirements with existing capacity and detect when capacity adjustments are needed.

OPERATIONS MANAGEMENT HIGHLIGHT 5.1

Source: Ambrose Greenway/Tony Stone Worldwide

A Resort Afloat: Capacity Utilization, Better Service, and Profits

A carefree cruise offers a relaxing holiday for vacationers and a first-class challenge for operations managers. Capacity on a luxury liner—its size and the allocation of space to various recreational and functional purposes—determines how many passengers can be accommodated. And, of course, more passengers onboard mean larger revenues: up to $1,500 per passenger for a four-day trip. With space at a premium, capacity decisions involve tradeoffs to balance the allocation of space among passenger cabins, recreation rooms, deck space, retail shops, and dining areas. Space allocations for essential services, however, are fixed: crew quarters, equipment, maintenance and storage, and kitchens.

Carnival Cruise Lines, the world's largest multiple-night cruise line, is expert in utilizing capacity to get the right balance between passenger bookings and quality service. With more than 780,000 passengers and revenues of $1.1 billion, Carnival Cruise Lines consistently operates its ships at over 100 percent of capacity (106.5 percent in 1989, 111.7 percent in 1988. For a cruise business, service is paramount, entailing seemingly endless luxury offerings: entertainment shows, bingo, casino, game rooms, skeet shooting, talent shows, child-care and entertainment, shops, swimming, sauna, and cabin attendants.

Of course, space for passengers and their entertainment is not the only capacity requirement. The crew, too, is crucial because services are so labor-intensive. Consider the dining room, central to a most prominent service. On the Mardi Gras cruise ship, the 600-seat dining room serves 1,200 passengers three main meals daily in two shifts. The lavish meals require more than 50 waiters, 50 table attendants, five head waiters, and a maitre d'. If served in one shift, the same meal would require double the dining room space and crew size, and a much larger kitchen. Two shifts, using smaller crews and space, increases passenger capacity without sacrificing service quality. And happy passengers are keeping Carnival's revenues on the upswing.

Sources: Standard & Poor's Corp., *Standard ASE Stock Reports* (August 16, 1990) 7458-59; "Real Maneuvering for a Fantasy Vessel," *Motor Ship* (May 1989), 35; "Paper Names Carnival Florida's Company of the Year," *Travel Weekly* (April 24, 1989), 5. David Lyons, "Carnival Cruise Lines Orders Big Liner," *Journal of Commerce and Commercial* (February 11, 1987), 22B

Decisions on expanding or reducing the capacity of this production line depend on marketing plans, product development, and product life cycles.
Source: **Ted Horowitz/The Stock Market**

Long-term Requirements Long-term capacity requirements are more difficult to determine because future demand and technologies are uncertain. Forecasting five or ten years into the future is a risky and difficult task. What products or services will the firm be producing then? Today's product may not even exist in the future. Obviously, long-range capacity requirements are dependent on marketing plans, product development, and the life cycles of the products.

Changes in process technology must also be anticipated. Even if products remain unchanged, the methods for generating them may change dramatically. Capacity planning must involve forecasts of technology as well as product demand.

STRATEGIES FOR MODIFYING CAPACITY

After existing and future capacity requirements are assessed, alternative ways of modifying capacity must be identified.

Short-term Responses For short-term periods of up to one year, fundamental capacity is fixed. Major facilities are seldom opened or closed on a regular monthly or yearly basis. Many short-term adjustments for increasing or decreasing capacity are possible, however. Which adjustments to make depend on whether the conversion process is primarily labor- or capital-intensive and whether the product is one that can be stored in inventory.

Capital-intensive processes rely heavily on physical facilities, plant, and equipment. Short-term capacity can be modified by operating these facilities more or less intensively than normal. The costs of setting up, changing over, and maintaining facilities, procuring raw materials and manpower, managing inventory, and scheduling can all be modified by such capacity changes.

In labor-intensive processes, short-term capacity can be changed by laying off or hiring people or by having employees work overtime or be idle. These alternatives are expensive, though, since hiring costs, severance pay, or premium wages may have to be paid, and scarce human skills may be lost permanently.

Strategies for changing capacity also depend upon how long the product can be stored in inventory. For products that are perishable (raw foods) or subject to radical style changes, storing in inventory may not be feasible. This is also true for many service organizations offering such products as insurance protection, emergency operations (fire, police, etc.), and taxi and barber services. Instead of storing output in inventory, input can be expanded or shrunk temporarily in anticipation of demand. Several of the most common strategies are summarized in Table 5.2.

TABLE 5.2 Temporary capacity changes

Type	Action
Inventories	Stock pile finished goods during slack periods to meet later demand.
Backlogs	During peak demand periods, ask willing customers to wait some time before receiving their product. File their order and fulfill it after the peak demand period.
Employment levels	Hire additional employees or lay off employees as demand for output increases and decreases.
Work force utilization	Have employees work overtime during peaks and be idle or work fewer hours during slack demand periods.
Employee training	Instead of having each employee specialize in one task, train each in several tasks. Then, as skill requirements change, rotate employees among different tasks. This is an alternative to hiring and layoffs for getting needed skills.
Process design	Change the job content at each workstation to increase productivity. Use work methods analysis to redesign jobs.
Subcontracting	During peak periods, hire other firms temporarily to make the product or some of its subcomponents.
Maintenance	Temporarily discontinue routine preventive maintenance on facilities and equipment so that during peak periods the facility can be operated when it would otherwise be idle.

Long-term Responses: Expansion From World War II through the 1960s, the U.S. economy was one of abundance and growth. Since the 1970s, the United States has encountered problems of scarce resources and a more competitive economy. Organizations today cannot be locked into thinking only about *expanding* the resource base; they must also consider optimal approaches to *contracting* it. Let's consider the first of these long-run responses, expansion.

EXAMPLE

A warehousing operation foresees the need for an additional 100,000 square feet of space by the end of the next five years. One option is to add an additional 50,000 square feet now and another 50,000 square feet two years from now. Another option is to add the entire 100,000 square feet now.

Estimated costs for building the entire addition now are $50/square foot. If expanded incrementally, the initial 50,000 square feet will cost $60/square foot. The 50,000 square feet to be added later are estimated at $80/square foot. Which alternative is better? At a minimum, the lower construction costs plus excess capacity costs of total construction now must be compared with higher costs of deferred construction. The operations manager must consider the costs, benefits, and risks of each option.

The costs, benefits, and risks of expansion pose an interesting decision problem. By building the entire addition now, the company avoids higher building costs, the risk of accelerated inflation (and even higher future construction costs), and the risk of losing additional future business because of inadequate capacity. But there may also be disadvantages to this alternative. First, the organization may not be able to muster the financial investment. Second, if the organization expands now, it may find later that its demand forecasts were incorrect; if ultimate demand is lower than expected, the organization has overbuilt. Finally, even if forecasted demand is accurate, it may not fully materialize until the end of the five-year planning horizon. If so, the organization will have invested in an excess-capacity facility on which no return is realized for several years. Since funds could have been invested in other ways, the organization has forgone the opportunity of earning returns elsewhere on its investment.

EXAMPLE

Extol Corporation's competitive strategy capitalizes on not being a product innovator. Hence, it avoids the costs of extensive research and development. Instead, Extol adopts its competitors new product developments and quickly adapts its production capabilities. Handsome financial returns can be realized with this strategy, but everything depends on the timing of introducing products in the marketplace. Accordingly, Extol intentionally overbuilds its physical facilities by 20 percent of expected capacity to avoid lost sales, which are likely to be far more costly than the cost of the additional 20 percent of capacity.

The general patterns of capacity utilization costs and incremental expansion can be seen in Figure 5.1. The first curve shows the optimal rate p_i of output in units per time period for an existing facility at time 1. Production can fall temporarily to a lower level p_1^-, but if it does, machine and labor resources will be under-utilized and unit costs will therefore increase. Output could be increased to p_1^+, but unit costs would also increase because of excessive overtime, inadequate preventive maintenance, and higher congestion in existing facilities.

If a firm anticipates that demand will be permanently higher, it could expand the facility and reap the benefits of economies of scale. Typically, expansion occurs in increments over time rather than in a single lump. The series of curves in Figure 5.1 shows optimum output rates for each stage of expansion assuming demand increases as expected. Capacity could be expanded in one step, from p_1 to p_4, but the risk of overexpanding is increased.

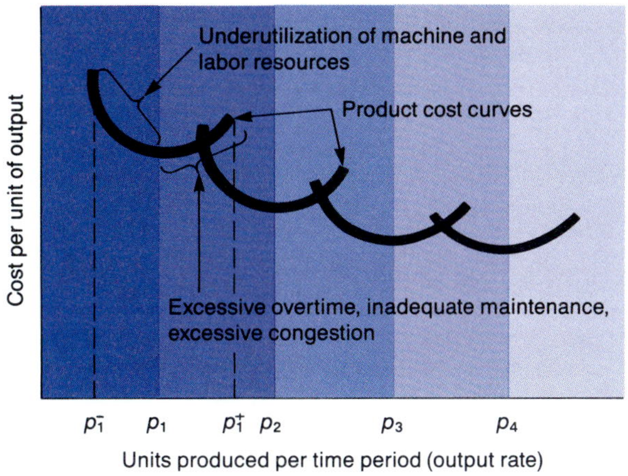

FIGURE 5.1 **Product costs related to facility capacity**

The financial and technical requirements of expansion go beyond facilities and equipment, as described in Operations Management Highlight 5.2.

Long-term Responses: Contraction and Constant Capacity Capacity contraction most often involves selling off existing facilities, equipment, and inventories, and firing employees. As serious declines in demand occur, we may gradually terminate operations. Permanent capacity reduction or shutdown occurs only as a last resort. Instead, new ways are sought to maintain and use existing capacity. Why? Because a great deal of effort, capital, and human skills have gone into building up a technology. Often this technology and skill base are transferable to other products or services. As one product reaches the decline phase of its life cycle, it can be replaced with others without increasing capacity (see Figure 5.2). This phasing in and out of new and old products is not by accident. Staff for product research and development and market research engage in long-range planning to determine how existing capacity can be used and adapted to meet future product demand.

CAPACITY PLANNING MODELING

MODELING ALTERNATIVES

Several models are useful in capacity planning. *Present value analysis* is helpful whenever the time value of capital investments and fund flows must be considered. (See the Supplement to Chapter 2.) *Aggregate planning models* are useful for examining how best to use existing capacity in the short term (see Chapter 10). *Breakeven analysis* can identify the minimum breakeven volumes when comparing projected costs and

OPERATIONS MANAGEMENT HIGHLIGHT 5.2

Source: Schmid, Langsfeld/The Image Bank

Keeping an Eye on the "Systems Side" of Expansion

When a company expands its capacity, it encounters much more than just physical changes. As the people at Zetaco will tell you, management systems and control procedures have to be upgraded to the newer conditions. This Eden Prairie, Minnesota, company makes computer-related equipment and data storage

revenues. In the following pages we present two useful models for evaluating short-term capacity utilization: *linear programming* and *computer simulation.* Then we apply a third model, *decision tree analysis,* to the long-term capacity problem of facility expansion. Although we could discuss even more models, these three models serve to illustrate the diversity of capacity problems confronting the operations manager.

products. As so often happens to companies facing continued expansion, Zetaco had to find out how to keep up with the increasing pressure on all aspects of its business: production, finance, engineering, sales and marketing, and inventory and production control. Expansion for Zetaco meant finding new ways to integrate production operations with all other parts of the business so that customers get served better, rather than getting lost and pushed aside during the bustle of growth.

Zetaco managers understand that physical expansion requires a corresponding increase in the company's "business systems" capacity. Greater numbers of customer orders mean greater effort to ensure that the time between taking an order and shiping it stays competitive. Additional orders also mean closer attention to inventory control so that excessive inventories don't let operating costs get out of hand. Finally, more orders mean more materials, and that means more purchase orders and receipts have to be expedited and processed.

Recognizing these needs, Zetaco adopted a team approach in its capacity planning. A group of employees from throughout the company selected a new business management system. They adopted an integrated minicomputer system that handles today's enlarged information requirements. The system's flexibility allows upgrading for future expansions as well. The system gives Zetaco faster response rates than ever before. All aspects of the business are integrated for better tracking of costs, materials, jobs, and profitability. And, perhaps most important, overall communications are improved: Everyone is sharing the same information. Rather than getting lost in the shuffle of expansion, Zetaco's customers are receiving closer attention than ever before.

Source: **"UNIX-Based System Solves Problem,"** ***P&IM Review*** **(September 1989), 40.**

LINEAR PROGRAMMING APPLIED TO PRODUCT MIX AND CAPACITY

Our first example of model applications illustrates the difficulties of measuring capacity in a multiproduct firm. As we discuss MultiBand's situation, we'll show you a way of finding the best use of capacity during a short-term planning horizon.

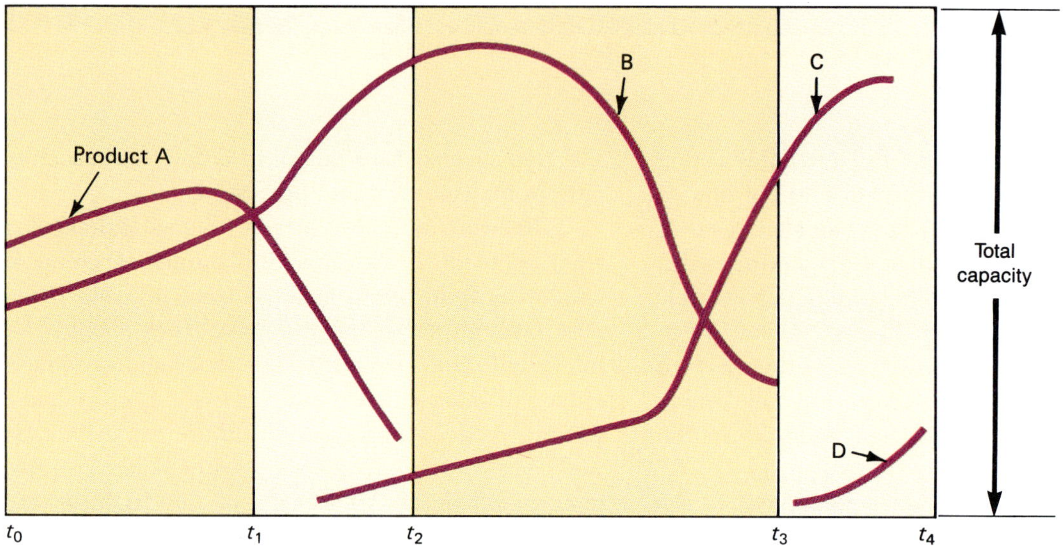

FIGURE 5.2 **Use of existing capacity by time-phasing products**

EXAMPLE

MultiBand Enterprises manufactures two products, a portable radio (PR) and a citizens band radio (CB). The marketing manager states, "We can sell all that can be produced in the near future." She then asks the operations manager, "What is your production capacity per month?" The operations manager replies that capacity depends on which product is produced.

"Our two products each require different amounts of three kinds of labor: subassembly, assembly, and inspection labor. Next month we will have available 316 hours of subassembly labor, 354 hours of assembly labor, and 62 hours of inspection labor. So capacity depends on which products we produce."

The operations manager knows that each CB requires .4 hours of subassembly labor, .5 hours of assembly labor, and .05 hours of inspection labor. Each portable radio requires .5 hours of subassembly labor, .3 hours of assembly labor and 0.10 hours of inspection labor.

The vice president says, "We know that each CB sold contributes $50 toward profit and overhead. Each PR sold contributes $40 toward profit and overhead.

What is MultiBand's capacity next month, and what mix of CBs and PRs should be manufactured next month?

Product mix problem A decision situation involving limited resources that can be used to produce any of several combinations of products.

The *product mix problem* is faced whenever a firm's limited resources can be used to produce any of several combinations of products. MultiBand's product mix problem is summarized in Table 5.3.

MultiBand's capacity depends on the product mix. If all resources next month are devoted to producing CBs, available subassembly labor can produce

$$316 \text{ hours} \div .40 \text{ hours/unit} = 790 \text{ units}$$

TABLE 5.3 **MultiBand's available resources and possible uses**

Resource	Resource Needed to Produce One Unit of Product (in hours)		Resource Available (in hours)
	CB	PR	
Subassembly labor	.40	.50	316
Assembly labor	.50	.30	354
Inspection labor	.05	.10	62

Available assembly labor can produce

$$354 \div .50 = 708 \text{ units}$$

Available inspection labor can produce

$$62 \div .05 = 1{,}240 \text{ units}$$

Since a CB requires all three kinds of labor, the maximum possible number of CBs is the smallest of these quantities, 708 units. On the other hand, we could produce only PRs. If each resource is devoted totally to PRs, available subassembly, assembly, and inspection labor can produce 632, 1,180, and 620 PRs; the maximum possible number of PRs is thus 620.

MultiBand's capacity alternatives are (1) 708 CBs produced by using all available assembly labor; (2) 620 PRs produced by using all available inspection labor; or (3) some combination of PRs and CBs. What is the *best mix* of CBs and PRs to produce? In other words, what is the best way to use existing capacity in the short run? This question can be answered by using a *linear programming* model, which is described and applied to the MultiBand problem in the supplement to this chapter. Several steps must be taken to apply this method.

Linear programming Mathematical method for selecting the optimal allocation of resources to maximize profits or minimize costs.

First, the decision variables must be identified. For MultiBand there are two decision variables—the number of CBs (labeled c) and the number of PRs (labeled p) to be produced next month.

Second, the criterion for measuring the "goodness" or "badness" of each decision alternative must be identified. MultiBand's criterion is the total contribution margin (TCM) as shown in Equation 5.1.

$$\text{TCM} = \begin{array}{l}\text{Contribution}\\ \text{margin from CBs}\\ \text{produced}\end{array} + \begin{array}{l}\text{Contribution}\\ \text{margin from PRs}\\ \text{produced}\end{array} \tag{5.1}$$

$$\text{TCM} = (\$50) \times \begin{array}{l}\text{(number}\\ \text{of CBs}\\ \text{produced)}\end{array} + (\$40) \times \begin{array}{l}\text{(number}\\ \text{of PRs}\\ \text{produced)}\end{array}$$

$$\text{TCM} = (\$50)\,c + (\$40)\,p$$

The TCM depends on how many CBs and PRs are produced. MultiBand needs to find values for c and p so that TCM is as large as possible; that is, it needs to maximize TCM.

Third, the restrictions limiting the number of products that can be produced must be identified. The restrictions for c and p are as follows:

Resource	Resource Used (in hours)	Resource Available (in hours) (resource restriction)
Subassembly labor	$.40\ c + .50\ p$	$\leq$ 16
Assembly labor	$.50\ c + .30\ p$	$\leq$ 354
Inspection labor	$.05\ c + .10\ p$	$\leq$ 62

Fourth, a systematic procedure to evaluate possible combinations of products must be applied. The combination of values for p and c that yields the highest value of TCM without violating the resource restrictions is the one that is selected. By applying a linear programming procedure, we find that the optimal solution for MultiBand is to produce 632 CBs and 126 PRs next month. This results in a contribution margin of:

$$\begin{aligned} \text{TCM} &= \$50(632) + \$40(126) \\ &= 31{,}600 + 5{,}040 \\ &= \$36{,}640 \end{aligned}$$

This product mix will consume all available subassembly and assembly labor, leave about 18 hours of unused or idle inspection labor, and provide a higher total contribution margin than any other combination of CBs and PRs. It represents the optimal use of existing capacity.

COMPUTER SIMULATION USED TO EVALUATE CAPACITY

In many systems, proper scheduling of the conversion facilities can lead to better use of existing capacity. Sometimes a careful analysis reveals a greater output rate than was thought possible. Such an analysis was performed at the University of Massachusetts Health-Service Outpatient Clinic.[4] The clinic's waiting rooms were overcrowded and confusing, and the professional staff felt overworked and harassed. During days when few walk-in patients came and appointment patients failed to appear, physicians were sometimes idle. On other days, physicians were still seeing patients up to an hour past closing time.

A team of analysts set out to find better ways to use the existing capacity. Their strategy was to build a Monte Carlo simulation model (see Chapter 10) of the clinic and to use the model experimentally to improve the clinic operations. First, they examined clinic records to estimate the demand on the system—the number of patient visits per week during regular clinic hours. The pattern of patient arrivals was examined by day of week and by time of day. This pattern included both periods of slack and periods of very high patient loads. The analysts used the simulation model to test experimentally the effects of various patient scheduling policies.

The recommendations of the simulation experiment were actually implemented at the clinic during the following year, and several improvements in its operation resulted. Patient waiting time was reduced; the number of patients seen by physicians increased more than 13 percent; and the average time that a patient spent with a

[4]This case history is based on the study of E. J. Rising, R. Baron, and B. Averill, "A Systems Analysis of a University-Health-Service Outpatient Clinic," *Operations Research* 21, no. 5 (September-October 1973), 1030–47.

physician went up by 5 percent. The number of hours physicians worked decreased by 5 percent. Less overtime was required, and staff morale improved. Clearly, the clinic's existing capacity increased because resources were scheduled and used more wisely.

DECISION TREE ANALYSIS APPLIED TO CAPACITY EXPANSION

Linear programming and computer simulation models focus on the short-term question of how to use existing capacity; but the planner also faces long-term decisions. One such decision has to do with capacity expansion. One technique for analyzing this and other sequential decisions is *decision tree* analysis.[5]

Decision tree A diagram used to structure and analyze a decision problem; a systematic, sequential laying out of decision points, alternatives, and chance events.

Chance event An event leading potentially to several different outcomes, only one of which will definitely occur; the decision maker has no control over which outcome will occur.

Decision tree analysis comprises the following steps:

1. Tree diagramming
   (a) Identify all decision points and the order (sequence) in which they occur
   (b) Identify alternative decisions for each decision point
   (c) Identify the *chance events* that can occur after each decision
   (d) Develop a tree diagram showing the sequence of decisions and chance events
2. Estimation
   (a) Estimate the probability for each possible outcome of each chance event
   (b) Estimate the financial consequence of each possible outcome and decision alternative
3. Evaluation and selection
   (a) Calculate the expected value of each decision alternative
   (b) Select the decision alternative offering the most attractive expected value

Let's use an example to help make a risky, long-run decision about expanding the capacity of an existing facility.

EXAMPLE

The city transit system in Smalltown operates its bus system at a $400,000 deficit annually. The city council has decided to raise bus fares to help offset the deficit. The director of city transit believes the fare increase will decrease ridership unless transit system capacity is expanded. The director suggests that expanded services be offered simultaneously with the fare increase to offset negative community reaction and perhaps increase ridership. He admits that, even with expansion, it is possible that ridership may only be sustained and may even decrease.

An influential council member suggests an alternative plan. She would increase the fare now but delay the capacity expansion decision for two years. If expansion is delayed, the director is sure that ridership will either decrease or be sustained at current levels. If service is expanded two years after the fare increase, ridership may increase,

[5] An example of extensive use of decision trees yielding substantial economic benefits is presented in T. J. Madden, M. S. Hyrnick, and J. A. Hodde, "Decision Analysis Used to Evaluate Air Quality Control Equipment for Ohio Edison Company," *Interfaces* 13, no. 1 (February 1983), 66–75.

be sustained, or decrease. If service is not expanded in two years, however, the most optimistic estimates are that ridership will either be sustained or decrease, not increase. The director has decided to use a decision tree analysis to evaluate this problem for an eight-year time horizon (the desired length of the planning period).

Tree Diagramming Figure 5.3 shows the director's initial tree diagram. The sequence of decisions and chance events flows from left to right. At the left side of the diagram, we see the first decision point (represented by a square) and its two alternatives, each represented by a branch emanating from the square. If service is expanded now (alternative B), the decision will be followed by a chance event (circle), which can lead to any of three outcomes: annual ridership during each of the next eight years will either increase, be sustained, or decrease. If service is not expanded now (alternative A), annual ridership during the next two years is expected to either decrease or be sustained. After two years, a second decision must be made: either

FIGURE 5.3 Decision tree diagram for a city transit system

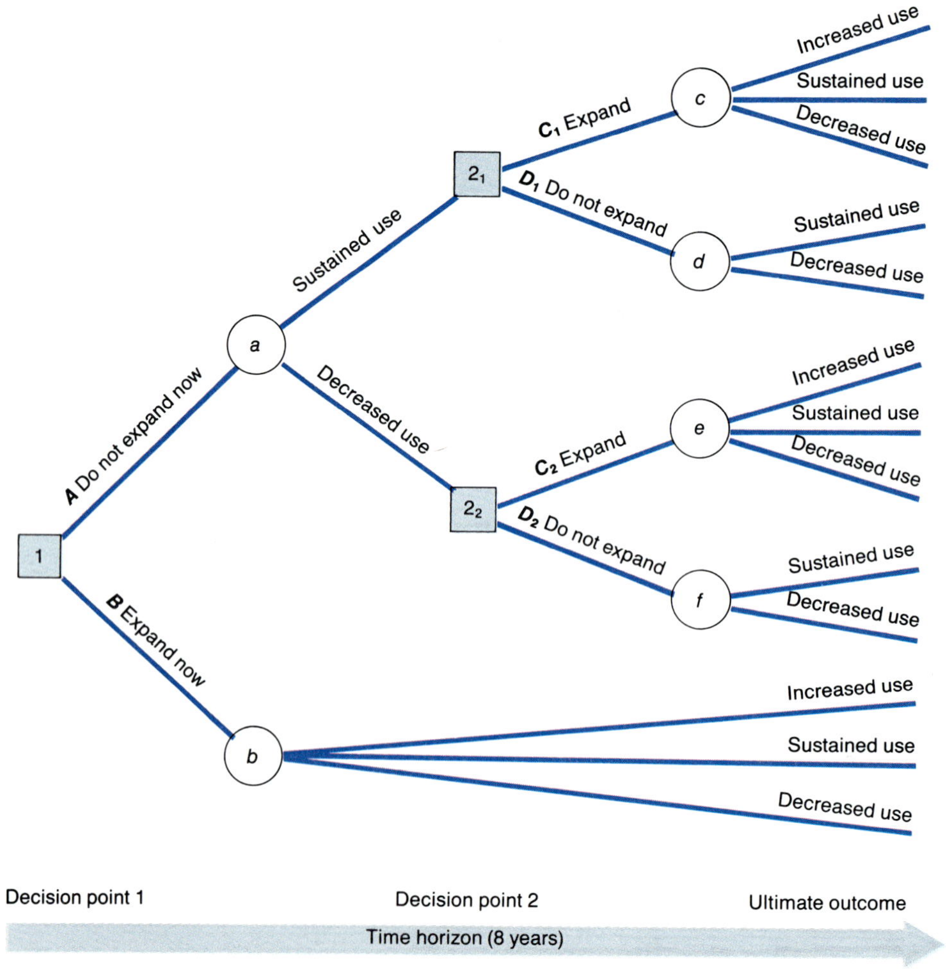

expand (alternatives C_1 and C_2) or do not expand (alternatives D_1 and D_2). If service is not expanded, ridership during the next six years will either be sustained or decrease. If service is expanded, ridership will either increase, be sustained, or decrease.

Estimating The next stage of the decision tree analysis involves estimating the outcomes and probabilities of chance events. Probability estimates are needed *wherever a chance event appears* in the diagram. Notice that probabilities of the outcomes for each chance event (Figure 5.4) sum to 1.0. This is because one and only one of the outcomes must occur.

For chance event *b*, the director believes that by expanding services now, the probability for increased ridership is 0.2, for sustained ridership 0.5, and for reduced ridership 0.3 for each of the next eight years. Similarly, probabilities have been estimated for each possible outcome for the chance events that follow alternatives A, C_1, C_2, D_1, and D_2. Probability estimates are shown in Figure 5.4, as are the cost consequences of all outcomes and actions.

Evaluating and Selecting The final phase of the analysis is to calculate expected values of all possible actions. We begin by calculating expected cost of nodes at the right side of the diagram, at the last stage of the problem, and then work backward.

Look at Figure 5.4 again. Suppose the city choses alternative A, ridership is

FIGURE 5.4 **Tree diagram with probabilities, outcomes, and costs (cost figures in \$ thousands)**

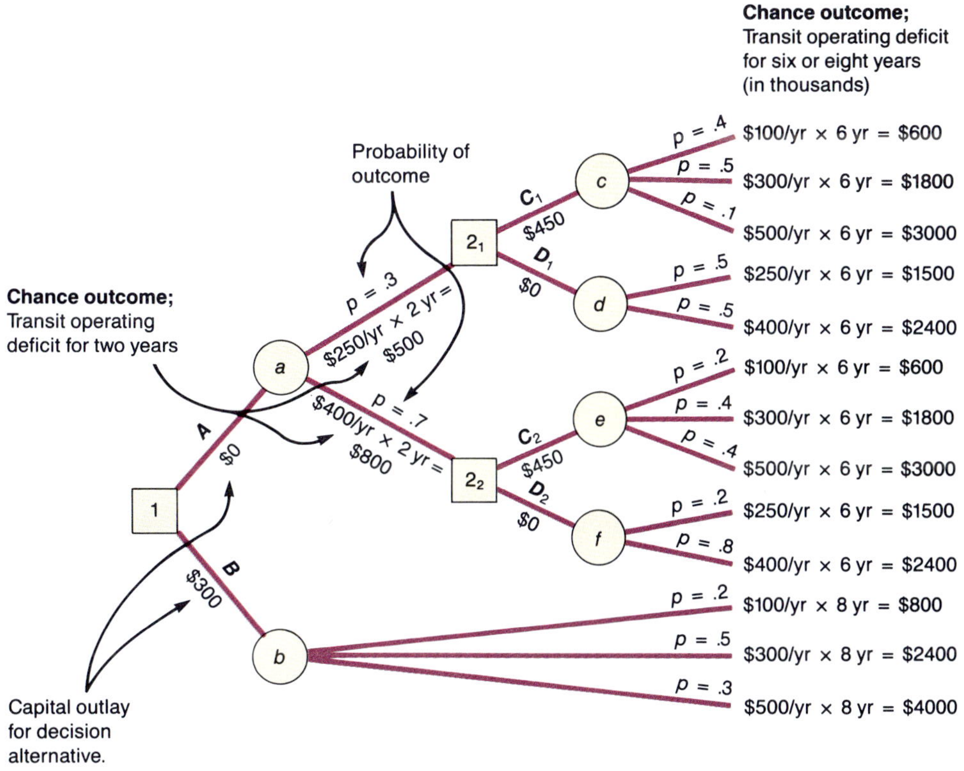

sustained, and the city chooses alternative C_1. Now chance event *c* poses three possible outcomes and the operating deficit for each. Given the probability of each outcome, we can calculate the *expected cost (EC)* associated with *c* as the sum of the products of probabilities and deficits:

$$\begin{aligned} EC_c &= (.4)(\$600) + (.5)(\$1{,}800) + (.1)(\$3{,}000) \\ &= 240 + 900 + 300 \\ &= \$1{,}440 \end{aligned}$$

Thus, the expected cost associated with *c* is \$1,440. We can similarly calculate the expected costs associated with events *b, d, e,* and *f* and record these costs for each node in Figure 5.5.

Now compare the expected costs of events *c* and *d* in Figure 5.5. Node *c* appears more desirable because its expected cost is lower than that of *d*. We now move to the left in the diagram to determine what decisions have to be made to reach nodes *c* and *d*. Decision alternative C_1 (cost \$450) precedes event *c* (cost \$1,440). The overall expected cost, then, of C_1 is \$450 + \$1,440 = \$1,890. Similarly, the overall expected cost of D_1 is \$0 + \$1,950 = \$1,950. Using the expected value criterion, you should pick alternative C_1 (expand service) rather than D_1. Alternative D_1 has been crossed out, indicating it is less desirable than alternative C_1.

Let us now repeat this analysis for decision square 2_2. If we find ourselves located at decision node 2_2, the desired course of action is alternative D_2, whose expected cost of \$2,220 is lower than the expected cost of alternative C_1, \$2,490.

The expected cost of event *a* is the sum of the weighted costs of its possible

FIGURE 5.5 **Decision tree showing expected costs and best decision strategy (cost figures in \$ thousands)**

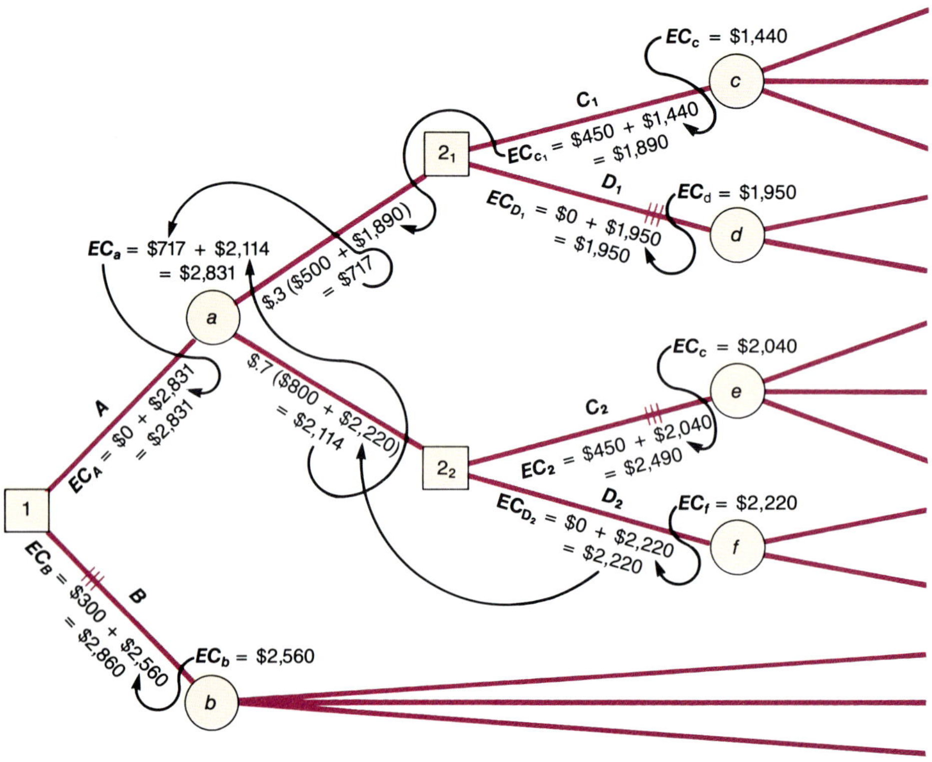

outcomes. If ridership is sustained (p = .3), the operating deficit is \$500 and the following expected cost is \$1,890 (knowing alternative C_1 will be selected. Likewise, if ridership decreases (p = .7) the operating deficit is \$800 and the following expected costs is \$2220 (knowing alternative D_1 will be selected). Thus, the expected cost of event a is:

$$\begin{aligned} EC_a &= (.3)(\$500 + \$1{,}890) + (.7)(\$800 + \$2{,}220) \\ &= 717 + 2{,}114 \\ &= \$2{,}831 \end{aligned}$$

The expected cost of decision alternative A is, then, \$2,831.

The expected cost for node b is \$2,560. In order to reach node b, decision B must be made initially at an additional cost of \$300. The expected cost of decision alternative B, then, is \$300 + \$2,560 = \$2,860. We have now determined the best course of action for the entire problem. First, the decision should be made not to expand the transit services initially (decision alternative A). If ridership is sustained during the years 1 and 2, the system should be expanded (decision alternative C_1). If ridership decreases during years 1 and 2, the system should not be expanded (decision alternative D_2). The expected cost of this course of action is \$2,831 thousands, as shown in Figure 5.5.

MODEL SELECTION

As you can see, the three types of modeling—decision tree analysis, linear programming, computer simulation—should be used selectively. The proper choice among them depends on the type of capacity problem. Other models, too, are sometimes beneficial. Selecting and using models for managing capacity requires a good understanding of the environment within which the organization is operating, including current demands on existing operations, and a vision of future business conditions.[6]

SUMMARY

In this chapter we focused on *capacity* as the maximum rate of productive or conversion capability of an organization's operations. Capacity planning decisions involve assessing existing facilities, estimating future needs, identifying and evaluating capacity alternatives (strategies), and selecting a best alternative.

We noted that capacity is usually measured in terms of an output rate. For some companies with diverse products and for service organizations, however, we saw that the only measure of capacity is often the maximum inputs rather than outputs.

For estimating future capacity needs and evaluating strategies for modifying capacity, our discussion illustrated how short-term and long-term time horizons must be considered. For making capacity decisions, such modeling approaches as linear programming, computer simulation, and decision tree analysis were discussed. Al-

[6]For further discussion of capacity change, see David A. Schilling, "Strategic Facility Planning: The Analysis of Options," *Decision Sciences* 13, no. 1 (January 1982), 1–14.

though modeling should not totally overshadow the behavioral implications of capacity decisions, we saw that capacity planning benefits significantly from the logical analysis in modeling. Product characteristics, economic factors, and processing technology were shown to be paramount in the capacity planning process.

CASE

Paradise Land Management Company

Paradise Land Management owns and operates hotels and apartment complexes near a major metropolitan area. They want to expand operations in the near future, the goal being to increase net earnings before taxes. Two alternative expansion opportunities are under consideration: the Densmore complex and the Highgate project. Both projects involve the purchase of land on which apartment buildings would be constructed and operated.

The site for the Densmore complex is situated in a respectable, quiet, sparsely populated residential neighborhood. Land for the 70-unit complex can be purchased for $60,000. Building costs are estimated at $1,680,000. Annual maintenance costs would amount to $30,000. Apartment units would rent for $410 per month. Paradise is also considering constructing a recreation facility nearby. It would cost $100,000 and would service both Densmore residents and the residents of the company-owned Paradise West, the only existing apartment complex in the neighborhood. Paradise West, with 120 units renting for $290 per month, has had an average occupancy rate of 84 percent for the past three years. The addition of Densmore and the recreation facility are expected to increase Paradise West's occupancy rate to 90 percent (probability .6) or 95 percent (probability .4). Densmore's occupancy rate is expected to be 90 percent (probability .5), 85 percent (probability .3), or 80 percent (probability .2).

The Highgate project calls for 400 units to be constructed on land costing $220,000 in a high-density population neighborhood with many competing apartments. Building costs would be $4,200,000. Rental revenue per unit would be $240 per month; annual operating costs would be $150,000. Highgate's occupancy rate is expected to be 90 percent (probability .2), 80 percent (probability .5), or 70 percent (probability .3).

What factors should be analyzed in making this capacity decision?

REVIEW AND DISCUSSION QUESTIONS

1. Define and give examples of normal and maximum measures of capacity.
2. Define and describe the operating capacity of a college of business administration. How should its capacity be measured?
3. Discuss the fundamental differences in short-term and long-term capacity decisions. What are the major considerations in each?
4. Outline the merits and drawbacks of incremental capacity changes and large lump changes.

5. What problems might you encounter securing and using data in a decision tree analysis?
6. How is product mix related to the capacity utilization decision?
7. What costs would be affected if you closed one of several warehouses (capacity contraction) in a distribution system? How might revenues be affected?
8. What analytical approaches and models are useful in making capacity decisions? Under what circumstances would each model be most beneficial relative to the others?
9. Capacity will be modified in response to demand. Demand will be modified in response to capacity. Which of these two statements is correct? Why?
10. Suppose you were considering expanding the local fire fighting system. Show what factors should be considered and how you would relate them to one another in your analysis.
11. Explain the relationship between capacity planning and location planning. To illustrate, select a service business and explain the relationship for that business.
12. How would the results of a decision tree analysis be affected if people made erroneous probability estimates? Demonstrate with an example.
13. Briefly describe a practical approach toward managing capacity change. Would it be important for a person wanting to be a general manager, not an operations manager, to understand this process? Why or why not?

PROBLEMS

SOLVED PROBLEMS

1. Annual demand for a manufacturing company is expected to be as follows:

Units demanded	8,000	10,000	15,000	20,000
Probability	.5	.2	.2	.1

Revenues are \$35/unit. The existing manufacturing facility has annual fixed operating costs of \$200,000. Variable manufacturing costs are \$7.75/unit at the 8,000 unit output level; \$5.00 at the 10,000 unit level; \$5.33 at the 15,000 unit level; and \$7.42 at the 20,000 unit output level.

An expanded facility under consideration would require \$250,000 fixed operating costs annually. Variable costs would average \$9.40 at the 8,000 unit level; \$5.20 at the 10,000 unit level; \$3.80 at the 15,000 unit level; and \$4.90 at the 20,000 level.

To maximize net earnings, which size facility should be selected?

Expected net revenue of existing facility

$$
\begin{aligned}
\text{Expected variable cost} &= [(\$7.75)(8{,}000)(.5) + (\$5.00)(10{,}000)(.2) \\
&\quad + (\$5.33)(15{,}000)(.2) + (\$7.42)(20{,}000)(.1)] \\
&= \$71{,}830 \\
\text{Expected total cost} &= \text{fixed cost} + \text{variable cost} \\
&= \$200{,}000 + \$71{,}830 \\
&= \$271{,}830
\end{aligned}
$$

$$\begin{aligned}\text{Expected revenue} &= \$35\ [(8{,}000)(.5) + (10{,}000)(.2) \\ &\quad + (15{,}000)(.2) + (20{,}000)(.1)] \\ &= \$385{,}000 \\ \text{Expected net revenue} &= \text{revenue} - \text{total cost} \\ &= \$385{,}000 - \$271{,}830 \\ &= \$113{,}170\end{aligned}$$

Expected net revenue of expanded facility

$$\begin{aligned}\text{Expected variable cost} &= [(\$9.40)(8{,}000)(.5) + (\$5.20)(10{,}000)(.2) \\ &\quad + (\$3.80)(15{,}000)(.2) + (\$4.90)(20{,}000)(.1)] \\ &= \$69{,}200 \\ \text{Expected total cost} &= \$250{,}000 + \$69{,}200 = \$319{,}200 \\ \text{Expected net revenue} &= \$385{,}000 - \$319{,}200 = \$65{,}800\end{aligned}$$

The existing facility maximizes expected net earnings.

2. Solve the decision tree shown in Figure 5.6, in which costs are shown at the ends of the branches.

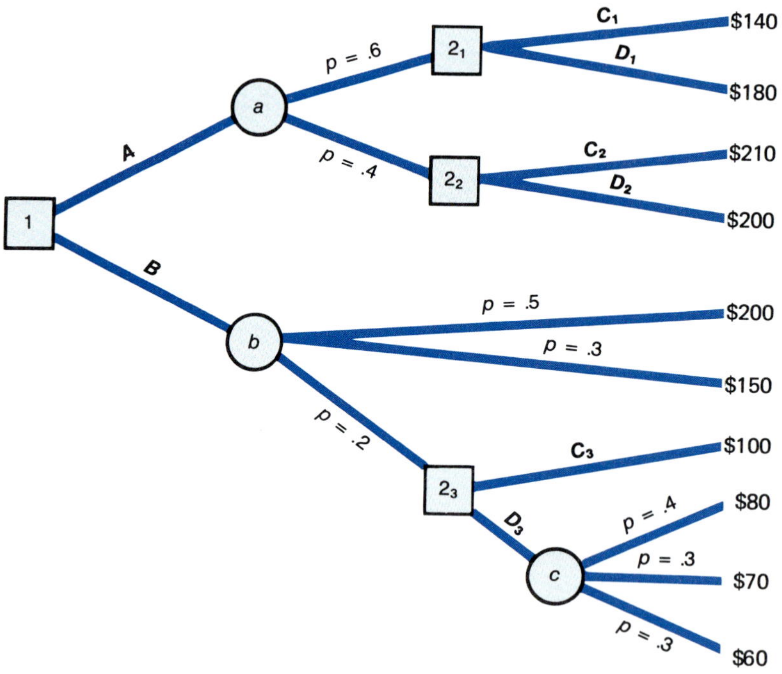

FIGURE 5.6

The solution, shown in Figure 5.7, is found by first calculating the expected cost of chance event *c*. Next calculate the expected cost of decision alternative D_3, which is simply the expected cost of *c*. Now eliminate the most expensive

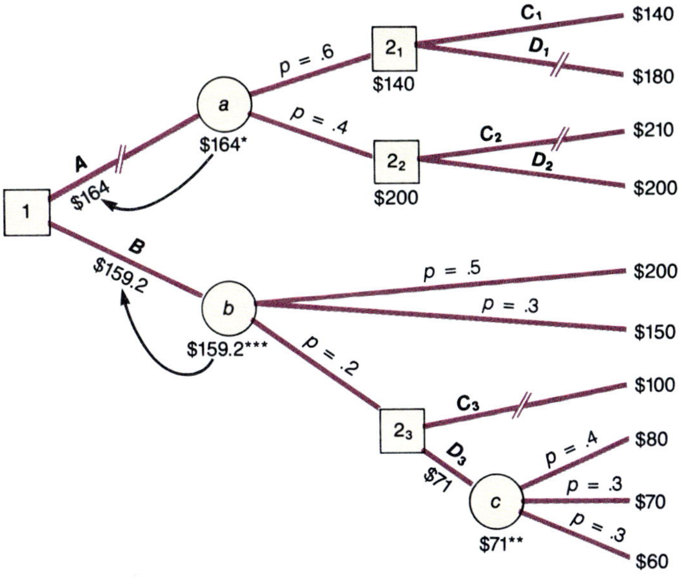

$^*EC_a = (.6)(\$140) + (.4)(\$200) = \$164$

$^{**}EC_c = (.4)(\$80) + (.3)(\$70) + (.3)(\$60) = \$71$

$^{***}EC_b = (.5)(\$200) + (.3)(\$150) + (.2)(\$71) = \$159.2$

FIGURE 5.7

alternatives (branches) for decision nodes 2_1, 2_2, and 2_3. Next, calculate the expected costs of chance events *a* and *b*. Since the expected cost of decision alternative *A* is simply the expected cost of *a*, and the expected cost of decision alternative *B* is simply the expected cost of *b*, choose the least expensive *B*.

REINFORCING FUNDAMENTALS

3. A manufacturer of dishware is considering three alternative plant sizes. Demand depends upon the selling price of the product; costs of manufacture depend on the size of the plant selected. Demand is expected to be as follows.

Demand probabilities

	Selling Price/Set of Dishware		
Annual Demand (in sets of dishware)	$60	$42	$40
10,000	.2	.1	.05
20,000	.4	.4	.25
30,000	.3	.4	.40
40,000	.1	.1	.30

Anticipated operating costs for the three plant sizes for different levels of operation are:

Variable manufacturing cost/unit

Level of Plant Operation (in units of output)	Plant Size		
	Small	Medium	Large
10,000	$ 21	$ 25	$ 32
20,000	16	14	18
30,000	19	13	12
40,000	26	18	14
Annual fixed cost of operation	$400,000	$420,000	$500,000

Which alternative is most attractive on the basis of annual net earnings?

4. How would your answer to Problem 3 change if variable manufacturing costs were changed to those shown below?

Variable manufacturing costs/unit

Level of Plant Operation (in units of output)	Plant Size		
	Small	Medium	Large
10,000	$21	$20	$25
20,000	19	16	18
30,000	19	15	10
40,000	23	18	12

5. Evaluate the decision tree shown in Figure 5.8. Costs are shown at the branch ends.
6. Management, facing a two-stage decision problem (see Figure 5.9), wants to pick a sequence of actions to maximize profits. The first decision (1) has three alternatives: *A*, with a profit of $20; *B*, with a profit of $30; and *C*, with a profit of $40. The chance event following the initial decision has either two or three possible outcomes, depending on the initial decision. The probability of each outcome is shown in Figure 5.9. Thereafter, a second decision, resulting in further profits, must be made. What is the best decision sequence?

CHALLENGING EXERCISES

7. Micro Distributors is considering an addition of 500,000 square feet of warehouse space to an existing facility during the next two years. Three expansion proposals are being considered: (1) add 100,000 square feet now and 400,000 square feet two years from now; (2) add 200,000 square feet now plus 300,000 square feet in

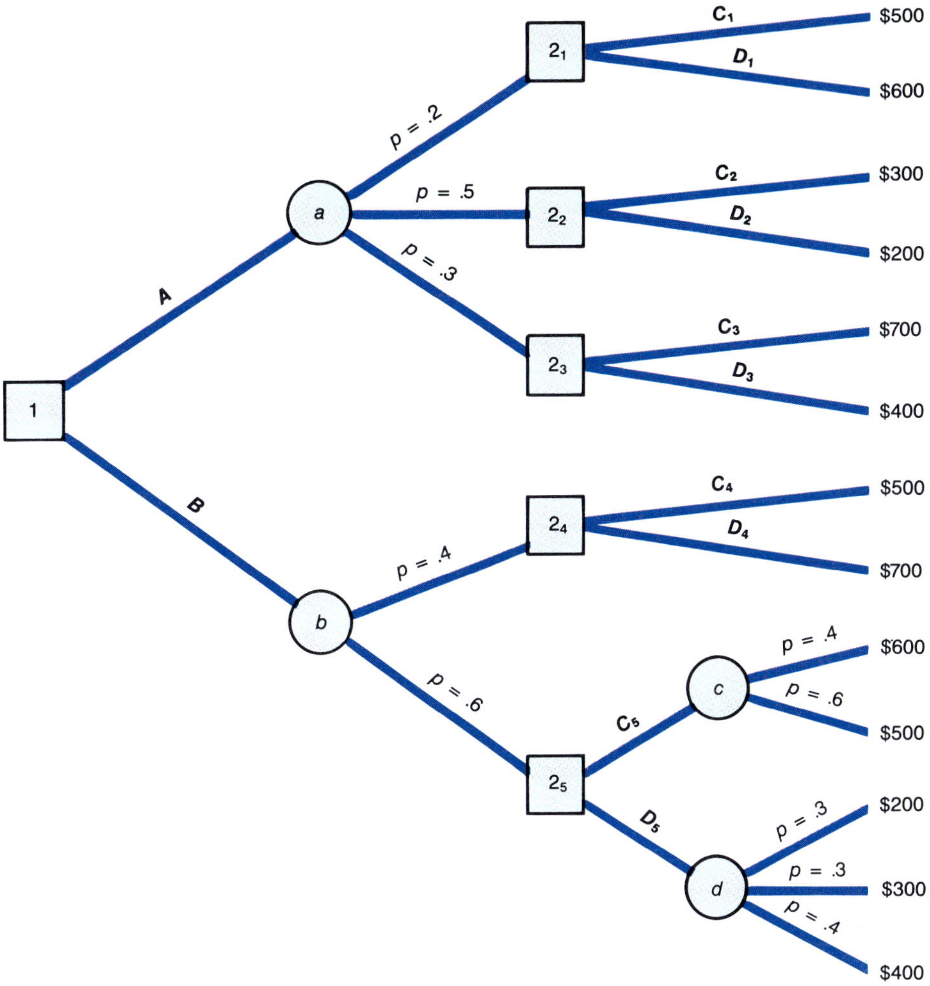

FIGURE 5.8

two years; or (3) do the entire addition now. Construction estimates show considerable cost savings for making the additions as soon as possible.

Construction estimates

	Now		Two Years From Now	
Alternative	Amount of Expansion (in thousands of square feet)	Cost (in $ millions)	Amount of Expansion (in thousands of square feet)	Cost (in $ millions)
1	100	1.00	400	3.2
2	200	1.75	300	2.6
3	500	3.30	—	—

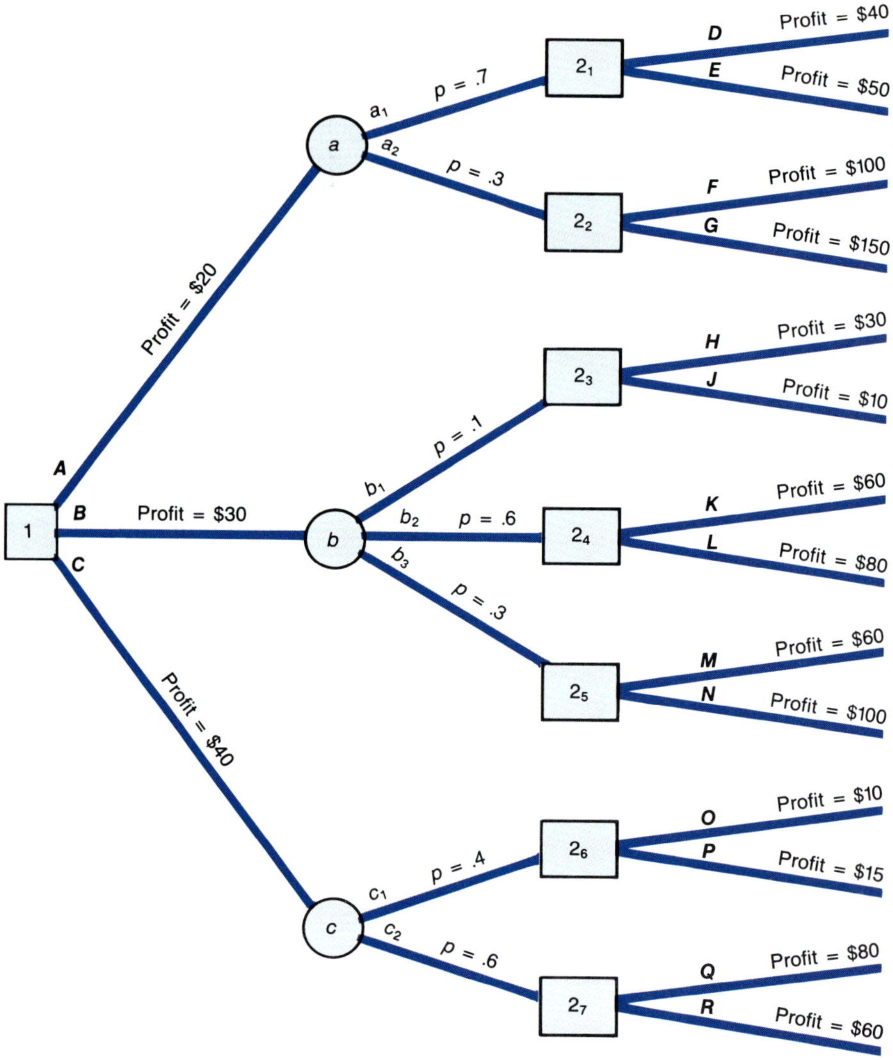

FIGURE 5.9 **Two-stage decision problem**

Micro's marketing personnel suggest a wait-and-see approach with incremental expansion: they favor alternatives 1 and 2. Although expansion is expected to create additional demand, other forces outside Micro's control may result in lower demand, in which case Micro would be left with excessive, unproductive warehousing capacity. A mild expansion now would permit a two-year observation of demand before deciding on additional expansion.

A ten-year planning horizon was chosen. Estimates of demand and net operating revenues obtained are as follows:

Estimates for first two years

	Alternative 1		Alternative 2	
Level of demand	Low	High	Low	High
Total net operating revenue ($ millions)	1.0	1.3	.8	1.4
Probability	.4	.6	.3	.7

Estimates for years 3–10

	Alternative 1				Alternative 2			
	If Expanded After 2 Years		If Not Expanded After 2 Years		If Expanded After 2 Years		If Not Expanded After 2 Years	
Level of demand	Low	High	Low	High	Low	High	Low	High
Total net operating revenue (in $ millions)	2.4	7.2	3.8	5.8	2.4	7.2	3.2	6.4
Probability (if demand was high in years 1 and 2)	.2	.8	.3	.7	.2	.8	.3	.7
Probability (if demand was low in years 1 and 2)	.3	.7	.8	.2	.4	.6	.7	.3

For alternative 3, ten-year operating revenue is estimated at $9 million with probability .5, $6 million with probability .3, and $2 million with probability 0.2. Which alternative is best? Justify your recommendation. For simplicity, ignore the time value of money.

8. The Reliable Storage Company has a large warehousing operation. In developing long-range plans, they are considering expansion of storage capacity. Estimates of future storage demand, increased revenues, and costs of expansion have been obtained for the ten-year planning horizon. Management has narrowed the expansion alternatives to three choices: (1) expand now by adding 100,000 square feet of storage space; (2) add 40,000 square feet now and 60,000 square feet three years later; or (3) add 40,000 square feet now and nothing later.

   If the entire expansion is done now, construction costs will be lower than they will be later. Further, there will be a greater chance for higher business revenues since enough space will be added to take in new business. There is a chance, however, of overexpanding; if the entire expanded facility is not needed, idle capacity will result. The more conservative alternatives are to expand modestly now or to wait and see if demand continues to increase as expected, and then expand or not accordingly. Both alternatives reduce the risk of investing funds in an idle, overexpanded facility. However, they have two disadvantages. First, limited storage capacity in the first three years may result in lost opportunities for more business. Second, future construction costs are expected to be considerably higher than those at present levels. Estimates of relevant factors for this decision are shown in Table 5.4.

TABLE 5.4 Data for expansion decision of Reliable Storage Company

Decision Alternative	Cash Outlays for Expansion: Expansion Cost Now	Cash Outlays for Expansion: Expansion Cost 3 Years From Now	Expected After-tax Cash Flow/Year, Years 1–3: If Demand Is High	Years 1–3: If Demand Is Low	Years 4–10: If Demand Is High	Years 4–10: If Demand Is Low
Full expansion now	100,000 sq ft × \$16/sq ft = \$1,600,000	-0-	\$180,000	\$90,000	\$240,000	\$120,000
Expand 40,000 feet now and 60,000 feet in 3 years	40,000 sq ft × \$18/sq ft = \$720,000	60,000 sq ft × \$24/sq ft = \$1,440,000	75,000	36,000	210,000	120,000
Expand 40,000 feet now; no further expansion	40,000 sq ft × \$18/sq ft = \$720,000	-0-	75,000	36,000	75,000	36,000

For years 1–3, it is estimated that the probability of high annual demand is .7; the probability of low demand is .3. For years 4–10, the probability of high demand is .6, and the probability of low demand is .4. Which decision is best? For simplicity, ignore the time value of money.

9. Watersight Tours, Inc., is deciding whether to hire an additional boat mechanic or to just keep their one current mechanic. Their two tourist boats have daily failure probabilities of .04 and .08, respectively. With one boat out of commission, the company loses \$400/hour; the operating loss is \$900/hour when both boats are inoperable. The time for a mechanic to repair one boat is four hours. Two mechanics working together can repair a boat in three hours. The second mechanic can be employed at a daily wage of \$200. Should Watersight hire the second mechanic? If so, how should the mechanics be used if both boats fail simultaneously?

KEY TERMS

Capacity 163
Chance event 177
Decision tree 177
Linear programming 175
Product mix problem 174

SELECTED READINGS

Buffa, E. S., *Meeting the Competitive Challenge.* Homewood, Ill.: Richard D. Irwin, 1984, 65–82.

Goldhar, Joel D., and Mariann Jelinek, "Plan for Economies of Scope," *Harvard Business Review* 61, no. 6 (November–December 1983), 141–48.

McLeavey, D. W., and S. L. Narasimhan, *Production Planning and Inventory Control.* Boston: Allyn & Bacon, 1985, 360–69.

Schilling, David A., "Strategic Facility Planning: The Analysis of Options," *Decision Sciences* 13, no. 1, (January 1982), 1–14.

Schmenner, Roger W., *Production/Operations Management: Concepts and Situations.* Chicago: Science Research Associates, 1981, 297–332.

Schroeder, Roger W., *Operations Management: Decision Making in the Operating Function.* New York: McGraw-Hill, 1981, 239–40.

Skinner, Wickham, *Manufacturing in the Corporate Strategy,* New York: John Wiley, 1978, 111–13 and 121–22.

SUPPLEMENT TO CHAPTER 5

LINEAR PROGRAMMING: THE GRAPHICAL AND SIMPLEX METHODS

The purpose of this section is to present the mathematical optimization technique called linear programming. We'll consider two linear programming (LP) methods: graphical and simplex. (A third method, the transportation or distribution method, can be used only on a special type of problem with particular characteristics; it is presented as a supplement to Chapter 6.) The graphical method is of limited practical value but is helpful for visualizing the underlying concepts of LP. The simplex method can be used to solve any LP problem.

In general, linear programming can be applied to decision problems with these characteristics.

Decision variable A numerical, controllable parameter that, if modified, yields a variety of results.

Objective function A mathematical equation that measures the value of all proposed decision alternatives; a linear programming equation.

Restrictions Restraints on the values of the decision variables of a linear programming problem.

1. *Decision variables.* The problem can be stated in terms of decision variables. A decision variable is a numerical parameter under the decision maker's control that, if modified in a variety of ways, yields a variety of results.
2. *Objective function.* The decision variables can be related by an objective (criterion) function, a mathematical equation that can predict the outcome of all proposed alternatives. In LP, the objective function must be linear, as you will see below.
3. *Restrictions.* Restraints on the values of decision variables can be specified.
4. *Goal.* The goal in solving the problem is to find values for decision variables that will maximize (or minimize) the objective function.

THE GENERAL LINEAR PROGRAMMING PROBLEM

The following is a statement of the general linear programming problem.

Maximize

$$Z = C_1X_1 + C_2X_2 + \dots + C_nX_n$$

where the $X_1, X_2, \dots, X_n$ is a set of variables whose numeric values are to be determined, and the $C_1, C_2, \dots, C_n$ are numeric coefficients. Notice that Z is a linear function of the variables X_i: when the value of X_i increases by 1, the value of Z increases by C_i; when X_i increases by 2, Z increases by $2C_i$, and so on.

Subject to constraints

$$
\begin{array}{l}
A_{11}X_1 + A_{12}X_2 + \ldots A_{1n}X_n \leq B_1 \\
A_{12}X_1 + A_{22}X_2 + \ldots A_{2n}X_n \leq B_2 \\
\vdots \\
A_{m1}X_1 + A_{m2}X_2 + \ldots A_{mn}X_n \leq B_m \\
X_1X_2, \ldots, X_n \geq 0
\end{array}
$$

Where each inequality constrains the value of the variable the $A_{11}, A_{12}, \ldots, A_{mn}$ are numeric coefficients, and the $B_1, B_2, \ldots, B_m$ are number constants. Notice that each constraint is a linear inequality: when X_k increases by 1, each sum of $A_{ij}X_j$ increases by A_{ik}; when X_k increases by 2, each sum of $A_{ij}X_j$ increases by 2 A_{ik}, and so on.

A more compact notation for the statement of the general linear programming problem is as follows.

Maximize

$$\sum_{j=1}^{n} C_jX_j$$

Subject to constraints

$$\sum_{j=1}^{n} A_{ij}X_j \leq B_i, X_j \geq 0 \text{ and } i = 1, 2, \ldots, m \quad j = 1, 2, \ldots, n$$

GRAPHICAL METHOD

The graphical method will help you grasp the basic concepts used in the simplex technique. To use the graphical method:

1. Identify the decision variables
2. Identify the objective (or criterion) function
3. Identify resource restrictions (constraints)
4. Draw a graph that includes all restrictions
5. Identify the feasible decision area on the graph
6. Draw a graph of the objective function, and select the point on the feasible area that optimizes the objective function
7. Interpret the solution

In explaining these steps, we repeat the case of MultiBand Enterprises used in Chapter 5.

EXAMPLE

MultiBand Enterprises manufactures two products, a portable radio (PR) and a citizens band radio (CB). The marketing manager states, "We can sell all that can be produced in the near future." She then asks the operations manager, "What is your production capacity per month?" The operations manager replies that capacity depends on which product is produced.

"Our two products each require different amounts of three kinds of labor: subassembly, assembly, and inspection labor. Next month we will have available 316 hours of subassembly labor, 354 hours of assembly labor, and 62 hours of inspection labor. So capacity depends on which products we produce."

The operations manager knows that each CB requires .4 hours of subassembly labor, .5 hours of assembly labor, and .05 hours of inspection labor. Each portable radio requires .5 hours of subassembly labor, .3 hours of assembly labor and 0.10 hours of inspection labor.

The vice president says, "We know that each CB sold contributes $50 toward profit and overhead. Each PR sold contributes $40 toward profit and overhead.

What is MultiBand's capacity next month, and what mix of CBs and PRs should be manufactured next month?

Step 1: Identify Decision Variables CBs and PRs can be manufactured by MultiBand. *These are the two decision variables.* The problem is to decide how many CBs and PRs to produce. As before, we let c stand for the number of CBs and p stand for the number of PRs.

Step 2: Identify Objective Function Each CB contributes $50 to profit and overhead, and each PR contributes $40. MultiBand's total contribution margin is:

$$TCM = (\$50)\ c + (\$40)\ p \qquad \text{(S5.1)}$$

This *linear objective function* states that total gain (or total contribution margin (TCM) depends on the decision as to how many CBs and PRs to produce. MultiBand would like total contribution to be as large as possible; it wants to *maximize* TCM.

Step 3: Identify Resource Restrictions To produce radios, MultiBand needs three types of labor: subassembly, assembly, and inspection. The available quantities of these three resources are 316 employee hours of subassembly labor, 354 hours of assembly labor, and 62 hours of inspection labor. A CB requires .4 hours of subassembly labor, .5 hours of assembly labor, and .05 hours of inspection labor. A PR requires .5 hours of subassembly labor, .3 hours assembly labor, and .1 hours of inspection labor. Thus we have three restrictions, one for each labor resource. The restrictions on the use of these three resources are expressed as linear inequalities.

Resource	Resource Used (in hours)		Resource Available (in hours)
Subassembly labor	$.4\ c + .5\ p$	$\leq$	316
Assembly labor	$.05\ c + .3\ p$	$\leq$	354
Inspection labor	$.05\ c + .1\ p$	$\leq$	62

Step 4: Draw a Graph of All Restrictions Look at Figure S5.1. The horizontal axis of the graph shows various quantities of CBs that could be produced. The vertical axis shows quantities of PRs. The *solution space* the part of the graph where the answer to the problem can be found) consists of all points on or to the right of the vertical axis and on or above the horizontal axis, since negative values of c or p have no meaning. Each point in this space represents some combination of p and c.

Solution space The possible (meaningful) values of variables in a linear programming problem.

Let's draw the line for the subassembly labor restriction. If the entire 316 subassembly hours are devoted to producing CBs, how many could be produced? Since each CB requires .4 hours, 316 hours ÷ .4 subassembly hours per CB = 790 CBs. This

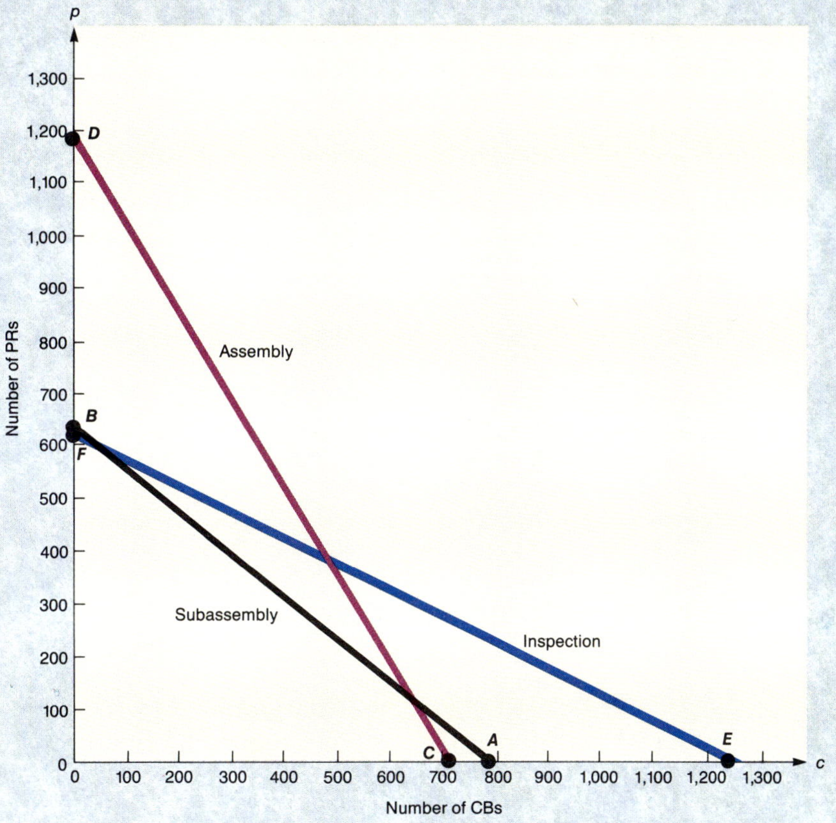

FIGURE S5.1 **Restrictions for MultiBand Enterprises**

combination of producing 0 PRs and 790 CBs is plotted as point *A* on the graph. Another alternative is to produce no CBs. In that case, we have enough subassembly labor to produce 316 hours ÷ .5 subassembly hours per PR = 632 PRs. This combination of products (0 CBs and 632 PRs) is represented by point *B* on the graph. Now, since all restrictions are linear, the line can be drawn connecting points *A* and *B*. Each point on this restriction line represents some combination of CBs and PRs that totally consumes all subassembly labor time. Points in the solution space that fall above or to the right of line *AB* are called *infeasible solutions* since they require more than 316 hours of subassembly. Points in the solution space that fall in, below, or to the left of the line AB are called feasible solutions.

Feasible (infeasible) solutions Solutions that satisfy (do not satisfy) the restrictions of a linear programming problem.

In a similar manner, line *CD* is the assembly labor restriction line, and line *EF* is the inspection labor restriction line.

Step 5: Identify Feasible Decision Area When management decides how many PRs and CBs to produce, they must adhere simultaneously to all three relevant restrictions. The feasible solutions lie within the shaded area (Figure S5.2) bounded by the corner points 0, *F, G, H,* and *C*.

Step 6: Draw Objective Function and Select the Optimum Point Although all points in the shaded area are *feasible* decision alternatives, some provide a greater total contribution than others. At point *C* (708 CBs, 0 PRs), for example, total contribution is ($50)(708) + ($40)(0) = $35,400. But 300 CBs and 300 PRs would

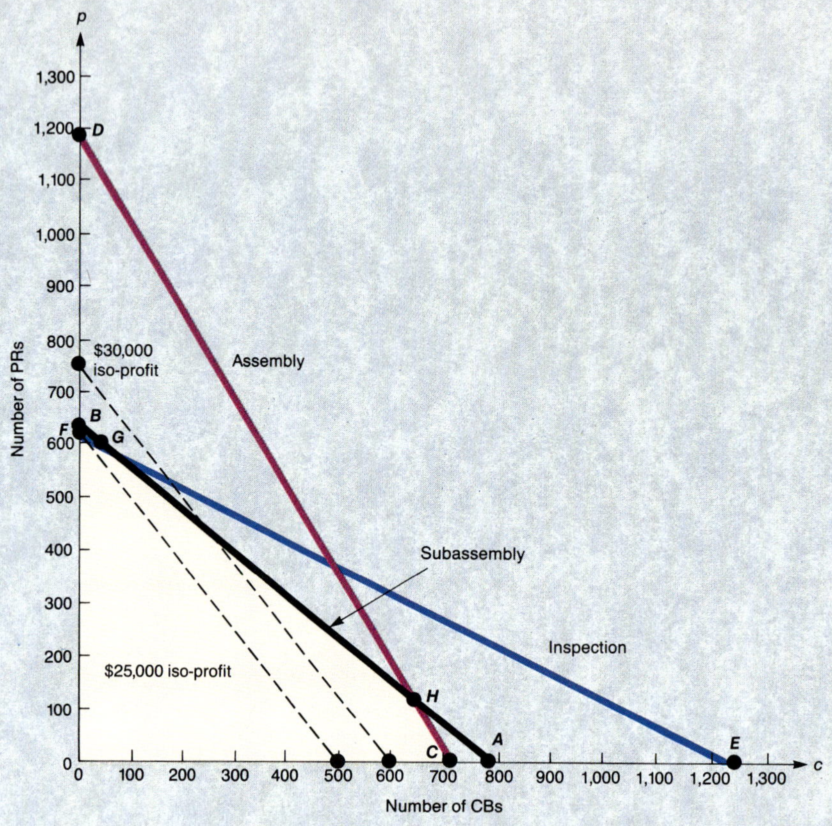

FIGURE S5.2 **Area of feasible solutions for MultiBand Enterprises**

only give a total contribution of ($50)(300) + ($40)(300) = $27,000. We must now pick out the *best* point from among the infinite number of points in the feasible area. Our task is simplified, however, because the *best point will lie at one of the corner (extreme) points of the feasible area.* Therefore, one of points 0, *F, G, H,* or *C* is optimal. We could calculate the total contribution for each of these five points and select the one that has the highest value.

Iso-profit line Points in the solution space of a linear programming problem whose corresponding profits are identical.

A graphical procedure also exists for finding the best point. It requires adding one more line to the graph, an *iso-profit,* or *constant-profit,* line. On an iso-profit line, all the points give the same profit. Suppose we want to find the iso-profit line representing a $25,000 contribution. Using Equation S5.1, we find:

$$\$25{,}000 = (\$50)c + (\$40)p$$

On Figure S5.2, we have drawn a dotted line connecting all the points at which a $25,000 profit would be contributed. You can see, for example, that a combination of 0 CBs and 625 PRs would contribute $25,000. In fact, even greater profits can be achieved. Look at the $30,000 iso-profit line. Some of the points on this line fall outside the feasible area and thus are not legitimate alternatives. Other parts of the line, however, fall in the shaded area. A $30,000 contribution is therefore attainable.

Two features of these iso-profit lines are particularly noteworthy. First, they are parallel to each other. Second, the farther the lines are removed from the origin of the graph, the greater the contribution they represent. Since all the lines have the same slope, our final step is to continue constructing iso-profit lines that are successively farther away from the origin. This procedure stops when any further movement away from the origin would cause the iso-profit line to lie entirely outside the feasible area. In our example, such a line would pass through point *H*. This point gives the *maximum* contribution; it is the *optimal* decision. When the problem is to maximize the objective function, the iso-profit curve should be the furthest from the origin; when the problem is to minimize it, the iso-cost curve should be the closest one to the origin.

The optimal decision at point *H*, interpolated from the graph, calls for the production of about 630 CBs and 125 PRs. The approximate value of this decision is

$$TCM = (\$50)(630) + (\$40)(125) = \$36{,}000$$

A more precise evaluation of the solution is obtained by noting that the optimal point *H*, lies simultaneously on two restriction lines, the subassembly labor line and the assembly labor line. By using simultaneous linear equations, we find the values for p and c that satisfy both equations. This occurs when $p = 126.15$ and $c = 632.31$. The value of this decision is:

$$TCM = (\$50)(632.31) + (\$40)(126.15) = \$36{,}661.06$$

Step 7: Interpret the Solution The optimal number of PRs and CBs is now known. How much of our three resources will be used for this product mix? Will any of the resources be unused? We can answer these questions both graphically and algebraically. Observation of the graph shows that the optimal point *H* lies on both the subassembly and assembly labor restriction lines, which represent the *maximum* amounts of these resources that are available for use. Therefore the maximum amounts of these two resources are being used in the optimal solution. There is no unused subassembly or assembly labor. Now consider the usage of inspection labor. The optimal solution falls below the inspection labor line. This means that all available inspection labor is not used in the optimal solution; some amount of inspection labor will be unused or idle. We can algebraically compute the unused labor:

Unused inspection labor	=	Available inspection labor	− Used inspection labor
	=	62 hours	− [(.05 hours/CB)(632.31 c) + (.10 hours/PR)(126.15 p)]
	=	62	− (31.62 + 12.62)
	=	17.76 hours	

Similarly, we confirm that subassembly and assembly labor are fully utilized, as follows:

Unused subassembly labor	=	Available subassembly labor	− Used subassembly labor
	=	316 hours	− [(.4 hours/CB)(632.31 c) + (.5 hours/PR)(126.15 p)]
	=	316	− (252.92 + 63.08)
	=	0 hours	
Unused assembly labor	=	Available assembly labor	− Used assembly labor
	=	354 hours	− [(.5 hours/c)(632.31 c) + (.3 hours/p)(125.15 p)]
	=	354	− (316.16 + 37.84)
	=	0 hours	

The graphical method can be used for problems with two or three decision variables. Since most operations management applications involve larger problems, the graphical method is of limited utility. It is useful, however, for visualizing the basics of linear programming.

SIMPLEX METHOD

Simplex method An algorithm for solving a linear programming problem by successively choosing feasible solutions and testing them for optimality.

Initial solution The feasible solution tested first using the simplex method in solving a linear programming problem.

The simplex algorithm is a mathematical procedure for finding the optimal solution to a linear programming problem. It begins with an initial solution, which is progressively improved in a series of stages. To use this procedure, the analyst should:

1. Set up the problem in a linear programming framework
2. Create an *initial solution*
3. Evaluate the existing solution
4. Evaluate variables that could be introduced to improve the solution
5. Select the most advantageous variable to introduce
6. Determine which variable is to leave the solution
7. Revise the solution matrix
8. Repeat steps 3–7 until no further improvement is possible

Step 1: Setting Up the Problem A standard format, a statement of the objective function and constraints, is used to set up the problem. In general form, the LP model is a maximization problem of *n* variables and *m* restrictions set up as follows:

Maximize

$$Z = C_1X_1 + C_2X_2 + \dots + C_nX_n$$

Subject to constraints

$$\begin{aligned} A_{11}X_1 + A_{12}X_2 + \dots + A_{1n}X_n &\le B_1 \\ A_{21}X_1 + A_{22}X_2 + \dots + A_{2n}X_n &\le B_2 \\ \vdots \qquad \vdots \qquad\quad \vdots \quad &\quad \vdots \\ A_{m1}X_1 + A_{m2}X_2 + \dots + A_{mn}X_n &\le B_m \end{aligned}$$

Once again, let us use this general model to express the facts of the MultiBand Enterprise situation.

Maximize

$$Z = \$50\,c + \$40\,p$$

Subject to constraints

$$\begin{aligned} .4\,c + .5\,p &\le 316 \text{ Subassembly labor} \\ .5\,c + .3\,p &\le 354 \text{ Assembly labor} \\ .05\,c + .1\,p &\le 62 \text{ Inspection labor} \end{aligned}$$

Slack variable A variable in a linear programming problem representing the unused quantity of a resource.

The restrictions above are stated as *inequalities.* The simplex procedure requires that each restriction be converted into an *equality*. This is accomplished by adding a *Slack variable* (S_i) to each restriction.

$$
\begin{aligned}
A_{11}X_1 + A_{12}X_2 + \ldots + A_{1n}X_n + S_1 &= B_1 \\
A_{21}X_1 + A_{22}X_2 + \ldots + A_{2n}X_n + S_2 &= B_2 \\
\vdots \qquad \vdots \qquad \qquad \vdots \quad \vdots \quad &\vdots \\
A_{m1}X_1 + A_{m2}X_2 + \ldots + A_{mn}X_n + S_m &= B_m
\end{aligned}
$$

S_1 is the slack variable representing the unused or idle quantity of the first resource. It is that portion of B_1 which is not devoted to real products $X_1, \ldots, X_n$. Similarly, S_2 is the amount of resource 2 that is not used. One slack variable is uniquely associated with each resource that is converted from an inequality to an equality. In the simplex procedure, each slack variable has a zero coefficient in the objective function. In the formulation above, therefore, the problem has a total of $n + m$ variables.

In formulating the problem, the conventional practice is to restate the objective function and restrictions so that each includes all of the slack variables. Let's express the MultiBand Enterprise example in the format described below, so that every variable appears in all the equations.

Maximize

$$Z = (\$50)c + (\$40)p + \$0S_1 + \$0S_2 + \$0S_3$$

Subject to constraints

$$
\begin{aligned}
(.4)c + (.5)p + 1S_1 + 0S_2 + 0S_3 &= 316 \\
(.5)c + (.3)p + 0S_1 + 1S_2 + 0S_3 &= 354 \\
(.05)c + (.1)p + 0S_1 + 0S_2 + 1S_3 &= 62
\end{aligned}
$$

Step 2: Creating an Initial Solution An initial solution is created by forming the matrix (table)shown in Table S5.1. We begin at the origin, with no real variables and only the slack variables in solution.

TABLE S5.1 Initial solution matrix for MultiBand Enterprises

C_i	In Solution (basis)	\$50 CB	\$40 PR	\$0 S_1	\$0 S_2	\$0 S_3	(B_i) Production
\$0	S_1	.4	.5	1.0	0.0	0.0	316
0	S_2	.5	.3	0.0	1.0	0.0	354
0	S_3	.05	.1	0.0	0.0	1.0	62
	Z_j	\$0	\$0	\$0	\$0	\$0	\$0
	$C_j - Z_j$	\$50	\$40	\$0	\$0	\$0	

(Annotations in table: X_j pointing to column variables; A_{ij} pointing to coefficients; B_i pointing to production values.)

Within the dotted rectangle are the coefficients, A_{ij}, of the variables in the restriction equations, *i* referring to a row and *j* to a column. At the top of each column is the decision variable, X_j or S_j, depending upon the column to which the coefficients in that column apply. For example, the variable c has coefficients .4, .5, and .05 in restriction equations 1, 2, and 3, respectively. In the first row of the dotted rectangle are the coefficients of the five variables in the first restriction equation. Notice the zero coefficients for S_2 and S_3 in the first row. These mean that S_2 and S_3 do not consume any subassembly labor, since they are slack variables for assembly and inspection.

Around the outer perimeter of the dotted rectangle we find some additional notation. The column headed In Solution (basis) lists the *variables that are in the initial or first-stage solution. The number of variables in solution (in the basis) is equal to the number of restrictions.* This is also true for each succeeding stage of the problem. The production column shows the quantity of each variable that is in solution. Thus the initial solution shows 316 units of S_1, 354 units of S_2, and 62 units of S_3 being produced. Since those are fictitious variables, nothing is really being produced. The next step clarifies this point.

Step 3: Evaluating the Existing Solution Refer again to Table S5.1 and find the C_j values representing the objective function coefficients of each variable. These are used to evaluate the existing solution. The value of the objective function for the existing solution is:

$$\begin{aligned} Z &= (\$50)(0) + (\$40)(0) + (\$0)(316) + (\$0)(354) + (\$0)(62) \\ &= \$0 \end{aligned}$$

This initial solution leaves all three resources idle, since none of the resources is used for real products. The economic value of this solution is recorded at the bottom of the production column.

Step 4: Evaluating the Effects of Introducing Other Variables into Solution Is it possible to improve upon the initial solution? It might be if a new variable is introduced into the solution. Before introducing a new variable, however, we need a procedure for evaluating the economic effects of each variable that could be introduced. This is the purpose of the Z_j and $(C_j - Z_j)$ rows of Table S5.1. C_j represents the amount of *increase* in the objective function if one unit of variable j is added into the solution. Z_j represents the amount of *decrease* in the objective function if variable j is introduced. $(C_j - Z_j)$ is the net increase. At the bottom of Table S5.1, beneath each variable, the $(C_j - Z_j)$ for each variable is recorded. The C_j values are obtained readily from the objective function, but determination of the Z_j values requires some explanation.

Z_j is obtained by considering the *substitution* rates between variable j and the variables that are currently in solution. These substitution rates are given by the coefficients under variable j in Table S5.1. Consider the CB radio column. If one CB is introduced, .4 subassembly hours, .5 assembly hours, and .05 inspection hours can no longer be idle. Each unit of CB that is added requires "giving up" .4 of an S_1, .5 of an S_2, and .05 of an S_3, that is currently being produced. If we give up the production of S_1, S_2, or S_3, how would the value of the objective function be changed? Since \$0 is contributed by each unit of S_1, S_2, and S_3, the amount of decrease in the objective function is:

$$Zx_1 = Z_{CB} = (\$0)(.4) + (\$0)(.5) + (\$0)(.05) = \$0$$

In a similar manner, the Z_j and $(C_j - Z_j)$ values for all variables in the MultiBand problem are recorded at the bottom of Table S5.1.

Steps 5-8: Finding the Best Variables The remaining steps of the simplex method, while cumbersome manually, can be executed quickly and accurately with readily available computer software packages. The remainder of our discussion uses QSOM, Version 2.0 (Quantitative Systems for Operations Management), a user-friendly system that includes several linear programming options, to illustrate the completion of the simplex method.[7]

Steps 5 and 6, selection of entering and leaving variables, are shown in Figure S5.3. Why did QSOM select CB as the entering variable? By examining the $(C_j - Z_j)$ row of the initial solution, we see that further improvement is possible. If we add a unit of CB into the solution, the objective function is increased by $50. Or, if we add a unit of PR, the solution is improved by $40. Additional units of S_1, S_2, or S_3 have no effect on the objective function, since each has a $(C_j - Z_j)$ value of zero. At each stage of the problem, we can introduce only one new variable. Each new variable must be evaluated so that the most attractive one can be chosen. In this case, CB is the most advantageous variable on a per-unit basis, so it is the one that should be selected.

Why was variable S_2 chosen to leave the solution? In this problem we can have only three variables in the solution at one time, one per constraint equation. If a new variable is introduced, an existing variable must leave the solution. Since we wish to introduce CB, either S_1, S_2, or S_3 must leave. To find the variable that should leave the solution, QSOM focuses on the substitution rates between CB and S_1, S_2, and S_3 (the variables in solution). Each CB requires giving up .4 S_1. There are 316 S_1's available to

FIGURE S5.3 **QSOM printout: Selection of incoming and outgoing variables (iteration 1)**

Iteration 1

		CB	PR	S1	S2	S3		B (i) / A (i, j)
Basis	C (j)	50.00	40.00	0	0	0	B (i)	
S1	0	0.400	0.500	1.000	0	0	316.0	790.0
S2	0	0.500	0.300	0	1.000	0	354.0	708.0
S3	0	0.050	0.100	0	0	1.000	62.00	1240
C (j) – Z (j)		50.00	40.00	0	0	0	0	
* Big M		0	0	0	0	0	0	

Current objective function value (Max.) = 0
(Highlighted variable is the entering or leaving variable)
Entering: CB Leaving: S2

[7]See Y. Chang 1991. *QSOM: Quantitative Systems for Operations Management* (Englewood Cliffs, N. J.: Prentice Hall, 1991). Readers who are interested in the manual procedure for the simplex method are referred to the management science selected readings at the end of this supplement.

give up. If we consider only subassembly labor, a maximum of 790 CBs can be introduced, as shown in the right column of Figure S5.3. If we consider assembly labor, a maximum of 354 ÷ .5 = 708 CBs can be put into solution. There are enough idle inspection hours (S_3) to allow 1,240 CBs to be introduced. Since *all* restrictions must be met, we can see that available resources are adequate for adding 708 units of CB into solution. If we do this, all assembly labor is used for producing CBs; none is idle. Thus assembly labor is the resource that keeps us from introducing more than 708 CBs; it is the *limiting resource* at this stage.

Let's summarize. QSOM adds 708 units of CB into solution. To do this, we must give up all 354 units of S_2; that is, we give up all the S_2's that were formerly in solution, and S_2 is the variable that leaves solution. In the revised solution, we are producing 708 CBs and no PRs. Graphically, this is shown as point *c* in Figure S5.2.

After introducing the new variable CB into solution, QSOM revises each row of the solution matrix to reflect the changes. The column headings are the same, but the row headings, restriction coefficients, and production quantities must be changed.[8] In terms of the graphical procedure, we are now moving *from the origin to an adjacent extreme point.* The resulting simplex tableau is shown in Figure S5.4.

Iteration 2

Basis	C (j)	CB	PR	S1	S2	S3	B (i)	B (i) / A (i, j)
		50.00	40.00	0		0		
S1	0	0	0.260	1.000	–.800	0	32.80	126.2
CB	50.00	1.000	0.600	0	2.000	0	708.0	1180
S3	0	0	0.070	0	–.100	1.000	26.60	380.0
C (j) – Z (j)		0	10.00	0	–100	0	35400	
* Big M		0	0	0	0	0	0	

Current objective function value (Max.) = 35400
(Highlighted variable is the entering or leaving variable)
Entering: PR Leaving: S1

FIGURE S5.4 QSOM printout: Selection of incoming and outgoing variables (iteration 2)

After completing the first iteration of the simplex method, the entire procedure is repeated using Figure S5.4 as the new starting point. Accordingly, QSOM has identified PR as the next entering variable, to replace S_1. Each entering PR will add $10 marginal contribution to profit, as noted in the $C(j) - Z(j)$ row, and there are sufficient resources to add 126.2 PRs, which consumes the 32.80 idle hours of

[8]The detailed procedures for making these changes are available in the reference books cited at the end of this supplement.

subassembly labor. After bringing variable PR into solution, QSOM again revises each row of the solution matrix to reflect the changes in the row headings, the production quantities, and the coefficients in the solution matrix. Graphically, QSOM has moved us to point *h* in Figure S5.2.

After completing the second iteration by bringing PRs into solution, the revised solution matrix (Figure S5.5) indicates that no further improvement is possible; all of the values in the $C(j) - Z(j)$ row are zero or negative. The optimal solution has been reached.

Final tableau (Total iteration = 2)

Basis	C (j)	CB 50.00	PR 40.00	S1 0	S2 0	S3 0	B (i)	B (i) / A (i, j)
PR	40.00	0	1.000	3.846	−3.08	0	126.2	0
CB	50.00	1.000	0	−2.31	3.846	0	632.3	0
S3	0	0	0	−.269	0.115	1.000	17.77	0
C (j) − Z (j)		0	0	−38.5	−69.2	0	36662	
* Big M		0	0	0	0	0	0	

(Max.) Optimal OBJ value = 36661.54

FIGURE S5.5 QSOM printout: Optimal solution for MultiBand

The summarized results are shown in Figure S5.6—632.3 CBs and 126.2 PRs will be produced to give $36,661.54 profit. All of the subassembly and assembly labor is fully consumed, but nearly 18 hours of inspection labor are unused. Consequently, some inspection workers might be moved to other operations where they can be productive. The opportunity cost for subassembly labor (S_1) shows the foregone profit

FIGURE S5.6 QSOM printout: Summarized results for MultiBand

Summarized Report For Multiband Page 1

Number	Variable	Solution	Opportunity Cost	Objective Coefficient	Minimum Obj. Coeff.	Maximum Obj. Coeff.
1	CB	+632.30	0	+50.00	+32.00	+66.66
2	PR	+126.15	0	+40.00	+30.00	+62.50

Maximized Obj. = 36661.54 Interation = 2

of not having one more hour of that resource; that is, if MultiBand had an additional hour of subassembly labor and used it properly, the resulting marginal contribution to profit would be $38.46. If, instead, we had an additional hour of assembly labor, the marginal contribution to profit would be $69.23.

Sensitivity analysis provides useful information for operations management. In the top half of Figure S5.7 you can see the original objective function coefficients for CBs ($50) and PRs ($40). We also see their minimum and maximum values within which the optimal solution mix remains the same. CBs, in other words, can have a contribution margin from $32.00 to $66.66 without changing the optimal solution mix (the solution remains at the same corner point, h, in Figure S5.2). The optimal quantities of CBs and PRs will remain unchanged, but total profit (Z), of course, will change. If the CB coefficient goes outside the stated range, the optimal solution mix will change and, to find it, the problem must be re-solved.

The lower half of Figure S5.7 shows the sensitivity of the right-hand side (RHS) for each restriction. In other words, how would the solution be affected if MultiBand had more or less of a resource than the original amount? Within the indicated range, the same variables remain in the optimal solution, but the optimal *quantities* of them change. If, for example, there were only 283.2 hours of subassembly labor (rather than the original 316 hours), the resulting optimal solution would still contain the same variables (CB, PR, and S_3). Outside the range, however, a different mix of variables would be optimal. An alternative interpretation is that within the indicated ranges, the opportunity costs of the solution variables remain as stated in Figure S5.6; otherwise, the opportunity costs change.

SOME ADDITIONAL CONSIDERATIONS

Minimization For purposes of illustration, we have used a maximization problem to present the simplex method. *Minimization* problems are also frequently encountered, and the same basic procedure is applied. The $(C_j - Z_j)$ values in step 4, however, have the reverse meaning in minimization problems; that is, as long as a negative $(C_j - Z_j)$

FIGURE S5.7 QSOM printout: Sensitivity analysis for MultiBand

Sensitivity Analysis for OBJ Coefficients							Page : 1
C (j)	Min. C (j)	Original	Max. C (j)	C (j)	Min. C (j)	Original	Max. C (j)
C (1)	+32.000000	+50.000000	+66.666664	C (2)	+30.000000	+40.000000	+62.500000

Sensitivity Analysis for RHS							Page : 1
B (i)	Min. B (i)	Original	Max. B (i)	B (i)	Min. B (i)	Original	Max. B (i)
B (1)	+283.20001	+316.00000	+382.00000	B (3)	+44.230766	+62.000000	+ Infinity
B (2)	+200.00002	+354.00000	+395.00000				

exists, further improvement is possible. The variable having the largest negative value is selected for introduction into solution. When all $(C_j - Z_j)$ are zero or positive, no further minimization is possible.

Artificial Variables Another circumstance arises when the problem restrictions are not of the less-than-or-equal-to variety used in our example. Two other types of restrictions are commonly encountered. First is the equality of the form:

$$A_1X_1 + A_2X_2 = B_1$$

In this case, a slack variable is not added since an equality already exists. However, a different kind of variable, an artificial variable, is added by QSOM to the left side:

$$A_1X_1 + A_2X_2 + A = B_1$$

The artificial variable serves computational purposes in the initial tableau. It is undersirable to have the artificial variable appear in the final solution. Therefore, the coefficient of A (called *Big M* at the bottom of the simplex tableaus in Figures S5.3, S5.4, and S5.5) in the objective function is made to be an arbitrarily large positive value in a minimization problem or an arbitrarily large negative number in a maximization problem. This ensures that A will be driven out of solution by the simplex procedure.

Surplus Variables Another type of restriction is the greater-than-or-equal-to restriction:

$$A_1X_1 + A_2X_2 \geq B_1$$

Both a surplus (negative slack) and an artificial variable are added by QSOM. The surplus variable converts the expression into an equality:

$$A_1X_1 + A_2X_2 - S = B_1$$

Then, since S has a coefficient of -1, an artificial variable must be added to the left side to create an identify matrix:

$$A_1X_1 + A_2X_2 - S + A = B_1$$

Once QSOM converts all the restrictions by adding the necessary artificial and slack variables, the previously described simplex procedure is executed.

REVIEW AND DISCUSSION QUESTIONS

1. Of what value is the graphic method of LP?
2. Define and illustrate the following:
    (a) Linear objective function
    (b) Linear constraint
    (c) Nonlinear objective function
    (d) Nonlinear constraint
3. What is meant by the term *feasibility area* (region of feasibility) in a linear programming model? What is the significance of the corner points?
4. In the simplex method, what is the standard format of problem formulation? Give an example.

5. What is a *slack variable?* Why is it used? How many will there be in an LP problem?
6. How many variables will be in solution at any stage of an LP problem?
7. What is the significance of the $C_j - Z_j$ row of the LP solution matrix?
8. After determining which variable to introduce next into solution, how do you determine how many units of that variable to introduce?
9. In the simplex method, what indicates that an optimal solution has been reached?
10. Define and illustrate
    (a) Artificial variable
    (b) Surplus variable
11. Under what conditions would an LP problem use artificial, surplus, and slack variables? Give examples of each.

PROBLEMS

1. Consider the following LP problem:
   Minimize $C = 16x + 10y$
   Subject to: $12x + 4y \geq 24$
   $6x + 12y \geq 36$
   (a) Using the graphic method, find the optimal solution.
   (b) If the objective function is changed to $C = 16x + 4y$, what is the optimal solution?
2. Solve the following problem using the graphic method of LP:
   Maximize $P = 2A + 2B$
   Subject to: $2A + 3B \leq 16$
   $2A + B \leq 8$
   If the objective function is changed to $P = 2A + 5B$, what is the optimal solution?
3. Product A offers a profit of $2.50/unit; product B yields $4 profit/unit. To manufacture the products, leather, wood, and glue are required in the amounts shown below.

Resources required for one unit

Product	Leather (in lb)	Wood (in board ft)	Glue (in oz)
A	$\frac{1}{2}$	4	2
B	$\frac{1}{4}$	7	2

Available resources include 2,000 pounds of leather, 28,000 board feet of wood, and 10,000 ounces of glue.
   (a) State the objective function and constraints in mathematical form.

(b) Find the optimal solution graphically.
(c) Which resources are fully consumed by the optimal solution?
(d) How much of each resource remains unused in the optimal solution?

4. Fatten Fast Feed Company produces a hog feed made from two basic ingredients, X and Y. A ton of Y can be purchased for $120; a ton of X costs $80. Each ingredient contains three types of nutrients, A, B, and C.

Nutrient content (units per ton)

	Nutrient		
Ingredient	A	B	C
X	450	73	69
Y	257	61	208

A ton of hog feed must contain at least 3,600 units of nutrient A, 730 units of nutrient B, and 1,250 units of nutrient C. What amounts of X and Y should be selected to minimize the cost of hog feed?

5. Quick Copy Service has a large backlog of printing jobs to be done. There are 10,000 standard lots of class A jobs and 18,000 standard lots of class B jobs. The cost of processing a standard class A job is $.72, of a class B job, $.33. The manager wishes to minimize processing costs for the coming month; however, some constraints must be met. First, the marketing department has requested that a minimum of 80 percent of the class A jobs and 60 percent of the class B jobs be completed this month. Second, wage payments are already committed for 4,200 direct labor hours for next month in the processing center. A class A job requires .16 labor hours, and a class B job requires .23 labor hours. The manager wants to fully utilize the direct labor during the month. How many jobs of each class should be processed?

6. Real Deal Distributors packages and distributes merchandise to retail outlets. A standard shipment can be packaged in small, medium, or large containers. A standard shipment of small containers yields a profit of $4; medium containers, $12; and large containers, $16. Each shipment is prepared manually, requiring packing materials and time. Each shipment must also be inspected.

Resource requirements per standard shipment

Container Size	Packing Time (in hours)	Packing Material (in pounds)	Inspection Time (in minutes)
Small	1.0	2.0	1.5
Medium	2.0	4.0	3.0
Large	4.0	7.0	3.0
Total amount of resource available	1,200	2,400	1,200

(a) Formulate this problem in a simplex format.
(b) What is the optimal number to produce of each container size?

7. Maxim, Inc., sends sales representatives to call on three types of clients: retail, industrial, and professional. Sales revenues of $2,000 result from calling on a retail client, $5,000 from an industrial contact, and $20,000 from a professional client. This month a total of 3,200 hours of sales representative time is available for calling on customers, and $10,000 is available for travel expenses. Management will not allow more than 20 percent of total sales force time to be devoted to retail clients, and they will not allow more than 30 percent of the travel expense budget to be used for calling on professional clients. Six hours of travel and selling time are required to call on a retail client, 11 hours for an industrial client, and 25 hours for a professional client. Travel expenses are $10 for each retail client, $14 for each industrial client, and $35 for each professional client. What is the optimal client mix for the coming month?
8. The Farmers Cooperative Oil Company produces two lines of motor oil and a special engine additive called New Motor. All three products are produced by blending two components. These components contribute various properties, including viscosity. (*Viscosity* is the thickness or tendency to flow.) The viscosity in the product is proportional to the viscosities of the blending components. The pertinent data appear in the table. Assume no limitation on demand. Set this up as a linear programming problem to determine how many barrels of each oil product Farmers should produce each week. Clearly define all variables. (Do not solve for the optimal solution.)

Blending Component	Viscosity	Cost Per Barrel (in $)	Availability (in barrels/week)
1	20	$14.00	8,000
2	60	$21.50	3,000
Product	**Viscosity Required**		**Profit Contribution (in $/barrel)**
30W oil	30		$23
40W oil	40		25
New Motor	50		30

9. Greenthumb Landscape Company employs senior and junior tree specialists who are assigned to various landscaping jobs. Daily wages are $70 for each senior specialist and $45 for each junior specialist. Working alone, a senior specialist processes an acre of work in four days. A junior specialist processes an acre of work in seven days. However, if both types of workers are assigned to a project, two days of senior work and three days of junior work will complete one acre. Greenthumb receives $600 for each acre it processes. Supervisory requirements depend on the type of tree specialist assigned to a project; .8 days of supervisor time is needed for each acre processed by a senior specialist; 1.0 days for an acre processed by a junior specialist; and 2.0 days for each acre processed by a junior and senior specialist working together. In total, 450 days of supervision, 1,200 days of junior specialist labor, and 1,000 days of senior specialist labor are available. How should the work force be utilized to maximize the profit?

10. Given the following simplex tableau:

C_j	In Solution	P_1	P_2	P_3	P_4	P_5	Production
		1	0	1	0	0	4
		0	1	0	1	0	6
		3	0	0	−2	1	6
	Z_j	0	5	0	5	0	30
	$C_j - Z_j$	3	0	0	−5	0	−30

(a) What variables form the basis solution? That is, what variables are in solution?
(b) What are the values of $C_1, C_2, \ldots, C_j$?
(c) Is this the optimal solution? Explain.
(d) Regardless of your answer in part (c), *assume* this is the optimal solution. Your supervisor says we *must* produce 2 units of P_1. What effect would this have on the objective function value of 30 units above?

11. Betherton Furniture Manufacturing has always used an outside carrier to make its deliveries. It is now investigating purchasing trucks and making its own deliveries. Betherton has available 220 workdays to use for the trucking operation, and $800,000 to invest in trucks. Due to loading restrictions and an unwillingness to become a totally owned private carrier, Betherton will purchase a maximum of 40 trucks; outside carriers will still be used a great deal. The three types of trucks under consideration have characteristics as shown in the table. Formulate, but do not solve, Betherton's situation as a linear programming problem.

Truck Type	Delivery Capacity (in ton-miles/day)	Operator Requirements to Meet Delivery Capacity (in workdays/vehicle)	Purchase Cost (in $)
A	8,400	3	16,000
B	10,000	6	26,000
C	14,500	7	30,000

OPERATIONS ANALYSIS USING QSOM, VERSION 2.0

12. Another department in MultiBand Enterprises (see Chapter 5 and the Supplement to Chapter 5) announces it will transfer 80 "free" labor hours next month to the department that produces CBs and PRs. These hours are in addition to those previously stated in the MultiBand example. How should the labor hours be used (due to worker training, the three types of labor are interchangeable)? Prepare your recommendation with supporting data.

13. Solve problem 4, the hog feed blending problem, using QSOM, Version 2.0. Print out your final tableau and the summarized results. Explain the results.

14. Formulate and solve problem 11 above, the Betherton Furniture Manufacturing Company, using QSOM, Version 2.0.

(a) Explain (interpret) the optimal solution in your own words.

(b) Which of the three constraints is loose? Explain.

(c) Truck supplier B has not received an order from Betherton. They inform you their price of $26,000 per truck is negotiable. Below what price would Betherton be interested in buying some B trucks? Explain how you determined this price.

KEY TERMS

Decision variable 192
Feasible solution 195
Infeasible solution 195
Initial solution 198
Iso-profit line 196
Objective function 192
Restrictions 192
Simplex method 198
Slack variable 198
Solution space 194

SELECTED READINGS

Anderson, D. R., D. J. Sweeney, and T. A. Williams, *An Introduction to Management Science,* 3rd ed. St. Paul, Minn.: West Publishing, 1982.

Bierman, H., Jr., C. P. Bonini, and W. H. Hausman, *Quantitative Analysis for Business Decisions,* 6th ed. Homewood, Ill.: Richard D. Irwin, 1981.

Chang, Y., *QSOM, Version 2.0: Quantitative Systems for Operations Management.* Englewood Cliffs, N.J.: Prentice Hall, 1991.

CHAPTER 6

LOCATING PRODUCTION AND SERVICE FACILITIES

Retailers and shopping center developers have learned by experience the truth of the familiar adage that the three secrets to success in retailing are location, location, and location.

Locational decisions are critical at several levels of geography. At the national level, retail analysts screen and select metropolitan and regional markets for new store entry. At the metropolitan level, not only are prime retail sites important but also an optimal distribution of those locations is needed to serve the marketplace. Distribution facilities must be properly sized and placed to ensure that goods can be efficiently linked between manufacturers, stores, and consumers. At a retail site such as a regional shopping center, store placement is best at the primary traffic entry point to the mall. Inside the mall a store location adjacent to the major pedestrian corridor contributes significantly toward higher store revenues.

Good retailers know their customers and competition and thus recognize market opportunities. Locational analysis includes careful evaluation of market factors such as competitor strength and locations, population growth, economic trends, highway developments, and demographic or socioeconomic patterns of consumers.

Serving the market from a good location can make the difference in a store's success.

Kenneth L. Wilkerson
Chairman
Robinson's
Los Angeles, California

This problem of how many facilities to have and where they should be located is encountered by service and product organizations in both the public and private sectors. Banks, restaurants, recreation agencies, and manufacturing companies are all concerned with selecting sites that will best enable them to meet their long-term goals.

The success of location planning both affects and is affected by organizing and control activities. Since the operations manager fixes many costs with the location decision, both the efficiency and effectiveness of the conversion process are dependent upon location. Leading to this decision are analyses with both modeling and behavioral dimensions. Let's examine the facilities location activity in more detail.

NEED FOR FACILITY LOCATION PLANNING

Revenues and costs are both affected by facility location. A technique called *break-even analysis* helps relate costs and revenues to facility location.

BREAK-EVEN ANALYSIS

Break-even analysis A graphical and algebraic representation of the relationships among volume of output, costs, and revenues.

Break-even analysis is a graphical and algebraic representation of the relationships among volume of output, costs, and revenues. As the volume of output from a facility increases, costs and revenues also increase. Costs can generally be divided into two categories: fixed and variable. Fixed costs are those incurred regardless of output volume. They include heating, lighting, and administrative expenses that are the same whether one or one thousand units of output are produced. Variable costs are those that fluctuate directly with volume of output: higher output results in higher total variable costs; lower output results in lower variable costs. Typically, they are the costs of direct labor and material. In Figure 6.1, total revenues and total costs are shown as linear

FIGURE 6.1 **Cost structures and break-even points for operations in two contrasting locations**

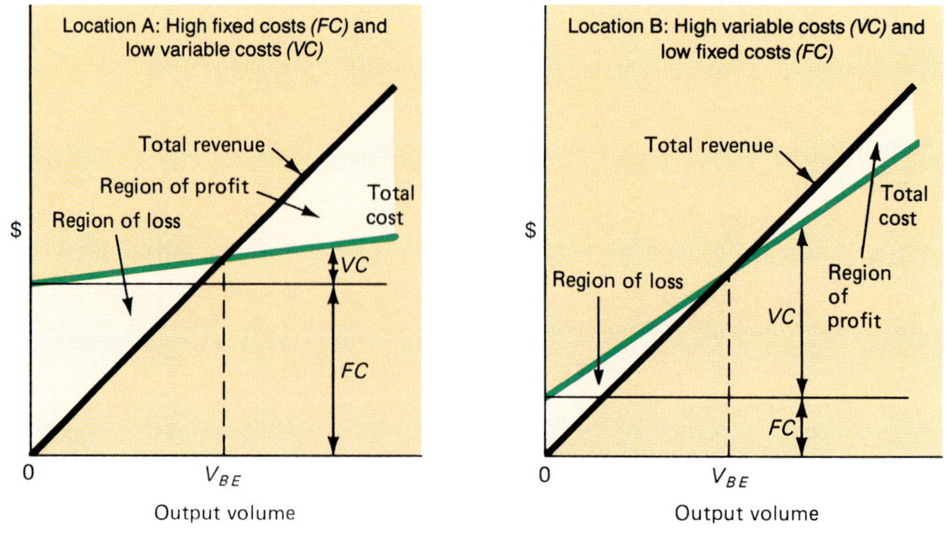

Break-even point The level of output volume for which total costs equal total revenues.

functions of output volume. Costs exceed revenues in the initial stages of output up to point V_{BE}. Point V_{BE} is the *break-even point:* the level of volume for which total costs equal total revenues. Thereafter, revenues exceed costs of operation.

Break-even analysis identifies the level of output that must be reached in order to recover through revenues all the costs of operation. The break-even point depends on the selling price of the product and the operating cost structure. Some conversion processes require high fixed costs—that is, large capital outlays and high overhead expenses—but low unit variable costs. They require a large volume of output to reach break-even, but once they have attained it, profitability increases rapidly. Other conversion processes have low fixed costs and high unit variable costs. Figure 6.1 shows both kinds of cost structures.

Break-even with Discontinuous Revenues and Costs Revenues and/or costs may be nonlinear rather than linear functions (with constant slope) of output volume, or the function may increase in jumps rather than smoothly. Indeed, a major purpose of break-even analysis is to reveal how the organization's costs and revenues change with volume of output.

Consider the situation in Figure 6.2. The organization has two facilities, A and B, which may be operated during the coming year. Facility A, working a single shift, has a break-even volume of V_{BE}(A) units. Thereafter, profitability increases up to the output

FIGURE 6.2 Break-even chart for operating one facility, two facilities, and two facilities on double shifts

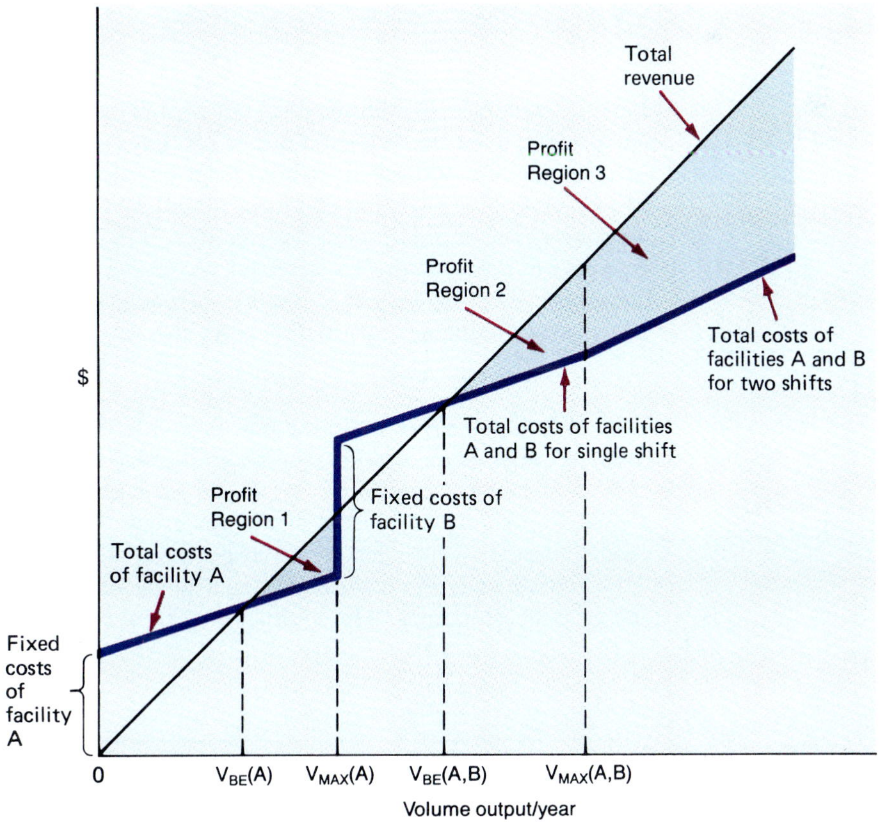

V_{max}(A). If greater profit is desired, facility B must be opened and additional fixed costs incurred. The overall operation (facilities A and B) will not be profitable until a volume of V_{BE}(A,B) units is achieved. Output volumes above V_{BE}(A,B) result in higher profit rates until volume V_{max}(A,B) is reached. To achieve outputs above V_{max}(A,B) a second shift is necessary, and variable costs increase accordingly. Beyond V_{max}(A,B), profits continue to increase, but at a slower rate as shown in profit region 3.

Information from the break-even chart can now be used for managerial decisions. Once the desired level of profitability for the year has been stated, we can show the volume of output required to achieve it. We can also identify how many facilities and shifts will be needed, and we can estimate operating costs and working capital requirements.

THE EFFECTS OF LOCATION ON COSTS AND REVENUES

Revenues In some industries, revenues depend on having the facility near potential customers. For example, for manufacturing firms that supply customers who are themselves manufacturers and assemblers, delivery time can be a crucial component of the strategic mission.[1]

For service industries, the situation is somewhat different. Location is not so important for *stored services,* those not directly consumed. Federal Reserve banks, automotive repair shops, and manufacturers who repair appliances are often quasi-manufacturers, and they don't necessarily have to be located near consumers. On the other hand, for firms that offer *directly consumed services,* location can be critical. Movie theaters, restaurants, banks, apartments, dry cleaning stores, and even public recreation areas obviously must be located conveniently to the public. Otherwise, consumers will go elsewhere, and revenues will decline.

Fixed Costs New or additional facilities entail fixed initial costs, usually incurred only once, which must be recovered out of revenues if the investment is to be profitable. Acquiring new or additional facilities involves costs for new construction, purchase and renovation of other existing plants, or rental. And once they're acquired, more money must be spent on equipment and fixtures. The magnitude of these costs may well depend on the site that is selected. A choice merchandising, corner location in downtown Washington, D.C., requires a totally different capital outlay from one in Greencastle, Indiana. Construction costs also vary greatly from one place to another.

Variable Costs Once built, the new facility must be staffed and operated, and these costs, too, depend on location. For labor-intensive conversion processes, the availability of labor and local expectations for wages are major concerns. Management must also consider proximity to sources of raw materials (inputs) and to markets for finished goods (outputs), which can vary transportation and shipping costs.

Seldom does an organization find a single site that is best in terms of all revenue and cost considerations. The location offering the highest revenue potential may also

[1]For a discussion of locational considerations in multiplant manufacturing strategies, see R. W. Schmenner, "Look Beyond the Obvious in Plant Location," *Harvard Business Review* 57, no. 1 (January-February 1979), 126–32.

Construction of this new facility in Saudi Arabia requires capital appropriations and expenditures that must be recovered out of revenues if the investment is to be profitable.

Source: Alastair D. Cook/Stockphotos, Inc.

incur higher costs. Tradeoffs must be made among fixed costs, variable costs, and revenue potential; the final choice of location should be the one that offers the best overall balance toward achieving the organization's mission. Staples stores, in Operations Management Highlight 6.1, is an example of such a balance.

In evaluating any potential site, then, we might consider all these revenue and cost factors using a break-even analysis (as in Figure 6.1). For location A, fixed costs are high and variable costs are low. The lower fixed costs of location B are offset by its higher variable costs.

REASONS FOR LOCATIONAL CHANGES

In addition to the need for greater capacity, there are other reasons for changing or adding locations.

1. Changes in resources may occur. The cost or availability of labor, raw materials, and supporting resources (such as subcontractors) may change.
2. The geography of demand may shift. As product markets change, it may be desirable to change facility location to provide better service to customers.
3. Companies may merge, making facilities redundant.
4. New products may be introduced, changing the availability of resources and markets.
5. Political and economic conditions may change.

OPERATIONS MANAGEMENT HIGHLIGHT 6.1

Source: John Zoiner

Paper, Pens, and Staples Need To Be at the Right Location

Tom Stemberg sells office supplies the same way that Toys 'R Us sells toys—in large volumes at low prices. His Staples stores offer an innovative combination of wholesale-club low prices and a very broad selection of merchandise. Customers load their shopping carts with office machines, furniture, paper clips, computer software, or anything else for the office. The first Staples "superstore" opened in 1986, growing impressively and planning further expansion.

Facility location decisions are a major reason for Staples' success. They have located their stores in the toughest market areas, such as Boston, New York, and Washington, where wholesale clubs and traditional full-service office supply stores offer fierce competition. Labor, land, and advertising are all costly in these large urban areas. Since all the competitors face these same high costs of operation, Staples has created an advantage by building a separate central warehouse, located in rural Putnam, Connecticut, to serve all its stores in the Northeast.

Cheaper labor in Putnam makes it less expensive to price the merchandise and sort incoming goods at the warehouse, instead of at the stores in the cities. Merchandise stays in Putnam until the stores need it. Then, it goes directly to the shelves, so that most of the store space is used for selling rather than for storing. This translates into better and cheaper use of space. Customers get a broader selection of merchandise and Staples avoids the costs of excessive store space. In these high-priced real estate areas, Staples stores are smaller, with lower rents than their competitors, but offer comparable merchandise. Staple's location advantage means a healthy profit margin.

Shrewd location decisions are doubly beneficial: Customers get good service, and owners get financial success. Tom Stemberg is extending his successful strategy by opening stores in other areas where operating costs are high. Los Angeles is the next step for exploiting the competitive advantage he has created.

Sources: **Michael Barrier, "Tom Stemberg Calls the Office,"** ***Nation's Business*** **(July 1990), 42; Arthur Markowitz,** ***Discount Store News*** **(October 16, 1989), 8; Steven Flax, "Seeking Big Money in Paper and Pens,"** ***Fortune*** **(July 31, 1989), 173.**

GENERAL PROCEDURES FOR FACILITY LOCATION PLANNING

THE PRELIMINARY SCREENING

A preliminary screening to identify feasible sites begins the planning process. For some kinds of facilities, particular environmental or labor considerations are crucial. Breweries, for example, require an adequate supply of clean water. Aircraft manufacturers must be located near a variety of subcontractors; primary aluminum producers need electrical power.

Resources	Local Conditions
Labor skills and productivity	Community receptivity to business
Land availability and cost	Construction costs
Raw materials	Organized industrial complexes
Subcontractors	Quality of life: climate, housing, recreation, schools
Transportation facilities (highways, rail, air, water)	Taxes
Utility availability and rates	

Sources of Information After identifying several key location requirements, management undertakes a search to find alternative locations that are consistent with these requirements. Where does this information come from? Local chambers of commerce provide literature promoting expansion possibilities in various state and local communities. The *Wall Street Journal* and numerous trade publications contain advertisements placed by cities and communities hoping to attract new commerce. The National Industrial Conference Board, the U.S. Department of Commerce, the U.S. Small Business Administration, and the U.S. Census of Manufacturers are among the many sources that provide both general and detailed location information. Data include geographic breakdowns of labor availability, population, transportation facilities, types of commerce, and similar information.

DETAILED ANALYSIS

Once the preliminary screening narrows alternative sites to just a few, more detailed analysis begins. At each potential site a labor survey may be conducted to assess the local skills. Where community or consumer response is in question, pilot studies or systematic surveys may be undertaken. Community response is important, for example, in deciding where to locate a nuclear reactor, recreation area, commercial bank, state prison, or restaurant. For assessing community attitudes and for developing strategies to gain acceptance, survey research techniques can be very helpful. Among all the many considerations, each company must identify which ones are most pertinent for their location strategies.[2]

Factor ratings A decision procedure in which each alternative is rated according to each factor relevant to the decision, and each factor is weighted according to importance.

Factor Ratings *Factor ratings* are frequently used to evaluate location alternatives because (1) their simplicity facilitates communication about why one site is better than another; (2) they enable managers to bring diverse locational considerations into the evaluation process; and (3) they foster consistency of judgment about location alternatives.

Typically, the first step in using factor ratings is to list the most relevant factors in the location decision (column 1 in Table 6.1). Next, each factor is rated, say from 1 (very low) to 5 (very high), according to its relative importance, (column 2 in Table 6.1). Then, each location is rated, say from 1 (very low) to 10 (very high), according to its merits on each characteristic (column 3 in Table 6.1). Finally, the factor rating is multiplied by the location rating for each factor, (column 4 in Table 6.1), and the sum of the products yields the total rating score for that location. The total scores indicate which alternative locations are most promising, considerating of all the various location factors.

TABLE 6.1 **Factor ratings for location alternative**

Factor	Factor Rating	Location Rating	Product of Ratings
Tax advantages	4	8	32
Suitability of labor skills	3	2	6
Proximity to customers	3	6	18
Proximity to suppliers	5	2	10
Adequacy of water	1	3	3
Receptivity of community	5	4	20
Quality of educational system	4	1	4
Access to rail and air transportation	3	10	30
Suitability of climate	2	7	14
Availability of power	2	6	12
		Total Score	149

FACILITY LOCATION MODELS

Various quantitative models are used to help determine the best locations of facilities. Sometimes, models are tailor-made to meet the specific circumstances of a unique problem. In New York City, for example, a mathematical model was developed to

[2]See international differences in P. M. Swamidass, "A Comparison of the Plant Location Strategies of Foreign and Domestic Manufacturers in the U.S.," *Journal of International Business Studies* 21, no. 2 (2nd Qtr. 1990), 301–317.

determine the best locations of fire companies.[3] Public officials want to balance available fire fighting services to reduce risks of property damage and fatalities. Among the regions of the city are different compositions of residential and commercial structures, alarm rates, hazard ratings, and street configurations. Furthermore, since many of these factors change with time, the problem is dynamic: A good location pattern now may not be so good in the future. The mathematical model for evaluating fire company locations takes into account many of these factors, as well as size of the area to be served, number of fire companies in the region, and travel characteristics of the fire company. This specialized model may be highly effective for locating emergency services in an urban setting.

There are some widely known, general models that can be adapted to the needs of a variety of systems. In the sections below we briefly introduce three types of models that have been applied to the location problem: the simple median model, linear programming, and simulation. All these models focus on transportation costs, although each considers a different version of the basic problem.

SIMPLE MEDIAN MODEL

Suppose we want to locate a new plant that will annually receive shipments of raw materials from two sources: F_1 and F_2. The plant will create finished goods that must be shipped to two distribution warehouses, F_3 and F_4. Given these four facilities, shown in Figure 6.3, where should we locate the new plant to minimize annual transportation costs for this network of facilities?

FIGURE 6.3 **Sources of raw materials and distribution warehouses (origin of coordinate system is arbitrary)**

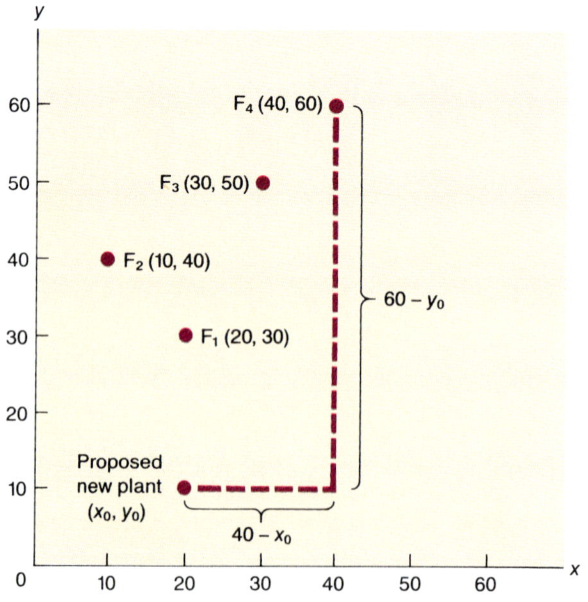

[3]This model is reported by K. L. Rider, "A Parametric Model for the Allocation of Fire Companies in New York City," *Management Science* 23, no. 2 (October 1976), 146–58.

Simple median model A quantitative method for choosing an optimal facility location, minimizing costs of transportation and based on the median load.

The Model The *simple median model* can help answer this question. This model considers the volume of loads transported on *rectangular* paths.[4] All movements are made in east-west or north-south directions; diagonal moves are not considered. The simple median model provides an optimal solution.[5]

Table 6.2 shows the number of loads L_i to be shipped annually between each existing facility F_i and the new plant; it also shows the coordinate location (X_i, Y_i) of each existing facility F_i, and the cost C_i to move a load one distance unit to or from F_i. We let D_i be the distance units between facility F_i and the new plant. The total transit cost, then, is the sum of the products $C_iL_iD_i$ for all i: cost times loads times distance.

$$\text{Total transportation cost} = \sum_{i=1}^{n} C_iL_iD_i \tag{6.1}$$

TABLE 6.2 Locations of existing facilities and number of loads to be moved

Existing Facility F_i	Annual Loads L_i Between F_i and New Plant	Cost C_i to Move one Load One Distance Unit	Coordinate Location (X_i, Y_i) of F_i (X_i, Y_i)
F_1	755	$1	(20, 30)
F_2	900	1	(10, 40)
F_3	450	1	(30, 50)
F_4	500	1	(40, 60)
	Total 2,605		

Since all loads must be on rectangular paths, distance between each existing facility and the new plant will be measured by the difference in the x-coordinates and the difference in the y-coordinates (see Figure 6.3). If we let (x_o, y_o) be the coordinates of a proposed new plant, then

$$D_i = |x_o - x_i| + |y_o - y_i| \tag{6.2}$$

Notice we calculate the absolute value of the differences, because distance is always positive. Notice too we could have written

$$D_i = |x_i - x_o| + |y_i - y_o|$$

Our goal is to find values for x_o and y_o (new plant) that result in minimum transportation costs. We follow three steps:

1. Identify the median value of the loads L_i moved.
2. Find the x-coordinate of the existing facility that sends (or receives) the median load.

[4]See. R. C. Vergin and J. D. Rogers, "An Algorithm and Computational Procedure for Locating Economic Facilities," *Management Science* 13, no. 6 (February 1967), 240–54.

[5]An alternative procedure, the center of gravity method, provides an approximate (but not necessarily optimal) solution and can be found in J. J. Coyle and E. J. Bardi, *The Management of Logistics*, 2nd ed. (St. Paul, Minn.: West Publishing, 1980).

3. Find the y-coordinate value of the existing facility that sends (or receives) the median load.

The x- and y-coordinates found in steps 2 and 3 define the new plant's best location.

Application of the Model Let us apply the three steps to the data in Table 6.2.

1. *Identify the median load.* The total number of loads moved to and from the new plant will be 2,605. If we think of each load individually and number them from 1 to 2,605, then the median load number is the "middle" number—that is, the number for which the same number of loads fall above and below. For 2,605 loads, the median load number is 1,303, since 1302 loads fall above and below load number 1,303. If the total number of loads were even, we would consider both "middle" numbers.
2. *Find the x-coordinate of the median load.* First we consider movement of loads in the x-direction. Beginning at the origin of Figure 6.3 and moving to the right along the x-axis, observe the number of loads moved to or from existing facilities. Loads 1–900 are shipped by F_2 from location $x = 10$. Loads 901–1,655 are shipped by F_1 from location $x = 20$. Since the median load falls in the interval 901–1,655, $x = 20$ is the desired x-coordinate location for the new plant.
3. *Find y-coordinate of the median load.* Now consider the y-direction of load movements. Begin at the origin of Figure 6.3 and move upward along the y-axis. Movements in the y direction begin with loads 1–755 being shipped by F_1 from location $y = 30$. Loads 756–1,655 are shipped by F_2 from location $y = 40$. Since the median load falls, in the interval 756–1655, $y = 40$ is the desired y-coordinate for the new plant.

The optimal plant location, $x = 20$ and $y = 40$, results in minimizing annual transportation costs for this network of facilities. To calculate the resulting cost, we use Equation 6.2 to calculate the distances D_i, and use these values in Equation 6.1:

$$\text{Total transportation cost} = \sum_{i=1}^{n} C_i L_i \left(|x - x_i| + |y - y_i|\right) \tag{6.3}$$

Total cost, $45,550, is shown in Table 6.3.

Some concluding remarks are in order. First, we have considered the case in which only one new facility is to be added.[6] Second, you should note an important assumption of this model: Any point in the $x-y$ coordinate system is an eligible point for locating the new facility. The model does not consider road availability, physical terrain, population densities, or any other of the many important location considerations. The task of blending model results with other major considerations to arrive at a reasonable location choice is a major managerial responsibility.[7]

---

[6]For adding multiple facilities, see R. A. Johnson, W. T. Newell, and R. C. Vergin, *Operations Management: A Systems Concept* (Boston: Houghton Mifflin, 1972).

[7]For a successful application that blends model results with other qualitative factors, see A. A. Aly and D. W. Litwhiler, Jr., "Police Briefing Stations: A Location Problem," *AIIE Transactions* 11, no. 1 (March 1979), 12–22.

TABLE 6.3 Calculation of total cost for optimal plant location ($x = 20$, $y = 40$)

Existing Facility F_i	x-coordinate x_i of F_i	y-coordinate y_i of F_i	Distance Between F_i and New Plant: x-direction: $\lvert 20 - x_i \rvert$	y-direction: $\lvert 40 - y_i \rvert$	Total distance D_i: $\lvert 20 - x_i \rvert + \lvert 40 - y_i \rvert$	Annual Load L_i Between F_i and New Plant	Cost to Move 1 Load 1 Unit Distance From F_i to New Plant (in $)	Annual Transportation Cost for F_i: $C_i \times D_i \times L_i$
F_1	20	30	0	10	10	755	1	7,550
F_2	10	40	10	0	10	900	1	9,000
F_3	30	50	10	10	20	450	1	9,000
F_4	40	60	20	20	40	500	1	20,000

Total transportation cost $= \sum_{i=1}^{4} C_i L_i D_i = \$45,550$

LINEAR PROGRAMMING

Linear programming may be helpful after the initial screening phase has narrowed the feasible alternative sites. The remaining candidates can then be evaluated, one at a time, to determine how well each would fit in with existing facilities, and the alternative that leads to the best overall system (network) performance can be identified. Most often, overall transportation cost is the criterion used for performance evaluation. A special type of linear programming called the *distribution* or *transportation* method is particularly useful in location planning.[8] The mechanics of this technique are omitted in the example that follows, but they are demonstrated in the supplement to this chapter.

EXAMPLE

Alpha Processing Company has three midwestern production plants located at Evansville, Indiana; Lexington, Kentucky; and Fort Wayne, Indiana. Five-year operations plans require that 200 shipments of raw materials be delivered annually to the Evansville plant, 300 shipments to Lexington, and 400 shipments to Fort Wayne. Currently, Alpha has two sources of raw materials, one at Chicago, Illinois, the other at Louisville, Kentucky. The Chicago source can supply 300 shipments per year and Louisville, 400. An additional source of raw materials must therefore be found. Preliminary screening by Alpha has narrowed the choice to two attractive alternatives: Columbus, Ohio, and St. Louis, Missouri. Each of these sites can supply 200 shipments per year. Alpha has decided to make its selection on the basis of minimizing transportation costs. Estimates of the cost per shipment from each source to each plant are shown in Table 6.4.

The cost analysis for Alpha Company proceeds in two stages. The first stage determines the number of shipments from each source to each plant that yields the lowest possible cost, assuming Columbus is the third source. The second stage

TABLE 6.4 Sources, destinations, and costs of raw material shipments

	Destination (cost per shipment)			
Source	Evansville	Lexington	Fort Wayne	Shipments Available
Chicago	$200	$300	$200	300
Louisville	100	100	300	400
Columbus	300	200	100	200
St. Louis	100	300[a]	400	200
Shipments needed	200	300	400	

[a]Cost to transport one shipment from St. Louis to Lexington.

[8]The simplex method of linear programming has also proved useful in location analysis. For an example of implementation for locating two new industrial production facilities, see R. F. Love and L. Yerex, "An Application of a Facilities Location Model in the Prestressed Concrete Industry," *Interfaces* 6, no. 4 (August 1976), 45–49.

determines the number of shipments yielding the lowest possible cost, assuming St. Louis is the third source. The minimum Columbus cost is compared to the minimum St. Louis cost, and the cheaper site is selected. A final solution for Alpha is shown in Figure 6.4.

If Columbus is selected, minimum annual shipping costs will be \$120,000. This occurs if 100 shipments go from Chicago to Evansville (costing \$200 each), 200 shipments from Chicago to Fort Wayne (costing \$200 each), 100 from Louisville to Evansville (\$100 each), 300 from Louisville to Lexington (\$100 each), and 200 from Columbus to Fort Wayne (\$100 each). These shipment quantities, shown beneath the diagonal lines in part (a) of Figure 6.4, satisfy the raw material needs of all three plants and fully uses the capacities of all three raw materials sources. Any other pattern of shipments will result in higher annual shipping costs.

Part (b) of Figure 6.4 shows that if St. Louis is selected, the minimum annual cost will be \$140,000. Columbus is therefore selected, at a cost of \$120,000 annually.

Notice that the linear programming model differs from the simple median model in two fundamental ways:

1. Number of alternative sites. The sample median model assumes that all locations are eligible to be the new location. The linear programming model, in contrast, considers only a few locations preselected from preliminary feasibility studies.
2. Direction of transportation movements. The simple median model assumes that all shipments move in rectangular patterns. The linear programming model does not so assume.

FIGURE 6.4 Evaluation of Alpha transportation costs

(a) If Columbus is third source

Source \ Plant	Evans-ville	Lexing-ton	Fort Wayne	Shipments available
Chicago	\$200 / 100	\$300	\$200 / 200	300
Louisville	\$100 / 100	\$100 / 300	\$300	400
Columbus	\$300	\$200	\$100 / 200	200
Shipments needed	200	300	400	

Minimum total annual cost = \$120,000

(b) If St. Louis is third source

Source \ Plant	Evans-ville	Lexing-ton	Fort Wayne	Shipments available
Chicago	\$200	\$300	\$200 / 300	300
Louisville	\$100	\$100 / 300	\$300 / 100	400
St. Louis	\$100 / 200	\$300	\$400	200
Shipments needed	200	300	400	

Minimum total annual cost = \$140,000

SIMULATION

Although several quantitative models like the ones we've discussed can handle location problems of limited scope, many real world problems are more complex than our examples. Some systems have multiple sources shipping to numerous plants; they in turn ship finished goods to warehouses from which further shipments are made to retailers. Multi-echelon (multilevel) production-distribution systems such as these pose formidable problems. Even with the simplest revision of this system, adding or deleting one network component, the combinatorial aspects of the problem make it computationally difficult. More realistically, we may want to consider more drastic changes, such as a total revision of the warehousing network. With problems of this complexity, no optimal solution is possible. Instead, approximation techniques like computer simulation are used.

BEHAVIORAL IMPACT IN FACILITY LOCATION

Our previous discussions of models focused on the *cost* consequences. But costs are not the whole story, and models can't account for aspects of a problem that are not quantifiable. New locations require that organizations establish relationships with new environments and employees, and adding or deleting facilities requires adjustments in the overall management system. The organization structure and modes of making operating decisions must be modified to accommodate the change. These hidden "system costs" are usually excluded from quantitative models, and yet they are very real aspects of the location decision.

CULTURAL DIFFERENCES

The decision to locate a new facility usually means that employees will be hired from within the new locale. It also means that the organization must establish appropriate community relations to "fit into" the locale as a good neighbor and citizen. The organization must recognize the differences in the way people in various ethnic, urban, suburban, and rural communities react to new businesses. Managerial style and organizational structure must adapt to the norms and customs of local subcultures. Employees' acceptance of authority may vary with *subcultures,* as do their life goals, beliefs about the role of work, career aspirations, and perceptions of opportunity. These cultural variations in attitude impact on-the-job behavior and talent.

Subculture Regional or ethnic variations of a culture.

At the international level are even greater cultural differences. Compare, for example, the Japanese work tradition with that of Western industrial society.[9] Japanese workers are often guaranteed lifetime employment. Management decisions usually are group rather than individual decisions. Employee compensation is determined by

[9]J. B. Keys and T. R. Miller, "The Japanese Management Theory Jungle," *Academy of Management Review* 9, no. 2 (April 1984), 342–53.

length of service, number of dependents, and numerous factors apart from the employee's productivity. Obviously operations managers in Japan face a very different set of managerial problems from their U.S. counterparts. Wage determination, employee turnover, hiring, and promotion practices are not at all the same.

The European social system, as another example, has resulted in a more "managerial elite" in their organizations than in U.S. organizations. Because of education, training, and socialization, including a lifelong exposure to a relatively rigid class system, lower subordinates are not prepared to accept participative managerial styles. This has resulted in organizations more authoritarian/centralized than participative/decentralized.

Locating a new facility in a new culture is not simply a matter of duplicating a highly refined manufacturing process. Merely transferring tools and equipment is not adequate. Managerial techniques and skills, in proper mixture, must be borrowed from the culture, and so must the cultural assumptions that are needed to make them work.[10] Clearly, the economic, political, and cultural makeup of a society has far-reaching effects on the technological and economic success of multinational location decisions.[11] Operations Management Highlight 6.2 shows how new economic and political changes can affect locational decisions.

JOB SATISFACTION

Job satisfaction Employee perceptions of the extent to which their work fulfills or satisfies their needs.

In recent years managers have been very concerned about employee *job satisfaction* because it affects how well the organization operates.[12] Although no consistent overall relationship between job satisfaction and productivity seems to exist, other consistent relationships have been found. As compared with employees with *low* job satisfaction, those expressing *high* job satisfaction exhibit the following characteristics:

Labor turnover A measure of the stability or change in an organization's work force; the net result of employee terminations and entrances.

1. Fewer *labor turnovers*
2. Less absenteeism
3. Less tardiness
4. Fewer grievances

Value system An individual's beliefs or conceptions about what is desirable, good, or bad.

These four factors can substantially affect both costs and disruptions of operations. But how is job satisfaction related to facility location? There is some evidence that satisfaction is related to community characteristics such as community prosperity, small town versus large metropolitan locations, and the degree of unionization. Accordingly, a company with facilities in multiple locations can expect variations in employee satisfaction due to variations in attitudes and *value systems* across locations.[13]

[10]L. R. Gomez-Mejia, "Effect of Occupation on Task Related, Contextual, and Job Involvement Orientation: A Cross-Cultural Perspective," *Academy of Management Journal* 27, no. 4 (December 1984), 706–20.

[11]For issues in international operations, see W. Skinner, *Manufacturing in the Corporate Strategy* (New York: John Wiley, 1978), chaps. 15–17.

[12]See R. M. Steers, *Introduction to Organizational Behavior* (Santa Monica, Calif.: Goodyear Publishing Co., 1981), chap. 13.

[13]See S. P. Robbins, *Organizational Behavior,* 2nd ed. (Englewood Cliffs, N.J.: Prentice Hall, 1983), 50–67.

OPERATIONS MANAGEMENT HIGHLIGHT 6.2

Source: Union Pacific Railroad

Free Trade and Location Alternatives

Goods flowing across the Canadian/U.S. border totaled $165 billion in 1988 alone. About 25 percent of U.S. exports go to Canada, and about 75 percent of Canada's exports go to the United States. To stimulate further commerce, the U.S./Canada Free-Trade Agreement took effect on January 1, 1989. The

CONSUMER CONSIDERATIONS

For many organizations, location planning must emphasize consumer behavior and proximity to customers. If primary product is a service to the public, the customer convenience may be the prime consideration. Theaters, banks, supermarkets, and agreement simplifies trade and investment across the border, and calls for phasing out tariffs over a ten-year period. Eliminating tariffs obviously saves the cost of the tariff. But it saves other operating costs as well by creating new location opportunities. The Gillette Company, for example, is closing two factories in Ontario because goods from the larger, high-volume U.S. plants can now be economically shipped to Canada. Many Canadian companies skillfully manufacture low-volume specialty products for U.S. markets. The Free-Trade Agreement will allow these companies to consolidate facilities in locations that are most beneficial; redundant facilities will be relocated or eliminated.

Decisions for new plant locations in coming years will consider new alternatives that high tariffs and limited markets had made economically infeasible. However, U.S. exporters will have to locate their plants carefully, depending upon where in Canada their markets are located. Among the Eastern provinces, for example, Newfoundland, Nova Scotia, New Brunswick, and Quebec are heavy importers of crude oil and natural gas. Saskatchewan and Manitoba, in contrast, import agricultural implements. In the Western provinces, construction and mining machinery are large import items for British Columbia and Alberta. Motor vehicles, parts, and accessories are substantial imports in nearly all provinces.

A great diversity of products are affected by the trade agreement. Tariffs were immediately eliminated on a wide range of products including animal feeds, snow skis, whiskey, vending machines, and motorcycles. For other products, such as paints, chemicals, and paper products, tariffs will be eliminated within five years. Tires, appliances, and steel are among the products for which tariffs will be eliminated within ten years. Meanwhile, of course, companies manufacturing the products have more time to plan out their location strategies to take advantage of the new, free-trade opportunities.

Sources: **Rachelle Garbarine, "Canada Pact Aids Upstate New York,"** ***New York Times*** **(August 1, 1990), D18; Dom Del Prete, "Free Trade Treaty Seen As Boom for Most U.S., Canadian Firms,"** ***Marketing News*** **(July 9, 1990), 6; Albert G. Holzinger, "A New Era in Trade,"** ***Nation's Business*** **(September, 1989), 67.**

restaurants heavily emphasize customer convenience when choosing a location. In fact, location convenience *itself* is often considered to be the service. For these reasons the location decision may be regarded as a responsibility of marketing staff instead of production/operations staff, especially as it affects revenues rather than costs.

Whether using manual typewriters and calculators or the latest in computer systems, employee job satisfaction directly affects operational performance by reducing labor turnover, absenteeism and tardiness, and grievances.

Source: Robert Kristofik/The Image Bank

Source: John Zoiner

SUMMARY

This chapter highlighted the problems of planning for facilities location, noting that the decision to change capacity often involves the location of new facilities or the dislocation of existing ones. Selecting a location requires consideration of costs and revenues. Preliminary studies gather information to identify feasible sites. Detailed studies use models to evaluate costs of alternative locations. Some models are simulation models, which can include many types of costs in complex, multilevel production-distribution systems; and simple median and linear programming models, which are particularly useful when there are substantial transportation costs among multiple facilities.

We saw that throughout the process of identifying and evaluating alternatives, management must consider the behavioral implications of location. The revenues of many service organizations depend upon a location featuring customer convenience. Organizations having less direct contact with the consuming public must recognize potential differences in employee behavior among various locations. Differences in lifestyles and values are necessarily carried over into the workplace, and these differences affect on-the-job behavior. Subcultural differences have implications for both job design (conversion technology) and managerial style.

At the international level, production/operations managers must recognize that locating in another country involves more than a simple transplanting of technology, and they must try to uncover "hidden" behavioral problems. Cultural differences, for example, may inhibit efficient operations.

CASE

Porta-Putt, Inc.

Porta-Putt, Inc., manufactures and distributes gasoline-powered outboard motors for boats. One of their three assembly plants, the St. Louis plant, is obsolete. The Los Angeles and Chicago assembly plants were recently renovated. Rather than continue operation in St. Louis, management is considering a new location for the third plant. This is an opportune time, because in two years the new Denver distribution warehouse will be opened. Since the new assembly plant could be the primary supplier of motors to the Denver warehouse, the new plant could be located to minimize shipping costs, which are a substantial part of Porta-Putt's operating costs.

Two types of shipping costs are incurred at the St. Louis plant. First, raw materials and subcomponents are shipped from Minneapolis and Seattle to the St. Louis facility. Then, after final assembly, the St. Louis plant ships the finished motors to the Denver distribution warehouse. Figure 6.5 shows the locations of the three facilities that ship to or from the St. Louis facility. Table 6.5 summarizes the annual number of loads shipped between St. Louis and each of the other three sites. The cost of shipping a load is estimated to be $.10/mile.

Management would like to find a location that would minimize the potentially high annual transportation costs. At the same time, however, there is some hesitation about moving away from metropolitan St. Louis, the original assembly plant established 35 years ago. Porta-Putt's experienced work force has survived many work methods and assembly line changes. From these refinements evolved an intricate assembly operation that efficiently produced quality motors—until recently, when the plant became

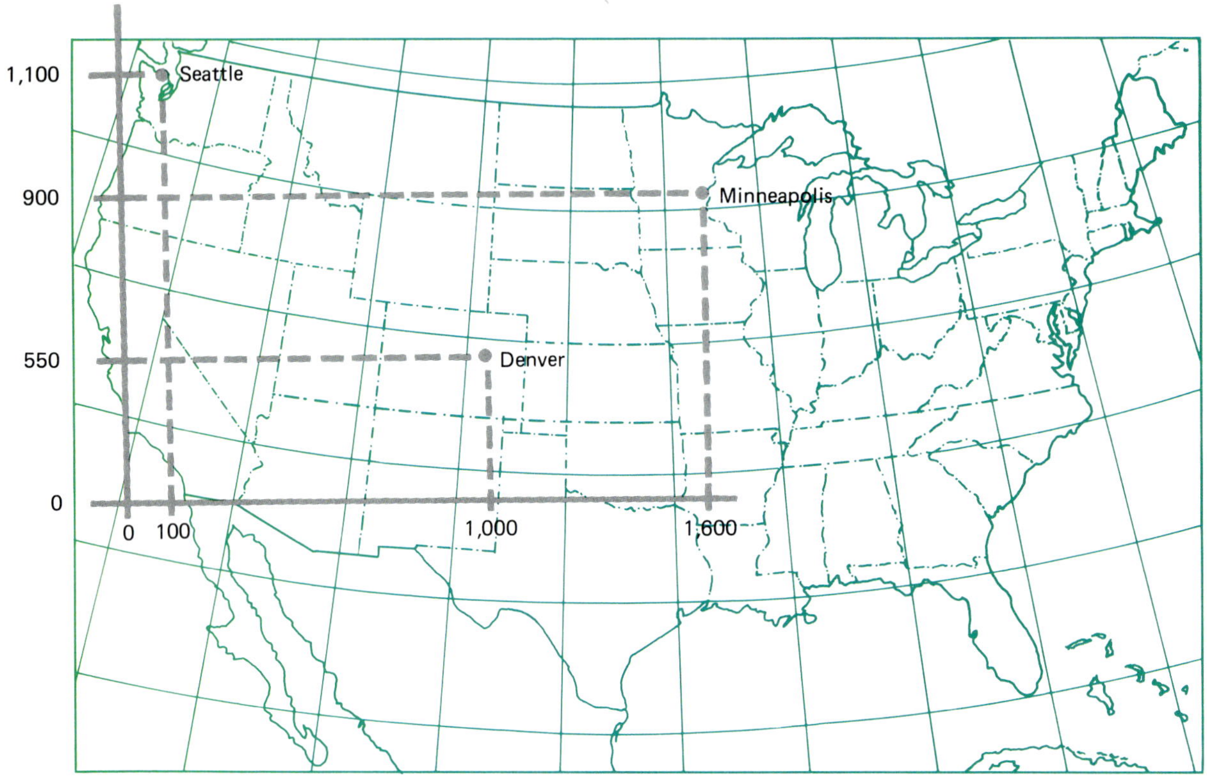

FIGURE 6.5 **Locations of shipping facilities for Porta-Putt, Inc.**

TABLE 6.5 **Loads between the St. Louis plant and shipping facilities for Porta-Putt**

Shipping Facility F_i	Annual Loads Between F_i and St. Louis	Coordinate location (x_i, y_i) of F_i (x_i, y_i)
Denver	10,000	(1,000, 550)
Seattle	8,000	(100, 1,100)
Minneapolis	4,000	(1,600, 900)

technologically obsolete. The vice president, who must make the location decision, feels that he should tell the St. Louis employees they might lose their jobs, but so far he has only discussed this possibility with several St. Louis managers. When the idea of relocation was introduced, these managers were dismayed at the prospect of leaving St. Louis. Present an analysis of the major factors in this decision and recommend a location.

REVIEW AND DISCUSSION QUESTIONS

1. Although facility location is a planning decision, it has implications for decisions in the organizing and controlling subfunctions. Explain.
2. Outline the factors that should be considered in locating a nuclear power generating plant. List these factors in order of priority.
3. Contrast the location problems of a manufacturing firm and a supermarket, showing the relevant considerations they share and those they do not.
4. Discuss the possible reasons for changing the location of an emergency services system, such as an urban firefighting company.
5. Suppose for economic reasons you want to locate your manufacturing facility in a small community that currently seems to be unfavorably disposed toward your industry. What strategies might you employ before making your decision?
6. Discuss the primary limitations of the simple median model. How important to the location problem are these limitations?
7. The simple median model is appropriate for some location problems; linear programming is appropriate for others. Identify the conditions of the location problem that would lead you to select one model over the other.
8. What aspects of different subcultures should be considered in location analysis?
9. If you expand your existing company by opening a new division in a foreign country, should the new division be staffed by local personnel or by personnel imported from the parent organization? Explain.

PROBLEMS

SOLVED PROBLEMS

1. Location A would result in annual fixed costs of \$300,000, variable costs of \$63/unit, and revenues of \$68/unit. Annual fixed costs at location B are \$800,000, variable costs are \$32/unit, and revenues are \$68/unit. Sales volume is estimated to be 25,000 units/year. Which location is most attractive?

   A break-even analysis is helpful for evaluating the two alternatives. The break-even points are found from:

$$V_{BE} = \frac{\text{fixed cost}}{\text{revenue/unit} - \text{variable cost/unit}}$$

$$V_{BE}(A) = \frac{\$300{,}000}{\$68 - 63} = 60{,}000 \text{ units}$$

$$V_{BE}(B) = \frac{\$800{,}000}{\$68 - 32} = 22{,}222 \text{ units}$$

At the expected demand of 25,000 units, profits (loss) for the alternatives are:

	Alternative	
	A	B
Revenue	$1,700,000	$1,700,000
Costs		
Variable	1,575,000	800,000
Fixed	300,000	800,000
Total	1,875,000	1,600,000
Profit (loss)	(175,000)	100,000

Location B is most attractive, even though annual fixed costs are much higher than for A.

2. A site is sought for a temporary plant to supply cement to three existing construction sites: downtown, at a mall, and at a suburb. The locations of the existing sites and the loads to be delivered to each are as follows:

Delivery Site S_i	Coordinate Location (x_i, y_i) (in miles)	Loads Li to New Plant	Cost C_i to move One Load One Mile
S_1 Downtown	(20, 10)	22	$10
S_2 Mall	(10, 40)	43	$10
S_3 Suburb	(40, 20)	36	$10
		Total 101	

Find the best site for the cement plant. What total shipping cost will result?

Using the simple median model, the median load is 51. To find the x-coordinate of the new plant, we begin at zero on the grid and move in the x-direction to the location that receives the 51st load (see Figure 6.6). At the first location ($x = 10$), 43 loads go to the mall. At the next location ($x = 20$), 22 loads go to downtown, and at this location the median (51st) load will have been delivered. Hence, the optimal x-coordinate is 20. In a similar fashion, the median load in the y-direction is delivered to the suburb site ($y = 20$). The resulting shipment costs, $22,300, are shown in the following table.

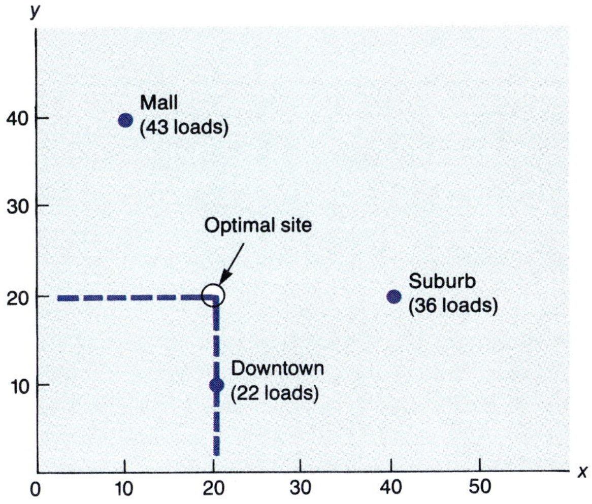

FIGURE 6.6 **Location grid**

Delivery Site S_i	Distance to New Plant: x-direction: $\|20 - x_i\|$	y-direction: $\|20 - y_i\|$	Total Distance (D_i)	Cost/Mile/ Load (C_i) to New Plant	Annual Loads (L_i) to New Plant	Annual Cost: $C_i \times D_i \times L_i$
S_1 Mall	$\|10 - 20\| = 10$	$\|40 - 20\| = 20$	30	$10	43	$12,900
S_2 Downtown	$\|20 - 20\| = 0$	$\|10 - 20\| = 10$	10	10	22	2,200
S_3 Suburb	$\|40 - 20\| = 20$	$\|20 - 20\| = 0$	20	10	36	7,200
						Total $22,300

REINFORCING FUNDAMENTALS

3. Bubble Breweries has two distribution warehouses on Highway 70. Warehouse A, located at mile zero, receives 3,000 standard beer shipments annually from the brewery. Warehouse B, located at mile 1,200, receives 1,000 standard shipments annually from the brewery. For these shipment patterns, what would be the better brewery location for minimizing annual transportation costs to warehouses?
4. Ontario Dairies, Ltd., is considering where to locate dairy processing centers to prepare milk products for regional markets in Canada. Locations and milk volumes are given below. Transportation costs are uniform throughout the area, at $.50/mile/100 pounds. Use the simple median model to find the best location. *Show your work.*

Location	Coordinate Location (x,y)	Milk Produced (in 100,000 pounds)
London, Ont.	(20, 0)	200
Cochrane, Ont.	(0, 400)	300
Toronto, Ont.	(140, 20)	800
Montreal, Queb.	(360, 80)	200

5. Bigtown is trying to find the best location for a master solid waste disposal station. At present, four substations are located at the following coordinate (x, y) locations: station 1 (40, 120), station 2 (65, 40), station 3 (110, 90), and station 4 (10, 130). The number of loads hauled monthly to the master station will be 300 from station 1, 200 from station 2, 350 from station 3, and 400 from station 4. Use the simple median model to find the best location.
6. Suresnap fishing reels require variable production costs of $12/unit. Fixed costs are $200,000 for first shift operations, which have a capacity of 30,000 reels. Distributors purchase reels for $20 each. Suresnap can double capacity by operating a second shift at an additional semifixed cost of $80,000. Using a schematic model, evaluate the alternative levels of plant operation.
7. First National Bank is considering building a new central processing facility (CPF) to process checks for four existing branch banks. This new facility will not be open to the public. Figure 6.7 shows the location of each branch. The main bank has coordinate (0, 0). The monthly volume processed from each branch is shown in the following table. The cost of transportations is $100/1,000 items processed/mile for each branch.

FIGURE 6.7

Branch	Volume (in 1000s)
A	60
B	50
C	10
D	100

The main bank wants to move all this volume to the new CPF.

(a) Locate the CPF using the simple median model. Show the CPF on the graph. Show your work.

(b) What will be the cost savings for processing branch C work at the CPF rather than at the main bank?

CHALLENGING EXERCISES

8. A company has conducted a comprehensive study of five cities, one of which will be selected as the site for a new facility. Annual operating costs for each city are estimated as follows:

Annual operating costs (in $ millions)

City	Labor	Transportation	Local Taxes	Power	Other
1	1.20	0.10	0.17	0.21	0.16
2	1.10	0.08	0.20	0.29	0.11
3	1.60	0.07	0.25	0.25	0.12
4	0.85	0.12	0.19	0.18	0.16
5	0.75	0.14	0.17	0.23	0.18

For each community, the company compiled subjective ratings of several important factors.

Ratings for factors

City	Receptivity of Community	Availability of Labor	Quality of Transportation	Quality of Life
1	very good	good	fair	acceptable
2	fair	very good	acceptable	fair
3	good	fair	outstanding	good
4	fair	outstanding	acceptable	very good
5	very good	acceptable	fair	outstanding

(a) On the basis of annual operating costs, which site is best?

(b) Devise a method for quantifying the intangible factors, and integrate them with the cost data into the overall evaluation. Which site is best now?

9. Highline Enterprises manufactures its products at plants in Los Angeles and Chicago. Shipments are then sent to customers in Denver, Seattle, and New York. The Los Angeles plant produces a maximum of 50 shipments annually, and the Chicago plant produces a maximum of 70 shipments annually. Costs/shipment from Los Angeles are $1,000 to Denver, $900 to Seattle, and $1,600 to New York. Costs/shipment from Chicago are $900 to Denver; $1,300 to Seattle; and $900 to New York. Next year, demand is expected to be for 60 shipments at Denver, 40 at Seattle, and 80 at New York. Highline will build a new plant at

either Dallas or Knoxville, and the plant will have an annual capacity of 60 shipments. At Dallas, manufacturing costs will average $100,000/shipment; at Knoxville, $80,000. Costs/shipment from Dallas is $600 to Denver; $1,000 to Seattle; and $1,400 to New York. Costs/shipment from Knoxville to Denver is $900; $1,200 to Seattle; and $700 to New York.

(a) Set up this problem in a linear programming framework.
(b) Outline the specific kinds of information you would expect from the linear programming model.
(c) What relevant information for this decision would not be provided by the model?

10. United American Savings and Loan has three processing facilities (Newburg, Central, and Wilmont) for 27 branch locations. A sudden increase in demand for processing has come about due to a new service—a customer draft-on-account, which is similar to a personal checking account in a commercial bank.

United American had closed the Newburg processing facility since the facilities at Wilmont and Central had enough capacity on one shift to handle demand. Now either the Wilmont facility must go to a second shift or the Newburg facility must be reopened. Revenue is expected to average $.20/item processed at each facility.

The Wilmont facility has been operating with fixed costs of $500,000 and variable costs of $.10/item, with an annual first shift capacity of 10 million items. Starting a second shift would increase variable costs for items processed on that shift to either $.12/item or $.14/item with probabilities of .6 and .4, respectively. Second shift annual capacity would be 10 million items.

The Newburg facility can be reopened for fixed costs of either $100,000 or $50,000, with probabilities of .3 and .7, respectively. Unit variable costs are expected to be $.12/item, and capacity is 7 million items annually.

As vice president of operations, you must prepare a recommendation for expanding capacity for an upcoming meeting with the president. In your analysis, prepare a decision tree for the president depicting this situation and a rough graph of costs and revenues for various volumes.

11. Revise the simple median model to reflect differences in transportation cost rates for loads shipped between the new facility and several existing facilities.

12. A company has three existing warehouses to which it will ship furniture from a new factory whose location must be decided. The factory will receive raw materials from its wood supplier and its fabric supplier. The annual number of shipments, shipment costs, and the locations of the suppliers and warehouses are shown below. Where should the factory be located to minimize annual transportation costs?

Existing Facility	Annual Loads to or from Factory	Cost/Load/Mile to or from Factory	Coordinate Location (*x*, *y*) (in miles)
Wood supplier	120	$8	(100, 400)
Fabric supplier	200	6	(800, 700)
Warehouse 1	60	5	(300, 600)
Warehouse 2	40	5	(200, 100)
Warehouse 3	70	5	(600, 200)

UTILIZING QSOM COMPUTER SOFTWARE

13. Reconsider Problem 12. What if building two small factories is an alternative to building one large factory? (Assume each small factory consumes one-half the total inputs and ships one-half the total outputs). What if three new small factories, each dedicated to supplying a warehouse, is an additional alternative? (Assume each small factory consumes inputs in proportion to the factory's share of total company outputs). Prepare your recommendations with supporting data.

KEY TERMS

Break-even analysis 212
Break-even point 213
Factor ratings 219
Job satisfaction 227
Labor turnover 227
Simple median model 221
Subculture 226
Value system 227

SELECTED READINGS

Aly, A. A., and D. W. Litwhiler, Jr., "Police Briefing Stations: A Location Problem," *AIIE Transactions* 11, no. 1 (March 1979), 12–22.

Buffa, E. S., *Meeting the Competitive Challenge.* Homewood, Ill.: Richard D. Irwin, 1984, 65–82.

Cole, J. J., and E. J. Bardi, *The Management of Logistics,* 2nd ed. St. Paul, Minn.: West Publishing, 1980.

Love, R. F., and L. Yerex, "An Application of a Facilities Location Model in the Prestressed Concrete Industry," *Interfaces* 6, no. 4 (August 1976), 45–49.

Schmenner, R. W., "Look Beyond the Obvious in Plant Location," *Harvard Business Review* 57, no. 1, (January–February 1979), 126–32.

Skinner, W., *Manufacturing in the Corporate Strategy.* New York: John Wiley, 1978.

Swamidass, P.M., "A Comparison of the Plant Location Strategies of Foreign and Domestic Manufacturers in the U.S.," *Journal of International Business Studies* 21, no. 2 (2nd Qtr. 1990), 301–317.

LINEAR PROGRAMMING: THE TRANSPORTATION METHOD

Transportation method
A special linear programming formulation for determining how sources should ship resources to destinations so that total shipping costs are minimized.

Homogeneous resources
Resources for which units supplied by one source are qualitatively equivalent to units supplied by any other source.

The *transportation* (or distribution) *method* is a special form of the general linear programming problem and must meet the general linear programming characteristics (see the supplement to Chapter 5). Additionally, the transportation method is applicable to problems with the following characteristics.

1. *Sources.* A finite number of sources can allocate resources in specifiable quantities.
2. *Destinations.* A finite number of destinations need these resources in specifiable quantities.
3. *Homogeneous units.* The resources are homogeneous—that is, one unit of resource supplied by a particular source is qualitatively equivalent to one unit supplied by any other source.
4. *Costs.* Each cost of allocating one unit of resource from a source to a destination is known and constant.

Although problems meeting these conditions can be formulated and solved by the simplex method, the transportation method is less cumbersome. The generalized transportation format consists of a source-destination matrix with m distinct sources (rows), each of which has A_i units of resource available, and n distinct destinations (columns), each in need of N_j units of resource. The cost of allocating one unit of resource from source i to destination j is C_{ij}. The problem is to allocate resources from sources to destinations so that the total cost of allocations for the system is minimized. The restrictions are:

1. Resource needs of each destination must be met.
2. No source can allocate more resource units than it has available, nor a negative number of resource units.

The objective, then, is to minimize total cost:

$$TC = \sum_{i=1}^{m} C_{i1}X_{i1} + \sum_{i=1}^{m} C_{i2}X_{i2} + \ldots + \sum_{i=1}^{m} C_{in}X_{in}$$

$$= \sum_{j=1}^{n} \sum_{i=1}^{m} C_{ij}X_{ij}$$

Where X_{ij} is the number of resource units allocated from i to j, subject to the restrictions (constraints) noted above.

THE TRANSPORTATION METHOD

We will use the Alpha Processing Company example (see page 224) to illustrate the transportation method. Alpha Processing's two raw material sources send shipments as needed to the various plants. The addition of a new raw material source at Columbus, Ohio, is being considered. We focus on this one alternative. Shipment costs, needs, and availabilities are summarized in Figure S6.1.

A five-step procedure is used to find the set of allocations that minimize total shipment costs:

1. State the problem so that the total number of shipments available equals the number of shipments needed.
2. Create an initial feasible solution.
3. Evaluate the solution for improvement.
4. Modify the solution accordingly.
5. Repeat steps 3 and 4 until no further improvement is possible.

Cost/shipment / shipment, allocated

Source \ Plant	P_1	P_2	P_3	Shipments available
S_1	\$200 / 200	\$300 / 100	\$200	300
S_2	\$100	\$100 / 200	\$300 / 200	400
S_3	\$300	\$200	\$100 / 200	200
Shipments needed	200	300	400	900 / 900

FIGURE S6.1 **Transportation matrix for Alpha Processing Company, adding the Columbus raw materials source (S_3), and initial solution**

1. Ensure That Availability Equals Need In Figure S6.1, the number of shipments available at the three sources (900) is equal to the number needed by the plants. Later we show how to adjust the matrix when this equality does not exist.

2. Create an Initial Feasible Solution A *feasible solution* is one in which the needs of all destinations are filled and the capacities of all sources are fully used. Many initial solutions are possible. By convention, we use the northwest corner rule to create an initial solution here. Allocate as many shipments as possible into the northwest cell of the matrix. In this example, 200 units can be allocated from S_1 to P_1, completely filling needs for P_1. Thereafter, allocations are made to adjacent cells to the east or south of the northwest corner. As shown in Figure S6.1, the next allocation is 100 shipments from S_1 to P_2. Now the shipping capacity of S_1 has been fully utilized. The third allocation is 200 shipments from S_2 to P_2. Next, 200 shipments are allocated from S_2 to P_3. Finally, 200 shipments are allocated from S_3 to P_3. These shipments are recorded beneath the diagonals in the appropriate cells. Overall, allocations of shipments are made from the northwest to southeast, without regard to costs. The resulting initial solution is feasible because all restrictions in the problem have been met. Using this solution, the annual cost is:

$$TC = (\$200)(200) + (\$300)(100) + (\$100)(200) + (\$300)(200) + (\$100)(200)$$
$$= \$170,000$$

3. Evaluate the Existing Solution Would a different solution yield lower total costs? This question can be answered by using the *stepping stone procedure.*

Stepping stone procedure An algorithm of the transportation method of linear programming that uses a set of occupied cells to evaluate the effect on costs if an empty cell was to become occupied.

First, the number of "used cells" in the solution must be considered. These are the cells in which shipping allocations occur. In general, the stepping stone procedure requires that there be $(m + n - 1)$ used cells, where m is the number of restrictions on sources and n is the number of restrictions on destinations. In Figure S6.1, there is one restriction for each source and one restriction for each destination, a total of six restrictions. Since there are five used cells, the $(m + n - 1)$ requirement is met, and we can proceed with the stepping stone procedure. [Later we consider what to do if the number of used cells is not equal to $(m + n - 1)$.]

We change the unused cells, one at a time, to see how the costs change. If several of these cells offer cost improvements, the most attractive one is selected, and the existing solution is modified accordingly. If none of these cells offers a cost improvement, the existing solution is optimal and the analysis ends.

We begin by changing the unused cell S_2 to P_1. If one shipment is allocated to this cell, the shipments in cell S_1 to P_1 must be reduced to 199. Otherwise, the P_1 restriction (200 shipments) would be violated. Next, shipments from S_1 to P_2 must be increased from 100 to 101 so that the S_1 restriction is met. Finally, the shipments from S_2 to P_2 must be reduced from 200 to 199. By making these changes, we have fully satisfied all restrictions. It is important to notice what has happened from a systems viewpoint. By making a change in allocations to *one* cell (S_2 to P_1), we need to make subsequent adjustments in *other* cells in the network so that the overall system adheres to the constraints. The cells requiring adjustment are shown in part (a) of Figure S6.2. The arrows indicate the *path of adjustment* for the four cells. Notice the pattern of alternating pluses and minuses from cell to cell throughout the path. A minus indicates that shipments are reduced in that cell, a plus that shipments are increased, to balance the network. This path is not arbitrarily selected; it is *unique.*

When the number of used cells in the solution equals $(m + n - 1)$, there is a unique adjustment path for each unused cell and several used cells. The used cells in the path are called the *stepping stones.*

How does one find the unused cell's unique stepping stone path? Beginning in the unused cell, move onto any used cell at right angles to the unused cell (no diagonal moves). Call it the used cell stepping stone 1, SS_1. Then move at right angles to the last

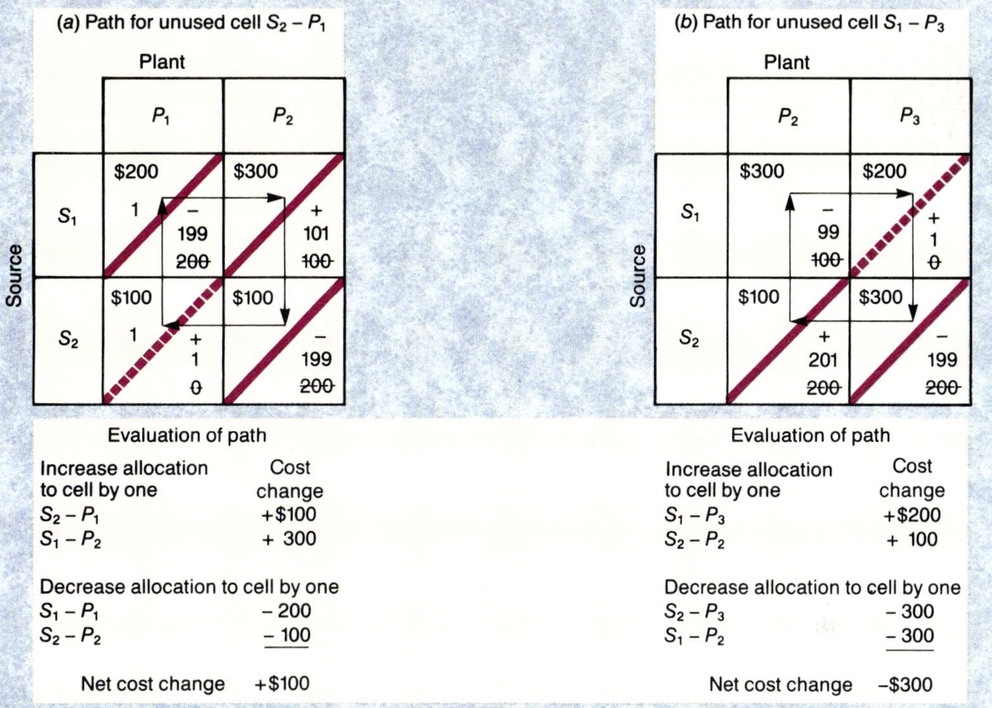

FIGURE S6.2 **Evaluating unused cells**

move, from SS_1 onto SS_2. From SS_2 move at right angles onto SS_3, and continue this process until a right angle move leads back to the unused cell from which the movements began. Be aware that each stepping stone must be a used cell. This series of rotations is clearly portrayed as a square path for cell $S_2 - P_1$.

If these changes are made, how will costs be affected? Relative to the initial solution, costs will be affected as follows: Costs will increase by $100, since a new shipment is allocated to cell $S_2 - P_1$; costs in cell $S_1 - P_1$ will decrease by $200, since one less shipment is allocated here; an additional shipment is allocated to cell $S_1 - P_2$, thus raising costs by $300; and costs for cell $S_2 - P_2$ will decrease by $100. Adding together all the increases and decreases, the overall net effect is a cost increase of $100. This path adjustment, summarized in part (a) of Figure S6.2, does not improve the solution. We now create a path adjustment beginning with a different unused cell.

The stepping stone path for unused cell $S_1 - P_3$ is $(S_1 - P_3) \rightarrow (S_2 - P_3) \rightarrow (S_2 - P_2) \rightarrow (S_1 - P_2)$. The clockwise direction of movement on this path, shown in part (b) of Figure S6.2, is irrelevant; it could just as well have been counterclockwise. This unique path shows that overall costs will be *reduced* by $300 if a shipment is allocated to cell $S_1 - P_3$. Instead of changing the initial solution to obtain this cost savings, we create a path adjustment beginning with each unused cell to see if even greater cost savings are possible.

Stepping stone paths have been created for each of the two remaining unused cells. Parts (c) and (d) show that costs will increase if shipments are allocated to either $S_3 - P_1$ or $S_3 - P_2$.

As you can see, only one of the four unused cells in the initial solution, cell $S_1 - P_3$, offers any cost reduction.

(c) Path for unused cell $S_3 - P_1$

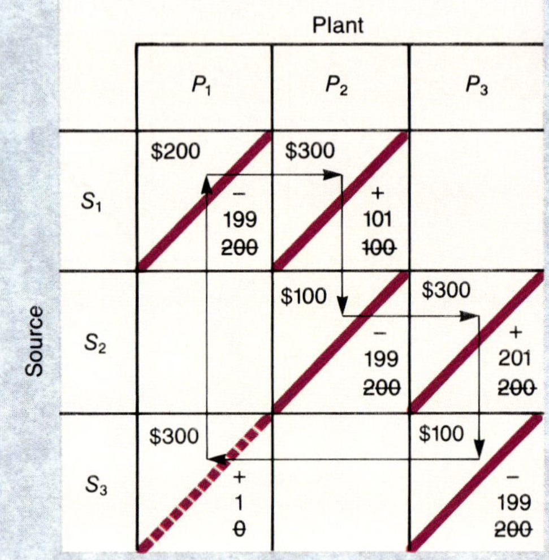

(d) Path for unused cell $S_3 - P_2$

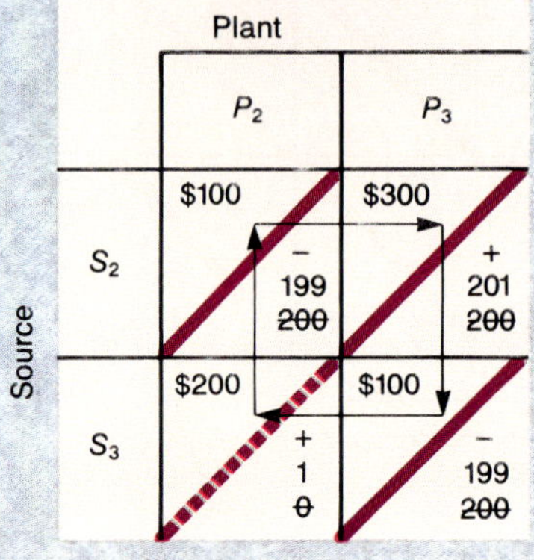

Evaluation of path

Increase allocation to cell by one	Cost change
$S_3 - P_1$	+$300
$S_1 - P_2$	+ 300
$S_2 - P_3$	+ 300
Decrease allocation to cell by one	
$S_1 - P_1$	− 200
$S_2 - P_2$	− 100
$S_3 - P_3$	− 100
Net cost change	+$500

Evaluation of path

Increase allocation to cell by one	Cost change
$S_3 - P_2$	+$200
$S_2 - P_3$	+ 300
Decrease allocation to cell by one	
$S_2 - P_2$	− 100
$S_3 - P_3$	− 100
Net cost change	+$300

FIGURE S6.2 —continued

4. Modify the Existing Solution The initial solution is modified by allocating shipments to cell $S_1 - P_3$. Furthermore, since $300 of cost savings result for each shipment, we allocate as many as possible. Examinating part (b) of Figure S6.2 reveals that no more than 100 shipments can be allocated, since no more than 100 can be removed from cell $S_1 - P_2$. Therefore 100 units are allocated to $S_1 - P_3$, and appropriate adjustments made in cells along the rest of the adjustment path. This new solution results in a cost savings of $300/shipment × 100 shipments = $30,000. The new solution is shown in Figure S6.3, part (a).

5. Reevaluate and Modify The new solution is now treated as an initial solution for which steps 3 and 4 are repeated. Applying the stepping stone procedure, we find that only one cell ($S_2 - P_1$) offers any cost reduction. This desirable change is highlighted in Figure S6.3, part (b). Therefore a second revised solution is created by allocating as many shipments as possible, 100, to $S_2 - P_1$ (see Figure S6.4).

(*a*) First revised solution

Plant

Source	P_1	P_2	P_3	Shipments Available
S_1	$200 / 200	$300	$200 / 100	300
S_2	$100	$100 / 300	$300 / 100	400
S_3	$300	$200	$100 / 200	200
Shipments needed	200	300	400	900 / 900

$TC =$ ($200) (200) + ($200) (100)
+ ($100) (300) + ($300) (100)
+ ($100) (200)
= $140,000

(*b*) Evaluation of unused cells of first revised solution

Plant

Source	P_1	P_2	P_3
S_1		+$300	
S_2	–$200		
S_3	+$200	+$300	

FIGURE S6.3 **Allocation in first revised solution**

Plant

Source	P_1	P_2	P_3	Available
S_1	$200 / 100	$300	$200 / 200	300
S_2	$100 / 100	$100 / 300	$300	400
S_3	$300	$200	$100 / 200	200
Needed	200	300	400	900 / 900

$TC =$ ($200) (100) + ($200) (200) + ($100) (100)
+ ($100) (300) + ($100) (200)
= $120,000

FIGURE S6.4 **Allocation in second revised (optimal) solution**

Evaluation of the unused cells of the second revised solution (see Figure S6.5) shows that no further cost reduction is possible. The optimal solution has been found. If the Columbus, Ohio, raw material source is added to the existing network, the best shipping allocation is 100 shipments from S_1 to P_1, 200 from S_1 to P_3, 100 from S_2 to P_1, 300 from S_2 to P_2, and 200 from S_3 to P_3.

Source \ Plant	P_1	P_2	P_3
S_1		+$100	
S_2			+$200
S_3	+$200	+$100	

FIGURE S6.5 Evaluation of unused cells of second revised solution

SOME ADDITIONAL CONSIDERATIONS

Inequality of Availability and Requirements We said earlier that the transportation method can be applied only when the resources available equal the resources needed. In the Alpha Company example, 900 shipments are needed and 900 are available. If the problem had originally stated that only 800 shipments were needed, an additional fictitious plant would be created and added to the matrix. This new plant P_4 would become a dummy column with a requirement of 100 shipments, creating the necessary equality. A cost of zero would be inserted in each cell of the dummy column to reflect the fact that allocations in these cells are fictitious, having no real cost. The use of a dummy row or column, whichever is needed, is equivalent to the use of slack variables in the simplex method.

Degeneracy A quality of a transportation linear programming problem such that there are too few occupied cells to enable evaluation of the empty cells.

Degeneracy A condition called *degeneracy* exists in a transportation problem when the number of used cells is less than $(m + n - 1)$. Degeneracy can occur at the initial or intermediate stages. When degeneracy exists, a unique stepping stone path cannot be created for an unused cell. A standard procedure for overcoming degeneracy places an arbitrarily small, fictitious allocation, symbolized θ (theta), in one of the unused cells. This cell is then treated as if it were a used cell during the current stage. *Theta* is not, however, a real allocation, and it does not result in any real cost. When θ is needed, it can be added to any unused cell, but time can be saved by adding it to an unused cell that will allow as many other unused cells as possible to be evaluated. *Theta* remains in the matrix until it is subtracted out, or until a real allocation is made to its cell. It then disappears from the problem.

Maximization Problems Sometimes the problem has a maximization rather than minimization objective. The same procedure is used in either case. In a maximization problem, the cell evaluations have a reverse interpretation. When maximizing, a positive cell evaluation indicates that further improvement is possible in that cell. A negative evaluation indicates that the cell offers no improvement.

Alternative Optimal Solutions The final optimal solution may not be unique. Alternative optimal solutions exist whenever any unused cells have zero cell evaluations. A zero evaluation means that although the existing solution mix can be changed, the criterion value will not change.

REVIEW AND DISCUSSION QUESTIONS

1. In general, how do you decide which cost elements to include in or exclude from the cells of a transportation LP problem?
2. What problem characteristics must exist to enable the use of the transportation method of LP?
3. Explain what is happening when you use the stepping stone procedure for cell evaluation.
4. What is meant by the property of *homogeneity?* Why is it important?
5. Identify the similarities and differences of the transportation and simplex methods of LP.
6. What is the significance of having $(m + n - 1)$ used cells in the solution? Will an optimal solution have $(m + n - 1)$ used cells?
7. Describe the northwest corner rule as a method for obtaining an initial feasible solution. Are there other ways of getting an initial feasible solution? Explain.
8. How do you know you have found an optimal solution? That an alternative optimal solution exists?
9. If the total resources available do not equal the total resources needed, what adjustments must be made in formulating the problem?
10. Why are dummy cells assigned a cost of zero? Can nonzero costs be used? Explain.
11. For an optimal solution matrix, give an economic interpretation of the cell evaluations.
12. What is the significance of degeneracy in transportation LP problems?
13. What types of location problems can be aided by the transportation method of LP?

PROBLEMS

REINFORCING FUNDAMENTALS

1. Consider the following problem, in which costs are recorded for allocating one resource unit from each source to each destination:

Source	Cost per resource unit A	B	C	Resource Available (in units)
1	$3	$5	$4	275
2	4	6	3	325
3	5	4	5	300
Resource needed (in units)	350	400	150	

(a) Use the northwest corner rule to obtain an initial feasible solution.
(b) What is the cost of this initial solution?
(c) Find the minimum cost solution.
(d) What is an optimal solution? What is its cost?
(e) Is there an alternative optimal solution?

2. Suppose the data matrix in problem 1 contained profit figures rather than costs. Find the solution maximizing profit.

3. The costs of shipping a unit from each source to each destination, and the resource restrictions, are given below.

Source	Cost per resource unit A	B	C	D	Resource Available (in units)
1	$7	$10	$8	$5	728
2	6	4	9	7	475
3	3	6	5	8	775
Resource needed (in units)	226	675	351	455	

(a) Find an initial feasible solution using the northwest corner rule.
(b) Find an optimal solution.
(c) Interpret your optimal solution.

4. The costs of shipping a unit from each source to each destination, and the resource restrictions, are given below.

Source	Cost per unit A	B	C	Resource Available (in units)
1	$4	$7	$3	250
2	5	6	2	150
3	3	7	5	250
4	6	1	4	200
Resource needed (in units)	350	300	200	

(a) Find an initial feasible solution using the northwest corner rule.
(b) Find an optimal solution.

5. Bill's Gravel Company operates three gravel pits from which loads of gravel are shipped to various construction sites. Pit 1 has a monthly capacity of 100 loads; pit 2, 85 loads; and pit 3, 145 loads. Requests for deliveries next month have come from four construction sites, site A (131 loads), site B (77 loads), site C (49 loads), and site D (104 loads). Bill's profits depend on which pit is used to supply each construction site.

Pit	Profit per load A	B	C	D
1	$24	$30	$27	$32
2	29	19	21	36
3	26	29	20	18

How should Bill allocate deliveries of loads?

CHALLENGING EXERCISES

6. Set up problem 1 in a simplex format.
7. Refer to Problem 9 at the end of Chapter 6. Solve the problem using the transportation method. Which site should be selected, Knoxville or Dallas? Explain.
8. A company has factories at cities V, W, and X. Management will add an additional plant at city Y or Z, with an annual capacity of 500,000 units of output. Capacities of existing plants are 722,000 at V, 510,000 at W, and 808,000 at X. City Y is attractive because labor costs will average only $5.10/unit, compared with $5.40/unit at city Z. Unit labor costs are $5.25 at V, $6.30 at W, and $5.70 at X. The factories annually ship output to wholesalers in cities A (615,000 units), B (961,000 units), and C (914,000 units), with shipping costs as follows:

Cost per unit

City	A	B	C
V	$1.10	$1.60	$1.35
W	1.35	1.40	1.20
X	1.00	1.25	1.45
Y	1.15	1.05	1.10
Z	1.05	0.90	1.20

Which city, Y or Z, is most attractive?

9. Solve problem 1 with QSOM.

10. Solve problem 5, Bill's Gravel Company, with QSOM. Interpret your results. How did QSOM address the issue that sources and destinations were not equal?

11. Solve problem 8 using QSOM, selecting site Y or Z. Yet another site is now a candidate, site T. Site T has 500,000 annual capacity and labor costs of $4.70/unit. The average cost of shipping one unit to wholesaler A is $0.90, B is $0.95, and C is $1.00. Is site T preferred to Y or Z? Explain.

KEY TERMS

Degeneracy 246
Homogeneous resources 240
Stepping stone procedure 242
Transportation method 240

SELECTED READINGS

Anderson, D. R., D. J. Sweeney, and T. A. Williams, *An Introduction to Management Science*, 3rd ed. St. Paul, Minn.: West Publishing, 1982.

Bierman, H., Jr., C. P. Bonini, and W. H. Hausman, *Quantitative Analysis for Business Decisions,* 6th ed. Homewood, Ill.: Richard D. Irwin, 1981.

CHAPTER 7

LAYOUT PLANNING

Planning the layout of machines and assembly lines has always been given priority in our operations.

International competition and technological advancements, though, have led to significant changes in the planning process. We use computers to create productive layout and design alternatives. For example, computer software packages are used to help determine total cost relationships, the materials department's most effective combination of "move and stores," and to reduce the cost of in-process materials.

Participative management and employee involvement have become an integral part of effective layout planning as well.

"Selling" new projects and effective implementation are the results of sound layout practices reflecting the everchanging workplace environment.

The tools for planning layouts discussed in this chapter are basic to the operations manager's job.

William W. Willoughby
Manager, Engineering Support
BOC Powertrain
General Motors Corporation
Flint, Michigan

Successful operations depend upon the physical layout of facilities. Flows of materials, productivity, and human relationships are all affected by the arrangement of the conversion facility. As we shall see, some modeling techniques are useful for layout planning, but behavioral factors must be considered too.

LAYOUT CONCEPTS

To see how layout planning affects operating efficiency and effectiveness, we need to examine how different types of layout designs apply to different situations.

TYPES OF MANUFACTURING AND SERVICE OPERATIONS

Intermittent operations Operations characterized by made-to-order, low volume, labor-intense products; by a large product mix; by general purpose equipment; by interrupted product flow; and by frequent schedule changes.

Continuous operations Operations characterized by standardized, high-volume, capital-intense products made to store in inventory, by small product mix; by special purpose equipment; and by continuous product flow.

The operations function in both manufacturing and service organizations can be divided into two basic types, intermittent and continuous, according to the volume and standardizing of the product or service.

Intermittent Operations Intermittent operations are characterized by made-to-order products, low product volume, general purpose equipment, labor-intense operations, interrupted product flow, frequent schedule changes, and large product mix.

Continuous Operations Continuous operations are characterized by standardized products made to store inventory, high product volume, special purpose equipment, capital-intense operations, continuous product flow, and small product mix.

BASIC LAYOUTS

Layout Physical location or configuration of departments, work centers, and equipment in the conversion process; spatial arrangement of physical resources used to create the product.

Process (-oriented) layout The arrangement of a facility so that work centers or departments are grouped together according to their functional type.

A *layout* is the physical configuration of departments, work stations, and equipment in the conversion process. It is the spatial arrangement of physical resources used to create the product.

We discuss three basic layouts: process-oriented, product-oriented, and fixed-position. These designs are differentiated by the types of work flows they entail; the work flow, in turn, is dictated by the nature of the product. Table 7.1 summarizes the differences among basic layouts.

Services have work flows, just as manufacturers do. Often the work flow is paper, information, or even the customers. We introduce layouts for manufacturers, then by example relate the layouts to services.

The right layout for an organization will improve productivity, the quality of the product or service, and delivery rates.

Process Layout A process-oriented layout is appropriate for intermittent operations when work flow is not consistent for all output. Variable work flow occurs when a variety of products or variations on a single product are produced. In a process layout, the work

TABLE 7.1 Characteristics of layout

Aspect of the Conversion Process	Layout Type: Product-Oriented	Layout Type: Process-Oriented	Layout Type: Fixed-Position
Product	Standardized product, large volume, stable rate of output	Diversified products using common operations, varying volumes, varying rate of output	Made-to-order, low volume
Work flow	Straight line of product; same sequence of operations for each unit	Variable flow; each order (product) may require unique sequence of operations	Little or no flow; equipment and human resources brought to site as needed
Human skills	Able to perform routine, repetitive tasks at fixed pace; highly specialized	Primarily skilled craftsmen; able to perform without close supervision and be moderately adaptable	Great flexibility required; work assignments and locations vary
Support staff	Large; schedule materials and people, monitor and maintain work	Perform tasks of scheduling, materials handling, and production and inventory control	Schedule and coordinate skillfully
Material handling	Predictable, flow, systematized and often automated	Flow variable; handling often duplicated	Flow variable, often low; may require heavy-duty, general purpose handling equipment
Inventory	High turnover of raw material and work-in-process inventories	Low turnover of raw material and work-in-process inventories; high raw materials inventories	Variable inventories and frequent tie-ups because production cycle is long
Space utilization	Efficient utilization, large output per unit space	Small output per unit space; large work-in-process requirements	Small output per unit space if conversion is on site
Capital requirements	Large investment in specialized equipment and processes	General purpose, flexible equipment and processes	General purpose, mobile equipment and processes
Product cost	Relatively high fixed costs; low unit costs for direct labor and materials	Relatively low fixed costs; high unit costs for direct labor, materials, and materials handling	Relatively low fixed costs; high unit labor and materials costs

Work center A facility, set of machines, or workstation that provides a service or transformation needed by a job (order).

centers or departments are grouped together according to their functional type. Distribution warehouses, hospitals, universities, office buildings, and job shops often use a process layout. Figure 7.1 shows a process layout for a medical clinic. Similarly, a manufacturer could have a process layout with *work centers* for welding, heat treating, painting, and so on.

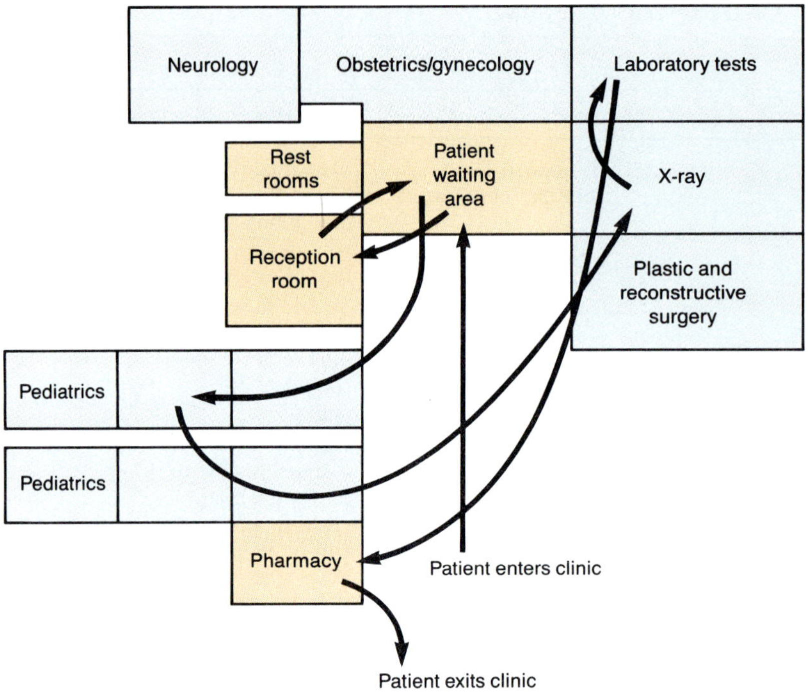

FIGURE 7.1 **Process layout for medical clinic**

Product (-oriented) layout The arrangement of a facility so that work centers or equipment are in a line to afford a specialized sequence of tasks.

Product Layout A product-oriented layout is appropriate for producing one standardized product, usually in large volume. Each unit of output requires the same sequence of operations from beginning to end. In a product layout, work centers and equipment are ideally arranged in a line to afford a specialized sequence of tasks. Each work center performs one highly specialized part of the total product buildup sequence. Automatic car washes, cafeterias, automobile makers, and beverage bottlers use product-oriented layout. Figure 7.2 illustrates a product layout for a manufactured product. Figure 7.3 illustrates a familiar product layout: an automated carwash.

Fixed-position layout The arrangement of a facility so that the product stays in one location; tools, equipment, and workers are brought to it as needed.

Fixed-position Layout A fixed-position layout is appropriate when, because of size, shape, or any other characteristic, it is not feasible to move the product. In a fixed-position layout, the product stays in one location; tools, equipment, and workers

FIGURE 7.2 **Product layout in manufacturing product #1735B**

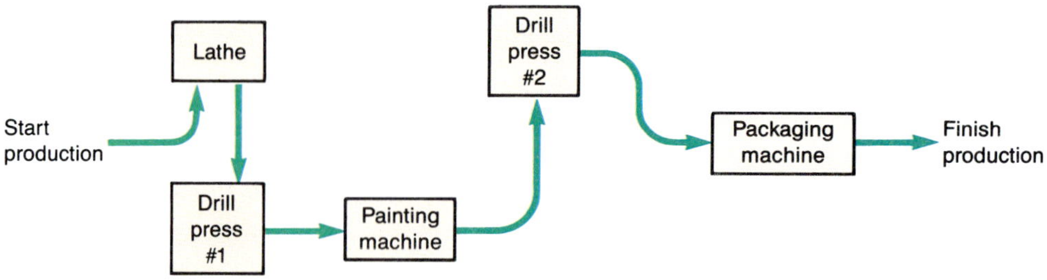

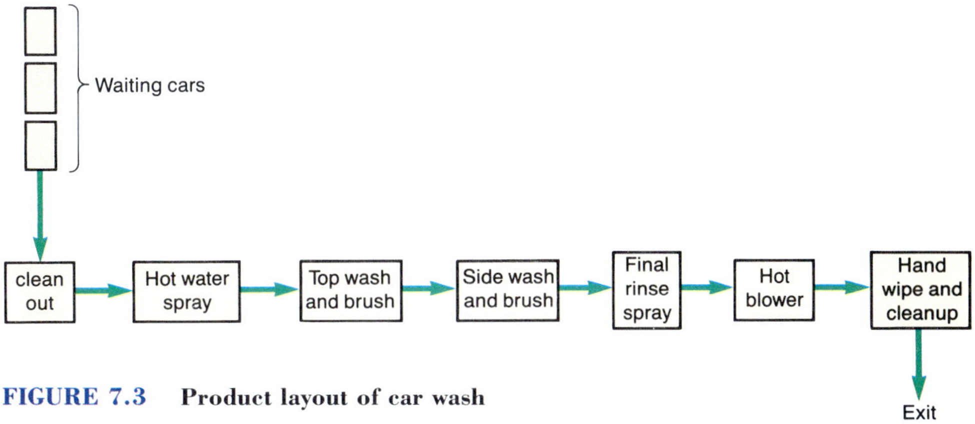

FIGURE 7.3 **Product layout of car wash**

In this fixed-position layout, the tools, equipment, and human skills are brought to the General Motors construction site in Hamtramck, Michigan, where Cadillacs will be made utilizing a product layout.

Source: **Junebug Clark/ Photo Researchers**

are brought to it, as needed. A home plumbing repair business, bringing skills and tools to the home, uses a fixed-position layout. Layouts for building ships, locomotives, and aircraft are often of fixed-position, as are agricultural operations, in which plowing, planting, fertilizing, and harvesting are performed as needed in the field.

Combination Layout Often a combination of layouts must be used. Most typically, a process layout is combined with a product layout.

EXAMPLE

Refrigerator manufacturers use a combination layout. First they use a process-oriented layout to produce various parts and subcomponents. Metal stamping may be one work center, welding another, and various heat-treating processes a third work center. For final assembly of the product, all these functions are brought together in a product-oriented layout.

DEVELOPING THE PROCESS LAYOUT: MODELS AND BEHAVIOR

PROCESS LAYOUT MODELS

Many models are useful in planning the process layout. Mathematical analysis can help managers conceptualize the problem; computer models can provide quick approximations of good layouts; and physical models (templates and scale models, among others) can help managers visualize the layout.

Templates
Two-dimensional cutouts of equipment drawn to scale for planning the facility layout.

Graphic and Schematic Analysis Perhaps the most common layout planning tool are *templates,* two-dimensional cutouts of equipment drawn to scale. These cutouts are moved about by trial and error within a scaled model of the walls and columns of the facility. Templates are used for all three types of layouts—process, product, and fixed. Similarly, computers can visually display layouts, and the "electronic templates" manipulated with a keyboard.

EXAMPLE

In designing and constructing a new manufacturing facility in Kentucky, the first task was to list and measure all the equipment for a boiler room, which was to be attached to the main building. This task had to be done first because only after the room had been sized could the price be negotiated with the general building contractor. Floor dimensions and heights of all boilers, air compressors, water pumps, and similar equipment were obtained from these vendors. Then, templates were cut to scale and arranged in an alternative layout. Upon review, an experienced maintenance foreman pointed out that to "rod-out" (clean) the boilers, a wall would have to be knocked out. To avoid having to knock a wall out, the boilers were turned in another direction on the template. A reasonable layout and size were decided upon, and the boiler room was constructed accordingly.

Load-Distance Model A facility using a process-oriented layout produces diversified products in variable work flows, and handles a relatively large amount of material. A special-order product might need to be moved through as many as 20 different work centers. All this movement costs money. People and equipment must be on hand, and space must be available for storing the product in between work centers. Since transporting adds no value to the product, managers seek layouts that minimize unnecessary flow among work centers.

The most commonly used quantitative, process layout model *minimizes* flow by considering the *number* of loads moved, and the distance between each pair of work centers.

Load-distance model An algorithm for laying out work centers to minimize product flow, based on the number of loads moved and the distance between each pair of work centers.

In this model, we minimize the cost C expressed as:

$$C = \left(\sum_{i=1}^{n} \sum_{j=1}^{n} L_{ij} D_{ij} \right) K \tag{7.1}$$

where n = the numbers of work centers
L_{ij} = the numbers of loads moved between work centers i and j
D_{ij} = the distance between work centers i and j
K = cost to move one load one distance unit

We assume the cost to move one load one distance unit is constant. If this cost varies, the expression for C can be modified by multiplying $L_{ij} D_{ij}$ by K_{ij}, where K_{ij} is the cost to move one load one distance one unit between work centers i and j.

We begin by estimating the number of loads we expect to move between each pair of work centers, say annually. These estimates can be summarized in a flow matrix like that in Table 7.2.[1]

TABLE 7.2 **Flow matrix showing estimated number of loads moved annually among work centers**

Work center	2	3	4	5
1	220	130	400	370
2		0	400	470
3			150	400
4				100

The next step is to determine the distance between each pair of work centers. These distances depend on the locations fixed by the layout. So propose an initial layout assigning space to each work center. Then, using Equation 7.1, calculate the cost of the initial layout. Finally, modify the initial layout to reduce costs. Repeat this process until you can improve no further.

Actually, the cost effectiveness of each possible layout need *not* be fully calculated with Equation 7.1. Although many different layouts are possible, many of them are equivalent, or nearly so, cost-wise, and their costs need not be calculated separately. Consider the situation shown in Figure 7.4. Six work centers could be spacially arranged in these three ways, among others. Geometrically, the three are nearly equivalent. In each design, these pairs of work centers are located as close to one another as possible: 1–2, 2–3, 4–5, 5–6, 1–4, 2–5, 3–6. Therefore, the evaluation criterion needs to consider only the flows between *nonadjacent* departments, 1–3, 1–6, 3–4, 4–6. *This means that the* $L_{ij} D_{ij}$ *computations following the initial evaluation for a layout design can be reduced just to those with nonadjacent flows.* The procedure is directed trial and error, and optimality is not guaranteed.

EXAMPLE

Greenwich Supply Company is a wholesale warehouse distribution facility. It receives into the shipping/receiving docks a variety of kitchen cabinets and appliances as

[1]The flow matrix in Table 7.2 is appropriate when the *direction of flow* between departments is immaterial. In some situations, however, a load from i to j may be more or less costly than a load moving from j to i. In these cases, an expanded flow matrix must be developed to identify the direction of flow. For a discussion of this expanded treatment, see Elwood S. Buffa, *Modern Production/Operations Management*, 6th ed. (New York: John Wiley, 1980).

1	2	3		4	5	6		4	5	3
4	5	6		1	2	3		1	2	6

FIGURE 7.4 Different but equivalent layout configurations

finished goods, and stores them by appliance in separate areas. Customers place orders for one or more kinds of appliances in various quantities. Loads of appliances are retrieved as needed to fill each order, then transported first to a packing area and then back to the shipping area. We will evaluate the warehouse layout to see if it can be modified to reduce materials handling costs.

The existing layout is diagrammed in Figure 7.5. Area 1 is the shipping/receiving dock, and area 9 is the packing area. The other 14 areas are the storage areas for the different types of appliances and cabinets.

	2	3	4	5	6
1 Shipping and receiving	7	8	9 Packing area	10	11
	12	13	14	15	16

FIGURE 7.5 Existing layout of Greenwich Supply Company's product storage areas (aisles omitted)

Materials handling flows occur between the packing area and the other 15 sections. Loads are hauled to area 1 from only one source, section 9. All other loads flow from the remaining sections *into* section 9. To simplify, we consider only loads moved to the packing area, area 9, from all areas except the shipping/receiving area, area 1; and loads moved to area 1 from area 9. The location of the shipping/receiving dock is fixed; it cannot be relocated. All other areas are eligible for relocation.

Records for the last two years reveal that the average annual loads from each area to area 9 are: 2–500, 3–80, 4–320, 5–140, 6–150, 7–160, and 8–330, 10–250, 11–100, 12–140, 13–240, 14–100, 15–240, and 16–500. From 9 to area 1 average annual loads are 2,500. We now use Equation 7.1 to calculate the cost of the existing layout. Table 7.3 shows the calculations for both adjacent and nonadjacent areas, a total cost of \$12,300 (K). Since K is a constant, we can compare the *load-distance rating,* that is, the factor 12,300, against another layout's load-distance rating and choose the layout on the basis of load-distance rating rather than actual cost.

To improve the layout, we try to move areas with heavy load flows between them closer together. The packing area, for example, can be moved closer to the shipping dock. We could also relocate area 16 closer to the packing area, and area 14 to a more

TABLE 7.3 **Load-distance model: calculation of layout cost**

Adjacent Work Centers			
Work Center Pair (i, j)	Distance D_{ij} Between Work Centers i and j	Loads L_{ij} Between Work Centers i and j	Load-distance Rating $(L_{ij}D_{ij})$
3,9	1	80	(80) (1) = 80
4,9	1	320	(320) (1) = 320
5,9	1	140	(140) (1) = 140
8,9	1	330	(330) (1) = 330
10,9	1	250	(250) (1) = 250
13,9	1	240	(240) (1) = 240
14,9	1	100	(100) (1) = 100
15,9	1	240	(240) (1) = 240

$$C = \left(\sum_{i=1}^{n} \sum_{j=1}^{n} L_{ij} D_{ij} \right) K$$

$$= \$1{,}700\ (K)$$

Nonadjacent Work Centers			
Work Center Pair (i, j)	Distance D_{ij} Between Work Centers i and j	Loads L_{ij} Between Work Centers i and j	Load-distance Rating $L_{ij}D_{ij}$
2,9	2	500	(500) (2) = 1,000
6,9	2	150	(150) (2) = 300
7,9	2	160	(160) (2) = 320
11,9	2	100	(100) (2) = 200
12,9	2	140	(140) (2) = 280
16,9	2	500	(500) (2) = 1,000
9,1	3	2,500	(2,500) (3) = 7,500

$$C = \left(\sum_{i=1}^{n} \sum_{j=1}^{n} L_{ij} D_{ij} \right) K \text{ for}$$

$$= \$10{,}600(K)$$

Total cost for all work centers = $1,700 + 10,600 = $12,300(*K*)

remote space. A revised layout incorporating these and other changes is shown in Figure 7.6. Overall, the layout has reduced load-distance by 20 percent, as shown in Table 7.4.

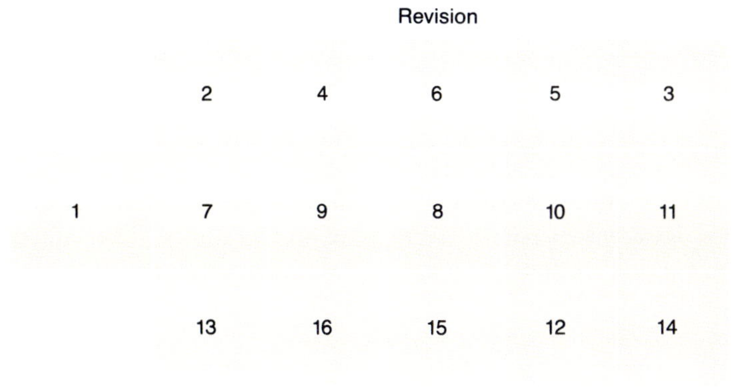

FIGURE 7.6 **A revised layout with load/distance ratings computed**

TABLE 7.4 Revised layout cost

Adjacent Work Centers		Nonadjacent Work Centers	
Work Center Pair	Load-Distance Rating	Work Center Pair	Load-Distance Rating
2,9	500	9,1	5,000
4,9	320	3,9	240
6,9	150	5,9	280
7,9	160	10,9	500
8,9	330	11,9	300
13,9	240	12,9	280
15,9	240	14,9	300
16,9	500		
	Subtotal 2,440		Subtotal 6,900

Total load-distance rating = 2,440 (K) + 6,900 (K)
= 9,340 (K)
Percent improvement = 20.4%

Some Limitations At best, the load-distance model is a starting point, yielding a layout that can be modified to account for additional complexities. Often the sizes or shapes of all work centers are not uniform. Moreover, we often must consider space for electrical wiring, and plumbing, and complications such as limited-access work centers and a variety of materials handling method. One layout might need to account for noisy work not being adjacent to audio testing. Another might need to account for dusty, dirty work not being adjacent to expensive, dirt-sensitive instruments. Finally, the number of loads moved between work centers might be very large. For these reasons, layout models are often used.

Computer Models Many computer-based layout models have been developed. These models fall under the general category of computer-aided-design (CAD). We will briefly discuss only one of them, CRAFT, the Computerized Relative Allocation of Facilities Technique.[2] Using criteria similar to the load-distance model, CRAFT finds a *satisfactory* layout by evaluating thousands of alternative layouts extremely quickly.

CRAFT can handle facilities comprising up to 40 work centers of different shapes and sizes, and can account for mobile and immobile work centers. These features take into account realistic restrictions imposed by the construction of buildings. CRAFT also considers differences in types and costs of materials handling methods among work centers. To use CRAFT, the analyst must provide an initial layout, a matrix identifying the number of loads moved among work centers, and a matrix identifying the cost of transporting loads among work centers.

After calculating the effectiveness of the initial layout, CRAFT exchanges the locations of pairs or triplets of work centers. The effectiveness of each exchange is evaluated, the best of these exchanges adopted, and the entire process repeated. When

[2]Elwood S. Buffa, Gordon C. Armour, and Thomas Vollmann, "Allocating Facilities with CRAFT," *Harvard Business Review* 42, no. 2 (March–April 1964), 136–58; and Philip E. Hicks and Troy E. Cowan, "CRAFT-M for Layout Rearrangement," *Industrial Engineering* (May 1976), 30–35; for three-dimensional CRAFT see R. Johnson, "Spacecraft for Multi-floor Layout Planning," *Management Science* 28, no. 4 (April 1982).

total materials handling costs can be reduced no further or when a specified number of repetitions has been reached, the best available solution is printed out as a layout.

An updated version of CRAFT allows for multiple types of spaces to be considered,[3] so that architectural elements can be accounted for in the layout. In an office setting, for example, representations of individual work centers, circulation areas, and walls and doorways are allowed. CRAFT affords the operations manager additional detail in layout planning, and illustrates the continued use of computers and modeling to improve operations.

BEHAVIORAL ASPECTS OF PROCESS LAYOUT

Operations managers must consider individual and group behavior when planning a process-oriented layout, underscoring the importance of his or her problem-solving skills. Layout can affect both employee relationships and customer satisfaction.

The layout designer's role seems to have changed with the use of computers. Do computers provide superior layouts? Some studies suggest they may not. A study by Scriabin and Vergin found that people developed more economical layouts than did three of the more widely publicized computer models.[4] This was true for both large and small layout problems. Although modern technologists assume that computer models are superior, the experimental results do not support this assumption. The researchers offer the following possible explanation of their findings:

> It may well be that in problems of larger size the ability of man to recognize and visualize complex patterns gives him an edge over the essentially mechanical procedures followed by the computer programs. Such as explanation is supported by experience in other types of problem solving.[5]

Perhaps some combination of human and computer skills may lead to even better results, as illustrated by Operations Management Highlight 7.1.

Individual and Interpersonal Behavior of Employees We know that our environment afects how we feel about ourselves and react toward others. The layout can either help or hinder employees' relationships with one another, and either raise or lower employee satisfaction, motivation, and performance.[6] Especially in offices, layout facilitates or impedes professional interaction among employees.

A process layout groups workers according to skills. Each group establishes norms and affiliations that affect the productivity of its members. Often these norms are compatible with management standards, but not always. Redesigning a layout may disrupt group relationships. Employees may react badly, and absenteeism, turnover, and labor relations problems may all increase. Realignment of loyalties may lead to conflicts among groups. As a result, *managers must be particularly skilled at intergroup coordination.*

---

[3]F. Robert Jacobs, "A Layout Planning System with Multiple Criteria and a Variable Domain Representation," *Management Science* 33, no. 8 (August 1987), 1020–34.

[4]Michael Scriabin and Roger C. Vergin, "Comparison of Computer Algorithms and Visual Based Methods for Plant Layout," *Management Science* 22, no. 2 (October 1975), 172–81. For different results and conclusions, see Thomas W. Trybus and Lewis D. Hopkins, "Human vs. Computer Algorithms for the Plant Layout Problem," *Management Science* 26, no. 6 (June 1980), 570–74.

[5]Scriabin and Vergin, "Comparison of Computer Algorithms," 179.

[6]Randall S. Schuler, Larry P. Ritzman, and Vicki Davis, "Merging Prescriptive and Behavioral Approaches for Office Layout," *Journal of Operations Management* 1, no. 3 (February 1981), 131–42.

OPERATIONS MANAGEMENT HIGHLIGHT 7.1

Source: Four by Five

First Chicago, Quaker Oats, and Xerox Use Computers for Office Layout

Do offices have product, process, and fixed-position layouts? Do office-space planners use graphic, schematic, and load-distance models? The answer is yes, and the characteristics of office-layout planning make it easier than factory-layout planning for the beginning operations student to understand.

Office-space planners have an impressive assortment of computer-aided design (CAD) software and hardware at their disposal, with such peripherals as optic scanners and color electrostatic plotters.

At First Chicago Corporation, a major U.S. bank, the Vice President of Properties Management and his staff are responsible for 4 million square feet of space. That's equivalent to about 10,300 fifteen by twenty ft living rooms! The task is enormous. Over 60,000 work orders, costing $50 million, for remodeling and construction are placed annually. An extensive computer system monitors this activity, maintaining inventories, designing interior space, analyzing space needs, tracking equipment maintenance schedules—even keeping track of the extensive wiring for data and telecommunications systems, the nerve center of world-class money center banks today.

First Chicago's neighbor in downtown Chicago, the Quaker Oats Company used a CAD system to design its new home office. Winning the 1988 Electronic Office Design Competition, the layout featured sunny, flexible spaces. Good planning and construction performance carried the project to competion on schedule and within budget.

To plan its office space, Xerox-Canada chose to use a firm specializing in office design for its offices in Edmonton, Alberta. Xerox specified that all work centers be at right angles for maximum efficiency, that window glare be eliminated and that the environment suggest to customers a soft-sell approach. A great deal of attention was given to detail, comfort, and aesthetics in this office design.

Designing an office goes far beyond allocating space and selecting furniture. Noise control, aesthetics, information flow, and networked computer workstations have created complex challenges for today's office-space planner.

Sources: Patricia M. Fernberg, "Xerox Canada, Inc.: Bringing Quality and Service to Light," *Modern Office Technology* 33, no. 4 (April 1990), 88–92; Dave Solaz, "Space Planning as a Tool for the Modern Facility Manager," *Office* 110, no. 6 (December 1989), 46, 105–106; Lorel McMillan, "Fast Growth Keeps First Chicago Hopping," *Facilities Design and Management* 18, no. 5 (May 1989), 70–72; and Patricia M. Fernberg, "Focus on Facilities: The Quaker Oats Company," *Modern Office Technology* 33, no. 12 (December 1988), pp. 88–92.

Customer Behavior For some organizations, customer relations present special problems, especially when the customer is actually in the facility and takes part in the conversion process. For medical, dental, and legal facilities, welfare agencies, supermarkets, and banks, individual customers have individual needs, and they may be "processed" through different work stations accordingly. The layout can affect not only the quality and speed of service, but customer satisfaction as well. The layout of a bank, for example, must afford the walk-in customer convenience in withdrawals, deposits, and money orders. At the same time, areas for loan applications must be both quickly accessible and private. Data processing, maintenance, and administrative areas can be more remote. Overall, the layout must provide a balance between easy, quick service, customer convenience, and satisfaction on the one hand, and efficient flow of materials and information among employees on the other.

Measuring Subjective Criteria Sometimes subjective, rather than quantitative, criteria dominate. Quantitative methods can still be applied, though. For example, planners might use an arbitrary scale, say from 1 to 10, to rate the importance of having two work centers close together. Then these ratings could be used in Equation 7.1 as the value of L_{ij}, instead of the load measure. This procedure provides a quantitative way of accounting for subjective priorities, including behavioral objectives, in layout planning.

DEVELOPING THE PRODUCT LAYOUT: ASSEMBLY LINE MODELS AND BEHAVIOR

Organizations that produce large volumes of a single product benefit from a product-oriented (assembly line) layout. Early in the twentieth century, Henry Ford revolutionized an industry and the U.S. economy by mass-producing automobiles. Since each car was identical, the entire production sequence could be predetermined in careful detail. Each task was minutely studied by engineers and managers to find ways to make the sequence quicker and cheaper. Better work methods, specialized equipment and tools, and extensive employee training were used to increase speed. This, then, was the basic concept of the Ford assembly line. The product layout is as applicable today as it was in 1913. Later, we examine some contemporary behavioral considerations that were only of minor concern at the beginning of the century.

PRODUCT LAYOUT MODELS

Graphic and Schematic Analysis Assembly line layouts are most often designed by industrial engineers. Historically, they have used manual trial-and-error techniques and templates, drawings, and graphical procedures. For large facilities with many tasks and work centers, no mathematical procedures ensure finding the best possible design. Consequently, the quality of the design depends upon the experience and judgment of qualified designers.

Product layouts are ideally arranged in a U-shape flow line for producing these standardized food products in large volume.

Source: John Zoiner

1. Line employee at work; 2. Aisle; 3. U-shaped conveyors; 4. Food-work in process; 5. Food drying oven.

Heuristic A procedure in which a set of rules is systematically applied; an algorithm.

Modeling the Product Layout Mathematical and computer-based *heuristic* models can identify and evaluate alternative layouts far more rapidly than manual or intuitive methods. These models have been developed as much by observation and experimentation as by theory, and they are often specially adapted for a specific layout problem.

Defining the Layout Problem The fundamental problem of layout planning for assembly lines is to determine the minimum number of stations (workers) and assign tasks to each station so that a desired level of output is achieved.

Notice several important implications in this statement. First, the design focuses on achieving a desired level of productive capability (output capacity). Second, if tasks are to be assigned to stations, the *sequence* of tasks must be considered. Which tasks must be done first, and which ones may follow? Finally, our concern is with attaining desired output *efficiently,* without using unnecessary input resources.

Capacity, Sequencing, and Efficiency Let's illustrate these ideas with an example.

EXAMPLE

A manufacturer is developing plans for a facility to make aluminum storm windows. The desired minimum daily output capacity is 320 windows. Figure 7.7 and Table 7.5 show the tentative assembly line layout. The operations manager wants to know if this is a good design and if better designs are possible.

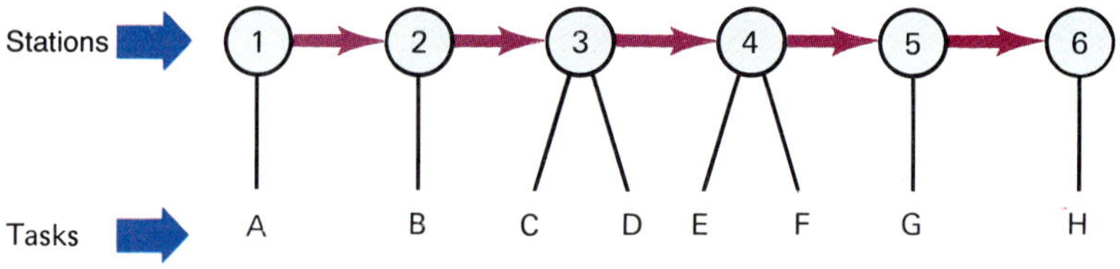

FIGURE 7.7 Diagram for storm window assembly line

This is a good design if the sequence and assignments meet the following criteria:

1. They produce the desired output capacity.
2. They are feasible.
3. They are efficient.

1. Is Capacity Adequate? The number of units this layout allows the company to produce each day depends on the station whose tasks take the longest time to perform. From Table 7.5 we know that the tasks assigned to station 1 require 70 seconds, and to

TABLE 7.5 Initial assembly line layout for aluminum storm windows

Work Station	Preceding Work Station	Task Assigned	Task's Required Predecessor	Task Time/Unit (in seconds)
1	—	A: Assemble frame	none	70
2	1	B: Install rubber molding	A	80
3	2	C: Insert frame screws	A	40
		D: Install frame latch	A	20
4	3	E: Install frame handle	A	40
		F: Install glass pane	B, C	30
5	4	G: Cover frame screws	C	50
6	5	H: Pack window unit	D, E, F, G	50
			Total	380

station 2, 80 seconds. Station 3 comprises two tasks: inserting frame screws (C) and installing the frame latch (D). Thus station 3 tasks require 60 (40 + 20) seconds. Tasks at stations 4, 5, and 6 require 70, 50, and 50 seconds, respectively. The longest time, then, is needed at station 2, 80 seconds. Since every unit passes through all stations, and each must spend 80 seconds at station 2, station 2 is the *bottleneck operation,* the station that restricts the rate of flow off the line. A finished window will flow off the end of the line every 80 seconds, no less, with this layout. This time is called the *cycle time* of the line.

Bottleneck operation The station on an assembly line that requires the longest task time.

With a cycle time of 80 seconds, how many windows are produced daily? If the operation runs for one 8-hour shift each day, the available productive time each day is 28,800 seconds (8 hours) × (3,600 seconds/hour). Therefore maximum daily output can be as follows:

Cycle time Time elapsing between completed units coming off an assembly line.

$$\text{Maximum daily output} = \frac{\text{available time}}{\text{cycle time/unit}} = \frac{28{,}800 \text{ seconds}}{80 \text{ seconds/unit}} = 360 \text{ units}$$

Since this assembly line can generate more than the required 320 units daily, capacity is adequate.

An alternative method for determining whether capacity is adequate calculates the *maximum allowable cycle time* given a desired capacity (320 units/day).

Maximum allowable cycle time Maximum time allowed to elapse between completed units coming off an assembly line, if a given capacity is to be achieved.

$$\begin{array}{c}\text{Maximum allowable cycle time}\\ \text{to produce desired daily output}\end{array} = \frac{\text{time available}}{\text{desired number of units}} = \frac{28{,}800 \text{ seconds}}{320 \text{ units}} = 90 \text{ seconds/unit}$$

This calculation shows that a layout whose cycle time is 90 seconds or less will yield the desired capacity. A layout whose cycle time is greater than 90 seconds will not yield adequate capacity.

Operations Management Highlight 7.2 describes a variety of assembly line balancing approaches.

2. Is the Sequence of Tasks Feasible? For now, we will assume that the proposed sequence of tasks is feasible. We will return to this question soon.

OPERATIONS MANAGEMENT HIGHLIGHT 7.2

Source: Derek Berwin/The Image Bank

North American Companies Balance the Line in a Variety of Ways

To design a product layout and balance the line, process engineers and managers often go beyond traditional analysis. Special purpose conveyors, automatic transfer equipment, and specially designed flexible manufacturing subsystems are becoming more prevalent in manufacturing, affording flexibility and making balancing the line easier. We explore contemporary line balancing more fully by examining flexible manufacturing in Chapter 4 and Japanese manufacturing practices in Chapter 15—such as Japanese U-shaped lines and just-in-time (JIT) manufacturing.

Diamond-Star Motors, a Normal, Illinois, automobile manufacturing facility, opened in 1988 to produce the Eclipse, Laser, and Talon models. Diamond-Star combines the best of Japanese and U.S. technologies. The facility has achieved balanced assembly lines through traditional analysis combined with a highly automated materials handling system and JIT scheduling. The major elements of this system are a car-on-track conveyor, automatic guided vehicles, an automated storage and retrieval system, robots, and conveyors—all balanced and then scheduled according to JIT. Modern analysis and equipment are but a part of making this 2 million square foot facility competitive worldwide: management has also adopted the Japanese concepts of Hito No Wa (harmony and teamwork among all people) and Kaizen (constant improvement).

Sun Micro-systems has expanded production facilities by establishing a plant in Milpitas, California. This facility balances lines with a more modular approach using a torque conveyor to drive the materials handling system. Materials and components move by this conveyor system, yet the line varies along the way from a job shop to a small, balanced assembly operation. Since installation, the productivity of the two main production lines has increased 164 percent and 345 percent, respectively.

A number of corporations have divided production into plants within a plant, including the Copeland Corporation of Sidney, Ohio, and Westinghouse Electric in Asheville, North Carolina. Copeland incorporated the concepts of Harvard professor Wickham Skinner in dividing the Sidney facility into two plants according to two distinct product lines. Productivity and quality increased for each product line. Interestingly, a plaque on the wall dividing the plant acknowledges the "Skinner Wall" and the date it was established.

At Asheville, Westinghouse has five separate assembly lines balanced by one common-feeder miniplant and one master storeroom. Plants within a plant seem to work especially well for large older facilities that tend to lose their identity (focus) over time. Most companies prefer more narrowly focused facilities with clear product or process layouts, making the assembly balancing problem less complex.

Sources: Karen A. Auguston, "East Joins West at Highly Automated Car Assembly Plant," *Modern Materials Handling* 44, no. 9 (September 1989), 68–71; Vinood Kapoor, "Mini-Plants: Injecting Competitive Strategies," *Automation* 35, no. 4 (April 1988), 34–37; and Kathleen M. Holmgren, "Workstation Producer's New Plant Provides Manufacturing Flexibility," *Industrial Engineering* (March 1988), 32–37.

3. Is the Line Efficient? The proposed layout has six stations, each manned by one employee. All six workers are paid for 8 hours daily. How much of our employees' time is spent productively, and how much idly? It depends on the pace of the line that management sets. The pace can be set anywhere between the 80-second cycle time and 90-second maximum allowable cycle time. In Table 7.6, we have calculated the efficiency of labor for cycle times of 90 and 80 seconds.

As you can see, idleness is higher for the 90-second cycle, 29.6% of the employees' total time, than for the 80-second cycle, 20.8%. Idle time amounts to 10 labor hours daily, for the 80-second cycle. If the hourly wage is $10, each day $100 is paid for unnecessary idleness. These excessive costs would eventually have to be passed on to the customer.

Line balancing problem Assigning tasks among workers at assembly line stations so that performance times are made as equal as possible.

Balancing the Line How can the cost of idleness be reduced? Perhaps the eight tasks (A to H in Table 7.5) can be reassigned so that more available employee time is used. Notice that if every station used up an equal amount of task time, no time would be idle time. The problem of equalizing stations in this way is called the *line balancing problem,* and solving it takes six steps:

1. Define tasks.
2. Identify precedence requirements.
3. Calculate the minimum number of work stations required to produce desired output.
4. Apply an assignment heuristic to assign tasks to each station.
5. Evaluate effectiveness and efficiency.
6. Seek further improvement.

Task The smallest grouping of work that can be assigned to a workstation.

For the example of the aluminum storm window facility, we have already taken the first step, defining tasks, shown in Table 7.5.

The second step reminds us that tasks must be done in a specific sequence. Certainly the window units, for example, cannot be packed until they are completely assembled. These sequence requirements are listed in Table 7.5 under the heading *Task's Required Predecessor.*

TABLE 7.6 Calculation of labor utilization efficiency for proposed 80- and 90-second lines

Station	1	2	3	4	5	6	Total Time/Cycle	Utilization of Employees (efficiency)
			Efficiency for 90-second cycle time (seconds)					
Employee time available (cycle time in seconds/unit)	90	90	90	90	90	90	540	
Productive time (task time) expended each cycle	70	80	60	70	50	50	380	380 ÷ 540 × 100 = 70.4%
Idle time each cycle	20	10	30	20	40	40	160	160 ÷ 540 × 100 = 29.6
			Efficiency for 80-second cycle time (seconds)					
Employee time available (cycle time in seconds/unit)	80	80	80	80	80	80	480	
Productive time (task time) expended each cycle	70	80	60	70	50	50	380	380 ÷ 480 × 100 = 79.2
Idle time each cycle	10	0	20	10	30	30	100	100 ÷ 480 × 100 = 20.8

Predecessor task A task that must be performed before performing another (successor) task.

Once the desired output is specified, we can calculate the *theoretical minimum number of stations required*, the third step in our solution. We do so by contrasting the time required to produce one unit with the time we can allow, given the daily output requirements. We have already calculated the time required, as the sum of the task times in Table 7.5: 380 seconds. And we have calculated the time allowable, as the maximum allowable cycle time: 90 seconds. Since just 90 seconds are allowed to produce one unit, 4.22 stations must operate simultaneously, each contributing 90 seconds, so that the required 380 seconds are made available, as required: (90) (4.22) = 380, or 4.22 = 380 ÷ 90.

$$\begin{aligned}\text{Theoretical minimum number of stations to produce 1 unit} &= \frac{\text{Time required/unit}}{\text{Time allowed/unit}} \\ &= \frac{380 \text{ seconds/unit}}{90 \text{ seconds/unit}} \\ &= 4.22 \text{ stations}\end{aligned} \quad (7.2)$$

Since only whole stations are possible, at least five stations are needed. The actual layout may use more than the minimum number of stations, depending on the precedence requirements. The initial layout in Table 7.5 uses six stations.

The fourth step assigns tasks to each station. The designer must assign eight tasks to five or more stations. Several assignment combinations are possible. For larger problems with thousands of tasks and hundreds of stations, we often use heuristics. We will apply a longest-operation-time heuristic to find a balance for the 90-second cycle time.

Longest-operation-time (LOT) rule A line-balancing heuristic that gives top assignment priority to the task that has the longest operation time.

The steps in the *longest-operation-time (LOT) rule* are:

LOT 1. Assign first the task that takes the most time to the first station. Maintain precedence requirements.

LOT 2. After assigning a task, determine how much time the station has left to contribute (time–task times).

LOT 3. If the station can contribute more time, assign it a task requiring as much time as possible. Maintain precedence relationships. Otherwise, return to LOT 1. Continue until all tasks have been assigned to stations.

To apply the rule, we first array the tasks in descending order of time. Tasks with their times in parentheses are: B (80), A (70), G (50), H (50), C (40), E (40), F (30), and D (20).

Following LOT 1 we try to assign B to station 1, since B has the longest time. However, B is ineligible because it must follow A (precedence requirement). Leave B and choose A, the task taking the next highest time. A is not proceeded by any task, so assign it to station 1. After A is assigned, station 1 has 20 seconds left to (LOT 2). Following LOT 3, we see that D is the first task on the list that takes 20 seconds or less, so we assign it to this station. Therefore, station 1 consists of tasks A and D for a total of 90 seconds operation time.

Now we begin again with LOT 1 and station 2. B takes the longest time, meets precedence requirements, and is therefore assigned to station 2. In LOT 2, we find the station has 10 seconds (90 − 80) left to contribute. Since all other tasks require more than 10 seconds, none is eligible to be assigned to station 2.

To station 3 we may assign C or E. Other choices would violate precedence requirements. We arbitrarily select C, with an operation time of 40 seconds. Remaining time at station 3 is therefore 50 seconds (90 − 40). Now E and G become eligible at this station. Since G takes the longest time, it is assigned. Thus station 3 consists of tasks C and G with a total performance time of 90 seconds (40 + 50).

This entire process, carried to completion, is summarized in Table 7.7 and shown in Figure 7.8: a five-station assembly line comprising 8 tasks.

TABLE 7.7 **Assigning tasks to stations using the longest-operation-time heuristic achieving a 90-second cycle time**

Heuristic Steps	Station	Eligible Tasks	Task Assigned	Task Time (in seconds)	Time Station Has Left to Contribute (in seconds)	Remaining Eligible Tasks
1	1	A	A	70	20	D
2	1	D	D	20	0	none
3	2	B,C,E	B	80	10	none
4	3	C,E	C	40	50	E,F,G
5	3	E,F,G	G	50	0	none
6	4	E,F	E	40	50	F
7	4	F	F	30	20	none
8	5	H	H	50	40	none

This layout is *effective* if it yields the desired capacity. It is efficient if it minimizes idle time. In the fifth step, we want to check both measures of performance. Figure 7.9 shows calculations of efficiency and effectiveness. The layout is more efficient than the one where efficiency is calculated in Table 7.6.

At this stage, we may be able to improve the layout by trial and error, step 6 of our station. In addition, many other heuristics may be used instead of the longest-operation-time approach. Several computerized heuristics are available, and since different heuristics can lead to different layouts, managers may want to try more than one approach.

FIGURE 7.8 **Revised storm window assembly**

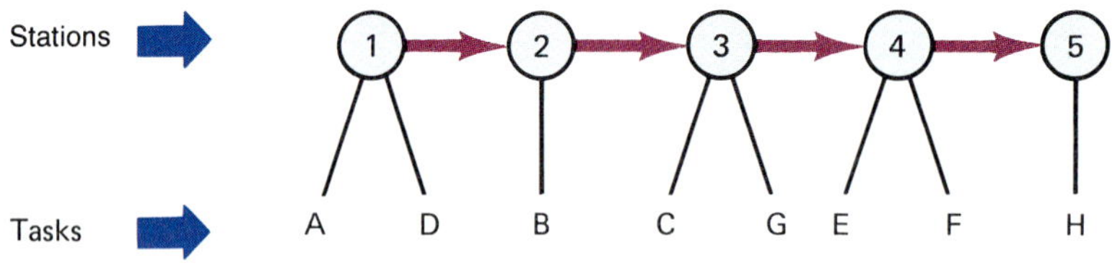

Task sharing Assigning one task each to two workers and assigning a third task to be shared between the two, thereby reducing idle time.

There are occasions when effectiveness and efficiency can be increased by deviating from the procedures we have presented. *Task sharing,* for example, occurs when there are three stations manned by workers, all of whom are sometimes idle. We can reduce idleness by eliminating one worker, and letting the other two take turns doing the task at the third station. Other improvements are possible if more than one worker can be assigned to a single station. Finally, if the desired output exceeds capacity, bottlenecks may be re-examined.

BEHAVIORAL ASPECTS OF PRODUCT LAYOUT

The major behavioral issues in product-oriented layouts involve employee satisfaction, motivation, interest, and productivity. Historically, the assumption has been that ever-increasing job specialization would lead to increased labor productivity. Experi-

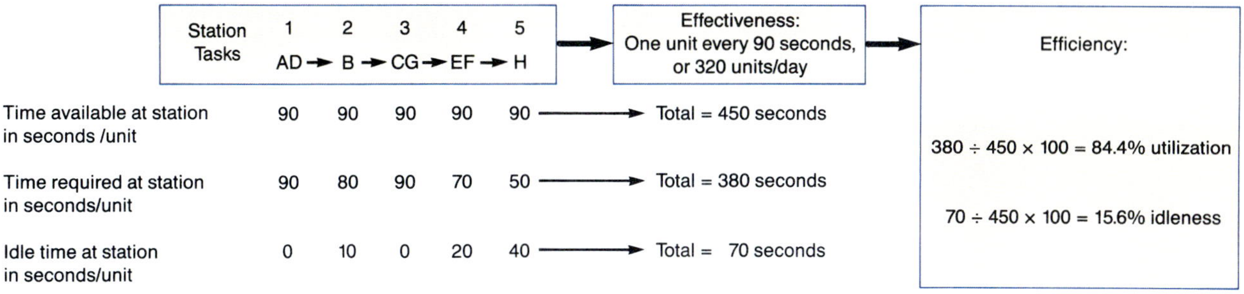

FIGURE 7.9 Assembly line design for 90-second cycle

ence has shown this assumption to be true, but only up to a point. Sometimes routinization leads to job dissatisfaction, absenteeism, and higher employee turnover. Often employees feel that as jobs become more highly specified, "something gets lost": the work tends to become meaningless. Responses to these problems include quality circles and job enlargement, enrichment, and rotation, all of which are discussed more thoroughly in Chapter 8.

MANUFACTURING CELLULAR LAYOUTS

Cellular layout The arrangement of a facility so that equipment used to make similar parts or families of parts is grouped together.

Group technology and *cellular layouts* can be combined and used to produce families of parts more economically than can traditional process or product layouts. In Chapter 4, group technology was described as a way of gathering data so that parts with similar characteristics, which are also manufactured similarly, could be identified. This identification and coding is the heart of group technology. The equipment to make these similar parts or families of parts is grouped together and designated for these parts. To some extent, a process layout, characteristic of job shops, is changed to a small well-defined product layout. This group of equipment is called a cell, and the arrangement of cells is called a *cellular layout.*

Figure 7.10 illustrates two alternative layouts for producing two parts. The parts are made from similar materials but one has two holes and the other just one, so they require different tooling. The part with two holes could be made in a job shop moving from machine A to C to D to E. Notice that in the job shop the machines are grouped together and the product moves about. Alternatively, these machines could be grouped in a line flow as shown in the cellular layout. Not every part has to have its own machine, as suggested in this cellular layout. Two parts might share, for example, machine D.

In order for a cell to be economical and practical in the long term, the machines must be closely grouped, and the cell must be flexible in its mix of capacity and must be big enough so any one absent employee does not shut it down, yet small enough for employees to identify with the cell and understand the products and equipment. Cellular layouts can be configured in many ways—in a line as in Figure 7.10, in a U as the Japanese have demonstrated, or in a C. Employees are often placed along U and C cells in such a way that they can attend several machines at one time.

Operations Management Highlight 7.3 explains how several companies profited from cellular layouts.

OPERATIONS MANAGEMENT HIGHLIGHT 7.3

Source: John Zoiner

Cellular Layouts Achieve Improved Performance

Modernizing a plant is a high risk/high reward task, as Caterpillar, Inc., is learning. Caterpillar has earmarked $1.8 billion for modernizing its plants by 1993. With more than $10 billion in annual sales, Caterpillar expects to reduce manufacturing costs by 20 percent, or about $1.5 billion, each year until the

Among the advantages of cellular layouts are lower work-in-process inventories, reduced materials handling costs, shorter flow times in production, simplified production planning (materials and labor), increased operator responsibilities, improved visual control, and fewer tooling changes (therefore quicker set-ups). Overall performance often increases by lowering production costs and improving on-time delivery. Quality revision is complete. Included in the company's plans are a worldwide information network, flexible manufacturing, and a cellular layout, in which workers will increase the range of tasks they perform.

For another U.S. company, cellular layout in conjunction with just-in-time (JIT) production transformed its classic job shop into a world-class manufacturing system. Machines had been grouped by process, but material movement was excessively slow, work-in-process inventories were too large, and quality was unacceptably low. Costs were increasing and market-share decreasing. In response, management first moved machines on one assembly line into an L-shaped cell; then they negotiated with union workers to accept group rather than individual incentives. Productivity improved. Lead time for the product was reduced from seven days to one day. Flexibility increased because every operator in the cell could perform all jobs. In every respect, the cellular layout was a success—for the employees and for management.

Cellular layouts often mean reduced annual inventory costs and improved productivity. Claims about improvements in quality are often made, but less often documented. Better documented is improved employee morale, an important result.

Sources: F. Frank Chen and Everett E. Adam, Jr., "The Impact of Flexible Manufacturing Systems on Productivity and Quality," *IEEE Transactions on Engineering Management*, 38, no 1 (February 1991), 33–45; Brian Bremner, "Can Caterpillar Inch Its Way Back to Heftier Profits?" *Business Week* (September 25, 1989), 75; 79; Thomas H. Goodrich, "Just-in-Time with an Emphasis on Group Technology," *Manufacturing Systems* 6, no. 7 (July 1988), 78–79; Timothy D. Fry, Martin G. Wilson, and Michael Breen, "A Successful Implementation of Group Technology and Cell Manufacturing," *Production and Inventory Management*, 28, no. 3 (3rd Quarter 1987), 4–6; and Barbara B. Flynn and Robert F. Jacobs, "An Experimental Comparison of Cellular (Group Technology) Layout with Process Layout," *Decision Sciences*, 18, no. 4 (Fall 1987), 562–81.

should increase as well, though that might take other interventions beyond the layout change.

Disadvantages include reduced manufacturing flexibility and potentially increased machine downtime (since machines are dedicated to cells and may not be used all the time) cells that become out-of-date as products and processes change, and the disruption and cost of changing to cells.

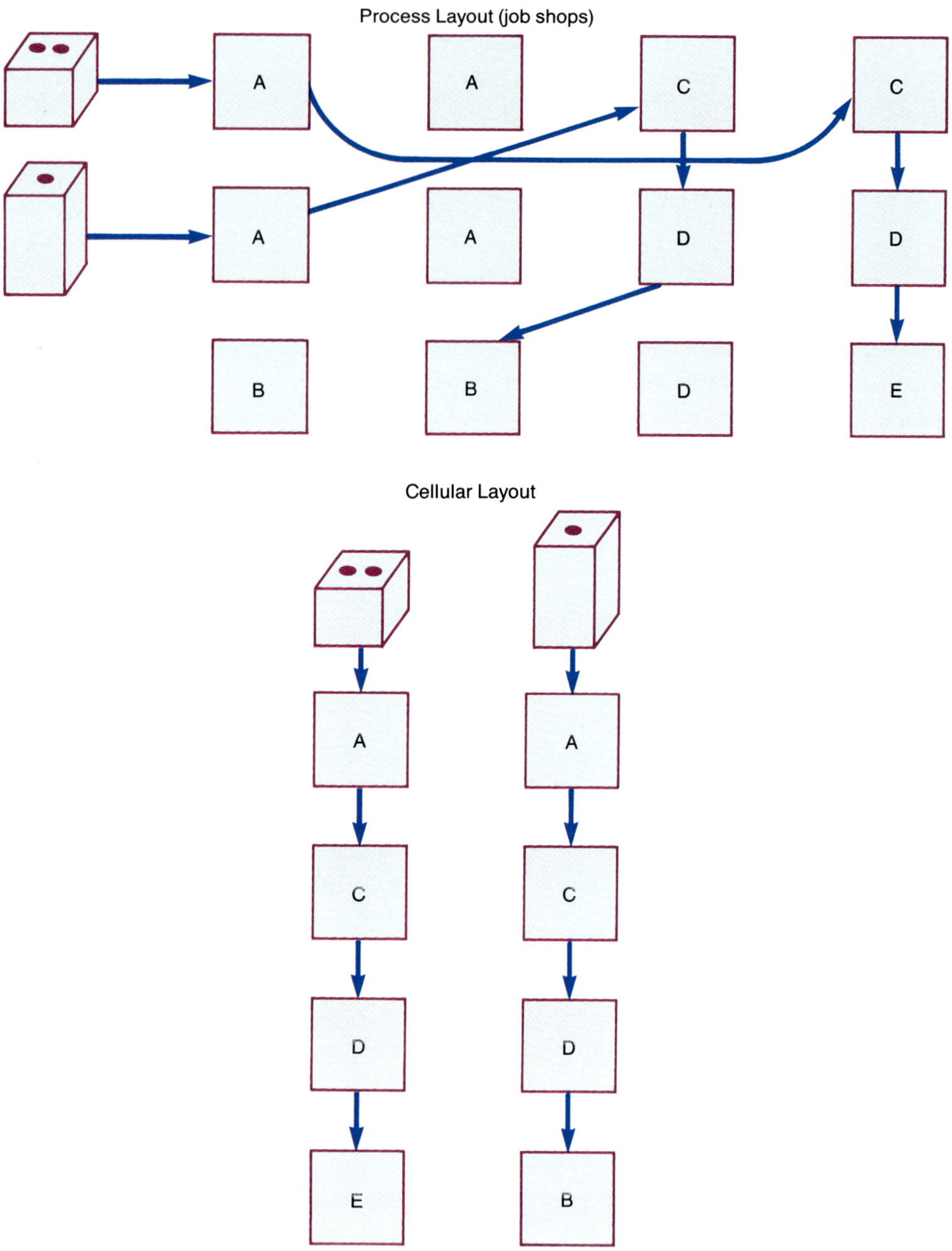

FIGURE 7.10 **Process versus cellular layouts**

Although *cellular layout* is a catchy new term, the phenomenon is not new. For decades, large job shops have grouped equipment for high-volume parts or special customers. Similarly, assembly lines may group machines by type to make or modify a variety of parts that "feed into" the main assembly line. When considering a "new" technique such as cellular layout, the astute manager will thoroughly look at past practices as a guide to changing the manufacturing environment.

THE JAPANESE APPROACH TO LAYOUT

Japan has taught the industrial world to rethink process layout, especially with the idea of work simplification and continuous improvement. Facility layout is one application where the Japanese change *both* the physical layout and the managerial system, which encourages employee involvement. Without getting into details, which we will present in Chapter 15 when we explain the Japanese manufacturing system, let's provide one example each of a physical and behavior contribution.

The Japanese use U-shaped assembly lines more often than straight lines so that workers on the inside of the U can reach a longer segment of the line. Moreover, tasks can be grouped, using fewer workers, and creating a more efficiently balanced line. The Japanese process layout is benefited, too, by an element of Japanese culture that encourages teamwork. In the United States, when equipment breakdowns cause an assembly line to stop, for example, workers typically wait for management, maintenance, or other staff to fix the problem. When a line stops in Japan, *all* workers act quickly to get it going again.

SUMMARY

Decisions about layout are made only periodically, but since they have long-term consequences, they must be made with careful planning. The layout design affects the cost of producing goods and delivering services for many years into the future. We discussed three traditional, basic layouts: process, product, and fixed-position. Process layouts arrange work centers according to function. Product (assembly line) layouts arrange work centers and equipment in a line so that a specialized sequence of tasks will result in product build-up. In a fixed-position layout, the product remains in one location, and resources are brought to it.

For process and product layouts, the design begins with a statement of the goals of the facility. Layouts are designed to meet these goals. After initial designs have been developed, improved designs are sought. This can be a cumbersome and tedious task because the number of possible designs is so large. For this reason, quantitative and computer-based models are often used. The models for process and product layouts are distinctly different: Process models generally minimize load (volume)–distance factors, and product models generally minimize idle labor time through a technique known as balancing the line.

CASE

Sonographic Sound Systems, Inc.

Sonographic Sound Systems, Inc., (SSS) is a small manufacturer of high-quality phonographs. For two years, SSS has produced its most popular portable phonograph on an eight-hour shift at a rate of 84 units/day. Management is satisfied with plant capacity but is concerned about the labor efficiency of its main assembly line. Fred Regos, operations manager, has asked his industrial engineer to recommend a redesign of the assembly line, because the vice president has established a goal of increasing labor utilization without decreasing the rate of output. This goal is consistent with the broader goal of reducing costs of the facility by 10 percent.

The current assembly line has seven stations at which a total of ten tasks are performed. The task descriptions, times, and precedence requirements are as follows:

Task	Description	Required Predecessors	Task Time (in minutes)
A	Load chasis frame	none	1
B	Insert gear assembly on frame	A	2
C	Install electric motor on frame	A	4
D	Assemble turntable stem to gear assembly	B	2
E	Install rubber bearing assembly onto gear assembly	B	1
F	Mount, fit, and fasten turntable mechanism to stem	D	5
G	Interconnect gear and motor assemblies	C, E	1
H	Install turntable	F, G	3
I	Install tone arm assembly	G	4
J	Install and fasten cover	H, I	3

Existing Assembly Line and Personnel

Station	1	2	3	4	5	6	7
Task	A and B	D and E	C and G	F	H	I	J
Worker	Alice	Tom	Bill	Debbie	Sam	Clorice	Ike

All employees have been with SSS two years or more. Tom finds that he has time on his hands and enjoys chatting with Alice. In all his time at SSS, Sam has never worked at another station. Although Bill doesn't like to perform task G, he takes great pride in his skill at doing C. Clorice and Ike agree that their jobs tend to get boring.

What changes would you recommend to Fred Regos? What reactions to these changes would you expect from the line employees?

REVIEW AND DISCUSSION QUESTIONS

1. Give examples of organizations that have predominantly product, process, and fixed-position layouts.
2. Compare and contrast the characteristics of intermittent and continuous operations.
3. Describe and illustrate the significant relationships between the capacity and layout decisions.
4. What relationships exist between the layout and location decisions?
5. To what extent do the quantitative layout models consider behavioral factors?
6. Compare the manual and quantitative models for product-oriented (assembly line) layout design. What are the advantages of each kind of model?
7. Identify and describe the different models used by a layout designer.
8. Identify the primary behavioral factors involved in process-oriented layout design. Give examples.
9. Explain the essential features of CRAFT.
10. Identify the primary behavioral factors involved in product-oriented (assembly line) layout design. Give examples.

11. Compare the manual and quantitative models for process layout design. What are the advantages of each kind of model?

12. Compare differences in design strategies for developing an initial layout design (for a new facility) and for developing a revised layout design (for an existing facility).

13. Some would contend that employees should not have a major voice in layout design. Others argue that the design process should be participatory, with major employees involvement. Discuss this issue.

PROBLEMS

SOLVED PROBLEMS

1. The assembly line shown in Figure 7.11 yields 120 units/day, the desired output rate for an eight-hour shift. Calculate the following: total time required to produce one unit, maximum daily output, minimum number of stations to produce one unit, and the efficiency of the line.

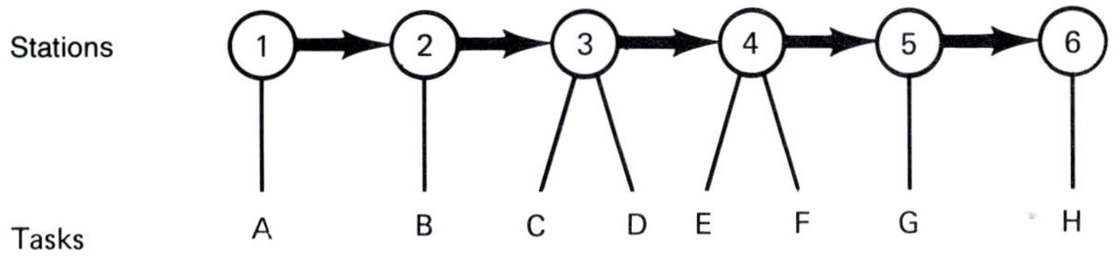

FIGURE 7.11

SOLUTION

We calculate the total time required as the sum of the task times:

$$\begin{aligned}\text{Total time required to produce one unit} &= 4 + 1.5 + 1.5 + 3.5 + 1.5 + 2.5 + 2 + 1.5 + 4 \\ &= 22 \text{ minutes/unit}\end{aligned}$$

The maximum daily output is the time available divided by the cycle time. The cycle time is 4 minutes, the largest work station time.

$$\begin{aligned}\text{Maximum daily output} &= \frac{480 \text{ minutes}}{4 \text{ minutes/unit}} \\ &= 120 \text{ units}\end{aligned}$$

The theoretical minimum number of stations required to produce one unit is the time required to produce one unit, divided by the time allowed to produce one unit. The time allowed is 4 minutes (time available ÷ desired output).

$$\begin{aligned}\text{Minimum number of stations to produce one unit} &= \frac{22 \text{ minutes/unit}}{4 \text{ minutes/unit}} \\ &= 5.5 \text{ or } 6 \text{ stations}\end{aligned}$$

Efficiency is a measure of employee utilization and employee idleness. Calculate employee utiiization as the ratio of the sum of task times for all stations, and the sum of available time for all stations.

$$\text{Utilization} = \frac{22 \text{ minutes}}{4 \text{ minutes} \times 6} = \frac{22}{24}$$
$$= 91.6\%$$
$$\text{Employee idleness} = 100\% - 91.6\%$$
$$= 8.4\%$$

2. Seven areas (see Figure 7.12) will receive incoming parts from a factory's receiving dock, which can be located at either position A or position B in the facility. The number of loads per month is shown in parentheses. The distances to A and B are given in brackets. Which position is best, A or B?

A	1 (90)	B
2 (60) [A:1; B:2]	3 (30)	4 (50) [A:2; B:1]
5 (40) [A:2; B:2]	6 (90)	7 (70) [A:2; B:2]

FIGURE 7.12

SOLUTION

Areas 1, 3, and 6 can be ignored since they are equidistant from A and B. Location A offers lower cost, as seen in the following table.

For A				For B			
Area	Distance from A to Area	Loads from A to Area	Loads Times Distance	Area	Distance from B to Area	Loads from B to Area	Loads Times Distance
2	1	60	60	2	2	60	120
4	2	50	100	4	1	50	50
5	2	40	80	5	2	40	80
7	2	70	140	7	2	70	140
		Total	380			Total	390

REINFORCING FUNDAMENTALS

3. A vacuum cleaner manufacturer incurs a variable cost of \$50/unit and receives revenues of \$70/unit. Two alternative layouts are being considered for finished goods storage and shipment. The first alternative involves loading finished products directly into trucks at the end of the assembly line. Annual fixed costs of operation of the large truck fleet would be \$350,000; materials handling costs would be \$150,000.

The second alternative involves storing finished products in a large warehouse near the assembly plant. The annual costs would be \$170,000 for a smaller truck fleet, \$195,000 in additional inventory costs, \$20,000 to cover damaged goods, and \$10,000 to load, operate, and maintain the conveyance equipment from the assembly plant to the warehouse.

Existing annual fixed costs of operation (in addition to the two layout alternatives) are \$400,000. What impact, if any, do the layouts have on the company's break-even volume of operation?

4. The university library is considering a new location for department 6, the book-purchase processing department. Library staff would like to exchange locations of department 6 and department 2 (2 being the social science reference staff). Given estimates as shown, what would be the impact of this change? Do you have a better recommendation? If so, show your work to support your recommendation.

Monthly book loads

Department	2	3	4	5	6
1	50	0	200	100	0
2		0	0	0	0
3			50	150	0
4				0	100
5					0

Current layout

1	2	3
6	5	4

5. Load shipments among work centers A through L, tentatively located as shown, are given in the table.

Annual loads (in units)

	To				
From	D	G	H	I	J
A	300	600			200
C	600	300	200		400
E	100				500

Layout (tentative)

A	B	C	D
E	F	G	H
I	J	K	L

(a) Assuming transportation cost of $1/distance unit for each load, find a good layout.

(b) Suppose the cost is $4/distance unit for each load from work center E and $1/distance unit for each load from A and C. Find a good layout.

6. A small printing shop wants to locate its seven departments in a one-floor building that is 40 units wide and 50 units long. Department sizes are as follows:

Department	Length (in units)	Width (in units)
Layout	10	10
Cutting	20	10
Shipping	10	10
Supply storage	20	15
Printing	25	20
Binding	20	20
Art	20	20

The expected average annual number of loads flowing between departments is given in the table. What is your layout recommendation?

	To Department						
From Department	Layout	Cutting	Shipping	Supply Storage	Printing	Binding	Art
Layout	—	700	—	—	—	—	—
Cutting	—	—	—	100	—	400	—
Shipping	—	—	—	500	—	—	—
Supply storage	—	600	100	—	400	100	—
Printing	—	—	—	—	—	1,200	100
Binding	—	100	1,000	—	200	—	—
Art	—	100	—	—	100	—	—

7. To help plan a new office layout, pairs of departments were rated according to how important it was to have the pair close to one another. On a scale of 1 (low importance) to 10 (high importance), ratings are given in the table below. Assume the overall space is three units wide and three units long; all departments are one unit by one unit. What is your recommended layout?

Importance of close proximity among service groups

Department	Design	Estimating	Accounting	Computer	Records	Sales Engineers	Management
Maintenance	—	—	—	—	—	—	—
Library	10	—	—	—	—	2	—
Design	—	9		6	6	10	6
Estimating	—	—	3	—	4	10	4
Accounting	3	—	—	4	8	5	3
Computer	—	—	—	—	4	6	3
Records	—	—	—	—	—	5	—
Sales engineers	—	—	—	—	—	—	10

8. Given the following tasks and requirements for an assembly line, what is the maximum daily output and efficiency?

Task	Task Time (in minutes)	Required Predecessors
A	5	F
B	2	F
C	3	E, G
D	7	A, B
E	8	D, H
F	4	—
G	6	D
H	3	D

9. Consider the following production line in which tasks A through H must be performed in alphabetical order:

Station	1 1	2	3 3	4	5	6
Task	A B	C	D E	F	G	H
Task time (in minutes)	2 1.5	4	2 2	3	2.5	3

(a) Identify the bottleneck operation.
(b) What is the minimum cycle time?
(c) Assuming an eight-hour work day, what is the maximum daily output?
(d) If the line uses one employee per station, how many hours of idle time are there daily? How many hours of productive time?
(e) Calculate the efficiency of the line.

10. Tasks, task times, and required predecessors are given in the table for a food processing plant. Assume the tasks cannot be split.

Task	Task Time (in minutes)	Required Predecessors	Task	Task Time (in minutes)	Required Predessors
A	3	none	E	2	A
B	6	A	F	4	C, B
C	7	A	G	5	C
D	5	A	H	5	D, E, F, G

(a) What is the theoretical minimum cycle time?
(b) Balance the line using the longest-operation-time (LOT) rule.
(c) Calculate the efficiency of the balanced line.

CHALLENGING EXERCISES

11. A group of physicians is considering forming a new medical clinic in a single-story facility in a suburban area. Although design plans are just underway, they have decided to have departments with relative sizes (space requirements) as given in the table immediately below.

Table A Department	Size (in square feet)	Department	Size (in square feet)
Laboratory	600	Neurology	600
Plastic surgery	600	Pediatrics	1,800
Patient waiting area	600	Pharmacy	400
OB/GYN	800	X-ray	600

The expected number of patients moving among pairs of departments during each month is given in the table below.

Department	Plastic Surgery	Waiting	OB/GYN	Neurology	Pediatrics	Pharmacy	X-ray
Lab	20	50	100	80	200		200
Plastic surgery		70		10		20	5
Waiting			400	100	900		50
OB/GYN					50	40	50
Neurology					10	20	80
Pediatrics						150	200
Pharmacy							30

The physicians are not yet concerned with the overall configuration of the building, just so all departments are on one floor. There is a direct relationship between number of patients and patient walking distances. What relative department locations do you recommend for minimizing patient flows (walking distances)?

12. An assembly line must be established to include the tasks as given in the table.

Task	Task Time (in seconds)	Required Predecessors	Task	Task Time (in seconds)	Required Predecessors
A	120	none	F	20	E
B	50	A	G	90	H
C	40	B	H	60	A
D	80	C, F	I	30	A
E	100	A	J	60	D, G, I

(a) Construct a sequence diagram for the tasks.
(b) To balance the line to a 120-second cycle time, what is the minimum number of stations required?
(c) Use the longest-operation-time (LOT) rule to balance the line to a 120-second cycle time.
(d) What is the efficiency of the line?

13. For the data in problem 12, redo parts (c) and (d) using the shortest-operation-time rule (the eligible task with the shortest time is assigned first). Compare your solution to using the largest-number-of-follower-tasks rule (the task with the largest number of follower tasks).

14. A toy company, Electro-Play, Inc., is interested in balancing a production line that will manufacture an electronic football game to compete with the successful pocket-calculator-size model of Mattel. Tasks, task times, and precedence requirements are given in the table.

Task	Task Time (in seconds)	Required Predecessors	Task	Task Time (in seconds)	Required Predecessors
A	40	none	G	10	C
B	20	A	H	10	E
C	15	B	I	10	E
D	60	none	J	5	F, G, H, I
E	20	D	K	10	J
F	10	C			

(a) Construct a sequence diagram for the tasks.
(b) To balance the line with a 60-second cycle time, what is the

theoretical minimum number of stations required? A seven-hour day is worked.

(c) Balance the line with the longest-operation-time (LOT) rule, balancing to a 60-second cycle time.

(d) What is the efficiency of the line?

(e) Many of the behavioral problems in assembly line balancing also apply to the more general problem of job design. What suggestions might you offer if you wanted to incorporate job enlargement/enrichment into the balanced line you constructed?

15. Able Manufacturing has an opportunity to bid on a contract to produce an electronic assembly. Able could use excess assembly capacity as its main production facility. The contract would require delivery within two years of 30,000 units. Able's engineers suggest an assembly line comprising nine tasks, as given in the table.

Task	Task Time (in minutes)	Required Predecessors	Task	Task Time (in minutes)	Required Predecessors
A	2	G	F	4	G
B	6	G	G	3	I
C	2	B, D	H	2	C, E
D	5	A, F	I	4	none
E	3	D			

Assembly would occur on one shift with average productive time of 7½ hours per employee daily (allowances for breaks, fatigue, shutdowns, etc.). There would be 22 productive days monthly. Direct labor costs are $9/hour; variable overhead is estimated at 10 percent of direct labor; direct materials are $12/unit; initial tooling for the project is $100,000, and semifixed costs of manufacturing for the assembly line are estimated at $7,000/month. For such contractual commitments, Able desires a 15 percent profit margin on the selling price. Should Able submit a bid and, if so, at what selling price?

UTILIZING QSOM COMPUTER SOFTWARE

16. Reconsider Problem 6. What if a proposed materials handling system will save 50 percent of the current handling costs on each load flowing from the binding department? Prepare your recommendations with supporting data.

17. Reconsider problem 14. What if the line is balanced to cycle times other than the 60-second cycle time? Prepare a report on the effects of various cycle times, with supporting data.

KEY TERMS

Bottleneck operation 267
Cellular layout 273
Continuous operations 252
Cycle time 267
Fixed-position layout 254
Heuristic 266
Intermittent operations 252
Layout 252
Line balancing problem 270
Load-distance model 257
Longest-operation-time rule (LOT) 271
Maximum allowable cycle time 267
Predecessor task 271
Process (-oriented) layout 252
Product (-oriented) layout 254
Task 270
Task sharing 272
Templates 256
Work center 253

SELECTED READINGS

Buffa, Elwood S., Gordon C. Armour, and Thomas Vollmann, "Allocating Facilities with CRAFT," *Harvard Business Review* (March–April 1964), 136–58.

Francis, Richard L., and John A. White, *Facility Layout and Location*, Englewood Cliffs, N.J.: Prentice Hall, 1974.

Fry, Timothy D., Martin G. Wilson, and Michael Breen, "A Successful Implementation of Group Technology and Cell Manufacturing," *Production and Inventory Management* 28, no. 3 (3rd Quarter 1987), 4–6.

Hicks, Philip E., and Troy E. Cowan, "Craft-M for Layout Rearrangement," *Industrial Engineering* 8, no. 5 (May 1976), 30–35.

Hyer, Nancy Lea, and Urban Wemmerlov, "MRP: GT A Framework for Production Planning and Control of Cellular Manufacturing," *Decision Sciences* 13, no. 4 (October 1982), 681–701.

Hyer, Nancy Lea, "The Potential of Group Technology for U.S. Manufacturing," *Journal of Operations Management*, 4, no. 3 (May 1984), 183–202.

Jacobs, F. Robert, "A Layout Planning System with Multiple Criteria and a Variable Domain Representation," *Management Science* 33, no. 8 (August 1987), 1020–34.

Johnson, R., "Spacecraft for Multi-floor Layout Planning," *Management Science* 28, no. 4 (April 1982).

McLeavey, D. W., and S. L. Narasimhan, *Production Planning and Inventory Control*. Boston: Allyn & Bacon, 1985, chap. 12.

Ritzman, Larry, John Bradford, and Robert Jacobs, "A Multiple Objective Approach to Space Planning for Academic Facilities," *Management Science* 25, no. 9 (September 1979), 895–906.

Schuler, R. S., L. P. Ritzman, and V. Davis, "Merging Prescriptive and Behavioral Approaches for Office Layout," *Journal of Operations Management* 1, no. 3 (February 1981), 131–42.

Trybus, Thomas W., and Lewis D. Hopkins "Human vs. Computer Algorithms for the Plant Layout Problem," *Management Science* 26, no. 6 (June 1980), 570–74.

PART III

ORGANIZING THE CONVERSION SYSTEM

Production and operations management activities

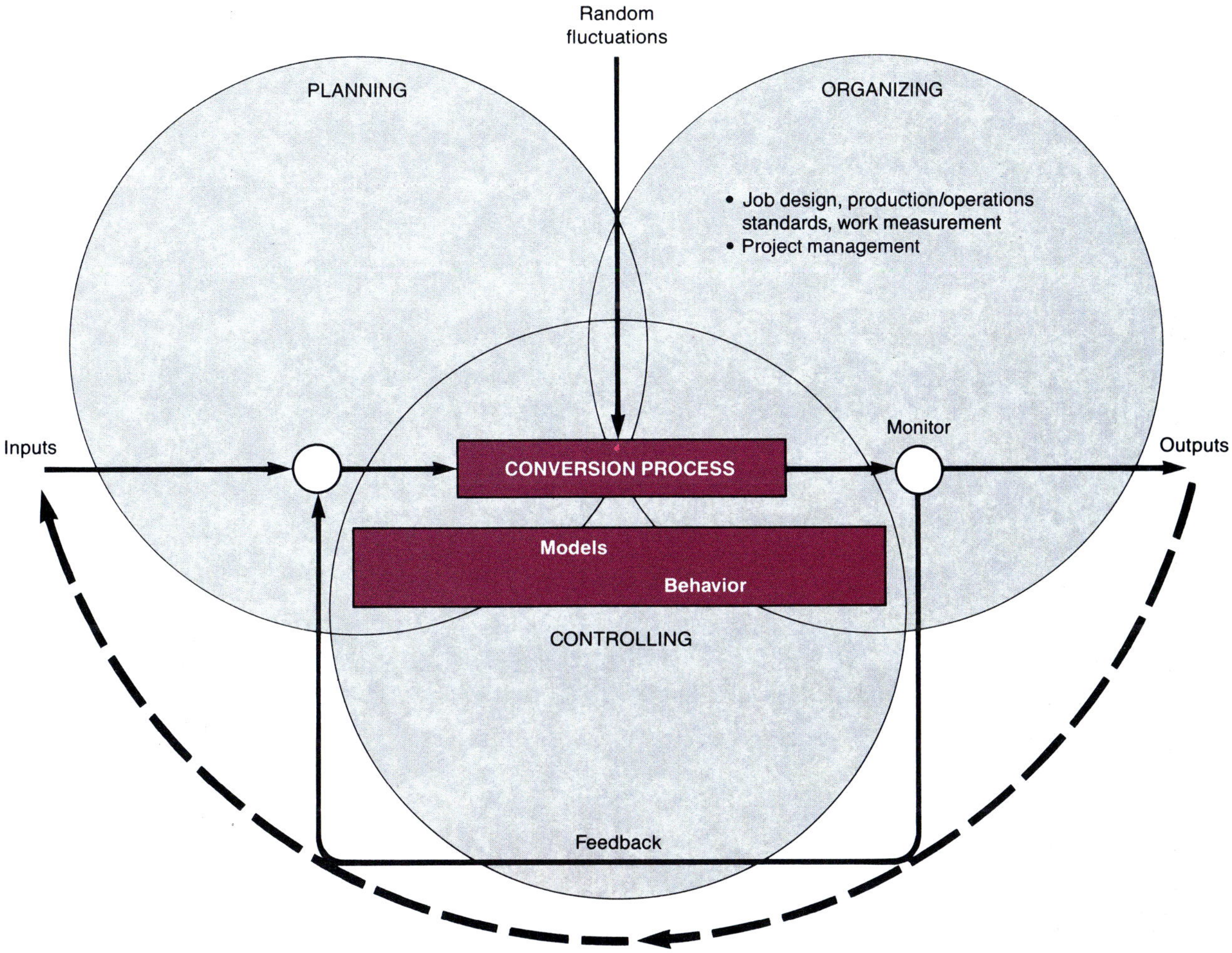

CHAPTER 8

JOB DESIGN, PRODUCTION AND OPERATIONS STANDARDS, AND WORK MEASUREMENT

Job design, job standards, and work measurement have always been important to 3M Company. Job design in particular is becoming ever more important and, I believe, is the most critical.

At 3M, the behavioral, human-factors element of job design is gaining in recognition and has resulted in the creation of a separate human-factors resource group for the corporation. I am glad to see that this chapter recognizes the importance of this factor. Job design must be considered in the very beginning of product design; too often we design products without giving thought to their manufacturability in human terms, and the affect that has on consistent quality.

At 3M Company, we have found that in labor-intensive areas, work standards and work measurement together increase productivity approximately 20 percent. As the chapter points out, many companies overlook or neglect this important element of operations. While money has to be spent to ***develop*** standards and measure the work, and money must continue to be spent to ***maintain*** these standards and measurement, 3M has found that this always pays off. The return on investment is generally more than 3:1. Work standards and work measurement must be evaluated carefully for their effect on quality—factors often overlooked in the past.

A challenge for operations management in the future is to develop effective design, standards, and measurement for white-collar jobs. Although difficult, this is not impossible. Because of automation, the percentage of blue-collar workers at 3M, and in business as a whole, is gradually declining. As a result, improving white-collar productivity is becoming increasingly important and needs to be seriously addressed. I believe much can be accomplished in this area through applying the principles and methods described in this chapter.

C. W. Pipal
Staff Vice President, Retired
3M Company
St. Paul, Minnesota

We hope the benefits of work standards and measurements cited by Mr. Pipal—productivity increases of 20 percent and returns on investment of up to 3:1—encourage you to grasp the fundamental issues and techniques we discuss in this chapter.

Job A group of related tasks or activities that needs to be performed to meet organizational objectives.

This chapter focuses on people at work. The basic building block in a manufacturing or service organization is the *job,* a group of related *tasks* or activities that need to be performed to meet organizational objectives. Jobs are then grouped into larger units called *departments,* and departments are grouped into basic *functions* such as marketing, engineering, and production. Consider an example. The elements of placing a washer on a bolt, placing a nut on a bolt, and tightening the nut firmly with an automatic wrench constitute a *task.* Repeating this and similar tasks constitutes a *job* in the motor assembly *department,* which is in the production *function* of an *organization* that finances, markets, and produces washing machines.

Two basic developments have characterized organizations in modern industrialized societies. First and most significant was scientific management's focus on the logic of the production process, particularly people and machines at work on a job. This follow-up of Adam Smith's concept of *labor specialization* has led to logical approaches to *job design,* individual and group standards for performance, and techniques for measurement of work. A good bit of the development in industrial engineering over the last century has been devoted to this rational, scientific, and logical approach to job analysis.

More recently, human relations and behavioral science studies of jobs have come about. The development of the behavioral approach has tended to moderate scientific management's rational approach to jobs. Behavioralists have provided clear evidence that people have multiple needs, feelings, and personal goals that are not always consistent with jobs designed and measured by rational techniques. Clearly, the modern production and operations manager must be aware of and respond to the worker as an individual human being.

In job design, we use methods analysis to establish the general work flow in the facility. Once the general work flow has been established, specific jobs can be designed and standards established to ensure that the jobs are being performed properly. Establishing a standard, however, requires an understanding of work measurement. We want to emphasize that work measurement *follows* methods analysis. Only after we have established the proper method for getting the job done (job design) can we be concerned about measuring it (setting the standard through measurement). Obviously, setting a standard for an existing job and then redesigning it constitute wasted effort. Let's begin our discussion of these three related areas with the one that comes first, job design.

JOB DESIGN

Job design Activities that specify the content of each job and determine how work is distributed within the organization.

In production and operations, *job design* follows the planning and designing of product, process, and equipment. Job design specifies the content of each job and determines how work is distributed within the organization. Just as an architect can build (design) a house many different ways with many different materials, so can a manager build (design) a job with many different parts (tasks). A combination of creativity and adherence to basic goals is critical to both the architect and the manager.

TRADITIONAL ENGINEERING DIMENSIONS OF JOB DESIGN

Often managers, responsible for many subordinates and equipment, feel overwhelmed by details. Couldn't we be more efficient if we improved our jobs? But how can we improve them when we hardly know what the jobs consist of? One answer to the managers' dilemma is offered by the scientific approach. It urges managers to do the following:

1. Identify the general operations problem and the jobs that seem to be contributing to or causing the problem.
2. Carefully analyze and document how work is being performed (established industrial engineering techniques are available to help analyze and document).
3. Analyze the tasks that the jobs comprise.
4. Develop and implement new work methods.

Specialization of labor Breaking apart jobs into tasks and assigning tasks to different workers according to their special skills, talents, and tools.

Jobs can be broken apart into tasks. If the tasks are assigned to different workers, each worker can perform fewer tasks but can perform them faster and perhaps under more specialized conditions (for example, with special tools or work benches). This basic concept, *specialization of labor,* has been very effective in increasing operating efficiency in manufacturing; it has been less effective, however, in the service industries.

Operation chart A graphic tool to analyze and time elementary motions of the right and left hand in performing a routine, repetitive task.

Work Methods Analysis Aids To help the manager or a staff analyst study a job once a problem has been identified, certain techniques have been developed. One of these uses *operation charts* to analyze the job in terms of elementary motions of the right and left hands—reaching, carrying, grasping, lifting, positioning, and releasing, for example. Often a time scale is placed in the middle of the operation chart so that it is clear how much time is taken by each hand to perform the associated motion. Operation charts are appropriate for routine, repetitive, short-cycle tasks producing low to moderate volume products.

Activity chart A graphic tool to analyze and time the small, physical actions of worker and machine in performing a routine, repetitive, worker-machine task so that idle time can be identified.

Activity charts segment tasks into small, physical actions, as listed in Figure 8.1, for example, of both the worker and the machine worked with. Each action, human or machine, is timed. In this way, the analyst can easily compute the percentages of productive and idle time and concentrate on methods of reducing idle time for the worker and/or the machine. Activity charts are appropriate for routine, repetitive tasks with worker-machine interaction. The activity chart in Figure 8.1 illustrates how a set of cards is loaded and unloaded for reading by an optical scanner. In this example, the analyst might improve efficiency by focusing on the first 10 seconds of idle machine

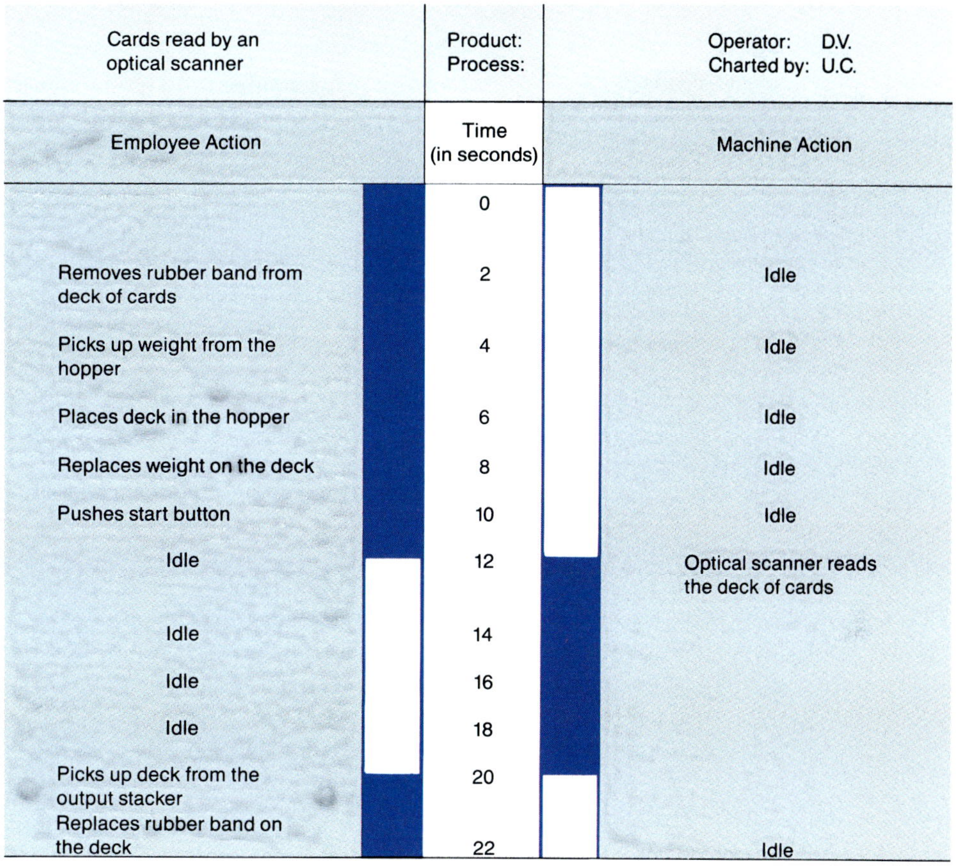

Summary

	Employee Time (in seconds)	Employee %	Machine Time (in seconds)	Machine %
Work	14	63.6	8	36.4
Idle	8	36.4	14	63.6

FIGURE 8.1 **Employee-machine activity chart**

time, the second 10 seconds of idle worker time, and the last 3 seconds of idle machine time.

Flow process chart A graphic tool to analyze and categorize interstation activities so that the flow of the product throughout the overall production process is represented.

Flow process charts analyze interstation activities, attempting to portray the flow throughout the overall production process. To capture this flow, analysts classify each movement of the product through the conversion process into one of five standard categories: operation, transportation, storage, inspection, or delay. Flow process charts are appropriate for visualizing the sequential stages of the conversion process. They help reveal unnecessary or duplicated effort whose elimination would improve efficiency. Flow process charts provide a broader level of analysis than operation or activity charts. Many jobs are examined, but none in depth. Descriptions of the five categories of product movement, and the icon for each, are:

○ *Operation:* Work performed in manufacturing the product; usually assigned to a single station.

⇨ *Transportation:* Movement of the product or its parts among stations.

▽ *Storage:* Intervals during which the product or its parts waits or is at rest. A *T* inside the triangle designates *temporary storage,* when the product is stored for a short time before the conversion process has been completed. A *P* inside the triangle designates *permanent storage,* when the completed product is in a storage facility more than a day or two.

□ *Inspection:* Work performed to verify that the product meets mechanical, dimensional, and operational requirements.

D *Delay:* Temporary storage before or after a production operation. When the temporary storage symbol is used, this category is often omitted.

EXAMPLE

A study was conducted to document the technical processing function of a major resource library.[1] The study was conducted in the early 1970s when computer use in libraries was in its infancy, yet it typifies studies we observe conducted today in private and public organizations. The purpose of the study was to provide a basis for specification of computer automation systems in technical processing. Figure 8.2 is a typical flow process chart. The following excerpt from the report illustrates this service sector application of traditional job design techniques.

> *Materials Flows and Procedures* This section presents the operations of the University of Missouri-Columbia Elmer Ellis Library's Technical Services Division in considerable detail. Because of the extensiveness of this description, a summary of the processing of materials is presented . . . The summary takes the form of "flow process charts" and "floor diagrams" describing the general operations and movements undergone by the broader categories of library materials. The "station" identifiers heading each column of the process charts refer to desk locations as marked on the accompanying floor diagrams.
>
> Flow process charts are in common use for describing processing of industrial materials, and they provide a convenient means of summarizing the numerous flow diagrams . . . The charts are easy to read once the following symbols and corresponding meanings are understood:
>
> ◎ Point of origination
>
> ○ Operation performed on an item or group of items
>
> ∘ Movement of an item or group of items from one location to another
>
> ▽ Delay
>
> ◇ Verification or check of some aspect of the item against a standard or other information
>
> The flow process charts presented technical procedures in enough detail that computer systems programmers could proceed with programming procedures for computers rather than continue with manual operations."

[1]S. Craig Moore, Everett E. Adam, Jr., Edward P. Miller, Daniel W. Doell, and Louis E. Fruend, *Library Studies Project*—Vol. I: *Technical Services in the UMC Library System* (Columbia: University of Missouri, 1973). See pp. 12–15, Vol. II.

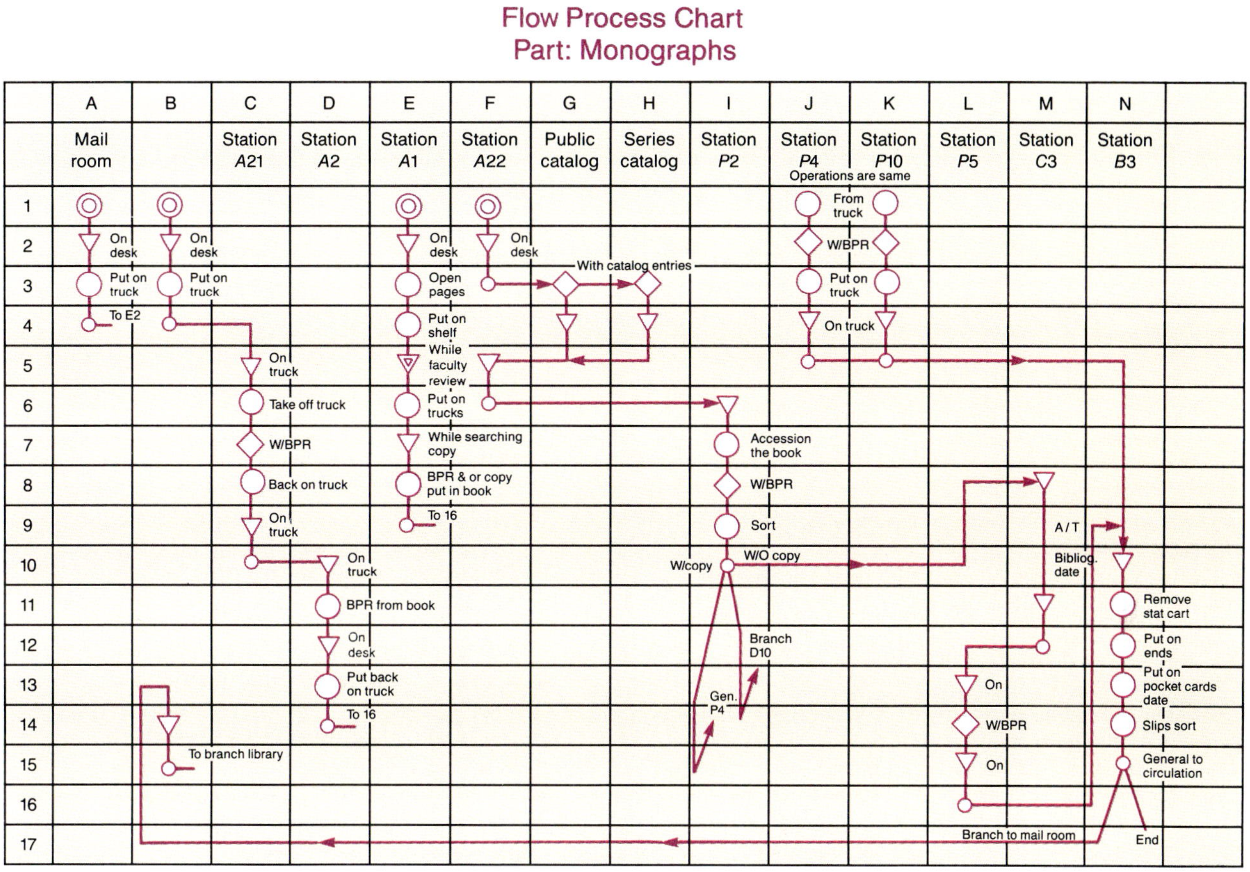

FIGURE 8.2 **Plan process chart of library operations**
Source: Craig Moore, Everett E. Adam, Jr., Edward P. Miller, Daniel W. Doell, and Louis E. Fruend, ***Library Studies Project***—Vol. I: ***Project Summary***, and Vol. II: ***Technical Services in the UMC Library system*** (Columbia: University of Missouri, 1973). See pp, 12–15, Vol. II.

Gang process chart A graphic tool to trace the interaction of several workers with one machine.

To trace the interaction of several workers with one machine, analysts may use *gang process charts.* A broad set of guidelines, called the *principles of motion economy,* may be used for analyzing and improving work arrangements, the use of human hands and body, or the use of tools to increase efficiency and reduce fatigue. Table 8.1 summarizes the application of these techniques to various kinds of work activities. Table 8.2 lists

TABLE 8.1 **Traditional analytic methods in job design**

Job	Analytic Method
Routine, repetitive tasks with short cycle times and low to moderate production volumes; worker at a fixed station	Operation charts, principles of motion economy
Routine, repetitive tasks with long cycle times and moderate to high production volumes; worker interacts with equipment or other workers	Activity charts, gang process charts
Overall conversion process; interactions of workers, stations, and work centers; flow of work	Flow process charts, floor diagrams

Principles of motion economy A broad set of guidelines focusing on work arrangements, the use of human hands and body, and the use of tools.

several principles of motion economy, many of which can be applied to both shop and office work.

Worker Physiology Over the years considerable effort has been devoted to studying people's physiology as it relates to their work. Statistics on reaching range, grip strength, lifting ability, and many other physiological factors have been reasonably well documented. Workplace arrangements, job design, and equipment design all require consideration of physiological factors. An industrial engineering handbook is a good source of information on the physiological capabilities of workers.

TABLE 8.2 **Principles of motion economy**

Using the Human Body the Way It Works Best	
1. The work should be arranged so that a natural rhythm can become automatic. 2. The symmetry of the body should be considered. The motions of the arms should be: (a) Simultaneous, beginning and completing their motions at the same time; (b) Opposite and symmetrical. 3. The human body is an ultimate machine and its full capabilities should be employed: (a) Neither hand should ever be idle. (b) Work should be distributed to other parts of the body in line with their ability. (c) The safe design limits of the body should be observed. (d) The human should be employed at its "highest" use.	4. The arms and hands as weights are subject to the physical laws and energy should be conserved: (a) Momentum should work for the body and not against it. (b) The smooth, continuous arc of the ballistic is most efficient. (c) The distance of movements should be minimized. (d) Tasks should be turned over to machines. 5. Tasks should be simplified: (a) Eye contacts should be few and grouped together (b) Unnecessary actions, delays, and idle time should be eliminated. (c) The degree of required precision and control should be minimized. (d) The number of individual motions should be minimized along with the number of muscle groups involved.
Arranging the Workplace to Assist Performance	**Using Mechanical Devices to Reduce Human Effort**
1. There should be a definite place for all tools and materials. 2. Tools, materials, and controls should be located close to the point of use. 3. Tools, materials, and controls should be located to permit the best sequence and path of motions. 4. The workplace should be fitted to the task and to the human.	1. Vises and clamps can hold the work precisely where needed. 2. Guides can assist in positioning the work without close operator attention. 3. Controls and foot-operated devices can relieve the hands of work. 4. Mechanical devices can multiply human abilities. 5. Mechanical systems should be fitted to human use.

Source: Frank C. Barnes, "Principles of Motion Economy: Revisited, Reviewed, and Restored," *Proceedings of the Southern Management Association Annual Meeting* (Atlanta, GA 1983), p. 298.

Working Environment Accounting for the physical environment is extremely important in designing jobs. Temperature, humidity, and air flow all affect work. If you've ever tried to mow grass or move furniture on a hot, humid day, you know how much harder high temperatures make your job. The same is true for less physically demanding work—typing, writing, and studying. These tasks are easier at temperatures a little warmer than those that are best for manual tasks, but are harder when temperatures are very high than when temperatures are moderate. A comfortable

In this office environment, variables such as light, temperature, air flow, and noise affect productivity, health, safety, and job satisfaction.
Source: Superstock

temperature might range from 65°F to 80°F (26.4°C to 38.4°C), the lower temperature better for physically demanding work.

Similarly, we know that noise, light, and many other environmental variables affect productivity. They also affect health and safety. Recognizing the lack of national uniformity in working conditions, Congress passed the Williams-Steiger Occupational Safety and Health Act of 1970. The act, which applies to every employer with one or more employees in a business concerned with commerce, established strict health and safety standards, and created the *Occupational Safety and Health Administration (OSHA)* to see that the standards are met.

Occupational Safety and Health Administration (OSHA) A division of the U.S. government created by the Williams-Steiger Occupational Safety and Health Act of 1970 to develop and enforce standards for job-related safety and health.

Although OSHA's success depends significantly on voluntary compliance, the program does provide enforcement measures and information to employers to help them understand and obey the law. OSHA inspectors now have the capability of identifying employers with the "worst" safety records and inspecting those locations first.[2] OSHA officials have accepted a "worst-first" scheduling rule. As best we can judge, inspections are based on a combination of worker complaints, target industries, random inspection, and worst-first analysis.

BEHAVIORAL DIMENSIONS OF JOB DESIGN

In the past, industries primarily used economic criteria in designing jobs. Economic criteria are still paramount. But behavioral criteria should be and are used as well. To ignore them is to bypass an opportunity for economic benefits in addition to those we achieve through traditional criteria. After World War II, managers and behavioral scientists developed an interest in industrial jobs in which workers had the "blue-collar blues." *Job rotation* and *job enlargement* techniques were responses to an overemphasis

[2]For initial development of the "worst-first" scheduling concept, see Everett E. Adam, Jr., "Priority Assignment of OSHA Safety Inspectors," *Management Science* 24, no. 15 (November 1978), 1642–49.

of scientific management. More recently *job enrichment* and the *redesign of job characteristics* have added to our abilities to improve jobs. Keeping in mind that our goal is to add further economic benefits, let's examine each of these behavioral techniques.

Job rotation Moving employees into a job for a short period of time and then out again.

Job Rotation Sometimes undesirable aspects of a job cannot be eliminated by redesigning or automating the job. An excellent way to approach such a job is to move employees into it for a short period of time and then move them out again.

Have you ever worked the graveyard shift (from midnight until morning)? Many people find it undesirable. Such service organizations as hospitals and police and fire departments, however, must have people on duty around the clock, and workers are moved into and out of the graveyard shift. Just as employees can move in and out of a shift that is undesirable, they can be rotated in and out of jobs that are undesirable. Rotating employees among different jobs can reduce boredom and monotony and expose the employee to a broader perspective of the entire production process.

Job enlargement Redesigning jobs to provide greater variety, autonomy, task identity, and feedback for the employee.

Job Enlargement Job enlargement proponents argue that we have simplified, specialized, and routinized jobs to the point that workers perceive them to be monotonous; workers are bored and dissatisfied. Because of boredom and job dissatisfaction, many workers withdraw from the organization, or the organization suffers from high levels of tardiness, absenteeism, and resignations (turnover). If managers would enlarge jobs by adding tasks, additional stimuli would reduce the ill effects of too simplified, too specialized jobs. Figure 8.3 illustrates the problem that job enlargement seeks to solve.

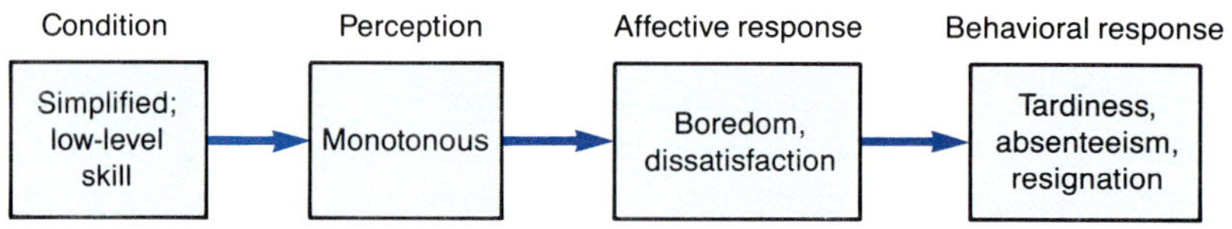

FIGURE 8.3 Assumptions behind job enlargement

Job enlargement offers the employee four opportunities:

1. Variety: the opportunity to use a variety of skills
2. Autonomy: the opportunity to exercise control over how and when work is completed
3. Task identity: the opportunity to be responsible for an entire piece or program of work
4. Feedback: the opportunity to receive current job performance information

A job may be enlarged in two basic ways. First, more tasks of a similar nature and skill level can be added. If a job consists of tightening one nut on one bolt, for example, it could be redesigned to consist of tightening four different nuts on four different bolts. The job would then be enlarged *horizontally*. Second, more tasks of a different nature but similar skill level can be added. Instead of tightening one nut on one bolt, the worker could assemble two pieces of metal and a piece of plastic, tighten a nut and bolt to hold the assembly together, and walk to a storage area to get more nuts and bolts. The job would then be enlarged *vertically*.

EXAMPLE

In a regional library, an analysis was made of all jobs. The five circulation clerks' duties included working at the circulation desk, shelving books, and maintaining a part of the collection (records, films, or young adult periodicals). The analyst discovered that the clerks felt the most rewarding and important part of their jobs was maintaining part of the collection. The routine, repetitious duties were merely receiving and checking out books at the circulation desk.

In their redesigned jobs, circulation clerks continued to shelve books and maintain a part of the collection, but they also performed some of the duties formerly done by a page. Time at the circulation desk was not allowed to exceed two hours at any one time, nor four hours a day. This essentially vertical redesign resulted in increased job satisfaction and reduced job turnover.

Attempts to enlarge blue-collar jobs, however, provide mixed results. It seems clear that for routine, repetitive jobs whose cycle times are less than two minutes, job enlargement can improve performance. Some studies have reported improved satisfaction without improved performance. Since workers who are more satisfied with their jobs tend to stay longer, reduced turnover may be the primary, or at least the most consistent, benefit of job enlargement programs.

Job enrichment
Redesigning jobs to give more meaning and enjoyment to the job by involving employees in planning, organizing, and controlling their work.

Job Enrichment Job enrichment is vertical change, similar to vertical job enlargement, yet different in that managerial tasks are added (rather than similar tasks in job enlargement). Proponents of job enrichment presume that many jobs are so highly specialized that workers can no longer visualize how their work contributes to the organization goals.

EXAMPLE

A manufacturing vice president for a leading foods manufacturer visited an operations management class and explained how job enrichment worked at his organization. The company produced corn flakes and was trying to sell its variety as the brand label for a larger grocery chain. Buyers from the grocery chain were at the corn flakes plant for the day. Two production workers were selected and brought directly into a conference room where boxes of competitors' and the company's corn flakes were available. These workers were asked, "Why are our corn flakes as good or better than the others'?" They answered by crunching various brands on the table and explaining in detail their jobs and quality control.

Two benefits resulted. First, the buyers were impressed with the workers' knowledge. Second, and most important, the workers returned to the workplace enthused about their contribution, and they spread this enthusiasm to other workers. They related their contribution in "selling the product." Their jobs were more meaningful to them, and their attitudes toward their jobs were improved.

Many managers feel that job enrichment and the goal of increased efficiency are not only compatible, they are necessary partners. They argue that it is impossible to sustain productivity without the conscious satisfaction that job enrichment helps create.

Two conditions are required for effective job enrichment:

1. Management must share information with workers on goals and performance.
2. Individual behavior must not be excessively controlled by the organization.

These two conditions can be met by reorienting traditional management thinking:

1. The organization must view each employee as a manager. Each must get involved in the management activities of planning, organizing, and controlling his or her own job. This is the basic goal of job enrichment.
2. The organization should strive to make work like play—to make the job fun. If a job can be designed so that it offers the rewards that a game does—visible and meaningful goals, immediate feedback, group cohesiveness, and people who are there because they want to be—then workers will enjoy their jobs.

Job Enrichment at General Foods The manufacturing vice president in the previous example told our class that his company's interest in job enrichment stemmed directly from a competitor's experience. In 1968 General Foods (the competitor) built a pet food plant in Topeka, Kansas. For workers at the plant, managers intended to emphasize new behavioral techniques that would develop skills, create challenging jobs, and encourage teamwork. The new job design focused on several basic features: autonomous work groups, challenging job assignments, job mobility and learning rewards, information availability, self-government, status symbols, and evaluation.

There were some start-up pains, but the first 18 months of the job enrichment effort generally yielded positive results. Fixed overhead costs were 33 percent lower than those of existing plants; quality rejects were reduced by 92 percent; the safety record was outstanding compared with other company plants; morale was high; absenteeism was 9 percent below the industry norm; and turnover was far below average.

Job Design in Sweden In the late 1960s and early 1970s, Saab and Volvo experimented with varying degrees of job enlargement, job rotation, job enrichment, and production "teams."[3] The results, though mixed, were generally positive. At one Volvo automobile assembly plant, for example, management combined job rotation and enrichment by having workers follow the same auto body through several stations. The job cycle time was increased six- or sevenfold, to some 20 minutes. Job turnover, the primary target for improvement, was indeed reduced from 40 to 25 percent. Absenteeism, however, nearly doubled. Increased absenteeism was attributed to government legislation enacted during the economic slowdown in Sweden at that time; it allowed workers to stay off the job with little or no effect on salary.

---

[3]Andrew S. Szilagyi, Jr. and Marc J. Wallace, Jr., *Organizational Behavior and Performance,* 2nd ed. (Santa Monica, Calif.: Goodyear Publishing, 1980), 173–77; W. F. Dowling, "Job Design in the Assembly-Line: Farewell to the Blue Collar Blues?" *Organizational Dynamics* (Spring 1973), 51–67; and C. H. Gibson, "Volvo Increases Productivity Through Job Enrichment," *California Management Review* (Summer 1973), 64–66.

Partial Solutions in Job Design Although not every job can be enriched, partial solutions for jobs that are hard to enrich are available. For routine, boring, and otherwise undesirable jobs, the following suggestions may alleviate the worst effects.

- Use the job as an entry job in the organization, with the understanding that the employee will be there only a short time. Occasionally a worker might even want to remain in the job.
- Post the job daily. Often you will get a few daily volunteers who are looking for a change but don't want the job permanently.
- Employ the mentally handicapped, fitting them carefully to these types of jobs. They often make excellent employees when adequately trained and properly matched to a job.
- Employ part-time workers. Especially if full-time work is not available, part-time workers may be happy to do work that they would dislike on a full-time basis.

Like studies of job enlargement, studies of job enrichment are not conclusive. These studies have generally concentrated on jobs lending themselves to enrichment. It is clear that if pay or supervision is a source of dissatisfaction, job enrichment will likely fail.[4] Some workers do not accept the middle class values and goals inherent in job enrichment; they "don't want to be a manager." For some workers, enrichment might reduce social interaction, a result many workers would find undesirable. And many employees prefer low expectations of competency, high security, and relative independence rather than the increased responsibility and growth that job enrichment entails.

Job enrichment does have promise, though, and has been successful in some situations. It works best in conjunction with, not *in place of*, sound work measurement and traditional job design methods.

Job Redesign and Employee Participation Recent research in job design suggests that certain *core dimensions* of jobs can be redesigned to improve employee performance. These dimensions include the variety, identity, significance, autonomy, and feedback mechanisms of the task. Conceptually, we can redesign these core dimensions so that they allow for individual differences in people's reactions to and feelings about their jobs. Researchers have not yet been able to answer some basic questions about job redesign: How do we identify and measure individual characteristics? Can we directly relate these characteristics to actual (not perceived) performance? Research does suggest that *individual differences* in employees must be accounted for if job redesign is to be effective. Furthermore, some employees may strongly resist job redesign.[5] Often, the general feeling is, "I know this job better than you do; who are you to be changing it?" It is much easier to bring about meaningful change in jobs if managers give workers the opportunity to *participate* in the change process.

---

[4]Raymond J. Aldag and Arthur P. Brief, *Task Design and Employee Motivation* (Glenview, Ill.: Scott, Foresman, 1979), 101.

[5]See Szilagyi, 160–68; Aldag, 81–105; Jon L. Pierce and Randall B. Dunham, "Task Design: A Literature Review," *The Academy of Management Review* 1, no. 4 (October 1976), 83–97.

Using their company's procedures manual, this small group is redesigning jobs in their work group. Participation can provide job enrichment and greater job satisfaction.

Source: Jay Freis/The Image Bank

EFFECTIVE JOB DESIGN: COMBINING ENGINEERING AND BEHAVIORAL APPROACHES

On the one hand are traditional, industrial engineering techniques for designing jobs, outgrowths of the scientific management approach. On the other hand are behavioral techniques, outgrowths of more recent organizational behavior research. What, then, is best? Let's try to relate these two approaches.

Figure 8.4, illustrates that *both* traditional engineering and behavioral techniques can be and are used to achieve the same expected outcomes. But in either case, the outcomes achieved depend on variable parameters of the external environment, the organization, and the individual employee. These variables moderate or intervene between *job design* technique and *expected outcome,* thus making effective job design highly complex, as Figure 8.4 suggests.

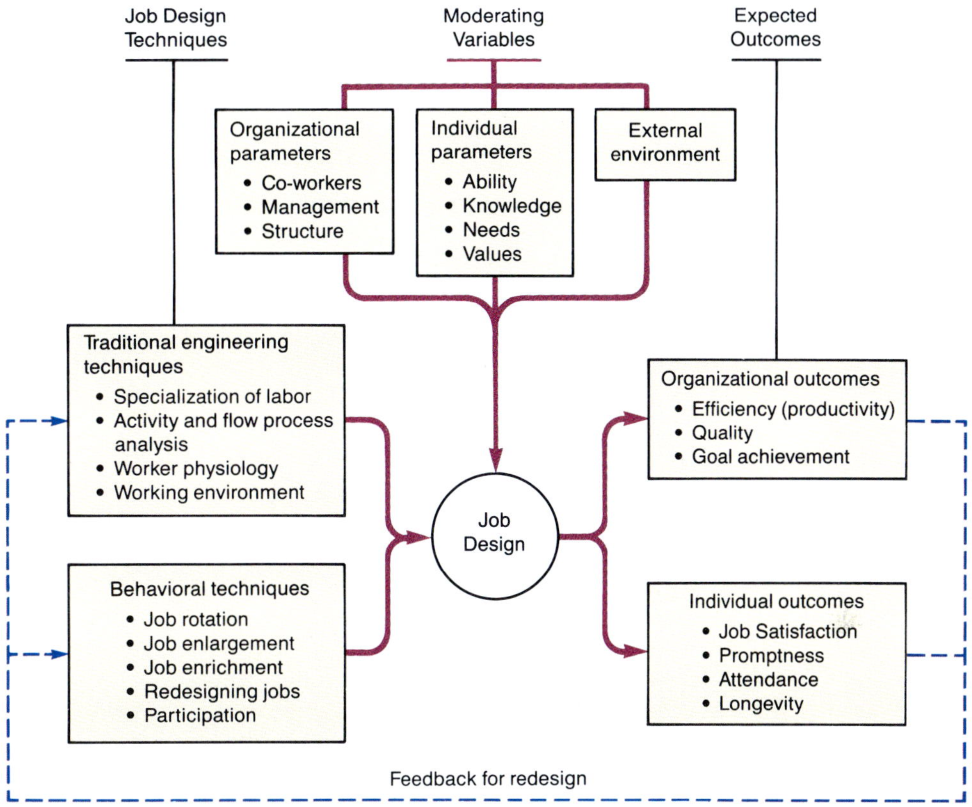

FIGURE 8.4 **Effective job design**

PRODUCTION AND OPERATIONS STANDARDS

Standard A quantitative criterion established as a basis for comparison in measuring or judging output.

To produce effectively and efficiently, management must establish goals for evaluating employee performance. These goals are translated into *standards.* A production and operations standard is a quantified criterion for measuring or judging output. The standard can be set for quantity, quality, cost, or any other attribute of output, and it is the basis for control.

STANDARDS AT VARIOUS LEVELS IN THE ORGANIZATION

Labor standard A quantitative criterion reflecting the output expected from an average worker under average conditions for a given time period.

Individual Standards The terms *standard, labor standard, production standard, labor time standard,* and *time standard* are often used interchangeably in operations management. A labor standard is simply the output expected from an average worker under average working conditions for a given time period. It is the concept of a "fair day's work." A standard for workers at the lowest level within the organization is expressed in terms of time allowed per unit of output or, conversely, output required per unit of time. A candy-making operation, for example, in which coconut is sprinkled on soft chocolate might have a standard of .01 minutes per piece or 100 pieces per minute.

In this labor-intensive assembly group, working in close proximity to one another, fair and accurate standards are essential for every individual as they assemble circuit boards. You can see how a team standard might be effective in this environment.

Source: Palmer/Kane/Tony Stone Worldwide

Departmental Standards Several workers may perform as a unit, thus forming a team-assembly operation. These teams may have one standard for the team's output. By adding all the individual and team standards together, managers can set department standards for quality, quantity, costs, and delivery dates.

In production and operations, one of the basic units of accountability is the department; the supervisor of the department is often evaluated in terms of his or her ability to manage the department efficiently. Frequently this evaluation is made against an expectation to operate at or near 100 percent *labor efficiency,* the comparison of "actual" labor hours to "standard" labor hours. For every actual labor hour used directly in operations, an expected number of pieces should be produced; this expected number is the standard. If this labor standard is achieved, we say 100 percent efficiency is achieved. If the standard is exceeded, more than 100 percent efficiency is achieved; and if the standard is not achieved, less than 100 percent efficiency is achieved.

Plant Standards At the plant, or comparable service unit (such as a hospital or a school), a specified volume of goods or services must be produced; labor, materials, and overhead standards must be maintained, and at the same time their costs must be controlled. If you are familiar with cost accounting systems, you realize the need for accurate cost systems for labor, materials, and overhead. Likewise, quality levels must be maintained commensurate with product objectives. The point is clear—operations managers have multiple goals, and they must account for them with multiple standards.

Surprisingly, labor time standards are used much less uniformly in the service sector than they are in manufacturing. Since the service sector is generally more labor intense, it could benefit most from labor time standards. If you find yourself employed in the service sector as an operations manager, you have an opportunity to bring great benefits to the largest labor sector of the economy by applying these scientific management techniques.

USES OF STANDARDS

As a basis for making operating decisions, labor time standards are used to evaluate the performance of workers and facilities and for predicting, planning, and controlling operations.

Consider two uses of time standards in shown Table 8.3: computing standard costs and estimating costs. Standard costs are computed in accounting as follows:

$$\text{Standard cost} = \text{Standard usage} \times \text{Standard labor rate} \tag{8.1}$$

TABLE 8.3 **Uses of labor time standards**

Evaluating Performance	Predicting, Planning, and Controlling Operations
Evaluating individual performance and subsequent compensation	Aggregate planning of work force levels and production rates
Evaluating department performance and subsequent supervisor compensation	Capacity planning and utilization
Evaluating process design, layout, and work methods	Scheduling operations; sequencing jobs
Comparing costs and revenues of equipment alternatives	Estimating cost of products and production lots
Calculating standard costs	Planning types of labor skills necessary and budgeting labor expenses

Standard usage An established industrial engineering time standard.

The *standard usage* is the industrial engineering established labor time standard; the standard labor rate is the accepted wage rate for the labor force that will be performing the work. If the standard usage—the labor standard—is incorrectly established, the standard cost will be in error. Standard costs are compared with actual costs, giving a *labor efficiency variance* where

$$\text{Actual costs} = \text{Actual usage} \times \text{Standard labor rate} \tag{8.2}$$

and

$$\text{Labor efficiency variance} = \text{Standard costs} - \text{Actual costs} \tag{8.3}$$

Key decisions are based on labor efficiency variances, so it is important that the data used to calculate the variance be correct. The following example illustrates how an error in establishing the labor standard carries through to the labor efficiency variance.

EXAMPLE

A manufacturing firm introducing a new product set a preliminary labor standard at 10 units/hour. The standard labor rate was $8/hour. During the third month of production, 800 units were produced using 90 labor hours. The labor efficiency variance is calculated as:

$$\begin{aligned}\text{Standard cost} &= (.10 \text{ hours/unit})\ (800 \text{ units})\ (\$8/\text{hour}) \\ &= \$640 \\ \text{Actual cost} &= (90 \text{ hrs})\ (\$8/\text{hour}) \\ &= \$720 \\ \text{Labor efficiency variance} &= \$640 - \$720 = -\ \$80\end{aligned}$$

Management was somewhat concerned about the negative variance, indicating actual costs are greater than standard costs, but decided to have industrial engineering thoroughly check the labor standard before taking corrective action. Engineering recommended the standard be established at 12 units/hour, and the labor efficiency variance was recalculated as

$$\begin{aligned}\text{Standard cost} &= (0.0833 \text{ hour/unit})\ (800 \text{ units})\ (\$8/\text{hour}) \\ &= \$533.12 \\ \text{Labor efficiency variance} &= \$533.12 - \$720 = -\$186.88\end{aligned}$$

The preliminary labor standard was in error by 20 percent (from 10 to 12 units/hour), and the corrected labor standard resulted in more than doubling the negative variance (from $-80 to −$186.88). Management now set out to find causes for the unfavorable variance.

FORMAL AND INFORMAL STANDARDS

There is no escaping the impact of the informal organization, with its own communication network, system of authority, leaders, and work standards. Standards of the informal organization may vary considerably from standards set by management, and operations managers should not ignore these informal organization standards. Rather, they must attempt to influence the informal organization to communicate in formal standards and at the same time attempt to influence the acceptance of formal standards by the informal work group.

THE ARGUMENT AGAINST STANDARDS

North American managers will, on occasion, argue that the wide use of labor standards is yet another nail in the coffin of American industry. Its tombstone epitaph would read "Not Competitive Worldwide." These managers insist that standards undermine the concept of *continuous improvement in all things.* The Japanese refer to this concept as *Kaizen.* The argument goes like this. A standard implies a quantified goal and when it is reached employees and managers alike will be satisfied and complacent. The focus should not be on a quantified goal expressed as a standard, but rather on *continuous improvement in performance,* to continually ask: Is there a better method? A better tool? Better instructions? Better training? With *Kaizen,* performance of today is measurement against performance in the past, not against a rigid or "absolute" number.

Kaizen The Japanese concept of continuous improvement in all things.

The philosophy esponsing standards and the philosophy esponsing *Kaizen* are not completely at odds. Both encompass a goal of improved performance and a way to measure whether the goal is achieved. The difference lies in how rigidly the goal is quantified. With standards, the quantification is fixed. With *Kaizen,* the quantification is continuously changing; the goal is to do better than before. As an operations manager you will need to reconcile or accommodate these philosophies. How you do so may well determine the competitive spirit of your employees.

WORK MEASUREMENT

A labor standard tells what is expected of an average worker performing under average conditions. There are two critical questions in establishing a labor standard:

1. How do we define "average" worker?
2. What dimension of performance should be measured, and in what units?

Work measurement The determination of the degree and quantity of labor in performing tasks.

After answering these questions, you can use *work measurement* techniques to establish labor time standards. Work measurement is the actual quantifying of performance dimensions.

THE AVERAGE WORKER

People vary not only in such physical characteristics as height, arm span, and strength, but in their working pace as well. To determine a labor standard, we need to find an "average worker." But how do we do that? Usually, the best thing to do is to choose a sample of workers and observe their performance. The costs of sampling and observing are traded off against the costs of inaccurate standards. The more workers sampled and observed, the costlier the sampling, but the closer the performance standard should be to true "average" performance, reducing costs associated with inaccurate standards. Then associated costs include the costs of inefficiency, distorted product costs, and costs related to all the operations activities listed in Table 8.3. In trading off the costs of sampling and the costs of inaccuracy, we can find a range of reasonably low total costs.

Once the average worker has been defined, we need to ask: Should the standard be the performance of the average worker or should the standard be set so that nearly everyone can be expected to achieve it? Table 8.4 shows a hypothetical situation in which workers are divided into five performance categories. Should the standard be set at 22.25 units per hour, the mean, or at 14 units per hour, a number that 95 percent of the workers can be expected to achieve? Some engineers feel that quoting a minimum standard, the second choice, encourages poor performance. They prefer to have about one-half the workers seeking but not attaining 100 percent of the standard; that is, they suggest setting the standard at the mean performance. Others feel that standards should be attainable by 90 to 95 percent of the workers. Both approaches can be used effectively.

TABLE 8.4 Distribution of 100 workers sampled

Number of Workers Sampled	Performance (in units/hour)	Frequency of Total Workers	Cumulative Frequency of Workers	Complementary Cumulative Frequency of Workers
5	10–14	0.05	0.05	0.95
20	15–19	0.20	0.25	0.75
45	20–24	0.45	0.70	0.30
25	25–29	0.25	0.95	0.05
5	30–34	0.05	1.00	0.00

PERFORMANCE DIMENSIONS

Managers generally consider *quantity* of input to be the primary dimension of performance to be measured. Quantity is usually measured as pieces per time period in manufacturing, and service units per time period in service industries. A lumber sawing operation, for example, might have a standard of 1,200 pieces sawed per hour; a bank might have a standard of 24 customers served per hour. Performance dimensions related to the quality of input are secondary. Quality standards are often expressed as the percent of output units that are allowable defective units. There are two key points in determining dimensions of performance:

1. The dimension must be specified before the standard is set.
2. The standard and subsequent actual performance must be measurable.

ACCURACY

How accurately can a work standard be set? Obviously, experienced engineers rating work can set a standard more accurately than can inexperienced raters. Although even experienced raters make errors, the standards they set are generally found to have lower variability than standards set using only historical data. We recommend that you use raters for work measurement, although you must be aware that because setting a standard is not a finely developed scientific procedure, there are bound to be some errors.

Work measurement techniques focus particularly on quantifying performance dimensions as a function of time.

WORK MEASUREMENT TECHNIQUES

There are six basic ways of establishing a time (work) standard:

1. Ignoring formal work measurement
2. Using the historical data approach
3. Using the direct time study approach
4. Using the predetermined time study approach
5. Using the work sampling approach
6. Combining approaches 2 through 5

Ignoring Formal Work Measurement For many jobs in many organizations, especially in the labor-intense service sector, formal labor standards are simply not set at all. The issue of a fair day's work for a fair day's pay is ignored. Even though there is no explicit basis for criticism, workers may be blamed for poor performance and inefficiency. Often, because management has not established a work (time) standard, some informal standard is established by default. Since this informal standard generally compares unfavorably with those set by other techniques, we do not recommend ignoring formal work measurement.

Historical Data Approach This method assumes that past performance is normal performance. In the absence of other formal techniques, some managers use past performance as their main guide in setting standards.

What are the advantages of this method? Basically, it is quick, simple, inexpensive, and probably better than ignoring formal work measurement altogether. The major disadvantage, as you can reason, is that past performance might not at all be what an average worker can reasonably be expected to perform under average working conditions.

Direct time study A work measurement technique that involves observing the job, determining the job cycle, stopwatch-timing the job cycle, and calculating a performance standard.

Direct Time Study Often called a *time study*, a *stopwatch study*, or *clocking the job*, this technique is certainly the most widely used method for establishing work standards in manufacturing. Perhaps you have observed a job being studied by an industrial engineer, clipboard and stopwatch in hand.

How does direct time study work? We won't go into all the fine points here, but basically there are six steps in the procedure:

1. Select the job to be timed. The direct time study approach depends upon direct observation and is therefore limited to jobs that already exist. The job selected should be standardized, in terms of equipment and materials, and the worker should be representative of all workers doing the job.
2. Select a job cycle. Identify the elements and tasks that constitute a complete cycle. Decide how many cycles you want to time with a stopwatch.
3. Time the job for all cycles and rate the worker. Workers behave in varying ways when their performances are being recorded; common reactions are resentment, nervousness, and slowing the work pace. To minimize these effects, repeated study, study across several workers, and standing by one worker while studying a job somewhere nearby, perhaps in another department, can be helpful. You can assign the worker a rating, as a percentage of the "normal" or average worker. Industrial engineers frequently use a rating factor when timing jobs. In essence the engineer is judging the worker as 85 percent normal, 90 percent normal, or some other rating depending on his or her perception of "normal." Obviously, ratings of this kind depend on subjective judgments.
4. Compute the *normal time* based on the average cycle time and the worker rating.
5. Determine the fraction of time available, making allowances for personal needs; delays, and fatigue.
6. Set the performance standard (standard time) based on the normal time and the allowances (steps 4 and 5).

Normal time The average cycle time for a job, adjusted by a **worker rating** to account for variations in "normal" performance.

Allowance fraction The fraction of time lost on a job because of workers' personal needs, fatigue, and other unavoidable delays; the remaining fraction of time is the **available fraction.**

Standard time The ratio of normal time to the available fraction of time.

To be more precise about the calculations of this procedure:

$$\text{Average cycle time} = \frac{\text{Sum of cycle times recorded}}{\text{Number of cycles observed}}$$

$$\text{Normal time} = \text{Average cycle time} \times \text{Worker rating}$$

$$\textit{Allowance fraction} = \text{Fraction of time for personal needs, fatigue, and unavoidable delays}$$

$$\text{Available fraction of time} = 1 - \text{allowance fraction}$$

$$\textit{Standard time} = \frac{\text{Normal time}}{\text{Available fraction of time}} \tag{8.4}$$

Operations Management Highlight 8.1 describes how several companies have effectively used work measurement techniques.

OPERATIONS MANAGEMENT HIGHLIGHT 8.1

Source: John Zoiner

Work Measurement Works

Work measurement at Ohio Edison Company, a regional utility, has resulted in a $1.4 million savings in just two years. Ohio Edison developed a comprehensive, computerized work measurement system to measure some 95 percent of their utility line work, delineating 265 "work packages"—such as installing a line pole—in the process. A computer report compared actual performance to the historical standard. Ohio Edison's goal was to improve communication between employees and management. That goal was achieved, along with a 7 percent increase in efficiency.

At Ford Motor Company are union members, engineers, and management sharing a common goal: a more competitive product through improved quality and productivity. Concomitant with this goal is Ford's Modular Arrangement of Predetermined Time Standards (MODAPTS), which provides a common language for work measurement and standards. MODAPTS is a part of Ford's $50 million per year involvement effort to get 110,000 automobile workers informed and participating in change. The application of MODAPTS has been successfully implemented in Ford's Norfork, Virginia, plant and is being expanded to other facilities.

Woolworth Holdings PLC and their national contract trucking carrier retained a United Kingdom management consulting firm to bring outside expertise to solving their delivery problems. The firm studied Woolworth's delivery systems, established new methods, set time standards, and created a new pay system for drivers. Schedules were set and a work measurement system established to assure Woolworth that their new store configuration investment would be supported by their contract delivery service. The result was an increased level of performance and an assurance that the service could be measured and monitored.

An unusual work measurement program at Clark Distribution Services Company in Chicago, ensures same-day filling of regular and rush orders for 1,200 equipment dealers. The activity card is the vehicle for change; computerized data from the card allows management to measure work and to respond immediately to bottlenecks or productivity slumps. The firm's President estimates the savings to be $1 million per year. The initial investment provides a 1000 percent annual return, quite acceptable by any yardstick.

Sources: Alex M. Stefanovic and Daniel C. Demko, "Ohio Edison's Line Work Measurement System Saves $1.4 Million a Year," *Transmission and Distribution* 41, no. 12 (December 1989), 54–59; Michael D. Shinnick and Walter W. Erwin, "Work Measurement System Creates Shared Responsibility Among Workers at Ford," *Industrial Engineering* 21, no. 8 (August 1989), 28–30; "Improving Store Delivery Schedules: The Woolworth Experience," *Retail and Distribution Management* (UK) 16, no. 2 (March/April 1988), 55–56; and Larry Beak, "Work-Measurement Program Saves $1 Billion Annually," *Modern Materials Handling* 42, no. 9 (August 1987), 68–71.

EXAMPLE

The time study of a machinery operation recorded cycle times of 8.0, 7.0, 8.0, and 9.0 minutes. The analyst rated the observed worker as 90 percent. The firm uses a .15 allowance fraction. Computing the standard time,

$$\text{Average cycle time} = \frac{8.0 + 7.0 + 8.0 + 9.0}{4} = 8.0 \text{ minutes}$$

$$\text{Normal time} = (8.0)(.90) = 7.2 \text{ minutes}$$

$$\text{Standard time} = \frac{7.2}{(1 - 0.15)} = \frac{7.2}{.85} = 8.47 \text{ minutes}$$

The standard time for this machinery operation would be set at 8.47 minutes, which is greater than the average cycle time observed. The average cycle time was adjusted for the rating factor (90 percent) and the allowance fraction (.15).

EXAMPLE

A laboratory research study required that a routine, repetitive task be designed so that quantity and quality could easily be measured. A collating task similar to such industrial jobs as collating sheets of paper for a promotional mailing, interleaving ash trays and paper in a packing operation, or collating papers for filing by an office file clerk was devised. For this collating task, a worker took one IBM data processing card from each of six boxes, examined each card for keypunching errors, and sequenced the cards in order, one from each box. A sequence of six good cards made one good set. The worker then stepped to another table and placed the set in a box of good units. If an error card was found, the worker placed the error card in an error box and returned to take another card from the box in which the error card had been found. The study required that the worker repeatedly collate good sets of six cards for several hours at a time.

A cycle consisted of completing one good set, placing the good set in the box, and returning to the six boxes to begin again. A time study was made by observing five different workers for 20 cycles each. The average cycle time for each worker is shown in the table. The average overall cycle time was 0.2247 minutes/cycle. (Another way of stating the standard is 4.4503 units/minute or, more commonly, 267 units/hour).

Direct time study for the quantity standard (expressed in minutes/cycle)

Observation	Single Card	Six Card-Set	Average Time
1	.0286	.1610	.1966[a]
2	.0255	.1540	.2287
3	.0166	.2089	.2804
4	.0276	.1616	.1831
5	.0292	.2096	.2345
Average	.0255	.1790	.2247

[a]Average of performance times for 20 cycles.

A question deserving an answer is: Why was the sample made up of five workers and 20 cycles? It was judged that this sample was of sufficient size to give a reasonably accurate estimate of average time, at a reasonable cost; in direct time study there is an accuracy/cost tradeoff.

Predetermined time study A work measurement technique that involves observing or thinking through a job, recording job elements, recording preestablished motion units, and calculating a performance standard.

Predetermined Time Study For setting standards for jobs that are not currently being performed but are being planned, the predetermined time study is helpful. A predetermined time study can also be applied to existing jobs as an alternative to a direct time study. The bases of this technique are the stopwatch time study and time study from films. Historical data have been accumulated on tens of thousands of people making such basic motions as reaching, grasping, stepping, lifting, and standing. These motions have been broken down into elements, each element timed, the times averaged to yield predetermined time standards, and the standards published in table form. The procedure for setting a predetermined time standard is as follows:

1. Observe the job or think it through if it is not yet being performed. It is best to observe under "typical" conditions: typical machine, materials, and worker.
2. Itemize the job elements. Do not be concerned about timing them; just thoroughly document all the motions performed by the worker.
3. From a table of predetermined time standards, record the standard for each motion units. Motion units are expressed in some basic scale (a Therblig scale is often used) that corresponds to time units.
4. Find the sum of the standards for all motions.
5. Estimate an allowance for personal time, delays, and fatigue, and add to the sum of standards. This total sum is the predetermined time standard for the job.

Details of this procedure are illustrated by reexamining the collating task discussed earlier.

The primary advantage of predetermined time studies is that they are not skewed by a typical performance of workers who are nervous because they are being timed: the timing has already taken place—away from the workplace in a logical, systematic manner. The basic disadvantage of this technique is that some job elements may not be recorded, or may be recorded improperly. Furthermore, if job elements can't be properly categorized and located in a table, a direct time study approach must be made instead of the predetermined time study.

EXAMPLE

Time measurement unit (TMU) A unit of time, equivalent to 0.00001 hours, used as a basis for *methods time measurement (MTM)*, a widely accepted form of predetermined time study.

For the collating job, a predetermined time standard was set. Table 8.5 shows the motions of the right and left hands and standards for each. The unit of measurement used is called a *Time Measurement Unit (TMU)*. One TMU is equivalent to 0.00001 hours. This technique is called *methods time measurement* (MTM) and is a widely accepted predetermined time study approach. The MTM procedure allows one to observe the task, breaking it down into movements that have been studied in depth and for which have a predetermined standard has been measured. For clarity, the MTM chart in Table 8.5 was broken into several blocks.

Notice toward the bottom of Table 8.5 the error allowance (placing an error card in the error box) of 3.2 TMU, and the allowance fraction of .15 for personal needs (fatigue and unavoidable delay). This allowance for personal needs is typical in industrial engineering.

Since one TMU equals 0.00001 hours, the total MTM time per cycle, 397.9 TMU, is converted to .23874 minutes/cycle. This is 4.189 units/minute, or 251 units/hour.

TABLE 8.5 Methods time measurement chart for collating job cycle

Right Hand	Standard (in TMU)	Left Hand
	14.2	Reach to cards
	3.5	Grasp a card
	10.6	Apply pressure to separate
	3.5	Turn card
	13.4	Move to focus eyes
Transfer card from other hand	5.6	
	50.8	Subtotal
	× 6	Multiplied by 6*
	304.8	Subtotal
	5.6	Transfer cards from other hand
	13.4	Move to final box
	4.0	Disengage cards
	15.0	Walk back to start again
	342.8	Subtotal
	3.2	Error allowance
	346.0	Subtotal
	× 1.15	.15 allowance fraction
	397.9	Total TMU

*Six good cards made one good set.

Work sampling A work measurement technique that involves defining the state of "working," observing the job over time, and computing the portion of time the worker is "working."

Work Sampling Work sampling does not involve stopwatch measurement, as do many of the other techniques; instead, it is based on simple random sampling techniques derived from statistical sampling theory. The purpose of the sampling is to estimate what proportion of a worker's time is devoted to work activities. It proceeds along the following steps:

1. Decide what activities are defined as "working." "Not working" comprises all activities not specifically defined as "working."
2. Observe the worker at selected intervals, recording whether a person is working or not.
3. Calculate the portion P of time a worker is working as:

$$P = \frac{\text{Number of observations during which working occurred}}{\text{Total number of observations}} \tag{8.5}$$

This calculation can then be used as a performance standard.

EXAMPLE

A library administrator was concerned about the amount of time a circulation desk clerk spent idly at the desk. "Working" for the circulation desk clerk meant only assisting a patron at the circulation desk. Working at a nearby desk, the information clerk was asked to record once every half-hour for a week whether or not the circulation clerk was "working." Results were as follows:

Day	Number of Observations	Number of Observations during which work occurred
Monday	16	8
Tuesday	15	8
Wednesday	20	12
Thursday	16	10
Friday	16	10
	Total 83	Total 48

The portion of the time spent working, as defined by the administrator, was

$$P = \frac{48}{83} = .578$$

The administrator concluded that the portion was low enough to warrant adding other clerical activities to this job.

Work sampling can also be used to set standards; the procedure is similar to the one used in direct time studies. We can determine normal time as shown below (Equation 8.6) and calculate standard times according to Equation 8.4.

$$\text{Normal time} = \frac{\text{Total observation time} \times \begin{array}{c}\text{Percent of time}\\ \text{worker observed}\\ \text{working}\end{array} \times \begin{array}{c}\text{Worker}\\ \text{rating}\end{array}}{\text{Number of units produced}} \tag{8.6}$$

Work sampling is particularly adaptive to service sector jobs such as those in libraries, banking, health care, insurance companies, and government. Accuracy of this technique depends keenly upon sample size.

Disadvantages of work sampling are that the analyst may not be completely objective or may study only a few workers, and that "working" is a broad concept not easily defined with precision. There are, however, some obvious advantages with work sampling: It is simple, easily adapted to service sector and indirect labor jobs, and an economical way to measure performance. In short, work sampling is a useful work measurement technique if it is used with discretion.

Combining Work Measurement Techniques Which work measurement technique should you use? In practice, they are used in combination, as cross-checks. One common practice is to observe a job, write down in detail all the job elements, and set a predetermined time standard. Then you can check the history of performance on this or similar jobs to verify that the predetermined standard is reasonable. To provide a further check, a direct time study can be made of the job by element and in total. No one work measurement technique is totally reliable. Because of the high skill level required in setting the standard, a cross-check is desirable whenever possible.

EXAMPLE

For the collating task we discussed earlier, the predetermined time standard was .2383 minutes/cycle. This was cross-validated by a direct time study, which provided a standard of .2247 minutes/cycle. Finally, in a previous study of this job under slightly different conditions, recorded time was .1954 minutes/cycle. The first two times are quite close, and the third was reasonably close, so the predetermined time standard was adopted.

An apparent oversight in the direct time study is the omission of the .15 allowance fraction used in the predetermined time study. If this allowance is deleted from the predetermined time study, the time is .2076 minutes/cycle, which is similar to the historically recorded time of .1954 minutes/cycle.

Work Measurement for White-Collar Workers Among the work measurement techniques presented, which appear most suitable for white-collar workers? Since white-collar jobs are typically labor intense and minimally automated, the same measurement techniques employed in the service sector would seem appropriate. We suggest a combination of historical data and work sampling. When a predetermined time study can be used—on more routine white-collar jobs—it can also be a useful approach.

Some experts have questioned the use of predetermined time standards in office settings.[6] Their argument is that office tasks are not repetitive and identical, as predetermined time studies require. Rather than focusing on measurement and a standard, these experts suggest more worker-management involvement, stressing participation and doing the task right the first time. To a great extent, that is the method recommended by the American Productivity and Quality Center (APQC) for white-collar productivity measurement and improvement.[7] The APQC method uses the nominal group method with the group involved in setting work processes and

[6]Robert L. DiGiacomo, "The Questionable Success of Conventional Clerical Work Measurement," *National Underwriter* 90, no. 2 (January 11, 1986), 13.

[7]"Measuring White-Collar Work," (parts 2 and 3), *Incentive* 162, no. 6 (June 1988), 58–61 and no. 7 (July 1988), 46–47.

measurement. The research behind this method was developed in part at Arizona State University and the University of Missouri–Columbia.[8]

In Operations Management Highlight 8.2 we examine how the proliferation of personal, mini, mainframe, laptops, and all manner of computers in offices of the 1990s is raising even more questions about work measurement techniques for offices, as well as questions these techniques may help to answer.

Current Uses of Work Measurement A comprehensive 1976 survey of U.S. and Canadian industries asked, "Are you using work measurement and, if you are, for what purposes?"[9] Responses were then compared with a similar survey *Factory* magazine had conducted in 1959. Of the nearly 1,500 usable responses in the 1976 survey, 89 percent reported they were using work measurement. This contrasts sharply with the 1956 survey, in which only 71 percent of the 785 respondents reported using work measurement. Correspondingly, the later survey found 53 percent of the respondents used work measurement to measure employee performance, compared with only 20 percent in the earlier survey. In the 1976 survey, work measurement was also used for estimating and costing (89 percent), establishing wage incentives (59 percent), and production scheduling (55 percent). As the survey makes clear, this traditional scientific management technique is by no means "dead" or "outdated" in industry; rather, it is apparently quite useful.

Another dimension of the 1976 survey involves setting standards. The question was asked "What conditions trigger revision of a standard?" Reasons most frequently cited were changes in methods and materials (75 percent), low performance due to a tight standard (65 percent), and high performance due to a loose standard (54 percent). The respondents were also asked, "How are standards established?" From Table 8.6 we see time study to be the most popular technique (89.5 percent). The percentages do not add to 100 percent, since often more than one technique is used to set a standard.

TABLE 8.6 How standards are established

Work Measurement Technique	Percent of Time Used
Time study	89.5
Predetermined approaches	
Standard data	61.4
Predetermined time standard system	32.2
Estimate based on historical experience	44.2
Work sampling	21.3
Others	3.0

Source: Rice, "Survey," 21. Reprinted with permission from *Industrial Engineering Magazine* (July 1977). Copyright Institute of Industrial Engineers, 25 Technology Park/Atlanta, Norcross, GA 30092.

[8]Everett E. Adam, James C. Hershauer, and William A. Ruch, *Productivity and Quality: Measurement as a Basis for Improvement*, 2nd ed., Research Center, College of Business and Public Administration, University of Missouri–Columbia, 1986.

[9]Robert S. Rice, "Survey of Work Measurement and Wage Incentives," *Industrial Engineering* 9, no. 7 (July 1977), 18–31.

OPERATIONS MANAGEMENT HIGHLIGHT 8.2

Source: Al Satterwhite/The Image Bank

Computerized Offices Are Changing the Nature of Work Measurement Techniques

Critics are suggesting that Barbara Garson's book ***The Electronic Sweatshop*** may be t' most provocative study of office computing to come along since personal computers became standard office equipment. Garson substitles her book "How Computers Are Transforming the Office of the Future into the

Factory of the Past," and claims that workers are continually paced and monitored by computers, making conditions similar to an assembly line. But computers go one better than the assembly line, affording constant, not periodic, and instant measuring of performance. Garson reports that 50 percent of all white-collar and clerical work is monitored by computer. Such electronic surveillance is accompanied by a constant state of tension; the potential human costs are easily deduced.

If the computer, as Garson suggests, has carried work measurement too far, the computer may also be the cause for new work measurement research. Computers and automation in the office create their own brand of fatigue. Repeated bouts with technical jargon, for example, is stressful and tension provoking. While many studies have focused on fatigue in the factory, few have set their sights in documenting the effects of fatigue in the office. One study to accept the challenge measured work output, heart rate, and brain wave activity of office workers who worked five hours without rest, comparing the same measurements with those of workers who were allowed to rest. The resulting data clearly confirmed that, without rest, white-collar performance sagged. More work measurement research is needed to better understand the computerized office environment and its effect on performance.

Sources: Tom Spain, "The Dark Side of Computing," *D & B Reports* 36, no. 3 (May/June 1988), 54–56; and O. Geoffrey Okogbaa and Richard L. Shell, *IIE Transactions* 8, no. 4 (December 1986), 335–42.

In 1986 within the Northamptonshire area of Great Britain, private and public organizations were surveyed about work measurement trends.[10] The most-used techniques were work sampling, time study, and a combination. The public sector clearly was increasing use of work measurement techniques, while the private sector appeared to have plateaued. There was no apparent decline in management's commitment to the techniques in either sector.

A broader survey conducted in 1986 in Japan, Europe, and the United States revealed that the productivity of companies using work measurement techniques was higher than companies not using them.[11] According to the survey, 83 percent of Japanese companies and 92 percent of European and American companies have set specific time standards and consider them a valuable tool. Japan tends to use more informal work measurement techniques, such as estimation by experience and measurement from historical business results. Regardless of culture, firms wanted higher accuracy with more simplicity. More broadly, 48 percent of Japanese firms see industrial engineers having expanded roles in decision-making, while 61 percent of European and United States firms thought so. We understand that industrial engineers and manufacturing engineers are more prevalent in Japan, which might explain this difference.

Two comments are in order. First, firms continue to report the usefulness of work measurement. Second, though productivity was higher for firms using work measurement than for those who did not, these same firms were likely to use other good management practices as well. Which practices, then, actually lead to higher productivity? Work measurement, job redesign, effective scheduling techniques, good strategic planning? Inconclusive studies such as this are common in business, and production/operations management is no exception. Using tenuous results to make decisions is, in part, what makes management more a "practice" rather than a "science."

COMPENSATION

In their desire to motivate employees and sustain high levels of performance and job satisfaction, production and operations managers establish compensation systems for jobs. Compensation typically is either a commonly used conventional system, resulting in a fixed hourly or monthly wage, or an incentive system, resulting in a variable wage. Table 8.7 summarizes such systems.

Managers view compensation as a way to influence behavior, whereas employees see it as a reward. Because of these different perspectives, the compensation system does not always provide the intended motivation, performance, satisfaction, and loyalty. Systems should be matched to objectives. If the organization values job experience, a seniority-based system might be best. Yet this might frustrate high achievers who would prefer incentive or merit-based systems. There seems to be a increasing interest in incentive systems of all types, but especially organization-wide (or plant-wide) systems called *productivity gain-sharing.* These are modifications of traditional plans, such as Lincoln or Scanlon plans, that have been available for some time. These compensation systems reward increases in group performance, usually sharing gains between the company and the employees equitably.

Productivity gain-sharing Rewarding employees for increases in organization-wide group performance.

[10]A.C. Cozens, "The Figure of Work Measurement in Northamptonshire," *Management Services* (UK) 32, no. 9 (September 1988), 20–22.

[11]Shigeyasu Sakamoto, "Key to Productivity: Work Measurement—An International Survey Report," *MTM Journal of Methods—Time Measurement* 13 (1987), 68–75.

TABLE 8.7 Summary of conventional and incentive pay systems

Conventional Systems	Incentive Systems
Job-based—Employee paid according to job characteristics; all employees on this job are given the same *rate* of pay. *Seniority-based*—Employee paid according to job characteristics and length of service; all employees on this job are given the same *range* of pay. Those with higher seniority are paid higher in the paid range. *Merit-based*—Employee paid according to job characteristics and performance; all employees on this job are given the same *range* of pay. Those who perform better are paid higher in the range. *Mixed-based*—Employee paid according to job characteristics and some combination of seniority, merit, and other.	*Individual*—Employee paid solely on the basis of measured performance; higher performance is tied directly and objectively to higher pay. *Group*—All employees in a work group are paid according to the performance of the of the group. *Organization-wide*—Employee according to some aspect of the organization-wide performance; cost savings or profit-sharing bonuses, awarded as supplements to conventional or other primary pay systems, are examples.

Source: Charles N. Greene, Everett E. Adam, Jr., and Ronald J. Ebert, *Management for Effective Performance.* (Englewood Cliffs, N.J.: Prentice-Hall, 1985), 118.

SUMMARY

This chapter highlighted a key function of production/operations management: to design jobs, establish job standards, and perform work measurement. In practice, job design is followed by work measurement (establishing the job standard through measurement).

We noted that traditional engineering approaches to job design have emphasized the use of operation charts, activity charts, flow process charts, and principles of motion economy. We showed that consideration must also be given to worker physiology and environmental conditions, as these affect job design. Such behavioral techniques as job rotation, enlargement, and enrichment, and involving employees in redesigning jobs were shown to enhance productivity and satisfaction. We learned that if managers use both traditional modeling and contemporary behavioral concepts in designing jobs, the results may be more efficient and effective performance than could be provided by either alone.

We emphasized the importance of standards. After the job has been designed, individual, department, and plant job standards must be established. Standards are used for evaluating the performance of employees and facilities and predicting, planning, and controlling operations.

Although work measurement techniques are not perfect, they were shown to yield results considerably more accurate than other alternatives may yield, such as relying totally on management's judgment. Work measurement techniques include using historical data, direct time study, predetermined time study, and work sampling. In practice, several techniques are used in combination to cross-validate the work that is measured.

CASE

First National Bank

Lock-box operations in large commercial banks process accounts receivable for customers. First National Bank has a major commitment to lock-box operations and is currently the regional processor for several major oil companies and national retailers, a large credit card company, and dozens of small regional companies. Customers of these companies mail their payments directly to First National, using a special zip code. Theoretically, First National is able to intercept the payment (shorten the mail time), process the paperwork, and credit the firm's account—all within a day from the time it receives the payment.

Lock-box operations are becoming a problem for First National. Every day it receives thousands of bills and payments for hundreds of accounts. Over the last few months, there have been as many as three days' backlog. First National is in jeopardy of losing two national accounts to competing banks, which are outperforming First National. First National has assigned a "breakthrough" team to set performance standards and study jobs within the Lock-box department.

The key job appears to be the account processor job. An account processor opens incoming mail, verifies payment with the bill, records payment by account number, separates payments and bills, and delivers each for further processing. An account processor must also encode the payments (usually checks) and send them to check processing so that they can clear the bank and First National can receive credit for the money it has credited to the national account customer.

The team performed both a direct time study and work sample for the account processor job, with the results shown below. The bank uses a .15 allowance fraction for all clerical jobs.

Management is concerned that setting a standard now will further damage performance. In fact, the day after the direct time study, 14 of the 35 second-shift workers were absent, a number much higher than the normal 10 percent. Jan Holms, an informal group leader who was one of the workers studied, told the analyst the company would "pay for this pressure." She was one of those absent the next day.

Frank Waring, the operations vice president, would like to change the entire work flow, dissolving the lock-box department as it is now organized and grouping lock-box and other operations functions by customer rather than product. Frank's counterpart at Citibank wrote an article for the *Harvard Business Review* explaining his bank's success with this "customer account focus," and Frank was most impressed. Although it seems an appropriate time to consider such a move, Frank is not gathering the support he had anticipated from his team of management subordinates.

Direct time study data: account processor job

	Processer 1					Processor 2				
Cycle time (in minutes)	0.5	0.7	1.0	1.3	1.5	0.5	0.7	1.0	1.5	2.0
Number of times observed	1	3	5	2	1	2	4	3	1	1
Performance rating			85%					80%		

Work sampling data: account processor job

	Processor 1	Processor 2
Number of payments processed	322	296
Length of time observed (in hours)	8	8
Performance rating	85%	80%
Idle time	25%	30%

REVIEW AND DISCUSSION QUESTIONS

1. Explain the difference between job design and job standards.
2. Discuss the relationship between work measurement and job design. Which typically follows the other? Why?
3. Contrast operation charts, activity charts, and flow process charts.
4. Contrast conventional compensation systems with incentive systems. As a beginning management trainee, which would you prefer? Why?
5. Explain how traditional engineering and behavioral job design can actually be used together (see Figure 8.4).
6. Contrast job enlargement and job enrichment. Are they mutually exclusive?
7. Discuss the assumptions behind job enlargement.
8. Explain how departmental and plant standards differ from individual job standards. Provide an example of each from an organization of your choice.
9. Select two uses of time (labor) standards. Explain how the time standard could help a municipal police department in a city of 40,000 persons for the two uses you have selected.
10. Explain the predetermined time study approach to work measurement.
11. Why would combining work measurement techniques be a good strategy in establishing a standard?
12. Discuss the current use of work measurement. What do you conclude?
13. Why are job standards important?

PROBLEMS

SOLVED PROBLEMS

1. In a candy factory a direct time study was made of the chocolate melting and pouring operation. Two inexperienced industrial engineers and one experienced engineer all made the study simultaneously. They agreed precisely on cycle

times (shown below) but varied on rating the worker. The experienced engineer rated the worker 100 percent, and the other engineers rated the worker 80 percent and 110 percent. The firm uses a .15 percent allowance fraction.

Cycle Time (in minutes)	Number of Times Observed
25	1
29	2
30	2
31	1

(a) Determine the standard time using the experienced industrial engineer's worker rating.

(b) Find the standard times using the worker rating of each inexperienced engineer. What is your interpretation when compared to part (a)? Are you sure the experienced engineer is correct? What could be done to enhance consistency in analyst performance ratings?

SOLUTION

Rating the worker at (100%):

$$\text{Normal time} = \frac{25(1) + (29)(2) + (30)(2) + 31(1)}{6}(100\%) = 29 \text{ minutes}$$

$$\text{Standard time} = \frac{29}{1 - .15} = 34.12 \text{ minutes}$$

Rating the worker at 110%:

$$\text{Normal time} = 29 \times 110\% = 31.90 \text{ minutes}$$

$$\text{Standard time} = \frac{31.90}{1 - .15} = 37.53 \text{ minutes}$$

Rating the worker at 80%:

$$\text{Normal time} = 29 \times 80\% = 23.20 \text{ minutes}$$

$$\text{Standard time} = \frac{23.2}{1 - .15} = 27.29 \text{ minutes}$$

Obviously, considerably different standard times are derived for different ratings. Although an experienced engineer could be wrong, we have more confidence in an experienced person. We could enhance consistency by training. Training films and short courses are available.

2. As a cargo loader for Southeastern Airlines, you are charged with the responsibility of setting a time standard (in minutes) for uploading refrigerated unitized loads. The following study was conducted over 300 hours with 900 uploadings performed.

Composite Worker Rating (in percent)	Activity	Number of Times Observed
80	Manually check and lift unitized load onto trailer	100
100	Tow loaded trailer with tractor to aircraft	300
120	Check electrical contacts holding pins and safety wires (called *wiring out;* this time will be reduced by 50 percent by an additional inspection during manufacture of the containers)	400
90	Correct any malfunctioning observed during wiring out	100
110	Load unitized load into plane bay with automatic lift	400
140	Return tractor and trailer to warehouse	300
	Personal or idle time	400

Official Southeastern personal time allowance fraction is .10 for an eight-hour work day *unless otherwise stated;* it is not otherwise stated here.

SOLUTION

$$\text{Average cycle time} = \frac{300 \text{ hours}}{900 \text{ uploadings}} = \frac{1}{3}\text{ hour} = 20 \text{ minutes}$$

Normal Minutes/Uploading

$$20 \times \frac{100}{2000} \times .80 = 8.0 \text{ minutes}$$

$$20 \times \frac{300}{2000} \times 1.00 = 3.0 \text{ minutes}$$

$$20 \times \frac{400}{2000} \times 1.20 \times 0.50 = 2.4 \text{ minutes}$$

$$20 \times \frac{100}{2000} \times .90 = .9 \text{ minutes}$$

$$20 \times \frac{400}{2000} \times 1.10 = 4.4 \text{ minutes}$$

$$20 \times \frac{300}{2000} \times 1.40 = 4.2 \text{ minutes}$$

Total normal time minutes/uploading = 22.9 minutes

$$\text{Standard time} = \frac{15.7 \text{ minutes/uploading}}{1 - .10} = 25.4 \text{ minutes/uploading} = .42 \text{ hours/uploading}$$

REINFORCING FUNDAMENTALS

3. **An experienced industrial engineer conducted a direct time study for an acid mixing operation. The analyst found cycle times as shown below, rated the observed worker at 80 percent, and used the firm's .10 allowance fraction. Determine the standard time.**

Cycle Time (in minutes)	Number of Times Observed
2.7	3
2.7	4
2.9	2
3.1	1
3.2	1

4. A speciality wood products company in eastern Kentucky manufacturers hand-made miniature wooden dogs. This Dandy Dogie product line is hand-carved, varnished, labeled, and boxed, all by the same person. But there are wide variances in quality and performance times, which management is no longer willing to accept. In the hope of establishing a standard time, management has done a direct time study focusing on the two-inch walnut beagle. The results are shown below. For now, hand-carving is being eliminated from the study. The firm's allowance fraction is .10. Establish a standard time for the remainder of the job.

Task times for Dandy Dogie (in minutes)

	Cycle				
Job Element	1	2	3	4	Worker Rating (in percent)
Varnish	5	4	5	4	105
Label	0.5	0.4	0.3	0.5	95
Box	2	2	1	2	95

5. American Commerce's labor standard for over-the-road truck drivers is 320 miles/8-hour shift. Current wages are $8/hour under a nationwide contract. The assigned drivers from the Cleveland terminal logged 31,525 miles the first week of April and recorded 822 hours of work. A no-overtime policy is in force for Cleveland-based drivers.
   (a) What is the labor efficiency variance for the first week of April?
   (b) The American Commerce shop steward (driver union representative) contends that since the drivers log primarily noninterstate miles, the standard should be 10 percent less, or 288 miles/day. Operating management would like a comparative labor variance for the first week in April. What do these labor variances actually mean to management?
6. A farming conglomerate has a large cow-calf operation. The manager expects the hay crew to place 1,750 bales of hay in the barn daily during harvest. The contract costs for labor only are $180/day (for a crew of four). In the past four days 8,100

bales have been harvested. What is the farm manager's labor efficiency variance for the hay crew? Would you suggest any action based on this figure?

7. Direct time study for a job resulted in the following times.

Cycle	Average Cycle Time (in minutes)
1	1.321
2	1.411
3	1.704
4	1.175

A predetermined time standard was set at 2,128 TMU/cycle, which converts to 1.275 minutes/cycle. What time standard would you recommend? Justify your choice.

8. Develop an employee/machine activity chart to show how a multipage term paper should be copied on a coin-operated photocopy machine. Use a layout diagram. Assume there are ample coins and that the stack of pages is unstapled at the start of the task.

9. Job analysis reveals that during a typical 8-hour workday a man-machine operation typically experiences various unavoidable delays totaling 40 minutes and one equipment setup changeover of 20 minutes. Operators need 20 minutes for personal time and take two 15-minute coffee breaks. Standard time per cycle (to produce one unit) is 10 minutes. How many units are produced by an operator rated at 85 percent? At 115 percent?

10. A student facing midterm exams decides to start studying in earnest. After one day in the library, the student is dismayed to find that, at her current rate of studying, she will not be ready to take the exams until four days after they are over. A friend volunteers to do a work sample and finds the following:

Study Period	Number of Observations	Number of Observations During Which Studying Occurred
1	11	8
2	23	11
3	7	3

As a percentage of her study period time, what portion of time is she studying?

11. Filing clerks in a state department of welfare were considered to be working any

time they had paper in their hands. Observations were made for seven days. Results are given below. What portion of time is spent in working? What work measurement technique is this? How might one alternatively define working?

Day	Number of Observations	Observations During Which Work Occurred
1	14	10
2	17	10
3	10	5
4	23	14
5	14	10
6	11	9
7	19	13

CHALLENGING EXERCISES

12. Several laboratory technicians in a hospital are responsible for running the highly automated "Chemistry 12" blood profile test. An experienced technician was monitored over a two-week period (70 hours). The analyst studying the job found that the technician performed 412 blood profile tests, working 60 percent of the time and idle the rest. Some idleness was due to waiting for the automated equipment to complete the test. The technician was rated at 85 percent, but the analyst was uncertain about this rating because of the automated equipment. Allowances are set at .10.

(a) Determine a standard time for a standard blood profile test.

(b) How could the analyst be more certain about the worker rating?

13. A manufacturer is considering buying one of two types of equipment, type A or type B. Initial equipment cost is $10,000 for either A or B. Operating costs are estimated as follows:

	A	B
Maintenance (per month)	$750	$500
Supplies (per unit)	0	.052
Operator (per hour)	9	9

The companies selling the equipment each arranged for experimental demonstrations, in which stopwatch time studies of operator/machine performance for five cycles were measured, with the following results:

	Task Times (in minutes) for A					Task Times (in minutes) for B				
	Cycle					Cycle				
Task	1	2	3	4	5	1	2	3	4	5
Load machine	0.32	0.29	0.28	0.31	0.30	0.30	0.27	0.25	0.22	0.21
Machine time (machine paced)	2.73	2.61	2.68	2.71	2.63	2.62	2.57	2.59	2.51	2.54
Unload machine	0.14	0.10	0.09	0.12	0.11	0.12	0.09	0.10	0.11	0.09
Inspect product	1.21	1.08	1.29	1.15	1.20	0.92	0.94	0.86	0.79	0.87
Apply label to product[a]	—	—	—	—	—	0.05	0.04	0.05	0.05	0.04

[a]Label application is automatic for A and manual for B.

The analyst rated the operator at 115 percent on equipment A and 110 percent on B. It is estimated that during their daily 8-hour shift, operators will receive two 15-minute coffee breaks. Unavoidable delays are estimated to be 40 minutes for A and 25 minutes for B daily. Evaluate the two alternatives and justify your recommendation of A or B.

14. A post office mail room receives mail and cancels the postage stamps. After first simplifying work, you make a direct time study of the simplified job and obtain the following times in minutes:

		Cycle				
Task	Description	1	2	3	4	5
1	Empty mail bags	.16	.31	.14	.15	.16
2	Sraighten mail	.60	.60	.60	.60	.60
3	Carry trays to reader	.34	.36	.35	.37	.38
4	Cancellation machine	.50	.50	.50	.50	.50
5	Empty trays	.24	.24	.48	.27	.25

You further determine the following information about this job:

(1) Tasks 2 and 4 are machine-controlled and cannot be speeded up by the operator.

(2) You observed two irregularities while timing the job. These task times vary by more than 20 percent of each task's average time.

(3) You rated the operator at 120 percent when he was working.

(4) Management and the worker's union have negotiated the following allowances for this job:

Personal—30 minutes/8-hour shift
Unavoidable delay—40 minutes/8-hour shift
Fatigue—.10

(5) An operator on this job earns $5/hour.
(6) Material cost per unit is $.50.
(7) Total overhead cost is added in at a rate of 150 percent of the sum of direct labor and material cost.

(a) How many pieces should each operator produce during an 8-hour shift?
(b) What is the total standard cost per piece?

15. As a bank officer assume you have your bank tellers count out $100 bank packs in denominations of six $10 bills, seven $5 bills, and five $1 bills. The purpose of this job is to supply your bank's night teller service with this bankpack. Suppose a continuous stopwatch time study yielded the following data:

Cumulative task times (in minutes)

		Cycle								
Task	Description	1	2	3	4	5	6	7	8	Worker Rating (in percent)
1	Count 6 $10s	.12	.66	1.24	1.95	3.26	3.91	4.52	5.05	110
2	Count 7 $5s	.27	.84	1.40	2.12	3.41	4.08	4.66	5.21	115
3	Count 5 $1s	.38	.96	1.51	2.20	3.52	4.18	4.74	5.29	105
4	Count $100	.56	1.09	1.80	2.41	3.80[a]	4.36	4.94	5.48	110
5	Place in chute[b]	—	—	—	3.13	—	—	—	—	90

[a]Teller had to recount because of error.
[b]Occurs once every 10 cycles.

The allowances for this job are set at .15.

(a) What is the normal time for this job?
(b) What is the standard time for this job?
(c) What is the standard output in terms of bankpacks/hours?
(d) How long (in terms of work hours) would it take to package 500 bankpacks, if the tellers assigned to the job worked at a pace on the average at 115 percent?

KEY TERMS

Activity chart 292
Allowance fraction 309
Direct time study 309
Flow process chart 293
Gang process chart 295
Job 291
Job design 292
Job enlargement 298
Job enrichment 299
Job rotation 298
Kaizen 306
Labor standard 303
Methods time measurement (MTM) 313
Normal time 309

SELECTED READINGS

Aldag, Raymond J., and Arthur P. Brief, *Task Design and Employee Motivation.* Glenview, Ill.: Scott, Foresman, 1979.

Barnes, Frank C., "Principles of Motion Economy: Revisited, Reviewed, and Restored," *Proceedings Southern Management Association.* Atlanta, 1983, 297–99.

Barnes, R. M., *Motion and Time Study: Design and Measurement of Work,* 6th ed. New York: John Wiley, 1968.

"Measuring White Collar Work," (parts 2 and 3), *Incentive* 162, no. 6 (June 1988), 58–61 and 162, no. 7 (July 1988), 46–47.

Rice, Robert S., "Survey of Work Measurement and Wage Incentives," *Industrial Engineering* 9, no. 7 (July 1977), 18–31.

Sakamoto, Shigeyasu, "Key to Productivity: Work Measurement, An International Survey Report," *MTM Journal of Methods—Time Measurement* 13, (1987), 68–75.

Szilagyi, Andrew S., Jr., and Marc J. Wallace, Jr., *Organizational Behavior and Performance,* 2nd ed. Santa Monica, Calif.: Goodyear Publishing 1980.

U.S. Department of Labor, Occupational Health and Safety Administration, *All About OSHA.* OSHA publication No. 2056.

CHAPTER 9

PROJECT MANAGEMENT

In the production department of Prentice Hall's college book division, our products are books, complicated books, books headed for the college market. Each book is a "project" that appears on the production editor's desk as a large pile of manuscript pages: a combination of typed copy, "tear sheet" copy of art and text from previous editions, figures drafted by the author, and other illustrations. These disparate elements are sent off in different directions for various treatments and must appear bound within covers and ready for sale approximately ten months later.

Planning for the production of a college text involves decisions about the book's specifications (size, color, paper, covers); design (typefaces, art); permissions (where and in what languages the book will sell); composition (setting the type); printing, and binding. Scheduling involves overlapping time frames so that some tasks can be done at the same time (editing and establishing costs, for example), while other tasks that depend on prior events occur later (paging and indexing, for example); and the schedule must end at a time advantageous to sales. Planning and scheduling for a specific book take place at a launch meeting, where activities are identified, the sequencing is established, and a time is set for each activity within the overall ten-month limit. The book's advance through the schedule is recorded and adjustments made as necessary. The production editor at Prentice Hall is able to carry a considerable number of books at the same time, very efficiently, thanks to the production schedule.

Susan J. Fisher
College Book Editorial Production
Prentice Hall
Englewood Cliffs, New Jersey

PROJECT PLANNING

PROJECT DEFINED

Ms. Fisher's commentary emphasizes a project orientation for creating and launching Prentice Hall's new products into the marketplace. The production editor plans, organizes, and controls the progress of each project (book) according to its unique production requirements. Project management in this environment is a way of life that calls for the coordination of numerous and diverse activities that are all interrelated. Project planning and scheduling are involved, and these require certain technical and behavioral considerations.

Project A one-time-only set of activities that has a definite beginning and ending point in time.

A *project* is a one-time-only set of activities with a definite beginning and ending point in time. The activities must be done in a particular order (they have precedence relationships). The key difference between project planning and other types of planning is that each project is a unique entity that occurs just once.

PROJECT PLANNING AND SCHEDULING

Project planning Activities that establish a course of action for a project.

Project planning includes all activities that result in a course of action for a project. *Goals* for the project, including resources to be committed, completion times, and activities must be set and their priorities established. Areas of responsibility must be identified and assigned. Time and resource requirements to perform the work activities must be *forecast* and *budgeted*.

Project scheduling Activities that establish the times and the sequence of project tasks.

Project *scheduling,* in contrast to project *planning,* is more specific. Scheduling establishes times and sequences of the various phases of the project. In project scheduling, the manager considers the many activities of an overall project and the tasks that must be accomplished and relates them coherently to one another and to the calendar.

EXAMPLE

Slick Wilson, a first-semester freshman at State, is receiving advice from his sophomore roommate on how to study for finals, which start in two weeks. Slick, who has ignored the entire problem until now, is advised to list all his courses and estimate how much time he needs to study for the final in each course. Next, Slick's roommate suggests that he should look in the final exam schedule. When he has determined the order in which he must take his finals, Slick should plan to study for the first one first, the second one next, and so on until he has prepared for all his exams. Slick prepares a study plan according to this advice, adding to the plan that, when he finishes his last final, he will throw the schedule away and forget about finals, school, and his introduction to (finals/project) scheduling.

The *project* in this example is to study for finals. The *beginning point* in time is now, two weeks before his first final. The *ending point* is the moment Slick steps in to take the last final. The project *activities* are studying for various courses. These activities must be *time sequenced* according to the order and dates he has to take the exams. Viewing final exam preparation as a project, you might use project management to improve the scheduling of your study time at the end of this semester.

PROJECT SCHEDULING MODELS

There are various methods for scheduling projects. In this section we look at two simple project scheduling models—Gantt charting and the Program Evaluation and Review Technique (PERT). Both are schematic models, but PERT also has some mathematical model adaptations.

These engineers are studying blueprints within a model of a paper mill. Large-scale projects such as this require project scheduling models for success.
Source: **Walter Bibikow/The Image Bank**

GANTT CHARTS

Gannt chart A bar chart showing the relationship of project activities in time.

A *Gantt chart* is a bar chart that shows the relationship of activities over time. Table 9.1 gives the symbols often used in a Gantt chart. An open bracket indicates the scheduled start of the activity, and a closing bracket indicates the scheduled completion. A heavy

TABLE 9.1 **Gantt chart symbols**

Symbol	Meaning
[	Start of an activity
]	End of an activity
[–]	Actual progress of the activity
v	Point in time where the project is now

line indicates the currently completed portion of the activity. A caret at the top of the chart indicates current time.

Figure 9.1 shows a Gantt chart of a student preparing for final exams. Project activities are listed down the page and time across the page. The project activities are studying for exams in English, history, math and psychology. Math is broken into two subactivities—studying concepts new since the last exam and studying concepts covered on previous exams, for review. By examining the horizontal time axis, we see that all activities must be completed in three and one-half weeks.

Studying English, for example, is scheduled to start at the beginning of week 1 and end after one and one-half weeks. The caret at the top indicates that one and one-half weeks have already passed. The heavy lines show how much of each activity has already been done. Students can use this chart to visualize their progress and to adjust their study activities.

As you can see, one of the strengths of project scheduling with Gantt charts is the simplicity of the schematic model.

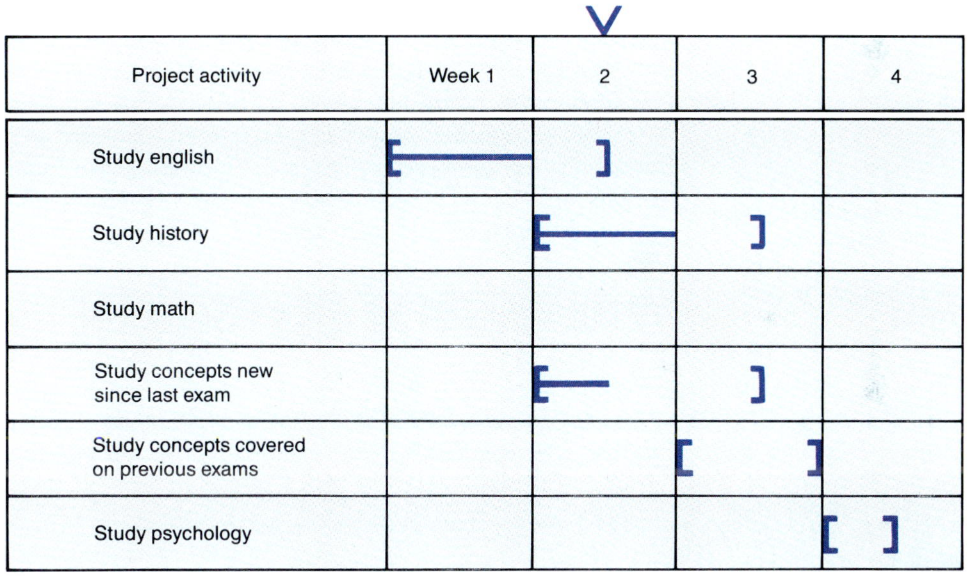

FIGURE 9.1 Gantt chart for project scheduling

EXAMPLE

A new manufacturing facility, which required a large expenditure in equipment, was built in Kentucky. The general contractor had had previous project experience, but the largest of his projects had been about half this size. He had never used formal scheduling techniques. To help him, the company representative drew up Gantt charts. These charts included both an overview chart listing major general and subcontractor activities and more detailed charts for critical activities from the overview chart. The charts forced the general contractor to plan in a way he hadn't done before. Later, the company representative saw him using the charts to communicate with his supervisors and subcontractors.

The Gantt charts were also valuable for the company representative, a recent business school graduate. The process of constructing the chart provided an understanding of project activities, their precedence relationships, and how in real time the project would be completed by the target date. The charts were a critical model for subsequent project control.

NETWORK MODELING

Network modeling Analyzing the precedence relationships of project activities and depicting them graphically.

Arc In network modeling, an arrowed line segment; the symbol for a project activity.

Node In network modeling, a circle at one end of an arc; the symbol for the beginning or ending of a project activity.

Network modeling allows us to address project scheduling a little more formally than we can with the Gantt chart. Although network models are based on rigorous theory and precise definitions, we discuss only a few terms and concepts here.

Figure 9.2 illustrates the essential features of network modeling. Each activity is symbolized by an *arc,* an arrowed line segment (or, simply, an arrow). Both the beginning and the ending of each activity are symbolized by a *node,* a circle at the beginning or ending of the arrow. The precedence relationship of the activities are represented by joint nodes: An arc whose ending node is the beginning node of a second arc represents an activity that must precede the second activity.

In Figure 9.2, there are six nodes, numbered 1–6. The arcs are named by their beginning and ending nodes: arc 1-2, 1-3, 2-4, 2-5, 4-6, and 5-6. The lengths of the arcs are of no significance. Nodes may be lettered, rather than numbered, or arcs as well as nodes may be numbered or lettered. Since arc 1-3 in Figure 9.2 ends at the node that begins arc 3-6, arc 1-3 represents an activity that must precede activity 3-6. In talking about networks, we may refer to arc 1-2, for example, interchangeably with activity 1-2.

PROGRAM EVALUATION AND REVIEW TECHNIQUE (PERT)

Program Evaluation and Review Technique (PERT) An application of network modeling originally designed for planning and controlling the U.S. Navy's Polaris nuclear submarine project.

Development of PERT In 1958 the U.S. Navy developed *Program Evaluation and Review Technique* (PERT) for planning and control of the Polaris nuclear submarine project. The results of using PERT in that application, in which some 3,000 contractors

FIGURE 9.2 Network of nodes and arcs

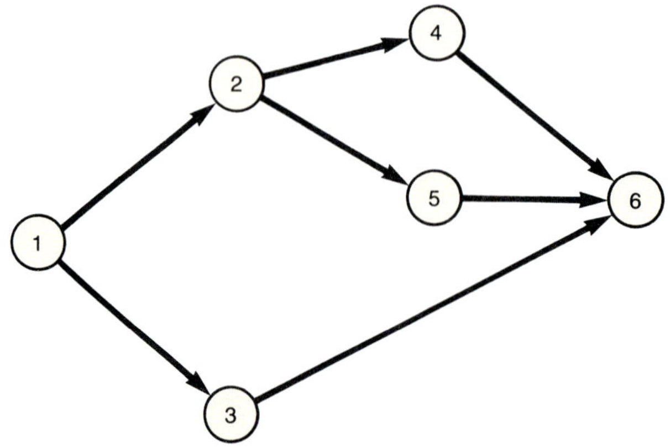

were involved, is generally reported to have reduced by two years the project completion time for the Polaris project. In both government and industry today, PERT is still widely used.

A similar modeling approach called the *Critical Path Method* (CPM) is also used by business and government. Since CPM and PERT are nearly equivalent, we will concentrate only on PERT.

PERT language The terms and symbols specific to PERT. An **activity** is project work needed to be accomplished, symbolized by an arc. A **dummy activity** is a fictitious activity consuming no time, symbolized by a dashed arc. An **event** is the beginning or ending of an activity, symbolized by a node. A **network** is the sequence of all activities, symbolized by nodes connected by arcs. A **path** is a portion of the network, including the first and last activities, for which each activity has a single immediate successor. A **critical path** is a path whose activities are expected to consume the most time.

Application of PERT First we should clarify the conditions under which PERT may be appropriately used. If your situation lacks the following features, PERT will yield little benefit. First, the project must be one whose activities clearly are distinct and separable. Second, the project and activities must all have clear starting and ending dates. Third, the project must not be complicated by too many interrelated tasks. Fourth, the project must be one whose activities afford alternative sequencing and timing.

Operations Management Highlight 9.1 reveals how PERT has been used successfully by different organizations.

Language of PERT The PERT language comprises simple symbols and terms. As described in Table 9.2, key symbols are those for *activity, dummy activity, event,* and *critical path* of the *network*. Since the critical path requires the longest time through the network, management should watch it most closely to avoid unnecessary project delays.

Logic of PERT How does PERT work? It works by following these steps:

1. Clearly identify all activities in the project.
2. Identify the precedence requirements of the activities.
3. Diagram the precedence requirements as a sequence of activities. (See Table 9.3 for typical sequences.)
4. Estimate the time each activity will take.
5. Calculate the critical path and other project performance criteria, creating the schedule and plan for subsequent control.
6. Reevaluate and revise as experience dictates.

(PERT language) **Optimistic time** (t_o) is the least amount of time an activity is expected to consume. **Pessimistic time** (t_p) is the greatest amount of time an activity is expected to consume. **Most likely time** (t_m) is the single best guess of the amount of time an activity is expected to consume. **Expected time** (t_e) is the amount of time an activity is expected to consume.

Time estimates are obtained from either past data or from people experienced in a particular activity. *Optimistic* t_o, *pessimistic* t_p, and *most likely* t_m times must be estimated so that the expected (average) time t_e can be calculated from the following equation.[1]

$$t_e = \frac{(t_o + 4t_m + t_p)}{6} \tag{9.1}$$

[1]Equation 9.1 is an approximation of the beta distribution, as is the variance calculation discussed next. Although these equations approximate the beta distribution, there is limited empirical evidence suggesting that activity times on projects are beta distributed. We accept these formulas based on practices and intuitive appeal, rather than evidence or statistical proof concerning the actual distribution of activity times.

OPERATIONS MANAGEMENT HIGHLIGHT 9.1

Source: Courtesy of Hewlett-Packard

Utilities and Aircraft Manufacturer Find PERT Useful

Pacific Gas and Electric (PG&E), General Electric (GE), and GTE Telecom are among the thousands of companies who successfully apply PERT to a variety of scheduling problems. PG&E uses personal computers with PERT to schedule projects varying in cost from $5,000 to more than $50,000,000. PERT has helped to design and construct facilities, prepare environmental studies, and conduct research and development.

At GE, PERT-based software was used to upgrade the U.S. Air Force's major ground support plane, the A-10 Thunderbolt II, also called the Warthog. Key to managing over 1,500 project activities, PERT helped GE win a $750,000 performance bonus. A time line criteria was essential to project completion and receipt of the bonus. The PERT-based software actually helped identify problems before they could delay production.

Telephone systems are often large, complex, costly-to-manage projects. Customers are not always sure about what they need and want, and telephone companies may promise too much too quickly. At GTE Telecom, the Systems Management Group uses a system known as Pertmaster to manage major telephone installation projects, from planning the project proposal through implementation. Replacing a manual Critical Path Method approach, computerized Pertmaster handles up to 2,500 activities and 29 different resources (labor skills, equipment types, etc). A telephone installation project at GTE Telecom may have as many as 1,600 activities, a complex project by any measure.

Sources: Earl Hazen, "Project Management Ensures On-Time Completion," *Transmission and Distribution* 41, no. 4 (April 1989), 24–27; Jim O'Hare, "Reworking the Warthog," *Manufacturing Systems*, 4 no. 8 (August 1986); pp 26–27 and "Saving Time and Money in Project Planning," *Telephone Engineer & Mangement* 90, no. 6 (March 15, 1986), 68.

TABLE 9.2 Program Evaluation and Review Technique (PERT) glossary

Symbol	Name	Meaning
——→	Activity	A task within the project that has a definite beginning and ending date or point in time. The activity consumes time. The length of the arrow is of no significance. Designated as an **arc.**
- - - - - →	Dummy activity	A fictitious activity consuming no time; necessary to preserve the unique identification of activities.
○	Event	The beginning or ending of an activity. A point in time. Each project has a distinct project beginning and project ending. Designated as a **node.**
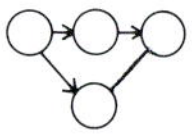	Network	The sequence of all project activities. The sequence obeys precedence requirements. Nodes connected by arcs.
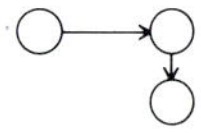	Path	Any one unique portion of the project sequence, beginning with the first activity and ending with the last activity, for which each activity has a single immediate successor. Each node pair has a single arc, an activity.
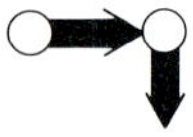	Critical Path	The path whose activities are expected to consume the most time.

Time Notation	Interpretation	Calculation
t_o	**Optimistic time:** The least amount of time an activity is expected to consume, possible only under extremely favorable conditions. Very little chance, say 1 in 100.	Assigned according to experience or past data.
t_p	**Pessimistic time:** The greatest amount of time an activity is expected to consume, possible only under extremely unfavorable conditions. Very little chance, say 1 in 100.	Assigned according to experience or past data.
t_m	**Most likely time:** The single best guess for activity completion time. The mode activity time.	Assigned according to experience or past data.
t_e	**Expected time:** The amount of time an activity is expected to consume, as likely to be exceeded as beaten. The mean activity time.	$t_e = \dfrac{(t_o + 4t_m + t_p)}{6}$
T_P	**Path time:** The amount of time expected to be consumed by activities on a path.	$T_P = \Sigma t_e$ for all activities on a path
T_B	**Expected beginning time:** The amount of time expected to be consumed before an activity can begin. The sum of expected times for activities preceding a node on a path.	$T_B = t_e$ for all preceding activities on a path
T_E	**Earliest beginning time:** The minimum amount of time that must be consumed before an activity can begin. The maximum expected beginning time.	$T_E = \max T_B$
T_C	**Expected completion time:** The amount of time expected to be consumed once an activity begins. The sum of expected times for activities succeeding a node on a path.	$T_C = \Sigma t_e$ for all succeeding activities

TABLE 9.2 continued

Time Notation	Interpretation	Calculation
T_L	**Latest beginning time:** The maximum amount of time that can be consumed before an activity begins, if the project is to be completed on time. The difference of the total time allowed for the project and the maximum expected completion time.	T_L = Time allowed − max T_C
T_S	**Slack time:** The amount of leeway time an activity can consume and still allow the project to be completed on time. The difference of the latest beginning time and the expected beginning time.	$T_S = T_L - T_E$

Let's use the six PERT steps in an example.

EXAMPLE

The Long-Term Care situation. Long-Term Care, Inc., is a Professional II nursing home aspiring to become a Professional I nursing home. It wants to provide the ultimate in nursing care for patients, but because of recent federal regulations it will need a new, specially designed facility. The administrator at Long-Term Care, Inc., must generate an overall project schedule.

The first thing the administrator must do is identify all activities. The administrator prepares the following list of long-term care activities:

A. Perform pilot services for six patients in new facility.
B. Build the facility.
C. Install all equipment and furnishings.
D. Recruit nursing home staff.
E. Train nursing home staff.
F. Pass safety inspection of Municipal Building Authority.

TABLE 9.3 Sample PERT networks

Network	Meaning
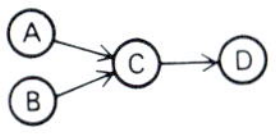	Represents activities AC, BC, and CD. CD may not begin until both AC and BC are completed. AC and BC may occur concurrently and are called *parallel activities.*
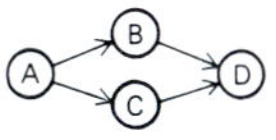	BD may not begin until AB is completed. CD may not begin until AC is completed.
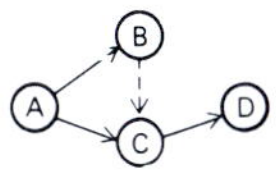	AB-BD and AC-CD are *parallel paths.* However, AC does not have to begin at the same instant that AB begins, although it may. Similarly, BD does not have to be completed at the same instant that CD is completed, although it may. Similarly, BD may be completed before AC is completed.
OR 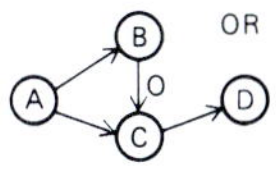	BC is a *dummy* activity, used when necessary to preserve the required sequence of the network. It may be symbolized in two ways, as shown. A dummy activity consumes no time. Using a dummy allows all activities to be identified by a unique pair of nodes. Activity CD cannot begin until activities AB and AC are completed. This network has two paths: AB-BC-CD and AC-CD.

Are these activities in the proper sequence? Suppose, as consultants, we encourage the administrator to establish clear precedence relationships. After some thought she identifies the necessary sequence of activities as shown in Table 9.4. (Time estimates are shown also.)

TABLE 9.4 Long-Term Care sequencing of activities

Activity	Required Predecessor	Time Estimates (in weeks) t_o	t_m	t_p
B. Build facility	None	20	24	30
F. Safety inspection	B	2	3	4
C. Install equipment	B	8	16	20
D. Recruit staff	None	2	2	3
E. Train staff	D	4	5	6
A. Perform pilot	C, E, F	4	5	9

Figure 9.3 accomplishes step 3 of PERT—diagramming the precedence requirements as a sequence. A coding scheme was adopted to identify nodes by numbers. Note that there must be a node to *begin* (node 1) and to *end* (node 6) the project.

A dummy activity is required in the diagram because activity A, which also can be called activity 5-6, must be preceded by activities E, C, and F. The only way we can logically arrange those precedents and have unique arc identities is to use the dummy activity, 4-5. Look at node 5. Before activity 5-6 can begin from the node, activities 2-5, 3-5, and 4-5 must be completed. If we did not use the dummy, activities C and F would both begin at node 2 and end at node 5; they would not have unique identities.

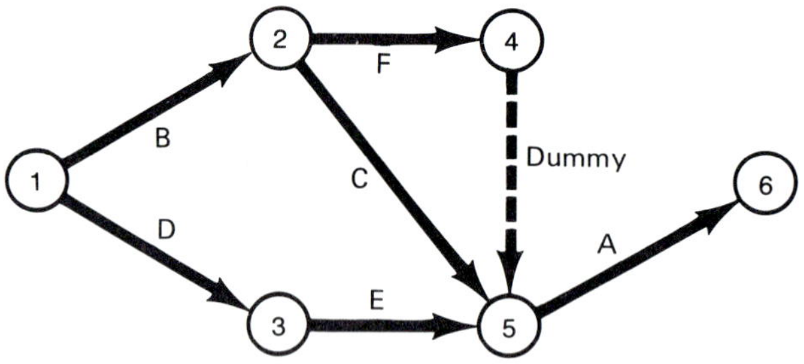

FIGURE 9.3 PERT diagram for Long-Term Care, Inc.

The next step for the administrator is to establish time estimates for each activity. Where can she find these times? She can ask building contractors, equipment manufacturers, and her own staff for their estimates of recruitment, training, and pilot program times. Time estimates are shown in Table 9.4.

Next is step 5, finding the critical path, critical path time, and slack times. First we calculate, using Equation 9.1, the expected time, t_e, for each activity. For activity 1-2, this calculation is as follows:

$$t_e = \frac{(t_o + 4t_m + t_p)}{6}$$
$$= \frac{[20 + 4(24) + 30]}{6} = 24.3 \text{ weeks}$$

Similar calculations are made for each activity, and the expected times are shown next to the arrows in Figure 9.4.

Which of the paths is the longest through the network? There are three paths: 1-2-4-5-6, 1-2-5-6, and 1-3-5-6. The total expected time for the first path is 24.3 + 3.0 + 0 + 5.5, or 32.8 weeks; for the second path 24.3 + 15.3 + 5.5, 45.1 weeks; and for the third path 2.1 + 5.0 + 5.5, 12.6 weeks. Therefore the critical path is 1-2-5-6, and the critical path time is 45.1 weeks. In Figure 9.4, we have shown the critical path on the PERT diagram.

Figure 9.4 also shows the earliest beginning times (T_E) and latest beginning times (T_L) *at each event,* allowing us to calculate the *event* slack time, the extra time available at each event if we arrive as soon as possible, leave as late as possible, and still finish the nursing home facility on schedule.

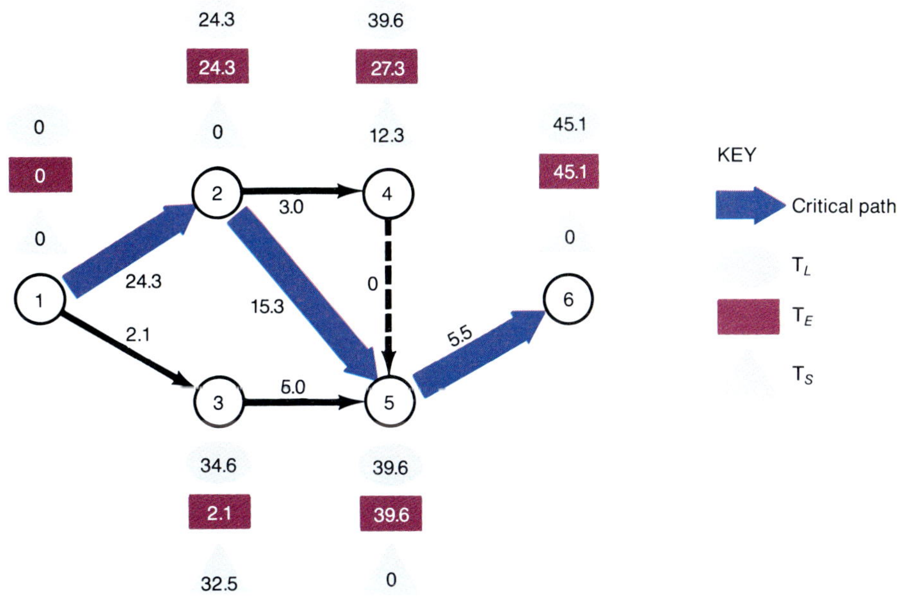

FIGURE 9.4 **Network for Long-Term Care, showing critical path and earliest beginning time T_E, latest beginning time T_L, and start time T_S for each node.**

Calculating these T_E and T_L is often a painstaking process, virtually impossible for complex projects without the aid of computers. It is important to understand the methodology, though, and so we will follow the process through. (Table 9.5 records all our calculations.)

To find the earliest beginning time T_E for a node, we must compare information about each path the node is on: For each path the node is on, we need to know the expected beginning time T_B at that node. We find each path's T_B at that node as the sum

TABLE 9.5 **Calculations of T_E, T_L, and T_S for nodes of the Long-Term Care network, in weeks.**

Node	Path 1 T_B	Path 1 T_C	Path 2 T_B	Path 2 T_C	Path 3 T_B	Path 3 T_C	T_E (max T_B)	T_L (T_{CP} − max T_C)[a]	T_S ($T_L - T_E$)
1	0	32.8	0	45.1	0	12.6	0	0	0
2	24.3	8.5	24.3	20.8	—	—	24.3	24.3	0
3	—	—	—	—	2.1	10.5	2.1	34.6	32.5
4	27.3	5.5	—	—	—	—	27.3	39.6	12.3
5	27.3	5.5	39.6	5.5	7.1	5.5	39.6	39.6	0
6	32.8	0	45.1	0	12.6	0	45.1	45.1	0

[a]T_{CP} is the critical path time, the shortest time the project can be completed under noncrash conditions, the time for all activities or the longest path through the network; 45.1 weeks.

(PERT language) **Latest beginning time** (T_L) is the maximum amount of time that can be consumed before an activity begins, if the project is to be completed on time. **Earliest beginning time** (T_E) is the minimum amount of time that must be consumed before an activity can begin. **Slack time** (T_S) is the amount of leeway time an activity can consume and still allow the project to be completed on time. **Expected beginning time** (T_B) is the amount of time expected to be consumed before an activity can begin. **Expected completion time** (T_C) is the amount of time expected to be consumed once an activity begins. **Path time** (T_P) is the amount of time expected to be consumed by activities on a path.

of the expected times for path activities preceding the node. Among all the path T_B then s at that node, we will choose the maximum T_B as the T_E for that node.

Let's begin with node 1. Node 1 marks the start of the project, and the beginning of activities 1-2 and 1-3. Node 1 is on all paths 1, 2, and 3, but no matter which path we consider, no activities precede node 1. We set our time at 0: the earliest beginning time T_E at node 1 is simply 0.

Move on to node 2. Node 2 is on path 1 (the top path) and path 2 (the middle path), but again the situation is greatly simplified because to calculate the T_E we are interested only in activities preceding the node. And whether on Path 1 or Path 2, the only activity preceding node 2 is activity 1-2. The expected beginning time T_B at node 2 for either path, then, is the just expected time T_E for activity 1-2: 24.3. Since the T_B at node 2 for either path is 24.3, the T_E for node 2 is 24.3.

For node 3, only one path, Path 3 (the lower path), contains node 3, and the only activity preceding node 3 is 1-3. The T_E for node 3 then is simply the t_e for node 1-3: 2.1.

Node 4 lies only on Path 1. The activities preceding node 4 are activities 2-4 and 1-2. The sum T_B of their expected times t_e is 3.0 + 24.3. The T_E for node 4, then, is 27.3.

Node 5 lies on all paths 1, 2, and 3. Consider the expected beginning time T_B at node 5 for each path in turn. On path 1, activities 4-5, 2-4, and 1-2 precede node 5. The sum T_B of their expected times t_e is 27.3. (Activity 4-5 is a dummy activity consuming 0 time.) On path 2, activities 2-5 and 1-2 precede node 5. The sum T_B of their expected times t_e is 39.6. On Path 3, activities 3-5 and 1-3 precede node 5. The sum T_B, of their expected times t_e is 7.1. The maximum T_B, or 39.6, is the T_E for node 5. We should pause now to note the rationale of our procedure. Three paths lead to node 5, three sequences of events running simultaneously. The greatest amount of time required along any one path up to node 5 is the minimum amount of time that must be consumed before beginning an activity at node 5. Hence this greatest amount of time, max T_B at node 5, is the earliest beginning time, T_E, for node 5.

Finally, at node 6 the project ends. You can see from Table 9.5, T_E will be 45.1. T_E is the earliest you can begin and complete on time. In this case it is the earliest we can complete node 5 (39.6) added to activity 5-6 (5.5).

Before moving on to the calculation of the latest beginning times T_L and the slack times T_S, we should notice that the T_B at each node along a path may be calculated cumulatively. The T_B at node 5 for path 1, for example, is the sum of the T_B at node 4 for Path 1—the immediately preceding node—and the t_e for activity 4-5—the activity connecting node 4 and node 5 on path 1. Similarly, the T_B at node 5 for path 3 is the sum of the T_B at node 3 for path 3—the immediately preceding node—and the t_e for activity 3-5—the activity connecting node 3 and node 5 on path 3. Computers, as you can guess, keep running tabs on T_Bs for hundreds of paths very efficiently.

So concludes the calculation of the T_E for each node. Calculating the latest beginning time T_L for each node is a similar, though reverse, process.

To find the T_L for a node, we must once again compare information about each path the node is on: For each path the node is on, we need to know the expected completion time T_C at that node. We find each path's T_C at that node as the sum of the expected times for path activities succeeding the node. Among all the path T_Cs, we will choose the maximum T_C, and find the difference of the total time allowed for the project and the maximum T_C as the T_L for a node.

Begin with not the first node, but the last: node 6. Since there are no succeeding activities, the T_L is set somewhat arbitrarily. We have defined "latest beginning time" as the maximum amount of time that can be consumed before an activity begins, if the project is to be completed on time. Since no more activities are beginning, we must only ensure that the T_L for node 6 does not exceed the total time allowed for the project. We assume here that the total time allowed for the project is exactly the critical path time, 45.1, and set the latest beginning time T_L for node 6 at 45.1.

Move to node 5. Node 5 lies on all paths 1, 2, and 3, but only activity 5-6 succeeds node 5. The expected time t_e for node 5 is 5.5, hence the T_C at node 5 for each path is 5.5. The T_L for node 5, then, is the difference between the total time allowed and 5.5, or 45.1 − 5.5, or 39.6.

Node 4 lies only on path 1. Activities succeeding node 4 on this path are activities 4-5 and 5-6. The sum T_C of their expected times t_e is 5.5 + 0, or 5.5 (recall that activity 4-5 is a dummy activity consuming no time). The T_L at node 5, then, is the difference of 45.1 and 5.5, or 39.6.

Node 3 lies only on path 3. Activities succeeding node 3 on this path are activities 3-5 and 5-6. The sum T_C of their expected times t_e is 5.0 + 5.5, or 10.5. The T_L at node 3 is the difference of 45.1 and 10.5, or 34.6.

Node 2 lies on path 1 and path 2. Consider the T_C at node 2 for each path in turn. For path 1, activities 2-4, 4-5, and 5-6 succeed node 2. The sum T_C of their expected times t_e is 3.0 + 0 + 5.5, or 8.5. For path 2, activities 2-5 and 5-6 succeed node 2. The sum T_C of their expected times t_e is 15.3 + 5.5, or 20.8. Among the path T_Cs, the maximum is 20.8. The T_L at node 2 is the difference of 45.1 and 20.8, or 24.3. As we did for calculating T_Es, let's pause to consider our rationale. Two paths lead out from node 2, two sequences of events running simultaneously. The greatest amount of time required along any one path following node 2 is the minimum amount of time that must remain before beginning an activity at node 2. Hence the difference between the amount of time available to the project and this greatest amount of time, max T_C at node 2, is the latest beginning time, T_L, for node 2.

Finally, node 1, which begins the project and lies on all paths. Since all activities succeed node 1, the T_C at node 1 for each path is identical to the path time T_P. In fact, the maximum T_C is the critical path time, 45.1, which we have somewhat arbitrarily used as the total time allowed. Thus the T_L for node 1 is exactly 45.1 − 45.1, or 0.

As before, we should notice that the T_C at each node along a path may be calculated cumulatively. The T_C at node 2 for path 1, for example, is the difference of the T_C at node 4 for path 1—the immediately succeeding node—and the t_e for activity 2-4—the activity connecting node 2 and node 4 on path 1. Similarly, the T_C at node 2 for path 2 is the difference of the T_C at node 5 for Path 2—the immediately succeeding node—and the t_e for activity 2-5—the activity connecting node 2 and node 5 on path 3. As for T_Es, the cumulative effect of T_Cs allow computers to perform calculations quite rapidly.

Having calculated the T_E and T_L for each node of the network, it is a simple matter to find the slack time T_S for each node. Slack time T_S for each node is the difference of T_L and T_E for each node. As we see from Figure 9.4, slack time for many nodes is 0. Node 3, however, has slack of 32.5 weeks, and node 4 has slack of 12.3 weeks. You will notice that for nodes on the critical path, slack time is 0. This is to be expected: on the critical path, there is no slack time. Activities must be carried out according to expected times or the project will fall behind schedule.

We may recruit workers, activity 1-3, as soon as we start to build, activity 1-2. If we start then, in 2.1 weeks we can expect to be finished recruiting workers. What is the very latest we need to start training the workers, activity 3-5? We must have the project completed in 45.1 weeks less 5.5 weeks for pilot runs and 5.0 weeks for training. Therefore we must begin training no later than at 45.1 − (5.5 + 5.0), or 34.6 weeks. *The slack time at event 3 is therefore the difference between latest beginning and earliest beginning times:* 34.6 − 2.1, or 32.5 weeks. Since management attention and resources may be shifted to the critical path from paths that have a good bit of slack, this is an important concept.

OPERATIONS MANAGEMENT HIGHLIGHT 9.2

Source: John Zoiner

Selecting A PERT Personal Computer Package

In 1986 International Data Corporation predicted that sales of PERT personal computer (PC) packages would grow an average of 40 percent annually, reaching $235 million in products shipped in 1990.

For six simple long-term care activities, we picked a rather sophisticated analytical technique (PERT) to do a simple scheduling job. Let's consider a real application of project scheduling in which a contractor was able to complete a hospital building project in 16 rather than 20 months.[2] The project included supplying the new hospital with all the required furniture and equipment. Using a computer package, the manager analyzed about 2,000 activities and 3,000 types of inventory items (furniture, etc.). As you can see, PERT works for simple and complex jobs as well. Once we conquer the basics, moving to computer software packages will be easy. Operations Management Highlight 9.2 addresses the selection of a computer software package.

[2]Avraham Shtub, "The Integration of CPM and Material Management in Project Management," *Construction Management and Economics,* (UK), 6, no. 4 (Winter 1988), 261–72.

This growth was realized, resulting in over 100 PERT computer-based packages from which you can now choose. What, then, are the choices? By what criteria should a choice be made? What package might a firm most likely be using (a firm, say, you want to join)?

Four types of software packages are available: low, middle, and high end PC packages, and mainframe packages. Low end PC packages require modest computer memory (256K–384K) and can analyze moderately large projects (one close to 1,000 activities and up to 20 resources). These packages are generally priced under $500. The high end PC packages cost from $2,000 to $6,000, but can handle much larger projects (up to 10,000 activities and 100 resources) that have higher computer memory requirements. Mainframe packages can cost over $100,000 and handle several hundred users simultaneously.

The most useful criteria in selecting a software package are: the size and complexity of the project in terms of activities, resources, and outputs. A variety of Gantt chart and PERT network diagrams are available. Other useful criteria are the needs of the project in terms of resource management, project costing management, and reporting. Finally one should consider how user friendly the purchase is and how well it interacts with data bases, spreadsheets, and word processors.

Constantly evolving computer technology makes calculating PERT packages difficult. But the serious buyers have plenty of literature available to help keep them abreast of new developments. The local library is an excellent place to begin scanning PC magazines, for example. Reviews of packages often appear, evaluating as many as 20 packages, then narrowing the field to the top three or four. Following up on the few packages that are repeatedly recommended will soon focus your sight on the best single choice for you.

Sources: Edward A. Wash and Arjana A. Assad, "Project Management and the PC: Software, Applications, and Trends," *Interfaces* 18, no. 2 (March-April 1988), 75–84; Lamong Wood, "A Manager's Guide to Computerized Project Management," *Manufacturing Systems* 7, no. 8 (August 1989), 18–24; L. Murphy Smith, "Using the Microcomputer for Project Management," *Journal of Accounting & EDP* 5, no. 2 (Summer 1989), 30–37; Michael Heck, "Harvard Project Manager Serves Pros, Casual Users," *InfoWorld* 11, no. 5 (January 30, 1989), 54–55; Michael Heck, "Micro Planning 6.10a: Project Management for Windows," *InfoWorld* 10, no. 41 (October 10, 1988), 71–72; Michael Heck, "Viewpoint: An Easy-to-Use Package for Large Projects," *InfoWorld* 10, no. 47 (November 21, 1988), 64–65; Mickey Williamson, "Project Management Software," *Computer World* 20, no. 49 (December 8, 1986), 55–61, 65–69.

Time/Cost Tradeoffs Managers often want to reduce critical path times, even if it costs extra money to make the reductions. Although we won't discuss these formal methods here, we consider basic time/cost tradeoff concepts.

Projects entail two kinds of time-related costs: *Indirect project costs* include overhead, facilities, and the opportunity cost associated with resources being used that can be eliminated if the project is shortened. Overhead costs of maintaining a house trailer at a construction site, for example, might be $1,100 per month for heat, light, telephone, clerical help, and other *indirect* construction costs. A second kind of cost is the *activity direct cost* of expediting (speeding up) the project. These expediting costs include overtime or extra labor, retaining an expeditor, and leasing more equipment.

The essence of the time/cost tradeoff is allocating resources (spending money) to reduce project time only so far as further direct costs do not exceed indirect project cost savings. Beyond this point, the cost of expediting exceeds the benefit of reduced indirect project costs.

PERT procedures for analyzing time/cost tradeoffs are useful and straightforward.

1. *Estimate costs.* For each activity, determine indirect project costs and expediting costs per time period.
2. *Estimate crash times.* For each activity, determine the shortest possible activity time.
3. *Identify activities on the critical path.*
4. *Evaluate the PERT network.* Reduce the critical path (CP) activity times by observing these restrictions: Expedite the CP activity that has the least expediting cost, continuing to the second least costly, and so on to the most costly, or until one of the following occurs:
   (a) The target expedited time has been reached.
   (b) The resources for expediting ($) have been exhausted.
   (c) The indirect project costs are less than the expediting costs for each activity on the critical path.

In this procedure, you must be careful to keep an eye on the critical path. As the path time of the original CP is reduced, other paths may become critical. Should two or more paths have to be expedited simultaneously, the procedure may become too costly. We look at an example to illustrate this procedure.

EXAMPLE

The facilities manager of Home State Insurance Company's new office wing finds that the air conditioning unit is not functioning. The compressor and the fan are out because the system was improperly wired. After much discussion, the general contractor has agreed to replace the whole system. Of course, the manager wants to know how quickly the job can be done. He has collected data as summarized in Table 9.6.

The manager has decided to construct a PERT diagram to help plan the work by finding the critical path time. He also intends to spend as much as $400 to expedite the project if it is economical to do so.

The manager is experienced in PERT diagramming and constructs the diagram in

Figure 9.5. The critical path comprises activities A, D, G, H, and I with a critical path time of 19 days. Steps 1 through 3 of the PERT time/cost tradeoff analysis are now completed.

To reduce the critical path time according to step 4, the manager can expedite only activity A at \$50/day for possibly 1 day and activity G at \$120/day for possibly 4 days. (When activity A is expedited for 1 day, the critical path has not changed, but project completion time has been reduced to 18 days. When activity G is expedited for 2 days, two paths become critical: path 1-2-5-6-7-8 and path 1-2-4-6-7-8, and project completion time has been further reduced to 16 days. The manager has spent a total of \$50 + \$120 + \$120, or \$290 of the \$400 allowable for expediting. To reduce the completion time by one more day, he must spend \$120 on G and \$80 on F (the cheaper of C and F) simultaneously. Therefore he must spend an additional \$120 + \$80, or \$200. He cannot do so, since total expenditure would exceed the \$400 budget limit.

TABLE 9.6 Home State Insurance Company data

Activity	Required Predecessor(s)	Expected Time t_e (in days)	Standard Deviation (σ_e) (in days)	Crash Time (in days)	Cost to Expedite (in \$/day)
A. Place order	—	3	1	2	50
B. Pull old compressor	A	4	0	2	100
C. Remove old fan	A	6	0	4	200
D. Build new unit	A	4	3	4	—
E. Remove old unit	B	5	5	2	400
F. Modify duct work	C	3	2	2	80
G. Ship new unit	D	7	1	3	120
H. Install new unit	F, G	3	2	3	—
I. Start up new unit	E, H	2	1	2	—

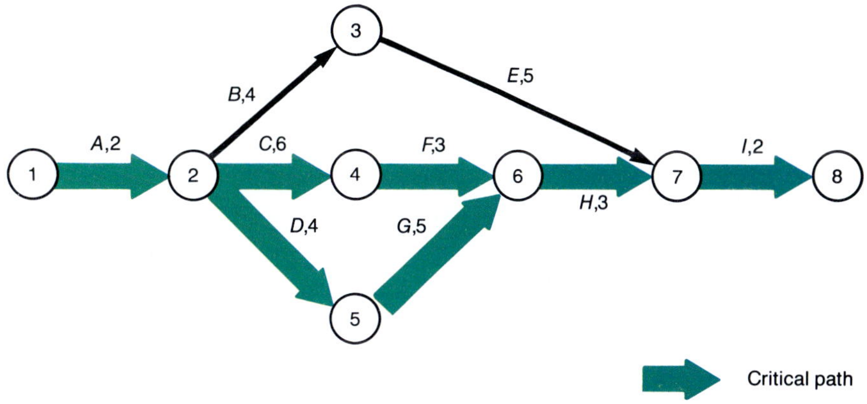

FIGURE 9.5 Home State Insurance Company PERT diagram

Probabilistic PERT A modification of PERT to consider the variance σ_e^2 and the mean μ_{cp} of the expected times.

Probabilistic PERT To estimate the probability of completing a project within some desired length of time, PERT can be used. We do this by considering the *variance* σ_e^2 as well as the mean μ_{cp} of the activity times. Standard deviation σ_e of an activity time is calculated as

$$\sigma_e = \frac{t_p - t_o}{6}$$

so the variance σ_e^2 is calculated as

$$\sigma_e^2 = \left(\frac{t_p - t_o}{6}\right)^2 \quad (9.2)$$

In using probabilistic PERT, we make the two assumptions that expected times are statistically independent and that project completion time is normally distributed. The assumption of independence allows us to add the activity time variances to find the total project time variance. The assumption of normality allows us to use the normal distribution in our analysis.

The mean of the distribution of project completion time is the sum of the individual t_e values on the critical path; it is the critical path time. The total variance σ_{cp}^2 for the critical path is the sum of the variances for all critical path activities.

$$\sigma_{cp}^2 = \sum_{i=1}^{n} \sigma_{ei}^2 \quad (9.3)$$

Consider the Home State Insurance Company example. In Table 9.5, the standard deviations for the critical path activities were 1 for A, 3 for D, 1 for G, 2 for H, and 1 for I. From Equation 9.3, we see the critical path variance (σ_{cp}^2) is:

$$\begin{aligned}\sigma_{cp}^2 &= \sum_{i=1}^{5} \sigma_{ei}^2 \\ &= 1^2 + 3^2 + 1^2 + 2^2 + 1^2 \\ &= 16\end{aligned}$$

The critical path probability distribution, then, has a mean μ_{cp} (the critical path time) and standard deviation σ_{cp} of:

$$\mu_{cp} = 19 \quad \sigma_{cp} = 4$$

Suppose now that the facilities manager wants the project to be completed by July 5, which is 16 days away. Using X to represent project completion time, he wants to find the probability P of $X \leq 16$:

$$P(X \leq 16)$$

The situation is illustrated in Figure 9.6. We can find the standard deviate Z by

$$\begin{aligned}Z &= \frac{X - \mu_{cp}}{\sigma_{cp}} \\ &= \frac{16 - 19}{4} = -0.75\end{aligned}$$

In the normal table (Appendix Table A), we find for $Z = -0.75$ the corresponding probability of 0.2734, which is the $P(16 \leq X \leq 19)$. Subtracting from the mean,

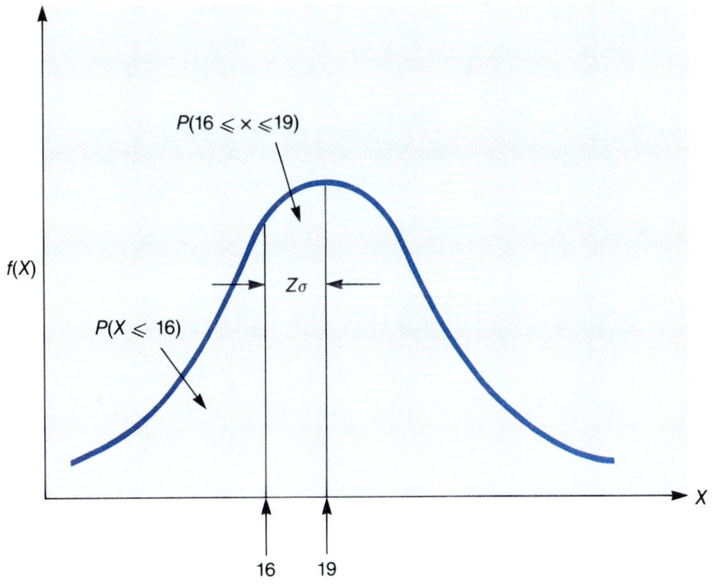

FIGURE 9.6 **Critical path time and variance for Home State Insurance Company**

$$
\begin{aligned}
P(X \leq 16) &= 0.5000 - P(16 \leq X \leq 19) \\
&= 0.5000 - 0.2734 \\
&= 0.2266
\end{aligned}
$$

The chance of finishing the project by July 5 is only about 22.7 percent. The manager might now want either to expedite or to generate some contingency plan.

Limited Resources PERT assumes that there are sufficient resources available to complete simultaneously all activities that are scheduled. This is often not the case. If there are conflicts, limited amounts of labor, for example, some rule is needed to allocate resources among competing activities. Although there are models for approaching this problem, simple heuristics are generally used in practice:

- Schedule the shortest activity first.
- Schedule the activity with the lowest variance (most certain) first.
- Schedule the jobs for a particular organization unit (division, department) first.
- Schedule the activity with the least slack first.

Numerous software packages are available to help analyze resources and plan their use judiciously. The approaches these packages involve may vary in detail, but you can use nearly any of them with confidence. Documentation accompanying the packages is almost always sufficient to get you going.

MANAGING THE PROJECT

Unlike routine, repetitive functions, project management presents some special challenges that require somewhat different talents and a unique management style. Getting the project launched and overseeing its completion have both technical and behavioral dimensions, as we see next.

PLANNING AND CONTROLLING THE PROJECT

Major projects pose real challenges in their planning and control. Two methodologies, work breakdown structures and progress reporting, can help.

Work breakdown structure (WBS) A methodology for the level-by-level breakdown of a project into successively more detailed subcomponent activities and tasks.

Work Breakdown Structure The *work breakdown structure* (WBS) is a methodology for converting a large-scale project into detailed schedules for its thousands of activities. The WBS is a level-by-level breakdown of project modules. The overall project is subdivided into major subcomponents that, in turn, are further subdivided into another, lower level of more detailed subcomponent activities, and so on. Eventually, all the tasks for every activity are identified, commonalities are discovered, and unnecessary duplication can be eliminated.

After the WBS is developed, it can be used to create segments of the network structure which, ultimately, are combined into the PERT network for the project. Let's examine the WBS methodology by continuing the Long-Term Care example.

EXAMPLE

Long-Term Care, Inc. intends to expand into a new, specially designed facility. Now, however, the administrator wants a more realistic project analysis for the new facility rather than the simplified preliminary analysis shown earlier. Consequently, the consultants developed a WBS that reveals several types and levels of activities that had been omitted in the preliminary analysis. Figure 9.7 shows selected portions of the WBS; only some of the level 3 and 4 activities are shown. In planning for level 2, some new activities were added that had been overlooked in the preliminary study: certification and long-term financing. At level 3, two special equipment needs were identified as were three different kinds of professional staff.

The administrator used the WBS to create segments of the network structure. From level 3, for example, she identified links among the tasks for hiring therapists and getting the two special pieces of equipment. As Figure 9.8 shows, the cardio-stress analyzer cannot be calibrated until the hydro-muscular bath is installed because the two systems work together. Similarly, the analyzer must be tested after the bath has been tested. Although therapists can be recruited earlier, their training cannot begin until the analyzer is calibrated: therapist training is geared toward the special equipment.

The administrator developed a complete PERT network (not shown) involving some 300 activities for the project. Start and finish dates for the activities were estimated along with their costs. From these data she developed project budgets that she used to monitor the project, stage by stage, as it progressed.

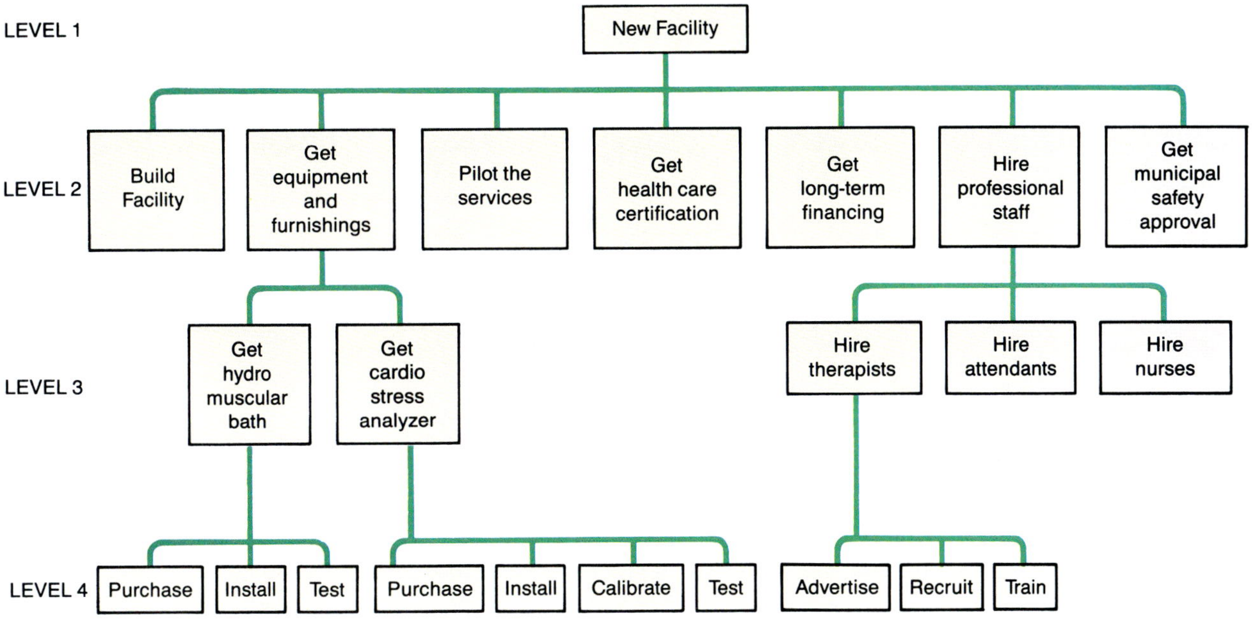

FIGURE 9.7 Work breakdown structure for Long-Term Care project

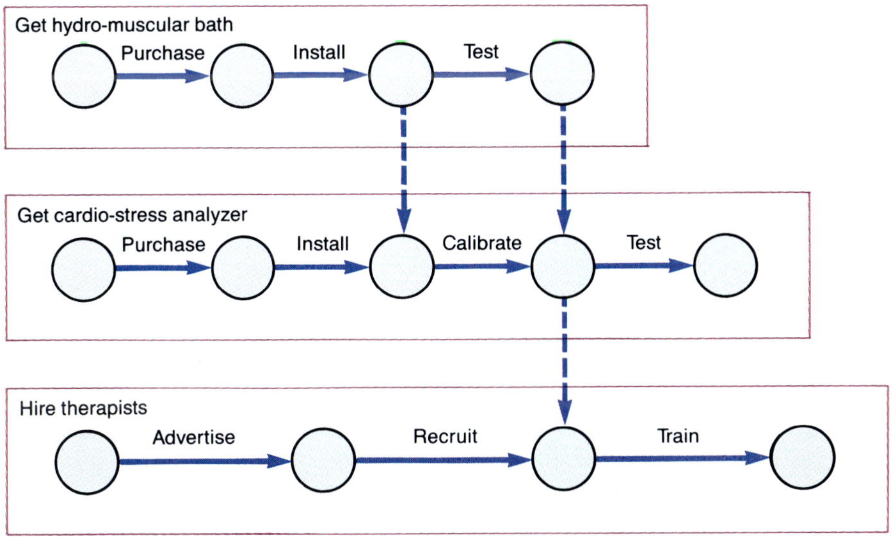

FIGURE 9.8 Creating network segments from work breakdown structures for Long-Term Care project

Progress reporting
Monitoring the time and cost variances during the progress of a project and depicting them graphically, including actual costs of work completed (ACWC), budgeted costs of work completed (BCWC), and budgeted costs of work scheduled (BCWS).

Progress Reporting Project management involves more than just planning; it also requires controlling: monitoring progress and taking corrective action when activities deviate from schedules or costs get out of line. Progress reporting helps managers control by showing cost variances (actual versus budgeted) and time variances (actual versus scheduled) during the project. Figure 9.9 shows how these time and cost variances can be consolidated into a visual progress report.

After the project began in January, the actual costs of work completed (ACWC) were tallied, month by month, into a cumulative total. As of the end of November (now), ACWC are $365,000. How do the actual costs compare with the budgeted costs for those same activities? The budgeted costs of work completed (BCWC) have been consistently lower than actual costs; cost overruns have been experienced. At the end of June, for example, the cost overrun for work completed was about $60,000, as indicated by the vertical distance between the ACWC curve and the BCWC curve. Corrective action is needed to contain the high cost variance.

The progress report also shows the budgeted costs of work scheduled (BCWS) in the project. These are the time-phased expenditures that were budgeted when the project was planned. If the activities had progressed as planned, expenditures would have occurred as indicated by the BCWS curve. At the end of November, however, $250,000 has been spent, which is the amount budgeted for work scheduled through September, not November: actual progress is lagging behind scheduled progress. The horizontal distance between the BCWS curve and the BCWC curve indicates the project is nearly two months behind schedule in terms of work completed versus work scheduled to date. Again, adjustments in work progress are required if the project is to be completed on schedule.

FIGURE 9.9

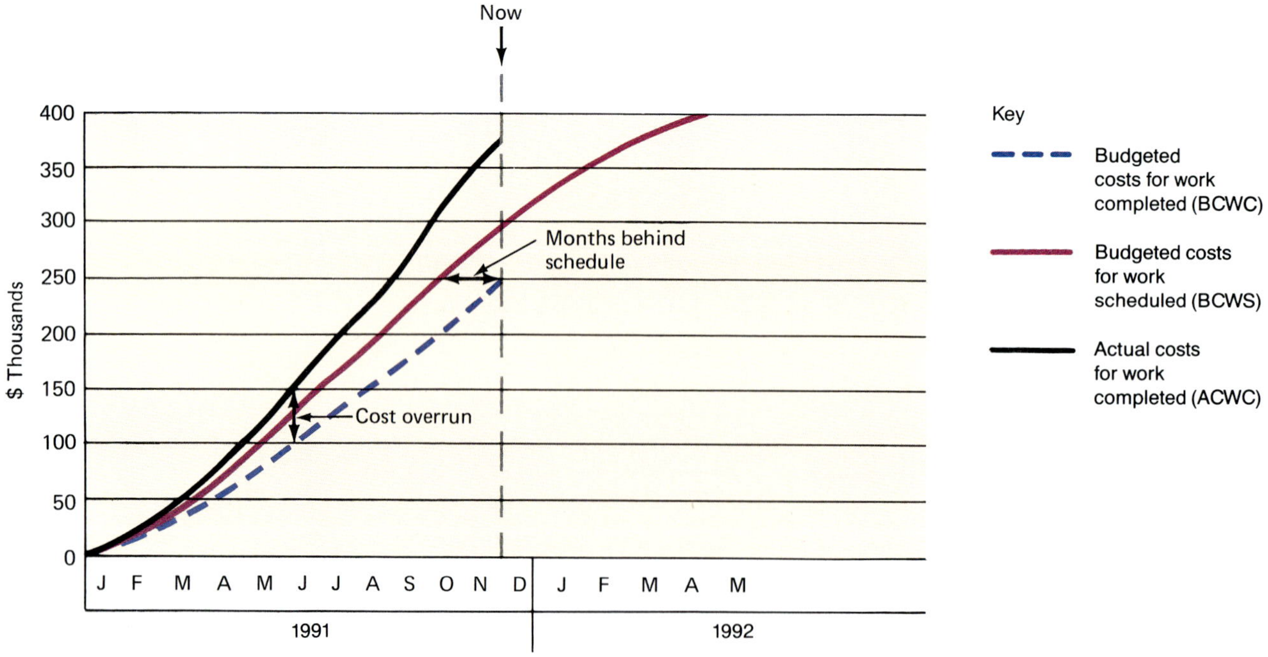

BEHAVIORS IN IMPLEMENTATION

Aside from the technical aspects of projects, project success usually depends upon a manager's organizational abilities as well. Some adjustments of the organization's structure are commonplace, as are the behavioral adjustments of managers and subordinates in project settings.

Matrix organization An organization that combines functional and project bases for groupings of organization units.

Matrix Organization The matrix organization is a team approach to special projects. When teams are established, the firm's organization departs from the conventional functional basis for organization—departmentalization. Figure 9.10 illustrates a project using a matrix organization. In this example, the "home" departments of the various team members are functional: engineering, production, and marketing, depending upon what skills are required for the particular project. Thus the vertical dimension of the matrix is the firm's usual organization and the horizontal dimension of the matrix is the project organization.

Today, project teams enjoy widespread acceptance in many of our major industries. They are especially effective in large companies that emphasize new product development and rapid launching of new products in the marketplace.

Several factors seem to have been responsible for this trend toward project teams. Rapid technological changes forced organizations to minimize development lead times, reduce costs, and avoid obsolescence. These pressures resulted in the need for a kind of organization that could cut across functional areas. The project matrix organization fills that need. Engineers, scientists, technicians, market specialists, and other skilled personnel can be effectively and efficiently loaned from their "home" unit to another unit for periods of time, thus avoiding duplicated skills and unnecessary costs.

FIGURE 9.10 **Project matrix organization**

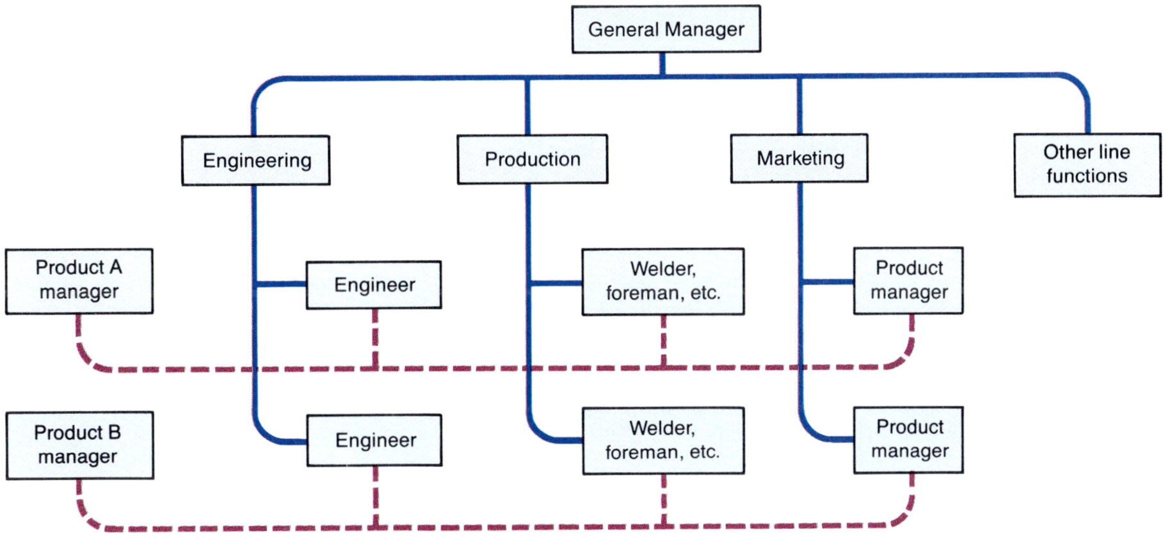

Comparing South Korean and U.S. PERT Applications Comparing results of recent surveys gives us insight into the patterns of project management practices used throughout the world.[3] Particularly interesting are recent surveys of Research and Development (R&D) units.

One survey, for example, reveals that R&D units in South Korea, a newly industrializing country, infrequently use Gantt chart or PERT and critical path method (CPM) techniques. The survey found that no South Korean company has fully adopted a matrix organization for its R&D unit. It may be inferred that, without formal techniques or a fully used matrix organization, South Korean R&D units operate with few restrictions and a great deal of flexibility.

R&D units in U.S. firms, on the other hand, report widespread use of Gantt chart and PERT and CPM techniques. PERT, for example, is used by 42 percent of the 50 R&D units surveyed. Another survey reported that PERT is used by 48 percent of the R&D units, and Gantt charts by 88 percent. These figures alone do not tell the story, though. Details of the survey reveal that even in the United States R&D project managers tend to opt for simplicity: They use PERT for time analysis, but often fail to use the cost and resource analysis features of their PERT software packages. No doubt, as managers become more comfortable and skilled using electronic technologies, they will find simplicity in these other PERT applications as well.

BEHAVIORS IN A PROJECT ENVIRONMENT

Project managers must not only be competent technically but must also be skilled in analysis, interpersonal relations, and decision making. Let's briefly examine a few key behaviors within project teams.

Communication Project leaders must be able to communicate freely with both team members and line employees who are not regular team members. Within the project team, communication is frequent and often involves intensive collaboration. Short daily meetings, written correspondence, and one-on-one problem-solving sessions are often necessary for the sorts of tasks required of project teams. The nonroutine, diverse, loosely structured tasks that project teams often engage in require flexible relationships and communication to avoid duplication of effort and costly project delays.

Motivation Project managers motivate team members in much the same way other managers motivate their staff. Motivation comes from either extrinsic or intrinsic rewards. One difficulty a project manager may face is they may not have sufficient latitude to give monetary rewards. They may be able, however, to give monetary rewards in the form of incentives for cost control and completion time. Or they may rely on intrinsic rewards, such as satisfaction from tasks accomplished, pride in quality

[3] Khaled A. Bu-Bushait, "The Application of Project Management Techniques to Construction and Research and Development Projects," *Project Management Journal* 20, no. 2 (June 1989), 17–22; Jinjoo Lee, Sangjin Lee, and Zong-tae Bae, "The Practice of R & D Management: An Empirical Study of Korean Firms," *R & D Management* (UK) 16, no. 4 (October 1986), 297–308; and J. C. Higgins and K. M. Watts, "Some Perspectives on the Use of Management Science Techniques in R & D Management," *R & D Management* (UK) 16, no. 4 (October 1986), 291–96.

In this architect's office, representatives from human resources and product management bring their skills together from their "home" departments to complete this facility expansion.
Source: Steve Dunwell/The Image Bank

workmanship, pleasure from job flexibility, and pride in the team effort. All of these can be fostered and encouraged by project managers.

Group Cohesiveness As the size of the project team increases, group cohesiveness decreases. The higher a group ranks in organization status (measured by project importance, skills required, and job flexibility), the more cohesive the group tends to be. If group members' social, economic, or psychological needs are met by a group, they tend to feel strong ties to the group. The more a project team fills these needs, the more cohesive the team. Finally, the closer group members work in close proximity to one another under stress conditions, the greater the group cohesiveness.

Overall, the more cohesive the group, the better the chances a project can be completed on budget and on time. Because of both the diversity of team members and the one-shot nature of the project, group cohesiveness is difficult to achieve in project teams. But project teams that are cohesive increase their chances of achieving their primary goals.

PROJECT ORGANIZATION ADVANTAGES AND DISADVANTAGES

Perhaps the one overriding advantage of project organization is that by grouping people and tasks, the organization can tackle unusual project opportunities on short notice. A key disadvantage, however, is that creating and dispersing project teams can be upsetting to the routine employees have developed. Furthermore, project managers often feel considerable constraints in having to accept responsibility for completing the project without being given line authority to control it.

SUMMARY

Project planning includes all those activities resulting in a course of action for a one-time-only venture with specific beginning and ending dates. Project scheduling is the time sequencing of the project activities. It can be viewed as a subphase of overall project planning. In project scheduling, the activities of the project are identified and related to one another and to the calendar.

Techniques for project scheduling include Gantt charts and PERT analysis. Gantt charts are visual aids whose strength lies in their simplicity and ease of understanding. Program Evaluation and Review Technique (PERT) analysis is an application of basic network analysis. Activities, represented as network arcs, are related sequentially to one another and represented diagramatically. Such statistics as critical path time, critical path variance, and event slack are calculated as a basis for project control. Other useful variations include cost/time tradeoff analysis and probabilistic PERT.

Planning for and monitoring the project is aided by work breakdown structures and progress reporting. A variety of computer software packages are available to assist in project planning, analysis, control, and reporting. Organizing by creating a project-oriented organization focuses on a matrix approach to grouping jobs. In a situation somewhat unique to projects, the project manager assumes responsibility for project goals without commensurate authority over line activities. Thus the project manager needs skills in communicating, coordinating, motivating, and maintaining a cohesive project team.

CASE

Electran Manufacturing, Ltd.

Electran Manufacturing, Ltd., is a diversified manufacturer in two primary fields: electronic applications and transportation equipment. In the transportation equipment field, Electran products are in the forefront of technological applications, especially in terms of electrical circuitry and component packages. Electran management takes great pride in its technological leadership and has decided to support a substantial research and development (R&D) effort.

Currently 74 persons are employed full-time in the R&D division, and at any one time at least twice that many more are involved to some degree in R&D projects. These employees are assigned primarily to engineering, finance, marketing, and production.

Electran organizes its R&D effort by functional area within the division. Engineers, scientists, and technicians are grouped separately. Additionally, within each of these technical specialties, employees are grouped and housed together. Electrical engineers, mechanical engineers, and metalurgical engineers, for example, are each grouped and located together. Projects rotate from group to group, depending upon what work needs to be accomplished. There is a department head for each of the engineering, science, and technical support areas, and three additional project managers have individual project responsibility. There is considerable pressure on project managers, but they have limited control over staff within the R&D division and even less control over the approximately 150 employees who assist the R&D division on an occasional basis. The R&D division manager has recently read a brief article about matrix organization. He wonders if matrix organization might be helpful in relieving some of the burden from his project managers and in increasing division productivity.

One of the three project managers is trying to grasp the basis of PERT. He has assembled the following data for a project soon to be started. He wants to establish a PERT diagram for the project, determine the earliest completion date from project start using expected times, and find the minimum cost plan. This project manager does not know whether he has enough data to proceed; even if he does have enough data, he does not know how to analyze them and apply the results.

Activity	Required Predecessors	Expected Time (in days)	Cost to Expedite (in $/day)
A-B	—	2	100
A-C	—	4	80
A-D	—	5	70
B-E	A-B, A-C	3	100
E-F	B-E	6	150
F-H	E-F	2	50
D-H	A-D	11	100
H-I	F-H, D-H	1	100

The project manager has budgeted $200 for expediting should he want to use it.

REVIEW AND DISCUSSION QUESTIONS

1. Differentiate between project planning and other types of planning.
2. Explain how project planning and project scheduling relate.
3. Provide an example, not given in this chapter, of a project. Describe the project, identifying the beginning and ending points, the activities, and the time sequencing of the activities in relation to each other and the calendar.
4. Discuss how a Gantt chart can be used as a scheduling tool. What type of model is a Gantt chart?
5. PERT has characteristics of both a mathematical model and a schematic model. Explain.
6. Explain how the scheduling and cost performance of a project might be measured. When might such a measure be useful?
7. Discuss the key behaviors exhibited with project teams. In your discussion, explain who exhibits each behavior, and explain the possible consequences of such behavior on reaching project goals.
8. Contrast the advantages and disadvantages of project organization.
9. Describe the conditions under which PERT may be appropriately used.
10. In PERT, the terms are important. Explain the difference between an activity and an event. What is a critical path?

11. Present the logic of PERT—that is, explain how PERT works.
12. Explain how a time/cost tradeoff could exist in a project involving the construction, staffing, and opening of a new clubhouse at an existing country club.
13. Managers often complain that statistical analysis is too complicated. Suppose that your supervisor feels this way, but he likes PERT. In minimally technical terms, explain the advantages of probabilistic PERT to your supervisor and try to convince him to accept it.
14. Your project is to design and build an insulated dog house for your favorite collie. Show how to use a work breakdown structure to develop the project network.

PROBLEMS

SOLVED PROBLEMS

1. Compute the values for the earliest beginning times (T_E) and the latest beginning times (T_L) for the network shown in Figure 9.11. The expected time is shown beside each activity. The solution is shown as Figure 9.12.

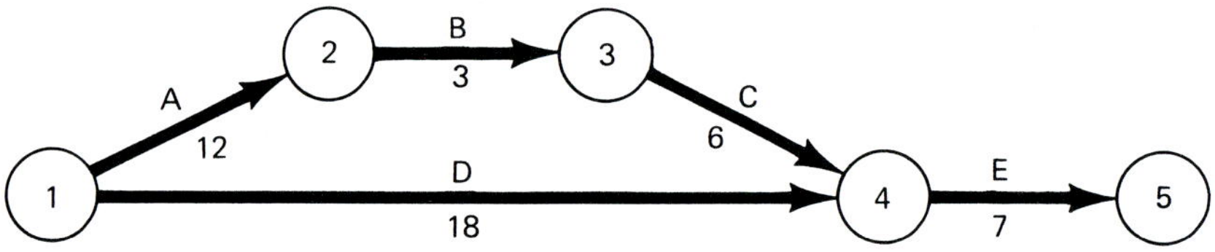

FIGURE 9.11

SOLUTION

Event	1	2	3	4	5
T_E	0	12	15	21	28
T_L	0	12	15	21	28

FIGURE 9.12

2. Determine the expected completion time and the variance of completion time for the network shown in Figure 9.13 (the optimistic, most likely, and pessimistic times are shown for each activity, in that order).

FIGURE 9.13

SOLUTION

Variable	Activity 1-2	Activity 2-3	Activity 3-4
t_e	$\frac{4 + 4(6) + 8}{6} = 6.00$	$\frac{7 + 4(11) + 13}{6} = 10.67$	$\frac{8 + 4(10) + 14}{6} = 10.33$
σ_e^2	$\left(\frac{8 - 4}{6}\right)^2 = 0.4444$	$\left(\frac{13 - 7}{6}\right)^2 = 1.000$	$\left(\frac{14 - 8}{6}\right)^2 = 1.000$

Expected completion time $= \Sigma\, t_e = 27.00$ weeks
Completion time variance $= \Sigma\, \sigma_e^2 = 2.44$

REINFORCING FUNDAMENTALS

3. A veterinarian would like to put a septic tank and drains for collecting animal waste in his animal shelter. He has identified the following activities and estimated their times (in days): planning (4), obtaining contractor (7), excavating (3), laying drainage tile (2), concrete work (4), landscaping (3). All activities are sequential except for laying the drainage tile and concrete work, which may be done simultaneously but only after excavating.
   (a) Prepare a Gantt chart.
   (b) Prepare a PERT diagram.
   (c) Which tool would be most useful for this project? Why?
4. Given the PERT diagram shown in Figure 9.14:
   (a) Compute the values for the earliest beginning times (T_E) and the latest beginning times (T_L).
   (b) Find the event slack at event 2.
   (c) The penalty cost per day for each day over 15 days is \$100. The costs of expediting, for those activities that allow it, are as follows:

Activity	Cost to Expedite (in \$/day)	Maximum Time That Expediting Can Reduce (in days)
2–4	70	2
3–4	60	1
4–5	150	3

Which activities (and by how many days), *if any*, would you expedite?

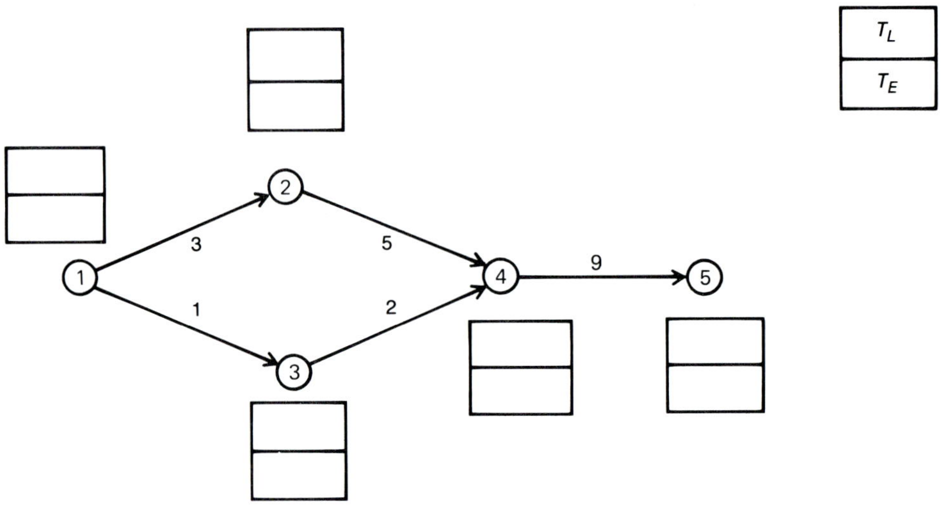

FIGURE 9.14

5. Given the PERT activities in Figure 9.15:
   (a) What is the critical path?
   (b) Construct a Gantt chart for this project.
   (c) Examine the activity variances. Which path through the network would you suggest that the project manager watch most closely? Why?

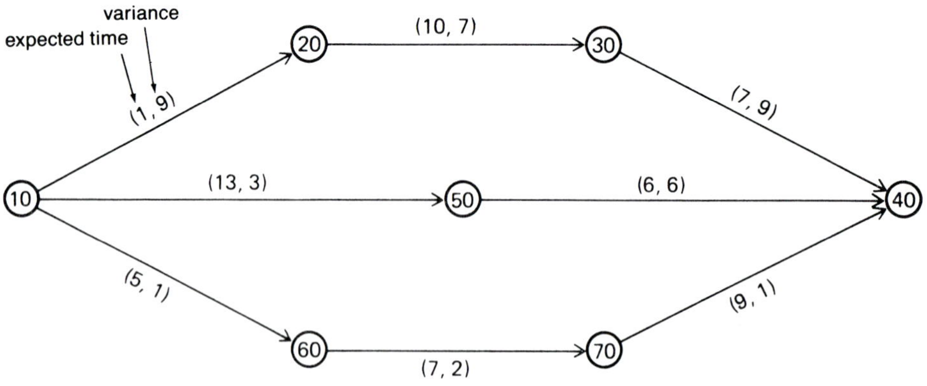

FIGURE 9.15

6. Given the data in Figure 9.16:

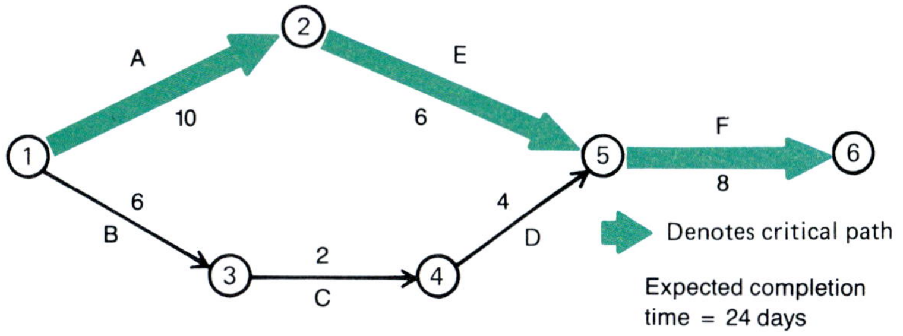

FIGURE 9.16

Activity	Expected Time (in days)	Cost to Expedite (in $/day)	Crash Time (in days)
A	10	$50	6
B	6	30	3
C	2	—	2
D	4	40	2
E	6	80	4
F	8	100	5

What is the minimum completion time (crash time) of the project and the associated expediting cost? Show your work by identifying all activity durations and expediting costs that minimize total expediting costs while still providing the minimum expected completion time for the project.

7. For the data given in problem 6, identify all possible expected project durations and the minimum total expediting costs of each. Develop a graph of this relationship, and identify the activity durations and the critical path activities for each point on the graph.

8. Consider the research and development project PERT diagram shown in Figure 9.17.

(a) Find the critical path and critical path time.
(b) What is the probability that the project will take more than 21 days to complete?
(c) A new activity is being considered: economic evaluations of pesticide application. This activity would precede activity DC and follow activities AB, AD, and AE. Draw the new PERT network. Identify the new activity on your network.

9. A market research project for Trademark Greeting Cards (TGC) is being planned as shown below. For the market research manager,

(a) Construct a PERT diagram.
(b) Explain the critical path concept and what the critical path is for this project.

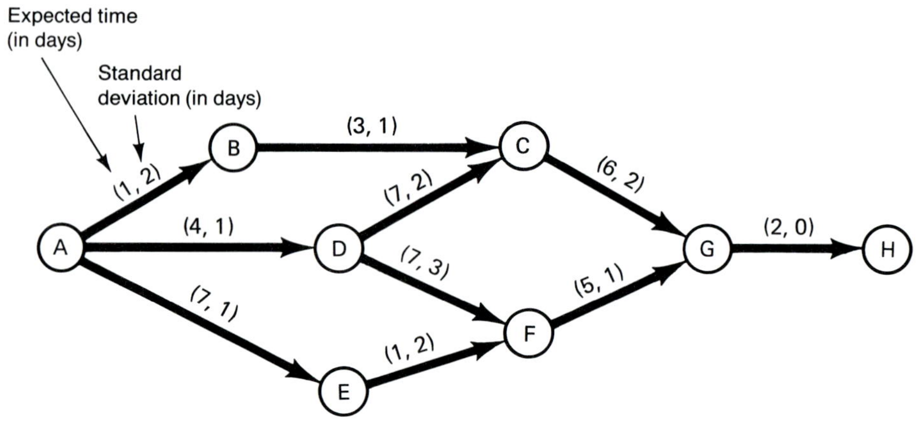

FIGURE 9.17

(c) Analyze costs and recommend action. The project has fixed costs of \$1,000/day; that is, each day the completion time is shortened from the expected time, the firm saves \$1,000.

Activity	Required Predecessors	Expected Time (in days)	Minimum Expedited Time (in days)	Cost To Expedite (in \$/day)
1	—	10	5	800
2	1	20	15	650
3	2	25	15	400
4	2	20	15	700
5	3, 4	15	13	900
6	5	15	10	1050
7	1	60	45	300
8	6, 7	5	4	850

10. A public accounting firm has described an audit program at a bank in terms of activities and events and has calculated the expected times (t_e) and their variances (σ_e^2) in days as shown in Figure 9.18 (e.g., activity 10–20 has $t_e = 8$ and $\sigma_e^2 = 3$).

(a) Find the critical path and the mean critical path time for the audit program.

(b) If activity times are assumed to be independent and normally distributed, what is the probability that the audit is completed in 22 days or fewer? Of what value is this information to a partner in the firm?

(c) What can you tell about activity 30-60 as it relates to the critical path?

(d) What is the event slack at event 50? Why?

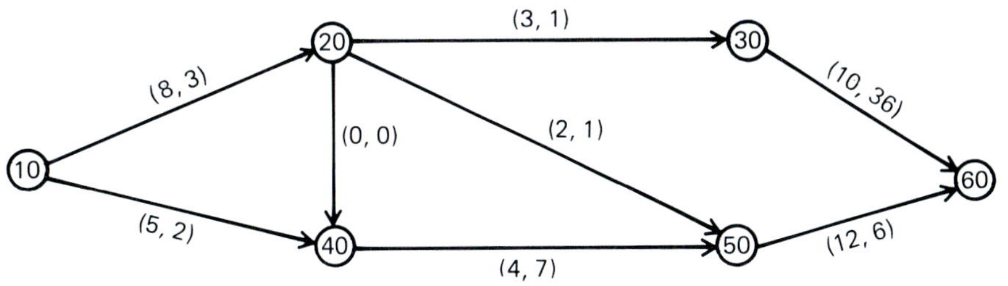

FIGURE 9.18

11. For an R&D project, the PERT network in Figure 9.19 was constructed. Activity times are in months.

(a) What is the critical path?

(b) What is the event slack at event 30? What does that mean?

(c) Two activities have to be added due to a change in project definition. An activity of two months must precede the entire project, and an activity of two months must precede activity 10-30. What impact, if any, will this have on the critical path and on the event slack at event 30?

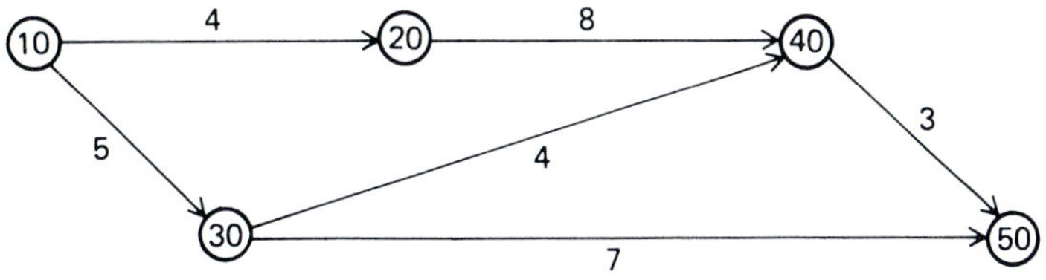

FIGURE 9.19

CHALLENGING EXERCISES

12. The data for a short project is shown in the table below.

(a) Construct a PERT diagram. Calculate the critical path time, and clearly designate the critical path.

(b) Calculate the earliest beginning time, the latest beginning time, and slack time at each event. Why is slack time always zero at each event on the critical path?

(c) Assuming independent activities that are normally distributed, what is the probability of completing the project in 19 days or fewer?

(d) If you chose to expedite only one activity, which would you choose? Why?

Activity	Required Predecessors	Expected Time (in days)	Variance	Cost to Expedite (in $/day)	Maximum Times That Expediting Can Reduce
A	—	6	2	100	3
B	—	11	9	50	1
C	—	13	5	200	2
D	A	6	4	—	—
E	C, F, G	4	4	300	1
F	D	4	1	150	1
G	B	7	3	200	2

13. A project manager for Electromagnet, Inc., has constructed the PERT network shown in Figure 9.20. Assist the manager by determining the following:

(a) Critical path and critical path time

(b) Probability of completing this project in 11 days or fewer and the probability of completing the project in 13 days or more (assuming independent activities and normally distributed completion times)

(c) Expected gain (or loss) from this project if completed, given the payoff table shown below:

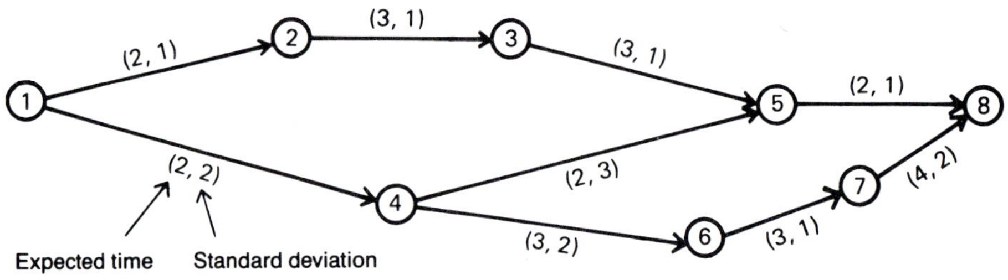

FIGURE 9.20

Alternatives	Finish in 11 Days or Fewer	Finish in 12 Days	Finish in 13 Days or More
Complete the project	+$800	+$200	−$100
Don't start the project	$0	$0	$0

14. A computer programming team has divided a project in terms of activities and events and has calculated expected activity times (t_e) and their variances (σ^2_e) in days, as shown in Figure 9.21. (For example, activity 10-20 has a $t_e = 8$ and $\sigma^2_e = 3$).

(a) Find the critical path and the mean critical path time for the project.
(b) If activities are assumed to be independent and normally distributed, what is the probability that all computer programming is completed in 17 days or fewer?
(c) Your goal is a lower project completion time. If you can spend \$500 and reduce activity 50-80 one day or \$600 and reduce activity 60-80 two days, which, if either, should you do?
(d) If the project requires more than 19 days, a penalty of \$300/day is assessed on the programmers. If the project finishes in fewer than 19 days, a bonus of \$300/day is given to the programmers. What is the expected payoff to the programmers?

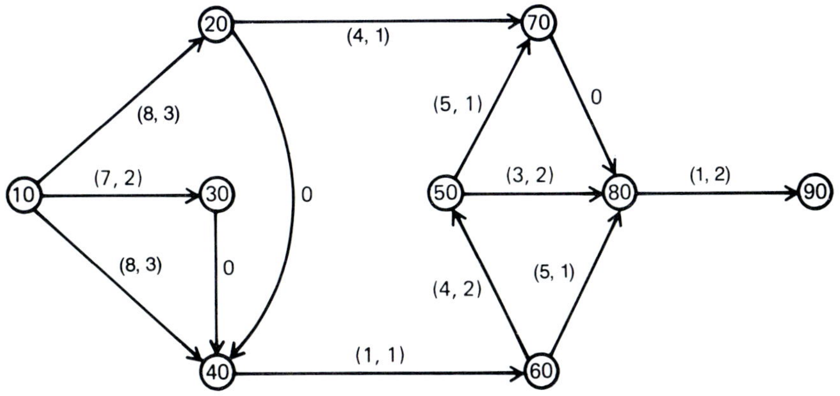

FIGURE 9.21

15. Temple Hospital is designing and implementing a wage incentive program. Included in the table of data below are the activities of this project and other project information. Activity times are independent and normally distributed.
(a) Construct a PERT network and mark the critical path.
(b) What is the probability of completion in more than 15 weeks?
(c) You have \$1,000 to spend expediting. Where would you spend it? Why?
(d) Develop a work breakdown structure (WBS) for the activities "structure internal wage program" and "finalize incentive program." You will need to be creative in identifying lower level activities. You might want to talk with a manager or visit the library for ideas.

Activity	Required Predecessors	Expected Time (in weeks)	Standard Deviation	Minimum Expected Time	Cost to Expedite (in $/week)
Project planning 1-2	—	3	1	3	—
Job analysis 2-3	1-2	5	2	2	500
Performance analysis 2-4	1-2	4	2	2	500
Market wage survey 2-5	1-2	7	3	6	300
Structure internal wage program 3-5	2-3, 2-4	3	2	2	1,000
Finalize incentive program 5-6	2-5, 3-5	4	2	4	—

UTILIZING QSOM COMPUTER SOFTWARE

16. Project data for renovating a building is shown below. Each activity whose most-likely time is 6 days or more can have its pessimistic time reduced by one day if you are willing to expend the resources to do so. Your client wants the renovation completed in 34 days or less and will pay you a $1,000 bonus for each day saved. You will be penalized $500 for each day in excess of 34 days. How much are you willing to pay to reduce the pessimistic times?

Activity	Required Predecessors	Time Estimates (in days)		
		Optimistic	Most Likely	Pessimistic
1-2	—	2	3	4
1-3	—	4	6	8
1-4	—	7	9	11
2-3	1-2	3	4	5
2-4	1-2	5	7	9
2-5	1-2	8	10	12
2-6	1-2	14	17	20
3-5	1-3, 2-3	7	9	11
3-6	1-3, 2-3	12	15	18
3-7	1-3, 2-3	8	11	14
4-5	1-4, 2-4	6	8	10
5-6	2-5, 3-5, 4-5	4	5	6
5-8	2-5, 3-5, 4-5	8	10	12
6-8	2-6, 3-6, 5-6	5	7	9
7-8	3-7	7	9	11
8-9	5-8, 6-8, 7-8	3	4	5

KEY TERMS

SELECTED READINGS

Cleland, D. I., and D. F. Kocaoglu, *Engineering Management.* New York: McGraw-Hill, 1981.

Davis, E. W., "Project Scheduling Under Resource Constraints—Historical Review and Categorization of Procedures," *AIIE Transactions* 5, no. 4 (December 1973), 297–313.

Moder, J. J., C. R. Phillips, and E. W. Davis, *Project Management with CPM, PERT, and Precedence Diagramming* 3rd ed. New York: Van Nostrand Reinhold, 1983.

Smith, Larry A., and Joan Mills, "Project Management Network Programs," *Project Management Quarterly* (June 1982), 18–29.

Weist, J. D., and F. K. Levy, *A Management Guide to PERT/CPM,* 2nd ed. Englewood Cliffs, N.J.: Prentice-Hall, 1977.

PART IV

SCHEDULING PRODUCTION AND SERVICE SYSTEMS

Production and operations management activities

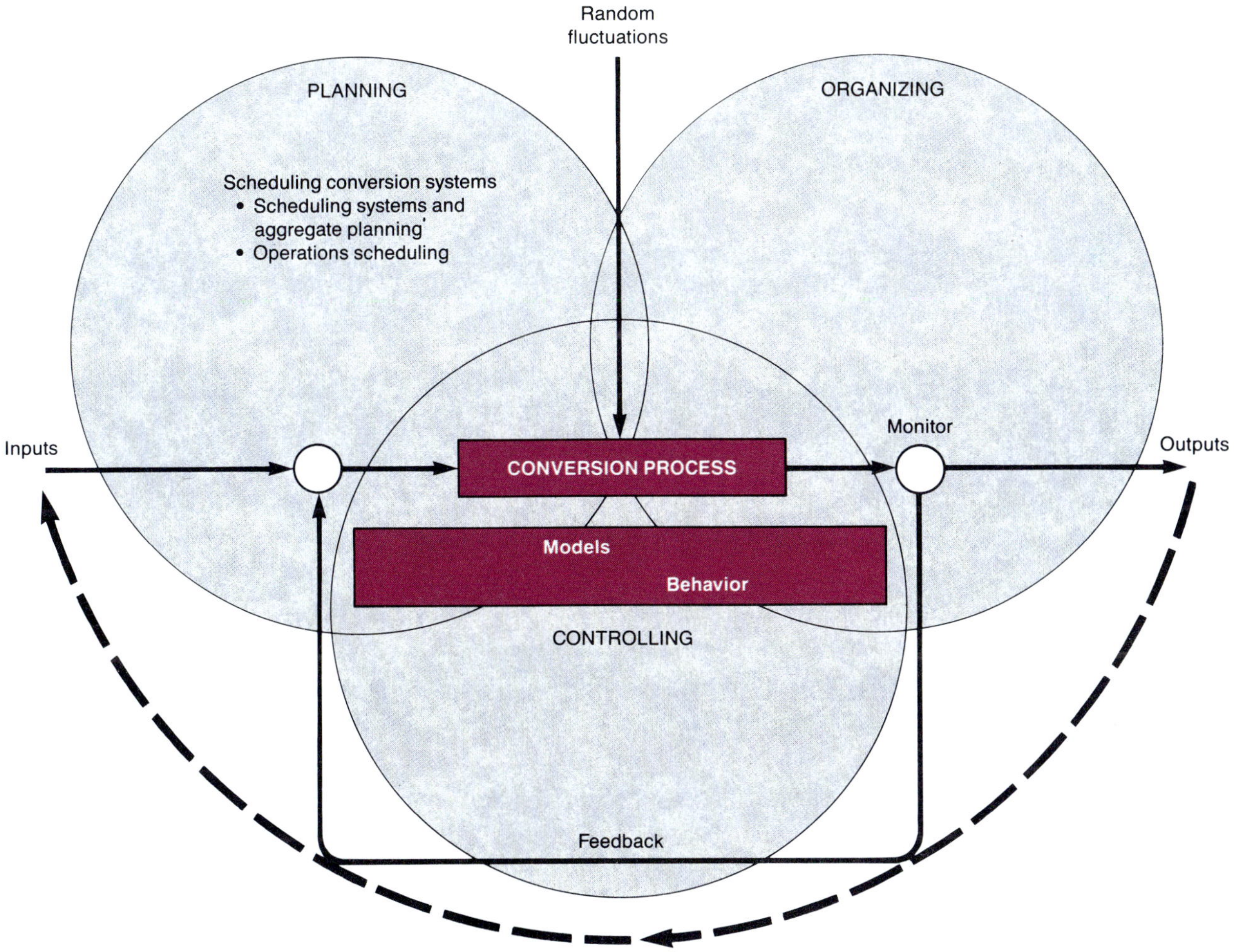

CHAPTER 10

SCHEDULING SYSTEMS AND AGGREGATE PLANNING FOR PRODUCTION AND SERVICES

Because the aircraft manufacturing industry is highly sensitive to fluctuating demands and to their corresponding impact on production costs, a thorough knowledge of scheduling systems is essential to our competitive position. A stable work force is a major goal of our aggregate planning process because of the added costs of erratic variations in the work force. Even minor changes, such as job transfers, multiply to many changes in a highly skilled and unionized environment. McDonnell Douglas Canada Ltd. uses several methods to maintain the delicate balance between short-term flexibility, necessary to meet changing market demands, and long-term production planning necessary to keep costs competitive. The effective use of suitable long-term planning horizons, inventories, reassigned employees, and level loading through finite capacity planning are some of the tools that help to temper the impact of change.

In an industry in which as many as 20,000 different parts (some of them used in large multiple quantities) are incorporated into a single aircraft component that has relatively long flow times, a disciplined approach to planning and scheduling systems is required.

Garret G. Ackerson, President
McDonnell Douglas Canada Ltd.
Toronto, Ontario, Canada

Imagine yourself in charge of a large facility, such as McDonnell Douglas Canada Ltd., that houses many types of equipment and people. How should you use these potentially productive resources during the next six months, year, or even longer? Your answer to this question, as Mr. Ackerson suggests, will directly affect the success of your organization. One source of guidance is provided through operations planning and scheduling systems. After presenting an overview of these systems, we will concentrate on two particular elements—aggregate planning and master scheduling—showing how they are used in both manufacturing and service operations.

OPERATIONS PLANNING AND SCHEDULING SYSTEMS

Operations planning and scheduling systems concern the volume and timing of outputs, the utilization of operations capacity, and balancing outputs with capacity at desired levels for competitive effectiveness. These systems must fit together activities at various levels, from top to bottom, in support of one another, as shown in Figure 10.1. Note that the time orientation ranges from long to short as we progress from top to bottom in the hierarchy. Also, the level of detail in the planning process ranges from broad at the top to detailed at the bottom.[1]

In this chapter we focus on the aggregate production and capacity plan and its decomposition down to the level of master production scheduling and rough-cut capacity planning. Let's begin with an overview of the entire system.

OVERVIEW OF THE OPERATIONS SCHEDULING AND PLANNING SYSTEM

Business plan A statement of an organization's overall level of business activity for the coming six to 18 months, usually expressed in terms of dollar volume of sales for its various product groups.

Product group (family) A set of individual products that share or consume common blocks of capacity in the manufacturing process.

The Business Plan The *business plan* is a statement of the organization's overall level of business activity for the coming 6 to 18 months. Developed at the top executive level, the plan is based on forecasts of general economic conditions, anticipated conditions of the industry, and competitive considerations; it reflects the company's strategy for competing during the coming year(s). It is usually expressed in terms of outputs (in dollar volume of sales), quarterly or sometimes monthly, for each of its broad *product groups* but not for the specific items or individual products within each group. It also may specify the overall inventory and backlog levels that will be maintained during the planning period.

The business plan, in a sense, is an agreement between all functional areas—finance, production, marketing, engineering, R&D—about the level of activity and the products they are committed to support. The business plan is not concerned with all the details and specific timing of the actions for executing the plan. Instead, it determines a feasible general posture for competing to achieve its major goals. The resulting plan guides the lower-level, more detailed decisions.

[1]Hierarchical planning and decisions are discussed in H. C. Meal, "Putting Production Decisions Where They Belong," *Harvard Business Review* 62, no. 2 (March-April 1984, 102-11).

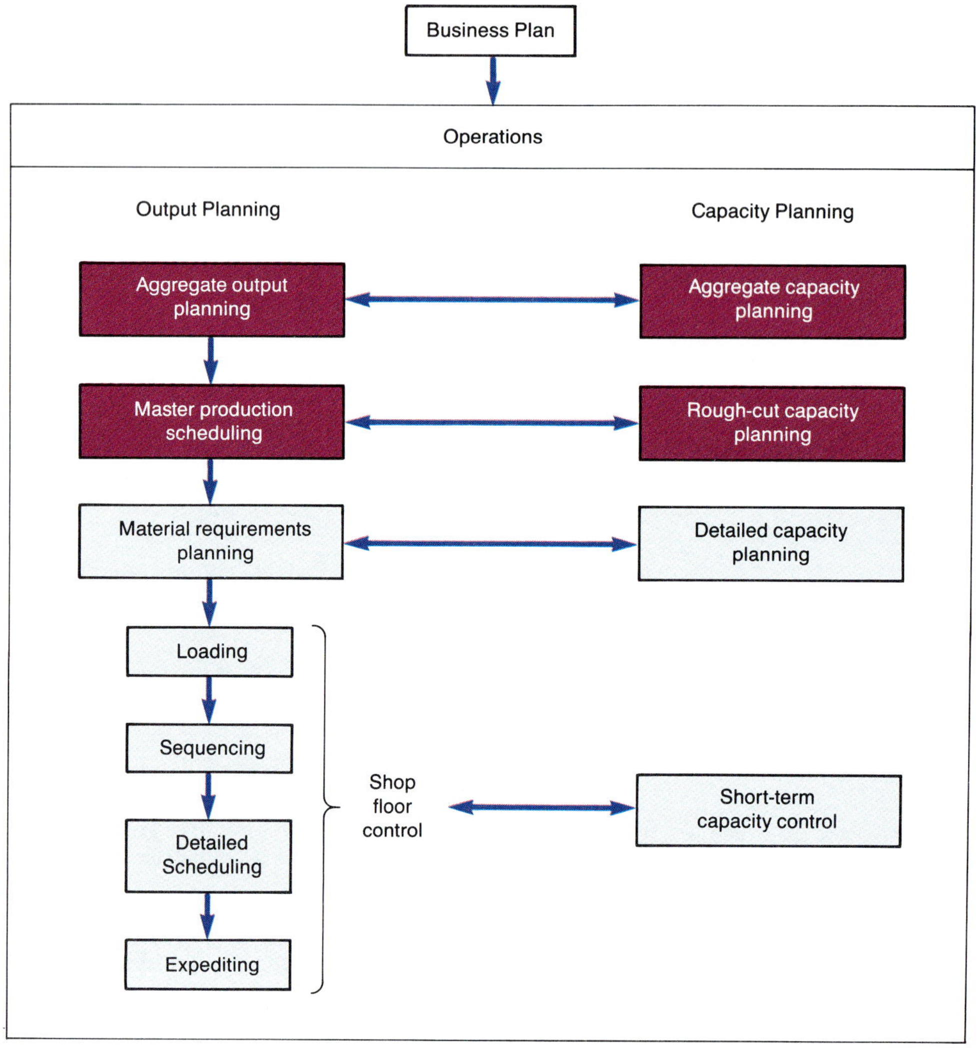

FIGURE 10.1 **The operations planning and scheduling system**

Aggregate output planning The process of determining output levels (units) of product groups over the coming six to 18 months on a weekly or monthly basis; the plan identifies the overall level of outputs in support of the business plan.

Aggregate capacity planning The process of testing the feasibility of aggregate output plans and evaluating overall capacity utilization.

Aggregate Production (Output) Planning This plan is the production portion of the business plan and addresses the *demand side* of the firm's activities by showing the outputs it will produce, expressed in numbers of units of its product groups or families. Since various product groups may be produced at diverse plants, facilities, or divisions, each of them needs its own production plan. The division's aggregate output plan covers the coming 6 to 18 months on a weekly or monthly basis. Planning at this level ignores such details as how many of each individual product, style, color option, or model to produce. The plan recognizes the division's existing fixed capacity and the company's overall policies for maintaining inventories and backlogs, employment stability, and subcontracting.

Aggregate Capacity Planning A statement of desired output is useful only if it is feasible. This is the role of aggregate capacity planning—to keep capacity utilization at desired levels and to test the feasibility of planned output against existing capacity.

Thus it addresses the *supply side* of the firm's ability to meet the demand. As for aggregate output plans, each plant, facility, or division requires its own aggregate capacity plan. Capacity and output must be in balance, as indicated by the arrow between them in Figure 10.1. A capacity plan translates an output plan into *input* terms, *approximating* how much of the division's capacity will be consumed. A product group, for example, usually consumes predictable amounts of capacity such as labor hours of assembly or machine hours for fabrication. Although these basic capacities are fixed, management can manipulate the short-term capacities by the ways they deploy their work force, by subcontracting, or by using multiple work shifts to adjust the timing of overall outputs. As a result, the aggregate planning process balances output levels, capacity constraints, and temporary capacity adjustments to meet demand and utilize capacity at desired levels during the coming months. The resulting plan sets limits on the master production schedule.

Master production scheduling (MPS) A schedule showing week by week how many of each product must be produced according to customer orders and demand forecasts.

Master Production Scheduling (MPS) The purpose of *master production scheduling* is to meet the demand for individual products in the product group. This more detailed level of planning *disaggregates* the product groups into individual products and indicates when they will be produced. The MPS is an important link between marketing and production. It shows when incoming sales orders can be scheduled into production, and when each shipment can be scheduled for delivery. It also takes into account current backlogs so that production and delivery schedules are realistic.

Rough-cut capacity planning The process of testing the feasibility of master production schedules in terms of capacity.

Rough-Cut Capacity Planning *Rough-cut capacity planning* (sometimes called *resource requirements planning*) is done in conjunction with the tentative master production schedule to test its feasibility in terms of capacity before the MPS is finally settled. This step ensures that a proposed MPS does not inadvertently overload any key department, work center, or machine, making the MPS unworkable. Although the check can apply to all work centers, it is typically applied only to the critical ones that are most likely to be bottlenecks. It is a quick and inexpensive way to find and correct gross discrepancies between the capacity requirements (in direct labor hours, for example) of the MPS and available capacity.

Material Requirements Planning The MPS is the driving force for *material requirements planning*. As discussed in Chapter 14, MRP shows the time-phased requirements for releasing materials and receiving materials that enable the master production schedule to be implemented.

Detailed Capacity Planning *Detailed capacity planning*, also called *capacity requirements planning*, is a companion process used with MRP to identify in detail the capacity required to execute the MRP. At this level, more accurate comparisons of available and needed capacity for scheduled work loads are possible. Detailed capacity planning is discussed in Chapter 14.

Shop floor control Activities that execute and control shop operations; includes loading; sequencing, detailed scheduling, and expediting jobs in production.

Shop Floor Control *Shop floor control* coordinates the weekly and daily activities that get jobs done. Individual jobs are assigned to machines and work centers (loading), the sequence of processing the jobs for priority control is determined, start times and job assignments for each stage of processing are decided (detailed scheduling), and materials and work flows from station to station are monitored and adjusted (expediting). Coordinating all of these activities into smooth flows, especially when unplanned delays and new priorities arise, often calls for last-minute adjustments of outputs and capacities, the *short-term capacity control*.

OPERATIONS MANAGEMENT HIGHLIGHT 10.1

Source: Robert Kusel/Tony Stone Worldwide

Scheduling for Small Airlines Has Its Ups and Downs

Commercial airlines plan and schedule at all levels, from aggregate planning down to detailed scheduling of hourly activities. The profitability of the airlines and the satisfaction of its customers ride in the balance in this risky and volatile industry. Especially for the smaller airlines—the commuter operations that fly passengers between major airports to more remote destinations—plans and schedules are essential.

Fast-growing Atlantic Southeast Airlines (ASA)

Several levels of scheduling at Atlantic Southeast Airlines are discussed in Operations Management Highlight 10.1. With this background on the entire production planning and scheduling process, let's take a closer look at aggregate planning and master scheduling.

fits the industry's trend of commuter lines forging relationships with the larger airlines. ASA has arranged with Delta Airlines that the large airline services the major airports like Atlanta and Dallas, and ASA services the small towns. Delta schedules its passengers onto connecting ASA flights to complete their trips from the major cities into small towns in Georgia, Texas, Oklahoma, Mississippi, and elsewhere.

ASA's plans and schedules, of course, are driven by Delta's plans and schedules. Aggregate capacity plans consider the number of planes, their size (in passenger seats), and the skilled human resources to operate them. The aggregate capacity is then allocated to serving the various cities and towns for selected days and times of the day. Schedules are prepared, too, for behind-the-scenes workers: ground crews and maintenance staff. And for companies in a rapid growth pattern, like ASA, increasing capacity requires better, bigger scheduling systems to cope with the uncertainties in this industry. Bad weather, for example, caused USAir alone to cancel 2900 flights in December 1989.

Unexpected events like bad weather complicate scheduling even more so for an airline like ASA, since these events affect not just ASA's schedule but the schedule of the "parent" airline, which in turn further affects the commuter airline. If Delta's on-time performance is bad, ASA suffers. Passengers cancel and operating costs increase. Connecting flights have to be rescheduled; old tickets become scrap paper, and new tickets have to be booked; and loaded luggage must be unloaded and reloaded. On-time operations, especially for connecting flights, provides good service, stable flight schedules, lower costs, and profitable operations. The effectiveness of airline scheduling is in part reflected in their records of on-time arrivals, as shown below, from November 1989.

Airline	On-time arrivals (in percent)
American	85.5
Delta	80.1
Continental	79.9
United	78.1
Northwest	76.7
USAir	68.4
Industry average	78.0

In aggregate planning, too, a commuter line must consider the risks of linking itself too closely with a larger airline. How will operations be adjusted if the larger airline falters? Braniff Express, a commuter line, was left with excess capacity and a disrupted scheduling system when Braniff shut down in 1989. Metro Airlines' capacity was suddenly underutilized when Eastern, its "big-brother" partner, had a prolonged strike in 1990. Small airlines that want to form alliances with the giants had better be prepared, in their planning and scheduling, to ride out the inevitable ups and downs of such an alliance.

Sources: Seth Payne, Chuck Hawkins, and Michael Schroeder, "The Best-Laid Plans of Ed Colodny Traffic Rises," *Wall Street Journal* (July 10, 1990), p. C12; Scott Ticer and James E. Ellis, "Small Planes, Tiny Towns, Big Bucks," *Business Week* (August 7, 1989), 64.

THE AGGREGATE PLANNING PROCESS

Developing an aggregate production plan involves four basic considerations: the concept of aggregation, the goals of aggregate planning, the forecasts of aggregate demand, and the options for adjusting short-run capacity.

An aggregate production plan for Purolator Courier involves measures of packages shipped, utilizes forecasts of package demand, and plans for airplane and ground truck capacities.

Source: **John Zoiner**

CONCEPT OF AGGREGATION

To develop an aggregate plan, managers must first identify a meaningful measure of output. This presents no problem for organizations with a single product because their outputs are measured directly by the number of units they produce. Most organizations, however, have several products, and a common denominator for measuring total output may not be so easy to find. A brewery manager, for example, can plan capacity in terms of gallons of beer produced, temporarily ignoring how that capacity will be distributed among various types of beer and packagings. A steel producer can plan in terms of tons of steel, and a paint producer, gallons of paint. Service organizations such as urban transit systems may use passenger miles as a common measure, health care facilities may use patient visits, and educational institutions may use faculty-to-student contact hours as a reasonable measure.

A meaningful measure can usually be found by identifying groups or families of individual products that, although different from one another, share common production processes or consume similar resources. Five models of electronic pocket calculators or six models of outboard boat motors are examples of two such product groups. In these cases it may be reasonable to plan in terms of units of the "representative" calculator or the "typical" outboard motor in the product group. You can see, then, that organizations strive for an overall measure of output that makes sense in the context of their unique production process and product mix.

GOALS FOR AGGREGATE PLANNING

The aggregate plan must simultaneously satisfy a number of goals. First, it has to provide the overall levels of output, inventory, and backlogs dictated by the business plan. If the business plan calls for inventory buildup in anticipation of a major promotional campaign, the aggregate plan should provide for the appropriate production support. Similarly, the business plan may call for seasonal buildup or reduction, and this too must be provided for in the aggregate plan.

A second aggregate planning goal is to use the facility's capacity in a manner consistent with the organization's strategy. Underutilized capacity can be an expensive waste of resources. Therefore, a firm's strategy may well be to operate at near full capacity for efficient operations. Another company, however (e.g., one competing on the basis of flexible service to customers), may keep a cushion of capacity for quick reaction to sudden surges in market demand. We can see, then, how the planned level of capacity use depends on the company's strategy.

Finally, the aggregate plan should be consistent with the company's goals and policies regarding its employees. A firm may emphasize employment stability, especially where critical job skills are scarce, and therefore be reluctant to hire or lay off employees. Other firms change employees freely as the output level is varied throughout the aggregate planning horizon.

FORECASTS OF AGGREGATE DEMAND

The benefits of aggregate planning depend on accurate forecasting. The forecasting models presented in Chapter 3 can be used to forecast demand for product groups as well as individual products.

INTERRELATIONSHIPS AMONG DECISIONS

Aggregate output plans are developed for periods of 6 to 18 months into the future. Why does the plan cover such a long time span? Because week-to-week and month-to-month activities are not independent of one another. In fact, they are closely interrelated, since management decisions about activities in one month determine which activities are available in subsequent months. Therefore, managers must consider the future consequences of current decisions.

EXAMPLE

As manager of a refrigerator manufacturing facility, you want to plan the level of output for February. At the end of January you observe 100 refrigerators in inventory. Twenty assemblers were on the payroll in January, each earning a salary of \$1600/month. On average, each assembler produces 10 refrigerators/month. You have just been informed that the demand for February is 200 refrigerators. Since you already have 100 in inventory, you decide to produce exactly 100 more during February so you can meet the February demand of 200 units. Since only 10 assemblers are required to produce February's planned output, you lay off 10 assemblers at an average layoff cost of $400/worker. One month later you face a similar decision. Demand for refrigerators in March is estimated to be 300 units. Since no refrigerators are left in inventory from February, the entire 300 units for March must be produced during March. To accomplish this, you must hire 20 additional assemblers at the beginning of March so that the work force (30 assemblers) can produce the required 300 units. The cost of hiring and training assemblers averages $300/assembler.

This is an example of planning with a one-month time horizon. If each month is treated separately and independently for planning purposes, what costs would result? Table 10.1 shows us.

TABLE 10.1 Costs using a one-month planning horizon

	Paid Employees			Laid-off Employees		Hired Employees		
Month	Number	Output (10/ employees)	Wages ($1600/ employees)	Number	Cost ($400 employees)	Number	Cost ($300 employees)	Total Cost
Feb	10	100	16,000	10	4,000	0	0	20,000
Mar	30	300	48,000	0	0	20	6,000	54,000
Total		400	$64,000		$4,000		$6,000	$74,000

Let's look at the same example using a two-month planning horizon. At the end of January you find out that demand is expected to be 200 units in February and 300 units in March. With this information you develop the plan (in Table 10.2) for both February and March. This plan calls for retaining all 20 assemblers for February and March and thereby avoiding the layoff and hiring costs of the first plan. This cost savings was accomplished by looking into the future and considering not only next month's expected demand but the demand for the following month as well. As you can see, aggregate plans should be developed not to minimize costs in each individual period but in the long run, since minimizing costs in the short run can create other costs in the long run.

We have seen that short time horizons can be undesirable. However, can we use a

TABLE 10.2 Costs using a two-month planning horizon

	Paid Employees			Laid-off Employees		Hired Employees		
Month	Number	Output (10/ employees)	Wages ($1600/ employees)	Number	Cost ($400/ employees)	Number	Cost ($300/ employees)	Total Cost
Feb	20	200	32,000	0	0	0	0	32,000
Mar	20	200	32,000	0	0	0	0	32,000
Total		400	$64,000		$0		$0	$64,000

horizon that is too long? From a practical standpoint, the answer is yes. By extending the planning horizon, we dramatically increase the number of alternatives. The costs of computation and the time required to find the best alternative can become prohibitive. Also, forecasts of demand usually become less accurate as we look farther into the future, and plans based on highly inaccurate forecasts may be of little value.

STRATEGIES FOR AGGREGATE PLANNING

AN AGGREGATE PLAN FOR A MANUFACTURER

Let's apply our knowledge of aggregate output planning to a simple graphical or manual approach. The goal is to find a cost-effective plan that meets expected demand over a 12-month horizon.

EXAMPLE

Go-Rite Company is a make-to-stock wagon manufacturer whose primary product group consists of three models of wagons. The annual business plan, based on marketing's sales forecasts, calls for wagon sales totaling $6,840,000 with quarterly sales as follows:

	Quarter			
	1	2	3	4
Forecasted sales for all product groups (in $)	1,080,000	2,640,000	1,960,000	1,160,000
Wagons (in units)	27,000	66,000	49,000	29,000
Labor (in hours)	21,600	52,800	39,200	23,200

The aggregate plan translated the business plan into manufacturing terms (wagon units and labor hours) using historical conversion factors. First, the typical wagon contributes $40 to sales revenue so the approximate number of wagons per quarter that must be produced to meet the business plan goal is shown in row 2. Since output, on average, is 10 wagons/day for each employee (or 0.8 labor hours/wagon), the estimated labor requirement in hours is shown in row 3. Forecasts of product-group demand (Figure 10.2) reflect a major peak in the spring and a minor peak in the fall. Lowest demand occurs during the winter months.

The first step in the analysis is to determine the production requirements the forecasted demand places on the facility. At first glance, May appears to be the peak month, with 24,000 units demanded. The number of productive days actually available must also be considered, however. Because of an annual vacation shutdown, for

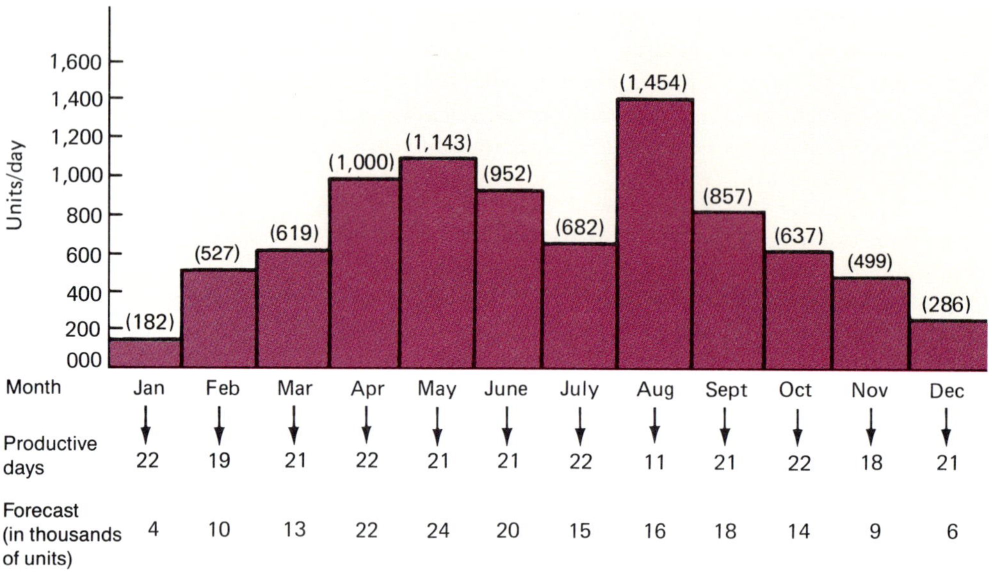

FIGURE 10.2 **Output rate (output per productive day) when monthly production meets monthly demand**

example, August has only 11 productive days. The output rates, output per available productive day, are shown in Figure 10.2. Let's examine three "pure strategies" that the planner could use to cope with these wide swings in monthly demand.

THREE PURE PLANNING STRATEGIES

Pure strategy Aggregate planning strategy using just one of several possible means to respond to demand fluctuations.

Several short-term capacity adjustments can be used to absorb monthly fluctuations in demand. Common in make-to-stock organizations are three such adjustments: work force size, work force utilization, and inventory size. Any one of these can be varied to meet varying demand without varying the other two (thus they can be called *pure strategies*). Usually, however, some combination of the three is better than just one. In addition, manufacturers often use subcontractors, rented or leased equipment, and other external resources for responding to periods of heavy demand.

Strategy 1: Vary the Number of Productive Employees in Response to Varying Output Requirements From historical data, management can estimate the average productivity per employee and thus determine the number of employees needed to meet each month's output requirement. When required monthly output declines, employees can be laid off. As it increases, the work force can be increased accordingly. In our example, productivity per employee is 10 wagons/day. Therefore about 18 employees would be needed in January, 53 in February, 62 in March, and so on.

Several disadvantages of this strategy are obvious. The wide swings in employment levels mean very high hiring and layoff costs. Also, indirect costs of training new employees and lowered employee morale during periods of layoff are common. In addition, required work skills may not be readily available when they are needed. Lead times necessary to hire and train employees must be accounted for in the planning horizon. Furthermore, community reaction to such a strategy may be negative. Finally, this strategy is not feasible for companies constrained by guaranteed wage and other hiring and layoff agreements with unions.

Strategy 2: Maintain a Constant Work Force Size but Vary the Utilization of the Work Force Suppose, for example, we chose the strategy of employing 70 workers per month throughout the year. On an average, this work force would be capable of producing 700 wagons each day. During the lean months (January, February, March, July, October, November, December), the work force would be scheduled to produce only the amount forecasted, resulting in some idle working hours. During high-demand months (April, May, June, August, September), overtime operations would be needed to meet demand. The work force would therefore be intensely utilized during some months and underutilized in other months.

A big advantage of this strategy is that it avoids the hiring and layoff costs associated with strategy 1. But other costs are incurred instead. Overtime, for example, can be very expensive, commonly at least 50 percent higher than regular-time wages. Furthermore, there are both legal and behavioral limits on overtime. When employees work a lot of overtime, they tend to become inefficient, and job-related accidents happen more often.

Idle time also has some subtle drawbacks. During slack periods, employee morale can diminish, especially if the idle time is perceived to be a precursor of layoffs. Opportunity costs also result from idle time. When employees are forced to be idle, the company foregoes the opportunity of additional output. While wages are still paid, some potential output has been lost forever.

Strategy 3: Vary the Size of Inventory in Response to Varying Demand Finished goods inventories in make-to-stock companies can be used as a cushion against fluctuating demand. A fixed number of employees, selected so that little or no overtime or idle time is incurred, can be maintained throughout the planning horizon. Producing at a constant rate, output will exceed demand during slack demand periods, and finished goods inventories will accumulate. During peak periods, when demand is greater than capacity, the demand can be supplied from inventory. This planning strategy results in fluctuating inventory levels throughout the planning horizon.

The comparative advantages of this strategy are obvious: stable employment, no idle time, and no overtime. What about disadvantages? First, inventories of finished goods (and other supporting inventories) are not cost-free. Inventories tie up working capital that could otherwise be earning a return on investment. Materials handling costs, storage space requirements, risk of damage and obsolescence, clerical efforts, and taxes all increase with larger inventories. *Backorders* can also be costly. Customers may not be willing to tolerate backordering, particularly if alternative sources of supply are available; sales may be lost, and lingering customer ill will may decrease future sales as well. In short, there are costs for carrying too much or too little inventory.

Backorders Outstanding or unfilled customer orders.

Mixed strategy Aggregate planning strategy that incorporates or combines some elements from each of the pure aggregate planning strategies.

Graphical planning procedure Two-dimensional model relating cumulative demand to cumulative output capacity.

A GRAPHICAL METHOD FOR AGGREGATE OUTPUT PLANNING

Usually, no pure strategy is best by itself; a mixture of two or three is better. The various alternative plans or "mixtures" involve tradeoffs. One way to develop and evaluate these alternatives is by using a *graphical planning procedure.* The graphical method is convenient, relatively simple to understand, and requires only minimal computational effort. To use the graphical method, follow these steps:

1. Draw a graph showing cumulative productive days for the entire planning horizon on the horizontal axis, and cumulative units of output on the vertical axis. Plot the cumulative demand data (forecasts) for the entire planning horizon.
2. Select a planning strategy, taking into account aggregate planning goals. Calculate and plot the proposed output for each period in the planning horizon on the same set of axes used to plot the demand.
3. Compare expected demand and proposed output. Identify periods of excess inventory and inventory shortages.
4. Calculate the costs for this plan.
5. Modify the plan, attempting to meet aggregate planning goals by repeating steps 2 through 4 until a satisfactory plan is established.

We will demonstrate steps 1 through 4 for three different aggregate plans. The fifth step, additional modification, is left for you to do as an exercise.

Level output rate plan An aggregate plan calling for a constant rate of output for all time periods of production.

A PLAN FOR LEVEL OUTPUT RATE

The first plan we demonstrate is a plan that calls for a constant rate of output throughout the planning horizon. Often such a plan is chosen when the costs of changing the rate of output, on a monthly basis, say, are deemed too high.

EXAMPLE

Step 1 of the graphical planning procedure for Go-Rite is to draw a graph of the demand data shown in Figure 10.2. This graph is the black curve in Figure 10.3. For step 2, we consider the fact that Go-Rite's business plan, and hence the goals of the aggregate plan, calls for output that meets forecasted demand throughout the planning horizon: Relying on backordering has been deemed too costly. We consider, too, that costs will be incurred if we change the output rate during the planning horizon: When the output rate is increased, additional employees must be hired and trained. When the output rate is decreased, some employees must be laid off and/or idle time occurs. The larger the increase or decrease in output rate, the greater the cost incurred. Table 10.3 shows the costs of changing output rates by different amounts. Output rates are expressed in terms of units (wagons) per day. The facility's maximum capacity is 100 employees (1,000 wagons/day) on a single shift. Capacity can be temporarily increased by using overtime with additional costs of $4/unit.

Thus, we select a planning strategy consisting of a constant output rate for each day throughout the planning horizon, one that allows cumulative output at least to meet forecasted demand throughout the planning horizon. To plot the curve of output, then, on the same set of axes we plotted forecasted demand, we must recognize that the curve should be a straight line—that is, a curve whose slope is constant, since we want the output rate to be constant. What slope should it have? What constant rate of output should we specify? Go-Rite's cumulative output line should be steep enough always to meet or exceed cumulative demand. But if the output line is too steep, excessive inventories are accumulated. Moreover, output rate cannot exceed the facility's maximum capacity: 1000 wagons/day, or 10 wagons/day for each of 100 employees. The desired line passes through the origin where output and days are both 0 (point A),

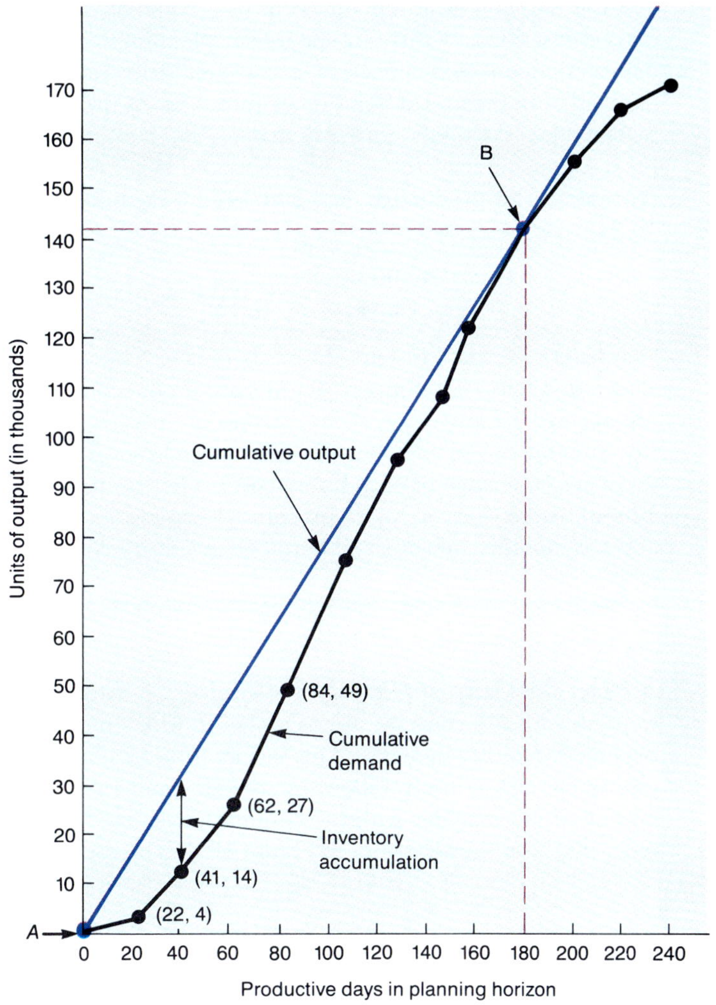

FIGURE 10.3 **Aggregate output plan and forecasted demand for level production**

TABLE 10.3 **Estimated cost for changing output rates**

Change in Output Rate from Previous Month (in units/day (increase or decrease))	Estimated Cost
1–200	$ 4,000
201–400	10,000
401–600	18,000
601–800	28,000

and the outlying point (point B) on the cumulative demand curve.[2] The cumulative output described by this line meets our planning requirements: Beginning on the first day production commences at a constant daily rate and total output exceeds total demand until the end of September (point B). At the end of September, units produced to date equal the total demanded to date. Thereafter, output exceeds expected demand for the remainder of the planning horizon. What is the constant output rate? Point B represents 180 productive days and 142,000 cumulative units of output (from Figure 10.2).

$$\frac{142{,}000 \text{ units}}{180 \text{ days}} = 790 \text{ units/day (approximately)}$$

Comparing the data in table form, as part of Step 3, the resulting monthly plans are shown in Table 10.4. Since 790 units are produced each day, and since each employee can average 10 units/day, 79 employees are needed. Step 4 requires that we calculate the costs for this plan. Since the daily output rate is unchanged from month to month, there are no change of output rate costs. The cumulative average monthly inventory is 120,405 units for the year. Inventory carrying cost is \$1/unit/month, based on the average monthly inventory. Therefore inventory costs are about \$120,405.

A Plan for Output Closely Following Demand (Chase Plan) An alternative to producing at a constant rate is a plan in which monthly output is geared to meeting expected monthly demand. This is sometimes called a *chase plan* because the output rate is chasing (closely following) the demand rate. When graphed, the cumulative output curve coincides with the cumulative demand curve. Therefore the daily output rates are those shown earlier in Figure 10.2. The resulting plan is shown in Table 10.5.

Variable output rate (chase) plan An aggregate plan that changes period-to-period output to correspond with the demand fluctuation.

TABLE 10.4 Monthly plan for level output rate

Month	Days	Output Rate (in units/day)	Output (in units)	Demand (in units)	Beginning Inventory (in units)	Net Additions (subtractions) to inventory (in units)	Ending Inventory (in units)	Average Inventory [(beginning + ending)/2] (in units)
Jan	22	790	17,380	4,000	0	13,380	13,380	6,690
Feb	19	790	15,010	10,000	13,380	5,010	18,390	15,885
Mar	21	790	16,590	13,000	18,390	3,590	21,980	20,185
Apr	22	790	17,380	22,000	21,980	(4,620)	17,360	19,670
May	21	790	16,590	24,000	17,360	(7,410)	9,950	13,655
June	21	790	16,590	20,000	9,950	(3,410)	6,540	8,245
July	22	790	17,380	15,000	6,540	2,380	8,920	7,730
Aug	11	790	8,690	16,000	8,920	(7,310)	1,610	5,265
Sept	21	790	16,590	18,000	1,610	(1,410)	200	905
Oct	22	790	17,380	14,000	200	3,380	3,580	1,890
Nov	18	790	14,220	9,000	3,580	5,220	8,800	6,190
Dec	21	790	16,590	6,000	8,800	10,590	19,390	14,095
							Cumulative average	120,405

[2]Passing the line through point A assumes no beginning inventory exists. If there are finished units on hand at the beginning of the planning horizon, the amount should be marked on the vertical axis and that mark, rather than point A, is the beginning point of the output line on the graph.

TABLE 10.5 **Monthly plan for variable output rate (chase plan)**

Month	Days	Change in Output Rate (in units/day)	Output Rate (in units/day)	Output (in units)	Demand (in units)	Beginning Inventory (in units)	Net Additions (subtractions) to inventory (in units)	Ending Inventory (in units)	Average Inventory[a] (in units)
Jan	22		182	4,004	4,000	0	4	4	2
Feb	19	+345	527	10,013	10,000	4	13	17	11
Mar	21	+ 92	619	12,999	13,000	17	(1)	16	17
Apr	22	+381	1,000	22,000	22,000	16	0	16	16
May	21	+143	1,143	24,003	24,000	16	3	19	18
June	21	−191	952	19,992	20,000	19	(8)	11	15
July	22	−270	682	15,004	15,000	11	4	15	13
Aug	11	+772	1,454	15,994	16,000	15	(6)	9	12
Sept	21	−597	857	17,997	18,000	9	(3)	6	8
Oct	22	−220	637	14,014	14,000	6	14	20	13
Nov	18	−138	499	8,982	9,000	20	(18)	2	11
Dec	21	−213	286	6,006	6,000	2	6	8	5
								Cumulative average	140

[a]Rounded to nearest whole number

Since monthly inventories are trivial, inventory costs for this plan are very low and backorders or stockouts are not permitted. The daily output rate is changed each month. February's output is 345 units per day greater than January's. From Table 10.3, we know that the cost of this increase is approximately $10,000. Similarly, we can calculate the cost of changing output rates for all the months in the planning horizon. Further costs are incurred for overtime work in May and August when output exceeds the fixed capacity of 1000 units/day. Overtime costs $4 per unit produced.

An Intermediate Plan As we have seen, excessive inventory and changes in output rates can be costly. We now develop a plan that changes output rates only occasionally instead of every month. The plan in Table 10.6 calls for a constant output rate of 548

TABLE 10.6 **Intermediate plan**

Month	Days	Output Rate (in units/day)	Change in Output Rate	Output	Demand	Beginning Inventory	Net Additions (subtractions) to inventory	Ending Inventory	Average Inventory
Jan	22	548		12,056	4,000	0	8,056	8,056	4,028
Feb	19	548	0	10,412	10,000	8,056	412	8,468	8,268
Mar	21	548	0	11,508	13,000	8,468	(1,492)	6,976	7,722
Apr	22	1,000	+452	22,000	22,000	6,976	0	6,976	6,976
May	21	1,000	0	21,000	24,000	6,976	(3,000)	3,976	5,476
June	21	1,000	0	21,000	20,000	3,976	1,000	4,976	4,476
July	22	1,000	0	22,000	15,000	4,976	7,000	1,976	8,476
Aug	11	689	−311	7,579	16,000	11,976	(8,421)	3,555	7,776
Sept	21	689	0	14,469	18,000	3,555	(3,531)	24	1,790
Oct	22	689	0	15,158	14,000	24	1,158	1,182	603
Nov	18	689	0	12,402	9,000	1,182	3,402	4,584	2,883
Dec	21	689	0	14,469	6,000	4,584	8,469	13,053	8,818
								Cumulative average	67,276

units/day during January, February, and March. This rate is boosted to 1000 units/day from April through July. Output is then decreased to 689 units/day for the remainder of the year. The inventory cost of this plan is $1/unit stored, or $67,276. Output rate changes cost $18,000 for the March–April change and $10,000 for the July–August change, for a total of $28,000.

Comparing the Plans The three plans are evaluated on the basis of total cost for the planning horizon. We have done this in Table 10.7. The level output plan has high inventory costs and no overtime or rate-change costs. The variable output plan has negligible inventory costs, high rate-change costs, and some overtime costs. These plans exemplify two of the pure strategies discussed earlier. The third (intermediate) plan incurs substantial costs of inventories and rate changes but has the lowest total cost. This plan reflects a mixed strategy, using moderate (not extreme) amounts of inventory and output rate changes to absorb demand fluctuations.

Production smoothing Production planning that reduces drastic period-to-period changes in levels of output or work force.

Our example shows why the aggregate planning process is sometimes called *production smoothing*. As demand decreases to lower levels, it is cheaper to decrease output rates (occasionally) than to continue to build up excessive inventories. If there is any one generalization that can be made about aggregate planning, it is this: *When planning production, smooth out the peaks and valleys to meet uneven demand because extreme fluctuations in production are generally very costly.*

TABLE 10.7 Operating costs (in dollars) for three plans

	Plan		
Type of Cost	Level Output Rate	Variable Output Rate (chase plan)	Intermediate
Overtime	0	31,988[a]	0
Inventory	120,405	139	67,276
Output rate change[b]	0	112,000	28,000
Total cost	$120,405	$144,127	$95,276

[a]May: 143 units/day × 21 days × $4/unit = $12,012. August: 454 units/day × 11 days × $4/unit = $19,976. $12,012 + $19,976 = $31,988
[b]From data in Table 10.3.

CAPACITY PLANNING

In evaluating the capacity *feasibility*, we see differences among Go-Rite's three aggregate plans. Neither the level plan nor the intermediate plan exceeds the facility's daily maximum capacity of 1000 units. The chase plan, however, exceeds maximum capacity in May and August and, accordingly, overtime or second-shift operations would be needed.

In terms of capacity *utilization*, the level plan consistently uses 79 percent of maximum capacity. The chase plan's utilization, in contrast, varies from only 18 percent up to 145 percent during the year. The intermediate plan uses 55 to 100 percent of maximum capacity. If these levels of utilization are unsuitable, either the demand for its products must be stimulated (to gain higher capacity utilization) or the capacity must be adjusted, by hiring more employees, for example.

MASTER SCHEDULING AND ROUGH-CUT CAPACITY PLANNING

The next step in the planning process is master production scheduling, which translates the aggregate plan into production schedules for individual products. As we illustrate master production scheduling, we will use the intermediate aggregate plan (Table 10.6) for the Go-Rite Company.

DISAGGREGATION OF AGGREGATE PLANS

Disaggregation The process of translating aggregate plans for product groups into detailed operational plans for individual products.

As contrasted with aggregate plans, the master schedule is more detailed: it deals with individual products (not just product groups) and when they will be produced week-by-week. How should our aggregate output be subdivided among each of the products we produce? What mix of these products should comprise our aggregate inventories? This process of translating aggregate plans into plans for individual products is called *disaggregation,* a problem that has received surprisingly little formal attention.[3] As a result, the dominant practice today involves disaggregation by cut-and-fit or trial-and-error procedures. Using forecasts of individual product demands, trial amounts of each product are scheduled week by week. The resulting weekly totals of output are then compared against aggregate requirements, checked for their capacity feasibility, and revised accordingly. You can see all of these steps in the discussion below as we develop a master schedule for the Go-Rite Company.

DEVELOPING A TRIAL MASTER PRODUCTION SCHEDULE

The master scheduler in our Go-Rite example has secured forecasts of weekly demands for the three wagon models (A, B, C). These forecasts are shown in Table 10.8 (forecasts beyond 16 weeks are omitted here for brevity). Each of the 16 weeks is 5 working days and thus, the forecast total, 44,970 wagons cover 80 productive days and match closely with the aggregate plan's overall demand of 45,000 wagons.

Next, a trial master production schedule is developed (Table 10.9). We can see that some of all three models are scheduled for production during the first week since no beginning inventories are available and Go-Rite's aggregate plan calls for no stockouts. After week 1, the master scheduler settles on a general pattern of producing wagons A and C in the same weeks while B is often produced alone. Through experience, by trying various combinations, the scheduler hopes to meet product demand, avoid excessive production setup costs, maintain appropriate aggregate inventory levels, and do all of this within planned capacity levels.

How well does this MPS match up with the aggregate plan? The schedule results in cumulative output that exceeds cumulative demand, as shown in Table 10.10. In addition, aggregate inventories after 8 weeks and 16 weeks closely parallel the levels sought in the aggregate plan. Thus the MPS is feasible insofar as the output desired in the aggregate plan is concerned.

[3]A review of the status of disaggregation is given in L. J. Krajewski and L. P. Ritzman, "Disaggregation in Manufacturing and Service Organizations: Survey of Problems and Research," *Decision Sciences* 8, no. 1 (January 1977), 1–18.

TABLE 10.8 Forecasts of weekly demand (in units) for individual products

	Week																
Product	1	2	3	4	5	6	7	8	9	10	11	12	13	14	15	16	Total
A	160	160	160	160	500	735	735	735	890	930	930	930	1,300	1,545	1,545	1,545	12,960
B	295	295	295	295	940	1,370	1,370	1,370	1,625	1,690	1,690	1,690	2,420	2,910	2,910	2,910	24,075
C	455	455	455	455	500	525	525	525	485	475	475	475	495	545	545	545	7,935
Total	910	910	910	910	1,940	2,630	2,630	2,630	3,000	3,095	3,095	3,095	4,215	5,000	5,000	5,000	44,970

TABLE 10.9 Trial master production schedule: units of output for each product for each week

	Week																
Product	1	2	3	4	5	6	7	8	9	10	11	12	13	14	15	16	Total
A	540	1,740	1,740	0	0	0	1,740	1,740	0	0	1,740	1,740	0	1,800	1,800	1,800	16,380
B	1,200	0	0	2,740	2,740	1,740	0	0	2,740	2,740	0	0	3,096	3,200	3,200	3,200	26,596
C	1,000	1,000	1,000	0	0	1,000	1,000	1,000	0	0	1,000	1,000	1,000	0	0	0	9,000
Total	2,740	2,740	2,740	2,740	2,740	2,740	2,740	2,740	2,740	2,740	2,740	2,740	4,096	5,000	5,000	5,000	51,976

TABLE 10.10 Comparing demand and output for trial MPS

		Week										
											Ending Inventory	
Product	Cumulative	1	2	3	4	5	6	7	8	16	Week 8	Week 16
A	demand	160	380	420	640	1,140	1,875	2,610	3,345	12,960		
	output	540	2,280	4,020				5,760	7,500	16,380	4,155	3,420
B	demand	295	590	885	1,180	2,120	3,490	4,860	6,230	24,075		
	output	1,200				3,940	6,680	8,420		26,596	2,190	2,521
C	demand	455	910	1,365	1,820	2,320	2,845	3,370	3,895	7,935		
	output	1,000	2,000	3,000			4,000	5,000	6,000	9,000	2,105	1,065
										Total	8,450	7,006
							Desired total from aggregate plan				8,468	6,976

ROUGH-CUT CAPACITY PLANNING

Is the MPS feasible from the standpoint of Go-Rite's capacity? Let's make some rough (approximate) checks to answer these questions.

We can check overall labor-hour requirements using accounting and engineering data. Suppose Go-Rite's labor standards (standard hours/unit) are 0.88, 0.66, and 1.08 hours for products A, B, and C, respectively.[4] Applying these standards to the 16-week (80-day) schedules, we see in Table 10.11 that the required labor hours are reasonably close to the planned available labor hours, overall, if employees work at the standard rates.

When discrepancies arise between available and required capacities they must be reconciled by revising the MPS or by adjusting the capacity.[5]

In summary, we can see how the goals of master scheduling and capacity planning become balanced by the process we've described. Capacity planning keeps capacity utilization at desired levels while master scheduling meets product demand.

TABLE 10.11 Rough-cut capacity test: Comparing labor requirements of the trial MPS and planned capacity

	Labor Requirements of 80-day MPS		
Product	Units	Standard Hours (in hours/units)	Labor Required (in hours) [units × standard hours]
A	16,380	0.88	14,414
B	26,596	0.66	17,553
C	9,000	1.08	9,720
		Total	41,687
		Total available labor (from aggregate plan)	41,581 hours[a]

[a]548 units/day × 62 days × 0.8 hours/unit + 1,000 units/day × 18 days × 0.8 hours/unit = 41,581 hours.

AGGREGATE PLANNING FOR SERVICE ORGANIZATIONS

Service organizations can also use aggregate planning. The typical service operation, however, is make-to-order rather than make-to-stock. Consequently, finished goods are not available for responding to demand fluctuations. Instead, backlogs of customer requests can be increased or decreased to utilize capacity at desired levels.

[4]The labor standards for the three types of wagons, when weighted by their historical proportions of total sales, result in an overall standard of 0.8 labor hours/wagon. The proportions of sales for the wagons are 35, 50, and 15 percent for models A, B, and C, respectively: .35 × .88 + .5 × .66 + .15 × 1.08 = .8.

[5]Further methods for rough-cut capacity planning are available in T. E. Vollmann, W. L. Berry, and D. C. Whybark, *Manufacturing Planning and Control Systems,* 2nd ed. (Homewood, Ill.: Richard D. Irwin, 1988). See also D. W. McLeavey and S. L. Narasimhan, *Production Planning and Inventory Control* (Boston: Allyn & Bacon, 1985).

Aggregate planning for this commercial-supplies distributor requires them to maintain the mix of labor skills, space, and the combination of supplies that meets their customers' requests. *Source:* **Four By Five**

Consider a city government's public roads department responsible for (1) repairing existing streets and roads (gravel, asphalt, concrete) and drainage systems, (2) building new roads, and (3) removing snow and ice. The department cannot build up inventories of these finished "products." It can, however, use the proper mixture of skilled and unskilled labor, equipment, supplies, and subcontractors that will meet the demand for various "products" (services).

EXAMPLE

In the past, the public roads department has had an experienced work force of about 400 people and, with an emphasis on stable employment, the director is reluctant to change the number of regular employees. The workers average 2000 miles of roads serviced/month. This figure is used to estimate the expected productivity: 5 miles/employee/month, or 0.24 miles/employee/day. Three sources are available for meeting excess demand:

1. The regular work force can work overtime. The overtime premium is 50 percent of the regular $1,500/month wage.
2. Subcontracting to private firms is available at an average cost of $400/mile. Contracts for these services must be arranged several months in advance.
3. Supplemental labor, up to a maximum of 100 workers, is available from May through September at a salary of $1,200/month. Hiring and layoff costs average $100/supplemental employee.

Among the three types of services, snow removal is given first priority due to its public safety implications. Second priority is new road construction because the department's crews work closely with subcontractors and the work has to be done during good weather. As the third priority, road repair and maintenance is used to absorb variations in the overall demand as long as the repair backlog does not get out of hand.

Currently, the director is evaluating two alternative plans for aggregate output and is dually concerned about their cost and service implications. Although minimizing cost is important, effective service to the public is a major concern to this highly visible operation.

Using miles of roads serviced as the common unit of measurement, the director has secured last year's aggregate (service group) demand and the demand for each type of service. With the existing 400 employees, the comparison between regular-time capacity and demand is shown in Figure 10.4. These data are then used to judge how the two new plans would have performed, in terms of backlogs and costs, if the plans had been in effect last year.

ALTERNATIVE PLANS FOR SERVICES

The first alternative, plan A, increases the work force to 480 full-time employees throughout the year. This provides a capacity of 115.2 miles/day and does not use subcontractors. As shown in Table 10.12, capacity in March and April is highly underutilized. However, the backlog at year end is small—less than one-half of one month's work. The ending backlog (967 miles) could be avoided by subcontracting during June through October, or using supplemental labor a portion of the year.

FIGURE 10.4 **Monthly demand and capacity for road services**

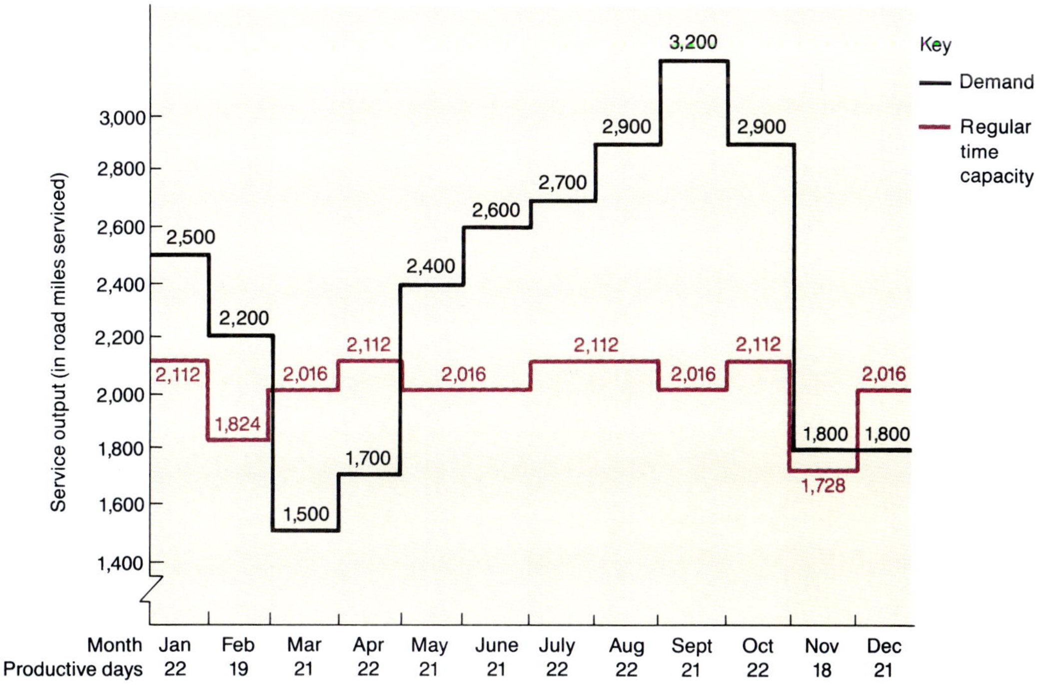

TABLE 10.12 Capacity and cost evaluation for Plan A

Month	Demand (in miles) Repair & Maintenance	Demand (in miles) Snow Removal & New Construction	Demand (in miles) Total	Capacity (in miles)	Backlog (−) from Capacity Shortage or Unutilized Capacity (+) Without Subcontracting (in miles)	Cumulative Backlog (−) (in miles)
Jan	850	1,650	2,500	2,534[a]	+ 34	0
Feb	870	1,330	2,200	2,189	− 11	− 11
Mar	1,000	500	1,500	2,419	+919	0
Apr	1,150	550	1,700	2,534	+834	0
May	1,300	1,100	2,400	2,419	+ 19	0
June	1,350	1,250	2,600	2,419	−181	− 181
July	1,350	1,350	2,700	2,534	−166	− 347
Aug	1,350	1,550	2,900	2,534	−366	− 713
Sept	1,300	1,900	3,200	2,419	−781	−1,494
Oct	1,150	1,750	2,900	2,534	−366	−1,860
Nov	800	1,000	1,800	2,074	+274	−1,586
Dec	600	1,200	1,800	2,419	+619	− 967

Costs (in dollars)	
Full-time employee	8,640,000
Subcontractors	386,800
Total	$9,026,800

[a]480 employees + 0.24 road miles/employee/day × 22 days = 2,534 road miles.

Plan B proposes 400 full-time employees throughout the year, 100 supplemental workers during May through September, and subcontracting in the peak months. The supplemental capacity for May through September (Table 10.13) would have reduced peak-season backlogs and left less than one month of unmet demand at year end. Subcontracting for 1,724 road miles during June through November would have satisfied the demand for services by year end.

COMPARING THE PLANS

Plan B, the lower-cost alternative, accumulates backlogs of road repair and maintenance in the early months of the year. Plan A, although more costly, avoids backlogs in the early months. It is risky, however, because it adds full-time employees who may have to be released later if future demand should diminish.

By now the fundamental considerations of the public roads department should be clear. See if you can find a good aggregate plan for its operations to assure yourself that you understand this planning procedure.

ADDITIONAL MODELS FOR AGGREGATE PLANNING

The graphical planning procedure is simple, easy to understand, and requires no special equipment. It can be done easily on a computer or manually. Its primary drawback is that the planner has no assurance that a "best" plan has been developed; it relies on the planner's experience and judgment. Other more sophisticated procedures, many beyond the scope of this book, have also been used to develop aggregate plans. Sophisticated or simple, all these models share several features. First, they all require the planner to specify a planning horizon and secure aggregate demand forecasts. Second, they all require the planner to explicitly identify decision variables. As we have discussed before, decision variables are the factors that can be varied to generate alternative plans: size of work force, output rate, overtime or idle time, inventory level, subcontracting, etc. Third, all models require the planner to estimate the relevant costs, including costs of wages, hiring/layoff, overtime, inventory, subcontracting, and so on.

OPTIMAL MODELS FOR AGGREGATE PLANNING

Linear Programming It is possible to formulate aggregate plans using linear programming.[6] The linear programming procedure then identifies the *optimal* plan for minimizing costs. This plan specifies the number of units of output to produce, how many shifts the manufacturing facility should operate, and how many units of inventory should be carried in each time period. One limitation of linear programming is its assumption of linear costs. As we see later, linear cost relationships are not always accurate representations of actual cost relationships.

[6] The application of linear programming to aggregate planning was pioneered by E. H. Bowman, "Production Scheduling by the Transportation Method of Linear Programming," *Operations Research* 4, no. 1 (February 1956), 100–103. An application of the simplex method to production planning by a truck manufacturer is given by J. A. Fuller, "A Linear Programming Approach to Aggregate Scheduling," *Academy of Management Journal* 18, no. 1 (March 1975), 129–36.

Table 10.13 Capacity and cost evaluation for Plan B

Month	Demand (in miles)					
	Repair & Maintenance	Snow Removal & New Contruction	Demand (in miles)	Capacity (in miles)	Backlog (−) from Capacity Shortage or Unutilized Capacity (+) Without Subcontracting (in miles)	Cumulative Backlog (−) (in miles)
Jan	850	1,650	2,500	2,112[a]	−388	− 388
Feb	870	1,330	2,200	1,824	−376	− 764
Mar	1,000	500	1,500	2,016	+516	− 248
Apr	1,150	550	1,700	2,112	+412	0
May	1,300	1,100	2,400	2,520[b]	+120	0
June	1,350	1,250	2,600	2,520	− 80	− 80
July	1,350	1,350	2,700	2,640	− 60	− 140
Aug	1,350	1,550	2,900	2,640	−260	− 400
Sept	1,300	1,900	3,200	2,520	−680	−1,080
Oct	1,150	1,750	2,900	2,112	−788	−1,868
Nov	800	1,000	1,800	1,728	− 72	−1,940
Dec	600	1,200	1,800	2,016	+216	−1,724

Costs (in dollars)	
Full-time employees	7,200,000
Seasonal employees	600,000
Hiring/layoff	10,000
Subcontractors	689,600
Total	$8,599,600

[a]400 employees × 0.24 road miles/employee/day × 22 days = 2,112 road miles.
[b]500 employees × 0.24 road miles/employee/day × 21 days = 2,520 road miles.

Linear decision rules (LDRs) A set of equations for calculating optimal work force, aggregate output rate, and inventory level.

Linear Decision Rules A well-known mathematical model provides a set of equations to calculate the best work-force size, output rate, and inventory level for each time period in the planning horizon. This set of equations has become known as the *linear decision rules* (LDRs).[7] The advantages of LDRs are that, like linear programming, they guarantee an optimal solution and save trial-and-error computations. In addition, they account for nonlinear cost relationships.

A disadvantage of LDRs is that they must be custom tailored for each organization. Using them requires a careful study of a company's cost structure, which must then be expressed in mathematical form. Next, a rather extensive mathematical analysis must be made to come up with the proper LDRs for that particular company. Whenever the cost relationships change—for example, when salaries increase—the LDRs must be derived anew.

A HEURISTIC APPROACH FOR AGGREGATE PLANNING

Management coefficients model A set of equations that represent historical patterns of a company's aggregate planning decisions.

A final class of aggregate planning models has evolved in recent years. These methods apply in situations in which management has done aggregate output planning on an intuitive basis. Best known among them is the *management coefficients model.* This procedure requires securing records of past work force, production, and inventory decisions. These data are analyzed by multiple regression techniques to find those regression equations that best fit the historical data. These regression equations are then used to make *future* planning decisions in much the same way that LDRs are used.

The advantages of the heuristic model are that the model is easy to construct if sufficient historical data are available and that insofar as it reduces the variability in decision making, its use can reduce costs. The heuristic model must be applied, however, with great caution. The fact that *past* decision-making tendencies have been successful does not necessarily mean they will be successful when they are applied mechanically to *future* circumstances. Furthermore, this procedure may yield a plan that is nowhere near optimal.

SEARCH PROCEDURES

Computer search A set of directions that systematically guides a computer in evaluating alternative aggregate plans.

Managers may use a *computer search* for the optimal aggregate plan. The computer tries many combinations of work force levels and output rates for each period in the planning horizon. Although the computer explores many possible combinations of these variables, it does not do so randomly. Very specific rules are built into the search procedure to guide the search in a systematic way. The search continues until no further improvement results or until a specified time of searching has elapsed.

A disadvantage of the computer search is that it may not yield the optimal plan. Although the computer explores and evaluates a large number of plans, it does not examine *all* possible plans.

The computer search is probably the most flexible of the optimum-seeking aggregate planning models. Cost functions need not be linear, nor do they need to be unchanging over time. Various types of costs and operating constraints can be incorporated in the model. When the tradeoffs for cost and accuracy are considered, the computer search is a very attractive approach to aggregate planning.

[7]The procedure for developing the LDRs is demonstrated by C. C. Holt, F. Modigliani, J. F. Muth, and H. A. Simon, *Planning Production, Inventories, and Work Force* (Englewood Cliffs, N.J.: Prentice Hall, 1960).

SELECTING AN AGGREGATE PLANNING TECHNIQUE

Few studies have compared these various techniques and models that range from simple graphical techniques to more complex mathematical models. A notable exception is the work of Lee and Khumawala.[8]

Lee and Khumawala compared the aggregate plans yielded by four models and the intuitive company decisions for a job shop manufacturing facility. A computer simulation was developed that closely followed the firm's operations and allowed the models to be compared. Models compared in the study are listed in Table 10.14. (Parametric production planning is another heuristic method.) As you can see, all models yielded higher annual profits than did the intuitive company decisions. The management coefficients model showed the least improvement, $187,000 (4 percent); the computer search showed the greatest improvement, $601,000 (14 percent).

TABLE 10.14 Comparative profit performance of selected aggregate planning models

Aggregate Planning Model	Annual Profit (in dollars)	Improvement Over Company Decisions (in dollars)
Company decisions	4,420,000	—
Management coefficients model	4,607,000	187,000
Linear Decision Rule	4,821,000	401,000
Parametric production planning	4,900,000	580,000
Computer Search	5,021,000	601,000

Source: William B. Lee and Basheer M. Khumawala, "Simulation Testing of Aggregate Production Planning Models in an Implementation Methodology," *Management Science* 20, no. 6 (February 1974), 906.

IMPLEMENTING AGGREGATE PLANS AND MASTER SCHEDULES

UNPLANNED EVENTS

Once the aggregate plan is developed, it must be continually updated to take into account unexpected events. Although January's forecasted demand may have been 4,000 units, at the end of January we may find that actual demand is above or below the forecasted amount, and ending inventory for the month may be at some level other than what we expected. Other unexpected events can also disrupt plans. Perhaps the planned output for the month is not achieved, or perhaps the work force does not

[8] W. B. Lee and B. M. Khumawala, "Simulation Testing of Aggregate Production Planning Models in an Implementation Methodology," *Management Science* 20, no. 6 (February 1974), 903–11.

produce at its average capability. Unexpected events must be taken into account by reusing the aggregate planning methods as before, except that we now use actual conditions, instead of forecasted conditions as input data to the model. Operations Management Highlight 10.2 features companies whose aggregate plans were revised according to a dramatic unexpected event: sweeping changes in scheduling technology.

When aggregate plans are updated, we can expect that corresponding changes will be needed in the master production schedule. In fact, MPS changes are often needed even when the aggregate plan remains fixed. MPS transactions, records, and reports are updated and reviewed periodically as forecast demand for individual products changes, when methods improvements or engineering changes modify the production process and performance times, and when materials are delayed or equipment fails. This periodic review and updating process, called *rolling through time,* exemplifies the dynamic nature of the planning and scheduling activities of operations management.[9]

BEHAVIORAL CONSIDERATIONS

Behavioral considerations enter into aggregate planning and scheduling both in the planning process itself and in attempting to implement the plan.

Behavior in the Planning Process Some important behavioral factors stem from the extreme complexity of the planning problem. Consider the time horizon that should be used for optimal planning. In some situations, a long horizon should optionally be used, but the complexities of planning increase accordingly. Do planners adopt a long enough horizon? Some experimental research reveals that they do not.[10] Although "short-sighted" plans based on judgment and experience result in operating costs that are higher than need be, the use of longer horizons apparently poses a difficult mental task. Fortunately, today's computers offer inexpensive, powerful assistance. Microcomputers with database software and electronic spreadsheets permit desktop convenience for exploring complex planning and scheduling problems quickly.

Behavioral Considerations in Implementation The implementation of a plan can affect organizational behavior in several ways. It signals the need for actions by other parts of the organization. Purchasing must plan to acquire necessary materials and resources. Arrangements may have to be made for retaining the services of subcontractors. Changes in work force must be closely coordinated with the personnel department so that appropriate human resources are available when needed. In short, the adoption of an aggregate plan initiates decision-making activities throughout the organization.

Implementation of a plan may also affect the organizational climate. Both motivation and job satisfaction can be affected. If the work force is decreased in successive time periods, when layoffs occur, or are anticipated, job security is threatened, and both morale and job satisfaction decrease.

---

[9]Rolling through time is discussed in Vollmann, et al., *Manufacturing Planning,* chap. 7.

[10]Time horizon and the effects of irrevelant information in intuitive planning are presented in the study by R. J. Ebert, "Environmental Structure and Programmed Decision Effectiveness," *Management Science* 19, no. 4 (December 1972), 435–45.

OPERATIONS MANAGEMENT HIGHLIGHT 10.2

Source: John Zoiner

New Technology Affords Better Scheduling for Deliveries

Over which routes and at what times should a company send its delivery trucks? How can it predict traffic bottlenecks in Chicago, St. Louis, Detroit, or Los Angeles? These and other questions plague schedulers of nationwide freight companies, the U.S. Postal Service, overnight delivery firms, and local carriers operating trucks and cars. Vehicle scheduling is a major economic and business activity. It determines the quality of delivery service to customers in terms of speed and reliability. It determines, too, how many trucks companies need: poor scheduling can mean idle trucks and drivers or unwise investments in extra vehicles to meet delivery commitments. Vehicles caught in traffic jams burn up gasoline nonetheless, and are manned by drivers who must be paid nonetheless, yet no benefit is returned to company or customer.

General Motors reports that more than 2 billion vehicle hours are lost each year in traffic delays. The cost is estimated at $70 billion in lost time. Leading the way toward improved traffic flows and, eventually, better vehicle routing and scheduling are the University of Michigan through its Intelligent Vehicle-Highway Systems (IVHS) program, General Motors through its IVHS program, the Federal Highway Administration, and the California Department of Transportation. The new idea is to equip large cities with automatic traffic-monitoring equipment that sends signals—information on congestion, accidents, and flow rates—to local control centers. Vehicles, too, would be equipped with tracking and communication devices so dispatchers at the local control center know the vehicles' locations at all times. Information about roads and vehicles would be processed by a computer, converted into recommended routes and transmitted to vehicles. A cellular phone, car radio, or dashboard CRT monitor might be the vehicle's information-receiving device.

In Berlin, traffic-monitoring equipment along 400 miles of roadway is already feeding traffic information into central computers. In conjunction with 70 universities and several European governments, the system has been in development since 1986. Some 700 vehicle owners are using the system to identify alternate, less-congested streets. By 1992 the system will be tested in London, Munich, Paris, and Turin.

The University of Michigan's Transportation Research Institute expects that by the year 2000 perhaps as many as 12 major cities will have invested in the computer systems for the new traffic management technology. And perhaps 50 areas will be so equipped by 2010. These new technologies will reshape production planning and scheduling for vehicle operations throughout the world. The result will be greater productivity, safer highways, and conserved energy.

Sources: **Julie Candler, "The Road Ahead for Trucking,"** ***Nation's Business*** **(July 1990), 34–35; T.A. Heppenheimer, "Street and Highway Smarts,"** ***Across the Board*** **(June 1989), 26–30.**

SUMMARY

We discussed in this chapter how operations planning and scheduling systems give coherence to production activities and, overall, direct them toward enhancing the organization's competitive effectiveness. These systems were shown to involve various hierarchical levels of activities that fit together from top to bottom in support of one another. The aggregate output plan focuses on the level of production activity for the coming 6 to 18 months, expressed in output of product groups, and supports the overall business plan. We learned that aggregate capacity planning emphasizes the availability of resources for achieving planned output. The two plans:—output and capacity—must be balanced at the aggregate level of analysis.

Next we gave a detailed analysis of master production scheduling, which deals with output and capacity in more detail. The master schedule shows week by week how many units of each item or end product must be completed based on customer orders and short-term forecasts of demand. Our discussion noted that to ensure the MPS is feasible, it must be developed in conjunction with rough-cut capacity planning. We saw that if scheduled production and capacity are mismatched, either the schedule must be modified or the capacity must be temporarily adjusted. The master schedule must be consistent with the aggregate plan from above and capable of guiding the more detailed scheduling activities later in the production process.

CASE

Chemtrol Pharmaceutical

Forecasts of Chemtrol Pharmaceutical's in primary product show seasonality of monthly demand as follows (in units/month): 400, 300, 500, 600, 500, 600, 500, 400, 200, 200, 300, 300. Currently, 300 units are on hand in finished goods inventory. Historically, the highly skilled work force has averaged .5 unit/person daily when 38 to 48 employees are operating. Average productivity drops to .416 units/person when fewer than 38 employees are working, and is .446 units/person with more than 48 employees. Standard materials cost $30/unit. Chemtrol's policy of producing 300 units/month during September through February and 500 units/month from March through August has led to predictable employment patterns for the local labor force. Wage rates average $10/hour, and the company operates an eight-hour shift on each of the 20 working days each month. Costs of hiring and training are estimated at $2,000/employee; a layoff costs $1,000/employee. Finished goods cost 4 percent of their value to store in inventory per month. Backorders are estimated to cost $15/unit/month.

Arlin Sprang, Production Manager, has been asked to find ways to reduce operating costs by at least 10 percent as part of Chemtrol's overall cost-reduction program. He wants to consider what possible efficiencies might result from alternative production scheduling policies.

REVIEW AND DISCUSSION QUESTIONS

1. Identify the relevant costs that should be considered in developing a plan for aggregate output and capacity.
2. Compare and contrast rough-cut with aggregate capacity planning. How are they similar and different?
3. What factors should be considered in selecting a planning horizon? Explain.
4. Outline the advantages and disadvantages of the three pure strategies of aggregate planning.
5. Compare and contrast three different methods of aggregate planning: graphical, linear programming, and heuristic.
6. What role does forecasting play in the aggregate planning process?
7. Aggregate plans and master production schedules are developed on the basis of demand forecasts. But after the forecasts have been made, actual demand often deviates from the forecasted amount. Explain how the aggregate planning process accommodates this deviation.
8. Explain how aggregate plans and master production schedules initiate functional activities of the organization.
9. Demonstrate how aggregate planning and scheduling costs are affected by forecast errors.
10. Discuss similarities and differences between the aggregate planning problems of service organizations and product organizations.
11. What situations cause master production scheduling to be so complex?
12. How might aggregate planning affect job satisfaction?
13. What situations cause aggregate planning to be so complex?

PROBLEMS

SOLVED PROBLEMS

1. A manufacturer has the following information on its major product:

Regular-time production capacity = 2,600 units/period
Overtime production costs = $12/unit
Inventory costs = $2/unit/period (based on the ending inventory)
Backlog costs = $5/unit/period
Beginning inventory = 400 units

Demand (in units) for periods 1, 2, 3, 4 is 4000, 3200, 2000, and 2800 respectively. Develop a level output plan that yields zero inventory at the end of period 4. What costs result from this plan?

Period	Demand (in units)	Output (in units)	Ending Inventory (in units)	Regular output (in units)	Overtime output (in units)
0			400		
1	4,000	2,900	− 700	2,600	300
2	3,200	2,900	−1000	2,600	300
3	2,000	2,900	− 100	2,600	300
4	2,800	2,900	0	2,600	300
Average	3,000		Total −1800		

$$\begin{aligned}\text{Total cost} &= \text{Overtime} + \text{Inventory} + \text{Backlogs}\\ &= (300 \times 4 \times \$12) + (0 \times \$2) + (1{,}800 \times \$5)\\ &= \$23{,}400\end{aligned}$$

2. A chair manufacturer who produces three different models (A, B, and C) has developed a master production schedule for the coming five weeks. Historically, worker productivity has averaged 8 units/week/employee based on the "typical mix" of chairs. The company employs 50 workers. The standard labor hours for chairs are 1.0, 2.0, and 1.5 hours for models A, B, and C, respectively. Evaluate the capacity utilization of the MPS.

	Master Production Schedule (in units)				
	Week				
Chair	1	2	3	4	5
A	200	0	200	0	100
B	0	0	0	200	100
C	100	300	100	0	0

Capacity is underutilized in weeks 1, 3, and 5; capacity is inadequate in week 2, as shown below.

	Labor Requirements for Week (in hours)				
Chair	1	2	3	4	5
A	200	0	200	0	100
B	0	0	0	400	200
C	150	450	150	0	0
Total	350	450	350	400	300
Total available labor	400	400	400	400	400

REINFORCING FUNDAMENTALS

3. Refer to problem 1. If you could adjust the beginning inventory (400 units) to any level you choose, what beginning level would minimize the annual operating costs?
4. Refer to problem 2. Develop a master planning schedule that improves the capacity utilization under the following conditions: Production during the five-week horizon must include 500, 300, and 500 units of chairs A, B, and C, respectively, and no more than two types of chairs can be scheduled in any week.
5. Reconsider the aggregate planning problem of the Go-Rite Company example presented in this chapter. If the beginning aggregate inventory is 5000 units (instead of zero), develop an aggregate plan that uses a level output rate. How do the costs of your plan compare with those of the level plan in Table 10.7?
6. Reconsider the aggregate planning problem of the Go-Rite Company example presented in this chapter. If the beginning aggregate inventory is 5000 units (instead of zero), develop an aggregate plan that uses a chase strategy. How do the costs of your plan compare with those of the chase plan in Table 10.7?
7. Refer to problem 6. Evaluate the capacity utilization that the new chase plan affords. Is the plan feasible in relation to capacity?
8. Randolf Corporation has estimated its aggregate demand for the coming year as follows:

Month	Productive Days	Demand (in units)	Month	Productive Days	Demand (in units)
Jan	22	8,000	July	22	26,000
Feb	19	12,000	Aug	11	16,000
Mar	21	18,000	Sept	21	18,000
Apr	22	20,000	Oct	22	14,000
May	21	28,000	Nov	18	9,000
June	21	25,000	Dec	21	7,000

Currently, there are 100 employees whose normal productivity is 12 units/day/employee. Daily capacity can be increased up to 30 percent by working overtime at an additional cost of \$2/unit. Regular time salaries average \$30/day/employee. Costs of storing units in inventory are \$2/unit/month. Inventory shortages cost \$10/unit short. Costs of hiring and training are \$300/employee, and layoff costs are \$200/employee. Additional capacity is available by subcontracting to a local manufacturer at a cost of \$8/unit. Currently, Randolf has 5000 units in inventory. Develop a good plan for next year's aggregate output.

9. An office equipment repair company has sales/service offices throughout North Carolina. The company services such products as typewriters, dictating equipment, photocopiers, and small computers. The following is the demand forecast for the next year in bimonthly groups. Each two-month period has 43 productive days.

Period	Forecasted Demand (in units of work)
Jan–Feb	210
Mar–Apr	245
May–June	260
July–Aug	250
Sept–Oct	235
Nov–Dec	220

(a) Graph the cumulative demand in relation to the cumulative productive days.

(b) Assume that an employee contributes 344 working hours each two months and that each unit requires 30 standard hours to produce. Assuming no overtime or part-time employees, calculate the number of employees required each period.

(c) The company employs enough people to meet peak demand without overtime, hiring, or firing to meet demand changes. With a current labor rate of $8.25/hour, what will be the bimonthly and annual labor costs? What is the extra cost incurred for this employment policy?

(d) Evaluate the costs of an alternative aggregate plan that allows hiring or firing a maximum of two times during the year. Assume hiring costs and firing costs are $2,300/employee, hired or fired. Would you recommend this plan over the plan in part (c) above?

10. Reconsider the two aggregate plans developed for the public roads department example in this chapter. Prepare for the director your recommendation for a better aggregate plan.

11. Reconsider the master production schedule for the Go-Rite Company (Table 10.9) in this chapter. Suppose the standard labor hours/unit are .80, .75, and .97 for models A, B, and C, respectively. Perform rough-cut capacity tests of the MPS under these new conditions, and compare your results with those in Table 10.11.

CHALLENGING EXERCISES

12. Reconsider the Go-Rite Company example in this chapter. Assume that customer backorders are now allowed and the backlog cost is $3/unit/month. Develop a good aggregate plan for wagon production.

13. Reconsider the Go-Rite Company example in this chapter. Suppose three months have elapsed since the initial aggregate planning and during that time actual demand was 5,000 units in January, 12,000 in February, and 14,000 in March. New sales forecasts for April through December are 24,000; 25,000; 21,000; 16,000; 16,000; 18,000; 14,000; 10,000; and 7,000. Develop a revised plan to take into account this new information.

14. Reconsider the Go-Rite Company example in this chapter:

(a) Develop an aggregate plan for the first 3 months of the year, ignoring the remaining months.

(b) Develop an aggregate plan for the first 6 months of the year, ignoring the last 6 months.

(c) Assuming your 6-month plan in part (b) is fully implemented, develop a good plan for the final 6 months of the year.

(d) Compare the costs of the 3-month, 6-month, and 12-month plans. Explain any differences among them.

15. A manufacturing firm is trying to schedule production for the coming three months. Product demand for each of the next three months is forecasted as 300, 250, and 325 units, respectively. Currently, 95 units are available in finished goods inventory at the factory. At the end of the three-month scheduling period, the company wants to have 120 finished units available and to have supplied all units demanded (backorders are not allowed). Regular shift operations are capable of producing 200 units/month at a cost of $10/unit. Overtime operations can supply up to 100 units/month at $15 cost/unit. Inventory costs are $2/unit/month for finished goods. Structure this scheduling problem in a transportation linear programming format. Create and interpret an initial feasible solution.

16. Reconsider the master production schedule for the Go-Rite Company (Table 10.9). The master scheduler wants to prepare a more detailed rough-cut capacity plan to see if the trial MPS is feasible at Go-Rite's four major work centers. The planned labor availability is as follows:

	Days 1–62		Days 63–80	
Work Center	Number of People	Standard Hours (in hours/week)	Number of People	Standard Hours (in hours/week)
Fabrication	19	760	35	1,400
Welding	16	640	30	1,200
Painting	6	240	10	400
Assembly	14	560	25	1,000

Each wagon is processed through all the work centers and, historically, the total work content in a typical wagon is distributed as follows: 35 percent in fabrication, 30 percent in welding, 10 percent in painting, and 25 percent in assembly. Evaluate the capacity utilization in the work centers that the trial MPS affords. Is the plan feasible in relation to capacity?

KEY TERMS

Aggregate capacity planning 374
Aggregate output planning 374
Backorders 383
Business plan 373
Computer search 397
Disaggregation 389
Graphical planning procedure 383
Level output rate plan 384
Linear decision rules (LDRs) 397
Management coefficients model 397
Master production scheduling (MPS) 375
Mixed strategy 383
Product group (family) 373
Production smoothing 388
Pure strategy 382
Rough-cut capacity planning 375
Shop floor control 375
Variable output rate (chase) plan 386

SELECTED READINGS

Berry, W. L., T. E. Vollmann, and D. C. Whybark, *Master Production Scheduling: Principles and Practice.* Falls Church, Va.: American Production and Inventory Control Society, 1979.

Buffa, E. S., and J. G. Miller, *Production-Inventory Systems: Planning and Control,* 3rd ed. Homewood, Ill.: Richard D. Irwin, 1979.

Holt, C. C., F. Modigliani, J. F. Muth, and H. A. Simon, *Planning Production, Inventories, and Work Force.* Englewood Cliffs, N.J.: Prentice Hall, 1960.

Krajewski, L. J., and L. P. Ritzman, "Disaggregation in Manufacturing and Service Organizations: Survey of Problems and Research," *Decision Sciences* 8, no. 1 (January 1977), 1–18.

Lee, W. B., and B. M. Khumawala, "Simulation Testing of Aggregate Production Planning Models in an Implementation Methodology," *Management Science* 20, no. 6 (February 1974), 903–11.

McLeavey, D. W., and S. L. Narasimhan, *Production Planning and Inventory Control.* Boston: Allyn & Bacon, 1985.

Meal, H. C., "Putting Production Decisions Where They Belong," *Harvard Business Review* 62, no. 2 (March-April 1984), 102–11.

Vollmann, T. E., W. L. Berry, and D. C. Whybark, *Manufacturing Planning and Control Systems,* 2nd ed. Homewood, Ill.: Richard D. Irwin, 1988.

CHAPTER 11

OPERATIONS SCHEDULING

First Express, a division of First Tennessee Bank, N.A., provides payment system services to financial institutions and corporations located nationwide. Each night, all across the nation, Federal Express airplanes fly to Memphis, and while Federal Express employees sort packages, First Express employees sort checks. Upon completion of the process and according to schedule, the airplanes fly from Memphis back to the originating cities and both the checks and packages are delivered to their appropriate destinations.

First Express provides this service because of the time value of money. When a check drawn on a Miami bank is deposited in a Seattle bank, the check must be sent from Seattle to Miami to be cashed. The time the check is in transit is called ***float*** time. Reducing the float time creates opportunities for a financial institution to produce additional business or produce income for itself. Let's assume the above mentioned check is for $10 million and that the normal float time is two days. If a service like ours can reduce the float time to one day, rather than two, the real value at today's rates is nearly $2,700. To the Seattle bank, this could be income that flows directly to the bottom line.

First Express provides this service. Intensive job shop and work center scheduling is required by many different organizations if the desired results are to be achieved. The Seattle bank must process and deliver the check to Federal Express before the plane departs. The plane must arrive in Memphis on time and be unloaded rapidly.

First Express's operation consists of receiving, sorting, reject processing, packaging, and reconciling. The inbound area requires more manpower initially as the boxes arrive quickly and receive priority sequencing at this point. This heavy work load moves to other departments as the evening progresses. Consequently, work schedules must accommodate each work center's highs and lows.

Personnel on the inbound side are cross-trained so they can be shifted to the outbound side later in the work cycle. Each step of this process is dependent on the successful completion of the preceding one. We have a narrow processing window; slackness in one area cannot be made up in another. With such little room for error, our employees must work quickly and accurately.

Packages arrive at First Express from 11:00 P.M. till 1:30 A.M. and begin to leave our facility at 2:05 A.M. The packages are loaded into the Federal Express airplanes and flown to the destination city, where a Federal Express employee immediately delivers the package to our clearing bank. The delivery must occur before that bank's deposit deadline or the availability of funds will not be "speeded up."

Many variables must be appropriately managed to provide our service. Every night, First Express puts into practical operation the concepts provided in this chapter.

Walter W. Stafeil
Senior Vice President & Manager
First Express
Memphis, Tennessee

Success at First Express depends on the ability to manage complex *intermittent operations systems.* In this chapter we examine the nature of intermittent systems and introduce some concepts, models, and behavioral considerations that enter into planning their use.

INTERMITTENT SYSTEMS

As we discussed in Chapter 10, conversion systems can be broadly classified as either *continuous* or *intermittent,* depending on the characteristics of the conversion process and the product or service. A *continuous* or *assembly-type system* is one in which a large or indefinite number of units of a homogeneous product is produced. An *intermittent system,* on the other hand, produces a variety of products one at a time (in which case they are custom made) or in batches to customer order. Many conversion facilities are neither strictly intermittent nor continuous but a combination of both.

MANUFACTURING

In a manufacturing context, intermittent systems are traditionally referred to as *job shops.* As work orders arrive, the work load on the facility increases. Some work centers may be idle at the same time that others are severely overloaded. A work center may experience a large buildup of orders awaiting processing. When one order is completed, the equipment may have to be reset or adjusted before the next order can be processed. The challenge is to manage these flows of orders through the shop.

The *sequence* in which waiting jobs are processed is critical to the efficiency and effectiveness of the intermittent system. Sequencing affects how many jobs are completed on time versus late, costs incurred for setup and changeover, delivery lead times, inventory costs, and the degree of congestion in the facility. Indeed, the scheduling of intermittent systems poses a challenging problem for operations managers.

BMW in Berlin, Germany, schedules this assembly line to produce the required numbers of this motorcycle during the different selling seasons.

Source: Four By Five.

SERVICES

Intermittent systems may be used in both product and service organizations. In restaurants and automobile repair shops, for example, conversion systems are similar in concept to those in manufacturing job shops. Operations Management Highlight 11.1 discusses the importance of work force considerations in scheduling Marriott's services.

INTERMITTENT SCHEDULING CONCEPTS AND PROCESSES

The stages of production planning we discussed in Chapter 10 apply to job-shop operations just as they do to continuous and assembly operations (see Figure 11.1). Guided by the business plan, aggregate planning reveals overall levels of planned output and capacity utilization. Then, customer orders and forecasts for specific products are incorporated into a master production schedule for the weeks and months

OPERATIONS MANAGEMENT HIGHLIGHT 11.1

Source: SuperStock

Scheduling Employees at Marriott Is Serious Business

While a student at the University of Utah, Bill Marriott, Jr., worked at a Marriott Hot Shop where he performed his daily duties as an ordinary Marriott Hot Shop worker. But, of course, as the son of Bill Marriott, Sr., who started the family business in 1927, Bill, Jr., was not an ordinary worker. Destined

ahead. This master schedule feeds the material requirements planning system (discussed in Chapter 14) that identifies when the products and components are due for completion. Then a transition occurs in the planning process; its emphasis shifts to even more detailed, day-to-day scheduling and control activities—shop floor control. As we to become chairman of Marriott, Inc., Bill, Jr., began early in his career to hone the skills he would eventually use to run a world-class service business. Chief among these skills is awareness of the capabilities, likes, and propensities of the extremely varied Marriott work force, and applying this knowledge to the critical task of scheduling.

Marriott's employees are among its most important resources. Their productivity and satisfaction on the job, according to company philosophy, are a key factor for success. Scheduling the working hours for such diverse service skills as housecleaning, maintenance, front desk, doormen, security, and others is no simple task, even in good times. But when business slackens, scheduling becomes even more difficult. In the 1980s, for example, the number of Marriott Hotel rooms increased more than 40 percent to 121,000, leaving the company with excess capacity. The 75-percent occupancy rate was still well above the industry average of 64 percent, but it was decreasing, creeping toward the industry's break-even occupancy level of 68 percent. Efficient scheduling becomes extremely important in a situation such as this; for example, although employee cutbacks can save costs, care must be taken so that customer services do not suffer correspondingly.

One important feature of Marriott's workforce scheduling is the use of part-time workers who know in advance that erratic hours may well be part of the job. Another feature is the increasing use of cross-training, enabling employees to learn multiple skills applicable to a wider range of jobs. Such flexibility is important when you have so many employees: Throughout all its operations—hotel and food services—Marriott employs 230,000 people. Management must be ever conscious of the need for consistency of service, though, and that means consistency of employee skills. Multiple-skilled employees afford flexibility in scheduling, but pose the potential for inconsistent, (that is, occasionally poor), service. For a business like Marriott, whose product ***is*** service, that could mean serious trouble. Hence the serious attention to employee training and well-conceived scheduling, a process that begins in the tradition of first-hand experience of its top executives as part of the workforce. Through successful scheduling of work shifts and activities, Marriott has been rated consistently among the best-run service businesses in the world.

Sources: Dean Foust and Mark Maremont, "The Baggage Weighing Marriott Down," _Business Week_, (January 29, 1990), 64–65; "How Master Lodger Bill Marriott Prophesied Profit and Prospered," _Fortune_ (June 5, 1989), 56–57.

discuss these activities in the context of job-shop operations, you'll see how they supplement the output plans and direct shop operations toward desired results. We discuss these concepts primarily in the context of manufacturing; for the most part, they apply to services as well.

Have you ever been sequenced behind several large special orders? If you were at the Varsity Fast Food restaurant in Atlanta, how long would you be willing to wait?

Source: **Janeart / The Image Bank**

OVERVIEW OF THE SCHEDULING AND CONTROL PROCESS

Output plans specify when products are needed, but these specifications must be translated into operational terms to be implemented on the shop floor. Included among these terms are loading, sequencing, detailed scheduling, expediting, and input/output control.

Routing The processing steps or stages needed to create a product or do a job.

Loading Each job (customer order) may have its unique product specification and, hence, its unique *routing* through various work centers in the facility. As new job orders are released, they are assigned or allocated among the work centers, thus establishing how much of a load each work center must carry during the coming planning period. This assignment is known as *loading* (sometimes called *shop loading* or *machine loading*).

Load The cumulative amount of work currently assigned to a work center for future processing.

Sequencing This stage establishes the priorities for jobs in the queues (waiting lines) at the work centers. Priority sequencing specifies the order in which the waiting jobs are processed; it requires the adoption of a priority sequencing rule, a concept we discuss later.

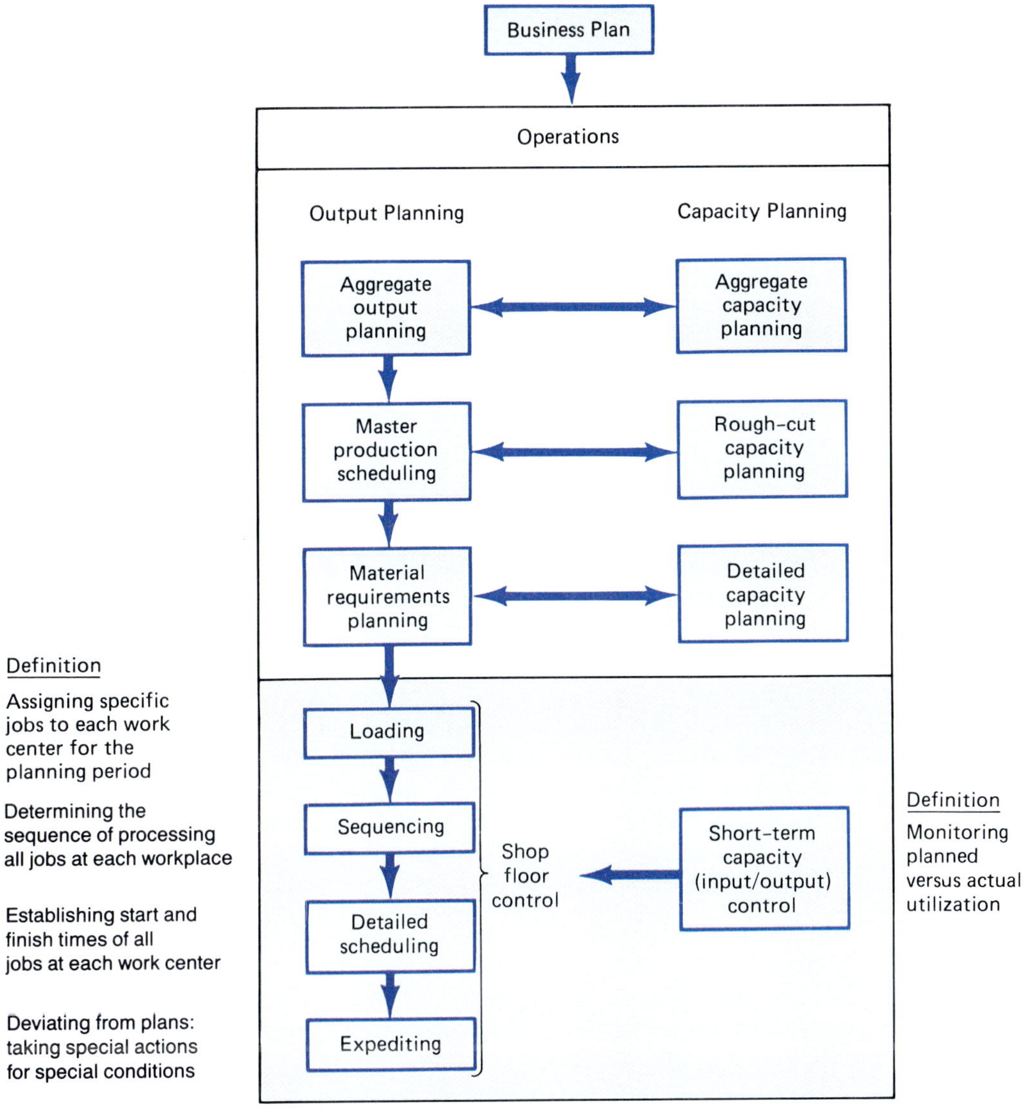

FIGURE 11.1 **The operations planning and scheduling system**

Detailed scheduling Determining start times, finish times, and work asignments for all jobs at each work center.

Detailed Scheduling Calendar times are specified when job orders, employees, and materials (inputs), as well as job completion (outputs), should occur at each work center. Detailed dates and times are usually not specified until after loading and sequencing. By estimating how long each job will take to complete and when it is due, schedulers can establish start and finish dates and develop the detailed schedule.

Expediting Tracking a job's progress and taking special actions to move it through the facility.

Expediting In tracking a job's progress, special action may be needed to keep the job moving through the facility on time. Manufacturing or service operations disruptions—equipment breakdowns, unavailable materials, last-minute priority changes—require managers to deviate from plans and schedules, and expedite an important job on a special-handling basis.

Input/output control Activities to monitor actual versus planned utilization of a work center's capacity.

Input-Output (Short-Term Capacity) Control Output plans and schedules call for certain levels of capacity at a work center, but actual utilization may differ from what was planned. Actual versus planned utilization of the work center's capacity can be monitored by using input-output reports and, when discrepancies exist, adjustments can be made.

Let's take a closer look at each of these activities to see what they involve and how they relate to one another.

LOADING

Planned order A customer order (job) that is on the books and planned for production but that has not yet been launched into production.

Open order A customer order (job) that has been launched into production and is in process.

Given several work centers, which jobs should be assigned to which centers? We know from the master production schedule which products are due for completion and when. Furthermore, we know from each item's routing which work centers will be involved. Although even the best production schedule can create imbalanced loads, either too heavy or too light, we can still manipulate and manage them at reasonable levels. Two approaches for doing so, infinite loading and finite loading, are used today. We will present infinite loading in the next section, but delay our discussion of finite loading. To best understand finite loading, you'll need an understanding of priority scheduling and detail scheduling. Therefore we'll address finite loading after presenting those topics. Our discussion of loading distinguishes between *planned orders*—that is, orders (jobs) that are on the books and are planned for production but that have not yet been launched into production—and *open orders*—that is, orders (jobs) that have been launched into production and are in process.

INFINITE LOADING

Infinite loading Assigning jobs to work centers without considering the work center's capacity (as if the capacity were infinite).

With an *infinite loading system,* jobs are assigned to work centers without regard to the work center's capacity; jobs are loaded from the production schedule into the work center as if its capacity were infinite. *Gantt load charts* and *visual load profiles* can be helpful for evaluating the current loadings, as can an *assignment algorithm.*

Gantt load chart A graph showing work loads on a time scale.

The Gantt Load Chart This graphical procedure is shown in Figure 11.2. An aircraft repair facility has four work centers through which five jobs must be processed. Aircraft A, B, C, D, and E require sheet metal and paint work, A, B, and D require electronics work, and C and E require hydraulics work. The chart shows the total estimated work load that the jobs require at all work centers. Thus 55 days of cumulative work lie ahead for the sheet metal center; the paint center faces a 32-day load, and so on. The chart does not specify which job will be completed at which time, nor does it show the sequence in which the jobs should be processed.

The Gantt load chart offers the advantages of ease and clarity in communicating important shop information. It does have some important limitations, however. The chart does not account for the vagaries of equipment (including breakdowns) and human performance. Moreover, the chart must be updated periodically to account for new jobs.

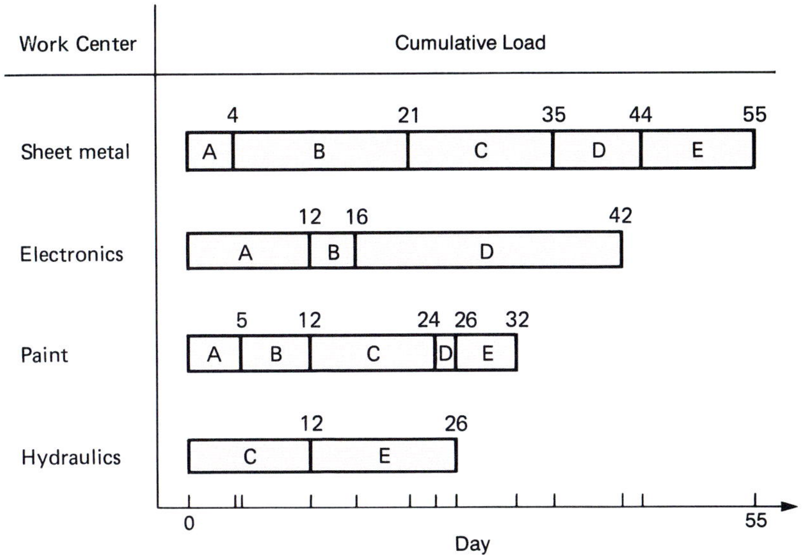

FIGURE 11.2 **Gantt load chart for aircraft repair facility**

The Gantt chart signals the need for reassigning resources when the load at one work center becomes too large. Employees from a low load center may be temporarily shifted to high load centers, or, alternatively, temporary employees can be hired. Multipurpose equipment can be shifted among work centers. If the waiting jobs can be processed at any of several work centers, some of the jobs at high load centers can be reassigned to low load centers. Later we will show how the Gantt chart can be applied to detailed scheduling as well as to loading.

Visual load profile A graph comparing work loads and capacities on a time scale.

Lot splitting Processing only part of a job at one time, then the rest of the job at a later time.

Operations splitting Processing part of a job at one work center and the rest at another.

Visual Load Profiles Since infinite loading ignores the capacity of the work center, the work center can be underloaded or overloaded. A *visual load profile,* like those shown in Figure 11.3, compares the load and the capacity.

In a manual scheduling system, Part (a) of Figure 11.3 the load consists of open orders (existing orders from customers) assigned to the work center. The load for week 1 exceeds capacity, but the future loads are well within capacity.

In a computer-based scheduling system, Part (b) of the figure, the load consists of open orders and planned orders (prospective orders from customers). We see that loads for weeks 3, 4, and 6 exceed capacity, even though loads for the open orders are feasible.

When confronted with critical overloads, we might shift some of the overload to alternative work centers. Or, we can use *lot splitting,* whereby a job order is split and only part of it is processed now, deferring the rest until later. Still another alternative is *operations splitting:* Part of the job is processed at one work center, and the rest is processed in another work center.

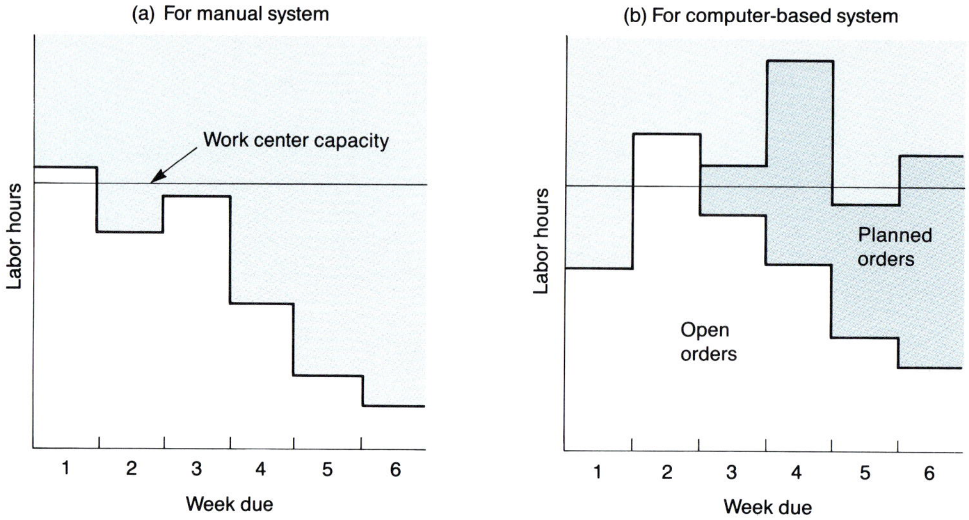

FIGURE 11.3 **Infinite loading for a work center: Visual load profiles**

Assignment algorithm A linear program to assign jobs so that a specific criterion is optimized.

The Assignment Algorithm Occasionally, linear programming can be useful for solving loading problems. Managers often have choices about which jobs should be assigned to which work center. Or perhaps the best center for the job is not available because it is already assigned a job and can process only one job at a time. The *assignment algorithm* is useful for solving these loading problems.

The method can be used when the number of jobs equals the number of work centers or machines the jobs require. This method also requires that each machine be assigned one and only one job. Furthermore, the "goodness or badness" of the assignments must be specifiable by some quantified criterion. The criterion might be profits, operating costs, or completion time. Finally, this method allows analysis of only one point in time. Thus, the method cannot be used if jobs are arriving continuously.

The assignment algorithm involves four simple steps that consider the *opportunity costs* of different assignments. To use the steps, we first make a matrix of the costs: the column entries are costs of each job at one work center; the row entries are costs of one job at each work center.

1. *Column reduction* For each column in turn, choose the least entry and subtract it from each entry in its column. Create a new matrix using these differences as its entries.
2. *Row reduction* For each row (of the new matrix) in turn, choose the least entry and subtract it from each entry in its row. Create a new matrix using these differences as its entries.
3. *Cover the zeros* Draw a vertical or horizontal line through all consecutive zeros and through all isolated zeros; use the minimum number of lines to cover all the zeros.
4. *Create new zeros* If the minimum number of lines is less than the number of work centers, choose the least nonzero entry from among all the entries, subtract it from each nonzero entry, add it to each zero entry at an intersection of lines, and leave all other zero entries unchanged. Create a new matrix using these results as its entries. Return to step 3.

5. *Make load assignments* If the minimum number of lines equals the number of work centers, the optimal assignments can be found at the zero entries in the matrix. Make load assignments as follows: First, does any row contain just one zero? If so, the job must be assigned to the work center at that zero location. The remaining assignments are found by examining the zero elements in the remaining rows. In the optimal solution, each job is assigned to one work center and each work center is assigned one job.

The following example illustrates that the assignment algorithm can be used by service organizations. Just remember to make analogies to the machine (server) and job (person served). The example we use is assigning customers to waitresses, but the algorithm could also be used to assign jobs to typists in a word processing center, inspection tasks to inspectors in a government health service inspection unit, and farm workers to farm work centers that have varying machine and labor skill requirements.

EXAMPLE

For the Beef Eater Restaurant, management must decide how to direct different types of customers into different waitress service areas. Management knows that various combinations of customer types and waitresses result in different service costs, owing to differences in customer traits and waitress skills and personalities. Let's use the assignment algorithm to determine a satisfactory load assignment. To begin, we create a matrix of costs. Rows correspond to customer types (jobs) and columns to waitresses (work centers).

Customer Type	Waitress		
	Sally	Wanda	Bertha
1	12.90	11.90	12.10
2	15.30	15.50	14.30
3	13.90	13.90	13.00

Performing step 1 of the algorithm, we work one column at a time. For each, we choose the lowest cost and subtract. The new matrix is on the left below. For step 2, we work one row at a time, choosing the lowest cost and subtracting. The new matrix is on the right below.

Customer Type	Waitress			Customer Type	Waitress		
	Sally	Wanda	Bertha		Sally	Wanda	Bertha
1	0	0	0	1	0	0	0
2	2.40	3.60	2.20	2	0.20	1.40	0
3	1.00	2.00	0.90	3	0.10	1.10	0

Performing step 3, we see that the minimum number of lines through the zeros is 2.

Customer Type	Waitress		
	Sally	Wanda	Bertha
1	0	0	0
2	0.20	1.40	0
3	0.10	1.10	0

Since 2 does not equal the number of waitresses (work centers), step 4 dictates that we choose the least entry, 0.10, subtract it from each nonzero entry, and add it to the zero entry at the intersection, row 1 column B. The other zeros are left unchanged. The new matrix is on the left below. Repeating step 3 yields the new matrix on the right below.

Customer Type	Waitress		
	Sally	Wanda	Bertha
1	0	0	0.10
2	0.10	1.30	0
3	0	1.00	0

Customer Type	Waitress		
	Sally	Wanda	Bertha
1	0	0	0.10
2	0.10	1.30	0
3	0	1.00	0

Now the minimum number of lines equals the number of waitresses, and we make load assignments accordingly: We see that customer type (row) 2 contains only one zero entry, so this customer must be served by Bertha. Next, for customer type 3 there are two zero elements (in columns 1 and 3). However, since Bertha already has an assignment, column 3 is no longer available. The only remaining zero element is in column 1, so Sally is assigned to customer type 3. That leaves customer type 1 for Wanda. The optimal load assignment is thus as follows:

Customer Type	Waitress	Cost
1	Wanda	11.90
2	Bertha	14.30
3	Sally	13.90

PRIORITY SEQUENCING

Priority sequencing rule A systematic procedure for assigning priorities to waiting jobs, thereby determining the sequence in which jobs will be processed.

When jobs compete for a work center's capacity, which job should be done next? *Priority sequencing rules* are applied to all jobs waiting in the queue. Then, when the work center becomes open for a new job, the one with the highest priority is assigned.

CHOOSING THE RIGHT SEQUENCING RULE

Many different sequencing rules are available, as we'll soon see, and the logical questions are "Which rule should I use?" "What difference does it make?" Your choice is important because a sequencing rule that performs well according to one criterion on one dimension, say minimizing inventories, may not do so well according to another, say minimizing setup costs. Some major criteria are the following:

Setup cost The cost of revising and preparing a work center for processing job.

- *Setup costs*
- In-process inventory costs
- Idle time
- Number or percent of jobs that are late
- Average time jobs are late
- Standard deviation of time jobs are late
- Average number of jobs waiting in the queue
- Average time to complete a job
- Standard deviation of time to complete a job

Three of the criteria (setup costs, inventory costs, and idle time) are primarily concerned with internal facility efficiency. The more these are minimized without jeopardizing service to customers, the better the use of limited resources and chances for improved profitability. Three of the criteria (percent of jobs that are late, average time jobs are late, and variance of time jobs are late) are more customer- or service-oriented than internal. To the extent that the values of these criteria increase, service to customers deteriorates. Finally, three of the criteria (number of jobs waiting, average time to complete a job, and variance of time to complete a job) reflect both customer service and internal efficiency. It is difficult, if not impossible, to find a sequencing rule that excels on all these criteria simultaneously.

SOME PRIORITY SEQUENCING RULES

The following rules are representative of the many used today in manufacturing and service industries:

First-come-first-served rule (FCFS) Priority rule that gives top priority to the waiting job that arrived earliest in the production system.

- *First come first served* (FCFS). As its name suggests, incoming jobs or customers are processed in their order of arrival. FCFS is commonly applied in service industries such as banks, supermarkets, etc.

Earliest-due-date rule (EDD) Priority rule that gives top priority to the waiting job whose due date is earliest.

Shortest-processing-time rule (SPT) A priority rule that gives top priority to the waiting job whose operation time at a work center is shortest.

Truncated-shortest-processing-time rule (TSPT) A priority rule that gives top priority to the waiting job that has waited longer than a predetermined **designated truncation time;** if no job has waited that long, the SPT rule applies.

Least slack rule (LS) A priority rule that gives top priority to the waiting job whose slack time is least; **slack time** is the difference between the length of time remaining until the job is due and the length of its operation time.

Flow time The total time that a job is in the system; the sum of waiting time and processing time.

- *Earliest due date* (EDD). Top priority is assigned to the waiting job whose due date is earliest. EDD ignores when the jobs arrive and the time each of them takes to process.
- *Shortest processing time* (SPT). The job that can be completed in the shortest time at this work center is processed next. The jobs' due dates and order of arrival are immaterial.
- *Truncated shortest processing time* (TSPT). Jobs that have waited longer than some predetermined *designated truncation time* are given highest priority and are processed next. If no jobs have waited that long, then the SPT rule applies.
- *Least slack* (LS). Highest priority goes to the jobs whose slack time is least. Slack is calculated as the difference of the length of time remaining until the job is due, and the length of its operation time. The order of arrival is ignored.

Let's examine some of these rules and illustrate how they work. We'll apply them to the five job orders waiting in the sheet metal work center of the aircraft repair facility we discussed earlier. Customers submitted these job orders during the past week. Rather than evaluating all of the 5 (1 × 2 × 3 × 4 × 5), or 120, different possible sequences for these five jobs, let's evaluate the sequences created according to the FCFS and SPT rules.

First-come-first-served (FCFS) Sequencing For convenience, we assume jobs arrived in alphabetical order, so that according to FCFS job A goes first, job B next, and so on. Customers requested their orders be completed by the due dates listed in Table 11.1.

The job *flow time* for this sequence is the total time each job is either waiting or being processed. Job B, for example, waits 4 days while A is being processed and then takes 17 days operation time. Job B is therefore completed in 21 days, its flow time.

Our FCFS sequence results in the following:

1. *Total completion time.* After 55 days, all jobs are completed.
2. *Average flow time.* The average flow time is 31.8, calculated by summing the flow times for all jobs and dividing by the number of jobs:

$$(4 + 21 + 35 + 44 + 55) \div 5 = 31.8$$

TABLE 11.1 **Sequencing data for a first-come-first-served (FCFS) priority rule**

Waiting Job (in FCFS sequence)	Processing Time (in days)	Flow Time (in days)	Due Date (in days from now)
A	4	4	6
B	17	21	20
C	14	35	18
D	9	44	12
E	11	55	12
	Total 55		

3. *Average number of jobs in the system each day.* The average number of jobs flowing in the system (waiting or being processed) from the beginning of the sequence through the time when the last job is finished is 2.89: For the first 4 days, 5 jobs are in the system; for the next 17 days, 4 jobs are in the system; for days 22 to 35, 3 jobs are in the system, and so forth. There are 55 total days for the sequence. Hence,

$$[5(4) + 4(17) + 3(14) + 2(9) + 1(11)] \div 55$$
$$= 2.89 \text{ jobs in the system/day}$$

4. *Average job lateness.* The average number of days that jobs are late is 18.6 days. The lateness of each job is the difference of its flow time and its due date. Flow time for job A, for example, is 4 days. Since its due date is 6 days, the difference is 4-6, or −2. Job A was finished 2 days earlier than required: no lateness. Flow time for Job B is 21 days, and its due date is 20 days; this job is one day late. Similarly, lateness for jobs C, D, and E is 17, 32, and 43 days, respectively. Average lateness is

$$(0 + 1 + 17 + 32 + 43) \div 5 = 18.6 \text{ days}$$

An advantage of the FCFS rule is its simplicity; moreover, it is "fair play" from the customer's viewpoint. However, some other rules are more desirable for effective and efficient operations.

Shortest Processing Time (SPT) The SPT rule assigns highest priority to the job order whose processing time is shortest.

The SPT rule yields the data in Table 11.2 and the following performance by using the sequence A, D, E, C, B:

1. *Total completion time.* After 55 days all jobs are completed.
2. *Average flow time.* The sum of flow times is (4 + 13 + 24 + 38 + 55) = 134. Average flow time is 134 ÷ 5 = 26.8 days.
3. *Average number of jobs in the system each day.* Over the entire span of 55 days, 5 jobs are flowing in the system for 4 days while job A is being processed; 4 jobs are in the system while job D is being processed for 9 days, and so on. Thus, the average number of jobs in the system each day is:

$$[5(4) + 4(9) + 3(11) + 2(14) + 1(17)] \div 55 = 2.44 \text{ jobs}$$

TABLE 11.2 **Sequencing data for a shortest processing time (SPT) priority**

Waiting Job (in SPT sequence)	Processing Time (in days)	Flow Time (in days)	Due Date (in days from now)
A	4	4	6
D	9	13	12
E	11	24	12
C	14	38	18
B	17	55	20
	Total 55		

4. *Average job lateness.* The lateness for jobs in this sequence are 0, 1, 12, 20, and 35 days, respectively. Average lateness is:

$$(0 + 1 + 12 + 20 + 35) \div 5 = 13.6 \text{ days}$$

CHARACTERISTICS OF THE SEQUENCING RULES

When we compare the performance of FCFS and SPT (see Table 11.3) we see that SPT is superior. Although total completion time is 55 days for both sequences, SPT affords a lower average flow time, so inventories are tied up to a lesser extent, and quicker service can be provided to customers. With SPT, the average number of jobs in the system is reduced, so the shop is less congested and inventory levels are lower. Finally, since average lateness is reduced, deliveries to customers are more prompt.

The superior performance of the SPT rule in our example was not an accident. For jobs processed in one work center, the SPT rule is consistently superior to other rules; it is optimal for minimizing average flow time, average number of jobs in the system, and average lateness.

TABLE 11.3 Comparison of SPT and FCFS rules

	Criterion			
Rule	Total Completion Time (in days)	Average Flow Time (in days)	Average Jobs in System Each Day	Average Lateness (in days)
FCFS	55	31.8	2.89	18.6
SPT	55	26.8	2.44	13.6

Of the five rules cited, only two—EDD and LS—are based on the due date. This criterion is especially appropriate for MRP scheduling systems because the MRP outputs identify scheduled receipts in weekly or even daily time periods that become the due dates for batches of component items.

SEQUENCING THROUGH MULTIPLE WORK CENTERS

Our discussion of sequencing, up to this point, has focused on processing jobs through a single work center and, for this simple problem, optimal analytical solutions are possible. For most facilities, however, jobs must be processed through many (often a hundred or more) work centers. Furthermore, the routing of jobs varies considerably: some jobs pass through a few work centers; others pass through many. As jobs arrive at facilities in a variety of patterns, so do they leave. Thus the composition of waiting jobs at a work center may change continuously, and priority sequencing becomes an ongoing process.

Queuing theory Concepts and models to describe and measure patterns of job arrivals and patterns of servicing customers and to evaluate the effectiveness of serving customers who wait in lines (**queues**) to be served.

For facilities like these, optimal analytic solutions do not exist. One approach by mathematicians and operations researchers has been to apply *queueing theory* to jobs as they "wait in lines" (queues) to be processed. The strength of queueing theory is that, potentially, it provides optimal solutions. Application of queueing theory is severely limited, however, because the mathematical complexity becomes overwhelming when assumptions about arrival times and processing times differ from a few well-known distributions (exponential and Poisson, for example) to more realistic empirical distributions.

SIMULATION OF INTERMITTENT (JOB-SHOP) SYSTEMS

Simulation techniques can be used to evaluate various sequencing rules in job-shop facilities. The following is list of data the modeler must be able to specify in order to stimulate the sequencing problem. The modeler can use historical data and patterns for this purpose, and during simulation can use the Monte Carlo method to randomly select portions of the historical data that the simulation requires as it runs.

1. *Work centers.* The number of work centers in the shop must be specified.
2. *Job arrivals.* The pattern and timing of jobs "arriving" at the facility must be specified.
3. *Job classification.* The processing requirements or routing of jobs must be specified.
4. *Processing times.* The time it takes to process jobs must be specified.
5. *Performance parameters.* Any number of parameters that gauge the performance at the facility can be incorporated into the simulation; the quantification of these parameters must be specified. Options include percent idle time, number of jobs in the queue, average waiting time, amount of inventory, average lateness of jobs, average job flow, and so on.
6. *Sequencing rule.* A sequencing rule must be specified.

The simulation known as a simulation run, is conducted over time. The simulation runs through a very large number of jobs, say 10,000 or more. The simulation generates new jobs arriving at various times, determines their routings, loads them to the appropriate work centers, sequences them according to the sequence rule, and determines their processing times. When a work center completes one job, it begins processing the next job in the queue, according to the sequence rule.

After all jobs have been processed, the simulation evaluates the performance of the facility according to the parameters specified. The performance statistics are saved for later comparison. The modeler may now run the simulation again, specifying a different sequence rule. When the simulation evaluates the performance of the facility accordingly, the results of both simulation runs can be compared. Any number of sequence rules may be evaluated and compared in this way.

Simulation Results for Job Flow Time One study tested ten sequence rules in six different job-shop configurations using computer simulation.[1] The results are based on processing over 2 million jobs through the simulated system. Our main interest in the results has to do with the *job flow performance* of the rules, an important concern to shop managers. Job flow is commonly measured in two ways: as the *average* flow time of

[1]See Y. R. Nanot, "An Experimental Investigation and Comparative Evaluation of Priority Disciplines in Job Shop-Like Queueing Networks." Ph.D. dissertation, UCLA, 1963.

jobs through the system; and as the *dispersion* of job flow times through the system (measured by a standard deviation or variance).

The simulation study found that average (mean) flow time per job was lowest (0.99) using the SPT rule; using other rules it was as high as 2.54. The standard deviation of flow time ranged from 1.55 to 5.43 using the various rules. Although the standard deviation of flow time was lower using two of the other rules, SPT did well on this parameter also. These results are not surprising when you consider how the SPT rule works. Since the highest priority job is the one whose processing time is shortest, this job does not have to wait long in the queue; its flow time (waiting plus processing time) is low.

Simulation Results for Job Lateness and Work-in-process Inventories

Using a computer simulation, another researcher examined how well 39 sequencing rules performed in terms of job lateness and inventories.[2] In terms of percentage of jobs late, SPT performed far better than most other rules tested. This same study found that the SPT rule was not optimal for minimizing in-process inventory, although its performance was still relatively good. The optimal rules were found to be *compound rules.* They require somewhat more complex calculations than does the SPT rule. These compound rules are a weighted combination of the SPT and other rules, all combined into one.[3] In short, the SPT, although not optimal, performed well, and it did so without requiring the extensive calculations of the more complex rules.

SEQUENCING PROCEDURES FOR OTHER CRITERIA

Additional sequencing rules are available for more specialized situations. First we examine sequencing when setup costs are the primary consideration. Next we look at a rule that minimizes the elapsed time to completion for the last job through two successive work centers.

Setup Dependence Sometimes the dominant consideration is the setup, or changeover, cost for processing the different jobs. Table 11.4 shows that total setup costs for the aircraft repair facility depend on the sequence in which the five jobs are processed. These data show the setup cost when job *j* is processed after job *i*. It assumes that job A is already being processed and jobs B, C, D, and E remain to be done. If we choose job B to follow A, a setup cost is high: ($29). If we choose job D to follow A, the setup cost is only $18. Which sequence of jobs minimizes total setup costs?

[2]See R. W. Conway, "Priority Dispatching and Job Lateness in a Job Shop," *Journal of Industrial Engineering* 16, no. 4 (July-August 1965), 228–37; idem, "Priority Dispatching and Work-in-Process Inventory in a Job Shop," *Journal of Industrial Engineering* 16, no. 2 (March-April 1965), 123–30.

[3]For examples of combination rules, see E. LeGrande, "The Development of a Factory Simulation Using Actual Operating Data, in *Readings in Production and Operations Management*, ed. E. S. Buffa (New York: John Wiley, 1966); also J. C. Hershauer and R. J. Ebert, "Search and Simulation Selection of a Job-Shop Sequencing Rule," *Management Science* 21, no. 7 (March 1975), 833–43.

TABLE 11.4 **Matrix of setup costs (in dollars)**

Predecessor Job	Successor Job A	B	C	D	E
A	0	29	20	18	24
B	0	0	14	19	15
C	0	35	0	37	26
D	0	15	10	0	10
E	0	18	16	40	0

Next best rule (NB) A priority rule that gives top priority to the wiating job whose setup cost is least.

The Next Best (NB) Rule One heuristic approach, the *next best* (NB) *rule* states, "Given that job *i* is being processed, assign highest priority to the job *j* where setup cost is least." For example, if job A is being processed, job D would be selected next, since it has the least setup cost for succeeding job A. After job D, job C or E ($10 setup cost) would be selected next. The NB rule would yield two sequences:

Sequence	Cost
NB_1: A-D-C-E-B	$18 + 10 + 26 + 18 = $72
NB_2: A-D-E-C-B	$18 + 10 + 16 + 35 = $79

NB_1 is preferred, since its cost is lower than NB_2. This NB_1 sequence is not optimal. A cost analysis of all 24 possible sequences, irrespective of the NB rule, shows that the optimal sequence is A-D-E-B-C, with a total setup cost of $60. However, NB_1 may be considered *satisfactory*, especially if we are dealing with larger problems for which complete enumeration of all alternatives is not feasible.

In this example, sequence NB_2 happens to be identical to the sequence according to the SPT (shortest processing time) rule. In general, however, sequences of the NB and SPT rules are not expected to coincide. If they do not, you must choose between the two rules. Your choice depends on the relative importance you place on costs of machine setup (NB) as opposed to the value of gaining overall shop effectiveness (SPT).

Sequencing Through Two Work Centers Imagine that all the jobs waiting must be processed through two successive work centers. Furthermore, suppose a customer wants you to get the entire set of jobs completed as rapidly as possible. You want to minimize the flow time of the last job in the sequence and an optimal procedure for doing so is available.

Suppose that jobs A through E in the aircraft repair facility must each pass through the sheetmetal center and then through the paint center. We wish to find the sequence that minimizes completion time of the last job. The processing time for each job in each center is shown in Table 11.5.

TABLE 11.5 Processing times (in days) for jobs at two work centers

Work Center	Job A	B	C	D	E
1	4	17	14	9	11
2	5	7	12	2	6

Since there are five jobs, there will be five positions in the processing sequence. These steps tell how to assign the jobs to the five positions in the sequence. We use the notation PT_{ij} to mean the processing time of job i at work center j. Here, i can be A, B, C, D, or E, and j can be 1 or 2.

1. Determine the minimum processing time PT_{ij} for all unassigned jobs.
2. If the minimum PT_{ij} is associated with work center 1, assign the corresponding job to the earliest available position in the sequence; if the minimum PT_{ij} is associated with work center 2, assign the corresponding job to the latest remaining position in the sequence. Eliminate this job and its processing times from further consideration.
3. If all jobs are assigned a sequence, quit. This sequence is the optimal sequence.
4. If jobs remain unassigned, return to step 1.

Using the data from Table 11.5, the assignments proceed as follows:

1. PT_{D2} is the minimum: 2 days.
2. Since PT_{D2} is associated with work center 2, job D is assigned to the last (fifth) position in the sequence.

Since job D has been assigned, job D and its processing time are eliminated.

3. Jobs A, B, C, and E remain to be assigned.
4. (Return to step 1.) Of the remaining eight PT_{ij}, PT_{A1} is the smallest.
5. (Repeat step 2.) Since job A's line is associated with center 1, job A is assigned to position 1 in the sequence. Job A and it's times are eliminated.
6. (Repeat step 3.) Jobs B, C, and E have yet to be assigned to remaining positions 2, 3, and 4 in the sequence.
7. (Repeat Step 1.) Of the remaining six PT_{ij}, PT_{E2} is minimum. Since it is associated with work center 2, job E is assigned to the last available position in the sequence (position 4).

Continuing in this manner, we find the finished sequence to be A-C-B-E-D. The time-phased flow of this sequence is shown graphically in Figure 11.4. Flow time of job D, the last job in the sequence, is 57 days, the minimum last-job flow time possible. It is important to remember that this rule applies when all jobs must be processed first on center 1, then on center 2.

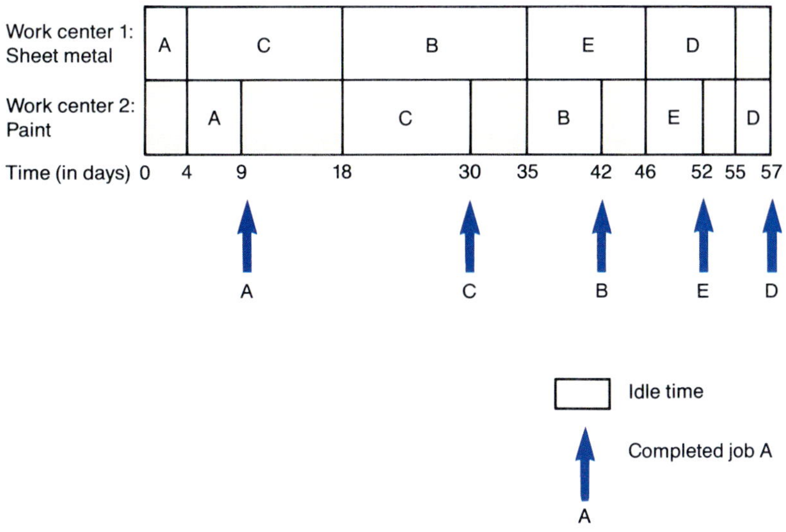

FIGURE 11.4 **Job flow for sequencing five jobs in two centers in sequence A–C–B–E–D**

In concluding our coverage of sequencing, you should note two of its overriding features. First, an abundance of sequencing methods is available; such methods can affect shop performance in different ways. Second, in choosing among these methods you should carefully evaluate them in terms of the criteria that are of greatest importance for your organization's competitive posture.

DETAILED SCHEDULING

Having discussed the loading and sequencing steps of scheduling intermittent systems, let's examine how detailed scheduling is accomplished. Operating personnel need detailed schedules so that they know when to start which job and when it should be finished.

Gantt scheduling chart A graph showing the time requirements of waiting jobs scheduled for production at machines and work centers.

Gantt Scheduling Chart We previously showed a Gantt load chart. Another version of the Gantt chart can be helpful for visualizing detailed scheduling. Figure 11.5 shows one possible schedule for jobs A through E in the aircraft repair facility. On the time scale, each pair of brackets denotes the estimated beginning and ending of a job. The solid bars beneath the brackets show the cumulative work loads at each work center. Overall, then, 55 days of job processing, 2 days of setup, and 19 days of idle time constitute the 76-day sheet metal schedule. As work is completed, the "Time now" arrow moves to the right, and a heavier or color-coded line may be used between the brackets to denote work actually completed. Scheduled and completed work can thus be compared.

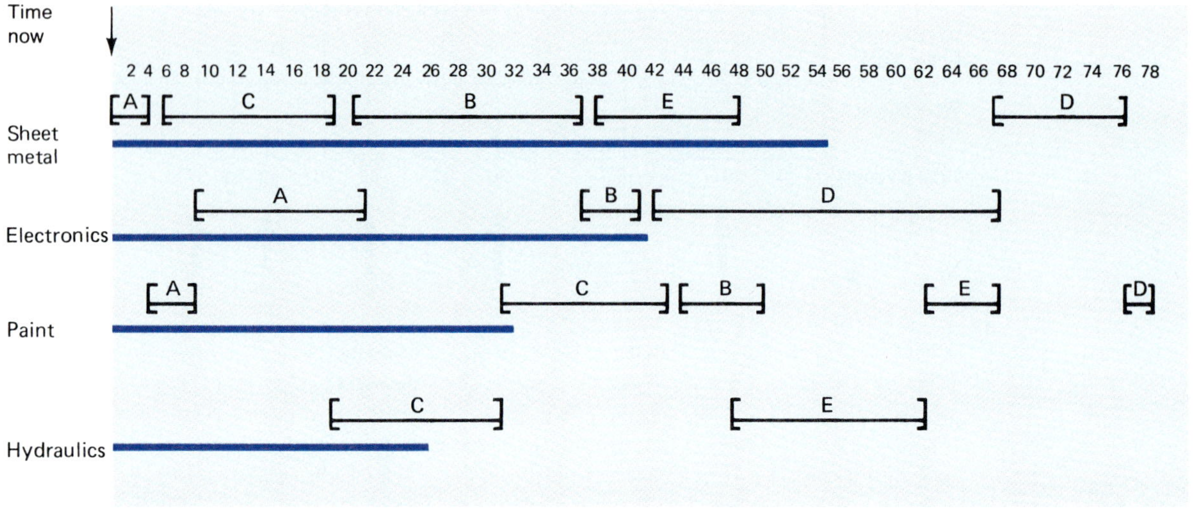

FIGURE 11.5 Gantt chart for order scheduling (job sequence: A–C–B–E–D)

FINITE LOADING

Finite loading A scheduling procedure that assigns jobs into work centers and determines their starting and completion dates by considering the work centers' capacities.

Finite loading is an alternative scheduling technique that combines into a single system the loading, sequencing, and detailed scheduling, which we have discussed individually. In contrast to infinite loading, finite loading systems start with a specified capacity for each work center and a list of jobs. The work center's capacity is then allocated unit by unit (e.g., labor hours) to the jobs by simulating job starting times and completion times. Thus the system creates a detailed schedule for each job and each work center based on the centers' capacities. Jobs are allocated to the centers according to their capacities hour by hour and day by day into the future. The resulting finite capacity load profile would resemble the one shown in Figure 11.6.

FIGURE 11.6 Finite capacity load profile for work center when capacity is 100 labor hours

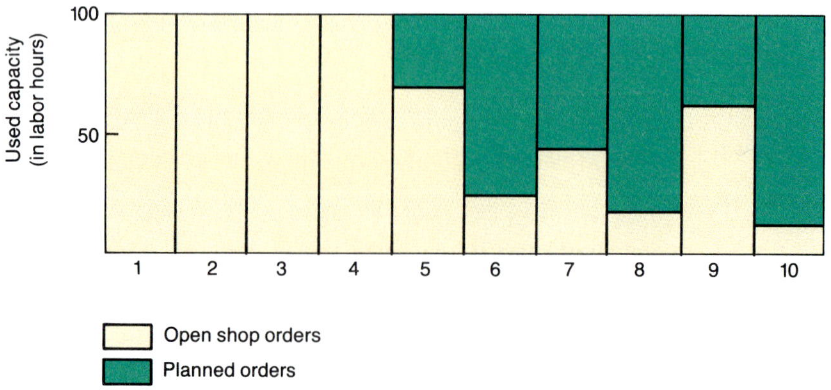

The sequencing rule is built into the simulation. Since inputs to the simulator (e.g., from an MRP system) specify job due dates (not start times or completion times), the jobs can be loaded using either *forward* or *backward scheduling,* as we see next.

FORWARD SCHEDULING

Forward scheduling Determining the start and finish times for waiting jobs by assigning them to the earliest available time slots at the work center.

Forward scheduling (or set forward) is commonly used in job shops where customers place their orders on a "needed-as-soon-as-possible" basis. Forward scheduling determines start and finish times for the next priority job by assigning it the *earliest* available time slot and, from that time, determines when the job will be finished in that work center. Since the job and its components start as early as possible, they will typically be completed before they are due at subsequent work centers in the routing. Consequently, the set-forward procedure accumulates in-process inventories that sit throughout the facility until they are needed at subsequent stations. While these excessive inventories are a drawback, *forward scheduling is simple to use, and it gets jobs done in shorter lead times, overall, than does backward scheduling.*

BACKWARD SCHEDULING

Backward scheduling Determining the start and finish times for waiting jobs by assigning them to the latest available time slot that will enable each job to be completed just when it is due, but not before.

Backward scheduling (or set backward) is often used in assembly-type industries and in job shops that commit, in advance, to specific delivery dates. Backward scheduling assigns the next priority job the *latest* available time slot that will enable the job to be completed just when it is due, but not before. Then the job's start time is determined by "setting back" from this finish date. *By assigning jobs as late as possible, backward scheduling minimizes inventories since a job is not completed until it must go directly to the next work center on its routing.* To gain these inventory efficiencies, however, a price is paid: Bills of materials and lead-time estimates must be accurately maintained for all work centers or else the system breaks down, due dates are violated, and delivery service to customers deteriorates.

EXAMPLE

The Hi-speed Machining Company has received two job orders, A and B, both of which require processing at machines 1 and 2. The first-come-first-served rule is used to sequence the jobs: Job A arrived in advance of job B. The sequence of routings for the two jobs, both of which are due in 8 hours, is given below. Each machine is available for 8 hours every day, and no other jobs are currently scheduled for them. We will develop schedules using the forward and backward procedures.

Route Sheet: Job A			Route Sheet: Job B		
Routing Sequence	Machine	Processing Time (in hours)	Sequence	Machine	Processing Time (in hours)
1	1	2	1	1	2
2	2	3	2	2	3
3	1	1			
		Total 6			Total 5

The forward schedule first assigns top-priority job A the earliest time slot available for the first machine on its routing; the first machine ismachine 1, for 2 hours. (See Figure 11.7). Then Job A is assigned for hours 3 through 5 on machine 2. Job A finishes on machine 1 at the end of hour 6, its earliest possible finish time. Next job B is assigned the remaining available time slots as early as possible. First it goes to machine 1 for hours 3 and 4. Then to machine 2 for hours 6 through 8.

Backward scheduling assigns the highest-priority job so that it finishes just at its due time. Therefore job A is assigned to the last machine on its routing, machine 1, for hour 8. Then it is assigned to the preceding machine on its routing, machine 2, for hours 5 through 7, again as late as possible. Similarly, job A is assigned to the first machine on its routing, machine 1, for hours 3 and 4. Now job B is assigned to the last machine on its routing, machine 2, for hours 8, 4, and 3. It is assigned to machine 1 for hours 1 and 2.

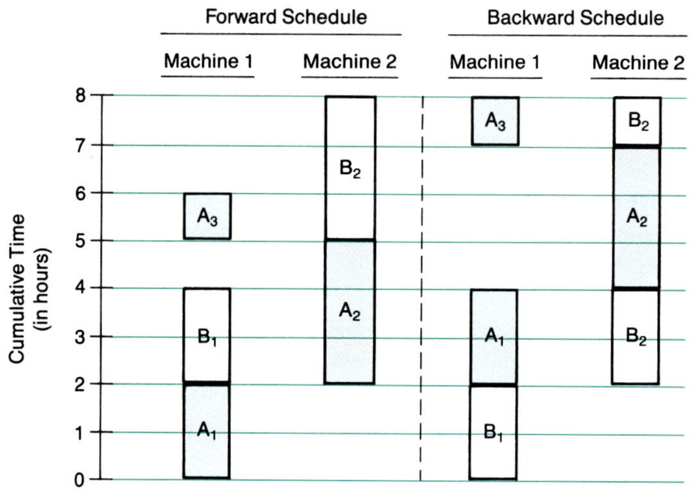

FIGURE 11.7 **Forward and backward schedules for Hi-Speed Machining Company**

You can see that the two procedures yield entirely different schedules for the two machines. In this example, both schedules allow both jobs to be completed by their due times, but this is often not the case, and overdue jobs, especially lower-priority jobs, will be the result. In our forward schedule, excess inventories accumulate: job A finishes two hours earlier than its due time, and job B finishes at the first machine in its routing one hour before it can go to the second on its routing. In the backward schedule, job B is interrupted at machine 2 in hour 4 to allow the higher-priority job A to pass through. Then job B resumes in hour 8.

USING FINITE VERSUS INFINITE LOADING

Finite loading has some drawbacks that lead its critics to conclude that it is an inappropriate control technique. Its schedules often become obsolete from unanticipated materials delays and inaccurate processing time estimates. Consequently, the finite loading simulation has to be rerun (updated) frequently, and these runs cost much more than does sequencing by priority rules for infinite loading systems. Advocates of finite loading, however, claim they get more accurate capacity load estimates for the very short term, the next few days, than they get from the infinite loading. Watervliet Arsenal, in Operations Management Highlight 11.2, is a successful user of finite loading.

EXPEDITING

Let's say that we have accomplished all the activities we've discussed so far. We have finished loading, sequencing, and detailed scheduling. But we are not done yet. Disruptions may prohibit our plans from being implemented to some extent. Necessary materials or manpower may not be available at the times planned; equipment may break down; a particularly important customer may ask for special treatment. Any of these and other contingencies may require rescheduling, a corrective action that is part of the *control* process. If the progress of a job is unsatisfactory, the job may be *expedited.* Special attention is devoted to it, and priorities may be shifted at work centers to "hustle the job through" ahead of others. Certainly, expediting is sometimes necessary; but caution should be exercised lest it be overused.

INPUT-OUTPUT (SHORT-TERM CAPACITY) CONTROL

Analyzing and reporting about input and output at a work center are helpful for monitoring and controlling the work center's performance. Specifically, reporting enables us to evaluate over time how well capacity is being utilized. In Table 11.6, labor-hour requirements of new jobs for the work center for each week are recorded in the first row as "planned input." The work center's "planned output" is the weekly work rate (hours of capacity to be expended each week) chosen by management. In Table 11.6, we see that planned output exceeds planned input, reflecting management's intentions to decrease the work center's backlog, week by week, from the beginning level of 300 units at week 0 down to 100 units (labor hours) by week 4.

OPTIMIZED PRODUCTION TECHNOLOGY (OPT)

An alternative to the production planning and scheduling approaches so far presented in this and other chapters is *Optimized Production Technology* (OPT) a computer-based system for planning production, materials needs, and resource utilization. It was first introduced in the United States in 1979 by Creative Output Inc., a consulting firm in

OPERATIONS MANAGEMENT HIGHLIGHT 11.2

Source: Reuters/Bettmann

U.S. Army Uses Big Guns to Plan and Schedule

Watervliet Arsenal in Albany, New York, is the U.S. Army's oldest active plant for manufacturing cannons. Founded in 1812, surprisingly it is still not out of date: In 1990 Watervliet Arsenal (WVA) received the Advanced Manufacturing Systems' World Class Manufacturing Award. To manage its 2700 employees

Milford, Connecticut.[4] The key feature of OPT is its emphasis on bottleneck work centers (people or machines). The OPT philosophy espouses that managing bottlenecks is the key to successful performance; total system output can be maximized, and in-process inventories reduced.

[4]See F. R. Jacobs, "OPT Uncovered: Many Production Planning and Scheduling Concepts Can Be Applied With or Without the Software," *Industrial Engineering* (October 1984), 32–41. See also R. E. Fox, "OPT—An Answer for America—Part IV," *Inventories & Production* 3, no. 2 (March-April 1983).

and 135 machine tools, WVA planned and successfully implemented a comprehensive computer-based production planning and scheduling system for the tank guns, artillery cannons, mortars, and recoilless rifles it produces. WVA's five-year plan is yielding reduced manufacturing lead times and processing costs, improved quality, and greater productivity.

The production scheduling system includes three steps: master production scheduling (MPS) followed by material requirements planning (MRP) followed by FACTOR, a computer simulation for detailed order scheduling. Waiting jobs are first evaluated in the MPS step to see if delivery dates can be met based on existing capacity constraints for key resources. Following this rough-cut capacity check, in the MRP step all the required component parts are identified, including their start and finish dates. The start and finish data are then fed into FACTOR to develop daily dispatch lists of priority jobs to be run for the day.

Finite loading is a main ingredient for the success of this system. It gives a realistic picture of available and utilized capacity as new jobs are loaded into production. FACTOR gives managers a picture of the entire production floor, rather than of just the one or few stages considered during manual scheduling. Managers can ask "what if" questions such as, "If I interrupt production by adding a new job today, what delivery time benefits for the new job will result, and what costs and delays will be created throughout the entire production system?" The simulation considers the interrelationships among all the machines, materials, and personnel in the plant. It can be used to run experiments on different ways for running the plant, according to different schedules on the shop floor. By evaluating alternative production opportunities when they arise, managers gain a clearer picture of the tradeoffs they face in their daily scheduling decisions. Armed with a top-flight scheduling system, this arsenal is loaded for more realistic delivery promises—and hence better customer service—and reduced unnecessary overtime and work-in-process inventories.

Sources: "Manufacturing Arsenal Implements Scheduling System," *P&IM Review* (August 1990), 40–41; "Four U.S. Facilities Earn World Class Status," *Modern Materials Handling* (March 1990), 12.

Optimized production technology (OPT) A production planning system that emphasizes identifying bottleneck work centers, and careful management of materials and resources related to those bottlenecks, to maximize output and reduce inventories.

The OPT software consists of four modules: (1) BUILDNET; (2) SERVE; (3) SPLIT; and (4) OPT. The starting module, BUILDNET, creates a model of the shop according to data provided by the user: how each product is made (its buildup sequence, materials, and routing through the shop), the product's time requirements (setup, run time, schedule delay), the capacity availability of each resource (work center, machine, worker), and the order quantities and due dates of work orders in the shop. The initial purpose of SERVE is to create a tentative schedule for the jobs waiting in the shop. Later, it creates a more refined schedule. The crucial information obtained from SERVE is an estimate of the percent utilization of the various shop resources.

TABLE 11.6 **Input-output report for work center 100 (report prepared after week 4)**

	Standard Hours/Week				
	1	2	3	4	5
Planned input	400	350	350	300	300
Actual input	400	350	350	300	
Cumulative deviation (actual − planned)	0	0	0	0	
Planned output	450	400	400	350	300
Actual output	440	410	405	330	
Cumulative deviation (actual − planned)	−10	0	+5	−15	
Planned backlog[a]	250	200	150	100	100
Actual backlog	260	200	145	115	

[a]Backlog at time 0 = 300 units.

The SPLIT module distinguishes critical from noncritical resources based on their percent utilizations calculated by SERVE. Resources that are near or above 100 percent utilization are the bottleneck operations. These bottlenecks, and the operations that follow them, are the "critical" operations; all others (those with lower percentage utilizations) are "noncritical." The OPT module reschedules the critical part of the network using forward scheduling. Then the program cycles back to SERVE to reschedule the noncritical resources.

The OPT package consists not only of software but of consulting services and training for implementation as well. The specific details of the procedure, especially of SERVE and OPT (the detailed scheduling modules), are proprietary (not published and available to the general public). Consequently, detailed comparative evaluations of its performance with that of other systems are not available.

BEHAVIORAL ELEMENTS IN INTERMITTENT SYSTEMS

The behavioral dimensions of intermittent systems relate to the sheer technical complexities of having many, perhaps thousands, of jobs flowing through many, perhaps hundreds, of work centers. Not only must all these jobs be processed, but customer deliveries must be on time, and the entire operation must be smooth and efficient. A single human being is incapable of accomplishing all this. Our limited mental capacities prohibit total awareness of current job status and how that status changes over time. For these reasons, the tools presented in this chapter have great value to managers of intermittent systems. Gantt load charts and scheduling charts, although simplistic in concept and appearance, serve as memory supplements. For decision making, priority sequencing rules play a similar role. By systematically applying priority rules, we get the simplified process we need. Although the rules do not ensure optimal system performance, they do help achieve satisfactory performance, and they are usually better than alternative approaches, including human intuition.

SYSTEM ORGANIZATION AND ROLE RELATIONSHIPS

Another behavioral factor is the intrarelationships of intermittent system employees, groups, and work centers or departments. All must be integrated in an effective system. Behavioral consideration specific to intermittent systems include those related to individual and group characteristics.

Individual Characteristics You may remember that intermittent systems, compared with continuous flow systems, comprise a variety of tasks. Different types of employee skills are necessary. Generally, jobs in intermittent systems are already "enlarged": tasks vary, and a higher degree of employee responsibility is emphasized in executing the tasks. In hiring, managers seek employees who are highly skilled and who can work independently without a great deal of supervision. Through monetary rewards, facilitating group relationships, and allocating work methodically, management can create a working environment that helps employees feel secure and fulfills their social needs. Doing so increases motivation in job performance.

Group Characteristics In discussing facility layout (Chapter 7), we pointed out that intermittent systems comprise work centers sharing common processes. A facility might have several work centers, each using workers skilled in machining, painting, and photography, for example. Group affiliations are often established among commonly skilled workers, machinists, for example. There are three reasons for these group affiliations: command structure, physical proximity, and shared craft interest. As a *formal* basis for group affiliation among machinists, for example, the organizational structure may specify that all machinists report to a machining foreman. Second, the physical proximity of machinists in the facility, since they usually work near one another, tends to facilitate interaction and communication, both work-related and personal. Since this is likely to occur on a regular basis, strong group bonds may form. Finally, an important shared interest—the craft or skill—is a basis for interaction. Unions facilitate this last affiliation; it is likely that in a unionized facility of any size, more than one union will represent differing groups of employees.

A work group significantly affects the operations of the system. Although a group usually adopts a set of group norms and strives to satisfy member needs, the group norms may or may not be consistent with management goals. Group norms can strongly influence its members' productivity, especially in highly cohesive groups. When the norms of these cohesive groups are consistent with management goals, the groups tend to produce at higher levels.

Centralized versus Decentralized Decision Making A decentralized scheduling system provides an important dimension of managerial discretion for the first-line supervisor: *The supervisor decides which employees will work on which job orders.* This prerogative does not exist in more centralized systems. In an environment in which wages are hourly and fixed, the decentralized system might be one of the few devices directly available to the supervisor for rewarding and motivating employees. In a more centralized system, job assignments are often depersonalized, handed out by the production control center. Gains in interdepartmental coordination can be offset by losses in employee satisfaction and/or productivity.

In many companies, bargaining between subordinates and foremen for job assignments is a traditionally accepted interpersonal process. Without it, the prestige of

The four specialists in the bank trading room have ample privacy to conduct trades individually, yet they can function as a group by communicating electronically or face-to-face.

Source: Leigh Simmons/The Image Bank

the supervisor and the experienced worker may both diminish. Unless other adjustments are made, this diminution can lead to frustration and defensive behavior on the part of supervisors and subordinates alike, followed by decreased productivity and quality.

SUMMARY

Intermittent systems have several distinctive characteristics. The types of processes, job orders, work flows, and human skills contrast sharply with those of continuous, or mass-production, systems. Generally, intermittent systems have to deal with diversified customer orders and irregular work flows. The intermittent scheduling process involves aggregate planning, master production scheduling, materials planning, loading, priority sequencing, detailed scheduling, expediting, and input-output control.

Concentrating on shop floor control, we showed how infinite loading systems allocate incoming jobs to work centers, and how Gantt charts and visual load profiles help evaluate current loadings. The assignment algorithm was also presented for loading in special circumstances. Then, the question of how to sequence jobs through the loaded work centers was considered. We saw how some rules performed well according to some parameters, but not so well according to others. The steps of detailed scheduling, expediting, and input-output control were also described and linked together with sequencing and loading.

Finite loading systems—those having integrated loading, sequencing, and detailed scheduling—were presented as an alternative to infinite systems. Finally, we concluded with some behavioral considerations of both individuals and groups for intermittent systems operation.

CASE

Newtone

In 1962 Bill Withers began to make custom furniture full time in his garage. Bill's work had been admired by friends and neighbors, who often asked him to make special pieces for them. In 1965, he expanded his operations by leasing a used facility and hiring two additional skilled workers: a woodworker and a leather specialist. By 1968, Newtone was incorporated and had 11 employees.

Today, Newtone serves a custom furniture market covering the northwestern region of the United States. Bill Withers, the president, has a staff of 37 employees. Custom-made furniture is the sole product line, and the company has prided itself on high quality and timely delivery services. Organizationally, Newtone has sales, purchasing, shipping, and design departments. Internal processing departments include wood framing, wood preparation, wood finishing, metal finishing, leather, glass, plastics, and cloth fabrics.

This past year, 250 to 300 jobs were processed in the facility on any given day. Although product quality remains high, on-time deliveries have deteriorated; the average job seems to be four to seven weeks late. Bill Arnold, an employee since 1967 and a special assistant to the shop manager, does the shop loading. His job also includes coordinating the overall shop efforts with those of the sales and design departments. He recently compiled data (shown in the table below) on waiting job orders for a typical day.

Detailed scheduling of orders has always been the responsibility of the three shop foremen. Larry Cline is foreman of the wood preparation, framing, and finishing departments. Isaac Trumbolt is foreman of the leather and cloth fabrics departments. Willie Heft is foreman of the metal, glass, and plastics departments.

Bill Withers is concerned about job lateness. He feels deteriorating customer service might well affect future sales. He has requested George Herring, whose primary experience has been coordinating a new physical distribution system, to analyze the current situation and recommend changes. George is uncertain which factors he should consider and how to proceed with the problem.

Number of Jobs Waiting at Newtone

Work Center	Total	Requiring *n* Work Centers								Not Late	Late (in weeks)		
		1	2	3	4	5	6	7	8		1–2	3–5	>6
Wood framing	314	—	—	63	69	47	44	44	47	261	44	9	—
Wood prep	409	—	—	98	86	74	45	57	49	61	147	119	82
Wood finishing	223	—	—	65	60	45	29	20	4	22	34	78	89
Metal finishing	71	—	—	—	7	32	25	7		55	16	—	—
Leather	157	—	—	—	—	44	61	23	29	135	19	3	—
Glass	63	—	—	19	22	16	6	—	—	63	—	—	—
Plastics	106	—	—	48	37	21	—	—	—	106	—	—	—
Cloth fabrics	198	—	—	—	41	74	53	30	—	133	45	20	—

REVIEW AND DISCUSSION QUESTIONS

1. What is a job shop (intermittent system)?
2. Outline and describe the critical parameters of the job-shop scheduling problem.
3. Identify elements of human behavior that are affected by job-shop scheduling.
4. Is job-shop scheduling a planning activity or a control activity? Explain.
5. Four activities of shop floor control are loading, sequencing, detailed scheduling, and input-output control. What are the distinctions among these four activities?
6. What are priority sequencing rules? Why are they needed?
7. Discuss the advantages and limitations of using the Gantt load chart and visual load profiles.
8. Discuss the significance of maintaining data integrity in computerized scheduling systems.
9. How does a Gantt chart for detailed scheduling differ from a Gantt load chart?
10. Why do most organizations settle for sequencing rules that yield satisfactory, but not optimal, system performance?
11. Outline and discuss major differences between finite and infinite loading.

PROBLEMS

SOLVED PROBLEMS

1. Five jobs await processing on a machine. The setup costs, shown below, depend on the sequence in which the jobs are processed. Apply the next best rule to determine the sequence for these jobs if job I is processed first.

Setup Costs (in dollars)					
Predecessor Job	Successor Job				
	I	II	III	IV	V
I	—	1,300	100	900	300
II	1,000	—	200	700	600
III	100	500	—	1,100	900
IV	500	800	900	—	400
V	800	200	600	300	—

Sequence: I-III-II-V-IV
Cost: \$100 + 500 + 600 + 300 = \$1,500

2. Jobs A, B, and C arrived in alphabetical order and are given priority on a first-come-first-served basis. Their routings and processing times are shown

below. Develop schedules for the jobs on the machines using the forward scheduling procedure.

	Route Sheet: Job A		Route Sheet: Job B		Route Sheet: Job C	
Renting Sequence Position	Machine	Time (in hours)	Machine	Time (in hours)	Machine	Time (in hours)
1	I	2	II	2	I	3
2	II	3	III	1	III	4
3	III	1	I	3	II	1

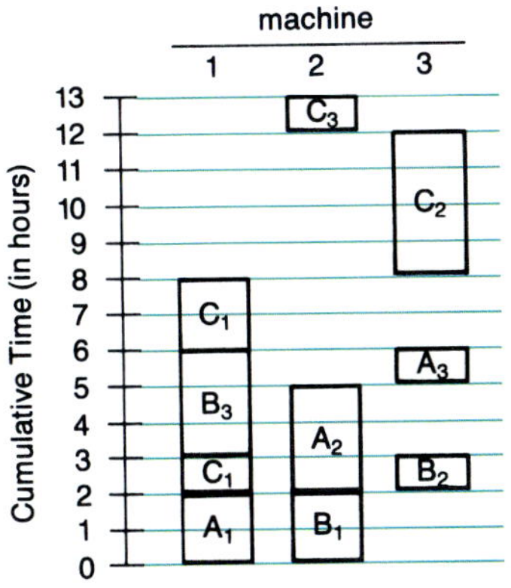

REINFORCING FUNDAMENTALS

3. Jobs arriving at Joanna's Downtown Upholstery Shop are processed and due as shown.

Waiting job (numbered in order of arrival)	317	318	319	320
Processing time (in days)	12	11	14	2
Due date (in days from now)	20	20	18	8

(a) How many processing sequences are possible for these four jobs?

(b) Apply the first-come-first-served priority sequencing rule, and calculate average job lateness. Now apply the shortest processing time rule, and calculate the average job lateness. Which rule is better in terms of average job lateness? Will that always be the better rule regardless of the data?

4. Given the following data for waiting jobs at a work center, calculate system performance using first-come-first-served, last-come-first-served, and shortest processing time sequencing rules.

Waiting job (alphabetically in order of arrival)	P	Q	R	S	T
Processing time (in days)	12	4	16	6	7
Due date (in days from now)	22	14	26	16	17

5. Suppose, for the waiting jobs in problem 4, setup costs incurred between any two jobs are as follows.

Predecessor Job	Successor Job				
	P	Q	R	S	T
P	—	$120	$90	$80	$30
Q	100	—	20	70	60
R	10	50	—	100	80
S	50	90	80	—	40
T	80	70	60	60	—

Assuming job P is being processed now, apply the next best (NB) rule and determine the resulting total setup cost. How does this setup cost compare with the setup cost resulting from the SPT rule?

6. Arline Industries is an intermittent manufacturing facility, processing jobs to customer order. Currently, eight open orders are awaiting processing. All jobs must be processed at the same facility.

Waiting job (alphabetically in order of arrival)	A	B	C	D	E	F	G	H
Processing time (in days)	23	16	5	31	11	20	2	27
Due date (in days from now)	28	35	15	40	30	45	8	50

(a) Develop a Gantt load chart for the facility.
(b) How many different processing sequences are possible?
(c) Develop a visual load profile for infinite loading; the work center's capacity is five days of processing per week.

7. (a) Apply the first-come-first-served (FCFS) sequencing rule to the Arline facility in problem 6. Calculate total completion time, average flow time, average number of jobs per day in the system, and average job lateness.
(b) Apply the shortest processing time (SPT) rule, and perform the same calculations as in part (a).

8. Apply the last-come-first-served (LCFS), earliest due date (EDD), and least slack (LS) rules to the Arline facility in problem 6. Compare these results to those from problem 7.

9. Data Systems, Inc., processes all incoming jobs through two work centers, A and B. Each job goes first through A, then through B. Five jobs await processing.

Waiting Job	S	T	U	V	W
Processing time (in days) in A	16	3	21	31	6
Processing time (in days) in B	7	9	5	17	13

Assign a job sequence that minimizes the flow time of the last job processed. What is the total flow time for this sequence?

10. Ten new projects await processing at Environmental Impact Affiliates. All projects must be evaluated first empirically and then legally. Estimates of processing times (in days) for the empirical and legal phases are:

Waiting project	A	B	C	D	E	F	G	H	I	J
Empirical phase	20	18	7	30	10	20	3	25	14	24
Legal phase	7	21	36	9	12	17	8	22	17	12

(a) Develop a Gantt load chart for the work centers (empirical and legal).
(b) Find the processing sequence that minimizes the flow time of the last project processed. What is this flow time?
(c) Draw the Gantt chart for scheduling based on the results for part (b).

11. First National Bank has four new tellers with varying skills who are to be assigned to the main bank or one of the branches. The criterion for assigning tellers to locations is minimal customer waiting time. Customer waiting time (in seconds) is shown in the table below for each of four locations and teller skills. Make teller assignments, using the assignment algorithm, that will minimize overall waiting time. What is the total waiting time index for the optimal assignment?

	Teller Skill			
Location	A	B	C	D
Main Bank	50	70	40	100
Southwest Branch	70	40	70	70
Clearwater Branch	90	70	50	50
Northgate Branch	80	60	70	50

CHALLENGING EXERCISES

12. Architectural Design Associates has six jobs to be assigned to six architects. The expected effectiveness of each architect on each job has been estimated on a rating scale from 1 to 100: a rating of 1 is high effectiveness; a rating of 100 is low effectiveness. Make the six assignments that will maximize overall effectiveness.

Effectiveness Ratings

	Architects					
Job	Louise	William	Ken	Mary	Carl	Patricia
1	33	40	19	24	58	36
2	57	61	8	29	3	24
3	25	56	12	20	10	14
4	44	72	22	37	47	27
5	62	42	31	20	10	33
6	49	33	30	15	22	41

13. At McFilly Corporation, eight jobs await processing at a single facility. After one job is finished, setup costs are incurred before the next job can be processed. Setup costs depend on the processing sequence.

Waiting job	A	B	C	D	E	F	G	H
Processing time (in days)	26	19	8	34	14	23	5	30
Due date (in days from now)	31	38	18	43	33	48	11	53

Facility Setup Costs (dollars)								
Predecessor Job	Successor Job							
	A	B	C	D	E	F	G	H
A	—	15	15	20	10	25	15	20
B	15	—	5	10	20	15	5	10
C	5	20	—	30	15	10	10	10
D	25	10	15	—	25	5	5	15
E	20	25	15	30	—	10	30	20
F	30	15	20	25	35	—	10	15
G	15	30	5	10	25	5	—	35
H	10	5	15	20	10	25	10	—

(a) Assuming job G is currently being processed, determine the sequence yielding the minimum total setup costs for processing the remaining jobs.

(b) For the sequence obtained in part (a), calculate total completion time, average flow time, average number of jobs per day in the system, and average job lateness.

(c) Assuming job G is processed first, calculate setup costs for the sequence resulting from the SPT rule applied to the remaining jobs.

14. Jobs A, B, and C arrive at a work center in alphabetical order and are given priorities on a first-come-first-served basis. The routings and estimated processing times through this work center's three machines are shown below. Develop schedules for the jobs on the machines using the forward and the backward scheduling procedures. Due times are hour 10 for job A, hour 16 for job B, and hour 14 for job C. How late are the jobs? How much excess inventory is there?

Routing Sequence Position	Route Sheet: Job A		Route Sheet: Job B		Route Sheet: Job C	
	Machine	Time (in hours)	Machine	Time (in hours)	Machine	Time (in hours)
1	I	3	II	3	I	4
2	II	3	III	2	III	4
3	III	2	I	2	II	2

15. Reconsider problem 14. Now, however, suppose job priorities are based on the SPT rule (not on the FCFS rule). Develop forward and backward schedules, and compare the results to those for problem 14. Now, instead of the SPT priorities, use earliest due date (EDD) priorities to develop forward and backward schedules; compare these results with your earlier results.

16. For the data in problem 10, suppose that each project must pass through both processing phases but does not have to be processed through them in any particular order. A project may go through either the empirical or the legal phase first, and then go through the other phase. Assume the projects are received in alphabetical order. Job due dates are: 60 for A, 75 for B, 32 for C, 85 for D, 70 for E, 95 for F, 25 for G, 110 for H, 130 for I, and 97 for J. Determine the processing sequence for the projects using the following sequencing heuristic:

(1) Assign an awaiting project to a work center whenever the work center becomes available.

(2) If both work centers become available simultaneously, the next assignment is made to the empirical research phase.

(3) At each work center, unstarted projects have priority over projects that have completed one phase of processing.

(4) Awaiting projects are assigned to work centers on a first-come-first-served basis.

(a) Determine the sequence in which projects are processed and completed.

(b) Calculate total completion time, flow times, average completion time, and average job lateness for the sequence obtained in Part a.

(c) Determine the sequence in which projects are processed and completed, using the following sequencing heuristic:

(1) Assign a project to a work center whenever the work center becomes available.

(2) If both work centers become available simultaneously, the next assignment is made to the empirical research phase.

(3) Projects are assigned to work centers on the basis of processing time; the awaiting project with the shortest processing time (SPT) is given highest priority, regardless of whether it has completed one phase of processing.

(d) For the sequence obtained in Part c, calculate total completion time, flow times, average completion time, and average job lateness.

(e) Compare the results of Parts b and d.

UTILIZING QSOM COMPUTER SOFTWARE

17. Z-Mat Manufacturing, Inc., utilizes a job shop in which jobs A, B, and C are performed. Machines 1 and 2 are required. Job A must first be processed on machine 1 for 3 days and then on machine 2 for 7 days. Job B is processed on machine 2 for 11 days. Job C is processed on machine 2 for 2 days and then on machine 1 for 6 days. Due dates (in days from day) for jobs A, B, and C are 6, 9, and 12 respectively.

Using QSOM's job-shop scheduling program with shortest processing time as the primary rule and first-come-first-served as the tie breaker, determine total completion time, mean completion time, maximum waiting time, mean waiting time, and mean lateness for completing jobs A, B, and C.

18. To demonstrate the power and utility of QSOM for job-shop scheduling, consider this situation, which is more complex than chapter examples.

In one particular machine shop, four jobs are processed on three machines (1-cutting, 2-grinding, 3-boring), as shown below.

Job	Machine Sequence (routing)	Process Times (in days)	Due Dates (in days from now)
A	1-2-3	2-1-1	7
B	2-3-1	10-8-6	16
C	1-3-2	4-7-1	4
D	3-2-1	8-1-6	17

Using SPT as the primary rule and FCFS as the tie breaker, with the QSOM job-shop scheduling program determine maximum completion time, mean completion time, and maximum waiting time for completing jobs A, B, C, and D.

KEY TERMS

Assignment algorithm 418
Backward scheduling 431
Detailed scheduling 415
Earliest-due-date rule (EDD) 422
Expediting 415
Finite loading 430
First-come-first-served rule (FCFS) 421
Flow time 422
Forward scheduling 431
Gantt load chart 416

Gantt scheduling chart 429
Infinite loading 416
Input/output control 416
Least slack rule (LS) 422
Load 414
Lot splitting 417
Next-best rule (NB) 427
Open order 416
Operations splitting 417
Optimized production technology (OPT) 435
Planned order 416
Priority sequencing rule 421
Queuing theory 424
Routing 414
Setup cost 421
Shortest-processing-time rule (SPT) 422
Truncated-shortest-processing-time rule (TSPT) 422
Visual load profile 417

SELECTED READINGS

Conway, R. W., W. L. Maxwell, and L. W. Miller, *Theory of Scheduling.* Reading, Mass.: Addison-Wesley, 1967.

Fox, R. E. "OPT—An Answer for America—Part IV." *Inventories & Production* 3, no. 2 (March-April 1983).

Hershauer, James C., and Ronald J. Ebert, "Search and Simulation Selection of a Job-Shop Sequencing Rule," *Management Science* 21, no. 7 (March 1975), 833–43.

Jacobs, F. R., "OPT Uncovered: Many Production Planning and Scheduling Concepts Can Be Applied With or Without the Software," *Industrial Engineering* (October 1984), 32–41.

McLeavy, D. W., and S. L. Narasimhan, *Production Planning and Inventory Control.* Boston: Allyn & Bacon, 1985.

Vollmann, T. E., W. L. Berry, and D. C. Whybark, *Manufacturing Planning and Control Systems,* 2nd ed. Homewood, Ill.: Richard D. Irwin, 1988.

Weeks, J. K., and J. S. Fryer, "A Methodology for Assigning Minimum Cost Due-Dates," *Management Science* 23, no. 8 (April 1977), 872–81.

P A R T V

CONTROLLING THE CONVERSION SYSTEM

Production and operations management activities

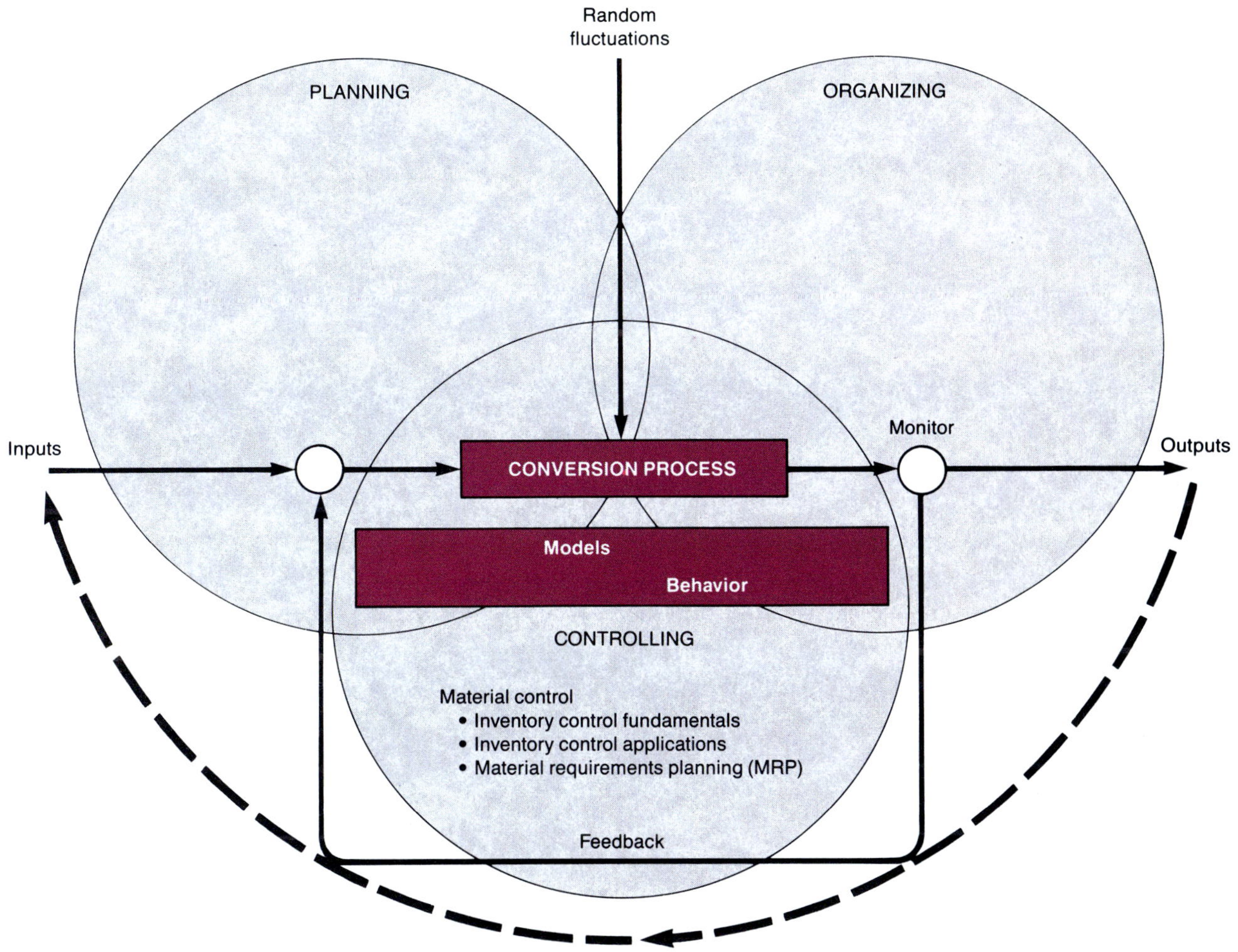

CHAPTER 12

INVENTORY CONTROL FUNDAMENTALS

Inventory control is vitally important to almost every type of business, whether product or service-oriented; in the business of water and electric utilities, inventory control touches almost every facet of operations. Raw materials such as coal and fuel oil must be scheduled and stockpiled for the production of electricity. Operating supplies such as hydrogen, chlorine, and fireside treatment chemicals must be delivered and on hand in the proper quantities for the operation of the power plant and the water treatment plant. Large stocks of materials such as poles, wire, valves, and pipe must be kept to operate, maintain, and expand the extensive distribution system required to deliver electricity and water to the customer. If the proper materials are not available when needed, construction crews will not be able to extend service to new customers in a timely fashion. During a loss of power or water pressure, the lack of a proper repair part could mean that a customer might be without service for an extended period of time. On a daily basis, even stocks of blank forms and envelopes must be kept on hand for the preparation of monthly bills.

Since the health and welfare of a community is involved, it would be easy to take the approach that large volumes of everything must be kept on hand to ensure that there will never be a shortage. But customers also like low rates, and the costs of inventory on hand can easily exceed 5 percent of the annual revenues of the utility. Thus the proper balance must be struck to maintain proper inventory with the minimum financial impact on the customer.

Richard E. Malon
Water and Light Director
City of Columbia
Columbia, Missouri

Production/operations managers are responsible for controlling costs of operations. One critical cost of operations is investment in raw materials, supplies, work-in-process, and finished products not yet shipped. If this investment becomes excessive, the results are high capital costs, high operating costs, and decreased production efficiency when too much space is used for inventory. Although these costs are apparent for manufacturing, it is easy to believe that service organizations do not have such inventory costs. Electricity is, after all, an "invisible" service we simply use when we turn on a switch. Yet, as Mr. Malon so aptly illustrates, inventory control is crucial to both efficiency and cost control in the generation and delivery of electricity and water to consumers who expect their public utility to provide good service at reasonable rates.

Operations managers usually develop a plan specifying desired amounts for materials, and they organize jobs to carry out this plan. Because of environmental influences, however, actual performance often does not conform to planned performance, and managers must exercise material (or inventory) control. Operations managers must monitor output, compare actual with planned output, and take corrective action through feedback mechanisms. This discussion is illustrated in the figure immediately preceding this chapter, where we are reminded again that inventory control relates closely to planning and organizing.

For most production/operations functions, there is somewhat of a balance between quantitative modeling and qualitative behavioral considerations. For inventory control, though, modeling has been developed so thoroughly by applied mathemati-

Source: Gary Gladstone/The Image Bank

The packaged warehouse inventory and the pre-packaged manufactured parts represent critical costs of operations for service as well as manufacturing industries.
Source: Jay Freis/The Image Bank

cians that one often is left in awe at the sophistication and completeness of the model. In this and the next chapter, we will focus on fundamental modeling, the richest approach for learning the basics of inventory control.

DEMAND AND CONTROL SYSTEM CHARACTERISTICS

INDEPENDENT AND DEPENDENT DEMAND

In Chapter 3 we made the distinction between independent and dependent demand. The current chapter and the next reflect inventory control systems for independently demanded items—that is, for items that are unrelated to one another. Before we turn to basic inventory concepts, let's briefly examine the elements of a control system in more detail than we have previously. Understanding control is important for managing inventories, but equally so for quality and overall cost control.

ELEMENTS OF A CONTROL SYSTEM

Controlling is a process by which some aspect of a system is modified to achieve a desired change in system performance. A homeowner, for example, may lower the thermostat setting at night to hold monthly heating bills within a budgeted amount. A manufacturer of luggage may decide to purchase leather from a new supplier when the manufacturer discovers that current suppliers are providing inferior leather. The purpose of the control process is to cause the system to perform true to company goals. Control is not an end itself but rather a means to an end: improving system operation.

Conceptually, many kinds of systems—biological, social, mechanical, political, and economic—have control subsystems that share certain elements. These include inputs, outputs, a *sensor*, a *comparator*, a *memory*, and an *activator*. The relationships among these subsystem elements are shown in Figure 12.1.

Information flow is essential to a control system. Without it, a system simply cannot work. In Figure 12.1, information flow is an information feedback loop, the basis for all control systems. Information about the output of the conversion process is transformed and fed back into the input of the process, in a steady flow. In this way, management is continually able to compare actual performance with planned results.

Although we may be unaware of them, control systems operate around us all the time. When the pupils in your eyes enlarge or contract as light intensity changes, your body is using a control system. Look again at Figure 12.1, and see if you can identify the subcomponents of this or another control system.

INVENTORY CONCEPTS

INVENTORY DEFINED

Inventories play a major part in the U.S. economy, as Table 12.1 shows. These data alone suggest that operating managers should find inventory management a fruitful area for lowering overall operations costs. From the firm's viewpoint, inventories

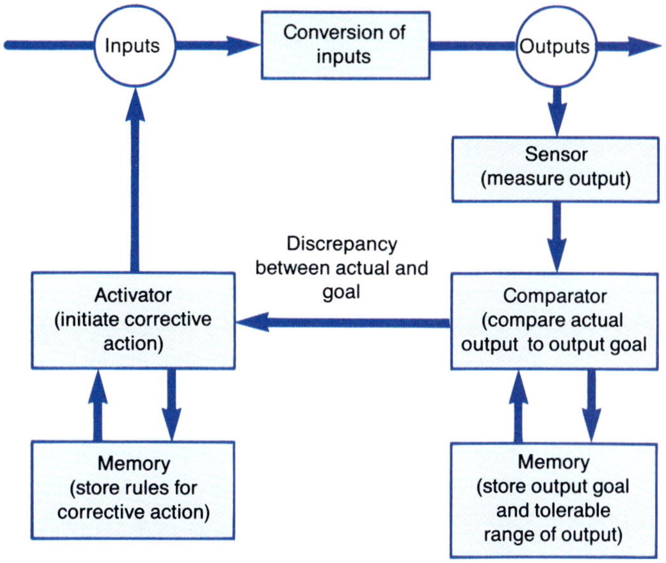

FIGURE 12.1 **Elements of the control subsystem**

Inventory Stores of goods and stocks, including raw materials, work-in-process, finished products, or supplies.

Stockkeeping item An item of inventory.

Stock (storage)point A location of inventory.

represent an investment; capital is required to store materials at any stage of completion.

Inventory is stores of goods and stocks. In manufacturing, items in inventory are called *stockkeeping items,* held at a *stock (storage) point.* Stockkeeping items usually are raw materials, work-in-process, finished products and supplies.

Inventory control is activities that maintain stockkeeping items at desired levels. In manufacturing, since the focus is on a physical product, inventory control focuses on materials control. In the service sector, since the focus is on a service (often consumed as generated), inventory control focuses less on materials and more on supplies.

TABLE 12.1 **U.S. Gross National Product (GNP) and inventories (in $ billions)[a]**

Year	GNP	Inventories	Inventories as a % of GNP
1950	1,203.7	278.1	23.1
1960	1,665.3	370.0	22.2
1970	2,416.2	571.1	23.6
1980	3,187.1	769.1	24.1
1985	3,618.7	833.3	23.0
1988	4,016.9	885.4	22.0
1990[b]	4,155.8	908.1	21.9

[a]Dollars are adjusted for 1982 value.
[b]Annual rate includes fourth quarter estimate.
Source: Economic Report of the President (February 1991), 288, 307.

EXAMPLE

First National Bank is a commercial bank with full-line services. The typical individual account involves various transactions: checking, savings, lock boxes, and loans. For the teller operation, the service is to convert labor and material into money management. Such materials as deposit slips, withdrawal slips, and loan payment coupons are more like operating supplies than raw materials. For the accounting operation, slips and coupons could be viewed as work-in-process, and monthly account statements awaiting mailing as finished goods (services).

Inventory control Activities that maintain stockkeeping items at desired levels.

For service organizations that are not highly labor-intense, inventories assume more importance. Transit systems maintain inventories of equipment and replacement parts. Local department stores maintain inventories of merchandise.

Production/operations management focuses on conversion of inputs into outputs of goods or services. This conversion process is reexamined to emphasize material input in Figure 12.2. Note that there may be stock points at the input (raw material), conversion (work-in-process), and output (product) stages.

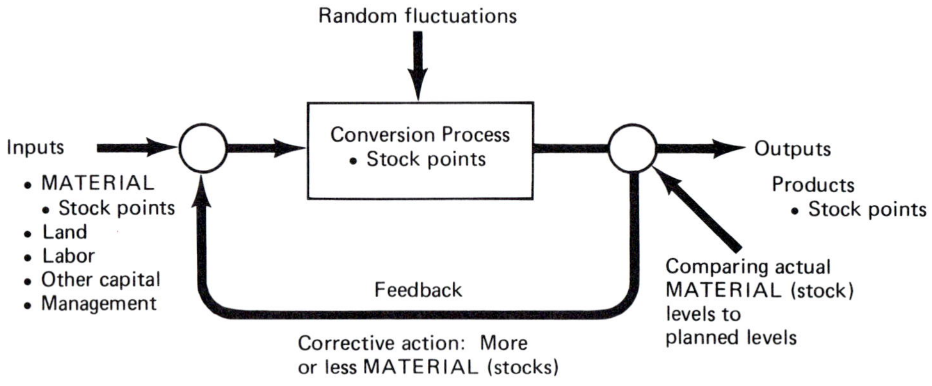

FIGURE 12.2 **The conversion process: materials conversion**

WHY INVENTORIES?

The fundamental reason for carrying inventories is that *it is physically impossible and economically impractical for each stock item to arrive exactly where it is needed exactly when it is needed.* Even if it were physically possible for a supplier to deliver raw materials every few hours, for example, it could still be prohibitively expensive. The manufacturer must therefore keep extra supplies of raw material inventory to use when they are needed in the conversion process. Other reasons for carrying inventories are summarized in Table 12.2.

Marginal efficiency of capital (MEC) A concept from finance espousing that a firm should invest in opportunities whose return is greater than the cost of capital.

Return on Investment and Turnover Inventory should be viewed as an investment and should compete for funds with other investment opportunities. If you have studied finance, you have been introduced to the concept of the *marginal efficiency of capital* (MEC). This concept holds that a firm should invest in those opportunities where return is greater than capital costs to borrow. Look at Figure 12.3, which shows a marginal efficiency of capital curve. This figure shows the rates of return on various inventory investment alternatives (shown as a percentage of total inventory investment

TABLE 12.2 **Why organizations carry inventory**

Level	Reason
Primary	Physical impossibility of getting right amount of stock at exact time of need
	Economical impracticality of getting right amount of stock at exact time of need
Secondary	Favorable return on investment
	Buffer to reduce uncertainty
	Decouple operations
	Level or smooth production
	Reduce material handling costs
	Bulk purchases

alternatives). The MEC curve for this firm shows that about 20 percent of the inventory investment alternatives will give a return on investment above the cost of capital. That is, about 20 percent of the firm's inventory alternatives will bring the firm more money than it would have to spend if it borrowed money. This 20 percent of investments should be accepted. The 80 percent of the investment alternatives that would bring in less than the cost of capital should be rejected. Inventory investment alternative A in Figure 12.3, for example, is an acceptable investment. If inventory cannot compete on this same basis with other uses of funds (plant, equipment, land, bonds, etc.), inventory should be reduced until it becomes an attractive alternative for the firm.

Both manufacturing and service firms are interested in return on investment, alternatively called *return on assets,* employed. Return on assets is the ratio of profits to assets. With a little thought we realize:

$$\frac{\text{Profits}}{\text{Assets}} = \frac{\text{Profits}}{\text{Sales}} \cdot \frac{\text{Sales}}{\text{Assets}}$$

Markup The ratio of profits to sales.

Turnover The ratio of sales to assets.

The ratio of profits to sales is *markup* and the ratio of sales to assets is *turnover*. Now we see that one way to improve return on investment is to increase turnover. We want to sell those assets that are in inventory over and over again in a reasonable time frame. One way to do this is to keep the assets in inventory low, thus improving the chance of high inventory turnover.

FIGURE 12.3 **Typical marginal efficiency of capital curve (MEC)**

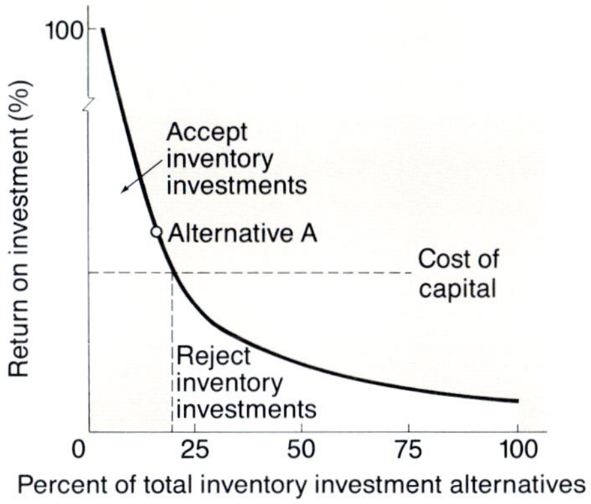

Buffer stock Inventories to protect against the effects of unusual product demand and uncertain lead time.

Buffer Stock When demand is unusually variable, some protection is needed against the prospects of high stockout costs. Inventory can be used to "buffer" against such uncertainties. Likewise, *lead time,* the time between ordering and receiving goods, is not always constant. Buffer stocks can be used to protect against stockouts from uncertain demand during lead time.

Lead time The time passing between ordering and receiving goods.

Decoupling Using inventories to break apart operations so that the supply of one operation is independent of the supply of another.

Decoupling Inventories are also useful when they *decouple* operations—that is, when they break operations apart so that one operation's supply is independent of another's supply. This decoupling serves two purposes. First, decoupled operations means that breakdowns, material shortages, or other production fluctuations at one stage of operation do not cause later stages of operation to shut down. A second purpose of decoupling through inventories is that one organizational unit can schedule its operations independently of another. In automobile manufacturing, for example, engine buildup can be scheduled separately from seat assembly, and each can be decoupled from final automobile assembly operations through in-process inventories.

Production Smoothing Inventories can also help to level production. When we examined aggregate planning and scheduling in Chapter 10, we noted that products can be built during slack demand periods and used in peak demand periods. Thus high costs of production rate and work force level changes can be avoided.

Material Handling For some operations, material handling costs can be reduced by accumulating parts between operations. This is particularly true of intermittent systems, since they involve less automation of material handling than do continuous systems. Parts can be accumulated and inventoried in tote boxes or baskets and transported by handjack dollies or forklift trucks much more economically than they can be carried by hand. In continuous manufacturing, automated material handling systems, are designed to reduce overall handling costs, resulting in less work-in-process.

Bulk Purchases With bulk purchases, quantity discounts can be arranged; thus a cost advantage of materials inventories is realized. Suppliers of materials that achieve economies of scale by producing or transporting large volumes often offer quantity discounts.

INVENTORY SYSTEM CONCEPTS

Multistage inventories Parts stocked at more than one point of the sequential production process.

Multistage Inventories When parts are stocked at more than one point in the sequential production process, there are *multistage inventories.* Since these parts must eventually come together into finished goods, it is an important problem to establish balanced inventory levels at each stage and for the system overall. Our treatment in this chapter focuses on inventory at a single stage, with little consideration of various stages. Material requirements for multistage dependence among inventories are discussed in Chapter 14.

Multiechelon inventories Products stocked at various levels—factory, warehouse, retailer, customer—in a distribution system.

Multiechelon Inventories Multiechelon inventories, illustrated in Figure 12.4, are inventories of products at the various levels, or echelons, in the distribution system. Our introductory discussion treats inventory at individual echelons.

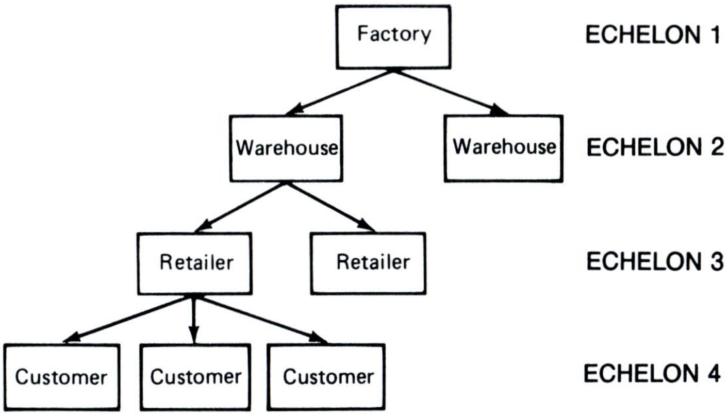

FIGURE 12.4 **Multiechelon inventory systems**

EXAMPLE

At a large medical center comprising of a hospital, a medical school, a school of nursing, and auxiliary research units, the annual expenditure for disposable surgical gloves exceeded $75,000. The stores clerk, who set reorder points and stock levels for the gloves, said she carried high volumes because demand on gloves at central stores was erratic, with occasional large withdrawals. Further examination uncovered two additional echelons of glove inventory in the hospital: the hospital floor or wing housing a surgery room and doctors' and nurses' offices and desks. Thus, demand on central stores was buffered by storerooms near surgery, and storerooms were buffered by emergency supplies in offices.

Reaction to Demand Changes An operations system should not have to react to increasing demand by increasing the levels of inventory in direct proportion to the increase in demand. As the hospital example illustrates, not reacting is sometimes complicated by multiechelon inventories. One statistical study of inventory-sales ratios in selected firms in Australia and the United States concluded that *an increase in demand can be accommodated by a less than proportional increase in inventories.*[1] The converse is also true: When demand decreases, inventories should not need to be decreased in direct proportion. Many firms became aware of this principle firsthand in the 1974–1975 and 1980–1982 recessions. As demand weakened during these periods, many firms reduced their inventories too much and suffered substantial increases in production costs as a result.

THE OPERATING DOCTRINE

Operations managers must make two basic inventory policy decisions: *when* to reorder stock and *how much* stock to reorder. These decisions are referred to as the inventory control *operating doctrine.*

Operating doctrine
Inventory control policies concerning when and how much stock to reorder.

[1]See J. M. Samuels and D. J. Smyth, "Statistical Evidence on the Relationship Between a Company's Sales and Its Inventories," *International Journal of Production Research* 6, no. 3 (1968), 249–56.

Multiechelon inventory in timber processing
Source: Richard Bullard/Tony Stone Worldwide

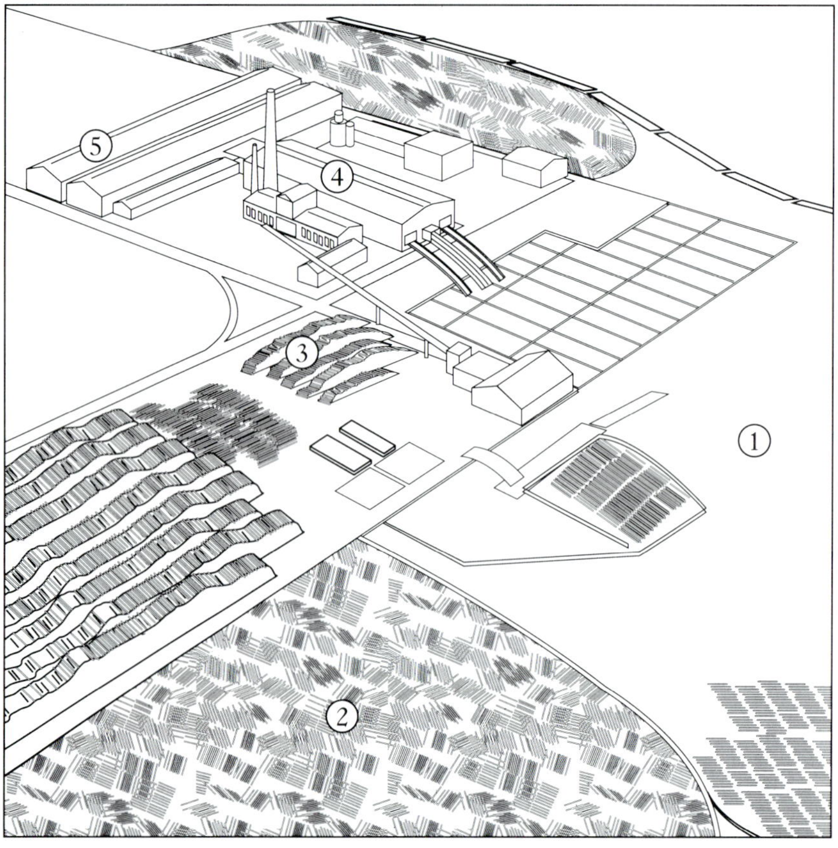

1. Ocean as a medium of transport; 2. Floating storage logs (raw materials); 3. Storage of in-process stripped logs; 4. Saw mill operation with in-process lumber; 5. Shipping dock for loading finished banded lumber.

Reorder point As part of the operating doctrine, the inventory level at which stock should be reordered.

Order quantity As part of the operating doctrine, the amount of stock that should be reordered.

The time to reorder is called the *reorder point.* A system signal, usually a predetermined inventory level, tells clerical or other responsible personnel when it is time to reorder stock. The amount that should be reordered is called the *order quantity. Both the inventory level that signals the reorder and the order quantity are economic decisions at the heart of the operations manager's inventory control function.* Although the manager may not actually operate the control system, he or she is responsible for setting the operating doctrine.

INVENTORY SYSTEMS

Q/R inventory system An operating doctrine for which an optimal reorder point *R*—the **trigger level**—and an optimal order quantity *Q*—the **economic order quantity** (EOC)—are fixed.

***Q/R* Inventory System** One practical way to establish an inventory system is to keep count of every item issued from inventory and place an order for more stock when inventories dwindle to a predetermined level, the reorder point. The reorder quantity, also called the economic order quantity, is fixed in size (volume), size having been predetermined. Figures 12.5 and 12.6 illustrate two such Q/R inventory systems. For the system shown in Figure 12.5, the demand for inventories, also called the *usage rate,* is known and constant. Replenishment inventories are assumed to be received at the stock point the moment they have been ordered. Notice that at the beginning of the time axis (far left), an order has just arrived. As time goes by, inventory is steadily depleted until a level of *R* units is reached. *R* is the reorder point, also called the *trigger level,* an order for *Q* units is placed. These units arrive at the instant they are ordered. Procurement lead time is zero. The usage pattern is then repeated, so again at level *R,* quantity *Q* is ordered. In a simple case like this, there would be no need to carry buffer stocks: Delivery is instantaneous, and the demand for the inventory item is known for certain. Thus *R* is set at zero units.

In a Q/R system, both the reorder quantity and the reorder point are fixed. For Figure 12.5, then *R* and *Q* are constant.

The inventory situation is slightly more complex for the system shown in Figure 12.6. Usage rate is variable; we do not know in advance how rapidly inventory will be depleted. As before, *R* and *Q* are constant; however, as you can see, somewhat different procedures are used to determine their values. It is difficult to establish the most

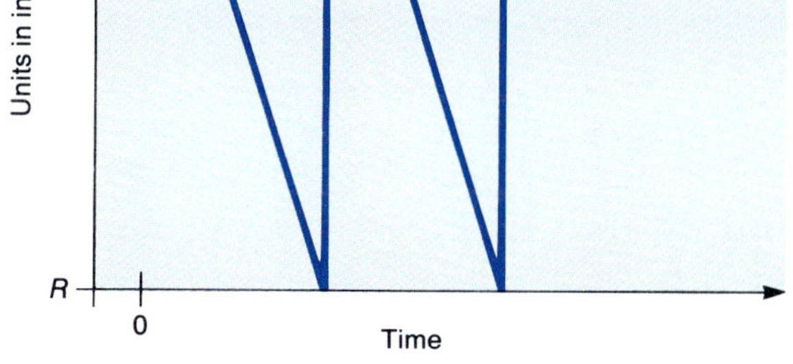

FIGURE 12.5 ***Q/R* inventory system: constant usage rate. *R* is the reorder point and *Q* the order quantity.**

The inventory level that signals the lipstick and cosmetic reorder and the reorder quantity are economic decisions at the heart of the operations manager's inventory control function—whether at the factory level as shown here or in the distribution chain.
Source: Superstock.

economical operating doctrine when demand varies, as it does here, and even more difficult when lead time varies too. Since lead time is the time between placing and receiving an order, it is shown as L_1 and L_2 on the graph. When either demand or lead time varies, the time interval between orders varies—but the order quantity always remains constant.

FIGURE 12.6 **Q/R inventory system: variable usage rate. *R* is the reorder point, *Q* the order quantity, and L_i the lead times.**

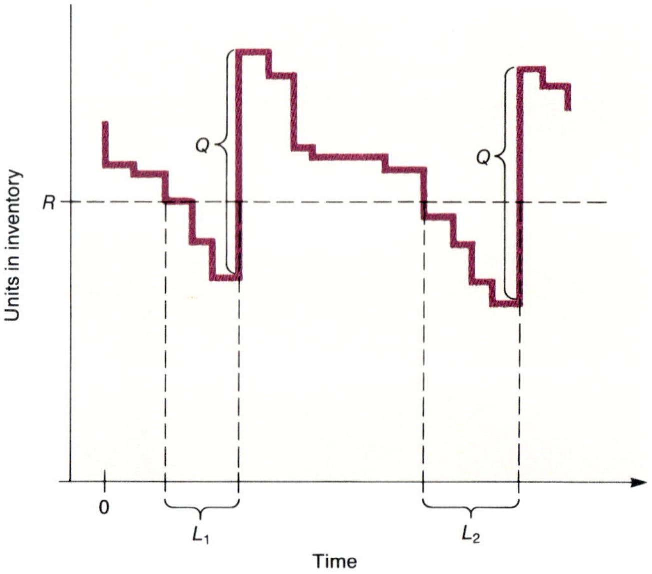

Periodic inventory system An operating doctrine for which reorder points and order quantities vary; stocks are replenished up to a fixed **base stock level** after a fixed time period has passed.

Periodic Inventory System Another practical inventory control method is to count inventories at set time intervals, periodically. With this method, the order quantity will be whatever is needed to bring the amount of inventory back up to some preestablished *base stock level.* As Figure 12.7 illustrates, the level of inventory is examined at times T, $2T$, and $3T$ and orders are placed for quantities Q_1, Q_2 and Q_3. The base stock level and the time T between orders are set by operations management and comprise the inventory system's operating doctrine. In the periodic system, T is constant, but Q_1 does not necessarily equal Q_2 or Q_3. Although Figure 12.7 shows constant demand within any one review period and zero lead time, these conditions could be relaxed and still allow the periodic inventory system concepts to be retained.

In this book, we emphasize Q/R systems. Although we concentrate on determining economic order quantities and reorder points, be aware that the procedures are similar for the periodic system. Economic order quantity in the Q/R system and base stock levels in the periodic system determine how much to order; reorder point in the Q/R system and time between orders in the periodic system determine when to order.

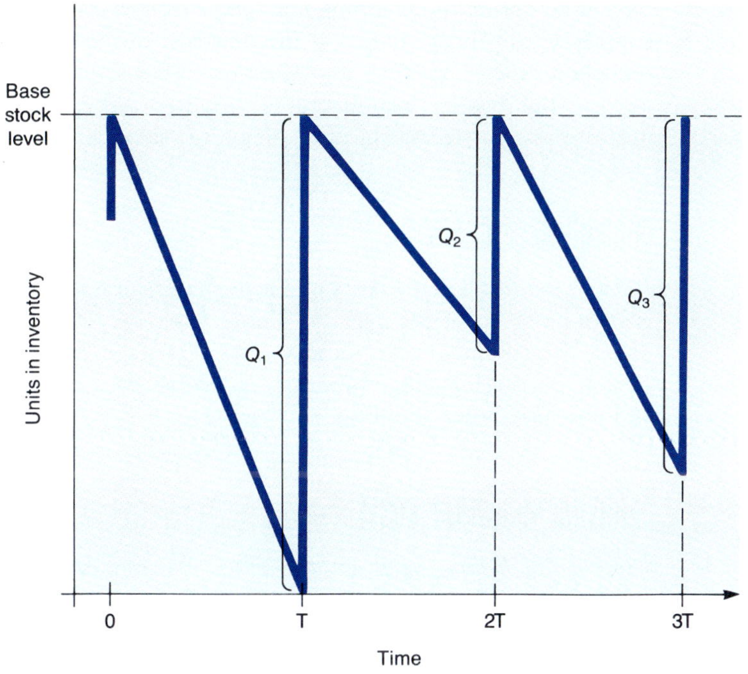

FIGURE 12.7 **Periodic inventory system. T is the time between orders and Q_i the order quantities.**

INVENTORY COSTS

In operating an inventory system managers should consider only those costs that vary directly with the operating doctrine in deciding when and how much to reorder; costs independent of the operating doctrine are irrelevant. Basically, there are five types of relevant costs:

1. Cost of the item
2. Cost of procuring the item
3. Cost of carrying the item in inventory
4. Cost associated with being out of stock when units are demanded but are unavailable (stockouts)
5. Cost associated with data gathering and control procedures for the inventory system

Often these five costs are combined in one way or another, but let's discuss them separately before we consider combinations.

COST OF ITEM

The *cost,* or *value,* of the item is usually its purchase price: the amount paid to the supplier for the item. In some instances, however, transportation, receiving, or inspection costs, for example, may be included as part of the cost of the item. If the cost of the item per unit is constant for all quantities ordered, the total cost of items purchased during the planning horizon is irrelevant to the operating doctrine. (See the supplement to this chapter.) If the unit cost varies with the quantity ordered, a price reduction called a *quantity discount,* this cost is relevant.

If the facility manufactures the item, the cost of the item is its direct manufacturing cost. Again, constant unit costs mean total costs are irrelevant.

PROCUREMENT COSTS

Procurement costs Costs of placing an order, or setup costs if ordered items are manufactured by the firm.

Procurement costs are the costs of placing a purchase order, or the setup costs if the item is manufactured at the facility. These costs vary directly with each purchase order placed. Procurement costs include costs of postage, telephone calls to the vendor, labor costs in purchasing and accounting, receiving costs, computer time for record keeping, and purchase order supplies.

CARRYING (HOLDING) COSTS

Carrying (holding) costs Costs of maintaining the inventory warehouse and protecting the inventoried items.

Carrying, or *holding, costs* are the costs of maintaining the inventory warehouse and protecting the inventoried items. Typical costs are insurance, security, warehouse rental, heat, lights, taxes, and losses due to pilferage, spoilage, or breakage. The cost of typing up capital in inventory is also considered a carrying cost.

STOCKOUT COSTS

Stockout costs Costs associated with demand when stocks have been depleted; generally lost sales or backorder costs.

Stockout costs, associated with demand when stocks have been depleted, take the form of lost sales or backorder costs. When sales are lost because of stockouts, the firm loses both the profit margin on unmade sales and its customers' good will. If customers take their business elsewhere, future profit margins may also be lost. When customers agree to come back after inventories have been replenished, they make backorders. Backorder costs include loss of good will and money paid to reorder goods and notify customers when goods arrive. As the next example shows, stockouts can and do occur in the service industries.

EXAMPLE

A customer at First National Bank had two unpleasant banking experiences this year. First, she went to a teller to get six rolls each of dimes and quarters. At this drive-in banking facility, the teller was out of rolls of dimes; he substituted two rolls of nickels but could spare no more. This forced the customer to make another stop at a competitor bank. The second experience was an attempt to obtain an $18,000 commercial rate loan to purchase land. The customer agreed to provide adequate stocks and bonds as collateral but was refused the loan because loan funds were not available, not because she was a bad risk. The customer received the loan at a competitor bank and thereafter did all her banking at the competitor bank.

COST OF OPERATING THE INFORMATION PROCESSING SYSTEM

Whether by hand or by computer, someone must update records as stock levels change. For systems in which inventory levels are not recorded daily, the cost is primarily incurred in obtaining accurate physical counts of inventories. Frequently, these operating costs are more *fixed* than variable over a wide quantity (volume) range. Therefore since fixed costs are not relevant to the operating doctrine, we will not consider them further.

COST TRADEOFFS

Our objective in inventory control is to find the *minimum cost operating doctrine* over some planning horizon. We need to consider all relevant costs—the cost of the item, procurement cost, carrying cost, and stockout cost. Using a one year planning horizon, these costs can be expressed in a general cost equation:

Total annual relevant costs	=	Cost of the items	+	Procurement cost	+	Carrying cost • Cycle stocks • Buffer stocks	+	Stockout cost • Lost sales • Backorders	(12.1)

Each cost in the equation can be expressed in terms of order quantity and reorder point for a given inventory situation. The solution method is then to *minimize* the total cost. This can be accomplished graphically; by tabular analysis using trial and error; or by using calculus, the most accurate method. Using calculus, operations researchers have developed a wide range of optimal formulas, which vary with changes in the actual inventory situation.

Graphically, minimizing total costs means cost tradeoffs. For a simple model in which cost of item and cost of stockouts are irrelevant, the tradeoff is between only two costs: procurement and carrying (see Figure 12.8). Notice that annual carrying costs increase with larger values of order quantity Q. This is logical; large values of Q result in large average inventory levels and, therefore, a large carrying cost. Likewise, when Q is large, fewer orders must be placed during the year so that the annual procurement cost decreases. Therefore, as shown in Figure 12.8, procurement cost decreases as carrying cost increases. There is a cost tradeoff between the two. If we add the costs graphically, we obtain a total cost curve. The optimal order quantity Q^* is the point at which annual

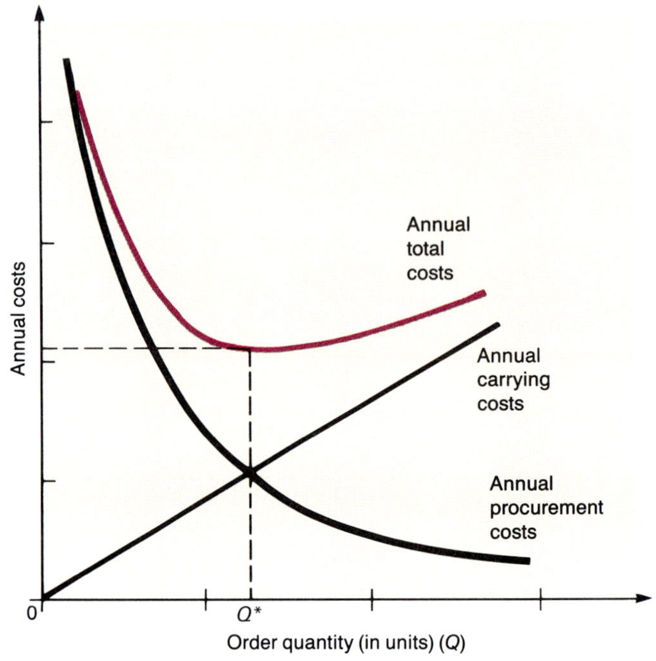

FIGURE 12.8 **Cost tradeoffs in inventory control. Q^* is the optional order quantity.**

total cost is at a minimum. For more complex situations, the cost curve becomes difficult to graph and analyze tabularly, *but the cost tradeoff concept remains.*

How could these costs tradeoff in actual application? Operations Management Highlight 12.1 helps us answer that question.

INVENTORY MODELING

Inventory modeling A quantitative method for deriving a minimum cost operating doctrine.

Deterministic model A model in which variable values are known with certainty.

Stochastic model A model in which variable values are probabilistic.

The purpose of modeling inventory situations is to derive an operating doctrine, and four simple steps are involved.

1. Examine the inventory situation carefully, listing characteristics and assumptions concerning the situation.
2. Develop the total annual relevant cost equation in narrative.
3. Transform the total annual cost equation from narrative into the shorthand logic of mathematics.
4. Optimize the cost equation, finding the optimum for how much to order (order quantity) and when to reorder (reorder point).

Inventory models can be classified as either *deterministic* (variables are known with certainty) or *stochastic* (variables are probabilistic). In this chapter we discuss two deterministic models, saving our discussion of a third deterministic model and

OPERATIONS MANAGEMENT HIGHLIGHT 12.1

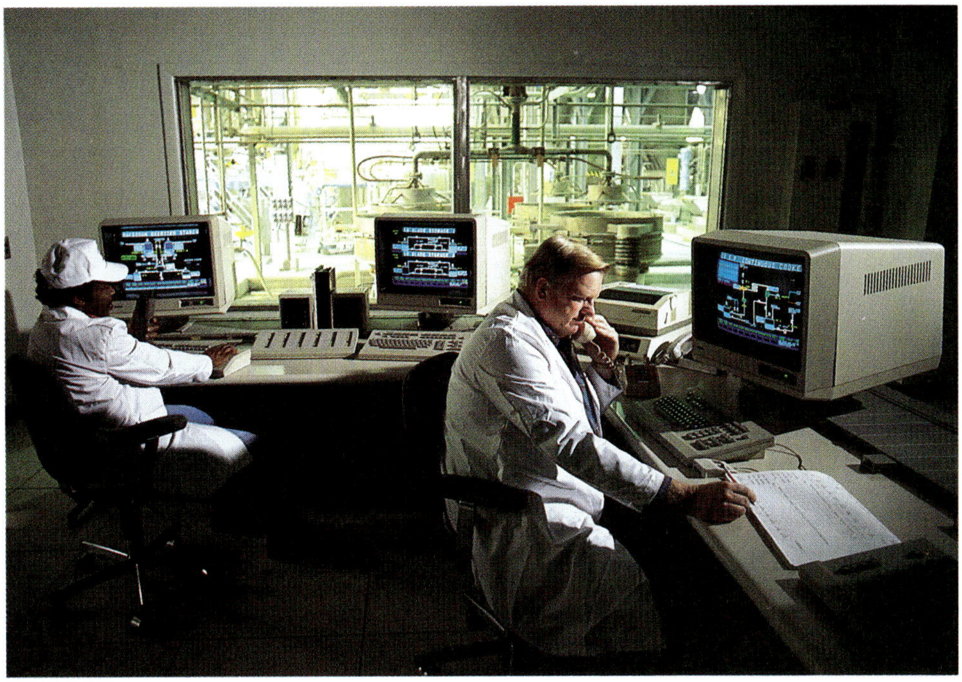

Source: John Zoiner

Inventory Modeling Saves Utility Industry Millions

The shocking oil spills during the Gulf War dramatically illustrated how very difficult the job of managing fuel supplies can be. On a smaller scale, the unpredictable nature of fuel supply and demand is made manifest continually. To manage supplies, utility companies must cope with equipment breakdowns and the vagaries of the weather, and more infrequently with strikes or natural disasters. To manage demands, utility companies must cope with extreme weather or an outage at a major nuclear plant.

In response to these difficulties, the Electric Power Research Institute spearheaded the development of a fuel inventory management model that has so far been used routinely by 74 utility companies. Integrating analytic and simulation methods, the model has advanced the state of inventory management to the tune of over $125 million in inventory costs savings.

Figure 12.9 illustrates the relationship of fuel supply actual plant operation, and customer demand (load). The crux of the analytical model is summarized for one utility in Figure 12.10. Total costs are a sum of burn costs, holding costs, and shortage costs. Holding costs and shortage costs vary according to

(continued)

Operations Management Highlight 12.1 (cont.)

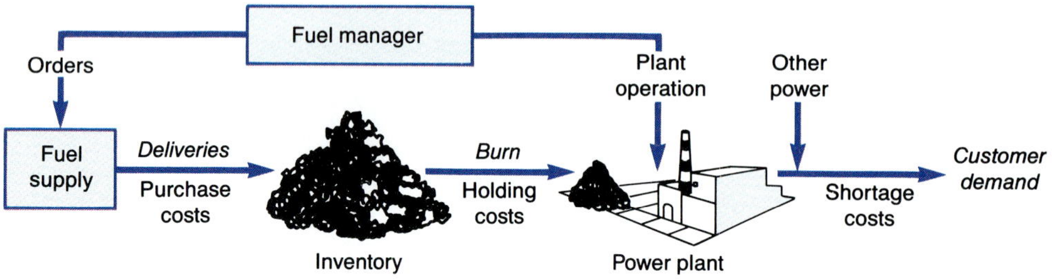

FIGURE 12.9 **Utility fuel management**
Adapted from Figure 1, Chao et al., *Interfaces*, 1989.

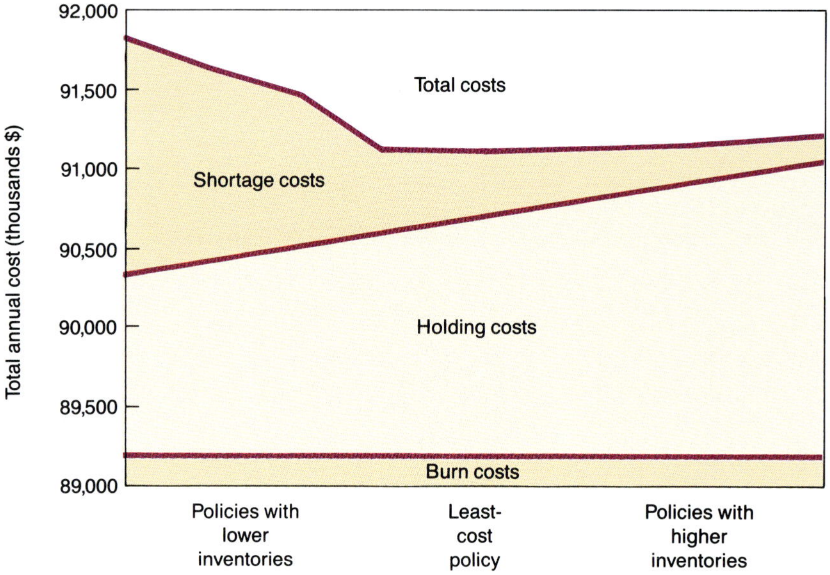

FIGURE 12.10 **Inventory Costs**
Adapted from Figure 4, Chao et al., *Interfaces*, 1989.

the policies of the operating doctrine. Notice a minimum total cost is achieved at roughly $91 million.

Utility companies currently using the model include Consumers Power of Jackson, Michigan; Tampa Electric; the Tennessee Valley Authority; San Diego Gas and Electric; and Kansas City Power and Light. At Consumers Power, three plants saved up to $10 million per year. The largest user to date is Southern Company, purchasing more coal than any other utility company in the United States: $2.2 billion worth of coal in 1987 alone. With the help of

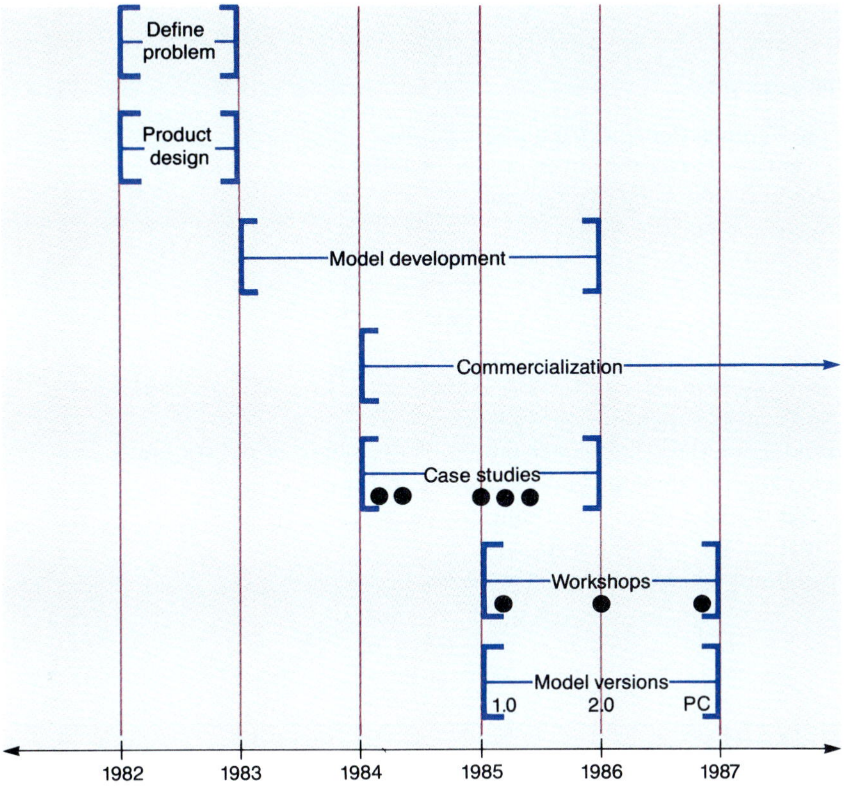

FIGURE 12.11 **Stages in development of the Electric Power Research Institute's fuel inventory management model**
Adapted from Figure 9, Chao et al., *Interfaces*, 1989.

the model, Southern Company was able to implement a new operating doctrine that allowed for lower-cost, plant-specific inventories, reducing inventories by $130 million annually and saving $20 million annually in the process.

These savings have not been realized without tremendous investment of research time and dollars. Figure 12.11 shows the stages of development since 1982 that were required to make the fuel inventory model a successful tool. Fuel (coal and oil) inventories for utility companies in the United States increased over 400 percent during the development of the model, reaching $9.3 billion and continuing to rise. Research time and dollars are well worth spending when so much is as stake. In the end, of course, it is utility customers that stand to gain. Money saved by better fuel inventory management can be passed on, reducing the $30 billion customers spend each year for electricity alone.

Source: Adapted from Hung-Po Chao, Stephen W. Chapel, Charles E. Clark, Jr., Peter A. Morris, M. James Sandling, and Richard C. Grimes, "EPRI Reduces Fuel Inventory Costs in the Electrical Utility Industry," *Interfaces* 19, no. 1 (January-February 1989) 48–67.

stochastic models until the next chapter. Also, as we mentioned previously, we will develop models only for the Q/R system, although the general method holds for the periodic system as well.

Variables in Inventory Models In developing and discussion models, we will use the following notation.

D = Total annual demand (in units)
Q = Quantity ordered (in units); order quantity
Q^* = Optimal order quantity (in units)
R = Reorder point (in units)
R^* = Optimal reorder point (in units)
L = Lead time (in time unit)
S = Setup or procurement cost (per order)
C = Cost of the individual item; cost per unit
I = Carrying cost per unit carried, expressed as a percentage of unit cost C
K = Stockout cost per unit out of stock
P = Production rate; output per time unit (in units); or delivery rate
d_L = Demand per time unit during lead time (in units)
D_L = Total demand during lead time (in units)
TC = Total annual relevant costs
TC^* = Minimum total annual relevant costs

DETERMINISTIC INVENTORY MODELS

THE SIMPLE LOT SIZE FORMULA

Simple lot size formula (Wilson formula) A deterministic inventory model characterized by one stock point, no stockouts, and constant and known demand, lead time, and unit cost.

The earliest derivation of what is often called the *simple lot size formula* was developed by Ford Harris in 1915.[2] Apparently, it was again independently derived by R. H. Wilson, who popularized it. In his honor, it is sometimes referred to as the *Wilson formula.*

The inventory situation is characterized thusly:

1. Inventory has one stock point.
2. Annual demand is constant.
3. No stockouts are allowed.
4. Lead time is constant and independent of demand.
5. Cost per unit is constant.

To simplify the case even further, lead time is assumed to be zero; that is, delivery is instantaneous.

What is the total annual relevant cost (TC) equation? Let's modify Equation 12.1 to fit this situation:

[2]Ford Harris, *Operations and Costs* (Chicago: A. W. Shaw Company, 1915), pp 48–52.

NCNB automatic teller.

Source: **Michael Quackenbush/The Image Bank**

$$\text{Total annual relevant costs} = \text{Procurement cost} + \text{Carrying cost} \qquad (12.2)$$

Stockouts are not allowed, and the cost of the items is excluded, since the cost per unit is constant. Only those costs that can be affected by our choice of Q are included. Expanding Equation 12.2,

$$TC = \begin{pmatrix}\text{Order}\\ \text{procurement}\\ \text{cost}\end{pmatrix}\begin{pmatrix}\text{Number of}\\ \text{orders}\\ \text{per year}\end{pmatrix} + \begin{pmatrix}\text{Cost of}\\ \text{carrying}\\ \text{1 unit}\end{pmatrix}\begin{pmatrix}\text{Average}\\ \text{number of units}\\ \text{carried per year}\end{pmatrix} \qquad (12.3)$$

$$= S\begin{pmatrix}\text{Number of}\\ \text{orders per year}\end{pmatrix} + IC\begin{pmatrix}\text{Average number}\\ \text{of units carried per year}\end{pmatrix}$$

The number of orders per year can be expressed in terms of annual demand and order quantity. Since

$$\text{Annual demand} = \begin{pmatrix}\text{Order}\\ \text{quantity}\end{pmatrix}\begin{pmatrix}\text{Number of orders}\\ \text{per year}\end{pmatrix} \qquad (12.4)$$

then

$$\text{Number of orders per year} = \frac{\text{Annual demand}}{\text{Ordered quantity}} = \frac{D}{Q}$$

How can we determine the average number of units carried in inventory per year? Look again at the constant usage situation in Figure 12.5. What is the maximum inventory, the highest that inventory will ever be? It is the order quantity, Q. What is the lowest inventory? Since we reorder when the stock is fully depleted, the lowest is zero. This pattern, in which inventories vary from maximum to minimum and then back to maximum, is called a *cycle*. For *any one cycle*, the average inventory is the average of the maximum inventory and the minimum inventory:

$$\text{Average inventory per cycle} = \frac{\text{Maximum inventory} + \text{Minimum inventory}}{2}$$

For the constant usage situation, then, average annual inventory per cycle is

$$\text{Average inventory per cycle} = \frac{Q + 0}{2}$$
$$= \frac{Q}{2}$$

Think about the several cycles of inventory orders in Figure 12.5. The average for any *one* of these cycles is $Q/2$, but what is the average inventory per year? Since for any time during any cycle, the average is $Q/2$, for any time at all during the year, the average is $Q/2$. *Average inventory is time independent,* as long as cycles during the year are the same.

EXAMPLE

Morrison, Inc., orders new trays and issues them to various cafeterias from central stores. If Morrison orders 1,000 trays eight times a year, what is the *annual average inventory* in trays, given all the assumptions for the simple lot size formula? The average inventory for the first, second, and so on to the eighth cycle is 1,000/2, or 500. Try to picture the cycling of inventories eight times and the annual effect of this cycling. For the *entire year,* the maximum is 1,000 and the minimum 0, and since the usage rate is constant average inventory is 500 trays.

Substituting our expressions for the number of orders per year and average inventory into Equation 12.3, our total cost equation is

$$TC = S\frac{D}{Q} + IC\frac{Q}{2} \tag{12.5}$$

From this total cost equation evolves the formula for the optimal order quantity Q^*, the quantity at the low point of the total cost curve in Figure 12.8 (To see how calculus is used to derive the formula, see the supplement at the end of this chapter.):

$$Q^* = \sqrt{\frac{2DS}{IC}} \tag{12.6}$$

Since delivery is instantaneous, the reorder point should be set at the lowest point possible, 0, to avoid carrying excess stock. The operating doctrine, then, is

$$\text{Order } Q^* = \sqrt{\frac{2DS}{IC}} \text{ units}$$
$$\text{When inventory reaches } R = 0 \text{ units}$$

EXAMPLE

Our Redeemer Catholic Church orders candles periodically, and delivery is essentially instantaneous. Annual demand, estimated to be 180 candles, is constant. Candles cost $8/dozen; the cost of placing the order is estimated to be $9; and the carrying charge is estimated to be 15 percent of the candle cost. What quantity should the church secretary order, and when? Calculate the economic order quantity:

$$
\begin{aligned}
Q^* &= \sqrt{\frac{2DS}{IC}} \\
&= \sqrt{\frac{2(180)(9)}{(.15)(8/12)}} \\
&= \sqrt{32{,}400} \\
&= 180 \\
&= 15 \text{ dozen}
\end{aligned}
$$

The church should order 15 dozen. Since delivery is instantaneous, the church secretary should order only when stock is completely depleted, which happens only once a year. The operating doctrine is $Q^* = 15$ dozen candles at the point $R = 0$.

In our example, the secretary orders periodically, perhaps intuitively. Possibly he considers that the reasonable cost of candles ($8/dozen) and the high cost of placing an order ($9) mean that he needn't order very frequently. This raises an important question. How *sensitive* are costs to optimal order quantity? How far away from optimal order quantity could the secretary be and still have total costs be reasonably close to minimum? Let's examine the sensitivity of the simple lot size formula.

Model Sensitivity We can compare the sensitivity of total costs (TC) for any operating system with the systems' minimum total costs TC^* with the ratio TC/TC^*. Recall that to find Q^* we examined the graph of TC, and chose Q^* as that value of Q that yielded the minimum TC, TC^*. Thus TC^* is computed by using Q^* as the value of Q in the equation for TC.

$$
\frac{TC}{TC^*} = \frac{S\dfrac{D}{Q} + IC\dfrac{Q}{2}}{S\dfrac{D}{Q^*} + IC\dfrac{Q^*}{2}} \tag{12.7}
$$

Substituting $\sqrt{2DS/IC}$ for Q^* into Equation 12.7 and solving algebraically, we find

$$
\frac{TC}{TC^*} = \frac{1}{2}\left[\frac{Q^*}{Q} + \frac{Q}{Q^*}\right] \tag{12.8}
$$

Note that the total cost ratio in this equation is expressed solely in terms of Q and Q^*. If our existing order quantity Q is very close to the optimal Q^*, the ratio TC/TC^* is slightly larger than one. As Q departs farther from Q^*, we expect TC/TC^* also to grow. Graphically, the relation between Q/Q^* and TC/TC^* for the simple lot size case (Equation 12.7) is shown in Figure 12.12. Note the flatness of the curve around the minimum point (1.0, 1.0). If Q is either twice or half as much as Q^*, costs increase only 25 percent. This has important practical implications. For cases that fit the assumptions of the simple lot size model, changing order quantities will not save much money.

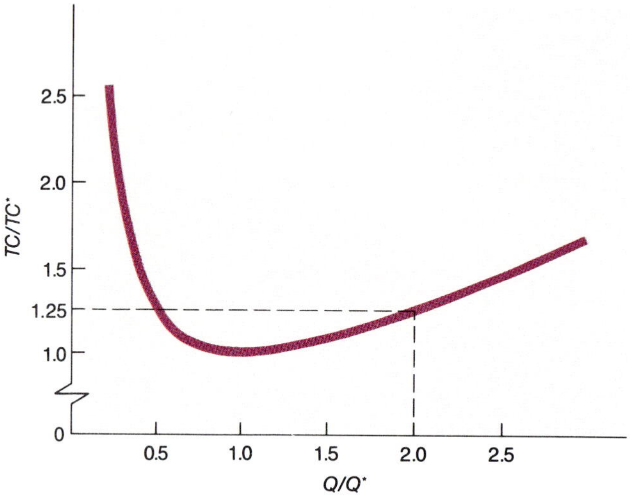

FIGURE 12.12 **Inventory sensitivity: simple lot size case**
Source G. Hadley and T. M. Whitin, *Analysis of Inventory Systems* (Englewood Cliffs, N.J.: Prentice Hall, 1963), 36.

EXAMPLE

Thompson Tooling has a Department of Defense contract for 150,000 bushings a year. Thompson orders the metal for the bushings in lots of 40,000 units from a supplier. It costs $40 to place an order, and the estimated carrying charge is 20 percent of the unit cost, which is $0.15. Thompson wants to know what percent their order quantity varies from optimal and what this variation is costing them, if anything. Finding optimal order quantity,

$$
\begin{aligned}
Q^* &= \sqrt{\frac{2DS}{IC}} \\
&= \sqrt{\frac{2(150{,}000)(40)}{0.2(0.15)}} \\
&= 20{,}000
\end{aligned}
$$

Comparing optimal order quantity Q^* with current order quantity Q:

$$
\begin{aligned}
\frac{Q}{Q^*} &= \frac{40{,}000}{20{,}000} \\
&= 2
\end{aligned}
$$

Comparing total costs:

$$
\begin{aligned}
\frac{TC}{TC^*} &= \frac{1}{2}\left(\frac{Q^*}{Q} + \frac{Q}{Q^*}\right) \\
&= \frac{1}{2}\left(\frac{20{,}000}{40{,}000} + \frac{40{,}000}{20{,}000}\right) \\
&= 1.25
\end{aligned}
$$

This calculation shows that even though order quantity is 100% higher than the optimal, costs are only 25 percent higher than the optimal. The excess (marginal) costs of the current order quantity can be found as follows:

$$\begin{aligned}\text{Marginal costs} &= TC - TC^* \\ &= 1.25\,(TC^*) - TC^* \\ &= 0.25\,(TC^*) \\ &= 0.25\left(S\frac{D}{Q^*} + IC\frac{Q^*}{2}\right) \\ &= 0.25\left[\frac{40(150{,}000)}{20{,}000} + \frac{0.2(0.15)(20{,}000)}{2}\right] \\ &= 0.25\,(300 + 300) \\ &= \$150\end{aligned}$$

Alternatively,

$$\begin{aligned}TC^* &= S\frac{D}{Q^*} + IC\frac{Q^*}{2} \\ &= \frac{(40)(150{,}000)}{20{,}000} + \frac{(0.20)(0.15)(20{,}000)}{2} \\ &= 300 + 300 \\ &= \$600\end{aligned}$$

and

$$\begin{aligned}TC &= \frac{(40)(150{,}000)}{40{,}000} + \frac{(0.20)(0.15)(40{,}000)}{2} \\ &= 150 + 600 \\ &= \$750\end{aligned}$$

Marginal cost of the current policy is \$750 − \$600, or \$150.

Notice from this example that for annual purchases valued at \$22,500, even though the difference of order quantity and optimal order quantity was *100 percent* of optimal, the cost to Thompson Tooling was only an additional \$150. You may also note that in calculating TC^*, we determined that ordering costs are equal to carrying costs when the value of Q is Q^* (each is \$300). This is just what we illustrated graphically (in Figure 12.8).

GRADUAL REPLACEMENT MODEL

Gradual replacement model A deterministic inventory model characterized by demand being withdrawn while production is underway; no stockouts, constant and known demand, lead time, and unit cost.

Sometimes, part of the order is delivered instantaneously, but the rest of the order is sent little by little over time. When the order is placed, the supplier begins producing units, which are supplied continuously to the purchaser. While these units are being added to inventory (causing it to grow), other units are being taken out of inventory (causing it to diminish). Consider the case in which replenishment rate (P) exceeds withdrawal rate (D). After some time, the order quantity has been produced, and net inventories have increased. The inventory level, however, never reaches the same high level as the simple lot size model, the order quantity. This situation is illustrated in Figure 12.13. During time T_P, the slope of inventory accumulation is not vertical, as it was in the simple lot size model. This is the case because the entire order is not received at one time. Since $P > D$, during the time T_P inventory is consumed as well as built up, and this situation continues until the initial order quantity, Q, has been produced and delivered. At that point, inventory, is at its maximum Q_{max}. Thereafter, during time T_D, units are being taken out of inventory but other units are not being added to it. The slope of inventory depletion corresponds to the withdrawal rate. At the

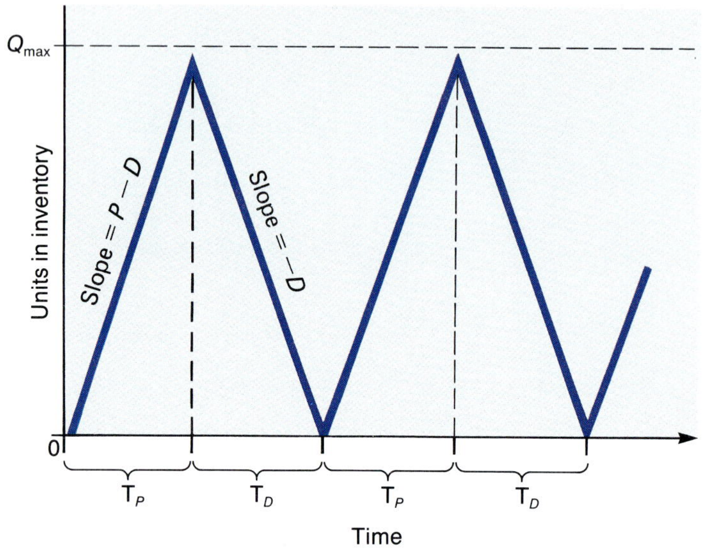

FIGURE 12.13 Gradual replacement (finite production rate) inventory situation

end of time T_D, another order for Q is placed, partial delivery is instantaneous, and the cycle repeats. The entire order is filled continually over time, not immediately as was the case with the simple lot size model.

Still applying the other assumptions of the lot size model, the total annual cost equation for this model is the same as Equation 12.2:

$$\text{Total annual relevant costs} = \text{Procurement cost} + \text{Carrying cost}$$

It can be written as follows:

$$TC = S\frac{D}{Q} + IC\left(\begin{array}{c}\text{Average number of}\\ \text{units carried per year}\end{array}\right)$$

As we have noted, maximum inventory Q_{max} never reaches Q but is always somewhat less. Therefore average inventory carried will not be $Q/2$. Realizing that the positive slope of the graph is $P - D$ and the negative slope is $-D$, we can find the maximum inventory, Q_{max} from

$$\text{Slope} = \frac{\text{Rise}}{\text{Run}}$$

$$P - D = \frac{Q_{max}}{T_P}$$

$$Q_{max} = (P - D)T_P$$

But the time T_P required to produce a lot Q is

$$T_P = \frac{Q}{P}$$

Substituting

$$Q_{max} = (P - D)\frac{Q}{P}$$

$$= Q\left(\frac{P - D}{P}\right)$$

Average inventory is then

$$\text{Average inventory} = \frac{\text{Maximum inventory} + \text{Minimum inventory}}{2}$$
$$= \left(\frac{Q(P-D)}{P} + 0\right) \div 2$$
$$= \frac{Q}{2}\left(\frac{P-D}{P}\right)$$

The total cost equation to be minimized in the gradual replacement correction model is

$$TC = S\frac{D}{Q} + \text{IC}\left[\frac{Q}{2}\left(\frac{P-D}{P}\right)\right] \tag{12.9}$$

which yields

$$Q^* = \sqrt{\frac{2DS}{IC}\left(\frac{P}{P-D}\right)} \tag{12.10}$$

Since production and resupply begins instantaneously, the optimal reorder point R^* would again be 0. Note that for this operating doctrine, the formula for Q^* is identical to Q^* for the simple lot size model (Equation 12.6) except for the *finite correction factor* $[P/(P-D)]^{1/2}$. Will this finite correction result in Q^* being greater here than in the simple lot size formula? Examine the factor and remember that $P > D$.

EXAMPLE

A large hotel serves banquets and several restaurants from a central kitchen in which labor is shifted among various stations and jobs. Salad consumption (demand) is virtually constant and known to be 30,000 salads/year. Salads can be produced at a rate of 45,000/year. Salads cost $0.40 each to make, and it costs $4 to set up the salad line. Carrying costs of salads, high because of spoilage, are estimated to be 90 percent of the cost of a salad. No stockouts are allowed. The hotel would like to establish an operating doctrine for salad preparation.

First, we can set the reorder point R^* at 0, because labor can be shifted to the salad operation instantaneously, and the production rate is greater than the demand rate. Finding Q^*,

$$Q^* = \sqrt{\frac{2DS}{IC}\left(\frac{P}{P-D}\right)}$$
$$= \sqrt{\frac{2(30{,}000)(4)}{0.9(0.4)}\left(\frac{45{,}000}{45{,}000 - 30{,}000}\right)}$$
$$= \sqrt{2(10)^6}$$
$$= 1{,}414$$

In the above example, an order should be placed for 1,414 salads when there are no salads on hand. When 1,414 salads are ordered, it takes about 11.5 days to produce them and about 17 days to consume them. Thus, some salads must be kept fresh for 5.5 days. The manager should therefore question whether it is feasible to do so. This situation illustrates how inaccurate costs or an inappropriate inventory model can distort reality. As the example shows, you should always make validity checks in applying inventory or other models to production/operations situations.

LEAD TIME IN DETERMINISTIC MODELS

Deterministic models can easily be adjusted for lead times known with certainty. The reorder point is calculated:

$$R^* = \text{Buffer stock} + \text{Demand during lead time} \qquad (12.11)$$
$$= 0 + D_L$$
$$= 0 + (\text{Lead time})\ (\text{Demand/unit time})$$
$$= L\ d_L \qquad (12.12)$$

The reorder point is now set and shown in Figure 12.14. At R^*, an order will be placed for Q^* units, which will arrive L units of time later. During the time between ordering and arrival, d_L units per time unit, D_L in total will be demanded, and inventory will be reduced accordingly.

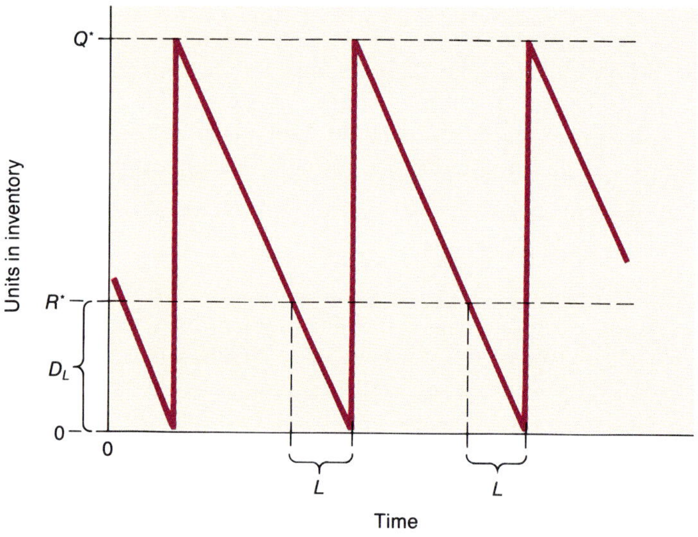

FIGURE 12.14 **Reorder points with lead times**

EXAMPLE

A fast-food chain has a local retail outlet that uses 730 cases of eight-ounce paper cups annually. Ordering costs are \$15; carrying costs are 30 percent of average inventory investment; and a case costs \$12. Delivery lead time is known with certainty to be five days. Establishing the optimal operating doctrine,

$$Q^* = \sqrt{\frac{2DS}{IC}} = \sqrt{\frac{2(730)(15)}{0.3(12)}}$$
$$= 77.99$$
$$\cong 78$$
$$R^* = L\ d_L$$
$$= 5d_L$$
$$= 5\left(\frac{730}{365}\right)$$
$$= 10$$

The operating doctrine would be to order 78 cases when stocks on hand reach 10 cases.

SUMMARY

In this chapter we illustrated that inventories are necessary for a number of reasons, the fundamental one being that it is physically impossible and economically impractical for every stock item to be delivered exactly when it is needed. In controlling inventories, we discussed that it is necessary to establish an operating doctrine, that is, policy decisions concerning *when* to replenish stocks and *how much* stock to replenish. These decisions are usually made within the framework of either a quantity/reorder (Q/R) inventory system or a periodic inventory system. In our analysis of the Q/R system, we noted that when stock is depleted to an established reorder point, a predetermined quantity is ordered. In the periodic system, after an established time interval has passed, stock is replenished up to a predetermined base stock level.

We defined the inventory costs that are relevant in selecting the operating doctrine—the cost of the item, and costs associated with procurement, carrying the item in inventory, and being out of stock when units are demanded. We learned that, formally or informally, inventory control decisions must account for these cost components and their tradeoffs.

For inventories with deterministic demands and lead times, some helpful models were presented: the simple lot size formula (Wilson formula) and the gradual replacement (finite correction) model. When demand and lead times are known, we noted that there is no need to carry buffer stock, since stockouts will never occur. This simplifies the models considerably.

REVIEW AND DISCUSSION QUESTIONS

1. Identify and describe the elements of control systems. Use a schematic diagram to assist in your discussion.
2. Give an example of a nonorganizational control system in science or engineering. Identify its goal, control elements, and information flows.
3. Give an example of an organizational control system. Identify its goals, control elements, and information flows.
4. Differentiate between multistage and multiechelon inventories. Must you have only one or the other? Explain.
5. What is meant by the inventory operating doctrine? For the operating doctrine, why are *two* decisions necessary?
6. Contrast the periodic and quantity/reorder inventory system operating doctrines.
7. Explain the steps in the modeling methodology for inventory situations. Why is the understanding of this methodology important to the practicing manager?
8. Define inventory control in the context of an automobile repair facility employing four mechanics. For any technical terms used in your definition, provide examples.
9. Refer to Figure 12.2 (the materials conversion process). For a general purpose farming operation, provide one example of a material item for each stock point.
10. Why are inventories necessary? Discuss.

11. What kinds of items should be selected when managers are attempting to improve inventory systems? Why?
12. Explain the cost tradeoffs of Equation 12.5 in essay form, using a graph if it is helpful.
13. Explain how the situation of the finite production (gradual replacement) rate inventory differs from the simple lot size situation. What impact does the cost of the item have on each situation? Explain.
14. In deterministic inventory models, total costs are relatively insensitive to deviations from the optimal operating doctrine. Explain.

PROBLEMS

SOLVED PROBLEMS

1. A television manufacturer requires 24,000 two-centimeter-long pieces of wire every month for assembly. Ordering costs are estimated at \$42, and the cost of carrying is 25 percent of the unit price, which is \$.08. Assuming delivery is instantaneous, find the reorder point and economic order quantity.

SOLUTION

$$D = (24{,}000)\ (12) = 288{,}000 \text{ pieces}$$
$$S = \$42$$
$$I = 25\%$$
$$C = \$0.08$$
$$Q^* = \sqrt{\frac{2DS}{IC}} = \sqrt{\frac{(2)\ (288{,}000)\ (\$42)}{(.25)\ (\$0.08)}} = 34{,}779.3$$

There should be 34,780 pieces/order; $R^* = 0$.

2. The Ohio State University location of McDonald's uses 120 six-ounce paper cups each day. McDonald's plans to be open 360 days a year. The cups cost \$.10/dozen; ordering costs are \$5/order; and carrying costs are 50 percent of the item cost (since space is a premium).
   (a) Find the economic order quantity if delivery is instantaneous.
   (b) Currently, cups are ordered every 30 days. Relate current ordering quantity, optimal order quantity, current total costs, and optimal total costs. What does this mean?

SOLUTION

For Part (a):

$$D = (120 \div 12)(360) = 3{,}600 \text{ dozen}$$
$$S = \$5$$
$$I = 50\%$$
$$C = \$.10$$
$$Q^* = \sqrt{\frac{2DS}{IC}} = \sqrt{\frac{2(3600)(\$5)}{0.50(\$.10)}} = 848.53 \cong 849 \text{ dozen}$$

For Part (b):

Current order quantity Q = 3600 ÷ 12 = 300 dozen
Current total costs:
Ordering costs = \$5 × 12 orders = \$60.00
Carrying costs = \$.05 × 150 (average inventory) = 7.50
Total current costs = \$67.50
Total Costs using Q^*:
Ordering costs = \$5 × (3600 ÷ 849) = \$21.200
Carrying costs = \$.05 × 424.5 = 21.225
Total costs using Q^* = \$42.425

Obviously, McDonald's can save \$25.075 by using the EOQ method rather than the current operating policy, a savings of more than 37 percent from current costs.

REINFORCING FUNDAMENTALS

3. A local bakery, Harry's, orders 100 50-pound bags of flour every three months.
   (a) What is the average inventory for three months (in bags)?
   (b) What is the average inventory for a year (in bags)?
   (c) What is the average monthly inventory (in pounds)?
4. Delicious Donut Shop requires 50 bags of flour every three months. The costs of ordering are \$12/order, and carrying charges are 22 percent of the flour cost. A bag of flour costs \$27. Flour can be delivered virtually instantaneously from a local warehouse. Determine the operating doctrine for a quantity/reorder point inventory system.
5. The owner of Delicious Donut Shop (see problem 4) has been ordering 100 bags of flour at one time.
   (a) What percentage is the owner away from optimal order quantity? How much is this deviation costing per year?
   (b) Considering the total cost of flour per year, what can you conclude about deviations from optimal order quantity? Should the owner continue to investigate similar situations? Why or why not?
6. Use the graphical method to estimate Q^* for the following situation, in which delivery is instantaneous and usage rate is constant throughout the year.

   D = 10,000 units, R = 0 units
   I = .25, C = \$100/unit
   Procurement cost/order = \$.50 + \$.50/unit in the order

7. A textile manufacturer is interested in optimally determined inventories for cutting operations for a children's product line. The production manager would like to establish the optimal reorder point and order quantity for each item in the line. Garment 78A201, a typical product, is demanded uniformly throughout the year; total annual demand is 14,000 items. The production rate is 2,000 items/month. Sewing, the operation following cutting, is staffed to meet annual demand exactly. Setup costs for cutting are \$240, and the cost of carrying one item for a year is \$.50. Since cutting and sewing are done in the same plant, delivery of cut items to sewing is essentially instantaneous. Determine the cutting operation operating doctrine for garment 78A201.

8. A missile manufacturer requires an electrically wired subassembly for final assembly. Annual subassembly demand is 480 "wire bundles"; order costs are \$85; carrying costs are 75 percent of average inventory investment; and bundles cost \$1,125 each. Delivery time is known with certainty to be 21 days. Establish the optimal operating doctrine.
9. Buster's, Inc., is interested in the economical order quantity for a production subassembly that is currently purchased from another company. The final assembly made by Buster's is for their parent company, under an annual contract, with the year's demand set at 125,000 units. Two purchased subassemblies are required for each final assembly. The cost of a subassembly is \$15, and the cost of placing an order with the supplier is \$35. The annual inventory holding charge is \$5. Buster's currently orders 1,500 units at one time. Can you save Buster's any money by recommending a new order quantity? If so, how much can be saved and what quantity should be ordered?

CHALLENGING EXERCISES

10. Ward Paper Box Company supplies a particular candy box to Russell Stover Candy Company, delivering 200 one-pound candy boxes/day. The machine that produces these boxes has a capacity of 1,000 boxes/day. In the past, Ward has always run the machine one day a week to satisfy the weekly demand of 1,000 boxes over a 5-day work week (50 weeks a year). Setup costs are \$100/run, and carrying costs are \$.05/box/day.
    (a) Find the economic order quantity for this candy box.
    (b) What is the cost savings in a year by ordering the economic order quantity rather than following current policy?
11. A fast-food outlet uses 220 breakfast paper cartons/day. The outlet plans to be open 365 days a year. The cartons cost \$.35/dozen; ordering costs are \$15/order; and carrying costs are 70 percent of the item (since space is a premium).
    (a) Find the economic order quantity if delivery is instantaneous.
    (b) Currently, cartons are ordered every 14 days. Relate current ordering quantity, optimal order quantity, current total costs, and optimal total costs. What does this mean?
12. A dairy that supplies a large number of retail outlets uses a certain ingredient at the rate of 1,500 pounds/day, 250 days/year. Delivery is virtually constant and requires two days. A two-day usage of safety stock is set by management and cannot be changed. Ordering costs are \$40/order, and the cost of carrying inventory charge is \$0.001/pound/day. Determine the following:
    (a) Economic order quantity
    (b) Reorder point
    (c) Maximum inventory level
    (d) Total annual carrying costs.
13. Often variances for production are computed and the results are used for subsequent production control.
    (a) Compute the raw material price and usage (quantity) variance and the direct labor quantity variance for Milton Industries' key product, shown below. State the variance as favorable or unfavorable.

	Standard for 1,000 Units	Actual for 1,000 Units
Raw materials:		
Price	$1.20/pound	$1.40/pound
Quantity	1 pound/unit	1,100 pounds
Direct labor:		
Price	$6.00/hour	$6.00/hour
Quantity	2.37 hour/unit	2,172 hours

(b) For each measure in part (a), would you take action as a manager? Why or why not?

(c) Write the general formula you used to compute this variance. (Note: We did not provide a formula in this chapter.)

14. A missile manufacturer (see problem 8) is investigating setting up a "bundle wiring" room and manufacturing the wire bundles for production. This would bring "in house," 480 items currently purchased at $1,125, generating some $540,000 of business a year. The method of production under investigation produces a maximum of 4 bundles/day over a 250-day year. Cost per item produced is estimated to remain at $1,125 each, but items can be delivered when they are produced rather than in the previously determined lot size. Ordering costs are expected to fall to $30/order, with carrying costs remaining 75 percent of inventory investment. The $1,125/item cost estimate would cover all fixed costs of the new production line and variable costs for this item only.

(a) For the Q^* of problem 8, find the total annual inventory cost when the items are purchased.

(b) Establish the Q^* for the manufacturer producing the wire bundle in house.

(c) For the Q^* in part (b), find the total annual inventory cost.

(d) Which do you recommend—purchase or produce? Why? What qualitative factors did you consider in your decision?

UTILIZING QSOM COMPUTER SOFTWARE

15. An auto parts outlet sells 120 spark plugs weekly and operates year-round less two weeks for holidays. The plugs cost $7/dozen, and the cost of placing an order is $12. Carrying costs are 30 percent of item cost. Using QSOM's inventory theory program and assuming delivery is instantaneous, determine Q^*, R^*, and order interval.

16. A general contractor uses 50,000 pounds of Portland cement each month. The 100-pound bags cost $8 each, and the contractor pays $15/order. Carrying costs are 25 percent of unit cost. Top management estimates that the shortage cost per bag per year would be $10, should such a situation occur. The supplier fulfills all orders in one month. Using QSOM's inventory theory program, determine the economic order quantity, reorder point, and the order interval for this contractor.

KEY TERMS

Buffer stock 456
Carrying (holding) costs 462
Decoupling 456
Deterministic model 464
Gradual replacement model 473
Inventory 453
Inventory control 454
Inventory modeling 464
Lead time 456
Marginal efficiency of capital (MEC) 454
Markup 455
Multiechelon inventories 456
Multistage inventories 456
Operating doctrine 457
Order quantity 459
Periodic inventory system 461
Procurement costs 462
Q/R inventory system 459
Reorder point 459
Simple lot size formula (Wilson formula) 468
Stochastic model 464
Stock (storage) point 453
Stockkeeping item 453
Stockout costs 462
Turnover 455

SELECTED READINGS

Buffa, E. S., and R. G. Miller, *Production-Inventory Systems: Planning and Control,* 3rd ed. Homewood, Ill.: Richard D. Irwin, 1979.

Hadley, G., and T. M. Whitin, *Analysis of Inventory Systems.* Englewood Cliffs, N.J.: Prentice-Hall, 1963.

Harris, F. W., *Operations and Costs.* Chicago: A. W. Shaw Company, 1915.

Starr, M. K., and D. W. Miller, *Inventory Control: Theory and Practice.* Englewood Cliffs, N.J.: Prentice-Hall, 1962.

SUPPLEMENT TO CHAPTER 12

OPTIMIZATION AND INVENTORY CONTROL

In this supplement we briefly present several optimization concepts from calculus and relate them to inventory control. If you have never studied calculus, you may not thoroughly understand these concepts; they are stated to provide a brief review for those who understand the basics of classical optimization.

The only inventory case derived here is the simple lot size formula, the first inventory model presented in the chapter. The derivation is started where the chapter stopped; development of the model terms are not repeated.

CLASSICAL OPTIMIZATION

The Derivative To find a derivative of a function is to differentiate with respect to a variable. Properties of derivatives we use in this supplement are:

$$\frac{d(a)}{dx} = 0$$

$$\frac{d(ax)}{dx} = a$$

$$\frac{d(y+z)}{dx} = \frac{dy}{dx} + \frac{dz}{dx}$$

$$\frac{d(x^n)}{dx} = nx^{n-1}$$

where a represents a constant and x, y, and z are variables.

Let's find the first derivative of the function $y = 3x^2 + x - 3$ with respect to the variable x:

$$\frac{d(y)}{dx} = \frac{d}{dx}(3x^2) + \frac{d}{dx}(x) - \frac{d}{dx}(3)$$
$$= 6x + 1$$

In this example, the first derivative of each term is used to find the first derivative $d(y)/dx$. The second derivative is found by taking the derivative of the first derivative:

$$\frac{d^2(y)}{dx^2} = \frac{d}{dx}(6x) + \frac{d}{dx}(1)$$
$$= 6$$

Optimization In the calculus, the derivative is taken to find the value of the decision variable that gives the largest or smallest value of a criterion function. The general procedure is to take the first derivative of a function with respect to a decision variable and set the result equal to zero. The equation is then solved for the decision variable in terms of the other parameters in the equation. To determine whether the optimal point is a maximum or a minimum, the second derivative is taken. If the second derivative is positive, the optimal point is a minimum. If the second derivative is negative, the optimal point is a maximum. If the second derivative is zero, the point is an inflection point.

In the previous example,

$$\frac{d(y)}{dx} = 6x + 1$$

The optimal value of x is found by setting this equation equal to zero and solving for x:

$$0 = 6x + 1$$
$$x = -\frac{1}{6}$$

When the second derivative was found, it was +6. Therefore $x = -1/6$ is a minimum point.

Partial Derivatives In finding a partial derivative, we hold all variables constant except one. Then we differentiate with respect to that one variable, treating all other variables as constants.

For example, if $y = zx^3 - x^2 + 2x$, let's find the first partial derivative of y with respect to x. To do this, we treat z as though it were a constant and differentiate:

$$\frac{\delta y}{\delta x} = \frac{\delta}{\delta x}(z\,x^3) - \frac{\delta}{\delta x}(x^2) + \frac{\delta}{\delta x}(2x)$$
$$= z\frac{\delta}{\delta x}(x^3) - \frac{\delta}{\delta x}(x^2) + 2\frac{\delta}{\delta x}(x)$$
$$= 3zx^2 - 2x + 2$$

Optimizing the Simple Lot Size Formula The total cost equation for the simple lot size formula was developed to be:

$$TC = CD + S\frac{D}{Q} + IC\frac{Q}{2}$$
$$= CD + SDQ^{-1} + \frac{IC}{2}Q$$

Taking the first partial derivative of total cost with respect to order quantity, Q:

$$\frac{\delta(TC)}{\delta Q} = 0 + (-SDQ^{-2}) + \frac{IC}{2}$$

Setting the first partial derivative equal to zero, and solving for Q:

$$0 = \frac{-SD}{Q^2} + \frac{IC}{2}$$
$$\frac{SD}{Q^2} = \frac{IC}{2}$$
$$Q^* = \sqrt{\frac{2DS}{IC}}$$

Taking the second partial derivative to ensure a minimum of the cost function:

$$\frac{\delta^2(TC)}{\delta Q^2} = \frac{\delta}{\delta Q}\left(-\frac{SD}{Q^2}\right) + \frac{\delta}{\delta Q}\left(\frac{IC}{2}\right) = -(-2)\frac{SD}{Q^3} + 0$$
$$= \frac{2DS}{Q^3}$$

A positive value results, thus ensuring a minimum. Notice that the term CD, the total cost of the items, dropped out when we found the first derivative. This illustrates that this cost component is constant with regard to changes in order quantity.

Again, we can see the power of the logic in calculus, but you need not be overwhelmed if you cannot follow all the mathematics. Clearly, the logic of mathematics is useful when applied to the many rational problems in productions/operations.

PROBLEMS

1. For the following total cost TC, find the optimal order quantity Q^*. A is a constant. Is this a minimum or a maximum cost point? Why?

$$TC = (27 + A)Q + \frac{100}{Q} + 274$$

2. Following are parameters of a given Q/R control system.
   (a) Delivery is instantaneous.
   (b) The vendor quotes a price c as twice the variable charge V plus the ratio of the fixed charge F divided by the order quantity Q.
   (c) The inventory storage rate i is applied to the value of the *maximum* inventory.
   (d) No stockouts are permitted.
   (e) The demand D per year and the cost S of ordering per order are both known. Define any additional notation used.
      (1) Explain the basic approach one should take in proceeding to analyze this type of system. Determinating the *optimal* operating doctrine is the goal.
      (2) Write a verbal total cost equation for the entire system.
      (3) Solve the system for the optimal operating doctrine (Q^* and R^*).

C H A P T E R 1 3

INVENTORY CONTROL APPLICATIONS

The Prime-Mover Company lives and dies in a very competitive industry that is truly global. Like all companies, to be competitive, Prime-Mover considers inventory management to be of major importance. At Prime-Mover we produce electric lift trucks predominantly used in narrow aisle, high rack/density storage systems. A typical customer is a grocery store using our product in its warehouse. Prime-Mover has in excess of 10,000 part numbers; we purchase parts and components from over 500 suppliers to support the manufacturing of ten products. These products have literally hundreds of variations and combinations as the product is customized to meet the needs of the customer.

In the Prime-Mover operation, quantity discounts for large volume purchases, variations in demand and lead time, and a requirement to provide excellent customer service are not only very real issues, but absolute facts of competitive survival. To achieve our objectives, we use a number of analytic techniques and highly computerized systematic inventory systems. In addition, we use less complex systems such as safety stock and two-bin systems, along with a variety of JIT techniques. This blending of computerization and manual systems allows Prime-Mover to manage a major asset in business: inventory size. Managing inventory is managing costs while serving customers well. The challenge of providing excellent delivery for whatever final configuration a customer requests, while minimizing inventory investment, is tremendous and continual, and we pride ourselves in meeting this challenge at Prime-Mover.

Dennis O. Wolfs
Executive Vice President
The Prime-Mover Company
Muscatine, Iowa

Mr. Wolfs brings to our attention that applying inventory fundamentals requires management to become involved in the total production system. Let's look at a few inventory situations that are slightly more complex and realistic than those in the last chapter, starting with quantity discounts, a technique utilized by the Prime-Mover Company.

DETERMINISTIC INVENTORY MODELS

QUANTITY DISCOUNTS

Quantity discount A policy of allowing item cost to vary with the volume ordered; usually the item cost decreases as volume increases due to economies of scale in production and distribution.

Each of us has purchased goods in larger quantities than we immediately need so that we could pay a lower unit price (dollars per pound, per gallon, etc.). When demand is known for certain, delivery is instantaneous (no stockouts), and item cost varies with volume ordered, the result is a modified simple lot size situation called the *quantity discount* case. Although the concept of quantity discounts is also applicable to other inventory situations, for our introductory treatment we will modify only the simple lot size situation discussed in Chapter 12.

Figure 13.1 illustrates the quantity discount concept, the basis of which is examination of price breaks. As volume ordered Q increases, the supplier can often produce and ship more economically. To encourage volume purchases, the supplier shares the economies of scale with the customer. In Figure 13.1, the solid lines represent average annual costs for various feasible order quantities. Note, however, that the solid lines are *discontinuous* at the price breaks; for different ranges of Q, different cost curves apply.

In the operating doctrine for quantity discounts, reorder point is still at zero inventory, since delivery is assumed to be instantaneous. The general procedure for determining the order quantity starts by checking the lowest cost curve for an optimal Q. If that is unsuccessful, each higher cost curve is systematically checked until optimal is found. Follow these steps:

1. Calculate the economic order quantity (EOQ) for the lowest unit price using the simple lot size formula.
2. Determine if the EOQ in step 1 is feasible by determining whether it is in the quantity range for that price.
3. If the EOQ in step 1 is not feasible, compute the total cost for the smallest *feasible* quantity at the lowest unit price.
4. If the EOQ for the lowest unit price is feasible, compute the total cost for this quantity at the lowest unit price, compute the total cost for the smallest feasible quantity at each unit price, and choose the quantity yielding the lowest total cost. Skip the remaining steps.
5. Repeat steps 1 through 4 for the remaining unit prices until a feasible EOC is found or all unit prices are evaluated. If the EOC for each unit price is not feasible, choose the price break with the lowest total cost.

Essentially, this procedure finds the quantity yielding the lowest cost on the lowest cost curve, checks its feasibility, and if it is not feasible, computes a cost at the price break

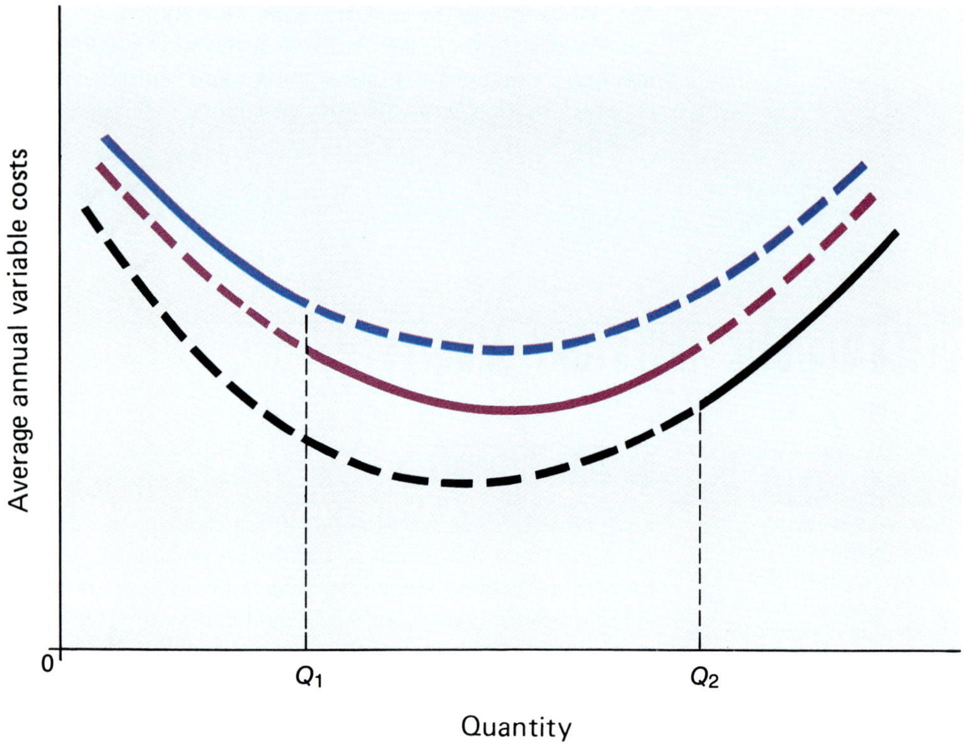

FIGURE 13.1 **Quantity discounts; price breaks are given at quantities Q_1 and Q_2**

that allows a feasible solution. Then we move to the next highest cost curve (see Figure 13.1) and repeat the procedures. In this way, all *minimum cost* EOQ's will be calculated, and all price breaks will eventually be checked, provided an optimal feasible solution is not discovered earlier. As in all inventory operating doctrines, the optimal order quantity is the *quantity that offers the lowest total cost.* An example should help clarify this procedure.

EXAMPLE

Consider an inventory situation in a medical center where disposable sanitary packs are ordered in boxes of 5 dozen/box. Annual demand is 400 boxes; the cost of placing an order is $12; and the inventory carrying charge is 20 percent. There are two price breaks: price per box is $29 for 1 to 49 boxes, $28.50 for 50 to 99 boxes, and $28 for 100 or more boxes.

To determine the optimal quantity, we begin on the lowest cost curve and compute Q^*_1 for a price of $28 per box.

$$Q^*_1 = \sqrt{\frac{2DS}{IC}} = \sqrt{\frac{2(400)(12)}{.2(28)}} = 41.40$$
$$= 41 \text{ boxes}$$

Since 100 or more boxes must be ordered to get a price of \$28 per box, our $Q^*_1 = 41$ is not feasible. Computing the total cost for the lowest feasible quantity (100) at this unit price, we get

$$\begin{aligned} TC &= CD + S\frac{D}{Q} + IC\frac{Q}{2} \\ &= 28(400) + 12\left(\frac{400}{100}\right) + .2(28)\left(\frac{100}{2}\right) \\ &= \$11{,}528 \end{aligned}$$

Moving to the next highest curve,

$$\begin{aligned} Q^*_2 &= \sqrt{\frac{2DS}{IC}} = \sqrt{\frac{2(400)(12)}{.2(28.5)}} = 41.04 \\ &= 41 \text{ boxes} \end{aligned}$$

The price of \$28.50 applies to orders of 50 to 99 boxes, so $Q^*_2 = 41$ is not feasible. Computing the total cost at the lowest feasible quantity (50) at this unit price, we get,

$$\begin{aligned} TC &= CD + S\frac{D}{Q} + IC\frac{Q}{2} \\ &= 28.50(400) + 12\left(\frac{400}{50}\right) + .2(28.50)\left(\frac{50}{2}\right) \\ &= \$11{,}638.50 \end{aligned}$$

Moving to the next highest and last cost curve,

$$\begin{aligned} Q^*_3 &= \sqrt{\frac{2DS}{IC}} = \sqrt{\frac{2(400)(12)}{.2(29)}} = 40.68 \\ &= 41 \text{ boxes} \end{aligned}$$

This is a feasible quantity, since \$29 is the price for an order of 1–49 boxes. Now we must compute the total cost for $Q^* = 41$:

$$\begin{aligned} TC^* &= CD + S\frac{D}{Q^*} + IC\frac{Q^*}{2} \\ &= 29(400) + 12\left(\frac{400}{41}\right) + .2(29)\left(\frac{41}{2}\right) \\ &= \$11{,}835.97 \end{aligned}$$

Comparing all total costs, we see that the lowest total cost is \$11,528 for an order quantity of 100. Therefore the operating doctrine for disposable sanitary packs is

$$\begin{aligned} Q^* &= 100 \\ R^* &= 0 \\ TC^* &= \$11{,}528 \end{aligned}$$

For the disposable sanitary packs, the quantity discount overcame higher carrying costs. The sum of ordering and carrying costs were \$328.00 for $Q = 100$, \$238.50 for $Q = 50$, and \$235.97 for $Q = 41$. However, the quantity discount of \$1 per box for 400 boxes (comparing $Q = 100$ with $Q = 41$) overcame the additional \$92.03 in ordering and carrying costs, making $Q = 100$ the more attractive choice.

In Chapter 12 and in the quantity discount situation above, we explained several deterministic models. In reality we rarely encounter the simplified conditions shown in these models. Let's now relax the deterministic conditions and examine some models of a more practical nature: stochastic inventory models.

STOCHASTIC INVENTORY MODELS

VARIABLE DEMAND, LEAD TIME, AND DEMAND DURING LEAD TIME

Variable Demand For simple inventory models, we assumed that future demand is known with certainty. Generally, however, this is not the case; demand must be estimated. The most common way to estimate demand is to collect data about past experiences and forecast future demand based on that data. Here is a summary of the most recent seven days' demand for a part used in manufacturing:

Range of Actual Daily Demand (in units)	Days Demand Fits Range	Relative Frequency: Percent of Total Days in Period
1–200	3	42.8
201–400	2	28.6
401–600	1	14.3
601–800	1	14.3
	Total 7	Total 100.0%

In the conventional method for measuring usage, we calculate (1) the average usage rate from historical data, and (2) the standard deviation of usage about the average. In the data for the manufacturing part, the usage rate intervals are very wide: Each interval is a 200-unit range. To obtain some very approximate indicators of the demand pattern, we calculate the mean and standard deviation of these data using only the midpoints of the intervals. Average, or expected, demand is calculated as 300 units/day $[(100\ (3) + \ldots + 700(1)) \div 7]$ with variability in demand calculated as a standard deviation of 214 units $[([3\ (100 - 300)^2 + \ldots + (700 - 300)^2] \div 7)^{1/2}]$. Figure 13.2 illustrates the frequency distribution of daily demand.

Lead Time Like demand, lead time is often uncertain rather than constant. If it is uncertain, the length of lead time takes on some distribution. Extending our manufacturing part example, we find that the distribution of lead times is as follows.

Actual Lead Time (in days)	Number of Lead Times	Relative Frequency: Percent of Total Number of Lead Times
2	2	28.6
3	3	42.8
4	2	28.6
	Total 7	Total 100.0%

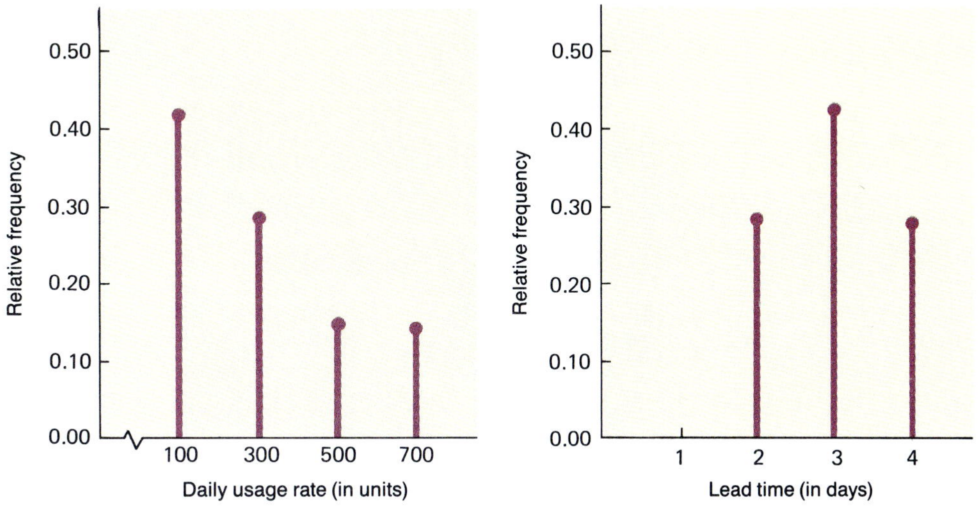

FIGURE 13.2 **Relative frequency distribution of daily usage and lead times**

The expected lead time is 3 days and the standard deviation of lead time is 0.75 days. Relative frequencies are shown in Figure 13.2.

Demand During Lead Time The two sources of demand variation during lead time, the length of lead time itself, and the demand per time period of lead time interact to determine *demand during lead time.* For our example we can determine "expected demand during lead time" (average demand). For the manufacturing part:

Lead-time demand Units of stock demanded during lead time; can be described by a probability distribution in stochastic situations.

$$\begin{array}{c}\text{Expected demand}\\\text{during lead time}\end{array} = (300 \text{ units/day})\ (3 \text{ days}) = 900 \text{ units}$$

If we had the lowest demand for each day (100) of the shortest lead time (2), we would have a low demand during lead time of 200 units. Likewise, if the most demanding condition prevailed, highest demand per day (700) and longest lead time (4), demand during lead time would be 2,800 units.

As you can see, between these extreme points, there can be various levels of demand. We can calculate all possible combinations of lead time and daily demand and see what values are possible for demand during lead time. We can also calculate the probabilities of these demands and use them to construct a probability distribution of demand during lead time. For larger problems involving many classification intervals of demand and lead time, hand calculations become tedious. An alternative method for generating the distribution of demand during lead time is to *simulate* the operation of the inventory system over time on the computer. By randomly selecting a lead time and a demand, computing a demand during lead time, and repeating the process dozens of times, we could classify the data into a distribution of lead-time demands and compute a mean and standard deviation to describe that distribution.

The instantaneous collection of grocery sales with optical scanners allows for more accurate estimates of demand, and when related to lead times, provides more accurate demand during lead time estimates and fewer stockouts for the customer.
Source: **John Zoiner**

Figure 13.3 illustrates how inventory levels are affected by variations in lead-time demand. After the first reorder, at time t_1, expected demand and expected lead time occur. After the second reorder at time t_2, the second lead time, L_2, occurs. Although L_2 is shorter than expected, daily demand during the lead time is considerably greater than expected; thus, overall lead-time demand is greater than expected. After the third

FIGURE 13.3 **Q/R system with varying demand and lead times. L_i is lead time and t_i is the time of order.**

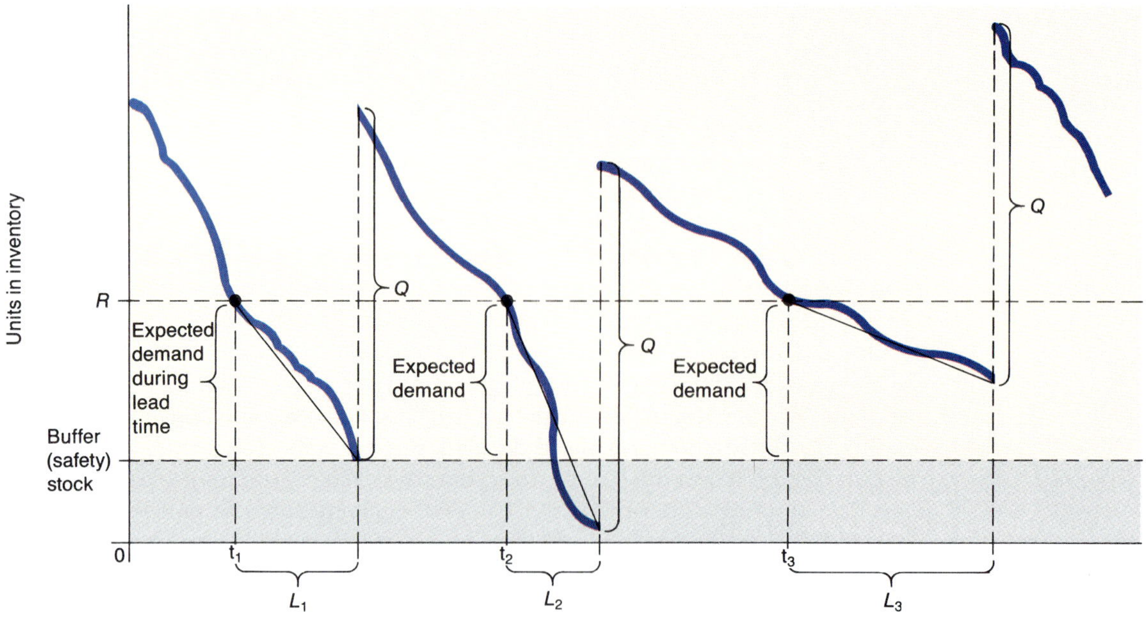

reorder at time t_3, both lead time, L_3, and daily demand are different from what was expected: Demand is much lower than expected, and lead time is much greater than expected. As the figure shows, the two variables, demand and lead time, interact. This interaction and the resulting variation is common in actual inventory situations.

Operations Management Highlight 13.1 details one such inventory situation: the managing of complicated spare parts inventories.

A MODEL FOR VARIABLE DEMAND AND CONSTANT LEAD TIME, WITH SPECIFIED SERVICE LEVEL

We now examine a moderately complex quantity/reorder point model in which lead time does not vary, but demand does. In this model, we want to find an operating doctrine that takes into account the possibility of a stockout. We want to establish buffer stocks that adequately protect service to customers when demand is uncertain.

We will define a few variables in addition to those defined in the previous chapter:

μ = demand during lead time, a random variable
σ_μ = standard deviation of demand during lead time
$\overline{\mu}$ = expected demand during lead time
$\overline{d}$ = expected average daily demand
$\overline{\sigma}_d$ = standard deviation of expected daily demand
$\overline{D}$ = expected annual demand
B = buffer stock
z = number of standard deviations needed for a specified confidence level

Look closely at the first cycle in Figure 13.3, noting several relationships. First, we can see that the expected lead-time demand $\overline{\mu}$ plus the buffer stock B equals the reorder point R. This general relationship holds:

$$R = \overline{\mu} + B \tag{13.1}$$

Second, we know that if lead time L is constant, which it is for the model being developed, expected lead-time demand equals expected demand times lead time:

$$\overline{\mu} = \overline{d}L$$

We also know that the buffer stock is the *protection* for the service level specified, $z\sigma_\mu$ units. Buffer stock is z standard deviates of protection for a given *variability* of demand during lead time. Substituting, the reorder point for our operating doctrine is now:

$$R = \overline{\mu} + B$$
$$R^* = \overline{d}L + z\sigma_\mu \tag{13.2}$$

The order quantity is simply the simple lot size formula with expected annual demand substituted for annual demand:

$$Q^* = \sqrt{\frac{2\overline{D}S}{IC}} \tag{13.3}$$

Using average demand in Equation 13.3 is appropriate for this model regardless of the shape of the demand distribution. Because of demand's variable nature, the demand distribution may take on many shapes. It may be a very unconventional empirical distribution, or it may be a normal distribution, Poisson distribution, or negatively exponential distribution. You may not be familiar with all of these distributions; we mention them only because they have been found to be reasonable representations of demand at various levels of production-wholesale-distribution

OPERATIONS MANAGEMENT HIGHLIGHT 13.1

Source: Lou Jones/The Image Bank

Spare Parts Inventory Important to After-Sales Service Strategies

More than likely, at one time or another you've had trouble getting "spares and repairs" for some product you own. Perhaps the proper service facility was hard to locate, or you found the facility only to be told the spare part you needed was out of stock. In the larger picture, the stockout could result from unexpected demand, an unexpectedly long delivery lead time, or some combination of the two. For the consumer, though, an out-of-stock spare part is simply frustrating. At times, we become convinced that the manufacturer is out of touch with customer needs. We become irritated at the manufacturer for failure, at the service facility for poor service, and at anyone else we can blame for our misfortune!

In establishing ***after-sales service strategies***, firms consider design, manufacturing, qualified service (repair) persons, and spare parts inventories. There is a clear relationship between perceived product quality and after-sales service. While adequate spare parts inventories are an important ingredient to a successful service strategy, managing these inventories often poses distinct challenges. Spare parts are often at the bottom of a multiechelon inventory system, a system that focuses first on purchased or manufactured parts, assembly, finished goods, and warehousing. To the contrary, firms that are best-in-class generally demonstrate a spare parts service strategy that provides them a competitive edge, even when their products are excellent before and during use. Examples of these best-in-class companies are Caterpillar and IBM—companies that thrive on their service image.

Let's consider IBM's National Service Division (NSD), a service group for some 1,000 different IBM products—in service with an installed population of tens of millions of individual items. These 1,000 products require over 200,000 numbered parts stored (1) in two central automated warehouses, (2) for 21 field distribution centers, (3) for 64 parts stations, (4) for 15,000 outside locations. Moreover, NSD's 15,000 customer engineers store spare parts in their car trunks and tool boxes. Managing spare parts inventory at IBM is a large, complex operations management task.

To help simplify the task, IBM developed Optimizer, a system for flexible and optimal control of service levels and spare parts inventory. The system handles over 15 million part-location combinations and billions of dollars in inventory. Though enormous in scope, the system is founded on a straightforward model that encompasses a reorder point and order-up-to a set level operating doctrine. The system allows alternative ordering for each part if demand and lead time require emergency backup and stock.

IBM's 1986 pre-implementation test led to changes that ensured later success. During 1987, implementation became a reality. Optimizer recommended stocking policies 20 to 25 percent below existing inventory and service levels—a potential inventory reduction of $500 million. Management decided to realize half this potential in cost savings, and half in improved service levels. Inventory was reduced by $250 million, but that still left room for some buffer stock to avoid stockouts and, hence, better service levels. The result was an operational savings of some $20 million per year, and a 10 percent improvement in parts availability at the lower echelons.

To you and me, these results mean a decrease in downtime on our IBM computers. If they fail, we can expect the right parts to be available to us through our local customer service engineer. At the same time, operational savings should ensure IBM's competitive position in the marketplace and that could mean lower prices as well.

Sources: Colin Armisted and Graham Clark, "After Sales Support Strategy." Paper presented at OMA-UK Conference on Manufacturing Strategy, Warwick, England, June 25–26, 1990; Morris Cohen, Pasumarti V. Kamesam, Paul Kleindorfer, Hau Lee, and Armen Tekerian, "Optimizer: IBM's Multiechelon Inventory System for Managing Service Logistics," _Interfaces_ 20, no. 1 (January-February 1990), 65–82; and Morris A. Cohen and Hau L. Lee, "Out of Touch with Customer Needs? Spare Parts and After Sales Service," _Sloan Management Review_, 31 (Winter 1990), 55–67.

systems. There is some evidence, for example, that the normal distribution describes many inventory situations at the production level; the negative exponential describes many of the wholesale and retail levels; and the Poisson describes many retail situations.[1]

EXAMPLE

Daily demand for product EPD101 is normally distributed with a mean of 50 units and a standard deviation of 5. Supply is virtually certain with a lead time of six days. The cost of placing an order is $8, and annual carrying costs are 20 percent of the unit price of $1.20. A 95 percent service level is desired for the customers who place orders during the reorder period. Backorders are allowed. Once stocks are depleted, orders are filled as soon as the stocks arrive. There are no stockout costs. We can assume sales are made over the entire year.

Determining the operating doctrine, we calculate order quantity as follows:

$$Q^* = \sqrt{\frac{2\bar{D}S}{IC}} = \sqrt{\frac{2(50)\ (365)\ (8)}{.2(1.20)}}$$
$$= 1{,}103$$

From the normal distribution, a 0.95 confidence level gives $z = 1.645$ (see Appendix A). Thus

$$R^* = \bar{d}L + z\sigma_\mu$$
$$= 50(6) + 1.645\sigma_\mu$$

From statistics, we know that for an independent variable the total variance is the sum of the individual variances. The variance of demand during lead time is as follows:

$$\sigma_\mu^2 = \sum_{i=1}^{6}\sigma_i^2 = 6(5)^2$$
$$\sigma_\mu = \sqrt{6(5)^2} = 12.2$$

Therefore,

$$R^* = 50(6) + 1.645(12.2)$$
$$= 300 + 20 = 320 \text{ units}$$

Our operating doctrine is to order 1,103 units when we reach an order point of 320.

In our example for product EPD 101, the operating doctrine accomplishes two things. First, it results in economical levels of cycle stocks because our choice of Q^* provides a proper balance between ordering costs and inventory carrying costs throughout the year. Second, it provides the desired level of customer service during lead times while we are waiting to receive a replenishment order from our suppliers. As illustrated in Figure 13.4, the 320 units we have on hand when we place an order provide a 95 percent assurance of being able to meet customer demand until the new shipment is received. We expect only 300 units to be demanded, but we carry an extra

[1]J. Buchan and E. Koenigsberg, *Scientific Inventory Control* (Englewood Cliffs, N.J.: Prentice-Hall, 1963).

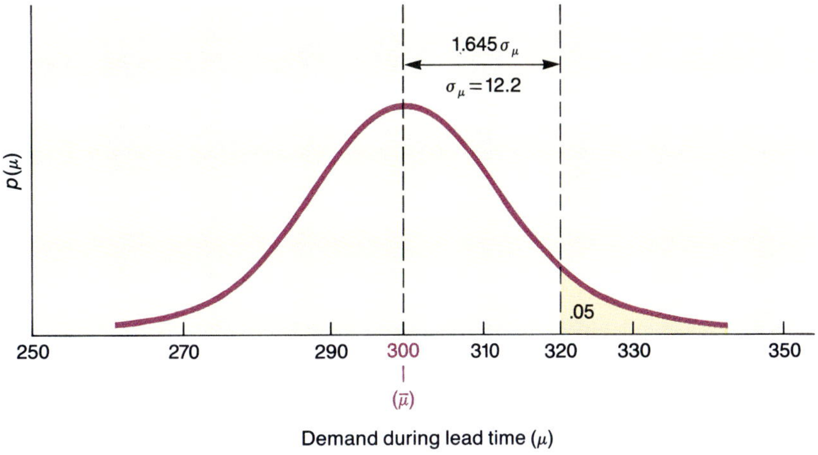

FIGURE 13.4 **Distribution of demand during lead time when lead time is six days and daily demand is normally distributed with mean of 50 units and standard deviation of 5 units.**

20 units of buffer stock to provide the desired service level. How much do we pay to obtain this extra level of production? Our average inventory levels for the year are 20 units higher than they otherwise would have been. Therefore the annual cost of carrying buffer stock is:

$$\begin{aligned} BIC &= (20 \text{ units})(.20)(\$1.20/\text{unit}) \\ &= \$4.80 \end{aligned}$$

Expected Stockout Cost and Expected Number of Stockouts At times demand is expressed as an empirical distribution, and lead time is constant. When this is the case, the density function $f(x)$, the cumulative function $F(x)$, and the complementary cumulative function $g(x) = (1 - F(x)$ can readily be found. *The complementary cumulative function also represents the probability of a stockout if that demand occurs.* The expected stockout cost, a key calculation in the total inventory cost, would be the expected probability of a stockout times the stockout cost that are incurred regardless of the number of units short. The complementary cumulative function can also be used to set buffer stocks for the allowable number of stockouts per year. The expected number of stockouts for any demand level is found by multiplying the number of orders in a year (D/Q) times the probability of a stockout. If the stockout cost is cost per unit short, then the calculation of stockout costs is more complex.

Variable Demands and Lead Times The basic procedure for finding operating doctrines when *both* daily demands and lead times vary is a convergence procedure; we use directed trial and error. For the quantity/reorder point model, we compute an order quantity assuming constant demand. Then we calculate a reorder point using the computed order quantity. We then use the computed reorder point to recalculate the order quantity and recalculate the reorder point. Eventually, the order quantity and reorder point converge to their optimal values. Another approach when both demand and lead time varies is an analytical calculation: complete enumeration of a joint probability distribution for demand during lead time. Similarly, one could use computer simulation to generate the joint probability distribution.[2] Although you should be aware of these models, their details are beyond our introductory treatment.

A SINGLE PERIOD MODEL FOR PERISHABLE PRODUCTS AND SERVICES

Products News vendors, produce managers, and owners of meat markets all must face the question "How much should I order, given that the product is perishable?" When the ordering situation is for the next period only, the critical costs are the costs C_u of being understocked and the costs C_o of being overstocked. The news vendor, manager, or owner is faced with minimizing overall costs when demand is not known with certainty.

Faced with the uncertainties of fast-food demand and many perishable items, inventory practices must minimize overall costs and maintain high service standards at the same time.

Source: **Gary Gladstone / The Image Bank**

Equation 13.4 suggests that the person ordering a perishable product or service should stock at the fractile (portion) of demand—the *critical fractile* CF—that is the ratio of the shortage (understock) cost to the sum of shortage and overstock costs.

[2]See Jack R. Meredith and Thomas E. Gibbs, *The Management of Operations* (New York: John Wiley, 1980), 437–44, for generating joint probability distributions.

Critical fractile The ratio of shortage costs to the sum of shortage and overstock for the perishable goods inventory situation.

$$CF = \frac{C_u}{C_u + C_o} \quad (13.4)$$

The *critical fractile* is the service level that maximizes profits for the perishable goods case.

EXAMPLE

A shop owner has four different retail locations, each featuring magazines as a major product line. The demand for a popular monthly magazine varies uniformly from 500 to 1,200 copies at all stores combined. Ordering is centralized and magazines can be moved easily from store to store. The magazines cost \$125/hundred and sell for \$2.25 each. When purchased in lots at this price, the publisher accepts no returns. What should be the ordering quantity for the next period?

$$\begin{aligned} CF &= \frac{C_u}{C_u + C_o} \\ &= \frac{(\$2.25 - \$1.25)}{(\$2.25 - \$1.25) + \$1.25} \\ &= \frac{1.00}{1.00 + 1.25} = \frac{1.00}{2.25} \\ &= 0.444 \end{aligned}$$

The manager would experience a loss in profit of \$1.00 per copy (\$2.25 − \$1.25) if he orders too few, but a loss of \$1.25 per copy if he orders too many. He should stock at 0.444 of the difference of 1,200 and 500 copies.

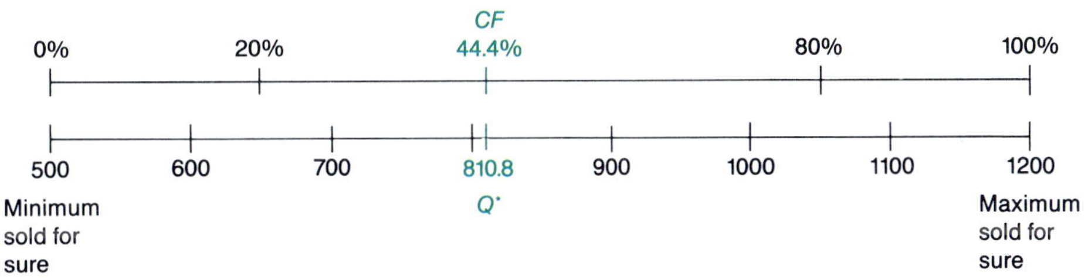

The economic order quantity (Q^*) is then

$$\begin{aligned} Q^* &= 500 + 0.444\ (1{,}200 - 500) \\ &= 500 + 310.8 \\ &= 810.8 \end{aligned}$$

Since orders must be in lots of 100, the order closest to optimal would be 800 copies of the magazine for next month.

Services This ordering rule holds for single service orders, just as for products. Consider, for example, the capacity planning question for service vendors such as accountants, cleaning services, and hotels: "How much capacity should be ordered for the next period if we know past demands, costs, and profits?" The assumption is that demand cannot be stored, just as in the perishable goods case.

EXAMPLE

The owner of a motel that has 32 rooms is trying to determine whether to build an addition or incur stockouts, referring customers to competitors when demand exceeds supply. The cost of maintaining a hotel room averages \$15/day. A typical room rents for \$45/night. During the last six months, demand has averaged as follows:

Range of Actual Daily Demand (in rooms)	Days Demand Fits Range
0–20	90
21–30	50
31–40	32
41 or more	10
	Total 182 days

The critical fractile, or optimal service level, is calculated as follows:

$$CF = \frac{C_u}{C_u + C_o}$$
$$= \frac{(\$45.00 - \$15.00)}{(\$45.00 - \$15.00) + (\$15.00)}$$
$$= \frac{\$30}{\$45} = 0.667$$

The demand distribution should be met up to the 0.667 fractile of the distribution to optimize profit. The fractiles are as follows:

Range of Daily Demand (in rooms)	Days Demand Fits Range	Cumulative Days	Cumulative Fractile
0–20	90	90	0.495
21–30	50	140	0.769
31–40	32	172	0.945
41 or more	10	182	1.000
	182		

It is optimal to have a capacity of rooms that is greater than 20 rooms and less than 31 rooms (0.667 is between 0.495 and 0.769). If 20 rooms were available, that demand would be met 49.5 percent of the time; if 30 rooms were available, that demand would be met 76.9 percent of the time. Since the motel currently has 32 rooms, its capacity should not be increased.

INVENTORY CONTROL IN APPLICATION

CONCEPTS FOR THE PRACTITIONER

Dynamic Inventory Levels The simple lot size formula

$$Q^* = \sqrt{\frac{2DS}{IC}}$$
$$= \sqrt{D}\sqrt{2S \div IC}$$

illustrates that the optimal order quantity Q^* varies directly with the square root of demand. Table 13.1 illustrates this relationship for several demand levels. Note that as demand increases 100 percent, inventory order quantity, and subsequently maximum inventory levels, increase only 41 percent. *Demand changes should not cause rapid, wide fluctuations in inventory.* If operations managers find that work-in-process and finished goods inventories are building rapidly, the problem may very well be caused by scheduling and loading difficulties, not by increases in demand.

TABLE 13.1 **Relationship between demand and order quantity in the simple lot size situation**

Demand (in units)	Change in Demand (in %)	Order Quantity (in units)	Change in Order Quantity (in %)
1,000	0	$31.62\sqrt{2S \div IC}$	0
1,500	50	$38.73\sqrt{2S \div IC}$	22
2,000	100	$44.72\sqrt{2S \div IC}$	41
3,000	200	$54.77\sqrt{2S \div IC}$	73
4,000	300	$63.24\sqrt{2S \div IC}$	100

Service level A treatment policy for customers when there are stockouts; commonly established either as a ratio of customers served to customers demanding or as a ratio of units supplied to units demanded.

Service Level *Service levels,* or treatment policies for customers when there are stockouts, can be established and measured according to several criterion. In this chapter we have focused on one criterion—the probability that there will be a stockout (of any size) during a lead time or cycle. Firms utilize at least two other common criteria as well:

1. Ratio of the number of *customers* receiving the product to the number of customers demanding the product
2. Ratio of the number of *units* supplied to the number of units demanded

Suppose four customers each demanded 100 units and demand was met. When a fifth customer demanded 200 units, however, demand was not met. In this case, service level as a customer ratio in this case is 4/5 or 80 percent serviced; service level as a unit ratio is 400/600, or 67 percent serviced. Our example in Figure 13.4 used the number of units as the service level criterion. Whether a firm uses a customer or a unit ratio depends on what use management wants to make of buffer stocks. As an operations manager, you must make sure that marketing and general management understand the way service level is being measured so that internal disagreements can be minimized.

SAVING MONEY IN INVENTORY SYSTEMS

Blanket rule A general policy for inventory control that can be modified as needed in light of total inventory costs.

Suppose your first assignment on your first job is to evaluate the current inventory system and procedures for a major distribution center of a national company. Where would you begin? What would you do? In this section, we hope to provide you with a general guide to saving money in inventory systems. Table 13.2 provides an overview of situations you might find in practice and the operating guides you could follow. There are two new concepts in the table: blanket rules and the ABC classification.

TABLE 13.2 A general guide for saving money in inventory control

Inventory Situation	Operating Guides
No priority for inventory items	Classify by ABC; examine high dollar volumes first, low dollar volumes last.
Blanket rules applied	Challenge on cost basis by examining items and families of parts; justify by return on investment.
Stochastic (variable) demand and lead times	Obtain estimates of mean and variance of demand, lead time, and especially demand during lead time; adjust buffer stocks, reorder point, and order quantity to avoid continued overstock or understock situations.
High stockout costs	Identify high stockout cost items by questioning staff; adjust buffer stocks on cost tradeoff basis.
Safety stocks	Evaluate reasons for safety stocks; levels should be based on demand, lead times, and cost tradeoff among ordering, carrying, and stockout costs; do not set intuitively.
Decoupling operations	Justify in-process inventory levels as basis for cost reductions and efficiency in operations; reduce levels if too much inventory results in inefficiencies due to space limitations.
Raw material and finished goods inventory	Examine physical inventories carefully; accept obsolescence write-offs but reduce future obsolescence through more careful scheduling and control; coordinate closely with purchasing on raw materials and marketing on finished goods inventories.

ABC classification Classification of inventory into three groups: an A group comprising items with a large dollar volume; a B group comprising items with moderate volume and moderate dollar volume; and a C group comprising items with a large volume and small dollar volume.

Blanket Rules *Blanket rules* are general rules such as "always carry a month's supply on all items," "reorder when you take out the last case of any item," and "don't order any inventory that won't fit in this room." These rules almost always afford an opportunity to evaluate the rule in light of the economics of total annual inventory costs.

ABC Classification We examine *ABC classification* closely since it holds considerable promise as a cost-saving technique. When an organization's inventory is listed by dollar volume, generally a small number of items account for a large dollar volume, and a large number of items account for a small dollar volume.

The ABC classification divides inventories into three groupings: an A grouping for those few items with large dollar volume; a B grouping for items with moderate unit and dollar volume; and a C grouping for the large number of items accounting for a small dollar volume. The A group might contain, for example, about 15 percent of the items, the B group 35 percent, and the C group 50 percent.

In construction projects there often is little room for too much or too little inventory. A shortage of structural steel can cause re-planning at high levels in the organization.

***Source:* LDG Productions / The Image Bank**

Table 13.3 lists a number of stock items according to decreasing dollar usage, and Table 13.4 groups these items into an ABC classification. The A items comprise 79.5 percent of the total dollar volume, the B items 17.6 percent, and the C items only 2.9 percent. Notice, however, that the number of A items is only 22.2 percent of the total number of items, the number of B items 22.2 percent, and the number of C items 55.6 percent. Figure 13.5 graphically illustrates the ABC classification for this example.

If you are trying to reduce costs in an inventory system, which class would you concentrate on? The high dollar volume group, the A group, should receive your attention first. One of the major costs of inventory is annual carrying costs, and your money is invested largely in class A. Tight control, sound operating doctrine, and attention to security on these items would allow you to control a large dollar volume with a reasonable amount of time and effort. Items in this class are usually either high unit cost items or high volume items with at least moderate costs. Class C items, the bulk of all items, should have carefully established but routine controls.

TABLE 13.3 Sample annual usage of inventory

Item Stock Number	Annual Dollar Usage	Percent of Total Dollar Usage
2704	125,000	46.2
1511	90,000	33.3
0012	32,000	11.8
2100	15,500	5.8
0301	6,200	2.3
0721	650	0.2
8764	525	0.2
7402	325	0.1
3520	300	0.1
	Total 270,500	Total 100.0

TABLE 13.4 Sample ABC classification of inventory

Classification	Item Stock Numbers	Annual Dollar Usage	Percent of Total Dollar Usage	Number of Items	Percent of Total Number of Items
A	1511, 2704	215,000	79.5	2	22.2
B	0012, 2100	47,500	17.6	2	22.2
C	0301, 0721, 3520 7402, 8764	8,000	2.9	5	55.6
Total		270,500	100.0	9	100.0

INVENTORY CONTROL PROCEDURES

Inventory control procedures vary in complexity and accuracy, from no noticeable control to computerized systems for distribution and production. In between these extremes are simple visual controls, the two-bin system, and cardex systems. We briefly examine here two of the systems: a cardex file and IBM's computerized MAPICS system. In Chapter 15 we discuss the Japanese just-in-time and kanban systems. The two-bin system, which needs no extended explanation, consists simply of filling two bins with units of the same item. One bin is used first; when it is empty, the quantity necessary to replenish the empty bin is reordered, and stock from the second bin is used.

Cardex file system A manually operated inventory control system in which an inventory card represents each stock item with transactions kept on the card.

Cardex File System The cardex file system has variations, but the essential features are as follows.

1. There is a card for every stock item; the cards are filed on a rotating drum or file cabinet in a central location.
2. On the top of each card is the computed operating doctrine. The supply source (vendor) may be listed here also.
3. The balance of the card is a ledger stating beginning inventory, orders placed, orders received, issues from stores, and current inventory levels. Each time a transaction is made, an entry with the corresponding date is recorded. When physical inventories are taken, cards are adjusted to reflect current actual inventories.

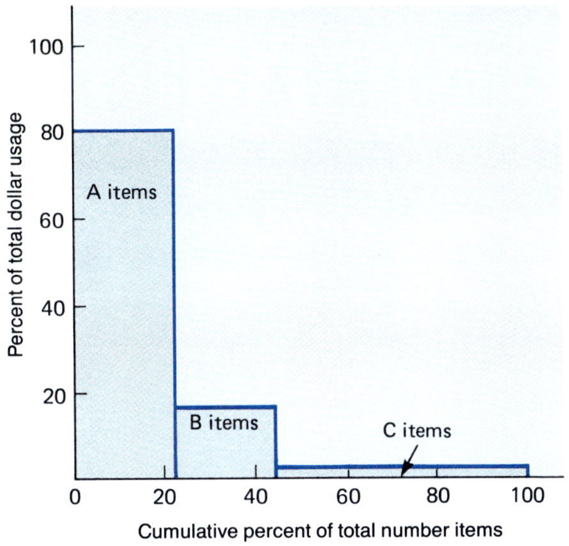

FIGURE 13.5
ABC inventory classification: percent inventory value versus percent of items

Even though simplicity is the main advantage, remote-terminal computers hooked into central processing computers have made this cardex procedure all but obsolete for multilocation distribution and manufacturing firms. Computers are less costly than cardex systems, especially when combined with automated identification such as bar-coders. Operations Management Highlight 13.2 addresses bar-coding in inventory management. Cardex files are still useful, however, for small and medium-sized organizations with limited computer access, even though microcomputers offer a good alternative for the progressive, small business owner.

Manufacturing Accounting and Production Information Control System (MAPICS) IBM's computerized common data base system for manufacturing information and control.

IBM's MAPICS *The Manufacturing Accounting and Production Information Control System* (MAPICS) is a series of modules for information and control in manufacturing.[3] Modules include financial, order processing and accounting, and manufacturing applications as well as a guide for implementation planning. The key module for control includes product data management, material requirements planning (MRP), inventory management, and production costing and control applications. IBM suggests that the benefits of the inventory management application include improved plant productivity, reduced time required of inventory personnel, reduced inventory investment and storage space, improved customer service, and establishment of the basic inventory data and status reports required for MRP. Production/operations managers will find computer and software companies eager to help them find a system that will fit their needs.

[3]See IBM's *Manufacturing Education Guide*, GH30-0241-0, and the *MAPICS Features Education Manual*, SR30-0369-1 (Atlanta, Ga., 1979).

OPERATIONS MANAGEMENT HIGHLIGHT 13.2

Source: Courtesy of Federal Express Corporation.

Manufacturers Realize Quick Payback for Bar-Code Technology

Automatic identification systems, also known as bar-coders, identify products using machine-readable binary codes. Bar-code technology allows faster, more accurate data entry, better document tracking, reduced inventory costs, and increased sales. Bar codes are the printed patterns of lines, spaces, and numerals you see today on most packaged products.

Bar codes are as useful to the manufacturer as they are to the retailer. The purpose is the same: to keep an accurate, current count of inventory items as they move past a scanner. In manufacturing, employees completing a step in the production process would typically pass the light wand over the bar codes that represent their employee number, the production

Source: Courtesy of Federal Express Corporation. All rights reserved.

process number, product (piece) number, and the quantity. This replaces manual inventory record-keeping as well as manual employee timekeeping. Many companies begin using bar-coding for inventory, then find applications to replace time clocks (employees check in with the wand), record billing time, manage assets, and other accounting activities.

Memorex Telex in Raleigh, North Carolina, uses bar-code technology to track the six-stage assembly of printed circuit boards. With bar-coding, the company has decreased inventory investment by 10 to 15 percent, reduced clerical errors to almost zero, and increased by virtually 100 percent its ability to give accurate inventory counts and product information to any department manager. Val Mode Lingerie, in New York City uses bar-coding in both the Prichard, Alabama, and Bridgeton, New Jersey, nylon garment assembly mills. Scanned production information is transferred to the company's vast IBM System 136 computer for tracking and analysis. Bar-coding systems such as those at Memorex Telex and Val Mode Lingerie find multiple uses and frequently pay for themselves within the first year of use.

Sources: Sharon Meatyard, "Track Lingerie 'As Smooth as Silk,'" *Manufacturing Systems* 7, no. 8 (August 1989), 52–53; Leila Davis, "Wider Uses for Bar Codes," *Nation's Business* 77, no. 3 (March 1989), 34, 36; Howard Abernathy and Benny Holder, "Bar Code System Provides Accurate Work in Process Count," *Industrial Engineering* 20, no. 10 (October 1988), 34–35; Stan Stec, "Information Please: What Are Some of the Applications of Bar Code Technology?" *Management Accounting* 69, 53; and "Bar Code System Gives Timely Information for Improved Cost Control," *Industrial Engineering* 19 (February 1987), 84–86.

Quantity/Reorder Versus Periodic Inventory Systems

To manage inventories of independent demand items, production/operations managers must select either a Q/R system or periodic inventory system. (Within an organization of any size, both systems exist, but in different settings.) The following facts are important to consider when choosing which system to use.

1. *The periodic system requires less employee time than the Q/R system.* In the Q/R system, each item must be counted as it is issued or demanded. In the periodic system, no person is required in the inventory area except at the end of the period, when a physical inventory count must be taken. The periodic system is especially good for raw material and supply inventories for which tight security is not necessary.
2. *The periodic system requires less calculating time than the Q/R system.* In the Q/R system, each issue or demand from stock must be subtracted to obtain net inventory. If this is not done, a reorder point might be skipped. *Systemic costs,* the costs of running the system, are generally less with the periodic system.
3. *The periodic system may require more buffer stock to protect against uncertain demand and lead time.* If order quantity and reorder point of the Q/R system and base stock and reorder time of the periodic system all are mathematically derived to minimize costs, there is no advantage to one system over the other. However, in the periodic system, the reorder time is often set to yield a nonoptimal weekly or monthly physical inventory resulting in higher costs.
4. *The periodic system may result in more stockouts when unusually high demand occurs.* When one or successive periods of unusually large demand occur, the Q/R system can react more quickly because it keeps track of net inventory with each unit demanded.

BEHAVIORAL PITFALLS IN INVENTORY CONTROL

Rational Decision Making Establishing the inventory operating doctrine involves a decision process that is rational, logical, and unemotional. As operations managers, you should be aware that people making inventory decisions interject their own biases and individual traits into the decision-making process from time to time. The people you work with are complex, with wants and desires of their own, and they should not be expected to behave like machines. The inventory management *process* is rational, but the people involved in the process are not always rational.

Feedback Operations managers must monitor inventory levels and make adjustments within the production planning and control process when they discover that actual output deviates from planned output. These adjustments might well involve decisions to build inventory, reduce inventory, or change inventory procedures and operating doctrines. Inventory cannot be controlled unless:

1. Performance and inventory levels are monitored.
2. Actual performance and material usage are compared with planned performance and usage.
3. Inputs to the conversion process, especially the capital inputs of inventory, are adjusted.

Performance should be compared using feedback in the form of status reports, prepared manually or by the computer, as well as first-hand impressions from touring the facility. There is no good substitute for walking through the conversion process yourself—whether your organization is a bank, restaurant, school, or manufacturing facility—so you can compare your first-hand observations with planned conditions and quickly make adjustments for discrepancies you may find.

Inventory Policy Often, top management adjusts aggregate inventory levels. These manufacturing and operations policy decisions should be well grounded in cost analysis. Top executives should guard against making frequent and drastic inventory policy changes; doing so might inadvertently increase overall production costs.

Individual risk-taking propensity The degree to which an individual tends to take or avoid risks.

Individual Risk-taking Propensity As you probably know from your own experience, people vary considerably in their tendencies to take chances. Some people thrive on taking risks; others are risk-averse. Any banker can tell you that among checking account customers are a certain percentage who keep far too many cash reserves in low interest-bearing accounts because they are afraid of future uncertainty. Operating managers can also be risk-averse. In their overreactions to the possibility of a stockout, they may carry excessive buffer stocks.

On the other hand, some people are high rollers, risk takers. As operations managers or supervisors, people who take excessive risks are just as damaging to inventory control as are people who are too risk-averse. They may allow inventory levels to vary drastically and cause stockouts, high costs, and adverse effects in other operations subsystems. Individuals' propensities to take risks controlling the organization's inventory should be assessed carefully. Extreme behaviors are costly to operations.

SUMMARY

In this chapter we continued our discussion of inventory control and stochastic (variable) inventory models, which are required when demand, lead time, or both are variable. We stressed that the operations manager is most interested in the distribution of demand during lead time, a critical factor in establishing buffer stocks and the reorder point.

We saw that money can be saved in inventory systems by evaluating the ABC classification, blanket rules, stochastic demand and lead times, high stockout cost items, and safety stocks. This chapter listed numerous inventory control procedures for practical application, among them the cardex file system and IBM's MAPICS.

Primarily, inventory control is a rational process that lends itself to logical procedures. Behavioral pitfalls in inventory control involve the irrationality of decision makers, lack of control, poorly established inventory policies, and the variability in people's propensity to take risks.

CASE

Good Shepherd Home

The Good Shepherd Home is a long-term care facility with an 80-bed capacity located in San Mateo, California. Mr. Scott, the administrator, is concerned about rising food costs. He questions whether administration is as efficient as it might be and realizes that food, a "raw material" for his food services, has increased in price significantly. Mr. Scott decides to investigate food services more closely.

Analyzing last month's purchased items, Mr. Scott summarizes a random selection of items. Mr. Scott wonders what interpretation he should make about these typical items. He has looked at 100 stock items and is considering tighter controls on the 40 stock items for which 400 order-units (dozens, cases, pounds, etc.) have been ordered.

Typical Inventory Items

Number of Stock Items	Quantity Ordered (in units)	Total Cost (in $)	Average Inventory (in $)
3	50	3,500	1,200
12	150	2,500	900
20	200	1,500	600
40	400	2,000	200
25	200	500	100

Of particular interest is a problem with a perishable good, bread. Since the home has residents in independent living units and eating at the home irregularly, bread demand is uneven. Bread is delivered daily and is used that day for table meal service only; the day-old bread is salvaged for dressing and similar dishes. Scott estimates the cost of bread to be $.75/loaf and the cost of day-old bread to be $.25/loaf. Scott says, "We should not be out of fresh bread at the table. Although man cannot live by bread alone, it is very important to our residents. I put a high cost on being out of bread—considerably more than the cost of a loaf. In fact, I think every time we run out of bread, it costs a dollar per loaf short in good will lost from our residents."

Knowing how Mr. Scott feels, the food services supervisor has a standing order for 30 loaves/day and twice that amount on Sunday. The demand for bread the last two weeks is shown below.

Bread Demand (in loaves)		
Day	Week 1	Week 2
Mon	20	19
Tue	15	27
Wed	21	20
Thu	30	32
Fri	31	27
Sat	19	16
Sun	42	39

In conversation with Mr. Scott, the supervisor says, "I recently heard about cost tradeoffs in food service inventory. I don't really see what item cost, carrying cost, ordering cost, and stockout cost have to do with proper nutrition. I try to buy good quality foods and spend less than $5/day on food for each resident. That's my objective."

Mr. Scott has heard, too, about cost tradeoffs, but he wonders what they mean and how they apply to a nursing home environment. To try to understand this better he talked to his bookkeeper. The supervisor says that she knows with certainty that demand for hamburger over a menu cycle is 200 pounds. Furthermore, the bookkeeper estimates it costs $12 to place an order and 20 percent of the hamburger cost to carry hamburger in inventory. Hamburger costs $1.55/pound. The dietitian says a menu cycle lasts two weeks, and Good Shepherd currently orders hamburger every week. Mr. Scott is puzzled by all this.

REVIEW AND DISCUSSION QUESTIONS

1. Explain three common criteria to measure and establish service levels, giving an example of each criterion.
2. What is meant by the ABC classification? How might an organization's inventory be analyzed using the ABC classification?
3. In Figure 13.1, why are the lines dotted? Is the optimal cost always associated with the lowest point on a cost curve? Why or why not?
4. Inventory control is a rational process in which decisions are often made irrationally. Explain.
5. Given a probability distribution of demand and a distribution of lead time, what alternatives exist for finding the probability distribution of demand during lead time? Select one alternative and explain how it works. Why is the distribution of demand during lead time important?
6. For Figure 13.3, explain how lead time and demand vary. What impact does such variation have on buffer stocks, if any?

7. Suppose a directive comes to a manufacturing facility from the controller strongly suggesting a 35 percent across-the-board reduction in inventory levels. The plant manager asks you to help explain the need for inventories in manufacturing. What points would you make in favor of inventories?
8. Select two general areas in which money might be saved in inventory control, and explain how you would plan a cost study for each.
9. Discuss the advantages and disadvantages of the periodic inventory system compared with the quantity/reorder inventory system.
10. Relate individual propensity for risk taking to decision making in inventory control.

PROBLEMS

SOLVED PROBLEMS

1. Actual daily demand and lead-time distributions are given below. What is expected demand during lead time? What is the minimum that demand during lead time will ever be?

Range of Actual Daily Demand (in units)	Days Demand Fits Range	Actual Lead Time (in days)	Number of Lead Times
1-5	2	2	2
6-10	6	3	3
11-15	2	4	2

SOLUTION

To find expected demand during lead time, we need first to find expected demand and expected lead time.

$$\text{Expected demand} = \frac{3(2) + 8(6) + 13(2)}{10} = 8 \text{ units/day}$$

$$\text{Expected lead time} = \frac{2(2) + 3(3) + 4(2)}{7} = 3 \text{ days}$$

$$\text{Expected demand during lead time} = 8 \times 3 = 24 \text{ units}$$

The minimum that demand during lead time will ever be is 3 units/day × 2 days = 6 units (not using midpoints for daily demand it *could* be 1 × 2 = 2 units).

2. Daily demand for mini wheels, a popular toy, is normally distributed with a daily mean of 60 cases and a standard deviation of 10 cases. Supply is virtually certain, with a lead time of three days. The cost of placing an order is \$6, and annual holding costs are 20 percent of the unit price of \$1.20. We want a 90 percent service level at our warehouse for customers who place orders during the reorder period. Service level is interpreted as the probability that there will be a stockout

of any size during lead time. Backorders are allowed. Once stocks are depleted, orders are filled as soon as the stocks arrive. We can assume orders arrive 200 days throughout the year. Determine the operating doctrine for mini wheels.

SOLUTION

$\bar{d}$ = 60 cases/day	L = 3 days
S = \$6	σ_d = 10 cases
I = .20	z = 1.282 for 90% service level
C = \$1.20	

Orders arrive 200 days throughout the year.

$$Q^* = \sqrt{\frac{2\bar{D}S}{IC}} = \sqrt{\frac{2(60)(200)(\$6)}{.20(\$1.20)}} = 774.59 = 775 \text{ cases}$$
$$\sigma_\mu = \sqrt{3(10)^2} = 17.32$$
$$R^* = \bar{d}L + z\sigma_\mu = 60(3) + 1.282(17.32) = 180 + 22.20 = 203 \text{ cases}$$

The operating doctrine for mini wheels is to order 775 cases when the on-hand inventory reaches 203 cases.

3. A Christmas tree supplier has evaluated weekly demand for November-December over the last seven years. Demand appears normally distributed with a mean of 350 trees demanded weekly and a standard deviation of 200. To ensure a fresh supply and maintain a reputation for quality, trees are cut weekly in anticipation of demand. A Christmas tree sells for an average \$6 wholesale locally and can be salvaged, if not sold locally, by shipping out of state at an average revenue of \$2 each (sold "not freshly cut"). Cost to raise and harvest a tree is \$3.75. What should be the weekly ordering (harvesting) quantity for the upcoming Christmas season?

SOLUTION

$$CF = \frac{C_u}{C_u + C_o}$$

If understocked, the lost sale cost is revenue less harvesting, \$2.25 (\$6.00 − \$3.75). If overstocked, the cost is harvesting less salvage, \$1.75 (\$3.75 − \$2.00).

$$CF = \frac{2.25}{2.25 + 1.75} = \frac{2.25}{4.00} = 0.5625$$

The optimal harvesting level will have 56.25 percent of the normal curve to the left of this stocking level. From Appendix A, we find that the area of the normal curve to be at Z = 0.157. Shown graphically in Figure 13.6, we need to find x, the ordering level.

$$x = \bar{\mu} + z\sigma_\mu$$
$$= 350 + 0.157\ (200) = 350 + 31.4 = 381.4$$

The supplier should harvest 381 trees a week, given these data, to optimize profits.

REINFORCING FUNDAMENTALS

4. A bookstore orders blue books (exam booklets) in boxes of one gross. Annual demand is even throughout the year and known with certainty to be 600 boxes. Lead time is known to be exactly one month. The cost of placing an order is \$16,

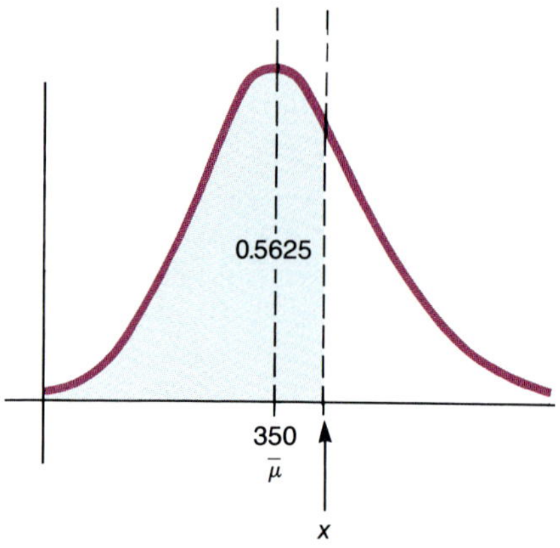

FIGURE 13.6

and annual carrying charges are 36 percent of the box price. The wholesaler gives the bookstore a quantity discount as follows:

Quantity (order in boxes)	Price/Box (in $)
1–49	7.50
50–99	7.35
100 or more	7.00

Establish the economic operating doctrine.

5. Actual daily demand and lead-time distributions are given below. What is expected demand during lead time? What is the minimum that demand during lead time will ever be?

Range of Actual Daily Demand (in units)	Days Demand Fits Range	Actual Lead Time (in days)	Number Lead Times
20–40	4	1	3
41–60	3	2	2
61–80	3	4	2

6. An electrical motor housing has an annual usage rate of 75,000 units/year, an ordering cost of $20, and annual carrying charge of 15.4 percent of the unit price. For lot sizes of fewer than 10,000, the unit price is $.50; for 10,000 or more, the unit price is $.45. Delivery lead time is known with certainty to be two weeks. Determine the optimal operating doctrine.
7. Daily demand for a manufactured part is normally distributed with a daily mean

of 80 cases and a standard deviation of 30 cases. Supply is virtually certain, with a lead time of three days. The cost of placing an order is \$15, and annual carrying charges are 20 percent of the unit price of \$6.50. We want a 90 percent service level at our warehouse for customers who place orders during the reorder period. Service level is interpreted as the probability that there will be a stockout of any size during lead time. Backorders are allowed. Once stocks are depleted, orders are filled as soon as the stocks arrive. We can assume orders arrive 200 days throughout the year. Determine the operating doctrine for this manufactured part.

8. The daily demand for a component assembly item is normally distributed with a mean of 120 and standard deviation of 15. Furthermore, the source of supply is reliable and maintains a constant lead time of four days. If the cost of placing the order is \$45 and annual carrying charges are \$0.75/unit, find the order quantity and reorder point to provide an 85 percent service level. Service level is interpreted as the probability that there will be a stockout of any size during lead time. Unfilled orders are filled as soon as an order arrives. Assume sales occur over the entire year.

9. A florist orders flowers weekly. Demand for carnations varies uniformly from 18 to 30 dozen a week. Carnations cost \$7/dozen and sell for an average price of \$11/dozen, some sold individually and some sold in arrangements. Salvage is virtually zero after a week's storage. Establish the ordering quantity for carnations. Explain your results in terms the florist will understand.

10. Daily demand for pickles for a local chain of fast-food restaurants is normally distributed with a mean of 30 jars and a standard deviation of 7. Supply is virtually certain with a lead time of two days; the cost of placing an order is \$2.50, and annual carrying charges are 80 percent of the unit price of \$.60/jar. A 98 percent service level is desired. Service level is interpreted as the probability that there will be a stockout of any size during lead time. The restaurant chain serves 365 days a year.

(a) Determine the operating doctrine for ordering pickles.

(b) Construct graphs similar to Figures 13.3 and 13.4 to portray this situation.

(c) What is the annual cost for pickle buffer stocks? Does this cost seem reasonable for a 98 percent service level?

11. For the fast-food restaurant chain in problem 10, suppose that exactly the same situation exists for coffee as did for pickles, except that coffee costs ten times as much per can as do pickles per jar.

(a) What is the operating doctrine for coffee?

(b) What is the annual cost for coffee buffer stocks?

(c) What conclusions can you reach concerning the effect price has on operating doctrine and buffer stocks (by comparing your answer with that of problem 10)?

12. For the fast-food restaurant chain in problem 10, suppose that exactly the same situation exists for chocolate syrup as did for pickles, except that chocolate syrup demand is 30 cans/day with a standard deviation of 28 cans.

(a) What is the operating doctrine for chocolate syrup?

(b) What is the annual cost for chocolate syrup buffer stocks?

(c) What impact does the variability of demand (the standard deviation) seem to have on buffer stocks (by comparing your answer with that of problem 10)?

13. Bilson, Inc., purchases all metal needed in bar stock form. With an annual demand of 4,500 units, an ordering cost of \$75, and storage costs of 25 percent of the unit cost, what is the optimal order quantity given these price breaks:

(a) 0–299, $60/unit
(b) 300–499, $50/unit
(c) 500 or more, $40/unit.

CHALLENGING EXERCISES

14. The demand per period for an important inventory item seems to have the following probability distribution:

Demand (in units)	Probability of Demand
5	.4
6	.2
7	.1
8	.3

All stock to meet the demand for a period must be acquired at the start of the period. The product costs $5/unit and sells for $8/unit. Any leftover units at the end of a period must be disposed of as "seconds" at a selling price of $4/unit. On the other hand, if the stock becomes depleted, there is no cost associated with the shortage.

(a) Under these conditions, is it more profitable to stock six or seven units at the start of each period?
(b) If there were a cost associated with a shortage and a probability of a shortage for each demand level, how would you modify your answer to part (a)?

15. Demand for the local daily newspaper at a newsstand is normally distributed with a daily mean of 210 copies and standard deviation of 70. A newspaper sells for $.25 cents and costs $.20 to purchase. Day-old newspapers are very seldom requested, and therefore they are destroyed. What should the newsstand's daily order be to maximize profits?

16. A bank purchases promotional ball point pens for $3 each. The company that supplies the pens suggests that if the imprinted pens were ordered in twice the quantity, a 35 percent discount could be arranged. At present the bank orders 100 pens every two months. Ordering costs are $12, and the bank's cost of money is 18 percent. What ordering policy should be followed? Show your analysis to support your decision.

17. Products in the Economize line of a hardware producer are so similar that they are grouped and viewed as one product. Daily demand for this group is normally distributed with a mean of 20 units and a standard deviation of 10. Supply is virtually certain with a lead time of five days. The cost of placing an order is $27.50, and carrying charges are 20 percent of the unit price of $94. Management wants a 90 percent service level for customers who place orders during the reorder period. Service level is interpreted as the probability that there will be a stockout of any size during lead time. Backorders are allowed. Once stocks are depleted, orders are filled as soon as the stocks arrive. Assume sales are made over the entire year.

(a) Find the optimal reorder point.
(b) Draw a units-in-inventory versus time graph of this inventory situa-

tion, identifying the optimal reorder point on the graph and identifying data given or calculated where possible.

18. At McDonald's on the Ohio State University campus, six-ounce paper cups are used at a rate of 120 cups/day and are ordered in lots of 850 dozen. McDonald's is open 360 days a year. After several months on the job, a business school student (employee) finds that lead time is virtually a constant three days, not instantaneous as was previously assumed, and that daily demand varies with a mean of 120 cups and a variance of 36 cups. The manager wants to run out of cups once every six months or less often (an average of two times a year). Establish an operating doctrine for management.

19. As operations manager of a group of stock market analysts for a small brokerage firm, you find yourself faced with the following problem. The company's market research group suggests you "follow" (analyze) some "risky" stocks, since some customers want this kind of investment. The research group estimates maximum demand from any one "high risk taker" to be in any one month:

Demand (in number of risky stocks)	Probability of Demand
2	.30
4	.20
5	.10
6	.30
8	.10

The group also assesses a cost associated with not being able to supply the number of risky stocks demanded to be \$100 (loss of customer possibilities) per request. Furthermore, you know that your unit costs per month (C) to "follow" stocks are:

$$C = \begin{bmatrix} \$25D \text{ for } D \leq 4 \\ \$15D \text{ otherwise} \end{bmatrix}$$

where D is the number of risky stocks demanded. How many risky stocks should you "follow" each month?

20. A bank is evaluating teller capacity. Daily demand for teller services is as shown below. The cost of not serving a customer or having the customer leave angry because of a long wait is estimated to be high and should be avoided. The cost of a teller is \$75/day. A teller typically generates \$250/day in revenue. Develop a decision rule for the bank to follow in comparing current capacity with the most economical capacity.

Average Daily Demand (in number of busy tellers)	Days Demand Fits Range
0	0
1–2	13
3–4	21
5–6	10
7 or more	6

21. You have a product whose average weekly sales are 600 units. By looking at records of past demand, you find that the demand pattern has followed the distribution below:

Weekly Demand Above (in units)	Percent of the Time Demand Above
400	100
450	90
500	79
550	64
600	50
650	22
700	8
750	3
800	0

The cost of carrying an item on inventory for one year is $1.30. Order cost is fixed at $72. Lead time is constant at one week. The stockout policy has been set to allow two stockouts/year on average. Determine the order quantity and the safety stock that minimize the variable costs.

22. Wendy's is interested in analyzing the ordering policy for some perishable items, including tomatoes. The daily demand for crates of tomatoes is shown below.

Actual Daily Demand (in crates)	Probability of Demand
2	.3
4	.4
6	.1
7	.1
9	.1

This cost of ordering tomatoes is small, estimated to be $.25 for a crate; a crate costs an average of $24. Carrying charges are 20 percent of the crate cost. The average shelf life of tomatoes is one day with zero salvage value. If a crate that is not on hand is demanded, the cost of being out of tomatoes is estimated to be $100. Lead time is known with certainty to be one day. To simplify ordering, management will only order lots of 2, 4, 6, 7, or 9 crates. Establish an optimal operating doctrine for Wendy's, which operates 365 days a year.

UTILIZING QSOM COMPUTER SOFTWARE

23. The manager of a health food outlet has determined that demand for her all-natural yogurt is approximately 20 quarts/week. The store operates 50 weeks/year. Her ordering costs are $25, and due to limited freezer space, carrying costs are $10/quart/year. The supplier offers 3 price breaks: Price/quart is $3.00 for 1–39 quarts; $2.90 for 40–79 quarts; $2.80 for 80–119 quarts, and $2.70 for 120 or more quarts. By means of QSOM's deterministic discount analysis submenu of the inventory theory program, determine the economic operating doctrine for the health food outlet. Use the "all units discounts" computer program option in the analysis.

24. A retailer has estimated that monthly demand for stone-washed jeans is 65 pairs. His ordering costs are $35, and carrying costs are $5/pair/year. The supplier offers 2 price breaks: $15/pair for 1–49 pairs, $14/pair for 50–99 pairs, and $13/pair for 100 or more pairs.

(a) Using QSOM's deterministic discount analysis submenu of the inventory theory program, establish the economic operating doctrine for this retailer. Use "all units discounts" in the analysis.

(b) Now assume that ordering costs drop to $15 and the supplier alters his discounts in the following manner: $15.00/pair for 1–49, $14.50/pair for 50–99, and $14.00/pair for 100 or more. How does this affect the economic operating doctrine?

(c) Refer back to the original data. Ordering costs are further reduced to $10, but as a result of fire losses in the warehouse, carrying costs skyrocket to $60/unit/year. How does this influence the economic operating doctrine? Why? (Use the original discount scheme.)

KEY TERMS

ABC Classification 502
Blanket rule 502
Cardex file system 504
Critical fractile 499
Individual risk-taking propensity 509
Lead-time demand 491
Manufacturing Accounting and Production Information Control System (MAPICS) 505
Quantity discount 487
Service level 501

SELECTED READINGS

Brown, R. G., *Decision Rules for Inventory Management.* New York: Holt, Rinehart & Winston, 1967.

Buchan, J., and E. Koenigsberg, *Scientific Inventory Control.* Englewood Cliffs, N.J.: Prentice-Hall, 1963.

Buffa, E. S., and J. G. Miller, *Production-Inventory Systems: Planning and Control,* 3rd ed. Homewood, Ill.: Richard D. Irwin, 1979.

Hadley, G., and T. M. Whitin, *Analysis of Inventory Systems.* Englewood Cliffs, N.J.: Prentice-Hall, 1963.

IBM, Manufacturing Accounting and Production Information Control System (MAPICS). Manufacturing Education Guide and MAPICS Features Education manual. (Order numbers GH30-0241-0 and SR30-0369-1). Atlanta, Ga., 1979.

Meredith, Jack R., and Thomas E. Gibbs, *The Management of Operations.* New York: John Wiley, 1980.

Sasser, W. E., R. P. Olson, and D. D. Wyckoff, *Management of Service Operations.* Boston: Allyn & Bacon, 1978.

Starr, Martin K., and D. W. Miller, *Inventory Control: Theory and Practice.* Englewood Cliffs, N.J.: Prentice-Hall, 1962.

Stevenson, William J., *Production/Operations Management.* Homewood, Ill.: Irwin, 1982.

CHAPTER 14

MATERIAL REQUIREMENTS PLANNING

As a real-life practitioner I can assure you that you are about to begin one of the most exciting chapters in this book. Material requirements planning (MRP) has become a centerpiece for all manufacturing systems. The key to successful production and operations management in a manufacturing company is the balancing of requirements and capacities. It's that simple and yet very challenging.

We at Hallmark Cards produce hundreds of products. About half of our annual sales volume consists of cards and the other half a wide variety of "social expression" products ranging from party goods, puzzles, pens, and pencils to mugs and stickers. In our card area, we produce 32 million cards a week. Without MRP, we would be totally out of control. This informative chapter will be one of the keystones of your professional career. To understand it is essential and to practice it can be a lot of fun. Remember what you are trying to do: Meet the needs of your customers. How? By having the product available when it is wanted. In production management, we do this by knowing in advance what our requirements are now and in the future and planning ahead to have the capacity available. We at Hallmark know this principle and practice it. It's not a theory—it's the real world.

Al Sondern
Corporate Vice President
Hallmark Cards, Inc.
Kansas City, Missouri

Material requirements planning (MRP) A system of planning and scheduling the time-phased materials requirements for production operations.

Mr. Sondern's remarks give clear evidence that managing conversion systems effectively entails attention to materials management, including procuring materials, coordinating materials availability, and controlling materials utilization. As a practitioner Mr. Sondern recognizes that the complexities of producing numerous different products can cause confusion, inefficiencies, and inferior customer service. Management is better able to control in such an environment if it gets timely and accurate information. A *material requirements planning* (MRP) system can provide this vital information.

PLANNING FOR MATERIALS NEEDS

In recent years material requirements planning systems have replaced reactive inventory systems (discussed in Chapters 12 and 13) in many organizations. Managers using reactive systems ask, "What should I do *now?*," whereas managers using planning systems look ahead and ask, "What will I be needing in the *future?* How much and when?"

Reactive systems are simpler to manage in many respects but have serious drawbacks, in particular, high inventory costs and unreliable delivery performance. The newer way, the planning system, is more complex to manage, but it offers numerous advantages. It reduces inventories and their associated costs because it carries only those items and components that are needed—no more and no less. By looking ahead to ensure that all materials are available when needed for product buildup, it reduces order processing delays. By setting realistic job completion dates, jobs get done on time, order promises are kept, and production lead times are shortened.

Improved customer service and other advantages come at a cost, however. They require a system for accurate inventory and product buildup information. They also require a realistic master production schedule (MPS) to specify when various quantities of end items will be completed. Finally, and perhaps most important, they require a certain *discipline,* a commitment by schedulers, supervisors, managers, and shop floor employees to make the system work. Once MRP job priorities and schedules are set, they must be adhered to. When discrepancies between planned progress and actual job progress arise, the system must be adjusted so that plans materialize. The key to getting this employee commitment is in keeping the system honest, accurate, and believable.

DEMAND DEPENDENCY

Demand dependency is an important consideration in choosing between reactive and planning systems. Recall from Chapter 3 that demand dependency is the degree to which the demand for some item is associated with the demand for another item. With *independent demand,* demand for one item is unrelated to the demand for others. In the *dependent demand* situation, if we know the demand for one item, we can deduce the demand for one or more related items. If, for example, the demand for an end product is known, we can calculate how many of its subcomponents are needed, because their demand is directly dependent on the end-item demand.

In the past, industry used reactive inventory control systems (such as the order quantity reorder point system) as the mainstay, ignoring the distinction between dependent and independent demand. More recently, however, we've learned that inventory planning systems such as MRP are more beneficial than reactive systems for dependent demand items. We don't need large safety stocks for dependent demand items because we usually know exactly how many will be needed. Furthermore, we don't need to accumulate excessive cycle stocks of dependent demand items in advance of when items are needed. Our MRP systems use accurate information about components as a substitute for excessive inventories of those components.

APPLYING MRP AS A SCHEDULING AND ORDERING SYSTEM

MRP is a system of planning and scheduling the time-phased materials requirements for production operations. As such, it is geared toward meeting the end-item outputs prescribed in the master production schedule as shown in Figure 14.1. MRP also provides information such as due dates for components that are subsequently used for shop floor control. Once this MRP information is available, it enables managers to

FIGURE 14.1 **The operations planning and scheduling system**

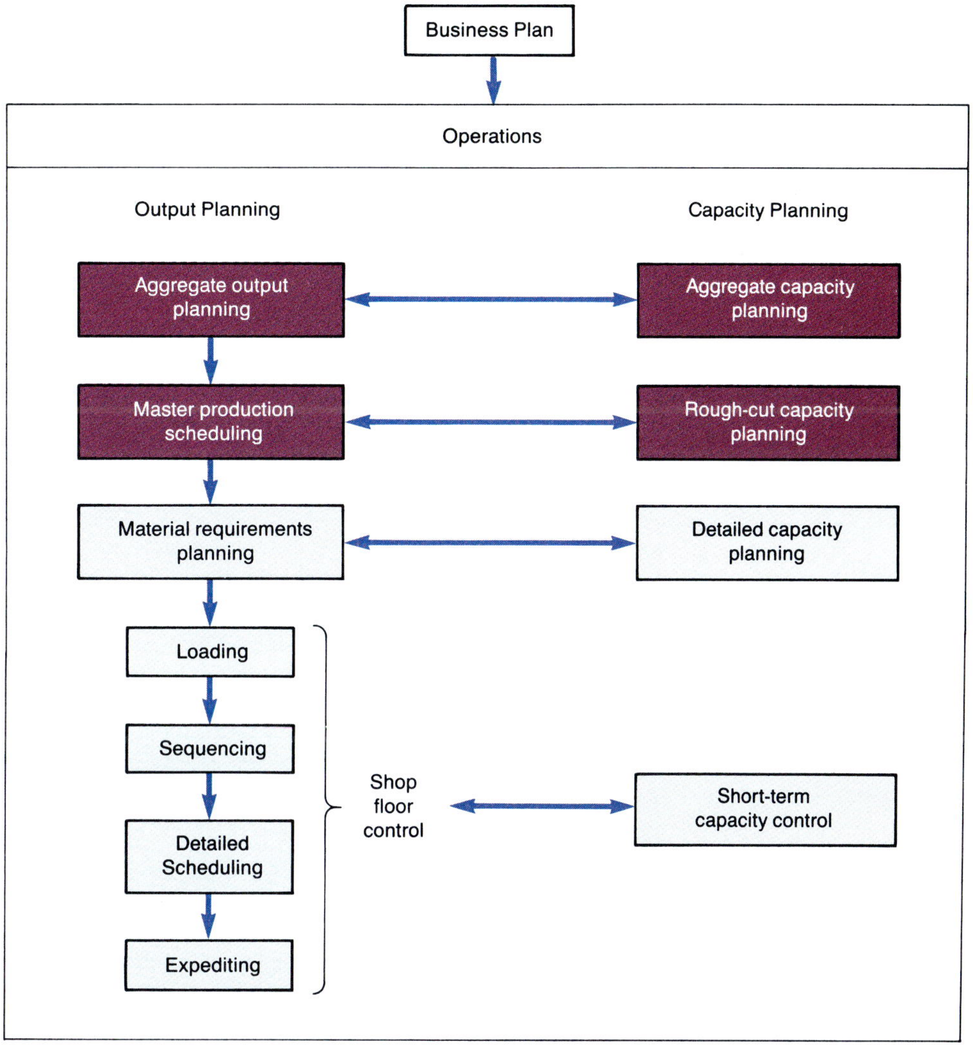

estimate the detailed capacity requirements for each work center. MRP's role in coordinating these activities becomes evident as we examine its objectives and methods in greater detail.

MRP OBJECTIVES AND METHODS

MRP provides the following:

1. *Inventory reduction.* MRP determines how many of a component are needed and when, in order to meet the master schedule. MRP enables the manager to procure that component as it is needed, thereby avoiding costs of excessive inventory.
2. *Reduction in production and delivery lead times.* MRP identifies materials and components quantities, timings, availabilities, and procurement and production actions required to meet delivery deadlines. By coordinating inventories, procurement, and production decisions, MRP helps avoid delays in production. It prioritizes production activities by putting due dates on customer job orders.
3. *Realistic commitments.* Realistic delivery promises can enhance customer satisfaction. By using MRP, production can give marketing timely information about likely delivery times to prospective customers. Potential new customer orders can be added to the system to show the manager how the revised total load can be handled with existing capacity. The result can be a more realistic delivery date.
4. *Increased efficiency.* MRP provides close coordination among various work centers as products progress through them. Consequently, production can proceed with fewer indirect personnel, such as materials expeditors, and with fewer unplanned interruptions because MRP focuses on having all components available at appropriately scheduled times. The information provided by MRP encourages production efficiencies.

MRP SYSTEM COMPONENTS

Figure 14.2 shows the basic components of an MRP system. Three major sources of information are mandatory in the MRP system: a master production schedule, an inventory status file, and a bill of materials file. Using these three information sources, the MRP processing logic (computer program) provides three kinds of information output for each product component: order release requirements, order rescheduling, and planned orders. Let's examine each of these information sources and outputs in more detail.

Master Production Schedule (MPS) The MPS is initially developed from firm customer orders or from forecasts of demand before the MRP system begins to operate. The MPS is an input to the MRP system. Designed to meet market demand, the MPS identifies the quantity of each end product (end item) and when it needs to be produced during each future period in the production planning horizon. Orders for replacement (service) components for customers are also entered as end items in the MPS. Thus, the MPS provides the focal information for the MRP system: the MPS ultimately governs the MRP system's recommended actions on the timing of procuring materials and producing subcomponents, which are geared to meeting the MPS output schedule.

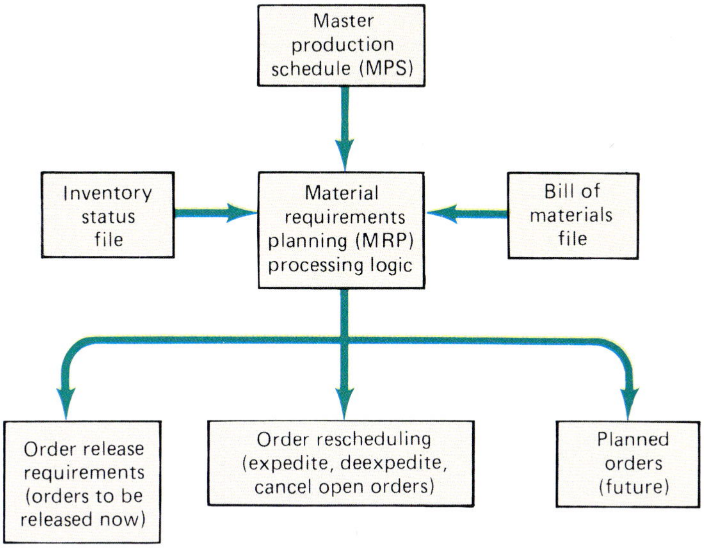

FIGURE 14.2 **Material requirements planning system**

Bill of materials A document describing the details of an item's product buildup, including all component items, their buildup sequence, the quantity needed for each, and the work centers that perform the buildup sequence.

Bill of Materials (BOM) The BOM identifies how each end product is manufactured, specifying all subcomponent items, their sequence of buildup, their quantity in each finished unit, and the work centers performing the buildup sequence. This information is obtained from product design documents, work flow analysis, and other standard manufacturing and industrial engineering documentation.[1]

Product structure The levels of components to produce an end product. The end product is on level 0, components required for level 0 are on level 1, and so on.

The primary information to MRP from the BOM is the *product structure,* an example of which is shown in Figure 14.3: One unit of end product A requires one unit each of components B and C. One unit of end product D requires one unit of component E and one unit of component F, which in turn requires one unit of component B and two units of component C.

[1]The central role of the bill of materials in MRP is discussed in Joseph A. Orlicky, George W. Plossl, and Oliver W. Wight, "Structuring the Bill of Material," *Production and Inventory Management* 13, no. 4 (1972), 19–42.

FIGURE 14.3 **Product structures for two assembled products**

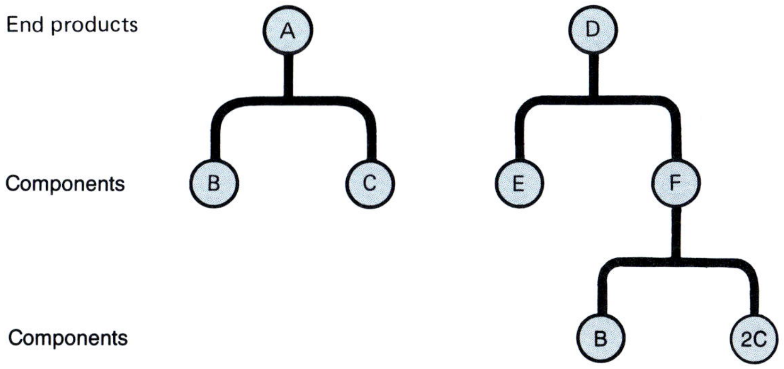

Item level The relative position of an item in the product structure; end items are upper-level; preliminary items in the product structure are lower-level.

In MRP terminology, A and D are *upper-level end items;* the components are *lower-level items.* By precisely identifying the levels in the product structure, we clearly show the relationships among the component items in all our end products. Each item in the product structure is given a unique identification number. Subsequently, by knowing the master schedule for end items, MRP can schedule and time-phase the orders for the correct lower-level component items in the product structure.

Inventory status file The complete documentation of the inventory status of each item in the product structure, including item identification, on-hand quantity, safety stock level, quantity allocated, and lead time.

Allocated quantity The quantity of an item in inventory that has been committed for use and is not available to meet future requirements.

Gross requirements The overall quantity of an item needed during a time period to meet planned output levels. Planned output for end items is obtained from the MPS. Planned output for lower-level items is obtained from the MRP.

Available quantity The quantity of an item expected to be available at the end of a time period to meet requirements in succeeding periods. Calculated as scheduled receipts plus planned order receipts minus gross requirements for the period, plus amounts available from the previous period.

Using this milling machine effectively depends on information from the master production schedule, the bill of materials (BOM) file, and the inventory status file so that the MRP processing logic can create proper order release requirements for the work that must be done.
Source: **Steve Dunwell/The Image Bank**

Inventory Status File The MRP system must retain an up-to-date file of the inventory status of each item in the product structure. This file provides accurate information about the availability of every item controlled by the MRP system which can then maintain an accurate accounting of all inventory transactions, both actual and planned. The inventory status file contains the identification number, quantity on hand, safety stock level, quantity disbursed (allocated), and procurement lead time of every item.

The MRP Processing Logic The MRP processing logic accepts the master schedule and determines the components schedules for successively lower-level items of the product structures. It calculates for each item in each product structure and for each time period (typically one week) in the planning horizon how many of that item are needed (*gross requirements*), how many units from inventory are already available, the net quantity that must be planned on receiving in new shipments (*planned order receipts*), and when orders for the new shipments must be placed (*planned order releases*) so that all materials arrive just when needed. This data processing continues until it has determined the requirements for all items used to meet the master production schedule.

Product structure (partial) for bicycle.
Source: Courtesy of Huffy Bicycles.

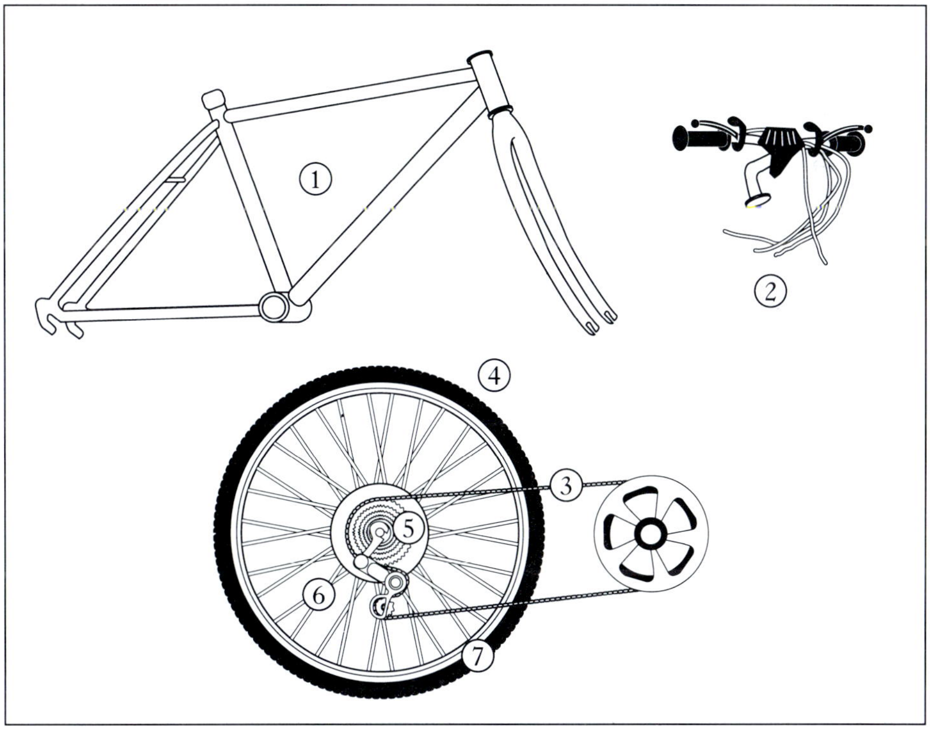

1. Level one: frame assembly; 2. Level one: control assembly; 3. Level one: drive chain assembly; 4. Level two: wheel subassembly (component of drive chain assembly); 5. Level three: axle (component of wheel subassembly); 6. Level three: spokes (component of wheel subassembly); 7. Level three: tire (component of wheel subassembly).

Planned order receipts The quantity of an item that is planned to be ordered so that it will be received at the beginning of the time period to meet net requirements for the period. The order has not yet been placed.

Planned order release The quantity of an item that is planned to be ordered and the planned period for releasing this order that will result in the order being received when needed. It is the planned order receipt offset in time by the item's lead time. When this order is placed (released), it becomes a scheduled receipt and is deleted from planned order receipts and planned order releases.

Scheduled receipts The quantity of an item that will be received from suppliers as a result of orders that have been placed (open orders).

Net requirements The net quantity of an item that must be acquired to meet the scheduled output for the period. Calculated as gross requirements minus scheduled receipts for the period minus amounts available from the previous period.

Management Information from MRP MRP output includes a report, similar to the sample in Figure 14.4, for each item in the product structure. The sample report shows that 400 units of this item are needed (gross requirements) in week 4 and another 500 are needed in week 8. No outstanding orders were previously placed, so there are no units of this item scheduled for receipt as of this time. There are, however, 50 uncommitted units of the item already available in inventory, and these will go toward meeting the week 4 requirement. Consequently, net requirements are 350 units for week 4 and 500 units for week 8. To meet these net requirements, the report indicates we should plan on receiving 350 units in week 4 and 500 units in week 8. Since this item has a three-week procurement lead time, the first order must be placed (released) in week 1 and the second order in week 5.

Item identification: #3201-Mounting bracket
Lead time: 3 weeks
Report date: week 0

		Week 1	Week 2	Week 3	Week 4	Week 5	Week 6	Week 7	Week 8
Gross requirements					400				500
Scheduled receipts									
Available for next period	50	50	50	50					
Net requirements					350				500
Planned order receipts					350				500
Planned order releases		350				500			

FIGURE 14.4 An MRP report for one item

This report clearly identifies the procurement actions required to keep production on schedule. It also gives suppliers advanced notification of the demands soon to be placed on them. As end-item demands change with time, modifications in the MPS will dictate corresponding adjustments of lower-level requirements. Weekly updating, for example, will revise schedules to reflect that an order must be received earlier (expedited), can be received later (deexpedited), or can even be cancelled. As you can imagine, this information system is especially valuable when there are many end items with hundreds or thousands of related subcomponents that must be coordinated among numerous suppliers and work centers. Table 14.1 defines some of the key terminology used in the MRP system and its component records.

THE MRP COMPUTATIONAL PROCEDURE

The MRP computational procedure uses the input information to calculate the current records for each component and item, as illustrated in the following example.

TABLE 14.1 Selected terminology of MRP component records

Allocated quantity: The quantity of an item in inventory that has been committed for use and is not available to meet future requirements.

Gross requirements: The overall quantity of an item needed at the end of a period to meet planned output levels. Planned output for end items is obtained from the MPS. Planned output for lower-level items is obtained from the MRP system.

Scheduled receipts: The quantity of an item that will be received at the beginning of a time period from suppliers as a result of orders that have already been placed (open orders).

Available quantity: The quantity of an item expected to be available at the end of a time period for meeting requirements in succeeding periods. It is calculated as scheduled receipts plus planned order receipts minus gross requirements for the period, plus amounts available from the previous period.

Net requirements: The net quantity of an item that must be acquired to meet the scheduled output for the period. It is calculated as gross requirements minus scheduled receipts for the period minus amounts available from the previous period.

Planned order receipts: The quantity of an item that is *planned* to be ordered so that it will be received at the beginning of the period to meet net requirements for the period. The order has not yet been placed.

Planned order release: The quantity of an item that is *planned* to be ordered and the planned time period for releasing this order that will result in the order being received when needed. It is the planned order receipt offset in time by the item's lead time. When this order is placed (released), it becomes a scheduled receipt and is deleted from planned order receipts and planned order releases.

EXAMPLE

Consider a company that makes kitchen chairs. Their simplest chair, model H, requires two subassemblies F and G, one for the seat and the front legs and another for the backrest and rear legs (see Figure 14.5). To assemble the seat to the front legs, a worker needs four fasteners. Similarly, to assemble the backrest to the rear legs, a worker needs four more fasteners. The two subassemblies are then attached to each other with four more fasteners. When the two subassemblies are combined, the chair is complete.

Figure 14.6 shows the *product structure tree* and component information including item identification, requirements for one parent item, lead time, and description. Each item in the product structure is categorized by a *level code.* The completed chair, item H, is the high-level item (level 0). Level 1 items are those whose parent is item H; these include items E, F, and G. Items A, B, C, D, and E are the individual components in level 2. Finally the lowest level (level 3) items are raw materials (RM) for the level 2 items.

Figure 14.7 shows a material requirements plan for shipping 500 chairs in week 8, and shipping 50 units each of items A and D in week 3 for replacing and repairing chairs in the field (raw materials have been omitted from the figure).

Without concerning ourselves with how this plan was developed, for the moment, let's concentrate on the information currently available for each item. We see that 100 units of H (finished chairs) are on hand prior to week 1. However, we need a safety stock of 50 units for unexpected demand. Thus, the net available for meeting the requirement of 500 units in week 8 is 50. Similarly, 200 units of G are on hand, but 30 units are for safety stock and 60 units were previously allocated to other job orders. Therefore, 110 units are currently available. For component A, there is a previous order (scheduled receipt) for 50 units that will be received in week 3.

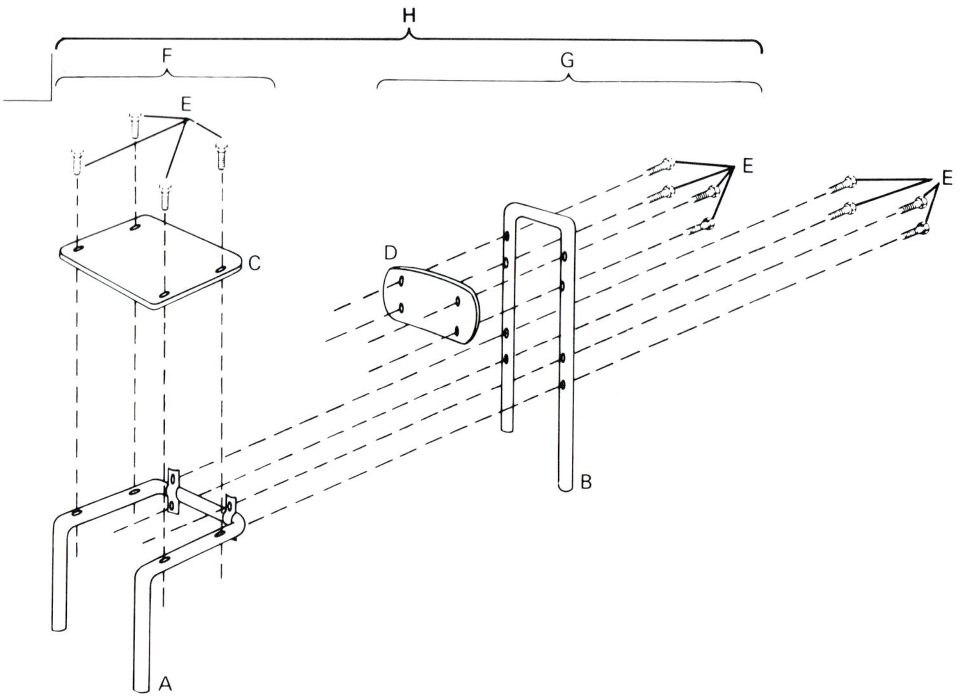

FIGURE 14.5 **Assembly diagram for chair model H**

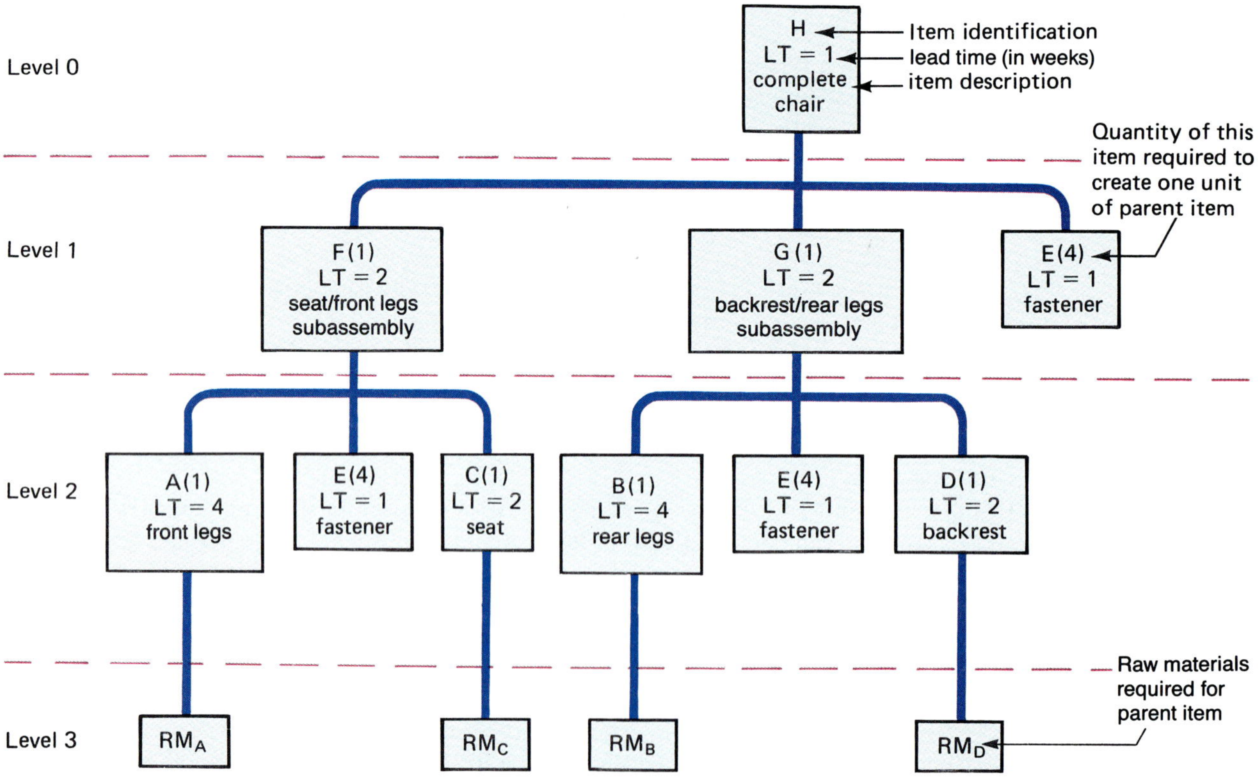

FIGURE 14.6 **Product structure tree and item information**

(Assumes lot-for-lot ordering)

Item ID	Low level code	Lead time (weeks)	On hand	Safety stock	Allocated			Week 1	Week 2	Week 3	Week 4	Week 5	Week 6	Week 7	Week 8	Notes
H	0	1	100	50	0	Gross requirements									500	from MPS
						Scheduled receipts										
						Available	50	50	50	50	50	50	50	50	0	
						Net requirements									450	
						Planned order receipts									450	
						Planned order releases								450		
G	1	2	200	30	60	Gross requirements								450		from H
						Scheduled receipts										
						Available	110	110	110	110	110	110	110	0		
						Net requirements								340		
						Planned order receipts								340		
						Planned order releases						340				
F	1	2	52	30	20	Gross requirements								450		from H
						Scheduled receipts										
						Available	2	2	2	2	2	2	2	0		
						Net requirements								448		
						Planned order receipts								448		
						Planned order releases						448				
A	2	4	50	20	30	Gross requirements				50		448				448 from F; 50: replacement parts ordered from field
						Scheduled receipts				50						
						Available	0	0	0	0	0	0				
						Net requirements				0		448				
						Planned order receipts						448				
						Planned order releases		448								
C	2	2	60	20	30	Gross requirements						448				from F
						Scheduled receipts										
						Available	10	10	10	10	10	0				
						Net requirements						438				
						Planned order receipts						438				
						Planned order releases				438						
B	2	4	150	20	30	Gross requirements						340				from G
						Scheduled receipts										
						Available	100	100	100	100	100	0				
						Net requirements						240				
						Planned order receipts						240				
						Planned order releases		240								
D	2	2	52	20	30	Gross requirements				50		340				340 from G; 50: replacement parts ordered from field
						Scheduled receipts										
						Available	2	2	2	0		0				
						Net requirements				48		340				
						Planned order receipts				48		340				
						Planned order releases		48		340						
E	2	1	500	300	150	Gross requirements						3152		1800		1800 from H×4; 3152 from G×4 + F×4
						Scheduled receipts										
						Available	50	50	50	50	50	0	0	0		
						Net requirements						3102		1800		
						Planned order receipts						3102		1800		
						Planned order releases					3102		1800			

FIGURE 14.7 Material requirements plan

Information Processing Sequence The MRP processing logic is applied first to the high-level items (end products) in the product structure, then to the items on the next lower level. It continues downward, level by level, until it has determined the requirements for all items in the product structure. In the chair assembly example, the completed chair H is the "level 0" (high-level) item requiring 500 completed units in week 8. All subsequent information processing is geared toward meeting this schedule. The inventory status file tells us that 50 units of H are currently available from inventory; these 50 units are carried forward as available at the end of week 7, resulting in a net requirement of 450 units in week 8. The MRP processing logic then calculates a planned order receipt in week 8 (at the time needed) for 450 units of H. When must this order be placed (released) so that it arrives when it is needed? The processing system answers this question by "offsetting" by the length of the lead time, one week as indicated in the inventory status file for H. This process is called *lead-time offsetting.* The result is the planned order release at the beginning of week 7, which, after the one week lead time, will result in a receipt of 450 units at the beginning of week 8.

Lead-time offsetting The process of determining the timing of a planned order release; backing off from the timing of a planned order receipt by the length of lead time.

Having determined requirements for all level 0 items, processing commences on the items in the next lower level, either F or G in the product structure at level 1 (item E at level 1 is a special case to be discussed soon). Level 1 items are considered next, because they are the only items needed to produce the level 0 item. The gross requirements for components G and F are determined by the planned order releases of the higher-level item H, 450 units in week 7. In general, the gross requirements for a lower-level item must include the planned order releases of the parent item for that time period. Then net requirements for F and G can be determined, and planned order receipts can be determined for the period. As was done for H, lead times are offset for F and G to determine planned order releases. The processing logic now proceeds to the next lower level of the product structure and determines requirements for items A–E. Then, raw materials requirements are determined.

Indented Bill of Materials To do its level-by-level calculations, the MRP processing logic obviously needs information about an end item's relationship to all its subcomponents. The *indented bill of materials* provides this information. Our model H chair (the end item) has an indented bill of materials (see Table 14.2) with the same information as its product structure tree, except it is now in a convenient computational format. We can see quickly how many of which components are required at each level for one complete chair.

Indented bill of materials A chart showing an end item's components, level by level, with increasing indentations to reflect the lower levels.

Product Explosion To create a parent item we often need multiple units of a lower-level item. One unit of H, for example, requires four units of E. Hence, the

TABLE 14.2 Indented bill of materials for Model H chair

Level	Quantity	ID	Description
.1	1	F	Seat/front leg subassembly
..2	1	A	Front legs
..2	4	E	Fastener
..2	1	C	Seat
.1	1	G	Back/rear leg subassembly
..2	1	B	Rear legs
..2	4	E	Fastener
..2	1	D	Back
.1	4	E	Fastener

Product explosion The process of determining from the product structure and planned order releases the gross requirements for components.

planned order releases of 450 units of H in week 7 must be multiplied by four ($4 \times 450 = 1{,}800$) to determine the gross requirements for E in week 7. This process is called *product explosion* or *bill of materials explosion.*

Low-Level Coding Often a single item is in the product structure of several end items, or it exists in several levels of one product structure. Item E, for example, exists at both levels 1 and 2 for end-item H. To make calculations efficiently for such an item, MRP by convention assigns the item to the lowest level in which it occurs in the product structure. Thus, E is treated as a level 2 item; gross requirements are determined from the planned order releases of its parent items F, G, and H.

USING MRP OUTPUTS FOR MATERIALS DECISIONS

Action bucket In the MRP record for the current week, a cell calling for immediate action to meet the MPS goal.

As we saw in Figure 14.7, in order to maintain the planned production schedule, planned order releases for items A, B, and D must be acted on in the current week, week 1. These cells are the *action buckets.* The action is to release (launch) an order for the quantities in the planned order release/week 1 cell. MRP merely indicates what actions are needed to meet the MPS goal; now management must act to "make things happen"—to cause (control) the productive system to execute so that management gets the results it wants.

KEEPING MRP CURRENT IN A CHANGING ENVIRONMENT

MRP is not static; it is responsive to new job orders from customers and current shop conditions, as well as changes anticipated for the future. Consequently the MRP system must be updated with current information and, at the same time, it must provide stability for production operations in the face of continual change. Four aspects of MRP—pegging, cycle counting, updating, and time fences—are vital elements in this dynamic environment.

Pegging The process of tracing through the MRP records and all levels in the product structure to identify how changes in the records of one component will affect the records of other components.

Pegging Materials plans can be disrupted in various ways. *Pegging* identifies which components are affected by such disruptions. Pegging shows the level-by-level linkages among components and their time-phased status in the MRP records. Figure 14.8 is an example; it shows the current records for an end-item A and for its subcomponents B and C at two lower levels in the product structure.

If we discover that the 20 units of C (scheduled receipts) for period 1 cannot be completed, plans for B and A are affected. The planned order release for B (20 units in period 1) should be cancelled because its supporting materials (C) will not be available. Consequently, the planned order release for 20 units of A in period 2 will be futile and should be cancelled unless special action is taken now to obtain the 20 units of B that are required for week 2. If no special action is taken, gross requirements for item A in periods 3 and 4 cannot be met.

Similarly, if the master scheduler were to increase week 7's gross requirements for A from 10 to 30 to meet a special customer order, the pegging procedure traces down through the records to identify associated changes at lower levels. The planned order release for A in week 6 is raised from 20 to 30 (because the planned order release will not cover the new demand). The associated requirements for B and C are changed accordingly. The pegging procedure shows exactly which items' plans must be changed.

Item A: Level 0; Q = 20; LT = 1	Period						
	1	2	3	4	5	6	7
Gross requirements	10	10	10	10	10	10	10
Scheduled receipts	20						
Planned order releases		20		20		20	

Item B: Level 1; Q = 20; TL = 1							
	1	2	3	4	5	6	7
Gross requirements		20		20		20	
Scheduled receipts							
Planned order releases	20		20		20		

Item C: Level 2; Q = 20; LT = 1							
	1	2	3	4	5	6	7
Gross requirements	20		20		20		
Scheduled receipts	20						
Planned order releases		20		20			

FIGURE 14.8 Pegging the MRP records

Cycle counting Counting on-hand inventories at regular intervals to verify inventory quantities shown in the MRP.

Cycle Counting Accurate records are a must in MRP; otherwise, production schedules cannot be maintained, deliveries will be missed, and labor and equipment will be inefficiently used. *Cycle counting* ensures that on-hand inventories correspond to the quantities shown in the MRP records. With cycle counting, components are counted, including deducting defective units, at each stage of production and in storage areas on a regular basis. Then the MRP records are updated, weekly or daily, to reflect these actual inventory counts. The updated records show excesses or shortages of components and hence indicate how production schedules at various work centers need adjustment.[2]

Regenerative method A procedure, used at regular intervals, to update the MRP by completely reprocessing the entire set of information and recreating the entire MRP.

Updating When new jobs arrive or other shop transactions take place, the MRP system must be updated. Changes can occur in the master production schedule, inventory status file (such as revised lead times), or product structure, when engineering changes the product design, for example. Two updating approaches are available: the *regenerative* and the *net change* methods. They differ in updating frequency. The regenerative method completely reprocesses the entire set of informa-

[2]Various methods for cycle counting are described in T. E. Vollmann, W. L. Berry, and D. C. Whybark, *Manufacturing Planning and Control Systems,* 2nd ed. (Homewood, Ill.: Richard D. Irwin, 1988), chap. 3.

This inventory manager ensures the integrity of MRP by validating accurate data records through cycle counting (by weight) to ensure that on-hand inventories match the quantities shown in the MRP records.

tion and recreates the complete MRP from beginning to end at regular intervals, often weekly.

Net change method Method for updating the MRP system in which only those portions of the previous plan directly impacted by informational changes are reprocessed.

The *net change method,* on the other hand, reprocesses only those portions of the previous plan that are directly affected by informational changes. It updates the MRP each time a change is posted and exploded throughout the system. The updated output contains those parts of previous plans that have changed. To do this, net change systems can require substantial computer access and rather elaborate computer programs. The net change systems do not seem to be as well received by managers.

Time fence A designated length of time that must pass without changing the MPS, to stabilize the MRP system; afterward, the MPS is allowed to change.

Time Fence As you can see, the dynamics of the MRP environment create potential confusion. If left unchecked, the changes can lead to unstable and erratic shop operations (called *system nervousness*). Stability is gained by using *time fences* in the MRP system. The time fence is incorporated into the MPS and is the shortest lead time from raw material to finished production for an end item. Within the time fence, the MPS is fixed; rescheduling is not allowed, except under unusual circumstances.[3] Thus, for the model H chair (Figure 14.6), the time fence is found by using the longest lead time at each level of product structure plus the longest lead time for purchasing raw materials (not shown in Figure 14.6). The longest lead times at levels 0, 1, and 2 are 1, 2, and 4

[3]System nervousness and time fences are discussed in D. W. McLeavy and S. L. Narasimhan. *Production Planning and Inventory Control* (Boston: Allyn & Bacon, 1985), chap. 8.

weeks, respectively, so the time fence will be 7 weeks plus the raw materials lead time. Within this time fence, the MPS becomes frozen and the planned order releases are called *firm planned orders.*

Firm planned order A planned order release scheduled within the MRP time fence.

LOT SIZING

The MRP system generates planned order releases, which trigger purchase orders for outside suppliers or work orders for internal component production. Associated with each order is a setup cost: all the costs of placing and receiving an order. This raises the question of how much to order; one must consider the tradeoff of ordering costs and holding costs. Various lot sizing policies are possible. In our example for the model H chair, we assumed *lot-for-lot ordering:* order quantity equals net requirements for a given period. In MRP systems, economic considerations often result in order quantities that are larger than a single period's net requirements so that holding and ordering costs balance out. The *EOQ technique, the Wagner-Whitin algorithm* (an optimal procedure), and others can be used, some of which are more elaborate and expensive than others.[4]

Lot-for-lot ordering A lot sizing policy in which order quantity equals net requirements for the period.

Part-period method A lot sizing policy in which order quantity varies according to a comparison of holding versus ordering costs.

One lot sizing method, the *part-period method,* does not provide an optimal lot size, but it is a low-cost method that approaches optimality.[5] It generates various order sizes by comparing holding versus ordering costs. In the top half of Table 14.3 we see a series of net requirements for an item; in lot-for-lot ordering, this would result in seven separate orders. Assume that ordering cost (setup) per order is $100 and holding cost is $0.50 per unit per period, based on ending inventory for that period. Using lot-for-lot orders, the total ordering cost for the horizon is $700, and, if the item is ordered and received at appropriate times, holding cost is zero, as shown in the lower half of the table.

Looking at the part-period method, we know that an order must be placed to meet the net requirement of 50 units for week 1. If we increase this order size to include the 80 units needed in week 2, we incur a holding cost of $40 (80 units × $0.50/week) to store the 80 units from week 1 until they are used in week 2. The 80 week-2 units are less costly to hold than to order, so the order size in week 1 should be increased from 50 to 130 units. Should it be increased even further? If it also included the 40 units needed for period 3, the additional holding costs of $40 (40 units × 2 periods × $0.50/unit/period) would raise cumulative holding costs to $80 for this order. Since the additional holding cost is less than the $100 additional ordering cost, the order size should increase to 170 units. Increasing the order size by still another 90 units (required for week 4) would require carrying these 90 units for three weeks at a cost of $135 (90 units × 3 periods × $0.50/unit/period). Since this $135 exceeds the $100 ordering cost, we cannot economically justify including these 90 units in the order to be received in week 1. We therefore order 170 units to be received in week 1, and this order meets our requirements for weeks 1, 2, and 3. We must place additional orders to meet the requirements of future weeks. Table 14.3 shows an example of the

[4]See William A. Ruch, "Economic Lot Sizing in MRP: The Marriage of EOQ and MRP." Paper presented at the 19th annual conference of the American Production and Inventory Control Society, Atlanta, October 1976. See also Harvey M. Wagner and Thomson M. Whitin, "Dynamic Version of the Economic Lot Size Model," *Management Science* 5, no. 1 (October 1958), 89–96. A comparative evaluation of various lot sizing and sequencing rules is given in Joseph R. Biggs, "Heuristic Lot-Sizing and Sequencing Rules in a Multistage Production-Inventory System," *Decision Sciences* 10, no. 1 (January 1979), 96–115. See also E. Steinberg and H. A. Napier, "Optimal Multi-Level Lot Sizing for Requirements Planning Systems," *Management Science* 26, no. 12 (December 1980), 1258–71.

[5]See W. L. Berry, "Lot Sizing Procedures for Requirements Planning Systems: A Framework for Analysis," *Production and Inventory Management* 13, no. 2 (1972), 19–34; Wagner and Whitin, "Dynamic Version."

TABLE 14.3 Order receipts and related costs (in dollars) for two lot sizing methods

	Period								
	1	2	3	4	5	6	7	8	Total
Net requirement	50	80	40	90	0	60	120	80	520
Order Receipts									
Lot-for-lot	50	80	40	90	0	60	120	80	520
Part-period	170	0	0	150	0	0	200	0	520
Holding Costs[a]									
Lot-for-lot	0	0	0	0	0	0	0	0	0
Part-period	60	20	0	30	30	0	40	0	180
Ordering Costs[b]									
Lot-for-lot	100	100	100	100	100	100	100	100	800
Part-period	100	0	0	100	0	0	100	0	300
Total Costs									
Lot-for-lot	100	100	100	100	100	100	100	100	800
Part-period	160	20	0	130	30	0	140	0	480

[a]Holding cost = $0.50/unit/period held
[b]Ordering cost = $100/order

order receipts pattern of the part-period method and its resulting costs, as compared with the lot-for-lot method and its resulting costs. Note that the part-period rule outperformed the lot-for-lot rule by $220 in this example.

Lot-sizing, along with many other MRP features, is illustrated by Dow Chemical's MRP system, which is discussed in Operations Management Highlight 14.1.

DETAILED CAPACITY PLANNING

Detailed capacity planning An iterative process of modifying the MPS or planned resources to make capacity consistent with the production schedule.

Route sheet A document that shows the routing of a component, including the work centers and operation times, through its production processes.

Each time the MRP system is updated managers must ask whether shop capacity is sufficient to implement the current plan. *Detailed capacity planning* (also called *capacity requirements planning)* is a technique that addresses this question and it does so in more detail than the rough-cut method presented in Chapter 10. New information from MRP permits refinements that were not possible at the rough-cut level. Let's see how this MRP information is used in detailed capacity planning.

We reconsider the chair manufacturer discussed previously and do a detailed capacity analysis for component A (the front legs) shown in the product structure tree, Figure 14.6. A *route sheet* (Table 14.4) has been developed for component A; it lists the

TABLE 14.4 Route sheet for component A

			Standard Times	
Operation Number Sequence	Work Center	Lead Time (in weeks)	Setup Time (in hours/batch)	Operation Run Time (in hours/unit)
1	Metal cutting	1	1.0	0.05
2	Metal forming	1	3.0	0.20
3	Drilling	1	0.5	0.04
4	Finishing	1	2.0	0.15

OPERATIONS MANAGEMENT HIGHLIGHT 14.1

Source: P. Tesman/The Image Bank

MRP Provides the Right Formula For Dow Chemical

As project manager in the business operations planning group, Kenneth Steele knew the problems and some potential improvements for Dow Chemical's decentralized methods for materials management. Each of Dow's commercial business units was organized along product lines resulting in many indepen-

operations sequence, work centers, lead times in each center, and standard times for setup and run. This routing information, obtained from engineering and production records, is used to evaluate the capacity requirements for item A.

Operation set-back chart A time-scaled chart showing the sequence, component by component, of product buildup.

To visualize the time-phased capacity requirements, we first construct the *operation set-back chart* for the end item, chair model H.[6] The abbreviated chart in Figure 14.9 shows details only for component A; details for the other components are omitted.

[6]Set-back charts are described in Vollmann, Berry, and Whybark, *Manufacturing*, Chap. 4.

dently managed inventory and distribution systems. Incoming shipments of materials for production and outgoing shipments of products for customers were frequent. Moreover, these materials flows were not coordinated among the business units. The result was complex and expensive logistics. Dow sought a system that would integrate materials and distribution flows.

A special management team of inventory and distribution managers opted for a new MRP/DRP (distribution resource planning) system that does everything from sales forecasting to master scheduling to inventory management to distribution planning. The DRP module enables Dow to plan its shipments and foresee potential problems earlier. Rather than just reacting when shipping problems arise, purchasing and shipping can take advanced action before problems erupt, which is usually less costly than reactive action, because distribution planning gives the advance information. Being alerted to potentially late shipments ahead of time, Dow can revise production schedules or reschedule vehicles and shipments methodically, instead of expediting or suddenly switching to more costly modes of transportation (such as air-freighting a needed shipment). One reason Dow can foresee these "downstream" logistics problems is DRP's linkage with MRP. The transportation program of DRP is integrated with MRP so that production schedules are connected into the transportation system, revealing what can be shipped and when.

Because people working in different functional areas all share the same set of data on shipments, production schedules, and materials status, they now have a better understanding of how their decisions affect other areas of the business. A proposed boost in production is translated immediately and concretely into increased demands on purchasing (and suppliers) for additional materials, adjustments in existing in-house inventories, equipment changeovers for production, and arrangements for shipping the finished goods to customers as promised. Employees now see how different parts of the business relate to each other and how interdependent their activities are.

In addition to improved communications, the MRP/DRP system has yielded other benefits as well. Dow is providing better service to their customers because manufacturing now has available the right materials at the right time. Production makes better lot sizing decisions because the computer system quickly evaluates the cost of alternative run sizes before production decisions are locked in. Inventory costs have been reduced 20 percent. Overall, for both internal operations and service to customers, MRP/DRP has proved to be a valuable tool for Dow Chemical.

Sources: Keith R. McKennon, "The Challenge of Attracting Professionals," *Transportation & Distribution* (September 1988), 54–58; "MRP/DRP Aids Dow Chemical," *P&IM Review with APICS News* (November 1988), 33–34.

We can see from the set-back chart that the capacity required of the four work centers by component A depends on the planned order releases of its parent item, component F. It also depends on how many component As, if any, are already finished and available in inventory. This information is provided in the current MRP record for component A, shown in Figure 14.10. The gross requirements for A were calculated from the planned order releases of its parent item, component F. We see that the planned order releases for A are desired in weeks 1 through 4. The labor hours (capacity) that these planned order releases of its parent item, component F. We see that planned order releases required at each work center are calculated from the standard times in the route sheet (Table 14.4) and recorded in Table 14.5.

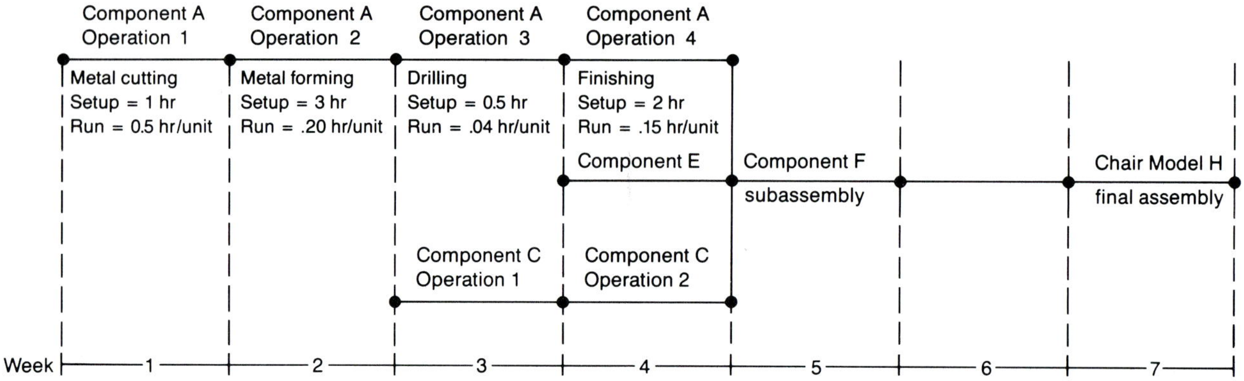

FIGURE 14.9 Partial operation set-back chart for chair model H

These capacity requirements take into account the projected availability of 10 units of component A for week 5; thus only 60 units, rather than the gross requirement of 70, require metal cutting capacity in week 1. Additional capacity at these four work centers will be required to produce component B, the rear legs, and from other chair models in the product line. By summing all the requirements from all sources (products), detailed capacity planning provides accurate estimates of the time-phased capacity demands on the work centers.

LIMITATIONS AND ADVANTAGES OF MRP

The limitations of MRP stem from the conditions that must be met before it can be used. A computer is necessary; the product structure must be assembly-oriented; bill of materials and inventory status information must be assembled and computerized; and a valid master schedule must be prepared. Another limitation has to do with data

		Period							
Component A (front legs) LT = 4		1	2	3	4	5	6	7	8
Gross requirements		80	90	90	90	70	70	70	90
Scheduled receipts		70	70	70	80				
Available	70	60	40	20	10	0	–	–	–
Net requirements		–	–	–	–	60	70	70	90
Planned order receipts						60	70	70	90
Planned order releases		60	70	70	90				

FIGURE 14.10 Current MRP record: component A

TABLE 14.5 Capacity requirements (in hours) at four work centers[a]

Work Center	Week 1	2	3	4	5	6	7
Metal cutting	4.0[b]	4.5	4.5	5.5			
Metal forming		15.0	17.0	17.0	21.0		
Drilling			2.9	3.3	3.3	4.1	
Finishing				11.0	12.5	12.5	15.5

[a]Setup + run times
[b]1hr/batch + 0.05 hr/uinit × 60 units = 4.0 hr

integrity. Unreliable inventory and transactions data from the shop floor can ruin a well-planned MRP system. Training personnel to keep accurate records is not an easy task, but it is critical to successful MRP implementation. In general, the system must be believable, accurate, and directly useful or else it will become an expensive ornament that is bypassed in favor of informal, ad hoc methods.

The dynamic nature of the MRP system is a vital advantage. It reacts well to changing conditions; in fact, it thrives on change. Changing conditions from the master schedule for several periods into the future can affect not only the end item but also hundreds, even thousands, of components. Because the production-inventory data system is computerized, management can make a new MRP computer run to revise production and procurement plans that react quickly to changes in customer demands as reflected in the master schedule.

MRP USER EXPERIENCES

In 1979, Anderson and Schroeder reported preliminary results of an MRP study sponsored by the University of Minnesota and the American Production and Inventory Control Society.[7] Questionnaires were mailed to approximately 1,700 industrial production/inventory control managers. The respondents' ideas about some major characteristics, problems, and benefits of MRP systems are shown in Table 14.6. Some users reported implementation problems—lack of communication about MRP within the company, lack of company expertise, and inadequate support from marketing and manufacturing personnel—all of which were viewed as more severe than computer hardware/software problems. When asked about the major problem in implementing MRP in their firm, the respondents most frequently answered "education of personnel" and "top management support."

Production/inventory control managers rated the accuracy of information in their production processes. These managers felt the least accurate information they had, overall, was on capacity (and capacity planning), market forecasts, and shop floor

[7]The data in this section are from John C. Anderson and Roger G. Schroeder, "A Survey of MRP Implementation and Practice," paper presented at 10th Annual Conference, American Institute for Decision Sciences, New Orleans, November 1979, and an earlier paper, "A Survey of MRP Implementation and Practice," MRP Implementation Conference sponsored by the Twin Cities APICS Chapter and the University of Minnesota, Minneapolis, September 1978. See also J. C. Anderson, R. G. Schroeder, S. E. Tupy, and E. M. White, "Material Requirements Planning Systems: The State of the Art," in McLeavey and Narasimhan, *Production Planning,* 277–91.

TABLE 14.6 Selected MRP system and environment characteristics (based on user responses)

Characteristic of System/Environment	Representative Measure of This Characteristic for All Respondents
Use regenerative updating method	70%
Use weekly updating of MPS	57%
Use pegging	55%
Use cycle counting	61%
Have automatic lot sizing by computer	45%
Use weekly time bucket	70%
Initiated MRP system after 1971	76%
Number of weeks in MPS	40 (average)
Installation cost (exclusive of operating cost)	$424,000 (average)
Estimated eventual system cost (exclusive of operating cost)	$715,000 (average)
Product data: produce both made to order and to stock	70%
Type of manufacturing: both assembly and fabrication	83%
Number of end items (per plant)	1,546 (average)
Number of components (per plant)	12,445 (average)
Number of levels in bill of materials (per plant)	6.2 (average)

Source: Anderson and Schroeder, "A Survey of MRP Implementation and Practice."

control. Their most accurate information was bill of materials records, followed by master production schedule and inventory records.

Finally, users assessed the benefits of MRP. They cited greater inventory turnover, shorter delivery lead time, better-kept delivery promises, fewer adjustments in internal production to compensate for unavailable materials, and fewer materials expediters.

It is evident from the results of this study that MRP is an improvement over previous production planning and control systems for many users. Its applications are growing as operations managers continue to develop better methods for materials management.

MANUFACTURING RESOURCE PLANNING (MRPII)

Historically, MRP systems typically were developed on a segregated basis, rather than as part of a highly integrated information system. More recently, however, companies are beginning to logically relate many of their information subsystems to the MRP system. Bills of materials data, for example, can be shared with an engineering information system data base; order release and order receipts data can be shared by the order billing and accounts payable information systems; and inventory status data from MRP can be part of marketing or purchasing information systems. This type of information integration, in fact, is exactly the impetus for a new generation of manufacturing planning and control systems.

Using telecommunications, information from the shop floor is instantaneously available in remote offices for Manufacturing Resource Planning.
Source: **The Image Bank**

Manufacturing resource planning (MRPII) An integrated information system that shares data among and synchronizes the activities of production and the other functional areas of the business.

Manufacturing resource planning (MRPII, or "closed loop" MRP) is an integrated information system that steps beyond first-generation MRP to synchronize all aspects (not just manufacturing) of the business. The MRPII system coordinates sales, purchasing, manufacturing, finance, and engineering by adopting a focal production plan and by using one unified data base to plan and update the activities in all the systems.[8]

As shown in Figure 14.11, the process involves developing a production plan from the business plan to specify monthly levels of production for each product line over the next one to five years. Since the production plan affects all the functional departments, it is developed by the consensus of executives and becomes their "game plan" for operations. The production department then is expected to produce at the committed levels, the sales department to sell at these levels, and the finance department to ensure adequate financial resources for these levels. Guided by the production plan, the master production schedule specifies the weekly quantities of specific products to be built. At this point a check is made to determine whether the capacity available is roughly adequate to sustain the proposed master schedule. If not, either the capacity or the master schedule must be changed. Once settled, the master schedule is used in the MRP logic, as previously described, to create material requirements and priority schedules for production. Then, an analysis of detailed capacity requirements deter-

[8]See V. Chopra, "Productivity Improvement Through Closed Loop MRP (Part 1)," *Production & Inventory Management Review and APICS News* (March 1982), 18–21. See also V. Chopra, "Productivity Improvement Through Closed Loop MRP (Part 2)," *Production & Inventory Management Review and APICS News* (April 1982), 49–51.

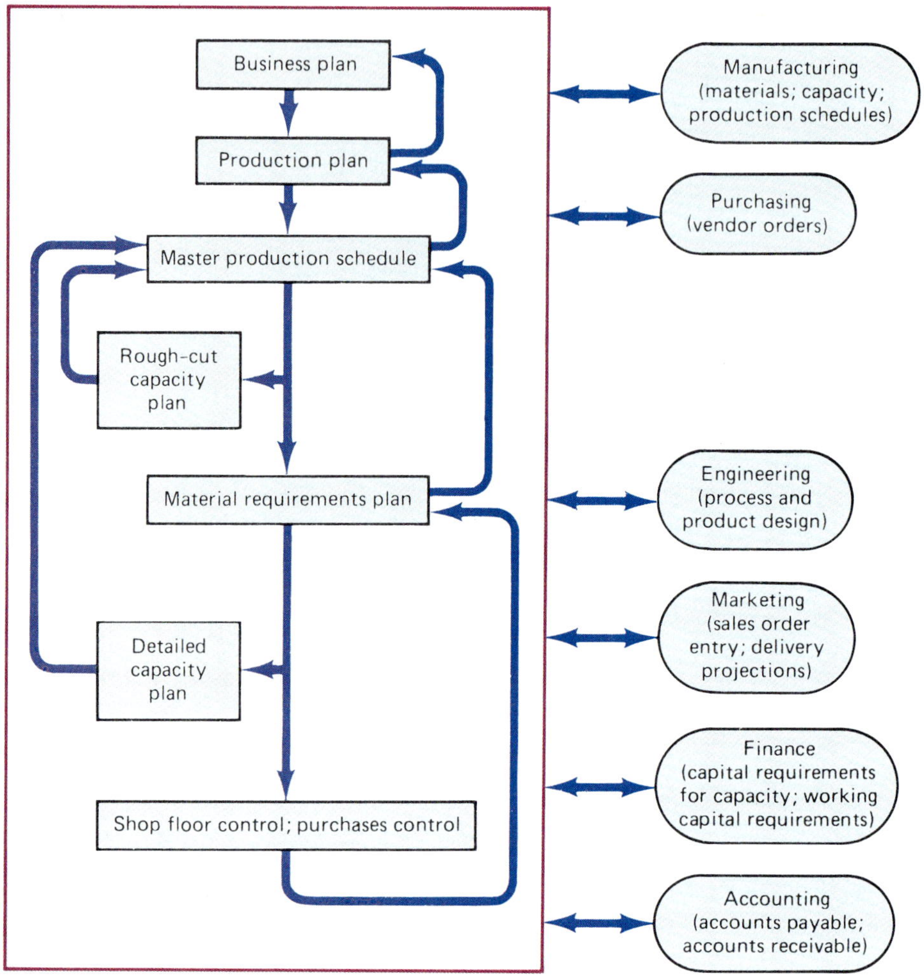

FIGURE 14.11 MRPII: An integrated system for planning and control

mines whether capacity is sufficient for producing the specific components at each work center during the scheduled time periods. If not, the master schedule is revised to reflect the limited available capacity. After a realistic, capacity-feasible schedule is developed, the emphasis shifts to *execution* of the plan: purchase schedules and shop schedules are generated. From these schedules, work center loadings, shop floor control, and vendor follow-up activities can be determined to ensure that the master schedule is met.

One use of the MRPII system is to evaluate various business proposals. If, for example, the output of product X increases by 20 percent in weeks 15 to 20 and that of Y decreases by 15 percent in weeks 10 to 15, how would operations and profitability be affected? The system can simulate how purchases and, hence, accounts payable are affected, when deliveries to customers and accounts receivable occur, what capacity revisions are needed, and so on. The company-wide implications of the proposed change can be evaluated, and various departments can be coordinated according to a common purpose. Operations Management Highlight 14.2 describes how Parke-Davis utilizes MRPII.

PURCHASING

Materials management Activities relating to managing the flow of materials into and through an organization.

Physical distribution Activities relating to materials management as well as to storing and transporting finished products through the distribution system to customers.

Purchasing Activities relating to procuring materials and supplies consumed during production.

Materials management brings together under one manager all the planning, organizing, and control activities associated with the flow of materials into and through an organization. *Physical distribution* is even broader, encompassing managing materials *flow into* the organization as well as managing materials *storage* and transportation *flow out* as finished products. In the context of operations management, we focus here on the narrower *purchasing function,* which provides materials, supplies, and services from outside vendors (suppliers). Accordingly, purchasing is an important boundary function that supports operations by acquiring major resources for the conversion process. For manufacturing firms involved in assembly, it is not unusual for the cost of purchased materials to exceed, as a percent of total product cost, the value added internally to the product through manufacturing and assembly. The importance of the purchasing function to the firm's performance and to operations performance is substantial.

PURCHASING OBJECTIVES

The objectives of purchasing can be summarized thusly: to efficiently provide fairly valued materials, supplies, and services in a timely manner. The following objectives are particularly important to operations:

1. *Good value.* Value is the combination of price and quality. Good value means a competitive price, though not always the lowest one.
2. *Reliable schedules.* On-time, just-in-time delivery means schedules are reliable, a crucial quality.
3. *Minimized investment.* Through careful analysis, the economics of order size, carrying costs, and stockout costs determine the investment level. For example, quantity discounts must justify the larger investment (for a larger order) or investment unnecessarily increases.
4. *Efficient administration.* Included here are executing a low-cost purchasing function, effectively coordinating activities with other internal functions (operations, engineering, etc.), and maintaining good relations with vendors.

EFFECTIVE PURCHASING

Effective purchasing means learning the purchase requirements, identifying qualified sources of supplies, minimizing the total cost of supplies and administering the purchase. Performing these tasks requires professional management skills, good computer resources, and recognition and support by executives throughout the organization.

Purchasing Requirements Typically, purchasing receives an item requisition that states quantity, description, and date needed. These internally generated requisitions are necessary because management allows only purchasing to deal with outside

OPERATIONS MANAGEMENT HIGHLIGHT 14.2

Source: SuperStock

Parke-Davis Is Looking Out for Your Health by Using MRP

Warner-Lambert has remained a tower of strength in the pharmaceutical industry by insisting on efficient, well-operated factories, including those of its Parke-Davis division. Producing products such as Tylenol, Parke-Davis must be able to trace materials, lot-by-lot, through the entire manufacturing system. Begin-

vendors—the proven, most efficient approach for acquisitions. Requisitions, however, are not always clearly written. Purchasing must seek clarification and understanding. At times purchasing may act as a facilitator between the vendor and the requisitioner so that the requisition is clearly communicated.

Sources of Supply Qualified sources of supplies are identified from salespersons, personal knowledge, advertisements, requisitioners, executives, trade and industry ning with raw materials receipts, through each stage of production, through final product shipment onto the retailers' shelves, tracing products is essential for consumer safety. This was never more true than during the tragedy involving contaminated Tylenol in 1983. Quickly identifying Tylenol batch numbers was possible only through extremely efficient tracing methods.

Parke-Davis is benefiting from an MRPII system at the Holland, Michigan, production facility that produces in bulk some 25 active ingredients. Inventory transactions can be more accurately traced throughout production since the facility switched to an in-house, microcomputer-based system (instead of a timeshared mainframe system). Delivery to customers has improved, and inventory turnover is approaching a new high level: 6.0 turns per year. Greater accuracy in tracing materials has also led to better process evaluations. Quality control and manufacturing staff now have useful historical information for identifying process improvements. These benefits arose, partially, by replacing the former time-lagged, overnight processing that left the plant up to three days behind in shop floor information.

Another reason for the plant's improvement in productivity however, is the employees' clearer perspectives on how their decisions affect other activities throughout the facility. The MRPII system has 14 interrelated modules that handle everything from incoming raw materials to inventory control, bill of materials, forecasting, production scheduling, product costing, and general ledger transactions. With a network of some 50 PC work stations, employees have accurate inventory and production information on which to base their decisions. They are making their decisions more carefully now because they can see directly how their decisions affect the plant. The plant as a whole is profiting, as are Parke-Davis customers.

Sources: John Merwin, "The Best Defense," *Fortune* (November 17, 1986), 178, 180; "Pharmaceutical Firm Employs Micro System for Lot Traceability," *P&IM Review with APICS News* (September 1989), 38–39.

associations, peers (other purchasing professionals), company records, and many other sources. Still, there are times when vendors must be developed to meet the specific needs of an organization. Quality, reliability, and understanding of the purchaser's business are all important parameters with which to evaluate a vendor. There is much to learn about developing vendor relationships from the Japanese, who use fewer vendors, develop "family" relationships, and make long-term commitments to the vendor.

Cost of Supply Useful approaches for evaluating supply costs include analyzing supply item histories, make-or-buy decisions, value analysis, traditional inventory economic analysis, and discounts. Also useful in cost control are evaluating the unit cost over time through simple historical statistical analysis of prices paid to vendor and evaluating vendor performance. Make-or-buy decisions focus on issues such as operations capability, need for production secrecy, investments required, volumes, importance to manufacturing, and so on. The analysis balances technical feasibility, capacity, and economic factors. Value analysis determines the required function of the item and then questions everything else, often ascertaining if less-expensive materials could be used. Traditional inventory analysis and quantity discounts were covered in detail in Chapters 12 and 13.

Prices and Value One of the functions of centralized purchasing is to get better prices than if purchasing were decentralized. Federal and state laws regulate pricing practices: price fixing, for example, is illegal, as is pricing differently the same item at the same quantity for different customers. Common sources for prices are lists, quotations, market prices, competitive bids, and direct negotiations.

Administering the Purchase Once purchase requirements are understood, costs evaluated, sources identified, and prices and values established, purchasing issues the supply order. Later the supplies are received, payments authorized, records kept, and in some cases orders expedited. These administrative functions must all be performed efficiently and in a timely manner to support operations, or the benefit of a centralized purchasing function is lost.

SUMMARY

This chapter introduced material requirements planning (MRP) as an information system that enables managers to improve the efficiency of operations, shorten delivery lead times to customers, and reduce inventory levels in many organizations today. We saw that MRP is applicable in environments where end items are produced from many demand-dependent components, assemblies, and materials with a known and stable sequence of product buildup. With information from bills of material, inventory status files, and the master production schedule, the MRP processing logic provides time-phased plans for procuring and utilizing materials. For each component in the product structure, MRP shows current and planned activities—open shop orders, planned order releases, scheduled receipts—for each period in the planning horizon.

MRP is especially useful in complex operations where new customer orders are arriving for a variety of products and where shop orders for various components are in different stages of completion. These numerous transactions are accommodated through periodic system updating with accurate shop status data. MRP procedures such as pegging, cycle counting, and time fences help stabilize a dynamic production environment by tracing which components are affected by change, ensuring that the availability of materials coincides with planned requirements, and freezing the short-term production plan so that imminent shop schedules are more predictable.

CASE

Solar Fabricators

Solar Fabricators, Inc., established in 1975, specializes in manufacturing components and supplies for residential construction. Its most successful product line is Solar Seal Window Assemblies, which consists of two independent products: a "main module" (one large standard-size window assembly) and a "secondary module" (one small standard-size window assembly). These and the other Solar products, including replacement and repair components, are sold directly to large building and construction contractors throughout the Sunbelt states. The master production schedule for these products specifies gross requirements of 2000 units in week 12 and 3000 units in week 16 for the main module; 1600 units in week 11 and 2500 units in week 16 for the secondary module; 400 units in week 7 for the installation tool for repairing the main module, and 600 units in week 4 for the measurement fixture replacing the secondary module. For all items, scheduled receipts, available units, safety stock, on-hand units, and allocated units are 0. Solar Fabricators wants to know which of two lot sizing methods, the lot-for-lot method or the part-period method, would be most advantageous for its material requirements planning. Production data are given in the accompanying table.

ID	Level	Description	Parent	Quantity Required (in units/unit of parent)	Supply Source	Lead Time (in weeks)	Ordering Cost (in $/order)[a]	Holding Cost (in $/unit/week held)
A	0	Main Module			SFI[b]	1	$ 400	$1.00
B	1	Packing container	A	1	OS	2	100	0.10
C	1	Window set	A	1	SFI	3	2,100	0.80
D	2	Measurement fixture	C	1	OS	3	1,800	0.10
E	2	Installation tool	C	1	OS	2	200	0.05
F	2	Framed window	C	1	SFI	3	1,600	0.60
G	3	Frame screw	F	4	OS	1	300	0.10[c]
H	3	Rubber gasket seal	F	1	OS	3	700	0.10
I	3	Glass panel	F	2	OS	4	1,200	0.30
J	3	Metal frame	F	1	OS	2	600	0.20
AA	0	Secondary Module	—	—	SFI	1	$350	$0.80
BB	1	Packing container	AA	1	OS	2	100	0.10
CC	1	Window set	AA	1	SFI	2	700	0.60
DD	2	Measurement fixture	CC	1	OS	3	1,800	0.10
E	2	Installation tool	CC	1	OS	2	200	0.05
FF	2	Framed window	CC	1	SFI	2	1,400	0.50
G	3	Frame screw	FF	4	OS	1	300	0.10[c]
HH	3	Rubber gasket seal	FF	1	OS	3	900	0.10
II	3	Glass panel	FF	2	OS	4	1,400	0.20
JJ	3	Metal frame	FF	1	OS	2	500	0.20

[a]Includes all costs of placing, processing, setup, and receiving an order. A purchase order for multiple items from a single supplier results in a 20 percent reduction of ordering costs per order.
[b]SFI means produced internally by Solar Fabricators; OS means purchased from outside supplier. Items B and BB are purchased from one supplier. Items D and DD are purchased from one supplier. All other items are supplied by different suppliers.
[c]Cost/10,000 frame screws/week held

REVIEW AND DISCUSSION QUESTIONS

1. Outline the purposes of MRP and explain how an MRP system can achieve these purposes.
2. Identify the basic issues of capacity management and describe how these are treated in detailed capacity planning.
3. Find or create example data illustrating inventory-related cost advantages of part-period versus lot-for-lot sizing policies.
4. Compare the cost tradeoffs involved in choosing among the following lot sizing rules: lot-for-lot, EOQ, and the part-period methods.
5. Explain the role of the master production schedule and how it relates to the other elements of an MRP system.
6. What is cycle counting? Explain how and why it is used in MRP systems.
7. Consider a product structure comprising four levels. Suppose, for one of the lower-level items in the structure, that a cycle count reveals that 10 fewer units are available than is shown in its current MRP record. Show how pegging is a useful procedure for this situation. Why?
8. Identify the pros and cons of frequent versus infrequent updating of MRP systems. What variables should the system designer consider in selecting an updating cycle?
9. How many time periods should be included in the time fence for an end item? Under what conditions should the time fence be violated by master production scheduling changes?
10. What information is needed for detailed capacity planning? Where does this information come from? Show how it is used in a capacity analysis.
11. Of what use are route sheets and operation set-back charts in MRP systems?
12. Within the context of overall planning and scheduling systems for operations, explain the role of MRP.
13. In what ways do material planning systems differ from reactive materials systems? Describe the advantages and limitations of each of these two types of systems.
14. Explain how the demand pattern for a component can be discontinuous or lumpy, even though the demand pattern for its parent item is smooth.

PROBLEMS

SOLVED PROBLEM

1. The product structures for end items A and S are shown in Figure 14.12. All items have a one-week lead time. Currently, there are 20 units of A available, 15 units of S, and 90 of C. The standard lot sizes are 50 for A, 35 for S, and 100 for C. The master production schedule calls for 20 units of item A and 15 units of item S for each of the next five weeks. An open order for 100 units of item C is scheduled for receipt in week 1. Create the MRP records for items A, S, and C.

Solved Problem

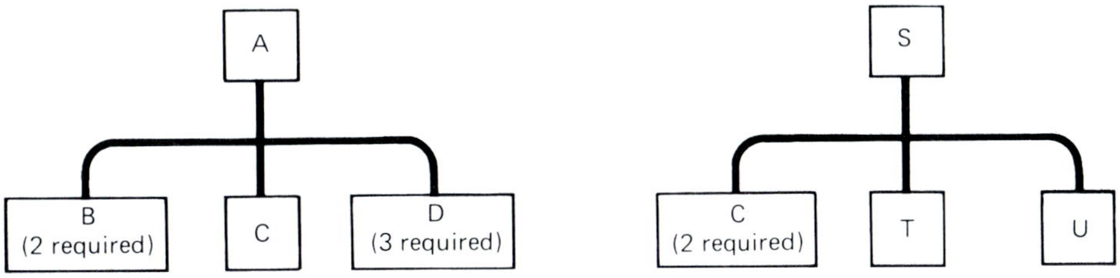

FIGURE 14.12

Item A		Week 1	2	3	4	5
Gross requirements		20	20	20	20	20
Scheduled receipts						
Available	20	0	30	10	40	20
Planned order releases		50		50		
Item S						
Gross requirements		15	15	15	15	15
Scheduled receipts						
Available	15	0	20	5	25	10
Planned order releases		35		35		
Item C						
Gross requirements		120		120		
Scheduled receipts		100				
Available	90	70	120	70		
Planned order releases			100			

REINFORCING FUNDAMENTALS

2. Creative Wood Products manufactures interior accessories for homes. One of their products, the Trophy Rack, is shown in Figure 14.13. Draw the product structure tree for the Trophy Rack, label it, and identify the low-level codes for its items.

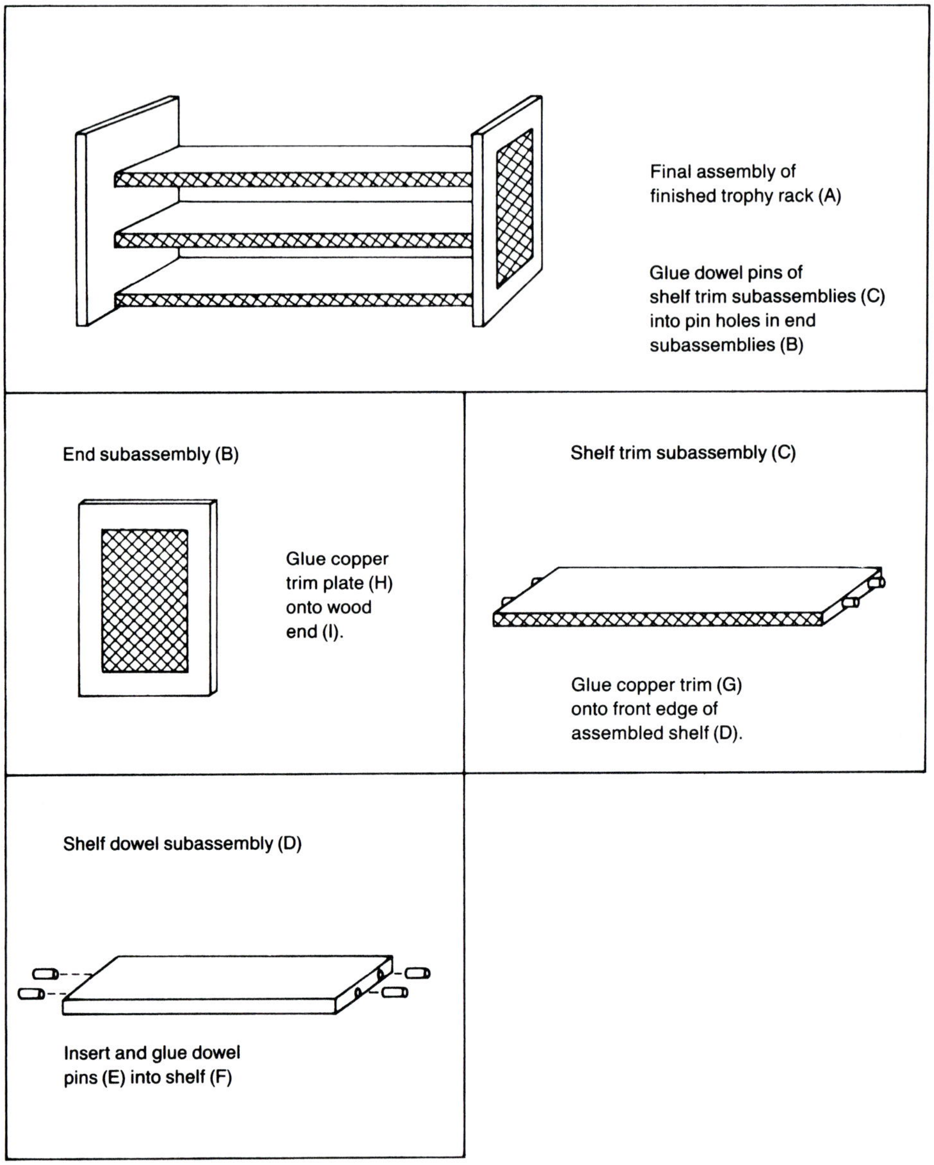

FIGURE 14.13 Trophy rack manufactured by Creative Wood Products

3. Product 800 is made from two 801 subassemblies, three 802 subassemblies, and two 803 subassemblies. An 801 subassembly consists of two units of component 406 and two units of component 407. The 802 subassembly is made from two units of component 205 and one unit of component 603. An 803 subassembly consists of one unit of component 407, one unit of 950 component, and three 747 subassemblies. A 747 subassembly is made from six units of item 910, three units of item 205, and one unit of item 942. Create a product structure tree for product 800, and determine how many units of each component is required to produce 150 units of product 800.
4. Create an indented bill of materials for product 800 in problem 3.

5. Each unit of end product X requires two units of subcomponent Z. The lead time for X is one week, the standard order quantity is 40 units, and current availability is 35 units. Gross requirements for the next six weeks are 25, 30, 20, 15, 15, and 20 units, respectively. For item Z, lead time is two weeks, standard order quantity is 80 units, and current availability is 90 units. A scheduled receipt for 80 Z's is due in week 1. Develop complete MRP records for X and Z.
6. Route sheets for components A and B are shown below. Planned order releases at the beginning of the current week are 60 units for item A and 40 units for item B. Each work center has an 8-hour capacity each day (5 days/week).
    (a) Create an operations set-back diagram for components A and B.
    (b) Determine the capacity requirements of the planned order releases for the current week.
    (c) In what sequence should the jobs be scheduled at each work center?

Component A: route sheet
Lead Time = 1 Week

Operation Sequence Number	Work Center	Lead Time (in days)	Standard Times: Setup Time (in hours/batch)	Standard Times: Operation Run Time (in hours/unit)
1	100	1	2	.1
2	200	1	1	.05
3	100	1	1	.05
4	300	1	2	.15

Component B: route sheet
Lead Time = 1 Week

Operation Sequence Number	Work Center	Lead Time (in days)	Standard Times: Setup Time (in hours/batch)	Standard Times: Operation Run Time (in hours/unit)
1	200	1	2	.15
2	100	1	1	.05
3	300	1	1	.10

7. Product 601 is made from three 740 subassemblies, two 810 subassemblies, and one 900 subassembly. A 740 subassembly consists of one unit of component 309 and two units of component 207. The 900 subassembly is made from two units of component 400 and one unit of component 782. An 810 subassembly consists of one unit of component 309, one unit of component 721, and two 682 subassemblies. A 682 subassembly is made from one unit of component 400 and one unit of component 207. Create a product structure tree for product 601 and determine how many units of each component are required to produce 150 units of product 601.
8. Determine the net requirements for items X and Y below:

	Item X	Item Y
Gross requirements	600	50
Scheduled receipts	100	0
Available	0	50
Planned order receipts	0	50
Planned order releases	700	0

9. Patterson Assemblies has a gear assembly that requires component GA211, with material requirements scheduled as shown below. Average demand is 83 units/week, the cost of placing an order (setup) is $200, and the inventory carrying charge is $1.50/unit/week. Holding costs are calculated on the basis of average inventory each week.

	Week								
	0	1	2	3	4	5	6	7	8
Requirements	—	20	120	80	0	160	194	20	70
Quantity ordered	—								
Beginning inventory	0								
Ending inventory	0								

Using the lot-for-lot method, complete the MRP record for part GA211. What action needs to be taken if it is now the beginning of week 1? Calculate the total of ordering and holding costs over eight weeks.

10. Refer to the data in problem 9. Use the Wilson EOQ formula to determine the lot size (deterministic case), then complete the MRP record. Calculate the total of ordering and holding costs over eight periods. What assumption is violated by using the EOQ formula in this case?
11. Refer to the data in problem 9. Using the part-period method, complete the MRP record. Calculate the total of ordering and holding costs over eight weeks.
12. Compare the total costs from the results of problems 9, 10, and 11. Which method appears best? Examining the cost components for each method, briefly explain the difference in the behavior of the various methods.
13. Carcord, Inc., has received an order for 200 units of product G to be completed eight weeks from now. The product structure tree is shown in Figure 14.14. There is no stock on hand (available) and none on order. Determine the order release data for all necessary orders.
14. Refer to the data in problem 13. Carcord has just been advised by the supplier of component L that a delivery delay of two extra weeks is expected because of equipment breakdown. What impact will this delay have on Carcord's deliveries of product G?

CHALLENGING EXERCISES

15. Carcord, Inc., has received an order for 150 units of product 501, whose product structure tree is shown in Figure 14.15. There is no stock on hand (available) and none on order. Determine the order release data for all necessary orders.

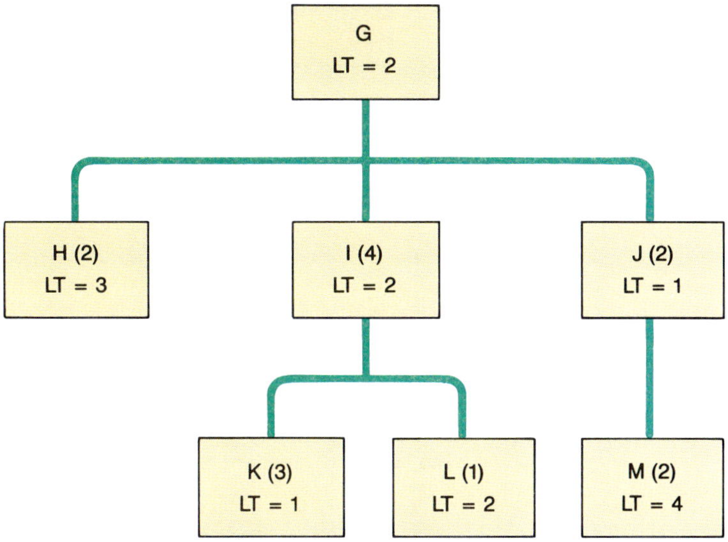

FIGURE 14.14 **Product structure tree for Carcord's product G. Lead times are in weeks.**

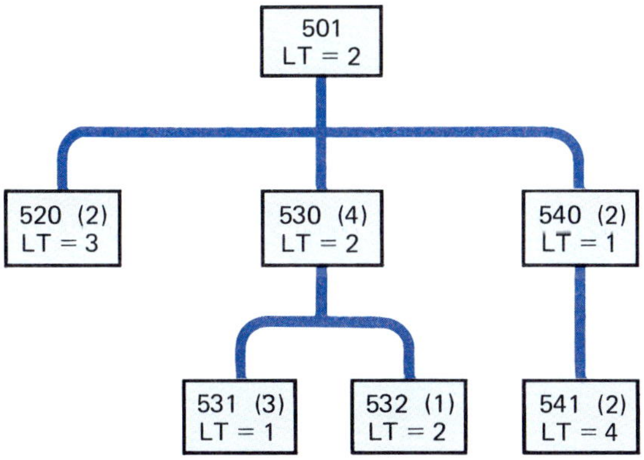

FIGURE 14.15 **Product structure tree for Carcord's product 501. Lead times are in weeks.**

16. Ambrex, Inc., has received an order for 70 units of product 20 and 50 units of product 40, to be delivered in 12 weeks. The product structure trees for products 20 and 40 are shown in Figure 14.16. Ambrex has on hand (available) 300 units each of components 31 and 37; there is no stock on hand or on order for other components. Determine the sizes and timing of planned order releases necessary to meet delivery commitments for products 20 and 40.

17. After planning for the conditions stated in problem 16, Ambrex receives a request for an additional order of 50 units of product 40. The Ambrex sales representative wants to know if she can promise delivery within 10 weeks, or earlier if

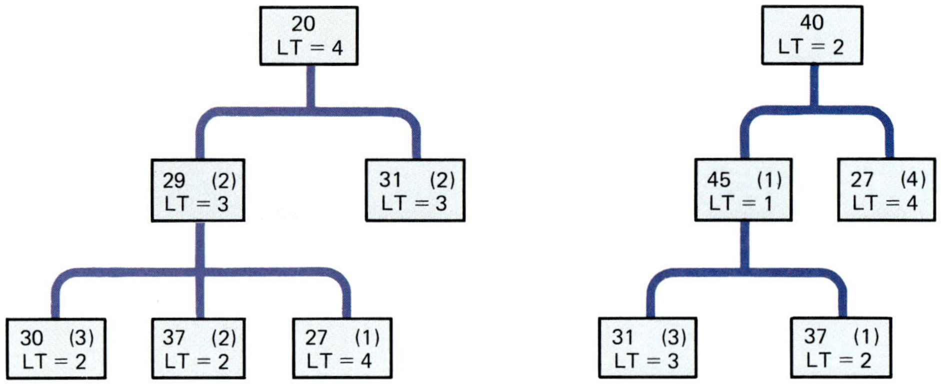

FIGURE 14.16 **Product structure trees for Carcord's products 20 and 40. Lead times are in weeks.**

possible, to the potential customer. As the production planner, realizing that your assembly operation can, at most, work on assembling 50 units of product 40 at any given time, what is your response to the sales representative's inquiry?

18. Components A and B are level 2 items in the product structure of the chair whose tree is shown in Figure 14.6. Their route sheets, current MRP records, and status reports on open orders are shown below.

Component A (front legs): route sheet

			Standard Times (hours)	
Operation Number	Work Center	Lead Times (weeks)	Setup Time/Batch	Operation Run Time/Unit
1	Metal cutting	1	1	.05
2	Metal forming	1	3	.20
3	Drilling	1	.5	.04
4	Finishing	1	2	.15

Component B (rear legs): route sheet

			Standard Times	
Operation Number	Work Center	Lead Times (in weeks)	Setup Time (in hours/batch)	Operation Run Time (in hours/unit)
1	Metal cutting	1	1	.07
2	Metal forming	1	1	.15
3	Drilling	1	1	.07
4	Finishing	1	2	.12

Current MRP records								
	Week							
Component A	1	2	3	4	5	6	7	8
Gross requirements	200	240	240	240	170	170	170	230
Scheduled receipts	170	190	200	230				
Available 140								
Planned order releases								
Lead time = 4 weeks Lot-for-lot ordering								
Component B								
Gross requirements	200	240	240	240	170	170	170	230
Scheduled receipts	190	200	240	240				
Available 50								
Planned order releases								
Lead time = 4 weeks Lot-for-lot ordering								

Status of open orders				
	Week			
Operations	1	2	3	4
Completed now	1,2,3,4	1,2,3	1,2	1
Remaining	—	4	3,4	2,3,4

(a) Complete the MRP records for items A and B.
(b) Prepare a capacity requirements report covering the next seven weeks for the four work centers.

19. Foley, Inc., has received an order for 70 units of product A and 50 units of product S, to be delivered in 12 weeks. The product structure trees for products A and S are shown in Figure 14.17. Foley has on hand (available) 300 units each of components C and E; there is no stock on hand or on order for other components.

(a) Determine the planned order releases for products A and S.
(b) After planning for the conditions stated above, Foley receives a request for an additional order of 50 units of product S. The Foley sales representative wants to know if she can promise delivery within

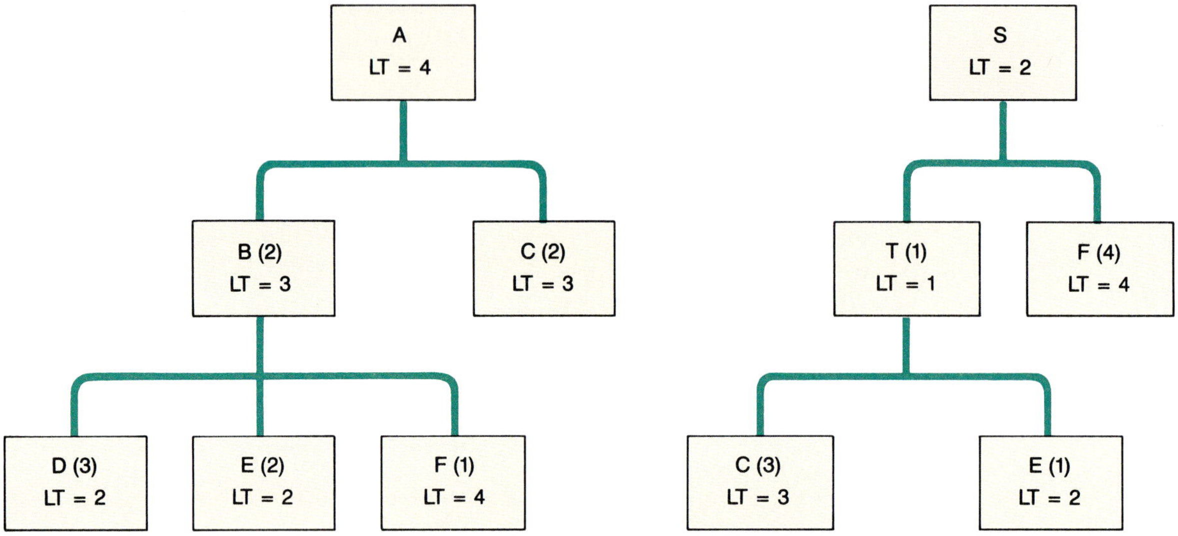

FIGURE 14.17 **Product structure trees for Foley's products A and S. Lead times are in weeks.**

11 weeks, or earlier if possible, to the potential customer. As the production planner, realizing that your assembly operation can, at most, work on assembling 50 units of product S at any given time, what is your response to the sales representative's inquiry?

KEY TERMS

Action bucket 533
Allocated quantity 526
Available quantity 526
Bill of materials 525
Cycle counting 534
Detailed capacity planning 537
Firm planned order 536
Gross requirements 526
Indented bill of materials 532
Inventory status file 526
Item level 526
Lead-time offsetting 532
Lot-for-lot ordering 536
Manufacturing resource planning (MRPII) 543
Material requirements planning (MRP) 522
Materials management 545
Net change method 535
Net requirements 528
Operation set-back chart 538
Part-period method 536
Pegging 533
Physical distribution 545
Planned order receipts 528
Planned order release 528
Product explosion 533
Product structure 525
Purchasing 545
Regenerative method 534
Route sheet 537
Scheduled receipts 528
Time fence 535

SELECTED READINGS

American Production and Inventory Control Society, *Capacity Planning and Control.* Washington, D.C.: APICS, 1979.

Berry, W. L. and D. Clay Whybark, "Research Perspectives for Materials Requirements Planning Systems," *Production and Inventory Management* 16, no. 2 (1975), 19–25.

"Computer Takes on MRP, Savings Multiply," *Industrial Engineering* 11, no. 3 (March 1979), 26–27.

McLeavey, D. W., and S. L. Narasimhan, *Production Planning and Inventory Control.* Boston: Allyn & Bacon, 1985.

Miller, Jeffrey G., and Linda G. Sprague, "Behind the Growth in Material Requirements Planning," *Harvard Business Review* 53, no. 5 (September-October 1975), 83–91.

Orlicky, Joseph A., *Material Requirements Planning.* New York: McGraw-Hill, 1975.

Peterson, L. D., "Design Considerations for Improving the Effectiveness of MRP," *Production and Inventory Management* 16, no. 3 (1975), 48–68.

Ruch, William A., "Economic Lot Sizing in MRP: The Marriage of EOQ and MRP." Paper presented at the 19th annual conference of the American Production and Inventory Control Society, Atlanta, 1976.

Vollmann, T. E., W. L. Berry, and D. C. Whybark, *Manufacturing Planning and Control Systems,* 2nd ed. Homewood, Ill.: Richard D. Irwin, 1988.

Wagner, Harvey M., and Thomson M. Whitin, "Dynamic Version of the Economic Lot Size Model," *Management Science* 5, no. 1 (October 1958), 89–96.

Whybark, D. C., and J. Gregg Williams, "Material Requirements Planning Under Uncertainty," *Decision Sciences* 7, no. 4 (October 1976), 595–606.

P A R T VI

MANAGING FOR WORLD CLASS COMPETITION

Production and Operations Management Activities

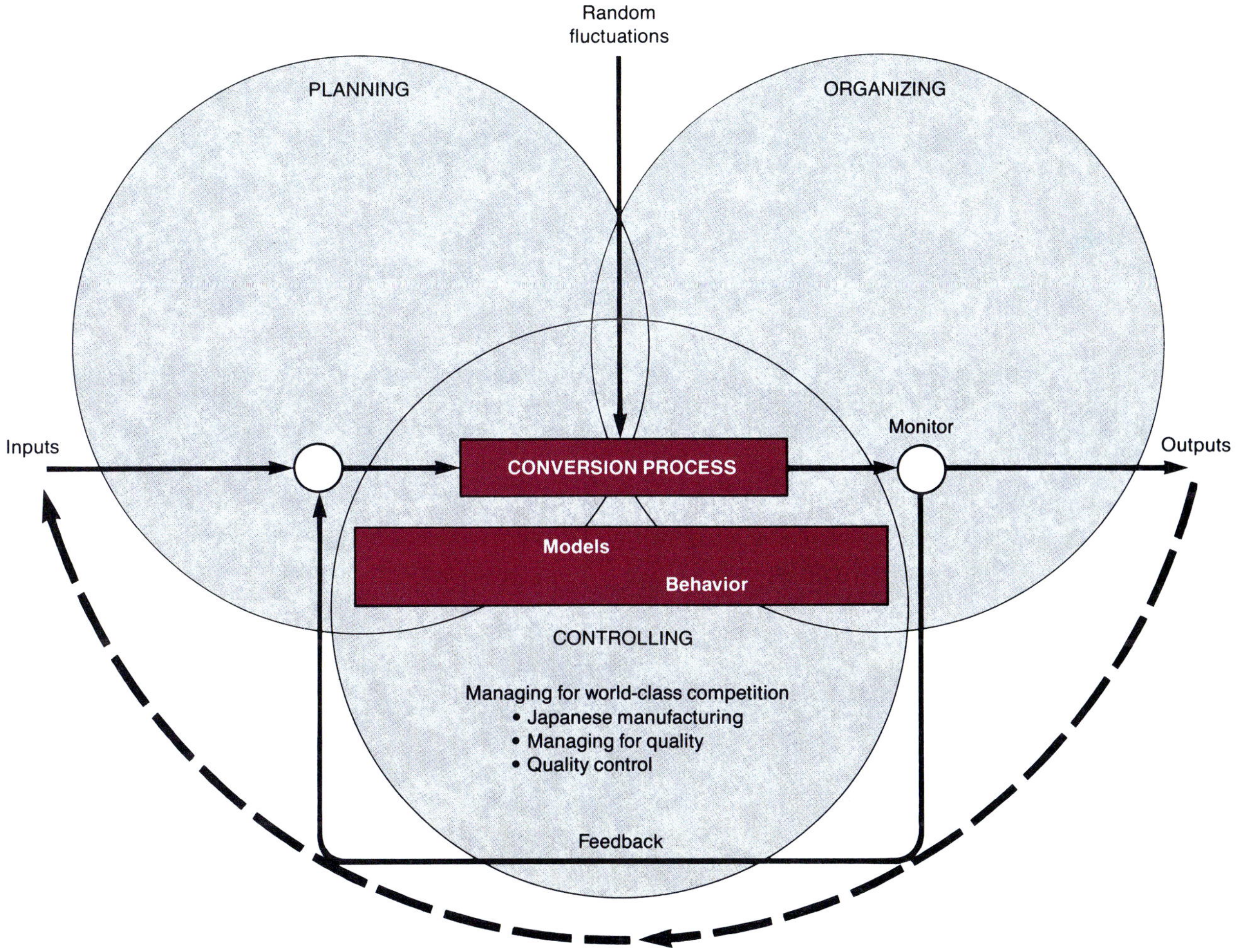

CHAPTER 15

JAPANESE CONTRIBUTIONS TO WORLD CLASS MANUFACTURING

Managing within a just-in-time (JIT) environment is challenging, and even more so when ownership is Japanese and the setting is a rural midwestern United States location. At Tri-Con we successfully apply many of the Japanese concepts and techniques introduced in this chapter in our seven North American facilities.

Tri-Con manufactures and supplies automotive seats, covers, and door panels for both American and Japanese manufacturers. At our Columbia, Missouri, plant we ship just-in-time deliveries eight times a day for Chrysler in St. Louis 125 miles away and several days ahead for Honda of America in Marysville, Ohio, some 500 miles away.

The information requirements from our customer, to our suppliers, and for our manufacturing systems differ considerably and provide a great opportunity for us to develop world-class information techniques. We have effectively integrated the computerized material requirements planning (MRP) you previously studied with the JIT you will study in this chapter. Keep in mind that MRP is basically a big calculator reacting to customer requirements and making recommendations for material to be purchased from other suppliers. The purchasing application accepts MRP recommendations to establish billing, ship to addresses, and place the order for item quantities and delivery dates. Accounts payable ensures that receiving quantities and prices are accurate. A material planner must continually analyze the database for accurate order policy codes, master level items, and leadtime offsets. This is no small challenge, and it offers an exciting opportunity for those involved in keeping a manufacturing plant in inventory, arriving JIT and never being short of parts.

John McMinn
Corporate MIS Manager
Tri-Con Industries, LTD.
Columbia, Missouri

Mr. McMinn's comments reflect Tri-Con's experiences and are representative of many other companies, as well. Prompt deliveries, reliable service, high-quality products, and close coordination with suppliers and customers, have become essential in many industries. Let's see how the Japanese approach to operations management can provide better manufacturing performance.

JAPANESE MANAGEMENT OVERVIEW

In recent years, operations management has experienced a revolution in manufacturing techniques and philosophies. New terms include *kanban,* just-in-time (JIT), and total quality control (TQC). How do these concepts become practices that have proven so successful in Japanese business? Today, a more widespread understanding of these Japanese approaches has led to their application throughout the world. It is to that understanding we direct our attention.

WHY STUDY THE JAPANESE?

Since the early 1970s managers in the United States have become acutely aware of a more competitive world-wide market. Foreign companies, particularly the Japanese, are competing more successfully in the North American markets. This increased competitive pressure has meant decreased market shares for U.S. and Canadian businesses. In response, they have renewed their emphasis on productivity, cost control, and in quality. The 1970s-1980s Japanese penetration into North American markets is now repeating itself in Western Europe. North American businesses are gaining a greater appreciation of the strengths exhibited by international competitors (see Chapters 1 and 2), especially Japanese manufacturers. Accordingly, it is important to understand the Japanese business environment and their manufacturing techniques.

HISTORICAL AND POLITICAL PERSPECTIVE

The history of Japan since World War II is the history of a developing economy, especially manufacturing.

Postwar Reindustrialization. After World War II, Japan was in a shambles. Property destruction was widespread, leaving only concrete or stone buildings in many of the major cities such as Tokyo, Osaka, Nagoya, and Yokohama. The Japanese economy, too, was ruined and faced the challenge of transition from a wartime to a peacetime economy with very few resources. This scarcity of resources was a key factor in the evolution of the just-in-time philosophy. In this same era, the Japanese government was restructured by the Allied Powers General Headquarters. Today, Japan is a country that uses centralized industrial planning, not a free market economy.

The Role of Government. Japanese companies, as compared to these in the United States, have at least one level of planning above the business plan: *governmental industrial planning.* This "guiding vision" for industry is provided by the *Ministry of International Trade and Industry* (MITI). MITI provides direction concerning which industries will flourish and which will decline and be phased out.[1]

Ministry of International Trade and Industry (MITI) The unit of Japanese government responsible for industrial planning for the activities that formulate industrial policy and determine the patterns of future growth and decline among the various industries comprising the Japanese economy.

Recent MITI policy has encouraged the expansion of research in solar energy, the development of fifth generation computers, and the production of experimental equipment for unmanned space flights. Table 15.1 illustrates the type of planning at the government level, predicting that by 2000, the Japanese will work largely in the service sector, an area where the United States currently holds a competitive advantage.

It is important to note several contrasts between U.S. government industrial policy and Japanese government industrial policy[2]:

1. The U.S. government emphasizes the regulation of industry. Japanese government is extremely cooperative with industry.
2. The U.S. Justice Department enforces U.S. antitrust laws that limit the

TABLE 15.1 **Comparison of Japan's Employment in 1980 and 2000 (in thousands of persons)**

	1980		2000		Annual Change (in %)
Primary Sector	5,770		3,080		−3.1
Secondary Sector	19,250		21,110		0.5
Manufacturing		13,770		14,200	0.2
Chemicals		1,750		1,450	−0.9
Primary Metals		670		540	−1.1
Machinery		5,380		8,930	2.6
Other		5,970		3,280	−3.0
Construction		5,480		6,900	1.2
Tertiary Sector	30,190		39,120		1.3
Utilities		300		330	0.4
Finance, Insurance, Real Estate		1,910		2,410	1.2
Transport and Communications		3,500		3,550	0.1
Service, etc.		24,480		32,830	1.5
Total	55,360		63,290		0.7

Source: From *Kaisha, The Japanese Corporation* by James C. Abegglen and George Stalk, Jr. Copyright © 1985 by Basic Books, Inc. Reprinted by permission of Basic Books, a division of HarperCollins Publishers, Inc.

[1]J. C. Abegglen and G. Stalk, *Kaisha, The Japanese Corporation* (New York: Basic Books, 1985), p. 33–34.

[2]Abegglen and Stalk, p. 33–34.

power and size of U.S. corporations by limiting market share. There are no similar restrictions on Japanese companies. Japanese corporations tend to compete by gaining market share and eliminating the competition.

3. U.S. policy rewards consumption. Japanese policy rewards savings, resulting in lower interest rates, which in turn lowers the cost of business capital.

MITI, however, is not without its critics in Japan. In his autobiography, Akio Morita, the chairman of Sony, refers to MITI officials as "bureaucrats" and suggests that MITI was an impediment in allowing Sony to compete in international markets during the company's early development.

JAPANESE MANAGEMENT

It is noteworthy that the initial interest in Japanese management centered on management-employee the interaction, rather than on manufacturing methods. For this reason we will first address Japanese management style and employee involvement. Our understanding of Japanese management style will provide a good platform for studying Japanese manufacturing techniques.

Japanese Management Style. North American managers are keenly interested in Japanese management style and in discovering what the Japanese do differently. Is Japanese success due to culture, environment, management skills, or beliefs about people? Management scholars and consultants are probing these issues and offering suggestions.

A popular view was presented in the early 1980s by William Ouchi. His analysis focused on characteristics of *organizations* as the basis for comparison.[3] Ouchi listed such distinguishing features of Japanese organizations as lifetime employment, slow evaluation and promotion, nonspecialized career paths, implicit control mechanisms, collective decision making, collective responsibility, and holistic concern for employees. In contrast, qualities inherent in American organizations include short-term employment, rapid evaluation and promotion, specialized career paths, explicit control mechanisms, individual decision making, individual responsibility, and a more segmented concern for workers.[4] Ouchi offered a new American approach, called *Theory Z.* He believes that some features of Japanese organizations could be successfully replicated in American organizations. *Theory Z* is a synthesis of the best aspects of both approaches.

Theory Z An approach to management proffered by William Ouchi that synthesizes traditional American and current Japanese methods, and stresses the contribution of every employee in solving problems through group consensus.

Richard Pascale and Anthony Athos, taking a different approach than Ouchi's, have developed a model that analyzes Japanese and American firms based on seven variables: the "hard Ss"—structure, strategy, and systems—and the "soft Ss"—skills, staff, subordinate goals, and style. Without elaborating on these concepts and the rationale behind them, it is difficult to evaluate the validity of Pascale's and Athos' argument that American firms are best at the "hard Ss" and Japanese firms are best at the "soft Ss."[5] The "soft Ss" involve people. Pascale and Athos, give Japanese

[3] William C. Ouchi, *Theory Z: How American Business Can Meet the Japanese Challenge* (Reading, Mass.: Addison-Wesley, 1981).

[4] This comparison is drawn from J. Bernard Keys and Thomas R. Miller, "The Japanese Management Theory Jungle," *Academy of Management Review 9*, no. 2 (April 1984), 342–53.

[5] Richard T. Pascale and Anthony G. Athos, *The Art of Japanese Management* (Warner Books, New York; 1981).

Asian cultures feature meticulous attention to detail. Computer-backups vary among cultures from adding machines and hand-held calculators to the abacus used here.
***Source:* AP/Wide World Photos**

managers high scores for their behavioral interactions with and treatment of employees. Many of Pascale's and Athos' conclusions stem from comparisons of a single Japanese firm, Matsushita Corporation, and a single American firm, ITT.

Other studies, too, clearly identify the setting in which Japanese firms are successful in dealing with people at work.[6] Cole, for example, offers excellent insights into why quality circles work well in Japan. Professor Cole has been studying and writing about the Japanese worker for over a decade, and he provides useful observations about Japanese behavior and culture.

Employee Involvement Openness and total employee involvement are important to the Japanese. With staff acting as coaches, all employees help solve production problems when they occur. Shop floor decisions benefit by input from employee relations, finance, and engineering personnel, all interacting with management and line workers. Japanese workers are especially well equipped to participate in this type of decision making because, in their careers, they commonly gain experience in a variety of different corporate disciplines.

One of the most often discussed aspects of Japanese management is lifetime employment. In his autobiography, Akio Morita shares these insights about lifetime employment:

> In Japan it was considered a serious thing to take a son, especially a first son, out of his home and family environment and bring him permanently into a new atmosphere

---

[6]R. E. Cole, *Work, Mobility, and Participation: A Comparative Study of American and Japanese Industry* (Berkeley, Calif.: University of California Press, 1979).

> in the world of business. . . . family background and recommendations and unspoken pledges of sincerity on both sides are indicated when a young man joins his business family. The commitments are genuine because they cover a working life, not just casual employment for a few years as in some countries where there is much more worker mobility.[7]

There are some indications, however, that job mobility is increasing as Japanese society becomes influenced by other cultures. Where it remains, lifetime employment has the effect of "driving out fear," allowing employees to take risks and offer suggestions that may radically improve operations.

Some Drawbacks of Japanese Management. Certain aspects of Japanese business practices, particularly in the areas of sexism and personal freedoms, would not be socially desirable or tolerated in North America. These points were made by Alan D. Hansen when he observed the Japanese economy on behalf of the U.S. government.[8] Following are descriptions of sexism and personal restrictions common in Japanese industries. It is important to note that some of these aspects of Japanese life are changing.

1. Women are often not considered part of the permanent work force. They are strongly encouraged to quit work when they get pregnant.
2. As the Morita quote alludes to, companies carry out extensive background checks on prospective employees, including interviews with family members, neighbors and teachers, and genealogical research to ensure that the candidate has the proper ancestry.
3. Lifetime employment is not available to women; even for men the lifetime ends, in many cases, with mandatory retirement at age 55.
4. Employees are strongly socialized to conform to company norms, which often discourage religious or social activities.
5. The Japanese government subsidizes industry through tax breaks and incentives and provides import barriers to protect Japanese industry.

JUST-IN-TIME MANUFACTURING

Just-in-time is both a philosophy and a set of methods for manufacturing. Although it has no single, agreed-upon definition, JIT emphasizes waste reduction, total quality control, and devotion to the customer.

ELIMINATING WASTE AND ADDING VALUE

Just-in-time requires a great deal of organizational discipline. As in the case of MRP, JIT requires not only changes in the way a company handles its inventory but also

[7]From the autobiography of Akio Morita, *Made in Japan* (New York: Dutton, 1986), 47.

[8]Alan D. Hansen, "Japanese Management: The Cherries and the Pits," *Exchange* (Spring 1983), 26–30.

changes in its culture. JIT also encompasses the Japanese managerial characteristics we have discussed in this chapter. Finally, JIT applies to all the functions of a company, not just operations.

Just-in-time (JIT) A manufacturing system whose goal it is to optimize processes and procedures by continuously pursuing waste reduction.

The definition of JIT that we adopt for our discussion is as follows: *JIT is a manufacturing system whose goal is to optimize processes and procedures by continuously pursuing waste reduction.*

Shingo's seven wastes Seven sources of manufacturing wastes identified by Shigeo Shingo as targets for reduction through continuous improvements in the production process.

The Seven Wastes. Shigeo Shingo, a recognized JIT authority and engineer at the Toyota Motor Company identifies *seven wastes* (see Table 15.2) as being the targets of continuous improvement in production processes. By attending to these wastes, improvement is achieved.

TABLE 15.2 The Seven Wastes

1. *Waste of overproduction.* Eliminate by reducing setup times, synchronizing quantities and timing between processes, compacting layout, visibility, and so forth. Make only what is needed now.
2. *Waste of waiting.* Eliminate through synchronizing work flow as much as possible, and balance uneven loads by flexible workers and equipment.
3. *Waste of transportation.* Establish layouts and locations to make transport and handling unnecessary if possible. Then rationalize transport and material handling that cannot be eliminated.
4. *Waste of processing itself.* First question why this part or product should be made at all, then why each process is necessary. Extend thinking beyond economy of scale or speed.
5. *Waste of stocks.* Reduce by shortening setup times and reducing lead times, by synchronizing work flows and improving work skills, and even by smoothing fluctuations in demand for the product. Reducing all the other wastes reduces the waste of stocks.
6. *Waste of motion.* Study motion for economy and consistency. Economy improves productivity, and consistency improves quality. First improve the motions, then mechanize or automate. Otherwise there is danger of automating waste.
7. *Waste of making defective products.* Develop the production process to prevent defects from being made so as to eliminate inspection. At each process, accept no defects and make no defects. Make processes failsafe to do this. From a quality process comes a quality product—automatically.

Source: Hall, R, *Attaining Manufacturing Excellence.* Homewood, Ill.: Dow-Jones-Irwin, 1987. p. 26.

Value-added manufacturing A method of manufacturing that seeks to eliminate wastes in processing, adhering to the edict that a stage of the process that does not add value to the product for the customer should be eliminated.

Value-Added Manufacturing JIT's seven wastes are at the root of what U.S. companies term *value-added manufacturing:* Any step in the manufacturing process that does not add value to the product for the customer is wasteful. Examples of wasteful steps include process delays, materials transport, storages, work-in-process (WIP) inventories, finished goods inventories, excessive paper processing, and many other activities that do not add value to the product. Wasteful tasks increase costs and reduce competitiveness. To identify and delete wastes, each aspect of manufacturing is analyzed to confirm or refute its value.

By applying the JIT philosophy, many companies are improving their productivity. However, incorporating JIT requires a heavy commitment of time and imposes a rigorous discipline upon the organization. Shingo states that it took 20 years for the

Toyota Motor Company to implement the JIT system and it will take most other companies ten years to obtain similar results.[9]

In the following sections, we discuss some special aspects of JIT and Japanese manufacturing: total quality control, pull coordination, *kanban,* setup time reduction, flexibility, preventive maintenance, and purchasing. When reading those sections, it will be helpful to keep in mind the following four points.

1. Not all Japanese companies practice JIT.
2. There are several different versions of JIT. Each company that practices the JIT philosophy does so a little differently.
3. Variations in cultures account for variations in JIT philosophies and techniques. For example, the *kanban* "card" system is natural to the Japanese, who generally enjoy playing cards. In the United States, the cards are often spurned and *kanban* squares, *kanban* lights, or yelling "Hey, Jack! Send me some more materials!" are used instead.
4. JIT is less a set of techniques and more an umbrella encompassing several techniques such as total quality control, total employee involvement, *kanban,* setup time reduction, zero inventories, and pull coordination.

JAPANESE MANUFACTURING TECHNIQUES

Professor Robert W. Hall, Indiana University, suggests these cornerstones to the Japanese manufacturing system.

1. Produce what the customer desires.
2. Produce products only at the rate the customer wants them.
3. Produce with perfect quality.
4. Produce instantaneously—with zero unnecessary lead time.
5. Produce with no waste of labor, material, or equipment; every move has a purpose so there is zero idle inventory.
6. Produce by methods that allow people to develop.[10]

Similarly, Richard J. Schonberger identifies nine simple—yet hidden—lessons from the Japanese.[11] These lessons focus on management technology, just-in-time production, total quality control, behavioral techniques, plant configurations, flexibility, purchasing, self-improvement of work quality, and striving for simplicity in all things.

How Japanese Manufacturing Ideally Works Although our example is oversimplified, ideally the Japanese approach to manufacturing would be as follows.

First, identify the customers' needs. Find out what customers require in terms of quantity, quality, and schedule. Know as much about the customer's needs as they do. Second, obtain the exact amount of material needed for today and process it piece by piece. The first person in the manufacturing process must perform their job and hand the piece to the next person. The piece must be correct or there will be delays all the way down the line. If there is an error and the next person cannot use the piece, it

[9]S. Shingo, *Study of Toyota Production System from Industrial Engineering Viewpoint.* (Tokyo: Japanese Management Association, 1981), foreword.

[10]Hall, *Zero Inventories,* p. 2.

[11]*Schonberger, Japanese Manufacturing Techniques.* Each lesson is a chapter in the book.

should be handed back with admonishment; it should be clear, though, that there is a willingness to help solve any problems so this will not happen again. There is no in-process inventory. Everything currently being made is needed by the customer, so no finished goods inventory exists.

Quality is perfect. Waste cannot be hidden—poor products that are 2, 3, or 4 percent defective cannot be made and put in storage to be sorted later. Finally, everyone is expected to be involved in discovering how to simplify the job, and management strives to aid all employees accomplish this goal. Cooperation, teamwork, and a striving for consensus in all decisions are foremost in management's mind.

Stockless production system A system of production that allows no (or as small as possible) inventories of raw materials, work-in-process, or finished goods; goes hand in hand with JIT philosophy.

Stockless Production In some leading Japanese manufacturing companies, a key element is "stockless" production. Everything is made as ordered, and delivered only as needed. Production is "just-in-time."[12] There is a necessary linkage between stockless production and quality—every item must be made correctly just in time and every time. There is no waste. Therefore labor, material, and tools are all used productively.

What can this stockless production do for a company? Table 15.3 illustrates spectacular results for four selected companies; benefits include savings in inventory, improvement in meeting schedules, and increased labor productivity.

The concept of zero inventories is very appealing, but we know that his approach is not always economically or practically feasible. It usually is feasible, however, for most firms to move closer to this goal.

TOTAL QUALITY EMPHASIS

Total quality control (TQC) The Japanese approach to quality control, stressing continuous improvement through attention to manufacturing detail rather than attainment of a fixed quantitative quality standard.

The term *total quality control* (TQC) originated with the book by that name, written by Armand Feigenbaum and first published in 1951. As applied by the Japanese, TQC is a detailed approach to quality and it relates to every facet of the business.

[12]For a synopsis of stockless/just-in-time systems, see Richard A. Schonberger, "Some Observations on the Advantages and Implementation Issues of Just-in-Time Production Systems," *Journal of Operations Management 3*, no. 1 (November 1982), 1–11; and Jinichiro Nakane and Robert W. Hall, "Manufacturing Specs for Stockless Production," *Harvard Business Review* 61, no. 3 (May–June 1983), 84–91.

TABLE 15.3 Results of stockless production programs in Japan[a]

Company	Duration of Program (in years)	Inventory Reduction (in % of original value)	Throughput Time Reduction (in % of original value)	Labor Productivity (in % increase)
A	3	45	40	50
B	3	16	20	80
C	4	30	25	60
D	2	20	50	50

[a]These data were collected in late 1981 by Professor Jinichiro Nakane, Waseda University, Tokyo. The companies did not wish to be indentified. The figures represent rough management estimates, as the rounded figures suggest. Labor productivity is estimated as sales in yen adjusted for inflation and divided by *total* employees.

Source: Hall, *Zero Inventories,* 24.

The TQC philosophy goes hand in hand with JIT since poor quality is seen as wasteful. With high quality, productivity improves by avoiding wasteful scrap and rework. By applying the techniques and philosophies discussed in this section, the Japanese have emerged as the world's quality leaders. They now have an image of quality that has become a powerful weapon in their competitive arsenal. As described in Operations Management Highlight 15.1, in a five-year period the Jidosha Kiki Company improved defect rates by a factor of 25 from suppliers and a factor of 33 times internally. Other JIT statistics improved as well.

To further illustrate Japanese success, consider these comparative levels of quality: While most U.S. companies measure quality in parts defective per hundred (e.g., 2 percent defectives), Japanese companies are achieving parts defective per million (e.g., 10 ppm's defective, or, 0.001 percent defectives). In effect, the Japanese have successfully combined the New World technology of mass production with the Old World ethic of craftsmanship. The historical underpinnings for this run deep, as illustrated by the fact that in the eighth century A.D., Japanese swordsmiths hammered the world's finest blades from 10,000 microlayers of steel.

Deming's Contributions to TQC Japanese competitiveness today relates directly to the influence of Dr. W. Edwards Deming, who has been closely associated with Japanese quality programs since 1950 when he was invited to address the Union of Japanese Scientists and Engineers about improving quality in industry. At the time, quality was poor in Japan. Deming contends that since production workers have little control over product design, process design, or the supply of raw materials, they are only minimally responsible for poor quality from production. He estimates that 85 percent of quality problems are assignable to management and the production systems they have created. Hence, to improve quality, Deming proffers 14 mandatory steps, called *Deming's 14 points for management*[13], that emphasize continuous improvement, better employee training, statistical analysis of work, and establishing inspection as an individual responsibility, and deemphasize fixed numerical goals that tend to limit improvement to merely meeting these fixed numerical goals.

Deming's 14 points for management Guidelines for improving quality, proposed by Dr. W. Edwards Deming, as part of total quality control.

Organizing for Quality Responsibility for quality in the Japanese organization is exemplified in four features: in-process inspection, visible control, line-stop, and the N-2 technique.

Work-in-process inspection is used instead of final inspection. (Chapter 17 discusses inspection in greater detail.) The following comments by Yoshimi Takemoto a vice president at Sanyo, illustrate the Japanese versus the U.S. approach:

> The American managers were proudly pointing out to me the spacious, well-equipped and well-staffed quality inspection section at the end of the assembly line. I wondered why they needed such an elaborate quality inspection station if they made their products properly in the first place. I told our workers to properly and carefully complete the assigned job, and not to send any slipshod work down the assembly line. In this way we cut the defect rate drastically.[14]

---

[13]H. Gitlow, and S. Gitlow, *The Deming Guide to Quality and Competitive Position* (Englewood Cliffs, N.J.: Prentice-Hall, 1987), 20.

[14]Yoshi Tsurumi, "Productivity, the Japanese Approach," *Pacific Basin Quarterly*, no. 6 (Summer 1981), 8.

OPERATIONS MANAGEMENT HIGHLIGHT 15.1

Source: Lou Jones/
The Image Bank

Japan's Global Power Is Growing

Until recently, Europeans have had far less economic interaction with the Japanese than with North Americans. For Europeans, the full force of the Japanese automobile onslaught will not be felt until the mid-1990s when the combined capacity at British plants of Honda, Nissan, and Toyota will be 500,000 cars per year. Europeans have seen the impact of Japan's imports on U.S. industry, and they are taking very seriously the imminent impact on their own countries. Japanese power is heatedly debated as revealed in a ***Business Week*** poll of executive opinions in Europe, Japan, and the United States. As we see from three poll questions, there is a great diversity of opinion about Japan's current and future economic power and about xenophobia (closed society).

How can judgment and perceptions vary so broadly? Which viewpoints are most accurate? There are many examples of American companies emulating Japanese manufacturing practices, but still only few descriptions of examples from Japan are available in translation. One of these few comes from Professor Robert Hall at Indiana University. His documentation of the impressive results achieved by the Jidoshi Kiki Company are given here.

Japan Isn't King of the Hill . . . Yet

Do you think Japan is the No. 1 economic power in the world today, or not?	U.S.	Europe	Japan
Is No. 1 economic power	28%	50%	13%
Isn't No. 1 economic power	72%	46%	84%
Not sure	0%	4%	3%

Japanese View the Future with Optimism . . .

In 10 years, do you think Japan's share of the global economy will have increased, decreased, or stayed about the same?	U.S.	Europe	Japan
Increased	25%	36%	54%
Decreased	47%	31%	13%
Stayed the same	27%	31%	31%
Not sure	1%	2%	2%

. . . And Consensus that Xenophobia Must End

To be successful in the 1990s, will Japan have to open itself to more cultural and ethnic diversity than it has in the past, or not?	U.S.	Europe	Japan
Will have to open itself	71%	65%	90%
Won't have to open itself	26%	32%	6%
Not sure	3%	3%	4%

Development of stockless production at Jidosha Kiki Company, Ltd.[a]

	Start of Program 1976	1981	
Inventory (days on hand)			
Raw material	3.1	1.0	
Purchased parts	3.8	1.2	
Work-in-process	4.0	1.0	
Finished goods	8.6	3.7	
Total	19.5	6.9	
Productivity index	100	187	
Defect rates			
From suppliers	2.6%	0.11%	
Internally (cumulative)	0.34%	0.01%	
Setup times			
Over 60 minutes	20%	0%	
30–60 minutes	19%	0%	
20–30 minutes	26%	3%	
10–20 minutes	20%	7%	
5–10 minutes	5%	12%	Single-digit setups
100 seconds–5 minutes	0%	16%	Single-digit setups
Under 100 seconds	0%	62%	One-touch setups

[a]These data were taken from a briefing by Jidosha Kiki executives during a visit on July 2, 1982. Jidosha Kiki, which supplies brakes and steering gear to the auto industry, learned its methods from Toyota, and their system is very similar.

Sources: "The Nasty Pileup in Europe's Auto Industry," *Business Week* (September 17, 1990), 48–49; "How Global Executives See Japan's Power," *Business Week* (September 3, 1990), 48–50; Robert W. Hall, *Zero Inventories* (Homewood, Ill.: Dow Jones–Irwin, 1983), 30.

While installing mufflers on automobiles, this line worker in Oppama, Japan, has a personal responsibility for quality and is authorized to stop the production line to prevent flaws and investigate problems.
Source: **AP/Wide World Photos**

Visible control A total quality control technique to make defects, as well as records of quality control, clearly visible to all employees so that company resources may be brought to bear on problems as they arise.

Andon A warning light used as a visible control technique in total quality control.

Poke a yoke Literally, "foolproofing." Total quality control techniques that foolproof production from defects.

Quality circle (QC) A small group of employees who meet frequently to resolve company problems.

Defects can go by unnoticed if they cannot be seen. The technique of *visible control* exposes problems by making them visible. For instance, when a product is to be packaged in a certain way, electronic sensors may be installed to detect steps that are not performed. A warning light, called an *andon,* flashes, immediately alerting the worker to an error. The Japanese call techniques like this *poke a yoke* or, in English, *foolproofing.*

Each line worker is authorized to make a *line-stop* whenever a flaw or error is detected. By pushing a button, the worker stops the production line, which usually sounds an alarm. Line workers, management, engineers, and others then examine the defect and determine ways to keep the problem from reoccurring.

In contrast to many U.S. companies, Japanese companies generally do not inspect incoming raw materials. When they do, they often use the *N-2 technique:* the first and last pieces in the lot are inspected and if they both are found to conform to requirements, then the entire lot is assumed to conform. Thus a sample size of only two (N-2) is all that is used.

Quality Circles *Quality circles* (QCs) were initially developed in Japan as employee participation programs to identify the variations in quality, and management programs to eliminate sources of those variations. Quality circles in Japan are usually small groups of employees (perhaps six to 12) who meet frequently and informally, often in an employee's home, to resolve company problems. Employees suggest to management potential solutions to problems, and then work as a team to implement the changes. Employees at all levels in the firm are trained in the basic skills of data charting, sampling, and control. These analytical and statistical skills have become a part of the Japanese general education curriculum and are widely reinforced by industry use. In 1980, quality control experts estimated that just under a million workers were involved

Fishbone (cause and effect) diagram A schematic model of quality problems and their causes; used to diagnose and solve these problems.

Quality loss function (QLF) A qualitative measure of the effectiveness of quality control, often in terms of the economic losses a customer suffers after purchasing an imperfect product.

in quality circles in Japan, but only as few as a hundred thousand workers were taking part in the programs in the United States. Those numbers are certainly larger today, as reflected by the increasing interest in the International Association of Quality Circles.

The Fishbone Diagram A *fishbone (cause and effect) diagram* is a schematic model of quality problems and their causes, and is frequently prepared by the consensus of a quality circle. Figure 15.1 illustrates a quality circle-prepared fishbone diagram for airline customer service. On the far left are listed the top four consumer complaint categories, as reported by the Civil Aeronautics Board.

Taguchi Method of Quality Control Dr. Genichi Taguchi is a past winner of the Deming Award for outstanding achievement in industrial quality, a past Director of the Japanese Academy of Quality, and currently an international consultant. He developed an approach to quality that has been gaining acceptance by a number of U.S. and foreign firms. Two features of Taguchi's method are its emphasis on quality design and the *quality loss function* (QLF). The QLF quantitatively measures the success or failure of quality control. Taguchi's QLF reflects economic losses that customers suffer when

FIGURE 15.1 **Fishbone diagram (cause and effect) of airline service quality**

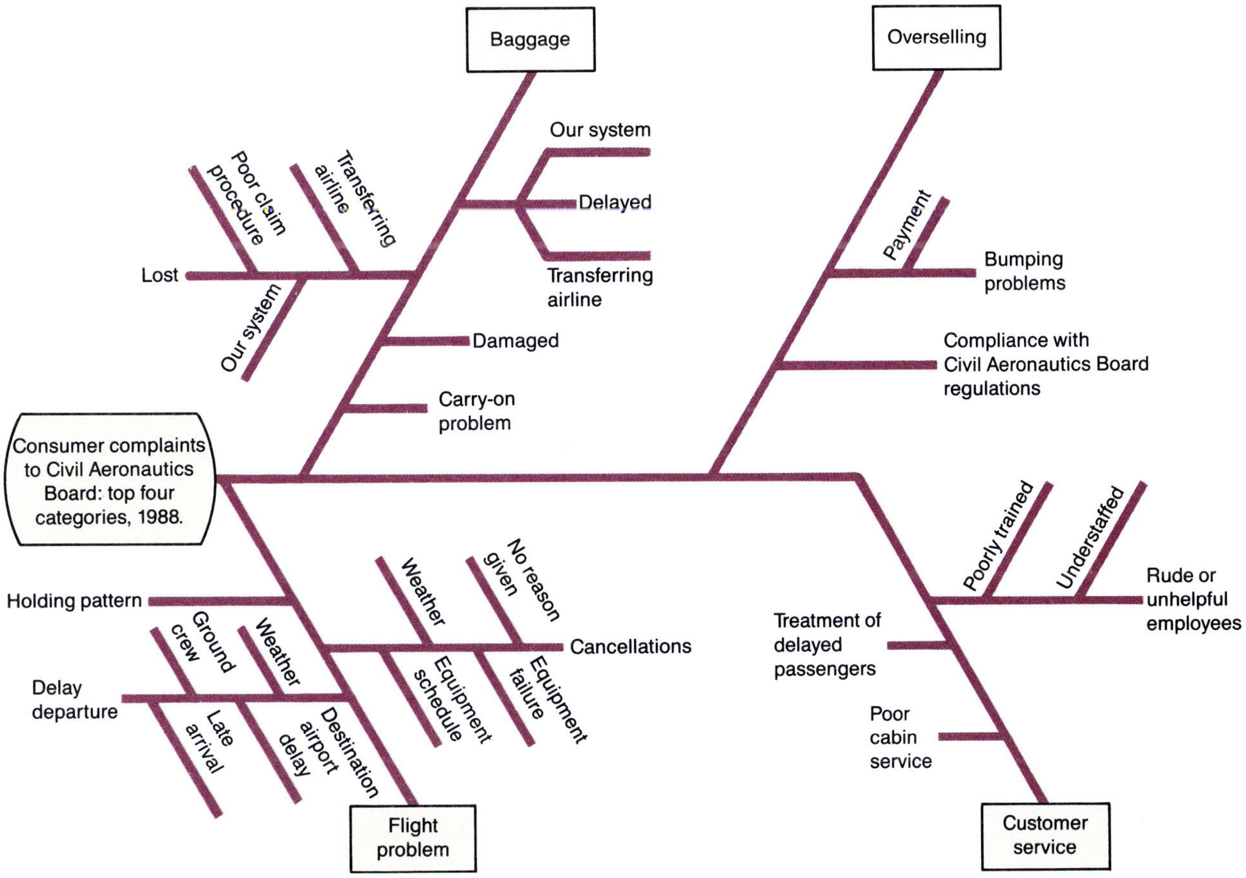

Taguchi method of quality control A method of controlling quality, developed by Dr. Genichi Taguchi, that emphasizes robust product design and the quality loss function.

they purchase an imperfect product. Losses include maintenance costs, failure costs, ill effects to the environment such as pollution, or costs of operating the product. Higher-quality products yield lower losses to customers.

The traditional concept is that any product that measures within specification limits is "good," and only those outside the limits are "bad": As long as the product measures better than the specification limits—*even though it may measure far short of the target specification*—no loss is assumed to occur. In contrast, Taguchi's QLF presumes that *any* deviation from the target specification is important because it means economic losses for the customer. Furthermore, the Taguchi method expresses quality in customer-based economic terms that are clear and understandable.[15]

Robust product A product that can perform under a wide range of environmental conditions without failing.

Quality design is another area in which Taguchi departs from traditional quality control. Focusing on customers, Taguchi methods place a premium on careful product design. Thus, in addition to quality control in production, Taguchi emphasizes quality control in four other functions: (1) product planning, (2) product design, (3) process design, and (4) production service after purchase. Products are designed so that they are *robust,*—that is, so they function under a wide range of environmental conditions without faltering. Further information about these methods for design quality is available from the American Supplier Institute, a nonprofit organization in Dearborn, Michigan, dedicated to communicating Taguchi's philosophy.

REPETITIVE MANUFACTURING: PUSH OR PULL?

Repetitive manufacturing processes are those that produce many units of one product or of several models of one basic product. Repetitive manufacturing is common in such industries as appliances, toys, and automobiles. Units of a given model can be visualized as progressing in a flow-oriented process through stages of product buildup. It may begin with fabrication of the basic components that are then built into subassemblies that are, in turn, combined in final assembly. The decisions of when and how many units to produce at each stage of processing vary considerably depending on the choice of a "push" versus a "pull" system for planning and control.

Push manufacturing system A system of production in which products are produced according to a schedule derived from anticipated product demand. An MRP-based or EOQ-based system.

Push Versus Pull Traditional Western perspective emphasizes a "push" system: nonstop adherence to a predetermined production schedule derived from anticipated demand for the products. Western industries tend to plan when final assembly will occur and, working backward toward earlier stages, identify how many subassemblies, fabricated parts, and purchased materials should be provided to accommodate the scheduled quantity of finished outputs. Thus, once the schedule is set into motion, the work at each stage proceeds in large lots or batches and, when completed, the subcomponents are pushed on through the system; they are either sent to the next department or are delivered to inventory where they wait for retrieval at the time they are needed at the next stage of processing. After a work center has met the schedule, its obligation to succeeding stages is fulfilled. Its subsequent activities are relatively independent of the other work centers because of the cushion of inventories. Thus the units progress in batches that are pushed through successive stages of buildup (even if they are not needed yet) until, finally, the required units of finished product are fulfilled.

[15]For more detail concerning the quality loss function see Genichi Taguchi, Elsayed A. Elsayed, and Thomas Hsiang, *Quality Engineering in Production Systems* (New York: McGraw-Hill, 1989).

Pull manufacturing system A system of production in which products are produced only as they are ordered by customers or to replace those taken for use. A JIT system.

The "pull" system of planning and control, popular in Japanese repetitive manufacturing, is quite different. It emphasizes simplicity, flexibility, and close coordination among work centers. Although final assembly schedules are developed, the manufacturer recognizes that actual demand will vary from what was anticipated and, consequently, is prepared to adapt production as these variations occur. The Japanese orientation is toward assembly-to-order rather than assembly-to-schedule. The upstream activities (subassembly, fabrication, purchasing of materials) are geared to match the final assembly needs for a relatively limited range of products. Consequently, the what and when of production in upstream departments is highly variable and is governed by what the downstream departments need. The subassemblies and component parts are thus "pulled" through the system by actual end-item demands in the specific models, sizes, or color combinations of the product demanded by consumers. The idea is that if units aren't needed now, don't produce them now or ahead of time; when they are needed, be prepared to create them rapidly in the required quantity.

OPERATIONS CHARACTERISTICS IN PUSH VERSUS PULL SYSTEMS

The design and operation of a conversion system take on quite a different flavor, depending upon whether it is geared toward a push or a pull orientation. The two approaches impose different types of equipment, machinery, and maintenance policies, as well as inventory postures, worker skills, support staffs, and management abilities.

Push System To accomplish its scheduled production in nonstop flows, the push system emphasizes predesigned and relatively fixed assembly line balances using dedicated single-purpose machines with high output capabilities. Abundant supplies of work-in-process inventories between stages facilitate nonstop production runs once they are started in downstream departments. Materials handling equipment shuttles parts and components to work areas from supplying departments or storage depots when scheduled by the materials control staff. The workers at receiving stations perform their specialized tasks repetitively on all units in the production lot. Work center management focuses on ensuring that the station is manned and has materials available and on motivating employees to meet scheduled output commitments. Long production runs avoid downtime and expensive setup and changeover costs.

Pull System Emphasizing flexibility and simplicity, the pull system uses cheaper, smaller, adaptable machines rather than one big expensive machine. Intricate tools and attachments permit rapid equipment changeovers as required for different models at each station. The goal of lotless (stockless) production in assembly is reflected in the closeness of work stations: each unit of product can be passed to the next station when the unit is completed, rather than accumulating in large batches after each stage. This gives station-to-station visibility of work progress, and it eliminates in-process inventories, inventory storage areas, inventory conveyance equipment, and materials control staff.

Diligent workers are the preeminent resource in the pull system. In addition to making the product, these workers adjust their own equipment for quick changeovers to different models. When low product demand warrants shutting down their production line, workers are reassigned to other lines, work on redesigning their own work stations and equipment to improve the production process, or do preventive maintenance. The pull system also demands more floor-level leadership from its supervisors, who must exercise problem-solving skills in balancing and rebalancing production line work daily to meet frequent variations in demand rather than adhering to nonstop predetermined schedules.

Workplace Layout: The U-Shape Flexibility in pull systems is exemplified by U-shaped, as opposed to straight-line, layouts. Consider, for example, the 13-station production work center in Figure 15.2. Suppose incoming materials are available to produce a small batch, say five units, of one product. If the 13 stations are positioned compactly, one or two workers can quickly set up all the machines without wasting much time moving between stations. Once production begins on the five-unit lot, the worker at location A can perform operations 1–3 and 11–13 on all the units, while the worker at B performs operations 4–10. As you can see, the U-shape offers more options for flexible work assignments than does a straight-line layout. A worker can operate both sides of the parallel legs or adjacent stations. When the demand for this work center's output declines, one operator alone can do the work at all 13 stations. When demand rises, the lone worker can be joined by another to respond rapidly with more output. The trick is to decide how many workers to use, how to distribute the work load, and what size the small lot should be.

KANBAN SYSTEM

Kanban Literally, a "visual record;" a method of controlling materials flow through a JIT manufacturing system by using cards to authorize a work station to transfer or produce materials.

The word *kanban* literally means "visual record." Usually, *kanban* is loosely referred to as a card system. *Kanban* is the production control system that "pulls" JIT production, allowing production with smaller inventories.

Two Card Kanban In the Toyota production system, for example, inventory is closely controlled at low levels by using a manual *two-card kanban system.* One kind of card, the conveyance *kanban,* is similar to a requisition, and authorizes the transference of materials from a supplying work center to a using work center. A second card, the

FIGURE 15.2 U-shape layout for a pull system work center

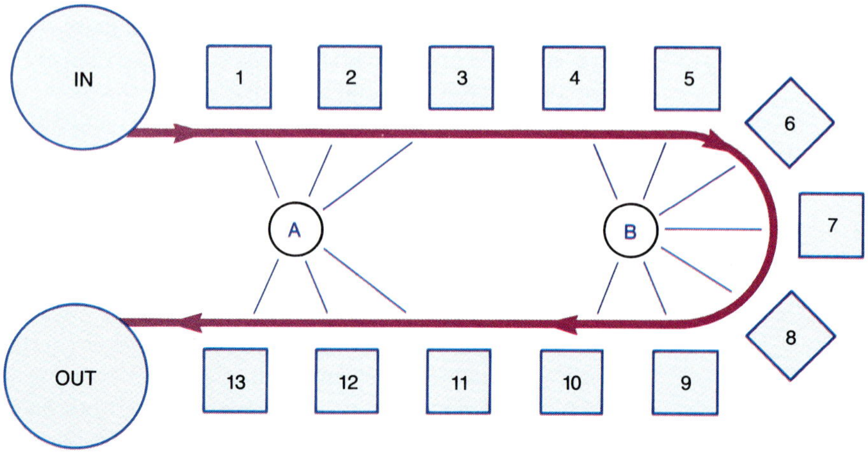

production *kanban*, authorizes the production of materials to replace those that were transferred earlier. Materials are transferred and produced in bins, and for each item in the production process are a prescribed number of bins in circulation at any one time. In addition, each bin houses a prescribed quantity, say four units, of materials. By choosing the number of bins and the prescribed quantities in them, inventories are carefully and visibly controlled on the shop floor. By reducing the number of cards circulating between two interacting work centers, in-process inventories approach zero and the needed parts arrive just in time. As a result, inventories of raw materials, component parts, or final products do not exist. Stockless production is a major feature in the pull system of planning and control.

Single Card Kanban In contrast to the two-card system, a *single-card kanban system* uses only a conveyance (or move) *kanban* and no production *kanban*. While Toyota and a few other companies use the two-card system, single-card *kanban* is the most often used.

Figure 15.3 illustrates a *kanban* control system operating between work stations 3 and 4. The bins with cards contain incoming materials. The bins without cards contain outgoing materials that are not yet allowed to be moved to the next work station. As soon as the operator in station 4 begins removing materials from bin A, she removes its *kanban* card and places it in the move card box (step 1). In step 2 the card is moved from the move card box and is attached to bin B, authorizing bin B be moved from station 3. In step 3, bin B is moved to station 4 replacing bin A just-in-time as it is moved back to station 3 to be filled again with materials at station 3.

While the kanban system is simple in design, it imposes strict controls on the production system: (1) No inventory is moved unless authorized to be so by a move card. (2) Each bin contains a fixed, exact quantity of inventory, no more, no less. (3) For each bin there is exactly one *kanban* card. (4) As soon as materials are removed from a bin, as in the case of bin B in our example, the *kanban* card is removed from the bin and placed in the move card box. (5) If all bins at a station contain the fixed inventory quantity, the operator stops production until another *kanban* card is received. (6) All bins are located in standard locations as is all equipment.

Measuring Kanban. Two commonly cited methods of measuring the performance of a manufacturing process are flow-through time and work-in-progress (WIP) inventory levels. As discussed in Chapter 11, flow-through time is the amount of time it takes one unit to pass through the entire process, from start to finish (on average). In the *kanban* system, both of these measures are at least partially dependent upon lot sizes. For example, if a *kanban* system uses 25 work stations and a lot size of 4, the average WIP will be near 100 units. If the cycle time for a balanced load is, say, two minutes per item (using the lot size of 4), flow-through time will be close to 200 minutes (allowing for some variation): one unit of product will flow through the system in 200 minutes.

EXAMPLE

The process for making component XY943 for the Digital Maestro CD Player involves five work stations. The cycle time is three minutes per item for every work station. This means that a *kanban* card will be returned from any particular work station to the previous work station, on average, every three minutes times the lot size. What would be the impact of reducing lot sizes from ten units to two? Using lot sizes of ten units and two units, average WIP inventory levels and flow-through times are calculated.

SOLUTION

WIP inventory levels:

Lot size = 10: Average WIP = 5 work stations × 10 units/lot = 50 units
Lot size = 2: Average WIP = 5 × 2 = 10 units

Process flow-through time (average):

Lot size = 10: Flow-through time = 5 work stations × 10 units/lot × 3 minutes/cycle
= 150 minutes
Lot size = 2: Flow-through time = 5 × 2 × 3 = 30 minutes

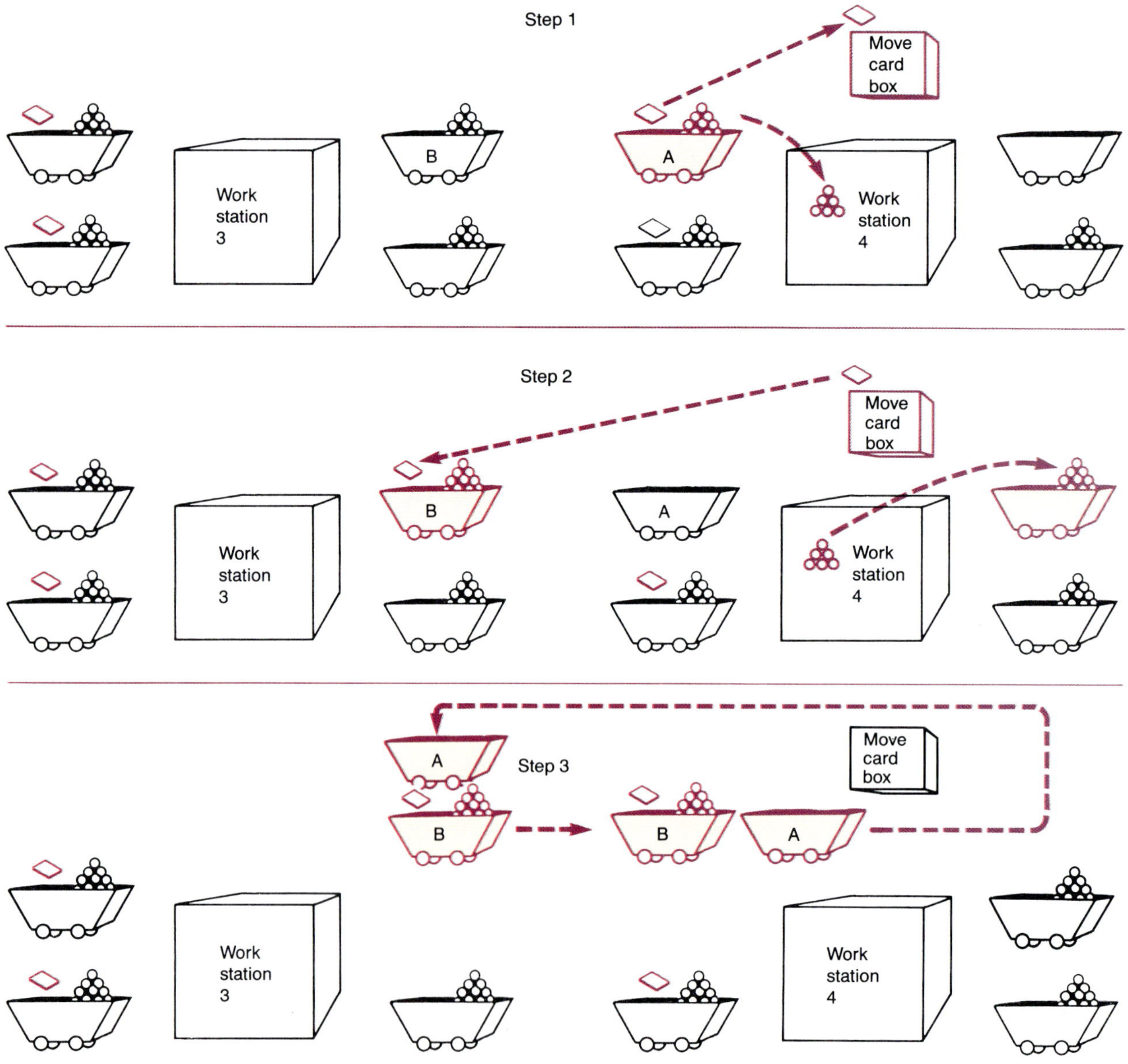

FIGURE 15.3 **Single-Card *Kanban* System.**

In the example, by reducing lot sizes from 10 units to 2 units the CD manufacturer was able to reduce WIP by a factor of 5, from 50 to 10 units, and flow-through time also by a factor of 5, from 150 to 30 minutes. Many companies have experienced similar drastic improvements through the introduction of *kanban*. For this reason, they are able to give better customer service (shorter production lead times) and have lower investments in inventories than do their competitors.

Uniform load scheduling (level scheduling) A method of scheduling in which small quantities of each product are produced each day, throughout the day.

Uniform Load Scheduling *Uniform load scheduling,* also referred to as *level scheduling,* is another scheduling method that is compatible with *kanban* and the JIT philosophy. It applies to mixed-model production lines where various products, rather than just one, are produced. According to Robert Hall, uniform load scheduling is best stated as "make a little bit of everything everyday." Doing so ties production closer to customer demand and avoids producing in large lot sizes (yielding larger inventories). Since uniform loads are expensive when they involve lengthy setup times, uniform load scheduling depends on finding ways to reduce equipment changeover times so that setup times are reduced. The next section explores some techniques for reducing setup times.

FLEXIBLE MANUFACTURING

Flexibility The capability of a manufacturing system to adapt successfully to changing environmental conditions and process requirements.

Through attention to detail and continuous pursuit of improvement, lot sizes can be reduced and a wider variety of products can be produced by the same line. We call such a production line "highly flexible." *Flexibility* is defined as the capability of a manufacturing system to adapt successfully to changing environmental conditions and process requirements.[16]

EXAMPLE

Flexibility takes many forms, depending on the manufacturing environment. One form is the ability to produce several products all on the same line. The General Motors Fairfax plant in Kansas City, Missouri, produces Pontiac Grand Prixs. Years ago, changing over from producing a car of one color to a car of another meant shutting down the painting area so it could be cleared of dust and scrubbed. Since this shutdown was time-consuming, it was advantageous to produce several car bodies of the same color before changing colors. Today, through the greater technology of airtight chambers and high powered vacuum suctions, the time it takes to change production from one color to another is greatly reduced. Grand Prixs are now produced in different colors, one car one color, a second car another color, without production line delays.

Another form of flexibility is the ability to respond quickly to increases in demand. Still another form is the ability to quickly develop new products and models to meet fast-changing consumer tastes.

Reducing Setup Time. As we have seen, complicated, time-consuming, and expensive setups discourage flexible manufacturing and JIT because producing in large

[16]P. Swamidass, *Manufacturing Flexibility: Monograph #2* (Waco, Tex: Operations Management Association, 1988).

lot sizes is more economical. The Japanese have concentrated on finding ways to reduce setup costs so that smaller lot sizes, and increased flexibility, become economically feasible. Table 15.4 describes some techniques for reducing setup time when the changeover from one product to another involves an exchange of die.

Shigeo Shingo states that OED is always preferred to IED and obviously, OTED is better than SMED. Without such techniques an exchange of die can often take many hours or, in some cases, days. The exchange of die techniques, however, requires a considerable investment in process design. These improvements, too, are the result of the Japanese attention to manufacturing detail. General Motors, in a joint venture with Toyota at the NUMMI (New United Motors Manufacturing Inc.) plant outside San Francisco, has installed a new press line with these die changing features.

Flexibility Without Automation Although automation can provide greater flexibility in production, automation is not mandatory. Making the production process flexible without automation has been referred to as "attaining the affect of automation without the expense."[17] Three methods for doing so are preautomation, modular design, and standardization. *Preautomation* attacks one of Shingo's seven wastes, the waste of processing itself. It makes no sense to automate a stage of a production process when that stage adds no value to the product. Before automating a process, preautomation studies can reveal unneeded equipment and activities that can then be eliminated rather than automated. Two other methods (discussed in Chapter 4), *modular design* and *standardization,* also help achieve some of the benefits of automation without the expense.

Preautomation An analysis that is performed before automating a production process, to reveal unnecessary equipment and activities so that they can be eliminated rather than automated.

Lot Size of One The ultimate flexibility is the ability to produce products from a family of products in lot sizes of one. By doing so, flow-through time is minimal and customer orders can be processed rapidly. Although achieving ultimate flexibility is difficult, trying to do so often is what separates run-of-the-mill manufacturers from world-class manufacturers.

SUPPORTING SERVICES FOR JIT

JIT's emphasis on a detailed, disciplined approach is reflected in strong supporting functions to bolster production. Preventive maintenance and purchasing are crucial examples.

[17]R. Hall, *Attaining Manufacturing Excellence*, pp. 117–48.

TABLE 15.4 **Exchange of Die Techniques**

IED:	(Inside exchange of die) To exchange the die, the machine must be stopped.
OED:	(Outside exchange of die) The die can be exchanged while the machine is running and another part is being processed.
SMED:	(Single minute exchange of die) The die can be exchanged in less than ten minutes.
OTED:	(One touch exchange of die) The die can be exchanged in less than one minute.

Source: Adapted from Shigeo Shingo, *Study of Toyota Production System* (Tokyo: Japanese Management Association, 1981).

Preventive maintenance (PM) JIT philosophy espousing daily, extensive checkups and repairs for production equipment, lengthening their useful life well beyond the traditional time frame.

Preventive Maintenance (PM) A distinctive feature of JIT environments is the constant attention to scheduled daily preventive maintenance of equipment. PM runs counter to the traditional philosophy that machinery depreciates to a value of zero over a number of years. Like a car, properly maintained manufacturing machinery can function in top shape for a number of years.

It is not unusual in a JIT environment for an entire plant to shut down production each day, for example, for four hours during the midnight shift for scheduled maintenance. Every machine is inspected and serviced. Machines are lubricated, parts are replaced, and tools and equipment are inspected for proper calibration.

JIT Purchasing JIT purchasing differs from and is changing the traditional North American perspective on purchasing. Japanese companies, for example, tend to adopt long-term relationships with fewer suppliers.[18] In exchange for long-term contracts, suppliers sometimes agree to special conditions such as locating the supplier plant within a certain radius of the JIT company, adopting total quality control techniques, and submitting to frequent inspections by company executives and quality specialists. Table 15.5 compares JIT and traditional purchasing in more detail.

APPLICATION OF JAPANESE MANUFACTURING IN THE UNITED STATES

While manufacturing methods such as JIT and TQC have met with great success in Japan, many of these methods are not culturally specific to the Japanese and need not be limited to them. Companies such as General Motors, Chrysler, RCA, Hewlett Packard, John Deere, General Electric, and Westinghouse have used JIT with varying degrees of success.

Operations Management Highlight 15.2 describes the success of five North American companies that have adopted Japanese manufacturing methods. Although the benefits these companies achieved are attractive, they do involve some risks. Rather than blindly adopting new manufacturing methods, operations managers must understand their industries and their companies' marketing needs, customers, and products. Only then can operations managers make appropriate process choices. Without much understanding, managers may choose inappropriate processes, and the company may become less competitive.

WHERE JIT MAY BE INAPPROPRIATE

Using JIT requires extraordinary discipline because JIT works but under stable, reliable operating conditions. For example, to use *kanban,* loads must not fluctuate by more than 10 percent and daily build schedules must not fluctuate.[19] If a company's

[18]Sang M. Lee, and A. Ansari, "Comparative Analysis of Japanese Just-in-Time Purchasing and Traditional Purchasing Systems," ***International Journal of Operations and Production Management*** (1985), 5–14.

[19]S. Aggarwal, "Making Sense of Production Operations Systems," ***Harvard Business Review*** (Sept.–Oct. 1985), 8–16.

OPERATIONS MANAGEMENT HIGHLIGHT 15.2

Source: Jay Freis

North American Firms Successfully Adopt Japanese Manufacturing Techniques

Richard Schonberger, in his book ***World-Class Manufacturing***, lists an honor roll of eighty-four companies that have benefited by adopting Japanese manufacturing techniques. We cite five examples to illustrate the variety of successes:

1. ***Inventory savings*** Hewlett Packard in Greely, Colorado: WIP cut from 22 days of on-hand inventory to one day.
2. ***Space savings*** Sperry in Minneapolis: Entire computer, from printed circuit

assembly to computer assembly, testing, packing, and crating, now made in one small room.

3. ***Leadtime and movement reduction.*** Omark in Guelph, Ontario: Lead time cut from 21 days to one day; flow distance cut from 2,620 feet to 173 feet.
4. ***Multiple improvements.*** General Electric in Louisville: Lead-time to build dishwashers cut from six days to 18 hours; raw and in-process stock cut by more than half; scrap and rework cut 51 percent; field service calls cut 53 percent.
5. ***Multiple improvements.*** Black and Decker/GE in Ashboro, North Carolina: Formerly made 10,000 coffee makers a day on three lines with three shifts and three months between model changes; now same volume but all models made daily on two mixed model lines with one shift and ***kanban*** squares for line stocking; space reduced by 52,000 square feet.

Source: Richard J. Schonberger, ***World-Class Manufacturing*** (New York: Free Press, 1986), 229–236.

TABLE 15.5 Comparative Analysis of Purchasing Practice: Traditional U.S. and Japanese JIT

Purchasing Activity	JIT Purchasing	Traditional Purchasing
Purchase lot size	Purchase in small lots with frequent deliveries	Purchase in large batch size with less frequent deliveries
Selecting supplier	Single source of supply for a given part in nearby geographical area with a long-term contract	Rely on multiple sources of supply for a given part and short-term contracts
Evaluating supplier	Emphasis is placed on product quality, delivery performance, and price, but *no* percentage of reject from supplier is acceptable	Emphasis is placed on product quality, delivery performance and price but about two per cent reject from supplier is acceptable
Receiving inspection	Counting and receiving inspection of incoming parts is reduced and eventually eliminated	Buyer is responsible for receiving, counting, and inspecting all incoming parts
Negotiating and bidding process	Primary objective is to achieve product quality through a long-term contract and fair price	Primary objective is to get the lowest possible price
Determining mode of transportation	Concern for both inbound and outbound freight, and on-time delivery. Delivery schedule left to the buyer	Concern for outbound freight and lower outbound costs. Delivery schedule left to the supplier
Product specification	"Loose" specifications. The buyer relies more on performance specifications than on product design and the supplier is encouraged to be more innovative	"Rigid" specifications. The buyer relies more on design specifications than on product performance and suppliers have less freedom in design specifications
Paperwork	Less formal paperwork. Delivery time and quantity level can be changed by telephone calls	Requires great deal of time and formal paperwork. Changes in delivery date and quantity require purchase orders
Packaging	Small standard containers used to hold exact quantity and to specify the precise specifications	Regular packaging for every part type and part number with no clear specifications on product content.

Source: Sang M. Lee, and A. Ansari, "Comparative Analysis of Japanese Just-in-Time Purchasing and Traditional Purchasing Systems," *International Journal of Operations and Production Management* 5, no. 4 (1985), 5–14.

master production schedule must be frequently updated, then *kanban* may not work because it does not adapt well to frequent scheduling changes. JIT also does not work well if suppliers and freight system are unreliable.

The clearest data about whether JIT is appropriate for a North American company might come from analyzing Japanese manufacturing plants located in North America. What do these plants' employees think of their jobs and employers? From limited data, we suspect these plants are productive and profitable while the American workers are not completely satisfied with their employers.[20] It will be interesting to watch developments, especially in the United States where individual freedom is highly valued. Cultural differences might account for fewer gains at their North American JIT plants than the Japanese enjoy with facilities in their homeland.

SUMMARY

Management students in Western societies often find the study of Japanese manufacturing techniques interesting because they have grown up with Japanese products and regularly hear about the threat the Japanese pose as awesome business competitors. Practicing managers in Western countries have an even deeper appreciation. In the 1970s, Western companies did not understand the challenge that the Japanese would come to pose. Many Western companies credited the Japanese success to cheap labor or government protection. Today, many of these same companies have lost market share and are now adopting a variety of JIT techniques.

Following World War II, the Japanese learned some important lessons from American industry and have since developed some unique manufacturing strengths. The Japanese have developed a system of manufacturing that works. Some important aspects of their approach are employee involvement, Japanese management principles, the just-in-time system, stockless production, total quality control, a pull versus push system, and the *kanban* system. The underlying philosophy of JIT is the continuous pursuit of waste reduction. Western businesses now can learn from the Japanese, adopting those techniques that will help them compete more effectively in worldwide manufacturing.

CASE The Bronson Insurance Group

COMPANY BACKGROUND

The Bronson Insurance Group was originally founded in 1900 in Auxvasse, Missouri, by James Bronson. The Bronson Group owns a variety of companies that underwrite personal and commercial insurance policies. Annual sales of the Bronson Group are $100 million. In recent years, the company has suffered operating losses. In 1990, the company was heavily invested in computer hardware and software. One of the problems the Bronson Group faced (as well as many insurance companies) was a conflict between established manual procedures and the relatively recent (within the past 20 years)

[20]See Joseph J. Fucini and Suzy Fucini, ***Working for the Japanese: Inside Mazda's American Auto Plant*** (New York: Free Press, 1990); David Gelsanliter, ***Jump Start: Japan Comes to the Heartland*** (New York: Farrar, Straus & Giroux, 1990); and "Japan Comes to Town, Reality Arrives Later," ***Business Week***, (August 20, 1990), 10.

introduction of computer equipment. This conflict was illustrated by the fact that much information was captured on computer but paper files were still kept for practical and legal reasons.

FILE CLERKS

The file department employed 20 file clerks who pulled files from stacks, refiled used files, and delivered files to various departments including commercial lines, personal lines, and claims. Once a file clerk received a request for a file, it usually took about two hours for the requester to receive the file. Clerks delivered files to underwriters on an hourly basis throughout the day. The average file clerk was paid $8,300 per year. One special file clerk was used full time to search for requested files that another file clerk had not been able to find in the expected place. It was estimated that 40 percent of the requested files were these "no hit" files requiring a search. Often these "no hit" files were eventually found stacked in the requester's office. The primary "customers" of the file clerks were underwriters and claims attorneys.

UNDERWRITING

Company management and operations analysts were consistently told that the greatest problem in the company was the inability of file clerks to supply files in a speedy fashion. The entire company from top to bottom viewed the productivity and effectiveness of the files department as unacceptable. An underwriter used 20–50 files per day. Because of their distrust of the files department, underwriters tended to hoard often used files. A count by operations analysts found that each underwriter kept from 100-200 files in his or her office at any one time. An underwriter would request a file by computer and work on other business until the file was received. Benson employed 25 underwriters.

MANAGEMENT INFORMATION SYSTEMS

Upper management was deeply concerned about this problem. The MIS department had suggested using video disks as a possible solution. A video disk system was found that would be sufficient for the companies needs at a cost of about $12 million. It was estimated that the system would take two years to install and make compatible with existing information systems. Another, less attractive alternative was using microfilm. A microfilm system would require underwriters to go to a single keyboard to request paper copies of files. The cost of a microfilm system was $5 million.

Case Questions

1. What do you recommend? Should the company implement one of the new technologies? Why or why not?
2. An operations analyst suggested that company employees shared a "dump on the clerks" mentality. Explain.
3. How would Japanese management handle this situation differently? Would W. Edwards Deming blame the clerks? Who would he blame for the problem?
4. Could you apply what you have learned in this chapter about lot size

reduction, WIP inventory reduction, and JIT to improve the files situation? Explain. What can you conclude about applying JIT in service settings?

CASE

Muzyx Corporation Final Assembly

The following is the final assembly process for the Maestro CD Player. The assembly line is well balanced with a cycle time of four minutes in each work station:

Work Station 1
Receive XT2 subassembly.
Remove XT2 from carton.
Inspect incoming materials for quality.
Work Station 2
Merge part XT2 with component R4 by fastening grommets.
Mark "X2" on part XT2 with a black magic marker.
Inspect part for quality.
Work Station 3
Align screws and fasten subassembly to chassis Z1.
Place elastic "retainer" band around assembly.
Inspect part for quality.
Work Station 4
Remove band from assembly.
Inspect assembly for defects.
Make sure all screws are tight on XT2, R4, and Z1.
Write workers initials on chassis Z1.
Replace band.
Work Station 5
Remove band from chassis.
Slide chassis into case Y6.
Close completed assembly by tightening four screws on the outer case Y6.
Perform quality check.
Work Station 6
Place completed assembly into carton to send to customer.

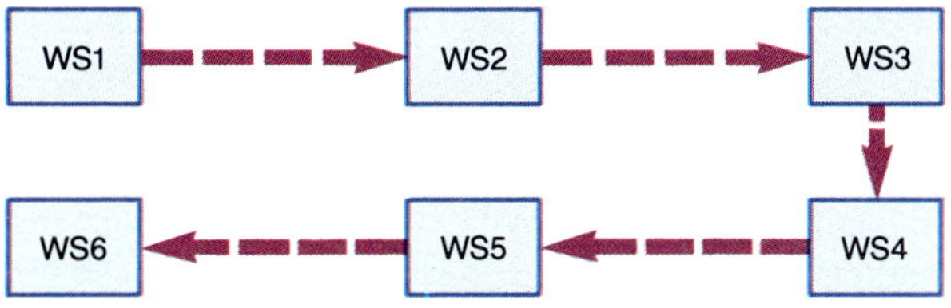

Layout

Applying what you have learned about waste reduction and value-added manufacturing, perform a value analysis of this assembly process, that is, logically identify and eliminate waste at each work station.

REVIEW AND DISCUSSION QUESTIONS

1. Given your current understanding of Japanese business practice, would you like to work for a Japanese corporation in your homeland? What would be the positive aspects? The negative aspects?
2. How do you suggest U.S. corporations effectively compete against the Japanese in (a) the world market? (b) the U.S. market?
3. The concept of economic order quantity was developed in Chapter 12. With your understanding of Japanese business practice, review the assumptions of the simple EOQ model. With which assumptions would the Japanese disagree?
4. There is a lot of discussion about but very few documented applications of JIT in services organizations. What JIT techniques would be valid in the following situations? Be prepared to explain your choices.
   (a) A bank
   (b) A restaurant
   (c) A copy center
   (d) A university
5. Review Shigeo Shingo's seven wastes (see Table 15.2). Which of these wastes are addressed by the following JIT techniques?
   (a) *Kanban*
   (b) Pull coordination
   (c) JIT purchasing
   (d) Flexible manufacturing
6. The role of Japanese governmental planning was discussed in this chapter. Would similar planning be of value in the United States? What is the current U.S. industrial policy? If you were in a position to establish U.S. industrial policy, what might you apply from your knowledge of the Japanese?
7. Why is it important to study Japanese manufacturing in a production and operations management course?
8. The Japanese tend to compete by establishing a competitive advantage and exploiting this advantage to increase market share. What are some advantages that U.S. companies enjoy that can be used to gain market share in response to the Japanese?
9. One of the much discussed aspects of Japanese management is their openness and willingness to share information. Indeed, it is striking that the Toyota Motor Company would share its production secrets with the rest of the world. In your view, does this openness help or hurt Japanese competitiveness? Does this create a psychological advantage for the Japanese? How?
10. Under what conditions should North American firms adopt Japanese manufacturing techniques? Should they "go Japanese" and adopt these techniques because of competitive fears? What must management understand about their own markets and companies before adopting Japanese manufacturing techniques?
11. Based upon your reading outside of the course, could a similar chapter be written about "German Contributions to World Class Manufacturing," "French Contributions . . ." or English Contributions . . . ?" What would some of these contributions be?
12. What are the contributions of the United States to world-class manufacturing?
13. Dr. W. Edwards Deming states that roughly 85 percent of poor quality can be attributed to management. Why is this? In a university setting, whose fault is it if a student fails? Is there a difference between manufacturing failures and those at universities? Explain.

14. When compared to their American counterparts, Japanese workers are seen as highly loyal to their employers. For instance, although unions exist in Japan, a workers' strike will consist of wearing black arm bands for a period of time. In contrast, what is it about North American management that suppresses employee loyalty?

15. Discuss preventive maintenance. In what ways is preventive maintenance absolutely necessary in JIT/*kanban*/pull manufacturing as opposed to push manufacturing?

16. How does flexibile manufacturing allow firms to introduce new products more quickly? How does flexibile manufacturing allow firms to reduce lot size? How does flexibile manufacturing reduce costs?

PROBLEMS

SOLVED PROBLEMS

1. *Kanban* bins circulating between two work stations each contain eight items. The cycle time is four minutes per item at the receiving work station. How often (average) will the supplying work station get a *kanban* card back from the receiving work station when the work stations are in operation?

SOLUTION

Materials in a bin will be consumed every 32 minutes (8 items/bin × 4 minutes/item) by the receiving work station. As a result, move cards will return to the supplying work station once every 32 minutes.

2. The process for making alarm clocks involves six work stations with cycle times of four minutes per item for every work station. The single-card *kanban* system uses ten units in each bin. The quality circle group has found a method to eliminate one stage of production, reducing the number of work stations to five. What are the reductions in work-in-process inventories and in flow-through time?

SOLUTION

Inventories and flow-through time for the five-station and six-station processes are compared.

WIP Inventory Levels

work stations = 6: Average WIP = 6 work stations × 10 units per lot = 60 units
work stations = 5: Average WIP = 5 work stations × 10 units per lot = 50 units
WIP reduction = 60 − 50 = 10 units

Flow-Through Time

work stations = 6: 6 work stations × 10 units/lot × 4 minutes/cycle
= 240 minutes
work stations = 5: 5 work stations × 10 units/lot × 4 minutes/cycle
= 200 minutes
Time reduction = 240 − 200 = 40 minutes

REINFORCING FUNDAMENTALS

3. The process for making a certain component involves seven work stations. The cycle time for all of the work stations is nine minutes. The current lot size is 25 units. What would be the effect on WIP levels and process flow-through times if the lot size were reduced to:
   (a) 19 units
   (b) 12 units
   (c) 5 units
   (d) 1 unit
4. Refer to the situation in Problem 3. The company's funds are rationed—that is, the company is having trouble getting financing. If the cost of each item in WIP inventory is $200, the company operates for 16 hours per day and 360 days per year, the cost of capital is 15 percent per year, and all finished goods can be sold, immediately, calculate the annual savings for each level of WIP you calculated.
5. It is important to most students to receive a class schedule that meets their academic program and personal needs. Yet student complaints about registration and advisors are often unheard. Problems or complaints could be divided into five categories: (1) unavailable or inadequate professional advice, (2) poor registration procedures, (3) unavailable classes, (4) too few sections for classes, and (5) inadequate information on registration procedures. Prepare a fishbone (cause and effect) diagram reflecting your experiences with these five complaint categories.
6. You've asked a friend for dinner and, afterwards, realized your spur-of-the-moment decision may have been bad judgment that you might regret. Now, you are studying fishbone (cause and effect) diagrams in operations management and decide to utilize this tool to help understand why the few times you have cooked, the meal never seemed to come out right—often with missing ingredients or a major sequencing problem. The upcoming meal will be simple: cold drinks, cheeseburgers, a tossed garden salad, and chocolate chip cookies. You have a charcoal grill—if you can find it. Prepare a fishbone diagram showing the necessary steps to prepare this meal.

KEY TERMS

Andon 574
Deming's 14 points for management 571
Fishbone (cause and effect) diagram 575
Flexibility 581
Just-in-time (JIT) 568
Kanban 578
Ministry of International Trade and Industry (MITI) 564
Poke a yoke 574
Preautomation 582
Preventive maintenance (PM) 583
Pull manufacturing system 577
Push manufacturing system 576
Quality circle 574
Quality loss function (QLF) 575
Robust product 576
Shingo's seven wastes 568
Stockless production system 570
Taguchi method of quality control 576
Theory Z 565
Total quality control (TQC) 570
Uniform load scheduling (level scheduling) 581
Value-added manufacturing 568
Visible control 574

SELECTED READINGS

Abegglen, J. C., and G. Stalk *Kaisha, The Japanese Corporation.* New York: Basic Books, 1985.

Cohen, S. S., and J. Zysman, *Manufacturing Matters: The Myth of the Post Industrial Economy.* New York: Basic Books, 1987.

Hall, R. W., *Zero Inventories.* Homewood, Ill.: Dow Jones–Irwin, 1983.

———, *Attaining Manufacturing Excellence.* Homewood, Ill.: Dow Jones–Irwin, 1987.

Heiko, L., "Some Relationships Between Japanese Culture and Just-in-Time," *The Academy of Management Executive,* 3, no. 4 (November 1989), 319–21.

Krajewski, L. J., B. E. King, and L. P. Ritzman, "Kanban, MRP, and Shaping the Manufacturing Environment," *Management Science* 33 no. 1, (January 1987), 39–57.

Lee, Sang, and A. Ansari, "Comparative Analysis of Japanese Just-in-Time Purchasing and Traditional Purchasing Systems," *International Journal of Operations and Production Management* 5, no. 4 (1985), 5–14.

Lubben, R. T., *Just-in-Time Manufacturing.* New York: McGraw-Hill, 1988).

Noori, H., "The Taguchi Methods: Achieving Design and Output Quality," *The Academy of Management Executive* 3, no. 4 (November 1989), 322–26.

Ouchi, W. O., *Theory Z.* New York: Avon Books, 1981.

Pascale, R. T., and A. G. Athos, *The Art of Japanese Management.* New York: Warner Books, 1981.

Schonberger, R.J., *Japanese Manufacturing Techniques.* New York: Free Press, 1982.

———, *World-Class Manufacturing.* New York: Free Press, 1986.

———, *World-Class Manufacturing Casebook.* New York: Free Press, 1987.

———, "The Transfer of Japanese Manufacturing Management Approaches to U.S. Industry," *Academy of Management Review,* 7, no. 3, (1982) 679–87.

———, "Some Observation on the Advantages and Implementation Issues of Just-in-Time Production Systems," *Journal of Operations Management* 3, no. 1, (1982), 1–11.

Shingo, S., *Study of Toyota Production System from Industrial Engineering Viewpoint.* Tokyo: Japanese Management Association, 1981.

Suzaki, K., *The New Manufacturing Challenge: Techniques for Continuous Improvement.* New York: Free Press, 1987.

Swamidass, P.M., *Manufacturing Flexibility,* Monograph No. 2. Waco, Tex.: Operations Management Association, 1988.

Taguchi, G., E. A. Elsayed, and Thomas Hsiang, Thomas *Quality Engineering in Production Systems.* New York: McGraw-Hill, 1989.

CHAPTER 16

MANAGING FOR QUALITY

At Ford Motor Company we have adopted an operating philosophy to establish and maintain an environment that will result in never-ending improvement in the quality and productivity of products and services throughout the Company, its supply base, and its dealer organizations. The new philosophy requires that the Company improve the quality and productivity of every element of the business from planning through field service. This includes—but is not limited to—all products and services, people relationships, attention to customers' needs, profits, shareholders' investments, and management approaches. In the final analysis, we are "customer-driven."

MISSION Our mission is to continually improve our products and services to meet our customers' needs, allowing us to prosper as a business and to provide a reasonable return for our stockholders, the owners of our business.

VALUES

- *People:* Our people are the source of our strength. They provide our corporate intelligence and determine our reputation and vitality. Involvement and teamwork are our basic human values.
- *Products:* Our products are the end result of our efforts, and they should be the best in serving our customers worldwide. As our products are viewed, so are we viewed.
- *Profits:* Profits are the ultimate measure of how efficiently we provide customers with the best products for their needs. Profits are required to survive and grow.

GUIDING PRINCIPLES

- *Quality comes first:* To achieve customer satisfaction the quality of our products and services must be our number-one priority.

- ***Customers are the focus of everything we do:*** Our work must be done with our customers in mind, providing better products and services than our competition.
- ***Continuous improvement is essential to our success:*** We must strive for excellence in everything we do: in our products, in their safety and value—and in our services, our human relations, our competitiveness, and our profitability.
- ***Employee involvement is our way of life:*** We are a team. We must treat each other with trust and respect.
- ***Dealers and suppliers are our partners:*** The Company must maintain mutually beneficial relationships with suppliers, dealers, and our other business associates.
- ***Integrity is never compromised:*** The conduct worldwide must be pursued in a manner that is socially responsible, and commands respect for its integrity and for its positive contributions to society. Our doors are open to men and women alike without discrimination and without regard to ethnic origin or personal beliefs.

The overall effort must mobilize the entire work force in the pursuit of specific Company goals aimed at satisfying customer requirements for quality, value, and delivery.

John A. Manoogian
Executive Director, Product Assurance
North American Automotive Operations
Ford Motor Company
Dearborn, Michigan

Performance quality is crucial to the long-term survival of most organizations. Each of us is aware, in varying degrees, of the international challenge to the North American automobile industry and the impact on quality and value. In the 1980s, John Manoogian had a significant hand in developing quality strategies and supporting improvement at Ford. It is interesting that his discussion about quality is in the context of Ford's mission, values, and guiding principles (the first of which is quality), and illustrates that quality is a major part of Ford's business objectives.

MANAGERIAL RESPONSIBILITY IN MANAGING FOR QUALITY

Managing for quality, the subject addressed in this chapter, begins and ends with managerial responsibility. Often managers have no great desire to improve quality. Managers seem to be unaware of the urgent need for quality improvement. Nationally, this need is increasing, and efforts to meet this need encounter many barriers. In this chapter we want to increase your *awareness* of the importance of performance quality in operations, and in both this and the next chapter to provide you with some alternative *analysis and program choices for improvement.* Should you become responsible for an operations function, the information in this and the next chapter on quality analysis and control will help you in your decision making as you seek quality improvement for your organization.

How important is quality to an organization or nation? Peters and Waterman, in the popular management book *In Search of Excellence*, point to quality as a characteristic repeatedly identified in excellent corporations throughout the United States.[1] What about quality in other nations? In thinking about this issue, we return to the Japanese experience since World War II. What qualities do consumers admire in Japanese products? The answer is that the Japanese understand and provide quality and value in their products. Let's first briefly discuss aspects of the concept of quality and then focus on managing for improving quality.

PRODUCT QUALITY

OUTPUT QUALITY

Design specifications The important, desired characteristics of a product or service specified in detail during the design phase.

The important characteristics of a product are specified when it is designed, prior to its manufacture. These characteristics are called the *design specifications.* After the product has been produced, we can observe the extent to which it conforms to or deviates from the design specifications. As we defined in Chapter 2, quality, or product quality, is the degree to which the design specifications for a product are appropriate to its function and use, and the degree to which the product conforms to its design specifications. Service quality is similarly defined, and we often generalize and use the term *output quality* to apply to either products or services. We will ask you to make inferences from the discussion of product quality to service quality in this and the next chapter.

In previous chapters we have focused on product and process design. However, in production and operations, we often have limited affect on design. This is unfortunate, because production must ensure that output conforms to design. For the most part, our discussion of quality is restricted to this narrower operations perspective involving conformance to a design. When output closely conforms to design specifications, output quality is high. When output deviates in an important way from design specifications, output quality is low. Output quality can be seen to fall on a continuum ranging from very low to very high, as Figure 16.1 shows.

Among popular alternative concepts of quality are the following:

- Quality is fitness for use.
- Quality is doing it right the first time—and every time.

FIGURE 16.1 Degrees of output quality

[1]Thomas J. Peters and Robert H. Waterman, *In Search of Excellence: Lessons from America's Best-Run Companies* (New York: Harper & Row, 1982).

- Quality is the customer's perception.
- Quality provides a product or service at a price the customer can afford.
- You pay for what you get (quality is the most expensive product or service).

Although each of these views have merit, they have shortcomings as well. In any case, little is accomplished by arguing over precise quality definitions or slogans. The first key to managing for quality is being aware of the need to improve; the second is selecting improvement techniques with the best chance for success. An understanding of product characteristics, product design, and process capability will help you become aware of quality issues in operations.

Product Characteristics All characteristics of the product are not equally important to our customers. Usually, only some characteristics need to be considered when assessing quality. But which ones? Weight? Size? Shape? Color? Functional performance? *The important product characteristics are determined by the specific market goals of the organization and by the technical requirements of the important stages of the conversion process.* Often we must compromise between these two sources of quality requirements.

Design Of two firms producing the same product, one may have to pay high costs to maintain an acceptable quality, while its competitor can maintain the same quality at a much lower cost. The difference is often a result of the emphasis placed on quality in the design phases of product development, prior to full-scale production. The old adage, "quality is *designed into* the product," holds true. The number of stages in the conversion process, the types of input resources needed, and the types of technical processes required to produce the output are all largely determined in the product design phase.

Process capability The ability of a conversion process to produce a product that conforms to design specifications; a range of variation from the design specifications under normal working conditions.

Process Capability *Process capability* is the ability of a conversion process to produce a product that conforms to design specifications. Since the performance of machines and people used in a conversion process varies from day to day, process capability is described by a range of variation from the design specification—the variation expected under normal working conditions. A statement about process capability is thus a statement about product uniformity: Instead of various parameters of the process—parameters of machines, workers, and so on—process capability relates to various parameters of the product.

A typical process capability, for example, might relate to the diameter of a component tube and be described by a range of diameters. Under normal working conditions, diameters of component tubes could be expected to measure within the range of process capability. Studies of the conversion process over time determine the variability of the process and hence the process capability. As an organization strives for continuous improvement, process capability should improve. We will return to the topic of process capability in Chapter 17.

Of course product and process design does not end when production begins. Design often continues throughout the product life in the form of various redesign activities. The need for redesign is signaled by reliability studies, quality assurance programs, warranty costs, and customer complaints.

MANAGING FOR QUALITY PRODUCTS AND SERVICES

Having discussed the concept of quality, let's ask how managers actually go about—or should go about—establishing and achieving the desired quality. There are several significant steps in effectively managing for quality. Figure 16.2 summarizes the activities operations managers must perform to establish an overall quality framework, as well as to carry out the details to achieve or improve quality.[2]

The manager must first determine how quality fits into the overall organizational strategy. Then, more specifically, he or she must determine the role that quality will play in the manufacturing (or operations) strategy; the approach used in production or

FIGURE 16.2 Managing for quality products and services

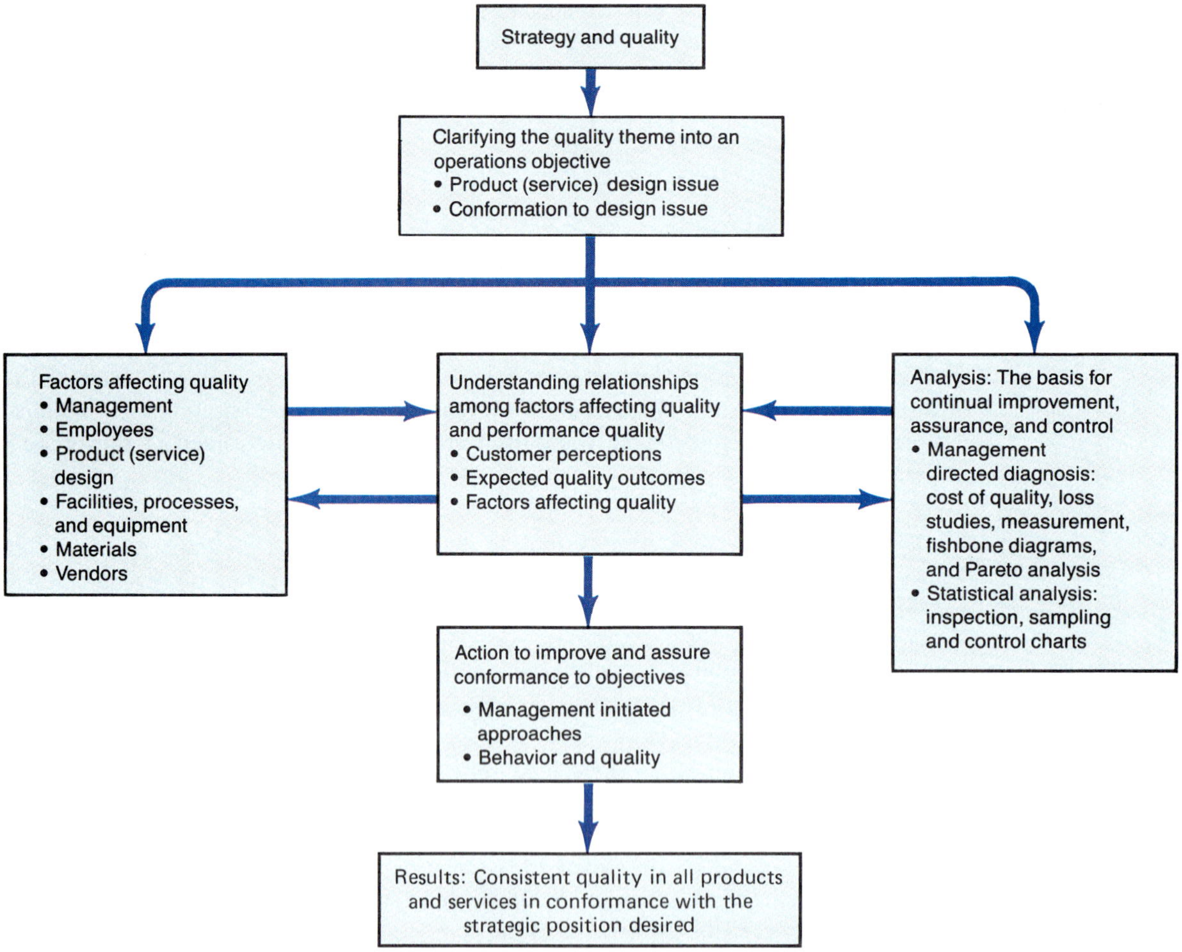

[2]For an alternative summary view prepared for operations executives and students, see Everett E. Adam, Jr., and Eugene M. Barker, "Achieving Quality Products and Services," *Operations Management Review* (Winter 1987), 1–8.

operations should complement the overall strategy of the organization. Next, the quality theme must be clarified: It is essential that individuals at all levels within the organization comprehend quality goals.

For any organization there are key elements that affect quality. Effective managers must be able to identify these elements—typically people, facilities, and materials—and seek to understand how they affect quality in their firm.

Once a strategy is developed and communicated and the key elements affecting quality are understood, the conversion process takes place: Products are manufactured, parts are made, services are generated, and customers are served. But, how do we know if we are conforming to plan? Are we seeking the continual quality improvement desired? With respect to quality, are processes under control? Are quality costs in line with expectations? Fortunately, there is a rich and thorough set of diagnostic and analytic techniques to help the operations manager answer these questions. Effective managers have found that statistical techniques, in particular, can be quite useful; these methods are stressed in Chapter 17.

Once managers have analyzed potential areas for quality improvement, they must give specific directions to ensure performance quality. A variety of programs and techniques can help bring behaviors and processes into conformance with expectations. We survey several major programs in this chapter. Finally, we can observe the long-term results: consistent quality in all products and services at levels in accordance with the organization's overall strategy. Let's now address each major block of Figure 16.2, with particular attention to quality analysis and action (programs); both are extremely significant in day-to-day operations management.

STRATEGY AND QUALITY

In developing an operations strategy, market potential (demand) is related to process capability. As product or service ideas emerge, a general production approach and sales plan are formed. Executives must develop and communicate an expectation of quality to guide the organization, defining the desired quality for each product or service, and setting quality standards for all activities that support the primary business goals—activities in accounting, finance, engineering, distribution, and administration.

This link between strategy and quality is crucial if the firm is to have a consistent purpose. Japanese managers understand the importance of this connection and North American managers seem to be catching on as well.

EXAMPLE

Company-wide quality control (CWQC) A management philosophy and set of activities characterized by mobilizing the entire work force in the pursuit of quality, by statistical thinking, and by preventing errors.

Japanese manufacturing firms have developed *company-wide quality control* (CWQC) that has evolved from inspection-oriented quality control (prior to 1945), through a statistical quality control growth phase (1945–1955) and a total quality control growth phase (1955–1970), into what is now CWQC with rapid growth (1970–present). As we described in Chapter 15, the typical Japanese firm promotes never-ending improvement in the effectiveness and efficiency of all elements of a business. The goal of CWQC is to mobilize the entire work force in a pursuit of specific company goals aimed at satisfying customer requirements for quality, price, and delivery. The CWQC organization improves the effectiveness and efficiency of every element in the business through statistical thinking, managing with facts, and preventing defects and errors and stresses these six elements:

1. Consider quality first in all business thinking and action.
2. Ensure the quality of new product development.
3. Make quality customer-oriented, not producer-oriented.
4. Consider the next step in any process as the customer.
5. Use a continuing "plan, do, check" action cycle in all business elements.
6. Respect humanity.[3]

There are certainly many companies that stress quality as a corporate strategy, among them Boeing, Caterpillar, Hewlett Packard, and IBM. For example, a survey by a major business publication asked CEOs which American companies have the highest quality products or services. Boeing was the top-rated company by these executives.

CLARIFYING THE QUALITY THEME

A key to achieving and maintaining high quality is first to set a strategy, and then effectively communicate this strategy as a theme to employees and customers. Refecting our definition of quality, both *product (service) design* and *conformance* to the design specifications must be clarified for engineering and operations. We have seen from several of the examples above the effort CEOs are taking in stressing a theme. As consumers we have seen the media presentations for products: Hallmark's "Mark of

After the quality strategy is established, supervisors must understand and communicate quality goals and expectations to employees on the shop floor.
Source: **Steve Dunwell / The Image Bank**

[3]Company-Wide Quality Control (CWQC)," Report of the NAAO Product Assurance Committee, February 13, 1984.

Excellence," Ford's "Quality Is Job 1," and General Electric's "Quality Is Our Most Important Product," to name but a few. Internally, companies also go to great lengths to stress the theme, goal, or quality thrust to employees. Some of the alternative "quality" definitions we explored stress this communication issue.

EXTERNAL AND INTERNAL ELEMENTS AFFECTING QUALITY

A systems viewpoint helps us understand the key elements, both external and internal, affecting quality. The organization as a system interacts externally with customers and vendors—two key elements that specify and affect quality at the boundaries of the firm. Customers' desires should be the basis for quality objectives. Often in service-oriented companies, customers also participate in generating the service—setting quality standards and making sure they are met. Examples include joint participation at self-service gasoline stations, cafeterias, and discount department stores. Customers, to a great extent, serve themselves—and quality can vary widely from individual to individual. It becomes a challenge to design service systems to meet a particular quality level in such a shared labor situation.

As the second key element, vendors are especially important to organizations that purchase a high percentage of their products. Progressive firms are moving toward vendor certification and away from incoming inspection. In essence, certification makes the vendor a part of the company team.

Internally, an organization's managers, employees, materials, facilities, processes, and equipment all affect quality. Dr. Joseph Juran and Dr. W. Edwards Deming, specialists on Japanese quality, suggest that as much as 85 percent of the quality problems are *management* problems.[4] Their view is that managers, rather than employees, have the authority and tools to correct most quality problems. *Employees* do have certain opportunities to affect quality, however, because some variations in quality are individually determined.

In a production environment, *materials* vary; high-quality materials are easier to work with than low-quality materials, and they often result in a labor savings. The key factor in production is often the degree of *variation*—there should be piece-to-piece consistency within a material lot and in subsequent lots. This is true for material used (inputs) as well as for products and services produced (outputs).

How do *facilities, processes,* and *equipment* affect quality? Tools wear out and break. Roofs sometimes leak and require fixing. Equipment needs to be in good repair so parts are made the same every time.

UNDERSTANDING RELATIONSHIPS AMONG FACTORS DETERMINING QUALITY

Customer Perceptions A progressive organization should have a well-established strategy for quality, one that is based on customer perceptions of quality. Customer service after the sale of a product is often as important as the quality of the product itself. A customer service audit is one way of identifying customer perceptions of

[4]W. Edwards Deming, "On Some Statistical Aids Toward Economic Production" *Interfaces* 5, no. 5 (August 1975), pp 1–15; J. Juran, *Upper Management and Quality,* 4th ed. (New York: Juran Institute, 1981).

quality. The audit is equally meaningful for services and products. It is also useful for all services performed internally (for others in the firm). The following example illustrates how Caterpillar emphasizes quality from a customer perspective.

EXAMPLE

Caterpillar Tractor Company's quality program is multifaceted, but each facet is unilaterally focused on customer perceptions of quality. For each purchase, two customer surveys are taken to identify quality problems: one after 300 hours of product use and one after 500 hours of use. Lists of identified problems are centrally compiled and maintained. Dealers, too, submit information by analyzing warranty and service reports and by conducting a quality audit as soon as the dealer receives product shipments. Dealers assess whether defects are created in assembly or in shipping. As part of its quality improvement program, Caterpillar guarantees 48-hour delivery of any part to any customer in the world, and encourages dealers to establish side businesses in rebuilding parts to reduce costs to customers and increase the speed of repairs.[5]

Expected Quality Outcomes Throughout this book we have emphasized that people skills, materials, and processes are blended together to provide products and services for customers. These products and services are of a certain quality, evaluated by how well they conform to expectations. We've emphasized that these expectations should be customer-based rather than internally based, that is, manufacturing- or engineering-based.

In reality, manufacturing and operations attempt to conform to internally based expectations. Thus, the design must ensure that these internally set specifications are consistent with customer expectations. Furthermore, design must also ensure that specifications are accurately translated into the language of manufacturing and operations—bills of materials, drawings, route sheets, procedures manuals, job descriptions, and so forth. In manufacturing, this is the work of manufacturing engineering. There must be a customer-product or customer-service link, a well-managed interface with clear instructions and feedback to operations, where the work is actually performed. This link is equally important for services and manufacturing organizations.

Factor Relationships To be more specific about the blending of people skills, materials, and processes, we ask: What are the key variables in operations that affect product or service quality?

Although our general answer is "it depends upon the manufacturing or service situation," we need to clarify. The way resources are blended (technology), the relative emphasis of one resource over another (cost structure), and the skills and abilities of people are all crucial. Competition, pride, knowledge—the list can go on and on as to what contributes to quality performance. At this point attempts to definitively model these interrelationships are speculative at best.[6]

[5]Hirotaka Takeuchi and John A. Quelch, "Quality Is More Than Making a Good Product," *Harvard Business Review* 61, no. 4 (July-August, 1983), 139–45.

[6]See, for example, a behavior-technology model of factors affecting quality in Everett E. Adam, Jr., James C. Hershauer, and William A. Ruch, *Productivity and Quality: Measurement as a Basis for Improvement,* 2nd ed. (Research Center, College of Business and Public Administration, University of Missouri-Columbia, 1986), 144–50.

Advances in product/service design, statistical thinking, planned change, and selected behavioral interventions hold the most promise for contemporary operations managers attempting to improve quality.

ANALYSIS FOR IMPROVEMENT, ASSURANCE, AND CONTROL

MANAGEMENT-DIRECTED DIAGNOSIS FOR QUALITY

Quality analysis includes techniques for diagnosis and improvement. Here we discuss diagnosis techniques; in the next chapter we discuss statistical analysis, a technique for quality control and improvement.

The Cost of Quality If organizations systematically examined the cost of poor quality, they would be amazed at how expensive it is. As a percentage of total cost of goods sold, poor quality is often well in excess of 20 percent of sales. What are the origins of such high costs? How can one document these costs? Why haven't otherwise successful companies reduced such costs? These and similar questions can be addressed by examining four broad cost categories: prevention, appraisal, internal failure, and external failure.

Internal failure costs Costs attributable to errors and defects in production at the plant.

Appraisal costs Costs of evaluating, measuring, or inspecting for quality at the plant and in the field.

Prevention costs Costs of planning, designing, and equipping a quality control program.

External failure costs Costs attributable to the failure of products in the field.

Internal failure costs are perhaps the most common and the easiest costs to document. Accounting systems identify and account for scrap, rework, and similar costs. To a large extent, *appraisal costs* can also be estimated. In the traditional organization in the United States, much of the inspection process is performed by an inspection staff and can be reflected as labor costs. Analyzing inspection costs is more difficult in a progressive, quality-oriented firm where every employee inspects his or her work as part of a job responsibility. However, even in this type of situation, costs can be estimated.

Prevention costs are more difficult to assess. Training, planning, measurement, vendor certification, equipment maintenance, and similar prevention activities can, however, be estimated. *External failure costs*—failures of the product or service after it leaves the facility and is being used or consumed—are much more difficult to assess. Field service costs, warrantee claims, and lost sales are all very real.

Although it may be a major effort for the accounting system to estimate costs, the results of such an effort are usually worthwhile. Regardless of the data collection method, *top management will certainly pay attention to a well constructed, reasonably documented total-cost-of-quality estimate.* It is an effective analytic tool, and can generate support for quality improvement efforts and expenditures. Evaluating the components of total quality costs can provide the astute operations manager with insight into areas with high potential for improvement. Can such a cost analysis be viewed positively? That is the question that Operations Management Highlight 16.1 examines.

Quality Costs and Assurance Quality assurance programs commonly involve systematic efforts to assess output quality. They determine current quality and trends in quality, and they make comparisons with the quality of competitors. This information is used in product and process redesign, market strategy, and product pricing decisions.

OPERATIONS MANAGEMENT HIGHLIGHT 16.1

Source: Lou Jones/The Image Bank

Does Quality Cost or Pay?

American manufacturers have embraced the concept of quality for over a decade now. Advertising campaigns promote superior quality. Experts such as Deming, Juran, and Crosby espouse quality techniques. Standards of excellence recognize outstanding quality achievements. Yet, what effect has attention to quality had on financial performance? Most managers admit that quantifying the costs and benefits of quality programs is difficult. Employee training and the price of not shipping defective products are usually regarded as two of the most important costs. The price of nonconformance—the cost of not doing things right the first time—and the return on investment are usually regarded as two of the most important benefits.

Examined below are the quality programs of four U.S. manufacturers, each of which has received the Malcolm Baldridge National Quality Award, to be discussed later in this chapter (see page 612). Of particular interest is how each of these companies defines the costs and benefits of its quality programs.

Milliken & Company This textile manufacturer, headquartered in Spartanburg, South Carolina, produces over 48,000 textile and chemical products. In 1981, Milliken initiated its Pursuit of Excellence program to create an overall commitment to customer satisfaction at all levels of the organization. As part of the program, Milliken reduced the number of management levels and dispersed authority throughout the company. Some 14,300 associates (employees) were reorganized into self-managed teams. The teams were formed to address business challenges and to respond to customer needs. Milliken's investment in training is substantial: approximately $1300 per associate in 1988. The company believes that the investment was worthwhile. The percentage of on-time deliveries increased from 75 percent in 1984 to an industry-leading 99 percent in 1988. The price of nonconformance has been reduced by 60 percent. Because of these improvements, Milliken has made significant inroads into the Japanese and Korean auto-manufacturing markets.

Motorola, Inc. This electronics manufacturer, headquartered in Schaumburg, Illinois, initiated its quality improvement program because of fierce competition from the Japanese. In 1981, Motorola set a goal to improve the quality of its products and services tenfold within five years. In 1987, after having achieved its initial goal, Motorola set two additional goals. One was to improve its quality tenfold within two years; the second was to improve quality one-hundredfold within four years. To reach its goals, Motorola established a training center and invested $170 million in training between 1983 and 1987. Data from employees, customer surveys, complaint hotlines, and other sources are used in quality improvement and product development efforts. Like Milliken, Motorola believes that the investment was worthwhile. The price of nonconformance has been reduced from 13 percent to 8 percent of annual revenues over the last three years, a savings of approximately $480 million. Motorola has also made significant inroads into foreign markets. In some markets, Motorola products enjoy a major share.

Globe Metallurgical, Inc. This metal-alloys manufacturer, headquartered in Ohio, initiated its quality improvement program in 1985. Faced with increasing amounts of lower-cost imports, Globe developed its program with one goal in mind: to become the standard of excellence in the metals industry. The quality program was based on three factors: quality, efficiency, and cost. Using computer-controlled systems and statistical process control, Globe monitors every aspect of the manufacturing process. In addition, quality committees were formed at every level of the organization to improve interlevel communication, determine the source of uncontrollable lapses in quality, review corrective actions, evaluate suggestions from quality circles, and address other quality-related issues. The result of these efforts are impressive: Worker productivity has increased, over 50 percent in some areas. Furnace productivity has also increased, reducing energy consumption. Customer complaints have decreased significantly as well.

Westinghouse Electric Corporation Commercial Nuclear Fuel Division (CNFD) The CNFD of Westinghouse realized early on that future business success depended on excellence in product quality. That is why the division set a goal to become the world's most efficient supplier of nuclear fuel. To reach its goal, the division adopted the total quality approach, based on four key imperatives: management leadership, product and process leadership, human resource excellence, and customer satisfaction. Employees monitor over 60 performance areas using statistical techniques. This information is used to set future goals. In the past three years, approximately 90 percent of the CNFD employees have received training. These efforts at improving quality have paid off for Westinghouse. The CNFD's on-time delivery rate now stands at 100 percent, and the fuel reliability performance rate at 99.995 percent. Quality improvements have enabled the CNFD to achieve a 40 percent U.S. and 20 percent worldwide market share.

It is interesting to note that not one of these award-winning companies provided precise figures for either the costs or benefits of their quality programs. This is true for other winners, such as Cadillac and Xerox, as well, underscoring the difficulty that even the very best American manufacturers experience when trying to quantify the effect that improved quality has on financial performance.

Sources: "A New Era for Auto Quality," *Business Week* (October 22, 1990), 84–96; Garrett DeYoung, "Does Quality Pay," *CFO* (September 1990), 24–34; "Malcolm Baldridge National Quality Award: Globe Metallurgical, Inc. & Westinghouse Electric Corporation—Commercial Nuclear Fuel Division," *Business America* (December 15, 1988), 6–7, 10–11; and Brad Stratton, "Xerox and Milliken Receive Malcolm Baldridge National Quality Awards," *Quality Progress* (December 1989), 17–20.

After product standards have been set by management, they must be checked. Since these product standards involve so many aspects of quality control, the costs of quality assurance are high. Prevention, appraisal, and internal and external failure costs previously discussed and outlined in Table 16.1 are all quality assurance costs.

Quality Cost Studies Once the costs of quality are understood, managers may conduct cost (or loss) studies to determine what actions should be taken, if any, to reduce costs. Consider, for example, the cost data collected and shown in Table 16.2. For a metal stamping company, the major cost categories are scrap, rework, in-process inspection, and customer returns—all failure and inspection costs. Two items, scrap and rework, account for $559,000 of the $889,700 total quality costs. Comparing prevention costs and failure cost would suggest whether more should be expended to prevent poor quality, and would be followed by more detailed cost analysis with recommendations for lower, overall costs for the coming six months.

ORGANIZING FOR QUALITY

Often, quality control in manufacturing firms is organized in a way distinctly different from the way it is organized in service firms. Usually, quality control in manufacturing is a staff function established specifically for that purpose, while in service firms, line managers and employees are typically responsible for quality control. One survey of quality control practices in manufacturing had 173 firms responding.[7] Firms were uniformly represented by size (number of employees), except for the 30 percent of respondents with between 1,001 and 5,000 employees. Two sizes of quality control

TABLE 16.1 Costs of quality assurance

Prevention Costs	Appraisal Costs	Internal Failure Costs	External Failure Costs
▪ QC administration and systems planning ▪ Quality training ▪ Quality planning (QC engineering work) Incoming, inprocess, final inspection Special processes planning Quality data analysis Procurement planning Vendor surveys Reliability studies ▪ Quality measurement and control equipment ▪ Qualification of material	▪ Testing ▪ Inspection ▪ Quality audits ▪ Incoming test and inspection and laboratory acceptance ▪ Checking labor ▪ Laboratory or other measurement service ▪ Setup for test and inspection ▪ Test and inspection material ▪ Outside endorsements ▪ Maintenance and calibration ▪ Product engineering review and shipping release ▪ Field testing	▪ Scrap, at full shop cost ▪ Rework, at full shop cost ▪ Scrap and rework, fault of vendor ▪ Material procurement ▪ Factory contact engineering ▪ QC investigations (of failures) ▪ Material review activity ▪ Repair and troubleshooting	▪ Complaints and loss of customer good will ▪ Warranty costs ▪ Field maintenance and product service ▪ Returned material processing and repair ▪ Replacement inventories ▪ Strained distributor relations

Source: Adapted from J. W. Gavett, *Production and Operations Management* (New York: Harcourt Brace Jovanovich, 1968), 401–402.

[7] Erwin M. Saniga and Larry E. Shirland, "Quality Control in Practice . . . A Survey," *Quality Progress* 10, no. 5 (May 1977), 30–33.

TABLE 16.2 Quality costs at metal stamping company (six months)

Quality Cost Category	Annual Quality Cost
Inspection expenses	
Raw material	$ 27,500
In-process and finished goods	111,000
Prevention expense	
Quality improvement project	7,500
Training new employees on quality	13,200
Tooling for quality improvement	3,500
Losses due to failure	
Down press time due to quality	74,000
Scrap	421,800
Rework	137,200
Customer returns	94,000
Total quality costs	$889,700

departments dominated: 36 percent of the respondents had 0–9 employees and 34 percent had more than 50 employees. Other department sizes were rather equally distributed.

Many managers today believe that quality control departments should be deemphasized and eventually disbanded. As employees who produce goods and services are trained in statistical processes and are given the tools to improve and control their own outputs, they should be accountable for quality. This shifts the responsibility directly to the source of good quality (as well as errors)—the employee and his or her manager. With this shift must come management support. The result of this change is inspection at the source of production by the participant in operations. There will no longer be a need for large quality control and assurance departments.

Sporadic problem A short-term problem that causes sudden changes for the worse in quality, usually addressed through control measures.

Chronic problem A long-term problem that causes continually poor qualty, usually addressed through breakthrough measures.

Breakthrough A solution to a chronic problem; a dramatic change for the better in quality, stimulated by concentrated, analytic, company-wide quality improvement programs.

Breakthrough versus Control When seeking quality improvement, a distinction is often made between *sporadic problems* and *chronic problems.* Sporadic problems are short term and cause sudden changes for the worse in quality; Chronic problems are long term and cause continually poor quality. Techniques for identifying and controlling sporadic problems are addressed in the next chapter. Chronic problems, on the other hand, require scientific problem solving to *break through* to attain a higher quality than the organization has been able to achieve for a *long time, often years.*[8]

Arriving at such a breakthrough requires convincing others of the need, identifying the few vital problem sources, organizing for new knowledge, analyzing, identifying resistance to change, acting to institute change, and freezing the change into place to gain lasting benefits. This process is very difficult to manage because chronic problems are often accepted as a way of life. Managers and employees are unwilling to admit to a better way of doing things, perhaps not even realizing there *is* a better way.

Japanese firms have demonstrated the usefulness of the breakthrough process, halving and then halving again the number of errors once accepted in manufacturing processes. They willingly aspire to attain levels of quality that many in North America and Europe have accepted as "unattainable." Now, many have come to realize that firms must have breakthroughs for quality to be competitive worldwide.

[8]See J. Juran and Frank M. Gryna, Jr., *Quality Planning and Analysis* (New York: McGraw-Hill, 1980), chap. 5.

Measurement of Services Generally, service characteristics are more complex than product characteristics. They are harder to identify and measure. Consequently, measuring and controlling quality are frequently ignored in services. Although service quality is important, the characteristics that determine customer acceptance are often intangible, complex customer perceptions such as timeliness, employees' attitudes toward customers, and the physical environment where the service is delivered.

Despite the difficulties, a procedure to measure service characteristics was developed and tested in the Federal Reserve banking system, and has since been applied by several large and medium-sized commercial banks and manufacturers, including Honeywell.[9] The procedure is participative: quality measures are developed by those involved in the delivery of services. A good bit of the procedure centers on definition—definition of process (system) boundaries, process components, and sources of variation (deviations). Measures include *quality indicators,* such as the number of errors or the percent defective, and conceptually innovative *quality productivity ratios,* relating outputs to resource inputs for quality. This measurement procedure has been used in a variety of service functions: personnel, check processing, transfer of funds (banking), data processing, and production planning.

PARETO ANALYSIS

Quality costs are not uniformly distributed. Almost without exception, only a few of the sources account for the bulk of the costs. This "maldistribution" of quality costs is illustrated by the frequency distribution shown in Table 16.3, often referred to in

Why have these customers selected live rather than automatic tellers (ATMs)? Measuring customer desires regarding timeliness, accuracy, friendliness, and availability of banking services is difficult, yet it is necessary to provide the service quality expected.
Source: **Jay Freis / The Image Bank**

[9]See Adam, Hershauer, and Ruch, *Productivity and Quality,* pp. 152–83, for details of the procedure, case applications, references for personnel and check processing studies, and related studies.

Pareto analysis Frequency distributions of quality cost sources.

Histogram A bar graph of frequency distributions.

quality diagnosis as a *Pareto analysis.* If we were to bar graph the table, it would be referred to as a *histogram.*

Examining Table 16.3, we see that operator errors contribute to photocopying quality costs as much as all other sources combined. Would a further examination of operator errors show a similar maldistribution of sources of error? Table 16.4 demonstrates this to be so. If we further break down regular operator large volume jobs in categories such as poor job instructions, inadequate attention to machine, and so forth, we would expect to find a *few vital sources* that primarily contribute to costs, rather than the *many trivial sources* that contribute much less to costs.

TABLE 16.3 **Quality costs in photocopying**

Class of Loss	Annual Quality Loss (in $)	Frequency of Loss (in %)	Cumulative Frequency of Loss (in %)
Operator error	500	50.0	50.0
Dirty, spotted drum or glass	225	22.5	72.5
Low ink level	125	12.5	85.5
Paper misfeed	75	7.5	92.5
All other sources	75	7.5	100.0

RECOGNIZING QUALITY ACHIEVEMENTS

The Deming Prize for Quality As we discussed in Chapter 15, Dr. W. Edwards Deming is perhaps the best-known American in Japan. His post–World War II teachings about statistical processes provided a methodology for the Japanese, and for his contributions the Deming Prize for Quality carries his name. The prize has been awarded annually since 1951 by the Union of Japanese Scientists and Engineers to companies that have demonstrated successful quality improvement programs. Very few firms outside Japan apply for the Deming Prize and as of 1991 the first and only non-Japanese winner is a U.S. utility, Florida Power and Light. Operations Management Highlight 16.2 describes the achievements that helped this company achieve such an honor. Other notable companies to receive the Deming prize include Toyota Motor, NEC IC/Microcomputer Systems, and Kansai Electric Power.

TABLE 16.4 **Operator error quality losses in photocopying**

Type of Job	Annual Operator Error Loss (in $)	Frequency of Operator Loss (in %)	Cumulative Frequency of Operator Loss (in %)
Regular operator error Large-volume jobs	325	65.0	65.0
Irregular (customer) operator error	100	20.0	85.0
Regular operator error Small-volume jobs	50	10.0	95.0
Substitute operator error	25	5.0	100.0

OPERATIONS MANAGEMENT HIGHLIGHT 16.2

Source: Peter Vandermark/Stock, Boston

American Company Awarded Deming Prize for First Time

In November 1989, Florida Power and Light (FPL) was awarded the Deming Prize For Quality and became the first American company to receive the prestigious award. FPL has 15,000 employees serving 3 million customer accounts with over $4 billion in annual sales. How did the nation's fourth-largest investor-owned supplier of electric utility services demonstrate a successful quality improvement program? An analysis of each of the four main types of quality improvement activities reveals how.

Senior Management Activity The involvement of senior management in award-winning companies is much more than that of other companies. In the early 1980s, Marshall McDonald, then chief executive officer of FPL, became convinced after a three-week visit to the Kansai Electric Power Company that quality improvement techniques could be successfully implemented in FPL. Kansai is one of Japan's largest utilities, and its total quality improvement program is the most emulated in the industry.

McDonald faced the task of convincing employees that quality improvement techniques could work for FPL. Senior management encouraged the formation of quality teams that used quality improvement techniques to solve specific problems. At the same time, senior management continued to visit Kansai and to seek advice from Kansai consultants.

Customer Satisfaction Activity To improve customer satisfaction, specific tasks and responsibilities are assigned to all departments within the organization because customer satisfaction depends on the participation of all departments. One measure of customer satisfaction in the utility industry is the number of complaints filed with the Public Service Commission. In 1984 over 2,000 complaints were filed against FPL (Figure 16.3). As part of the quality improvement program, FPL introduced the Trouble Call Management System (TCMS). A cross-functional system, TCMS tracks power outages and other customer problems. As a result of the new system several improvements have been achieved. By 1989 the number of complaints filed against FPL had declined to 900. Complaints filed in 1990 against FPL were running 13 percent to 16 percent lower than in 1989. Before TCMS, the delay between the time when a customer reported a problem to FPL and the time when the repair order was issued averaged 30 minutes. Today, that average has declined to six minutes. In the early 1980s, the length of time that a FPL customer was without service averaged 100 minutes per year. Today the average is 48 minutes.

Employee Involvement Activity Award-winning companies are consistently characterized by a high level of employee involvement. Managers assume the responsibility for total quality and for their employees who must become involved in the total quality program. FPL service managers use data obtained from the TCMS to analyze past problems. This information is used to predict where problems may occur in the future, enabling FPL to avoid service interruptions. One such case involved FPL employees who discovered that although lightning was thought to be the primary cause of service interruptions, the nature of the problem indicated the source

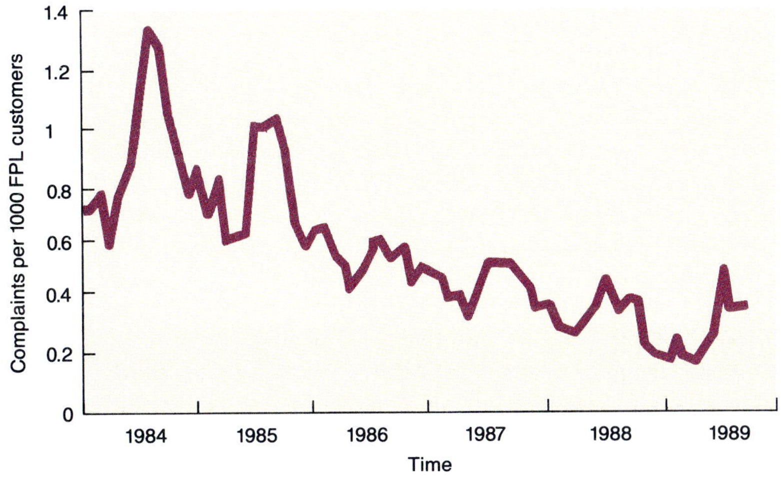

FIGURE 16.3 **The number of FPL consumer complaints to the Florida Public Service Commission has been on the decline since 1984.**

Source: Florida Power and Light Company; *Computerworld* (December 11, 1989. Copyright 1989 by CW Publishing, Inc., Framingham, MA 01701—Reprinted from Computerworld.).

(continued)

Operations Management Highlight 16.2 (continued)

was something else. The TCMS enabled FPL employees to discover that the source of the problem was inadequately grounded transformers. FPL corrected the problem and, today, fallen trees are the primary cause of service interruptions.

Training Activity FPL officials cite training as one of the most important factors in the success of their quality improvement program. Because FPL's employees were most familiar with the traditional American style of quality control, adopting the new quality improvement program required a "complete change of philosophy." Employees received training in two areas, in the concept of total quality and in the use of the more structured quality improvement techniques. FPL's quality improvement program is highly regarded within the industry. Once a month, FPL sponsors an orientation detailing how the utility operates. FPL has also established a subsidiary named Qualtec to provide quality improvement consulting services.

Although FPL has achieved its quality improvement objectives and has received the Deming prize, one official notes that "Quality improvement is never finished. It won't change as rapidly as it has over the last five years, but it won't stop."

Sources: George H. Labovitz, and Yu Sang Chang, "Learn From the Best," _Quality Progress_ (May 1990), 81–85; and Alan J. Ryan, "IS Strategies: Florida Power and Light—Where Quality Takes Command," _Computerworld_ (December 11, 1989), 95–100.

Certain characteristics are consistently evident in the quality improvement programs of award-winning companies: The programs are all clear, detailed, and well-communicated, they are based on time—usually three to five years—and they include both defensive and offensive quality improvement goals. Above all, top management assumes responsibility for total quality within the company. *Typically, the quality improvement programs of award winners detail four main types of quality improvement activity: senior management activity, customer satisfaction activity, employee involvement activity, and training activity.*

The Malcolm Baldrige National Quality Award The Malcolm Baldrige Award, established by the U.S. Congress, was first implemented in 1988 to recognize quality achievement and excellence of U.S. companies. The late Malcolm Baldrige was an industrialist and Secretary of Commerce under President Ronald Reagan. Categories of criteria for the award are shown in Figure 16.4 and Table 16.5. Note how many of the categories are "soft" (that is, involving management, employees, and customers) rather than "hard" (involving techniques and data analysis). The problems of quality are to a great degree behavioral, and these categories demonstrate this fact: leadership accounts for 10 percent of the possible award points, planning 6 percent, human resources 15 percent, and customer satisfaction 30 percent—nearly two-thirds in total.

Malcolm Baldrige Award winners include companies you might recognize—Westinghouse (1988), Xerox (1989), and Cadillac (1990)—as well as others you might not. Operations Management Highlight 16.1 focused on four winners. Award criteria are rigorously adhered to by independent examiners and judges from industry, government, and academics, who find two or three companies each year worthy of the award.

FIGURE 16.4 **Examination categories for the Malcolm Baldrige National Quality Award**

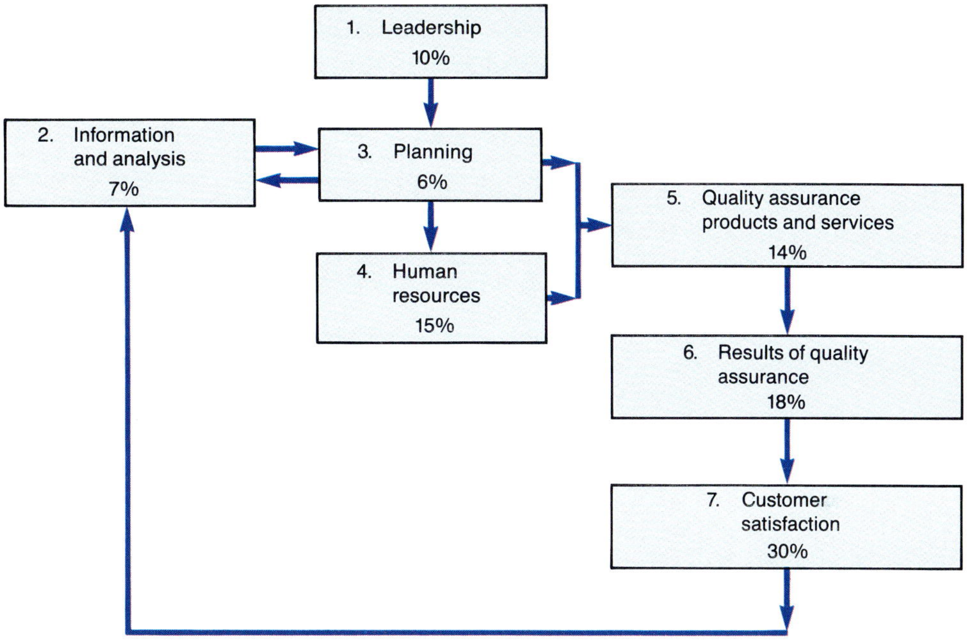

Industry segments are establishing their own quality awards. An example is *Distribution* magazine's annual *Quest for Quality* award, which identifies winners for different modes of transportation. A transportation segment such as less-than-truckload carriers would have a few winners who are highly rated by their customers on four criteria: service, convenience, price, and salesperson competency. Although this award doesn't carry the distinction of Deming or Malcolm Baldrige awards, it provides a useful benchmark and develops awareness of quality improvement. Such awareness is crucial for American industry in its push to be quality-competitive worldwide.

MANAGEMENT-INITIATED APPROACHES AND ACTIONS TO IMPROVE QUALITY

American companies are taking action to improve quality. Upon what research or premises are these companies basing their actions? What actions are the leading-edge companies taking? We now turn to these two questions.

TABLE 16.5 **Examination categories, items, and point values for the Malcolm Baldrige National Quality Award**

1991 Examination Categories/Items		Maximum Points
1.0 Leadership		100
1.1 Senior executive leadership	40	
1.2 Quality values	15	
1.3 Management for quality	25	
1.4 Public responsibility	20	
2.0 Information and Analysis		70
2.1 Scope and management of quality data and information	20	
2.2 Competitive comparisons and benchmarks	30	
2.3 Analysis of quality data and information	20	
3.0 Strategic Quality Planning		60
3.1 Strategic quality planning process	35	
3.2 Quality goals and plans	25	
4.0 Human Resource Utilization		150
4.1 Human resource management	20	
4.2 Employee involvement	40	
4.3 Quality education and training	40	
4.4 Employee recognition and performance measurement	25	
4.5 Employee well-being and morale	25	
5.0 Quality Assurance of Products and Services		140
5.1 Design and introduction of quality products and services	5	
5.2 Process quality control	20	
5.3 Continuous improvement of processes	20	
5.4 Quality assessment	15	
5.5 Documentation	10	
5.6 Business process and support service quality	20	
5.7 Supplier quality	20	
6.0 Quality Results		180
6.1 Product and service quality results	90	
6.2 Business process, operational, and support service quality results	50	
6.3 Supplier quality results	40	
7.0 Customer Satisfaction		300
7.1 Determining customer requirements and expectations	30	
7.2 Customer relationship management	50	
7.3 Customer service standards	20	
7.4 Commitment to customers	15	
7.5 Complaint resolution for quality improvement	25	
7.6 Determining customer satisfaction	20	
7.7 Customer satisfaction results	70	
7.8 Customer satisfaction comparison	70	
TOTAL POINTS		1000

Source: 1991 Application Guidelines Malcolm Baldrige National Quality Award, U. S. Department of Commerce, National Institute of Standards and Technology, Gaithersburg, MD. (1991), 5.

CONTEMPORARY MANAGEMENT-INITIATED APPROACHES TO IMPROVING QUALITY

The most popular approaches to quality improvement in the United States are based upon the teaching, writing, and consulting of Dr. W. Edwards Deming, Dr. Joseph M. Juran, and Philip B. Crosby. "Total quality control" programs exemplify the approaches of these men in varying blends. Let's briefly discuss each, providing references for the interested reader.

Deming's Statistical Thinking Dr. Deming's approaches to quality improvement, analysis, and statistics are widely accepted by Japanese business. As previously noted, the highest quality award in Japanese industry, the Deming prize, carries his name. What, then, does he propose?

Dr. Deming lays responsibility for quality improvement at management's doorstep. The *system* is generally the cause for inefficiency and low quality, according to Deming, and it is management's responsibility to *work on the system* (as workers work in the system). He stresses variation as a major manufacturing problem and proposes the use of control charts to assist in evaluating variation. Students of operations management can learn about Deming's philosophy by studying a set of video training tapes offered by the Massachusetts Institute of Technology's Center for Advanced Engineering Study or by studying Gitlow and Gitlow.[10]

Juran's Management Processes Through Quality Dr. Juran is a popular author, lecturer, and consultant. For decades, he has presented American managers his views on management's role in quality improvement. Juran has an international background, and his message is managerial in nature. He addresses American management on issues such as rationality, analysis, and management processes in order to get at problems in quality. Although he uses statistical analysis freely, his primary objective is to get top management to help the company's management team develop the *habit of annual improvement.* In Juran's approach, continuing improvement is supplemented with breakthrough, essentially an organized approach to problem identification, analysis, and change based on this analysis, which we presented earlier in this chapter. The key to the Juran message is that management can and must seek continual improvement. In doing so, quality will improve, along with other performance dimensions. Because competition among firms and nations is so great, *annual improvement, hands-on management,* and *training* to institutionalize improvement must all fit together to meet the competition for quality products and services.[11]

Juran has published a number of books, has contributed freely to professional quality journals, and has developed a set of lectures and video tapes to explain his approach. His message is well thought out and presented in a lively way.

[10]W. Edwards Deming, "On Some Statistical Aids Toward Economic Production," *Interfaces* 5, no. 5 (August 1975), 1–15; Myron Tribus, "Deming's Way" (M.I.T. Center for Advanced Engineering Study, April 1982); "Deming's Redefinition of Management" (M.I.T. Center for Advanced Engineering Study, Working Paper); Howard S. Gitlow and Shelly J. Gitlow, *The Deming Guide to Quality and Competitive Position,* (Englewood Cliffs, N.J.: Prentice-Hall, 1987).

[11]Joseph M. Juran, *Upper Management and Quality,* 4th ed. (New York: Juran Institute, Inc., 1983); idem, *Management of Quality,* 4th ed. (New York: Juran Institute, Inc., 1981); idem, *Quality Control Handbook,* 3rd ed. (New York: McGraw-Hill, 1974); idem, *Quality Planning and Analysis* (New York: McGraw-Hill, 1980).

Crosby's Concept of Free Quality As an experienced executive who for 14 years was corporate vice president and director of quality for ITT, Philip Crosby was involved in the initial phases of "zero defects" programs (presented later in this chapter). He is an active consultant, lecturer, and author of the popular quality books, *Quality Is Free* and *Quality Without Tears*. The concept of the first book, explains his overall approach:

> Quality is free. It is not a gift, but it is free. What costs money are the unquality things—all the actions that involve not doing jobs right the first time. Quality is not only free, it is an honest-to-everything profit maker. Every penny you don't spend on doing things wrong, over, or instead becomes half a penny right on the bottom line.[12]

Phil Crosby Associates (PCA) in Winter Park, Florida, has been involved in educating tens of thousands of executives from throughout the world in quality awareness as a means for improvement. The focus of this training is on conformance to requirements, prevention, the proper attitude toward quality, and measuring quality as a cost of quality. These "absolutes" are put together in an effective presentation package for corporations. Crosby's approach is based on attitudes and awareness; he focuses on management's role in using this approach to improve quality. Whereas Deming and Juran use analysis as a basis for their philosophies, Crosby's approach is behavioral. Evidently, his methods are quite effective. We are aware of individual quality assurance executives, as well as major corporations such as IBM, who have had good success with Crosby's approach.

EXPERIENCES OF LEADING-EDGE FIRMS

Although many companies claim to be taking forward strides in quality improvement, including such companies as American Express, Armco, Citicorp, Firestone, Hewlett Packard, Honeywell, IBM, and McDonnell Douglas, it is difficult to obtain documented and published details of successful corporate-wide quality programs. However, we do have a few well-documented examples. We now take a closer look at three organizations that have achieved high quality.

Toyota Motor Company Toyota has been a pacesetter for automotive companies throughout the world as a consistently low-cost, high-quality producer. The Toyota concept of stockless production provides high inventory turnover: an annual turnover of working assets of 62 times in 1970, compared with an annual turnover of fewer than ten times for typical U.S. firms.[13] Toyota also has several important quality features, including: (1) involvement of the work force in quality and productivity suggestions (quality circles), (2) inspection of supplier plants, and (3) the use of statistical methods and analysis at all levels in the company.

The involvement of the work force can be seen in Table 16.6, which is based on research by Robert Hall. Professor Hall notes that the great increase in 1973 resulted from a need to react effectively to the oil crisis. This event jolted Toyota into greater action. Managers should keep in mind that many small savings add up, and some proposals may lead to large savings. Project-by-project teams, often in the form of

---

[12]Philip B. Crosby, *Quality Is Free* (New York: Mentor, 1979), p. 2; see also Jay W. Leek, "Quality in Review, the PCA Experience," *Proceedings the World Quality Congress 1984* (Brighton, England, June 1984).

[13]Hall, *Zero Inventories*, 26.

TABLE 16.6 Number of annual proposals by workers at Toyota

Year	Total Number of Proposals	Number of Proposals per Person	Acceptance Rate
1965	9,000	1.0	39%
1970	40,000	2.5	70
1973	247,000	12.2	76
1975	380,000	15.3	83
1976	463,000	—	83
1977	454,000	—	86
1978	528,000	—	86
1979	576,000	—	91
1980	859,000	18.7	94

Source: Robert W. Hall, *Zero Inventories,* Homewood, Ill.: Dow Jones–Irwin, 1983) 27.

quality circles, account for many of the formal proposals and implementations. In contrast, the American worker simply doesn't have the opportunity or the perceived incentive to improve his or her own work. Using Toyota as a paradigm, it is clear that management must provide that environment.

Toyota and Nissan regularly inspect supplier plants. This practice is now being followed by U.S. auto manufacturers.[14] Ford's QI Preferred Quality Supplier Program is an example. Toyota, like many Japanese firms, depends upon workers at all levels to use statistical thinking (as Deming proposes).

Ford Motor Company In addition to employing Dr. Deming as a consultant, Ford has actively pursued the Japanese—and in general the foreign car maker's—quality lead in automobile production. Ford has developed an integrated business strategy to (1) actively pursue quality improvement, adopting many Japanese quality techniques, and (2) promote and advertise both the commitment to quality and actual achievements in quality improvement. Quality improvement is stated as the number one business priority at Ford.

Regarding the first part of Ford's strategy, Ford continues the process of renewing its use of statistical management methods to improve productivity and quality. Retired Ford Chairman Donald E. Peterson endorsed Dr. Deming's 14 points as the foundation for Ford's goal of never-ending improvement in quality and productivity.

The results of Ford's efforts are now being recognized by consumers. In the late 1980s Ford advertised that they are number one in quality among American automobile manufacturers; they cited independently collected data to support their claim.[15]

Xerox Corporation The segment of Xerox that produces copiers and duplicators has met extremely quick foreign competition, especially from Japanese manufacturers. This competition is directed at gaining market share with low-cost, high-quality

[14]Richard J. Schonberger, *Japanese Manufacturing Techniques* (New York: The Free Press, 1982) 58.

[15]For information about Ford's quality improvement, we are particularly indebted to Ford executives John A. Manoogian, Executive Director Product Assurance, North American Automotive Operations, and Dick Smith of his staff; James K. Bakken, Corporate Vice-President, Operations Support Staff; and William W. Scherkenbach, Director Statistical Methods.

products.[16] Xerox's response has been to completely reassess the way they have been doing business and learn to deal with issues involving quality and productivity in a different way. Xerox has implemented a number of new approaches that will enable long-term competitiveness.

Xerox, unique in its industry because it developed the product line that formed the industry, now has a basis for comparison with very *real* competitors who once did not exist. Xerox has three major phases underway:

1. *Competitive benchmarking.* Developing and implementing a continuous process of measuring Xerox products and services against the best and toughest competitors in the world—the best in any industry, not just copiers and duplicators. This led to action resulting in a 21 percent gain in customer satisfaction in one year.
2. *Employee involvement.* Getting the best from the minds and talents of Xerox employees at all levels. Problem-solving teams, quality circles, changing management style—over one-fourth of Xerox employees are involved in team activities aimed at improvement.
3. *Leadership through quality.* Exposing the very top executives to the work of Juran and Deming and sending them to Phil Crosby's Quality College in Winter Park, Florida, has led to the beginning of a total quality control process in all aspects of the corporation. Top management credibility has been established at Xerox.

From Xerox, we see how a U.S.-based company prepared to meet the quality improvement challenge. One result for Xerox has been recognition as a Malcolm Baldridge Quality Award winner. We see in Toyota, Ford, and Xerox several similar ideas and a return to the basic concepts and principles of leading worldwide quality experts. Why? Worldwide competition in terms of quality products and services seems to be the driving force.

BEHAVIOR AND QUALITY

Achieving desired quality depends upon appropriate human performance. In recent years much effort has been devoted to instilling a "quality orientation" in the people who work in the conversion process. Behavioral change procedures directed at changing performance quality *before* rather than after the fact, however, have met with limited success. We will discuss some of these attempts and the inherent behavioral problems that relate to quality in the following sections.

QUALITY/QUANTITY TRADEOFFS

Few studies have specifically investigated the relationships between quantity and quality of output. A popular view supported by Dr. Deming and Dr. Juran is that any decrease in quantity caused by greater attention to quality would be more than offset by

[16]This section is based on Frank J. Pipp, "A Management Commitment to Quality" (Keynote address, 37th Annual Quality Congress, American Society for Quality Control, May 1983).

the decrease in waste. A review of the literature suggests there is no simple relationship between these two factors. For routine, repetitive tasks such as typing, bank proofing, or collating, workers tend to emphasize one over the other. If quality improves, quantity decreases; if quantity increases, quality suffers. For tasks involving more complex and diverse physical and mental tasks, the relationship between quantity and quality is not nearly so clear. For these more complex tasks, when does the worker emphasize quality at the expense of quantity? When does the reverse occur? There is no simple answer to our questions. The quantity/quality tradeoff is usually determined by how the conversion processes are designed, staffed, and managed.

ZERO DEFECTS

Zero Defects A program to change workers' attitudes about quality by stressing error-free performance.

Zero Defects programs, which attempt to improve quality by changing workers' attitudes, were particularly popular in the 1960s and 1970s. Their theme, "Do it right the first time," stresses error-free performance. Unfortunately, however, production/operation processes inevitably result in some undesirable output. Error-free performance is, for most processes, economically and practically infeasible. Although many people assume that errors are made because employees are not conscientious enough about their work, attempts to change employee attitudes have met with very limited success. Banners, slogans, Zero Defect days, and the like generally improve performance only temporarily; in about six months, employees' performance returns to its previous level.

Achieving desired banking service depends specifically on individual human performance.

***Source:* John Zoiner**

QUALITY MOTIVATION

Quality motivation Programs to motivate workers to improve quality, including incentive and merit pay systems.

The American Society for Quality Control has a workbook that stresses the basic concepts of *quality motivation*. The idea is to apply techniques of motivation and management to obtain improved product quality. Contemporary views include a behavior-performance-reward-satisfaction sequence.[17] Organizations are becoming keenly aware of the alternative pay plans that can shape performance. Incentive and merit pay systems, for example, can include rewards for good quality.

BEHAVIORAL MODIFICATION IN QUALITY CONTROL

Operant conditioning A technique to modify behavior by direct rewards and punishments.

There have been several attempts to influence performance quality on routine repetitive tasks by employing *operant conditioning* procedures.[18] Operant conditioning assumes that behavior can be modified by a series of rewards. It appears that performance *quality* is more difficult to change than performance *quantity*. Second, it is clear that financial rewards more often motivate improved quality than do nonfinancial rewards. Once reasonable quality performance levels have been reached, however, continued financial rewards do not motivate significant additional quality improvement. Third, behavior is influenced more by direct rewards than by procedures to change attitudes. These procedures provide mixed results, at best.

EXAMPLE

In an attempt to influence quality in a diecasting department of some 36 workers, one company succeeded in obtaining a significant increase in quantity but no significant change in quality. Figure 16.5 shows weekly changes in the department as the result of a formal program involving weekly individual meetings between the supervisor and each employee. Quantity is measured as percent of standard, and quality is measured by percent defective. Overall, the company, with a $73,000 first-year cost reduction in this department, judged the program successful and implemented it in other departments. The fact remains, however, that quality did not improve, even though emphasis was given to performance quality at least weekly.

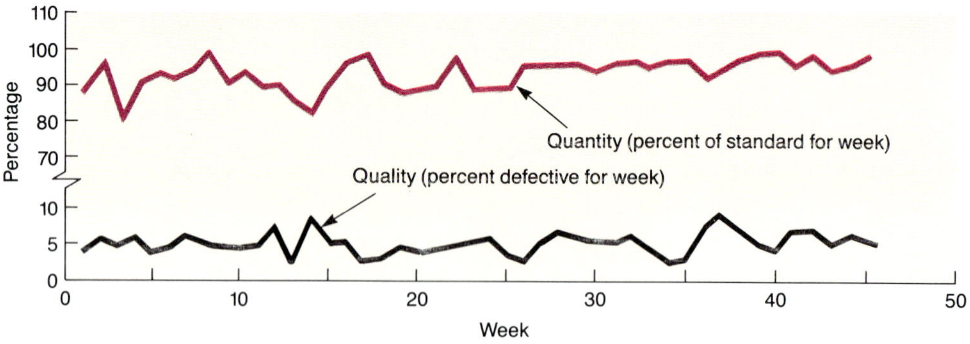

FIGURE 16.5
Weekly diecasting quality and quantity

[17]Charles N. Greene, Everett E. Adam, Jr., and Ronald J. Ebert, *Management for Effective Performance* (Englewood Cliffs, N.J.: Prentice-Hall, 1985), pp. 104–24.

[18]See Everett E. Adam, Jr., "Behavior Modification in Quality Control," *Academy of Management Journal* 18, no. 4 (December 1975), 662–79. This work provides references to the related works of George A. Johnson, William A. Ruch, William E. Scott, Jr., and James B. Shein, all of whom have contributed to quality motivation research. See also David A. Sprague, Barry Zinn, and Robert Kreitner, "Improving Quality Through Behavior Modification," *Quality Progress* 9, no. 12 (December 1976), 22–24.

Hair stylist quality specifically demands individual human performance.
Source: **Sobel / Klonsky / The Image Bank**

QUALITY CIRCLES

It was noted in Chapter 15 that *quality circles* (QCs) were initially developed in Japan as employee participation, quality improvement programs. Within the United States QCs have evolved into participative productivity improvement programs which focus on both performance quantity and quality. As in Japan, participation is voluntary. Employees are paid while participating during regular working hours or on overtime. A group leader is selected and trained for the leadership role by the organization. Then the participating group receives training in the methods of problem solving, analysis, and reporting. The group begins meeting to identify problems, collect and analyze the data, recommend solutions, and carry out management-approved changes. Many companies are testing this participative technique in a few locations with an eye toward wider application.[19]

[19]For discussions of quality circles and their applications, see A. V. Feignbaum, "The Internationalization of Quality," *Quality Progress* 12, no. 2 (February 1979) 30–32; Gerald E. Swartz and Vivian C. Comstock, "One Firm's Experience with Quality Circles," *Quality Progress* 12, no. 9 (September 1979) 14–16 (Westinghouse's experience); Charles A. Aubrey, II, and Lawrence A. Eldridge, "Banking on High Quality," *Quality Progress* 14, no. 12 (December 1981), 14–19 (Continental Bank's experience); George Munchus, III, "Employer-Employee Based Quality Circles in Japan: Human Resource Policy Implications for American Firms," *Academy of Management Review* 8, no. 2 (April 1983), 255–61; and John D. Blair and Kenneth D. Ramsing, "Quality Circles and Production/Operations Management: Concerns and Caveats," *Journal of Operations Management* 4, no. 1 (November 1983), 1–10.

Very few evaluations of the effectiveness of QCs are available. Most organizations report a ratio of savings to costs in a range of 3:1 to 6:1, clearly favoring the programs. Others simply accept quality circles as a management participative philosophy without documenting savings. One field study, however, did systematically evaluate QCs' effectiveness.[20] In this study empirical investigation of effective and less-effective quality circles was conducted in nine manufacturing plants of a large, midwestern company. Effective QCs reported higher group cohesion, performance norms, job satisfaction, intrinsic satisfaction, satisfaction with co-workers, self-monitoring, and organization commitment than did ineffective QCs. If an organization values the group's suggestions and values member satisfactions and feelings, the results of this study are that quality circles are effective. Another recent study, evaluated a few QC's in detail at two firms over two years and found them to be rather ineffective beyond the initial six months.[21] It is not clear that QC's are the best participative approach for quality improvement in the U.S. culture.

MANAGEMENT STYLE AND QUALITY CONTROL

Several writers suggest that a participative management style best enhances efforts to control and improve quality.[22] Focusing on the individual, these efforts—many of which are in services—emphasize involvement in setting quality goals, establishing quality measures, and designing jobs for enhanced quality. Managers are increasingly interested in quality, especially in *management techniques* to improve quality. Perhaps this managerial awareness is increasing because of the difficulties encountered recently by such basic U.S. industries as steel and automobiles. International competitors have challenged and sometimes outperformed their U.S. peers in productivity and quality.

SUMMARY

In this chapter on managing for quality, we have discussed concepts of product quality, factors affecting quality, management-directed diagnosis, contemporary management approaches to improving quality, and behavioral dimensions in quality. Quality improvement, assurance, and control can be facilitated by management's planning and organizing efforts. Operations managers must provide direction and establish control.

[20]Ricky W. Griffin and Sandy J. Wayne, "A Field Study of Effective and Less Effective Quality Circles," *Academy of Management Proceedings 1984,* 217–21.

[21]Everett E. Adam, Jr., "Quality Circle Performance" *Journal of Management* 17, no. 1 (March 1991), 25–39.

[22]See John R. Hinrichs, *Practical Management for Productivity* New York: Van Nostrand Reinhold, 1978). Hinrichs returned to field sites and interviewed participants in quality improvement studies (see Chapter 2, "Enhancing Product Quality," the original study by E. E. Adam, Jr., and Chapter 6, "Building a Participative Management System to Enhance Product Quality," the original study by F. B. Chaney and K. S. Teel). See also John C. Shaw and Ram Capoor, "Quality and Productivity: Mutually Exclusive or Interdependent in Service Organizations?" *Management Review* (March 1979), pp. 25–28, 37–39; G. M. Hostage, "Quality Control in a Service Business," *Harvard Business Review* 53, no. 4 (July–August 1975), 98–106; and A. V. Feigenbaum, "Quality and Productivity," *Quality Progress* 10, no. 11 (November 1977), 18–21.

However, they must be aware that all of these control procedures are used by people. Quality motivation and behavioral modification techniques are some methods operations managers can use to encourage employees to improve quality. The Japanese have taught us a good bit about high quality—both in analysis and managing people.

This chapter has presented the belief that the most important fundamental aspects of quality improvement are understanding concepts in quality, being able to apply basic analysis techniques, and understanding that quality improvement is behavioral as well as analytical. Once you have mastered these concepts, you will have a good grasp of the fundamentals of quality improvement.

CASE

Fast Break Markets

A small regional supermarket chain, Fast Break Markets, prides itself on being a high-service, full-line supermarket chain. A typical store has a flower shop, bakery, liquor store, post office, pharmacy, VCR movie rental, and tobacco shop as part of the overall market. Sales have been increasing 20 percent per year in the early 1990s, attributed equally to in-store sales and adding new stores.

The table below reflects customer complaints systematically collected at three typical stores over two months. The vice president of operations, Max Creach, is astounded by the number of complaints and the different types of complaints. He intends to get the manager of each of the 11 stores to organize the employees to address these complaints. Max would like to analyze the data and then suggest a method for each manager to follow. Although Max has heard of quality concepts such as quality cost studies, breakthrough versus control, fishbone diagrams, and Pareto analysis, he doesn't really know what to suggest to each supermarket manager when they meet.

Customer complaints in three stores for two months

Customer Complaint	Number of Times Made
Sanitation	27
Courtesy clerk (bagger)	21
Product quality	87
Product request	105
General	58
General service level	55
Checker	59
Human error	27
Queueing (waiting line)	33
Stock condition	166
Prices and price marking	45
Policy and procedures	40
Parking	18
Check cashing	15
All other	71
Total	827

CASE

Kitchen Appliance Quality

The production manager for the only facility of a small manufacturer of kitchen appliances is interested in getting management's attention on quality issues. He has allies in the marketing manager and accountant, but little interest from the president and the primary owner, both of whom are interested in production efficiency, sales volume, short-term profits, and growth. The production manager and his allies have the following data, but don't know how to organize the data into an effective presentation. From this information, put together the best case possible to impress management that quality is important and should be stressed.

Customer evaluations of top-selling product last year	
Style	Good
Price	Excellent
Reliability	Poor
Recommend to friend?	No
Percentive defective for top-selling product last year	
Fabrication	7.2
Assembly	11.5
Finished goods	9.8
Quality costs	
Training	$ 1,200
Vendor qualification program	500
Field testing	3,500
Quality measurement tools	400
Scrap (full cost less scrap value)	475,000
Inspection in plant	85,000
Field maintenance	15,000
Rework (full shop cost)	1,200,000
Warranty program	45,000
Processing and repairing returns	375,000
Laboratory testing	3,700
Financial results	
Annual sales	$10,000,000
Total cost of goods sold	7,000,000
Selling and admin expenses	1,300,000
Total assets in business	3,500,000
Estimated cost due to loss of distributors' good will	
Late deliveries	$ 50,000
Poor quality	200,000

REVIEW AND DISCUSSION QUESTIONS

1. If you were to design a portable radio, what product characteristics would you specify as critical for enhancing sales? What characteristics are less important?

2. What product characteristics and quality analysis procedures are important for a dormitory cafeteria? Which of these is most important? Which is least important?
3. Discuss the roles of the cost of quality assurance in quality planning.
4. Explain how strategy and quality interrelate.
5. Explain the interactions among the components in Figure 16.2, "Managing for quality products and services."
6. What is the difference between sporadic problems and chronic problems? How do these relate to quality improvement?
7. Managerial "breakthrough" is a process or approach to obtaining a higher level of quality. Explain this process.
8. How can Pareto analysis be used effectively as a diagnostic tool in quality improvement? Explain.
9. "If our employees are asked to increase output quality, the quantity of output is going to suffer." Discuss this statement.
10. Is operant conditioning an effective management technique for quality motivation in nonroutine, nonrepetitive tasks? Why or why not?
11. A manager is expected to become proficient in quality analysis techniques and to understand contemporary improvement programs and behavior. Are these expectations inconsistent? Explain.

PROBLEMS

REINFORCING FUNDAMENTALS

1. It is important to most students to receive a class schedule that meets their academic program and personal needs. Yet student complaints about registration and advisors are often unheard. Problems or complaints could be divided into five categories: (1) unavailable or inadequate professional advice, (2) poor registration procedures, (3) unavailable classes, (4) too few sections for classes, and (5) inadequate information on registration procedures. Suppose these problems caused the average student to lose 90 hours of personal time over a four-year period. Assume students could receive $5.00/hour working instead of being inconvenienced by poor registration and advice. Prepare a Pareto analysis for the quality loss in registration and advising, given the data below. Interpret your results—that is, explain where administrators should focus correction efforts.

Reason for Loss	Frequency of Reason (in %)
Advising deficiency	20.0
Poor registration procedures	15.0
Unavailable classes	20.0
Too few sections	30.0
Inadequate procedures	15.0
Total	100.0

Reason for Loss	Frequency of Reason (in %)
Too few sections:	
Unable to carpool	5.0
Cannot work part time	20.0
Loss of sleep—early classes	10.0
Cannot get preferred instructor	20.0
Extra summer or semester required	10.0
Unable to fit into schedule—miss education	20.0
Other reasons	15.0
Total	100.0

2. Quality losses due to employee performance in a fast-food facility were estimated as shown below. Complete a Pareto analysis for this data and interpret your results for management. For the largest dollar loss, prepare a Fishbone diagram with your thoughts on the reason for the cost.

Class of Loss	Loss One Shift (in $)
Prepare too much food	$150.00
Prepare wrong item	35.00
Incorrect order taken	30.00
Wrong change	50.00
Slow service	75.00
Impolite to customer	45.00
Other services	100.00
Total	$485.00

KEY TERMS

Appraisal costs 603
Breakthrough 607
Chronic problem 607
Company-wide quality control (CWQC) 599
Design specifications 596
External failure costs 603
Histogram 609
Internal failure costs 603
Operant conditioning 620
Pareto analysis 609
Prevention costs 603
Process capability 597
Quality motivation 620
Sporadic problem 607
Zero Defects 619

SELECTED READINGS

Adam, Everett E., Jr., and Eugene M. Barker, "Achieving Quality Products and Services," *Operations Management Review* (Winter 1987), 1–8.

Adam, Everett E., Jr., James C. Hershauer, and William A. Ruch, *Productivity and Quality: Measurement as a Basis for Improvement,* 2nd ed. Columbia, Mo.: Research Center, College of Business and Public Administration, University of Missouri, 1986.

Crosby, Philip B., *Quality Is Free.* New York: Mentor, 1979.

Deming, W. Edwards, "On Some Statistical Aids Toward Economic Production," *Interfaces* 5, no. 5 (August 1975), 1–15.

Gitlow, Howard S., and Shelly J. Gitlow, *The Deming Guide to Quality and Competitive Position.* Englewood Cliffs, N.J.: Prentice-Hall, 1987.

Griffin, Ricky W., and Sandy J. Wayne, "A Field Study of Effective and Less Effective Quality Circles," *Academy of Management Proceedings* (1984), 217–21.

Hinrichs, John R., *Practical Management for Productivity.* New York: Van Nostrand Reinhold, 1978.

Ishikawa, Kaoru, *Guide to Quality Control.* Tokyo: Asian Productivity Organization, 1976.

Juran, J., *Upper Management and Quality,* 4th ed. New York: Juran Institute, 1983.

Juran, J., and Frank M. Gryna, Jr., *Quality Planning and Analysis,* 2nd ed. New York: McGraw-Hill, 1980.

Munchus, George, III, "Employer-Employee Based Quality Circles in Japan: Human Resource Policy Implications for American Firms," *Academy of Management Review* 8, no. 2 (April 1983), 255–61.

Rosander, A. C., *Applications of Quality Control in the Service Industries,* 2nd ed. New York: Markel Dekker, Inc/ASQC Quality Press, 1985.

Takeuchi, Hirotaka, and John A. Quelch, "Quality Is More Than Making a Good Product," *Harvard Business Review* 61, no. 4 (July-August 1983), 139–45.

CHAPTER 17

QUALITY ANALYSIS AND CONTROL

At Monsanto Chemical Company we are changing corporate culture to more consistently meet agreed-upon customer requirements with each and every business transaction. The mechanism to bring about this change is a Monsanto Quality Improvement Process called Total Quality. The Total Quality Improvement Process is a systematic approach to problem solving based on the teachings of Messrs P. B. Crosby, W. E. Deming, and J. M. Juran.

A key component of the improvement process is statistical methods to achieve process stability. Chapter 17 illustrates how statistical methods can help determine the cause of process variations and the steps to control these variations.

At Monsanto Chemical Company a high priority for each process, whether it's manufacturing or service, is to achieve process stability. Statistical methods are widely used in making this priority a reality.

As worldwide competition grows, the company that does the best job of consistently meeting agreed-upon customer requirements with minimum hassles and rework will be the company of preference. We are committed to being one of the selected few companies of preference in those areas in which we choose to compete.

Fred L. Thompson
Director, Total Quality
Monsanto Chemical Company,
A Unit of Monsanto Company
St. Louis, Missouri

Mr. Thompson's comments are clear evidence that quality analysis and control play a central role in today's competitive environment. Analysis and control are the methods used to implement each organization's quality objectives. You will gain a clearer picture of why and how these tools can be beneficial after reading about process capability, statistical process control, inspection, and acceptance sampling. First, however, we examine process variation, one of the fundamental facts of life in production operations.

PROCESS VARIATION

Variation in all operating systems necessitates quality analysis and quality control. We need analysis and control because of the inherent conflict between these two facts:

- Variation (nonuniformity) is inevitable in every operating system: no two units of output are alike.
- The production and use of products and services are most economical when those products and services are of uniform quality.

Although variation cannot be eliminated, by learning more about it, reducing it, and controlling it, we can increase the number of products from the operating system that conform to usage requirements.

SOURCES OF VARIATION

Variations in any conversion process stem from the many sources that constitute the production system—people, materials, machines and equipment, and work methods. We could get uniformity of all the lead pencils we produce if all incoming wood had uniform texture, strength, and density; if all lead and other materials had uniform characteristics; if the tool setters and equipment operators had uniform behavior throughout the workday; if the equipment ran uniformly, without tool wear or breakdowns; and if the work environment had uniform lighting, humidity, temperature, and so on. However, since uniformity is impossible, the key questions become, "How much variation exists in the processes?" and "What can I do to control the nonuniformity in the processes?"

MEASURING NATURAL VARIATION: PROCESS CAPABILITY

Sampling The process of selecting and measuring representative units of output termed **sample units;** a set of sample units is termed a **sample.**

The first step toward control is to document the process's capability—its performance under chronic conditions in which sporadic variations do not exist. Many companies simply do not know what their processes are doing, or are capable of doing, and a capability study is a factual basis for gaining such an understanding. The *process capability study* begins with *sampling,* the process of selecting and measuring representative units of output called *sample units.* A set of sample units is thus called a *sample.* Sample units are measured according to some key product characteristic, and the

Sources of product variation in toy assembly operation.
Source: **Keith Dannemiller**

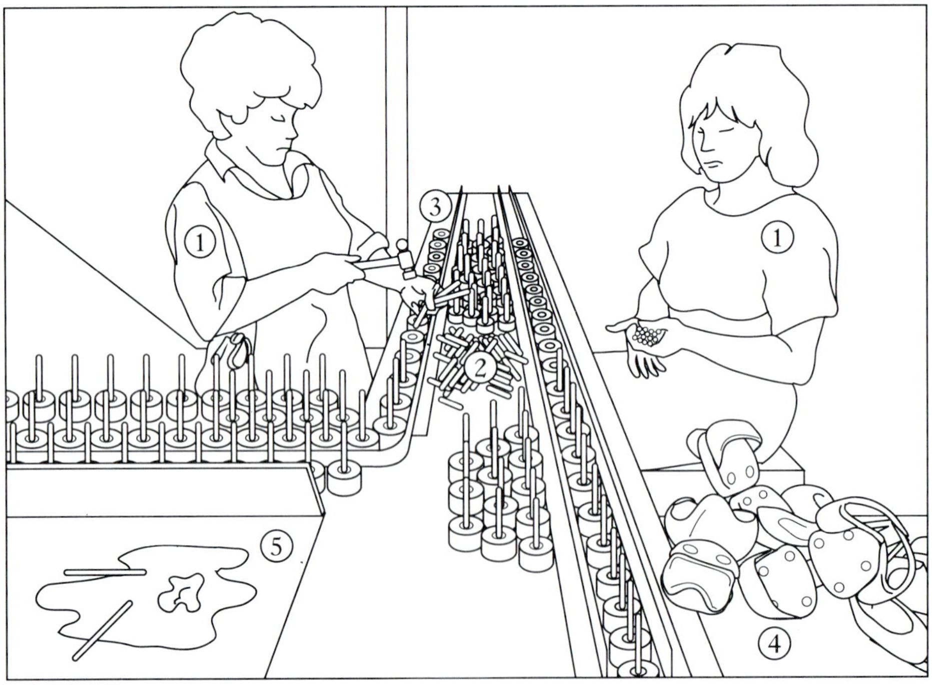

1. Each employee is different and might use different work methods; 2. Diameters and lengths vary from axle to axle; 3. Sizes of holes vary from wheel to wheel; 4. Poor stock damages some bodies but not others; 5. Dirt and debris interfere with assembly.

Variation in the service to these drive-through customers originates from the bank tellers, their equipment, and the work methods and materials they use.

Source: John Zoiner

results are summarized in a histogram. Then, the average X and standard deviation S of the distribution of sample unit measurements are defined by Equations 17.1 and 17.2.

$$\overline{X} = \frac{\sum_{i=1}^{n} X_i}{\text{n}} \tag{17.1}$$

$$S = \sqrt{\frac{\sum_{L=1}^{n} (\overline{X} - X_i)^2}{n-1}} \tag{17.2}$$

where X_i = Measurement for sample unit i
n = Number of units in the sample

EXAMPLE

Hardness is a critical characteristic of rubber seals for automobile windows. To determine the process capability of forming seals, 90 seals are randomly selected during production. A histogram of the measurements is shown in Figure 17.1. The average hardness, calculated using Equation 17.1, is $\overline{X}$ = 62.56. The standard deviation, calculated using Equation 17.2 with n = 90 observations, is S = 12.97. Three standard deviations (3S) above and below $\overline{X}$ are also shown.

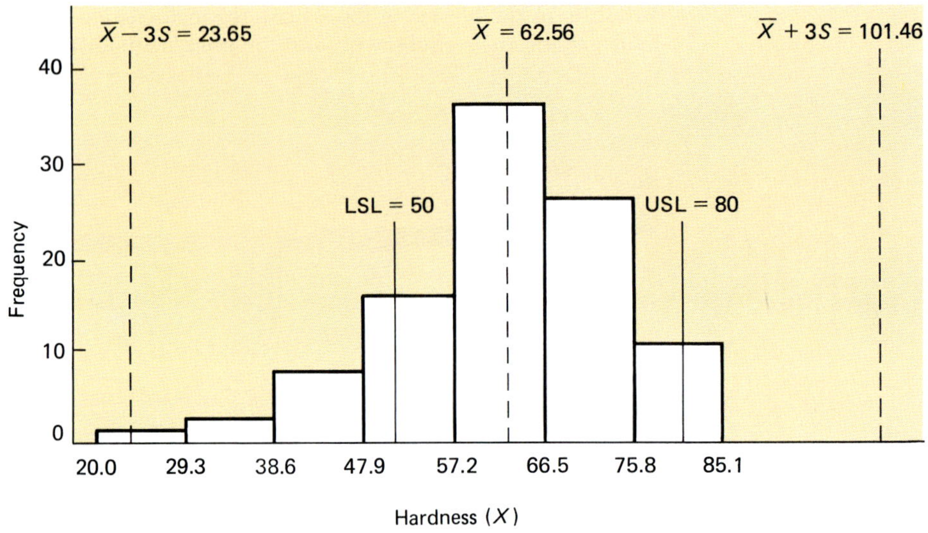

FIGURE 17.1 Histogram of rubber seal hardness for $n = 90$ observations

When sporadic problems are absent, the unit-to-unit variations will be random. Furthermore, most processes have a natural variation pattern that is bell-shaped or normally distributed. So, if the initial histogram is nonnormal, we have reason to suspect that sporadic conditions do exist, contrary to the investigator's initial beliefs, and consequently, the measurements may be contaminated and not reflect the process capability. Data that is not random must be screened out to get a true picture of the process capability. Another reason why the normal distribution is important will be seen later when we construct control charts. At this point we merely emphasize that nonnormality is a signal for caution and further investigation into the process. The data can be tested for normality using the Chi-square goodness-of-fit test or probability plotting paper.[1]

For the rubber seal example, the distribution in Figure 17.1 appears to be slightly skewed to the left but, overall, seems to approximate the bell-shaped pattern. The average and standard deviation from the 90 observations are our best estimates of the seal-forming process (the population of individual seals). The *"natural limits"* are three standard deviations from the average, and show that about 99.7 percent of the seals will have hardness values between 23.65 and 101.46 for the chronic condition of the seal-forming process.

Natural limits Three standard deviations above and below the average of sample unit measurements.

Specification Limits Capability histograms convey more information about process quality by comparing them with the product's specification limits. *Specification limits* are the boundaries between "good" and "bad" for a particular characteristic in terms of the product's fitness for use. A customer, for example, may specify the nominal resistance of 17 ohms for an electrical component, with an upper specification limit (USL) of 19 ohms and a lower specification limit (LSL) of 15 ohms. Figure 17.2 shows three

Specification limits (SL) **Upper (USL)** and **lower (LSL)** boundaries defining the limits of variation in a product characteristic such that the product is fit for use; output measuring outside these limits is unacceptable.

[1]See R. C. Pfaffenberger and J. H. Patterson, *Statistical Methods,* 3rd ed. (Homewood, Ill.: Richard D. Irwin, 1987); see also E. L. Grant and R. S. Leavenworth, *Statistical Quality Control,* 6th ed. (New York: McGraw-Hill, 1988).

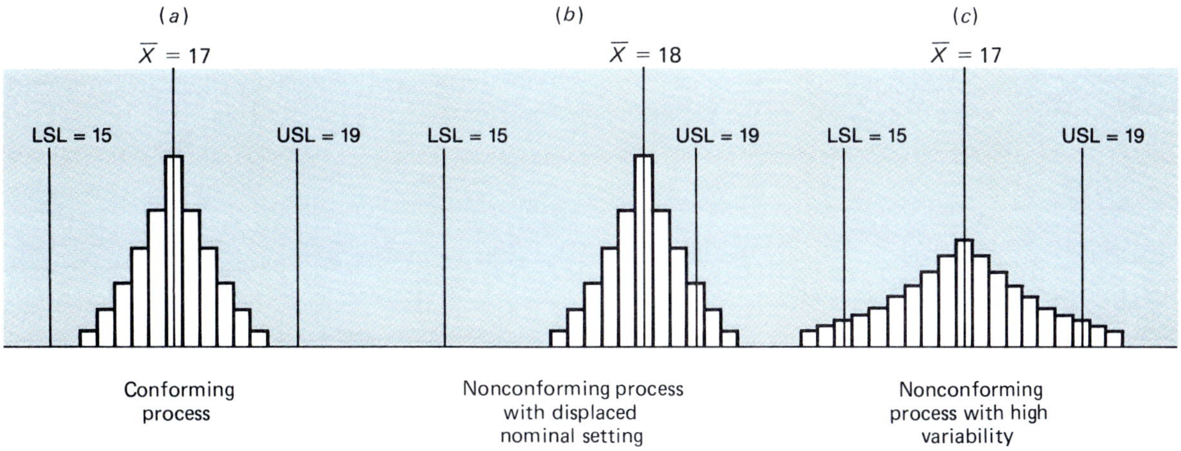

FIGURE 17.2 **Three process capability conditions**

contrasting process capability conditions for production of the electrical component. The chronic condition of an ideal process would have zero standard deviation. The chronic condition in part (a) is quite good, but not ideal; the process is conforming because the average actual, or observed, resistance coincides with the required resistance, midway between the upper and lower specification limits, and the process variability is low. The process variability in part (b) is low, but the displacement of the average actual resistance above the required resistance results in nonconforming output above the upper specification limit. This process should be monitored closely because nonconformance will increase if the average resistance shifts further upward or if variability increases. Part (c) has nonconformance due to high process variability. So long as this chronic condition persists, the company will incur costs associated with the existing levels of nonconformance. If, in addition, sporadic problems arise, causing a shift in the average resistance or increasing the variability, nonconformance will increase.

EXAMPLE

In Figure 17.1 the lower specification limit (LSL) indicates that seals whose hardnesses are under 50 are unsatisfactory, based on extensive performance tests in engineering. Similarly, the upper specification limit outlaws seals whose hardness is above 80. A comparison of the product specifications with the process distribution reveals a significant discrepancy: More than 11 percent (10 units) of the observed seals measure under the LSL and more than 5 percent (5 units) measure above the USL. Extrapolating further, if the process is normally distributed with an average hardness of 62.56 and standard deviation of 12.97, it can be shown (by using the normal distribution found in Appendix A) that about 16.6 percent of the seals produced in the future will measure under the LSL, and about 8.8 percent will measure above the USL.

The company can estimate the costs associated with this level of product nonconformance and, if justified, determine how to improve the chronic condition of the process through breakthrough and improvement programs.

Process capability analysis, then, describes what the process can do in its chronic condition, and predicts how much of the output will conform to specifications. Meanwhile, the analyst needs to watch for the onset of nonrandom (sporadic) variations in the process, as we see next.

STATISTICAL PROCESS CONTROL

Statistical process control (SPC) The use of sample statistics to detect and eliminate nonrandom (sporadic) variations in the conversion process.

In-control process A process for which all variations are random; if some variations are nonrandom (sporadic), the process is termed an **out-of-control process.**

Control chart A chart of sampling data used to make inferences about the control status of a conversion process.

Variable characteristic A product characteristic that can be measured on a continuum.

Attribute characteristic A product characteristic that can be measured by a rating of good or bad.

One approach to controlling nonuniformity, *statistical process control* (SPC), is to detect and eliminate nonrandom (sporadic) variations as they arise while the process is operating. The process is said to be *in control* when all variations are random and is *out of control* when some variations are sporadic. The process is monitored periodically by examining sample units of output. If measurement data for the critical characteristics have shifted away from a purely random pattern, the process is stopped until the causes of nonconformance are corrected. *Control charts* are the primary tool for SPC, and the selection of control charts depends on the type of measurements that are to be used.

MEASURING VARIABLES VERSUS ATTRIBUTES

Two different types of measurement, by variables and by attributes, are used in process control. In some situations, we must measure a product characteristic on a continuous scale, such as its length, weight, or volume, each of which is a *variable characteristic.* Alternatively, an *attribute characteristic* can be measured by a simple rating of good or bad, success or failure, etc.

Attribute measurements are quicker and easier to make, so they offer more economical data gathering and storage. Variable measurements, however, contain more potential information. Notice, for example, that we could not have constructed the process capability histogram for rubber seal hardness in Figure 17.1 if we merely had classified each of the 90 sample units as either acceptable or unacceptable. Variables measurements provide the capability data, and they also provide more powerful information for controlling the process.

CREATING CONTROL CHARTS FOR VARIABLES USING AVERAGES

Shewhart control charts are the workhorse of statistical process control.[2] The name of the chart honors Dr. Walter Shewhart of the Bell Telephone Laboratories, who is generally recognized as the "father" of statistical quality control. When a conversion process begins to shift out of control, we would like to know as soon as possible so we can initiate corrective action. Although one would think it would be a simple matter to detect a shift by observation, it usually is not. Occasionally, random variability in the process may make it seem that output quality is falling when actually there has been no basic change. At other times, real shifts are mistakenly interpreted as random variability. If a basic change occurs, we want to correct it so we can avoid costs of

[2]Dr. Walter A. Shewhart, *Economic Control of Quality of Manufactured Product* (New York: D. Van Nostrand Company, 1931).

producing faulty products. On the other hand, we do not want to waste resources trying to correct a process that is already operating properly. To help avoid interpretative errors and detect when real shifts have occurred, control charts are very useful.

$\overline{X}$-chart A control chart using sample averages.

Control limits (CL) Upper (UCL) and lower (LCL) boundaries defining the range of variation in a product characteristic such that the conversion process is in control.

The $\overline{X}$-chart Figure 17.3 shows a control chart for the temperature of a chemical plating operation. This chart, known as an $\overline{X}$-chart, has three important parameters determined from historical data: average temperature, *upper control limit* (UCL), and *lower control limit* (LCL). Control limits are boundaries defining a range of variation used to infer the central status of the conversion process. In the past, the average temperature for the process had been 86°C. The upper and lower control limits had been set at 89°C and 83°C. After the chart was constructed, four more days of operation transpired. Sample temperature readings for these days were measured and recorded on the chart. Temperature averages for the first two days were near the previous historical average; the third day's average was near the upper control limit. An operations manager could have glanced at this chart and said, "The process is in control based upon the last three days' performance." The average on day 4 was outside the control limits. The average had probably shifted above the historical average of 86°C. How can we draw this conclusion? Because of the central limit theorem, which we study next.

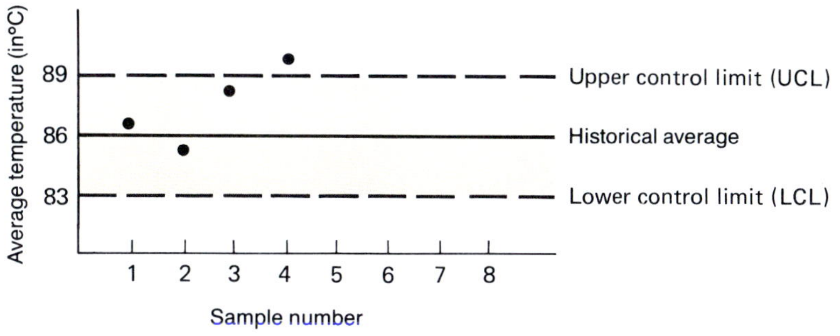

FIGURE 17.3 **Example $\overline{X}$ control chart**

Central limit theorem A statistical hypothesis that the sampling distribution approaches normality as the size of the samples increases, regardless of the distribution of the measurements of individual sample units.

Central Limit Theorem Predicting the performance of the conversion process by interpreting control charts makes use of a theorem of statistics known as the *central limit theorem.* This theorem allows us the convenience of using the standard normal distribution in making predictions about the process we are monitoring. With it, we can conveniently determine the chances that some important characteristic of our process has changed, and we can express these chances explicitly. To apply this theorem, we take a randomly selected sample of n units of output. For each sample unit we measure the critical characteristic, say its length, and compute the average of the n observed lengths. The central limit theorem specifies that if we compute averages for many such samples, then averages will be distributed approximately normally regardless of the distribution of individual lengths. The approximation to normality improves, and the standard deviation of the sampling distribution—that is, the distribution of the averages—diminishes, as the size of the samples is increased (see Figure 17.4).

The central limit theorem hypothesizes an important relationship between the

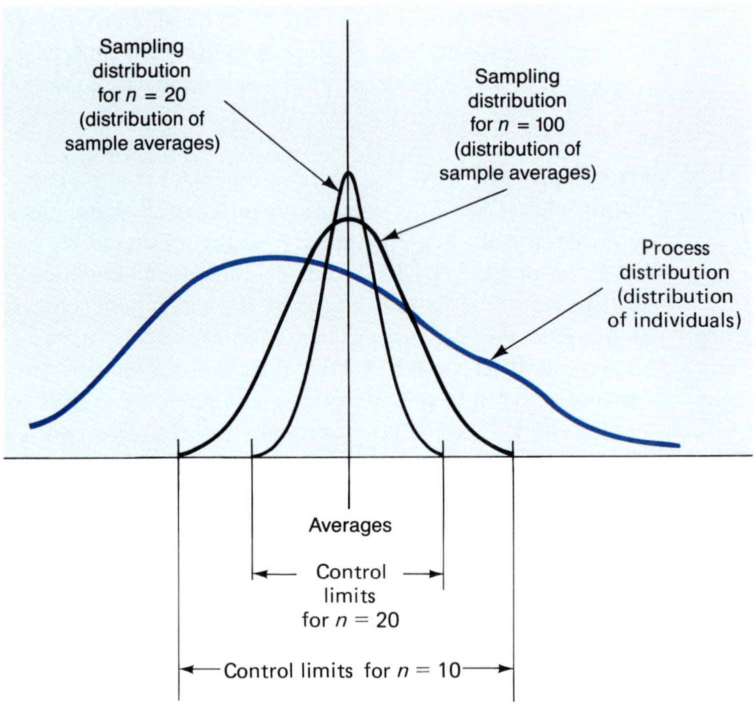

FIGURE 17.4 **Two distributions of sample averages taken from a process distribution**

standard deviation S of the distribution of individuals and the standard deviation $S_{\overline{X}}$ of the sampling distribution, as shown in Equation 17.3.

$$S_{\overline{X}} = \frac{S}{\sqrt{n}} \tag{17.3}$$

This relationship is helpful because it sometimes eliminates cumbersome calculations; if either standard deviation (estimated) is known, we can easily calculate the other standard deviation for any sample size n.

Steps in Developing Control Charts for Averages With this overview of control charts, let's examine the steps for constructing and interpreting them to control the average performance of a process. The following are the steps in developing control charts:

1. Partition the *historical data*. A control chart is constructed from historical data; future performance is compared with this past performance. You must have two distinctly different data sets, one for control chart construction and a second to reflect the most recent performance.
2. Using the data for control chart construction, *calculate* a process average and upper and lower control limits. The control limits are based on the sampling distribution.
3. Draw the control chart axes so that the y-axis represents the variable measurement and the x-axis represents the sequence of samples.

4. *Plot* the current or most recent sample average on the chart.
5. *Interpret* the chart to see if (a) the process is in control and no action is required, (b) the process is out of control and a cause should be sought, or (c) the process is in control but trends are occurring that should alert the manager to possible nonrandom conditions.
6. *Update* the control chart. Periodically, the control chart is reconstructed by returning to step 1. You can repartition the data by discarding the oldest historical data and replacing it with historical data collected since the last updating.

The calculations for the control chart use Equations 17.4–17.7, which define the sample average $\overline{X}$, that is, the average of the sample units (for some variable measurement); the average $\overline{\overline{X}}$ of the sample averages; the standard deviation $S_{\overline{X}}$ of the distribution of the sample averages; and the UCL and LCL.

$$\overline{X} = \frac{\sum_{i=1}^{n} X_i}{n} \tag{17.4}$$

$$\overline{\overline{X}} = \frac{\sum_{j=1}^{m} \overline{X}_j}{m} \tag{17.5}$$

$$S_{\overline{X}} = \sqrt{\frac{\sum_{j=1}^{m} (\overline{X}_j - \overline{\overline{X}})^2}{m-1}} \tag{17.6}$$

$$\begin{aligned} \text{UCL} &= \overline{\overline{X}} + kS_{\overline{X}} \\ \text{LCL} &= \overline{\overline{X}} - kS_{\overline{X}} \end{aligned} \tag{17.7}$$

where X_i = Measurement for sample unit i
n = Number of units in each sample
$\overline{X}_j$ = Average of the sample units in sample j
m = Number of samples
k = Constant; number of standard deviations

To calculate a sample average, let X_i be the measured value for the *i*th unit in a sample of size n. From Equation 17.4, $\overline{X}$ is the average of these n measurements. Now instead of sampling only once, suppose we conduct m samplings, always creating samples of size n, and obtain m sample averages. The sample average for the *j*th sample is then denoted by $\overline{X}_j$. We can then calculate the average $\overline{\overline{X}}$ of these m sample averages and the standard deviation $S_{\overline{X}}$ of their distribution. Equation 17.5 defines $\overline{\overline{X}}$, also called the process average, and its calculated value is graphed as the center line of the control chart. The standard deviation $S_{\overline{X}}$ of the sample averages' distribution, also called the sampling distribution, is used in Equation 17.7 to calculate the control limits for the chart.

EXAMPLE

Continuing with our earlier example, the automobile company wants to set up a chart for controlling the average hardness of the rubber seals for car windows. The 90 individual hardness measurements came from 18 samples in which five seals (n = 5) were measured in each sample. We first find the sample average $\overline{X}$ for each sample, using Equation 17.4, as shown in column 3.

Sample Number j ($j = 1 \ldots 18$)	Hardness of Unit X_i ($i = 1 \ldots 5$)	Sample Average $\overline{X}_i$
1	65, 70, 60, 50, 65	$310 \div 5 = 62.0$
2	70, 80, 70, 40, 60	$320 \div 5 = 64.0$
.		
.		
.		
17	60, 70, 85, 60, 60	$335 \div 5 = 67.0$
18	55, 75, 80, 40, 55	$305 \div 5 = 61.0$

Then we find the average $\overline{\overline{X}}$ of these sample averages by using Equation 17.5:

$$\overline{\overline{X}} = \frac{62.0 + 64.0 + \ldots + 67.0 + 61.0}{18} = 62.56$$

Next we calculate the standard deviation of the sample averages distribution using equation 17.6:

$$S_{\overline{X}} = \sqrt{\frac{(62.0 - 62.56)^2 + (64.0 - 62.56)^2 + \ldots + (67.0 - 62.56)^2 + (61.0 - 62.56)^2}{18 - 1}}$$

$$= 5.80$$

Finally, if we want control limits that are three standard deviations ($k = 3$) above and below the average of the sample averages, we apply Equation 17.7 as follows:

$$UCL = \overline{\overline{X}} + 3S_{\overline{X}} = 62.56 + 3(5.80) = 79.96$$
$$LCL = \overline{\overline{X}} - 3S_{\overline{X}} = 62.56 - 3(5.80) = 45.16$$

The resulting control chart for average hardness is shown in Figure 17.5.

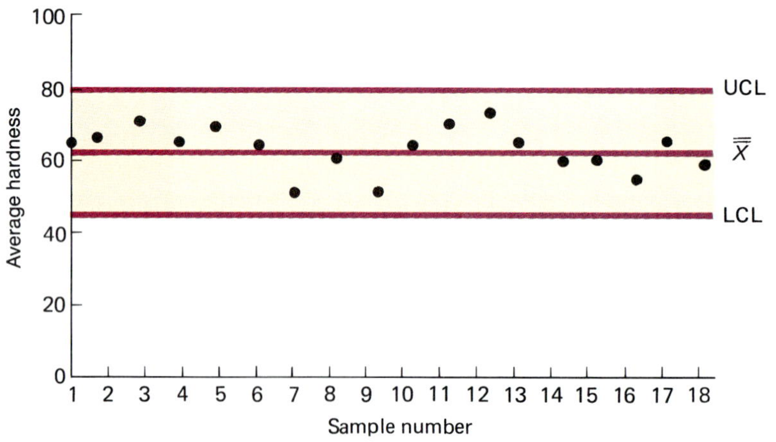

FIGURE 17.5 **$\overline{X}$ chart: Control chart for average hardness of window seals**

Although the example uses three standard deviations ($k = 3$) to set the control limits which is the dominant industry practice, some applications merit the use of wider or narrower control limits. The real issue is one of risk. Management must decide how certain they want to be that, when a process appears out of control, it really is out of control. Managers may want different degrees of certainty based on how important they believe an error to be. Common alternatives in setting the control limits are to set k at ± 1, 2, or 3. As shown in Figure 17.6, with narrow control limits ($\bar{\bar{X}} \pm 1S_{\bar{X}}$), there is a reasonable chance that when the process appears to be out of control, it may not actually be out of control (probability .317, or $1 - .683$). This probability is equal to the area outside the control limits in part (a) of Figure 17.6. With wider control limits ($\bar{\bar{X}} \pm 3S_{\bar{X}}$), there is little chance of such an error (probability .003). This is the area outside the control limits in part (b); when a sample average falls outside these limits, the process is very likely out of control.

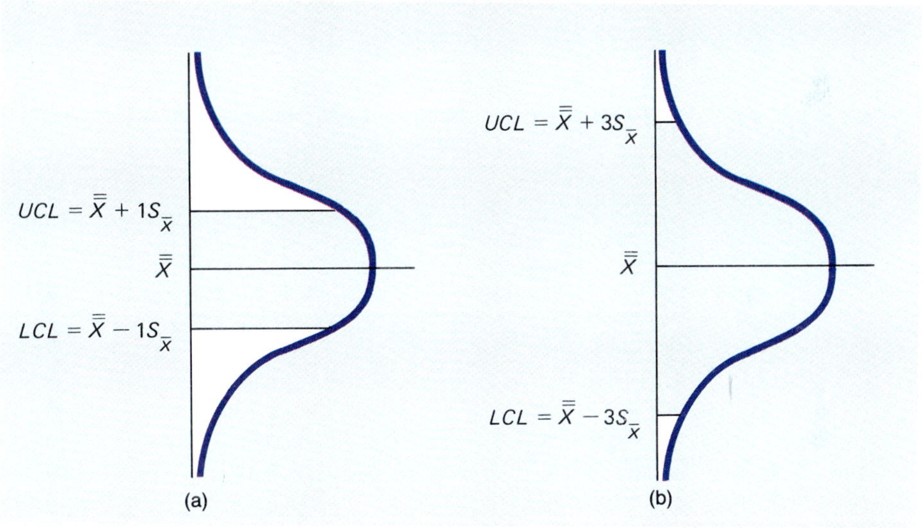

FIGURE 17.6 **Probabilities of α error for control limits using 1 standard deviation (a) and 3 standard deviations (b)**

Producer's risk (type I error) (α) The risk or probability of incorrectly concluding that the conversion process is out of control.

Consumer's risk (type II error) (β) The risk or probability of incorrectly concluding that the conversion process is in control.

The selection of control limits involves tradeoffs between two types of risks. With the first type, α, called the *producer's risk* or *type I error,* there is a possibility of concluding that the process is out of control when it is actually in a state of statistical control. (This is the same terminology used later in sampling plans.) The producer's risk is reduced by using wide control limits; it is increased by using narrow control limits.

With the second type of risk, β, called the *consumer's risk* or *type II error,* there is a possibility of concluding that the process is in control when it is actually out of control. The consumer's risk increases as the control limits are widened, and decreases as they are narrowed. Ultimately, in choosing control limits a manager must consider these risks and the costs associated with them. If the costs of undetected shifts are high relative to the costs of correcting the process, narrow limits (lower consumer risk) are appropriate. If the costs of restoring the process to the desired state are high compared with the costs of producing defective output, wider limits (lower producer's risk) are appropriate.

Sample range The arithmetic difference of the highest and lowest measurement for a sample.

Simplifying Chart Construction: Tabular Methods If performance data are normally distributed, we can use a tabular method rather than Equations 17.6 and 17.7 for constructing control charts.[3] The tabular method uses *sample ranges,* which can be calculated quickly, rather than standard deviations to determine the control limits. The sample range R_j of the jth sample is the arithmetic difference of the highest and lowest measurement for the sample. Thus the average $\overline{R}$ of the sample ranges is the sum of all the R_j, divided by the number of samples. To use $\overline{R}$ to determine control limits, predetermined factors must be used. These factors are given in Table 17.1. Thus, using the tabular method, the UCL and LCL are defined by:

$$\begin{aligned} \text{UCL} &= \overline{\overline{X}} + A_2\overline{R} \\ \text{LCL} &= \overline{\overline{X}} - A_2\overline{R} \end{aligned} \tag{17.8}$$

TABLE 17.1 **Factors A_2, D_3, and D_4 for $\overline{X}$ and R charts (for three-standard-deviation control limits)**

Number of Units in Sampling n	A_2 for $\overline{X}$ Chart	R Chart: D_3 for LCL	R Chart: D_4 for UCL
2	1.88	0	3.27
3	1.02	0	2.57
4	0.73	0	2.28
5	0.58	0	2.11
6	0.48	0	2.00
7	0.42	0.08	1.92
8	0.37	0.14	1.86
9	0.34	0.18	1.82
10	0.31	0.22	1.78
11	0.29	0.26	1.74
12	0.27	0.28	1.72
13	0.25	0.31	1.69
14	0.24	0.33	1.67
15	0.22	0.35	1.65
16	0.21	0.36	1.64
17	0.20	0.38	1.62
18	0.19	0.39	1.61
19	0.19	0.40	1.60
20	0.18	0.41	1.59

Source: Adapted from E. L. Grant and R. S. Leavenworth, *Statistical Quality Control,* 6th ed. (New York: McGraw-Hill Book Company, 1988), p. 670.

[3]If the process distribution is skewed, a median control chart, instead of an averages control chart, can be used to control the central tendency of the process. See Grant and Leavenworth, *Statistical Quality Control.*

EXAMPLE

Using the rubber seal hardness data, the range R_j of the jth sample of five measurements ($n = 5$) is calculated in the third column below.

Sample Number j ($j = 1 \ldots 18$)	Individual Hardness of Unit X_i ($i = 1 \ldots 5$)	Sample Range R_j
1	65, 70, 60, 50, 65	70 − 50 = 20
2	70, 80, 70, 40, 60	80 − 40 = 40
.		
.		
.		
17	60, 70, 85, 60, 60	85 − 60 = 25
18	55, 75, 80, 40, 55	80 − 40 = 40

The average $\overline{R}$ of the sample ranges is given by:

$$\overline{R} = \frac{20 + 40 + \ldots + 25 + 40}{18} = 28.89$$

The control limits, then, using Equations 17.8, are calculated as follows:

$$UCL = 62.56 + (0.58)(28.89) = 79.32$$
$$LCL = 62.56 - (0.58)(28.89) = 45.80$$

As you can see, the tabular method yields control limits that are very close to those we previously calculated. Based on the 18 historical sample averages, the process seems to be in a state of statistical control, but averages are not the whole story. What about the variability of the process? The answer to this question is examined next.

CREATING CONTROL CHARTS FOR VARIABLES USING RANGES

R chart A control chart using sample ranges.

In Figure 17.2, we saw how increases in process variability can result in nonconforming output. We want to be able to detect changes in variability, and we can do so by using a control chart based on control limits we calculate using the standard deviation or sample ranges. So far, we have plotted averages on our control charts. Here, we shift attention to the *R chart,* a control chart on which we plot ranges. The *R* chart is widely used in industry because it is computationally simple and easy to understand, and because tabular help (Table 17.1) is readily available. Again, as was the case with the averages chart, the tabular method is applicable only if the process is normally distributed.

The data for the *R* chart includes the range for each sample; each sample range is plotted on the chart. The average range $\overline{R}$ is also drawn on the chart. The control limits are calculated using Equations 17.9 below, along with the appropriate predetermined factors D_3 and D_4 given in Table 17.1. After the process demonstrates a state of statistical control, subsequent sample ranges can be plotted on the chart. When the new sample ranges are unusually high or low (outside the control limits), investigation is undertaken to find the cause of the nonrandom behavior.

$$UCL_R = D_4\overline{R}$$
$$LCL_R = D_3\overline{R} \qquad (17.9)$$

EXAMPLE

For the rubber seal hardness example, $\overline{R}$ of the 18 sample ranges is 28.89. From Table 17.1, for samples of size $n = 5$, we see that $D_3 = 0$ and $D_4 = 2.11$. The control limits, using Equations 17.9, are calculated as follows:

$$UCL_R = (2.11)(28.89) = 60.95$$
$$LCL_R = (0)(28.89) = 0$$

The lower control limit is set at zero on the hardness scale since the D_3 factor is zero for sample size below $n = 7$. The 18 sample ranges are plotted on the R chart in Figure 17.7.

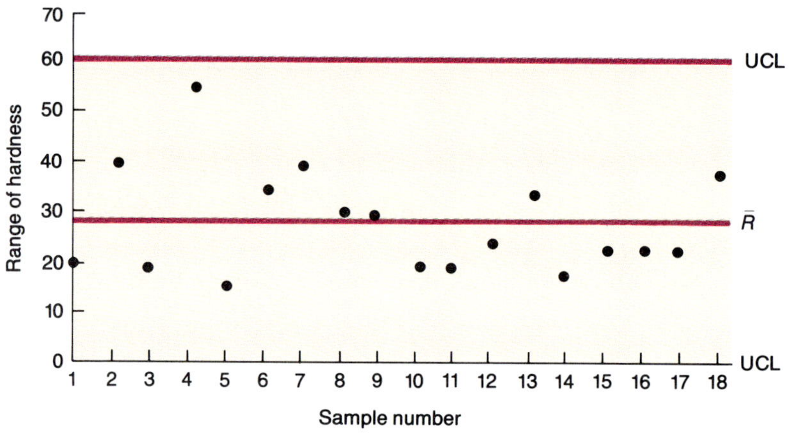

FIGURE 17.7 ***R* chart: Control chart for range of hardness of window seals**

INTERPRETING CONTROL CHARTS FOR VARIABLES

Up to this point we have completed steps 1 to 3 in developing c›ntrol charts; the historical performance has been plotted. But before we can begin using these tools to monitor future process behavior, we must first confirm that the historical data reflect the true chronic condition of the process, that only random variation is present. We so confirm by looking jointly at the two control charts ($\overline{X}$ and R), along with the process capability histogram (Figure 17.1). The comparison is essential because the three diagrams contain different information and this information must be consistent before we can conclude that the variation in the process is random.

The control charts show the time-phased pattern of sample averages and sample ranges. No predictable patterns are evident in the plotted points, and none falls outside the control limits. Consequently, we would like to conclude that the plotted points reflect random variation, but to do so we must first confirm that the process has a normal distribution. Why? Because the tabular factors for the control limits, and hence their validity, are based on the assumption of normality. If the process departs from a normal distribution, the control limits in Figures 17.5 and 17.7 are invalid and, consequently, we cannot tell if the process is in a state of statistical control. We validate the normality assumption now by observing that the histogram of individual measurements in Figure 17.1 closely resembles, although not perfectly, a normal distribution. A subsequent statistical test for goodness-of-fit supported the normality assumption. We thus conclude that the control limits are valid.

Next we use the control charts to confirm the validity of the histogram in Figure 17.1. The validation is needed because the histogram merely *summarizes* the 90 measurements; it may be masking sequential patterns (nonrandom variations). Perhaps, for example, the process average or standard deviation was shifting while the samples were being taken. If so, those shifts might not be evident from looking at the histogram, but the control charts would reveal such patterns. The control charts in Figures 17.5 and 17.7 do not show any obvious nonrandom patterns in the plottings, so we conclude that the histogram contains only random variations.

Our cross-checking sufficiently assures us that the chronic condition of the rubber seal process has been identified. Now we have created useful tools for statistical process control; we can go on to step 4 and plot future process data on the validated control charts.

Many of the procedures that were described previously for constructing variables control charts are also applicable for constructing control charts for attributes, as we see next.

CONTROL CHARTS FOR ATTRIBUTES USING FRACTION DEFECTIVE

Fraction defective The ratio of defective units to total units.

p chart A control chart using sample fractions defective.

When sample units are classified into one of two categories (good or bad, success or failure, etc.), measurement is by attribute. Suppose we observe sample units from some process and classify each as either defective or acceptable. We can calculate the fraction of defective units in the sample and compare it to the historical fraction defective in the process. Such a chart is called a *fraction defective chart* (or *p chart*). If the sample fraction defective p deviates widely from the historical process fraction defective $\bar{p}$, we may conclude that some change in the process has occurred, that the current fraction defective is either higher or lower than usual. If the process is under control, the sample fraction defective p is an estimate of the underlying process fraction defective $\bar{p}$. Several such sample estimates tend to be normally distributed.

To construct an attribute control chart, we begin by inspecting a sample of n units to determine what fraction of those units is defective. We do this with Equation 17.10, where x is the number of defective units:

$$p = \frac{x}{n} \tag{17.10}$$

If this process is repeated, say m times, we get several estimates of fraction defective. Then, using these m estimates of p, we calculate the historical *average* fraction defective $\bar{p}$ for the process using Equation 17.11.

$$\bar{p} = \frac{\sum_{j=1}^{m} p_j}{m} = \frac{\sum_{j=1}^{m} x_j}{nm} \tag{17.11}$$

where n = Number of units in each sample
P_j = Fraction defective for sample j
m = Number of samples
x_j = Number of units defective in sample j

The central limit theorem applies for fraction defective charts if that samples' p values have an approximately normal distribution (unless the sample size is small and $\bar{p}$

is close to zero). The standard deviation S_p of the distribution of p is given by Equation 17.12. In this equation, $\bar{p}$ is the average fraction defective, and n is the size of each sample,

$$S_p = \sqrt{\frac{\bar{p}(1 - \bar{p})}{\text{n}}} \tag{17.12}$$

The control limits are calculated from Equation 17.13.

$$UCL_p = \bar{p} + kS_p \tag{17.13}$$

$$LCL_p = \bar{p} - kS_p$$

EXAMPLE

A visual inspection for scratches (each unit is judged good or bad) on a decorative paint trim operation produced the following data for last week. For each sample, 30 units were inspected.

Sample Number $j(j = 1 \ldots 10)$	Number x_j of Units *Defective*	Sample Number $j(j = 11 \ldots 20)$	Number x_j of Units Defective
1	5	11	5
2	4	12	7
3	4	13	4
4	5	14	5
5	7	15	4
6	4	16	5
7	5	17	5
8	6	18	7
9	4	19	6
10	5	20	4

This week 30 pieces were again sampled on each of two occasions. On Monday, six pieces were found defective in the first sample, on Tuesday nine were found defective in the second sample. As operations manager, you want to know if the process is in control this week.

To find a solution, construct a fraction defective control chart with two-standard-deviation limits based on last week's typical process performance. Last week's data are used to calculate average fraction defective ($\bar{p}$), the standard deviation S_p of the distribution of average fraction defective, and the control limits UCL and LCL. Then the fraction defective for this week's samples are plotted against last week's control chart. The required calculations are shown here.

$$\bar{p} \text{ for last week} = \frac{\sum_{j=1}^{20} x_j}{nm} = \frac{101}{(30)(20)} = .168$$

$$S_p = \sqrt{\frac{\bar{p}(1 - \bar{p})}{n}} = \sqrt{\frac{(.168)(1 - .168)}{30}} = .0683$$

$$UCL = S_p + 2S_p = .168 + 2(.0683) = .305$$

$$LCL = S_p - 2S_p = .168 - 2(.0683) = .031$$

Fractions defective in second week:

$$p_{21} = \frac{6}{30} = 0.20; \; p_{22} = \frac{9}{30} = .30$$

Now you can construct the resulting control chart as shown in Figure 17.8. Monday's fraction defective is close to the historical process average. Tuesday's sample indicates that the process is still in a state of control. If a future fraction defective falls outside the control limits, the operating manager can be quite confident (95.4 percent) that nonrandom variation has arisen in the paint trim process.

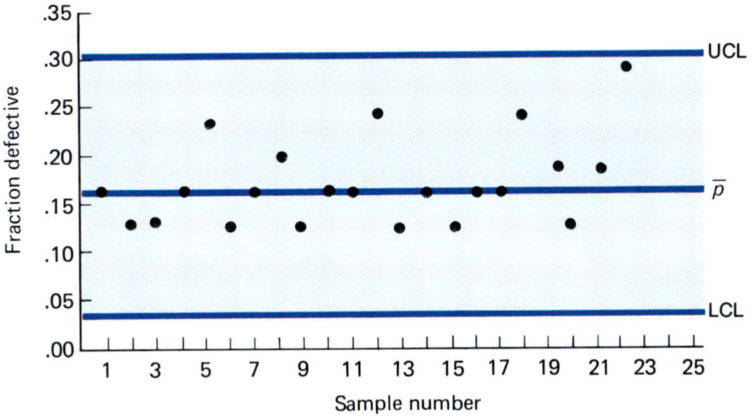

FIGURE 17.8 **Fraction defective control chart (p chart); $n = 30$**

Although our discussion has focused on fraction defective control charts, other attributes also can be used to make control charts, some of which are summarized in Table 17.2. Operations Management Highlight 17.1 discusses the implementation of p charts in health care. Other examples and methods for using these attribute control charts can be found in the quality control references at the end of this chapter.

TABLE 17.2 **Types of attributes control charts**

Name of Chart	Symbol	Attribute Measured
Fraction defective	p	Fraction of nonconforming units in a sample
Number defective	np	Number of nonconforming units in a sample
Nonconformities	c	Number of nonconformities in one unit
Demerit score	D	Weighted sum of demerits for different nonconformities in one unit

Adapted from Grant and Leavenworth, *Statistical Quality Control,* 670.

OPERATIONS MANAGEMENT HIGHLIGHT 17.1

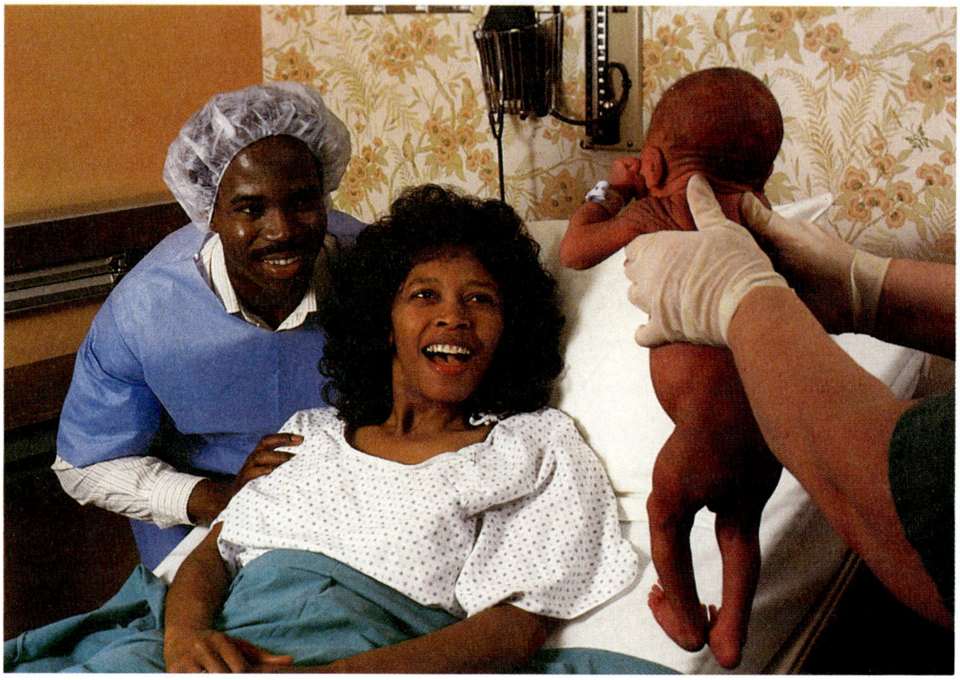

Source: Joseph Nettis/Photo Researchers

Statistical Quality Control Can Be Good for Your Health

More and more, hospitals and clinics are using statistical quality control for improving their health care services. Better quality care for patients is certainly one goal. Insurance companies and government agencies, too, hope that SQC can contain the spiraling costs of health care. The American Institute

OTHER CONTROL CHART CONSIDERATIONS

As Figure 17.9 shows, graphs of control chart data can have many shapes. Notice that when the process is in its chronic condition, data are randomly scattered around the central value of the chart. When successive data points form an identifiable pattern or fall outside the control limits, very likely something other than randomness is in effect.

of Medical Law (AIML), for example, has incorporated an eight-hour quality assurance module into its 120-hour program for risk management certification. The AIML emphasizes the use of statistical analysis for process control and improvement. The Florida Department of Insurance has recognized the growing importance of the SQC approach and, accordingly, has approved the AIML certification program for state licensing of all health care risk managers.

In the AIML program, Shewhart control charts are used to demonstrate how to reduce what are known as adverse patient outcomes (APOs), and the losses they cause. Medication errors in the hospital, for example, can be analyzed by using a *p*-chart. For each department, such as pediatrics, the ratio of patient-days with medication errors to the total patient days is the sample fraction defective. To make employees aware of their performance, the charts are made visible to all. The source of each medication error—the nurse, the physician, the pharmacy, or the laboratory—can be pinpointed. Out-of-control incidents are investigated for correction and improvement. In addition to medication errors, other types of APOs, too, can be controlled using Shewhart charts. The accuracy of hospital admissions procedures, on-time performance of respiratory therapy, incidence of drug and transfusion reactions, and incidence of repeat x-rays are just a few examples of APOs that can be monitored and controlled with SQC.

As is typical of any change, SQL tools, and other data-based process analysis using statistics, are meeting resistance in health care organizations. However, the counterpressures are even greater: three hospitals in Massachusetts, for example, closed in the last six months of 1989 and six to ten others were expected to close their doors by 1991. Sixty percent of hospitals in Massachusetts were operating at a deficit in 1990. Similar trends exist all across the United States.

As SQC gains acceptance in health care organizations, there is growing hope that it will result in better patient care and in financially healthier clinics and hospitals, too.

Sources: **Glenn Laffel, "Implementing Quality Management in Health Care: The Challenges Ahead," *Quality Progress* (November 1990), 29–32; M.P. Demos and N.P. Demos, "Statistical Quality Control's Role in Health Care Management," *Quality Progress* (August 1989), 85–89**

Subsequently, management should launch an investigation to determine the cause of this nonrandom behavior.

Step 6 in the construction of control charts, you may remember, is updating the charts. When the charts are periodically updated, they become dynamic rather than static. The control limits and/or the central tendency of the chart change over time. Charts must be updated whenever breakthrough and quality improvement programs

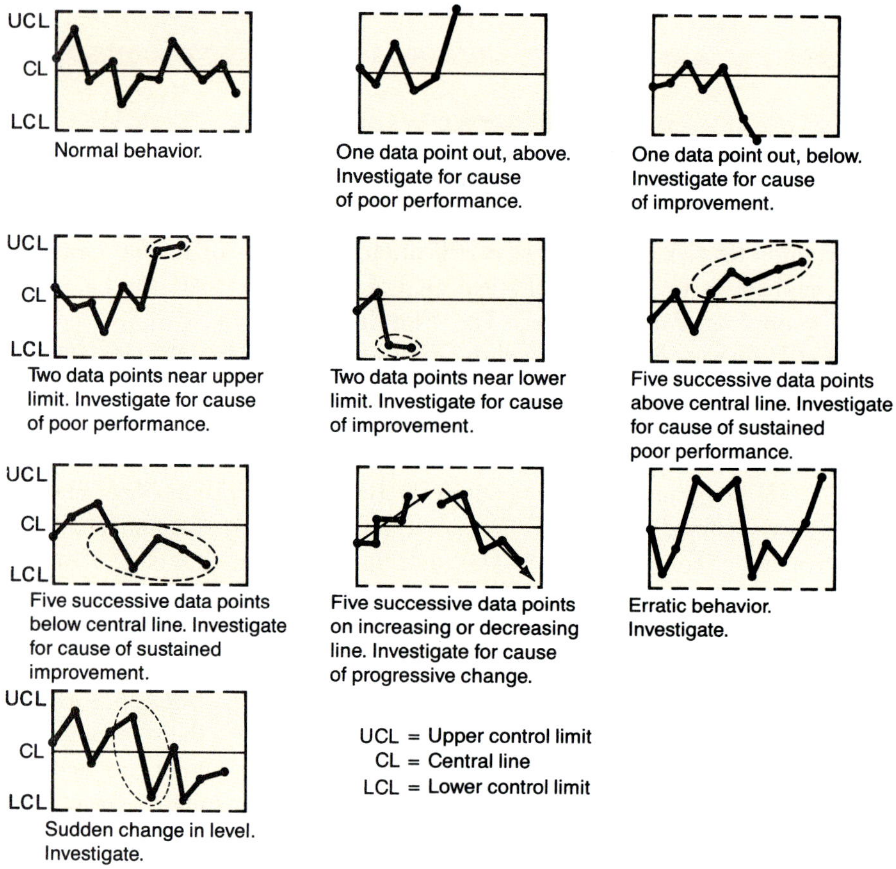

FIGURE 17.9 **Control chart evidence for investigation**
Source: Bertrand L. Hansen, *Quality Control: Theory and Applications*, © 1963, p. 65. Reprinted by permission of Prentice-Hall, Inc., Englewood Cliffs, N.J.

are implemented, or when other significant changes occur in the people, methods, machines, or materials in the process.

After we have identified the product (or process) characteristic to be controlled, we must resolve a number of other control questions. What sample size should be used? How often should a sample be taken? What control limits should be selected? To what degree do we want to emphasize detection and control versus prevention? The answers to these and other questions are important because they determine both the effectiveness and the cost of the control process. Specific answers to these questions depend to a great extent on the specific organization, on the nature of its processes and products. In general, choices among alternative statistical parameters involve tradeoffs among opposing costs and risks that must be evaluated.

One reason for the increased use of control charts is the growing number of user-friendly and powerful software packages, such as *SQCpack*-PLUS that can be used right at the work stations on production or service lines.[4] But even with manual systems, control charts are used in some form in many manufacturing facilities, for example, automobile manufacturing, appliance production, diecasting operations, pet food

[4]*SQC pack*-PLUS (Dayton, Ohio: P-Q Systems, 1990).

production, metal stamping, and petroleum refining. Recently, service industries have adopted this useful technique in various settings; accident rates measure goodness of traffic control processes, numbers of robberies measure public safety systems, sickness rates measure health care systems, and accident rates measure safety in ski slope recreation systems. Banks, hospitals, and other service organizations make use of control charts, too.

INSPECTION

Inspection The observation and measurement of inputs and outputs.

Inspection of raw materials, work-in-process, and finished products provides the basic data for documentation and evaluation in the control process. Inspection, as we have already implied in our examples, is the observation and measurement of the conversion process outputs and inputs. Inspection can be done either visually or mechanically; its purpose is to see whether the physical characteristics of the product or service conform to specifications. Inspection is commonly divided into three areas: receiving inspection, work-in-process inspection, and finished goods inspection.

Receiving Inspection Generally, output quality can be no better than the input quality. Inputs are often built up, over a succession of stages, into the final product. At the end of this progression, we sometimes find that defective inputs used in initial stages result in an unacceptable final product. This means costly repair, which could have been avoided. To do so, management often provides for inspection of inputs prior

Careful inspection of these rocket fuses provides the basic data for documenting quality and for evaluating the quality control process.
Source: **Steve Dunwell / The Image Bank**

Receiving inspection The inspection of inputs.

to their use. At *receiving inspection,* incoming shipments of raw materials, subcomponents from vendors, or other inputs are observed and evaluated against predetermined quality standards. These materials are often physically separated from work-in-process materials and are only released to operations after passing the initial inspection. It is best to eliminate receiving inspection, moving inspection to the vendor's facility, but only if a working relationship of trust can be established with the vendor.

Work-in-process inspection The inspection of a product at one or more stages of production.

Work-in-Process Inspection The employee who produces an item should be responsible for inspecting it to ensure its quality. When someone other than this employee needs to inspect work, management can provide for *work-in-process inspection.* The outputs of one or more stages of production are screened before they are used in subsequent operations. The intensity of inspection depends on the volume of output, the cost of inspecting, and the cost consequences (in subsequent stages) of not inspecting.

Percent defective The percent of units that are defective.

Critical ratio The ratio of inspection costs to percent defective.

An important decision for the operations manager is how many inspection stations to have and where to locate them. A very simple heuristic can be used to help make this decision. Two key factors must be considered: the *percent defective,* that is, the percent of output expected to be defective at each stage of the conversion process, and the *cost* of inspection. Ideally, you would want to inspect at locations where inspection costs are low and percent defective is high. This would give a small *critical ratio,* the ratio of cost to percent defective. We can use a simple three-step procedure for selecting the locations of inspection stations:

1. Identify all stages of the conversion process that are potential locations for inspection stations. For each potential location estimate the inspection costs and gather historical percent defective data.
2. Compute the critical ratio for each potential inspection station.
3. Rank the inspection stations by critical ratio. The smallest critical ratio is the most desirable location; the highest critical ratio is the least desirable, and so forth. With limited resources, place inspection stations until funds are depleted.

EXAMPLE

A process has three potential locations for inspection: locations A, B, and C. Percents defective are 10 percent for location A, 5 percent for location B, and 6 percent for location C. The cost of inspection at location A is \$150, at B \$200, and at C \$100. Critical ratios are:

$$\text{A}\ \frac{\$150}{.10} = \$1{,}500$$

$$\text{B}\ \frac{\$200}{.05} = \$4{,}000$$

$$\text{C}\ \frac{\$100}{.06} = \$1{,}667$$

Inspection stations should be placed first at location A, second at location C, and finally at location B. If funds are limited, place stations in this order until funds for inspection are depleted.

Finished Goods Inspection Various testing procedures can be used to determine whether the final product conforms to functional and appearance standards. If it does not, sources of discrepancy must be identified, and corrective measures must be initiated. Finished goods inspection should be a verification stage as the management focus should be *prevention* early in the operations process, not detection at this stage.

ACCEPTANCE SAMPLING

Acceptance sampling A statistical quality control technique used in deciding to accept or reject a shipment of input or output.

Acceptance sampling is an important statistical application in quality control.[5] Acceptance sampling is based on a systematic plan that prescribes how to sample finished production and how to use the sampling data to maintain quality at desired levels. It is often used to monitor the quality of incoming materials and parts, or for any other situation that requires a decision to accept or reject a large shipment or batch of items. Acceptance sampling, in contrast to ongoing statistical process control, is an "after-the-fact" procedure: It is applied *after* production has ended.

We'll focus on acceptance sampling as it applies to receiving inspection. When a large shipment of a purchased item arrives, someone must decide whether to accept or

Acceptance sampling of these castings for chain saws uses the sampled data to determine whether to accept the shipment of castings or to reject them. ***Source:*** **Steve Dunwell / The Image Bank**

[5]See Erwin M. Saniga and Larry E. Shirland, "Quality Control in Practice . . . A Survey," *Quality Progress* 10, no. 5 (May 1977), 32, who found that over 70 percent of responding firms used sampling and control charts. About a third of the respondents judged quality control techniques moderately useful, a third fairly useful, and a third of great consequence. Few rated the techniques of little consequence.

reject the shipment. We have a range of choices, from inspecting all units in the shipment to sampling just a few units. A systematic *sampling plan* can provide the information needed for the accept/reject decision for the entire shipment. Thus the time, effort, and cost of 100 percent inspection are avoided. Of course, there are some risks involved because of possible sampling errors.

Sampling plan A plan for acceptance sampling specifying the number of units to sample and the number of sample units that must conform to specifications if the shipment is to be accepted.

SAMPLING ERRORS

Two kinds of errors can result from sampling. A shipment of good quality can be mistakenly rejected if a disproportionately large number of defective units from the shipment is selected at random. It is also possible to select at random mostly good units from a shipment of poor quality overall. As we discussed earlier, the first type of risk is α (type I error), the *producer's risk;* the second is β (type II error), the *consumer's risk.* We want a sampling plan that assures that each of these risks is no greater than a specified chosen level.

SAMPLING PLAN ALTERNATIVES

Single sampling Acceptance sampling based on a single sample.

Acceptance number The number of sample units specified in a sampling plan that must conform to specifications if the shipment is to be accepted.

Double sampling Acceptance sampling based on a first, small sample and, if results are inconclusive, a second, larger sample.

Multiple sampling Acceptance sampling based on many small samples.

Three classes of sampling plans are most commonly found in industrial applications. With a *single sampling* plan, a randomly selected sample of n units is taken from the shipment, and the quality of each sampled unit is determined. If more than c of the sampled units are nonconforming, the entire shipment is rejected. If c or fewer items are nonconforming, the entire shipment is accepted. The number c is called the *acceptance number.* Notice that the decision is based solely on the results from a single sample of n units. *Double sampling* is a two-stage process in which the first, smaller sample may result in a clear accept or reject decision, or in an inconclusive result that calls for a second sample. After measuring the second sample, the cumulative evidence from both samples lead to either an acceptance or a rejection. The total number of units needed to make a decision, on average, is smaller with double sampling than with single sampling. *Multiple sampling* is a further extension of the double-sampling concept in which many samples, each of a very small size, may be taken from the shipment until the cumulative evidence is conclusive enough to warrant acceptance or rejection. In most applications, multiple sampling requires fewer sample units than double sampling to arrive at the accept/reject decision. Although double- and multiple-sampling require fewer sample units, they are also more cumbersome to design, implement, and understand. These factors may explain why single sampling, which is discussed in greater detail below, is so frequently encountered in practice.

OPERATING CHARACTERISTIC CURVES

For large shipments consisting of many units, say 5,000, we must determine a sample size n and an acceptance number c such that we are sufficiently assured that our accept/reject decision, based on the sample, is correct. The choices for n and c determine the characteristics of our sampling plan. Standard procedures are available for determining the sampling plan parameters, n and c, that will meet the performance requirements specified by the user. The performance requirements include the following four items of information: AQL, a conventional notation standing for "acceptable quality level" or "good quality"; LTPD, standing for "lot tolerance percent defective" or "poor quality level"; α, the producer's risk; and β, the consumer's risk. Assigning numeric values to these four parameters is largely a matter of managerial judgment. As soon as their numeric values have been assigned, values for n and c can be determined.

EXAMPLE

A large medical clinic purchases shipments of pregnancy test kits (PTKs). A shipment contains 10,000 PTKs. It is important that the chemical composition of the PTK shipment be evaluated so that prescribing physicians are assured of valid tests.

Physicians have agreed that a shipment has acceptable quality if no more than 2 percent of the PTKs in the shipment have an incorrect chemical composition. They consider shipments having 5 percent or more defective PTKs to be an extremely bad quality shipment. We want a sampling plan that affords a .95 probability of accepting good shipments but only a .10 probability of accepting extremely bad shipments. These performance specifications for the sampling plan are summarized on the left side of Table 17.3. A sampling plan was derived to meet these performance requirements. The plan calls for 308 PTKs to be sampled from each shipment (right side of Table 17.3). If more than ten of these PTKs are defective, the entire shipment is rejected. If ten or fewer PTKs are defective, the shipment is accepted. In this way a shipment having 2 percent defective PTKs has only 5 chances out of 100 of being rejected, whereas a shipment having 5 percent defective has only ten chances out of 100 of being accepted. This sampling plan includes procedures for determining the probability of accepting the shipment if its percent defective is between 2 and 5. These probabilities are shown in Figure 17.10.

TABLE 17.3 Sampling plan and specifications for PTKs

Performance Specifications	Parameters of Sampling Plan
Good quality (AQL) = .02 or fewer defectives	
Desired probability of accepting a good quality shipment = .95	n = 308
Risk: probability of α errors = .05	c = 10
Bad quality (LTPD) = .05 or more defectives	
Desired probability of accepting a bad quality shipment = .10	
Risk: probability of β errors = .10	

Operating characteristic (OC) *curve* Given a sampling plan, the graph of the probability of accepting a shipment as a function of the quality of the shipment.

The curves in Figure 17.10, called the *operating characteristic curves* or OC curves, reveal how sampling plans discriminate among shipments. If a shipment is of high quality (low percent defective), a good sampling plan yields a high probability of accepting the shipment. If a shipment is of poor quality (high percent defective), the plan yields a low probability of accepting the shipment.

You can see from the black OC curve in Figure 17.10 that the desired probabilities of accepting good and bad quality PTK shipments have been obtained. The second OC curve represents a different sampling plan, $n = 154$ and $c = 5$, that does not meet desired performance specifications: It offers only a .88 probability of accepting a good quality shipment, and a .22 probability of accepting a bad shipment.

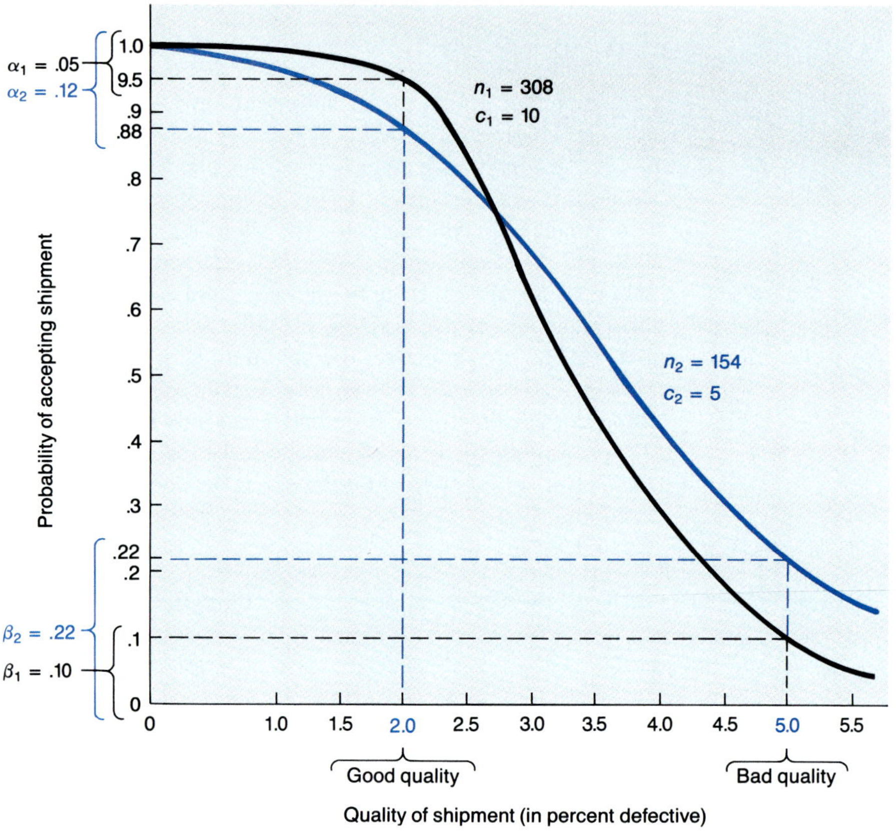

FIGURE 17.10 **Probabilities of accepting a PTK shipment; OC curves**

***General Effects of* n *and* c** A sampling plan specifying a unique pair of n and c has a unique OC curve. Sampling plans calling for a large sample size are more discriminating than plans calling for a small sample size. Figure 17.10 shows OC curves for two sampling plans with different sample sizes and acceptance numbers. Comparing plans, the ratio of the acceptance number c and the sample size n is constant. For plans with larger n's the probability of accepting good quality lots is higher than for plans with smaller n's; similarly, for plans with larger n's the probability of accepting bad quality lots is lower than for plans with smaller n's. Of course, these benefits are not obtained without incurring the higher inspection costs associated with large sample sizes.

The effect of increasing the acceptance number c (for a given value of n) is to increase the probability of accepting the shipment for all levels of percent defective other than zero (Figure 17.11). By increasing c, more defective units are allowed to pass inspection. By decreasing c, inspection is tightened.

In general, higher values of c allow "looser" performance, increasing the probability of accepting a shipment with a given percent of defective units. Increasing n results in greater confidence that we have correctly discriminated between good and bad shipments. However, inspection costs are also increased with larger values of n. The task of quality management is to find the proper balance between the costs and benefits of alternative sampling plans.

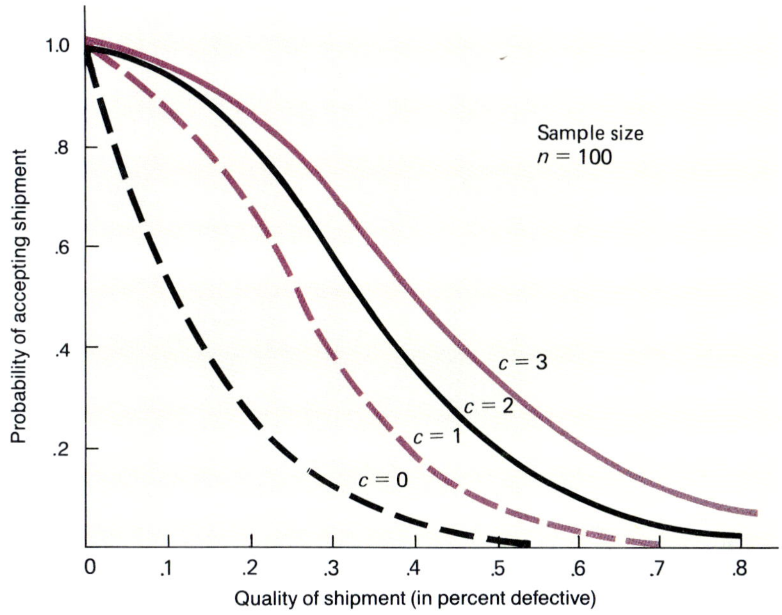

FIGURE 17.11 Effect of variations in c on OC curve

Establishing Policies on Good and Bad Quality Choosing what percent defectives constitute good and bad quality is a vital management decision. The sampling plan is designed around this decision. If managers are too stringent in defining good quality, the costs of obtaining (purchasing) such high quality shipments can become exorbitant. At the other extreme, accepting a high percent defectives can result in conversion disruptions, high scrap and rework costs, and higher costs of customer ill will. If it is possible to negotiate good and bad quality levels when purchasing shipments from suppliers, you can arrange for the supplier's finished goods inspection to use the same sampling plan that your receiving inspection uses. Such an arrangement simplifies matters considerably. Operations Management Highlight 17.2 describes how Tandy uses sampling inspection to improve quality for their customers.

Constructing OC Curves The sampling plans discussed here are based on the Poisson approximation to the binomial probability distribution. We assume a random sample of size n taken from a Poisson population that has an average percent p

OPERATIONS MANAGEMENT HIGHLIGHT 17.2

Source: Jeff Smith/The Image Bank

Quality Control at Tandy Means Reliability for Customers

When Wells Fargo Bank upgraded their integrated office support system in 1988, they chose Tandy computers. Why? Because Tandy has a very good price-performance ratio and are devoted to good customer service. Installing and servicing a network of personal computers at 286 Wells Fargo work

of defective units. Then we use tables or graphs to calculate the probability of c or fewer defective sample units, or the probability of more than c defective sample units. This general approach is adopted here to show how data is obtained for any OC curve.

The chart shown in Figure 17.12 is a convenient substitute for extensive stations would test the reliability of its computers, and Tandy was ready to meet the challenge. The reliability of the PCs, located at 24 Wells Fargo branches, has improved productivity and increased the accuracy of documentation for loans—all of which stems directly from Tandy's concern for quality control during production.

Since streamlining their quality control program during the mid-1980s, Tandy is shipping its customers more and more good computers and fewer defective ones. The number of "dead-on-arrival computers"—computers that fail when they first reach the customer—has dropped from 10 percent to less than 0.9 percent. The average time a Tandy computer will operate before it fails has increased to 33,000 hours for the Tandy 1000 computer and 58,000 hours for the Tandy 3000.

Numerous quality control tests have been the key to improved manufacturing. Incoming materials and manufactured parts must pass functional tests to ensure that the mechanical components as well as electromechanical systems function properly. Tandy computers must also withstand destructive testing that goes well beyond the typical physical demands of normal use. For environmental testing, Tandy computers are exposed to extreme temperatures, ranging from −40°F to +165°F, replicating the range of climates encountered during shipment. For operating testing, the electrical power supply is varied, with volts ranging from 105 to 135, because such variations are encountered in the diverse locals of Tandy customers. Vibration and shock testing, too, are essential to ensure the final packed computer withstands the rigors of cross-country shipment, including bumpy roads and accidentally dropped freight.

Once a shipment leaves the factory, it is appraised by an independent Tandy quality department. Representing the customer, this department evaluates each shipment with acceptance sampling. This screening step is completed before any shipment is allowed to go into any of the 7,000 Radio Shack stores, or before any materials from vendors are allowed into production. All of these steps, together, enable Tandy to better serve their industrial customers, such as Wells Fargo Bank, and their retail customers, too.

Sources: Keith Denton, "Reducing DOAs (and other Q.C. Problems)," _P&IM Review_ (December 1989), 35–36; Julie Pitta, "Wells Fargo Exec Locks in PCs, Seeks Bulletproof Reliability," _Computerworld_ (July 11, 1988), 35, 40.

probability computations. Each diagonal curve represents an acceptance number c for the sampling plan. Then, for any proposed percent defective p and any sample size n, the resulting pn is used to find the probability of acceptance (for c or fewer defects) from the left side of the chart. Data points for an OC curve are obtained by using different p values (quality levels) while holding n and c constant.

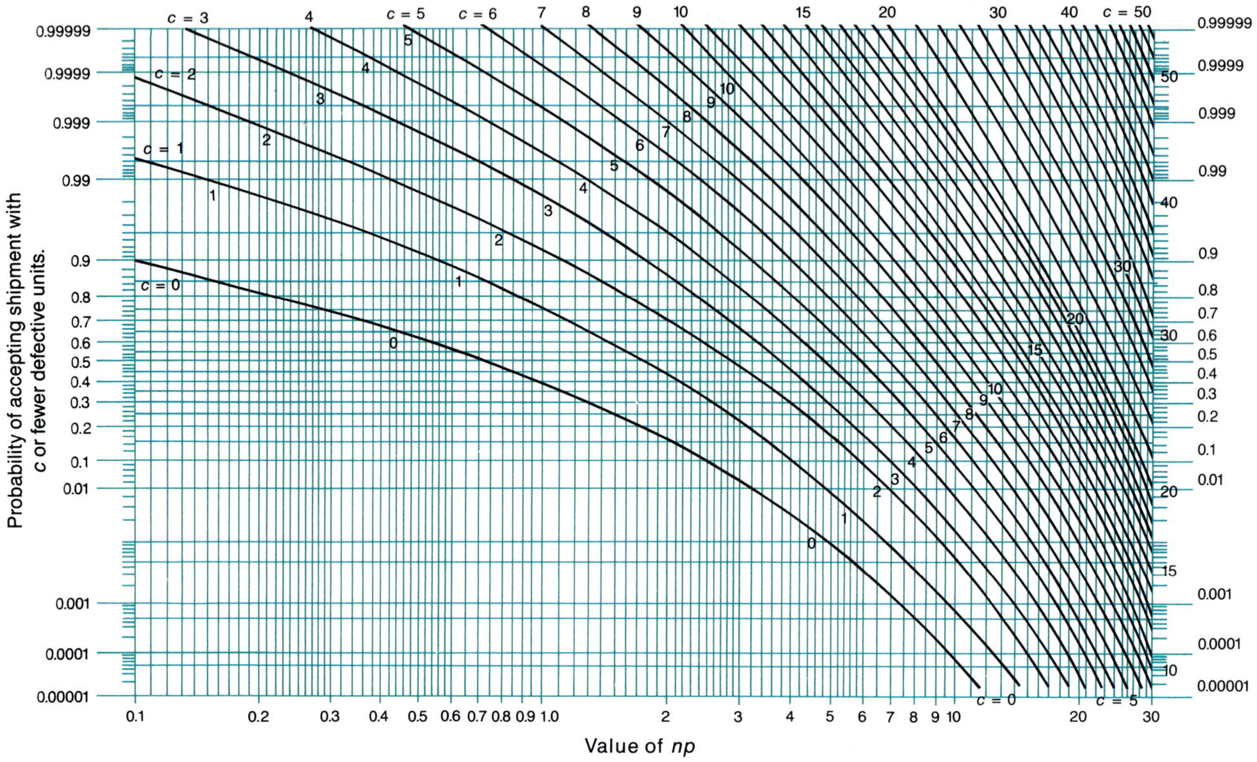

FIGURE 17.12 **Probability curves for Poisson distribution**
Source: H. F. Dodge and H. G. Romig, *Sampling Inspection Tables* (New York: John Wiley, 1959).

E X A M P L E

We want to construct the OC curve for a single sampling plan that has an acceptance number $c = 2$ and a sample size $n = 30$. For each of 12 assumed values of fraction defective p, the probability p of acceptance is estimated using Figure 17.12, yielding the following data for the OC curve:

p	n	pn	P	p	n	pn	P
.01	30	0.30	.995	.11	30	3.30	.370
.02	30	0.60	.973	.13	30	3.90	.270
.03	30	0.90	.930	.15	30	4.50	.180
.05	30	1.50	.800	.17	30	5.10	.130
.07	30	2.10	.650	.19	30	5.70	.090
.09	30	2.70	.520	.21	30	6.30	.050

The resulting OC curve is shown in Figure 17.13.

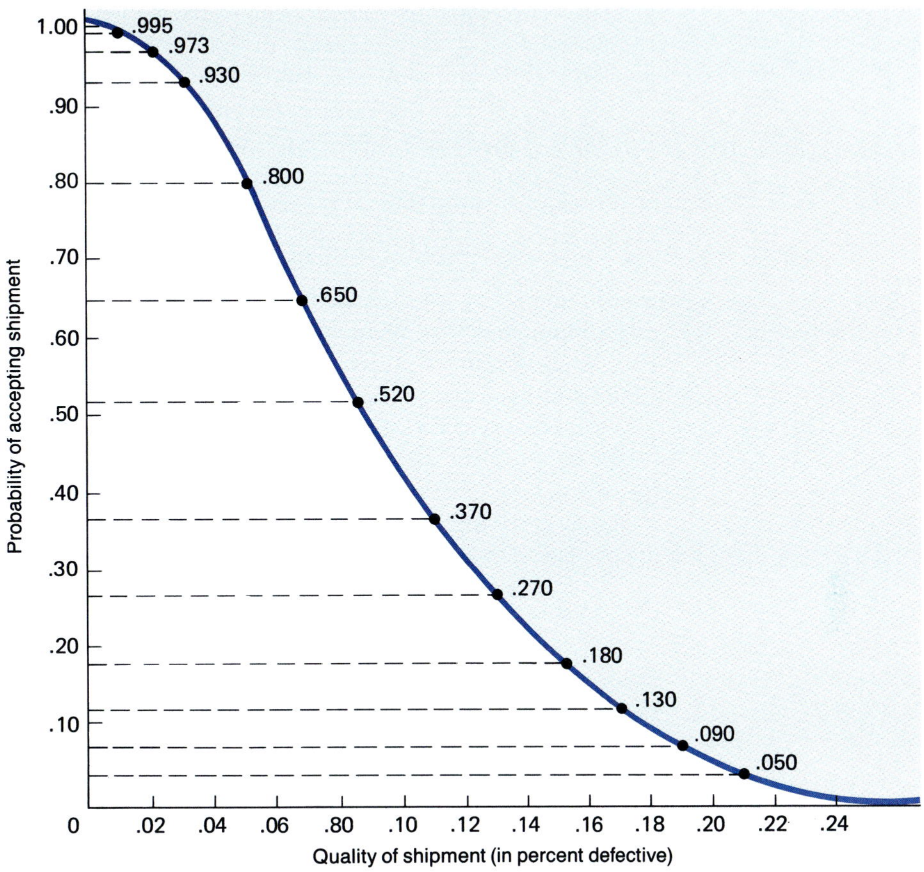

FIGURE 17.13 **OC curve for $n = 30$, $c = 2$**

You may experiment, then, using various combinations of n and c to obtain an OC curve (and the associated sampling plan) that gives the desired levels of assurance for accepting good quality shipments and rejecting bad quality shipments. More formalized approaches to constructing sampling plans are discussed in books on quality control referenced at the end of this chapter.

SUMMARY

The need for quality analysis and control arises from the fact that output quality varies in every operating system, and this variation increases the costs of operations. Through process capability studies, we can better understand and control variation, and thus increase output quality. The capability study measures process performance under chronic conditions, in the absence of sporadic variations. It provides an estimate of the process's ability to produce output that meets specifications.

Statistical process control (SPC) seeks to detect and eliminate nonrandom (sporadic) variations as they arise while the process is operating. The process is monitored periodically by examining sample units of output. The critical characteristics of the samples are recorded on control charts to determine if they have shifted away from a random pattern. If so, action is initiated to eliminate the causes of the sporadic behavior in the system. Variables control charts, such as $\overline{X}$ and R charts, are used to control the variability of characteristics, such as length or weight, that can be measured on a continuum. Attributes control charts, such as the p chart for fraction defective, are used when a unit of output can be classified good or bad, according to whether it exhibits or does not exhibit a certain characteristic.

Inspection is the set of procedures for observing quality characteristics and for gathering the data for quality analysis and control. Both input and output can be inspected, either visually or mechanically. Inspection is most commonly encountered in materials receiving, work-in-process inspection during conversion, and finished goods after conversion is completed.

Acceptance sampling is a statistical plan for deciding to accept or reject a shipment (or lot) of a product. Rather than inspecting the entire shipment, a random sample of several units is the basis for the decision on the entire lot. The choice of how many to inspect and the limits for nonconformances depends on the tolerance for sampling errors and the desired quality levels. Operating characteristics (OC) curves show the risks of each sampling plan, along with its ability to discriminate accurately between good and bad quality lots.

CASE

Hydrolock, Inc.

In 1978 George Thrall founded Hydrolock, Inc., a manufacturing company producing small rubber gaskets used in hydraulic systems. His gaskets were simple in design and relatively easy to produce in large quantities. In 1990, gross sales from servicing customers throughout North America with large quantity shipments reached $8 million. A very autocratic management style exists throughout the company.

Demand for Hydrolock products has increased so rapidly that the manufacturing facility is constantly under pressure to increase output around the clock. Customers and sales personnel in the field often call the home facility to determine estimated lead times for prospective orders and estimated delivery times for existing orders. In response, production supervisors continually emphasize to employees the need for increasing output to meet demand.

In late 1990, George Thrall encountered a new problem: an increase in customer complaints about the quality of shipments being received. Plant supervision insisted the problem was twofold and that nothing could be done about either: (1) workers were asked to produce at maximum efficiency, so quality suffered; and (2) workers had absolutely no motivation for high quality performance. George decided to add a quality control analyst to the Hydrolock staff in hopes of finding and correcting the sources of customer dissatisfaction.

In his first two weeks the quality analyst uncovered some data that a production supervisor had recorded two years previously.

Data for Gasket YB4 (1988)

Sample Number*	Number of Units Defective
1	6
2	1
3	0
4	2
5	1
6	4
7	3
8	2
9	6
10	0
11	3
12	2

*40 units inspected in each sample

The analyst began gathering data on current production of the same gasket. Samples were taken once each day for five consecutive work days with these results.

Data for Gasket YB4 (1990)

Sample Number*	Number of Units Defective
1	4
2	8
3	6
4	2
5	8

*40 units inspected in each sample

If you were the new analyst, what would be your ideas for getting to the bottom of George Thrall's quality problem? Of what value are the data at hand? Does management have a style and outlook toward employees that enhances quality performance? What would you recommend?

REVIEW AND DISCUSSION QUESTIONS

1. Discuss the steps in a process capability study.
2. What are the "natural limits" of a process? How do they relate to product specification limits?

3. Select a convenient operation and identify its sources of variation. Describe how each source can result in variability of output quality.
4. Identify different types of inspection and discuss their roles in the quality assurance and control process.
5. What is the relationship between inspection and acceptance sampling?
6. How does variable measurement differ from attribute measurement?
7. What is an acceptance sampling plan? How does it work? What factors must be considered in designing it? What costs are incurred in using it?
8. What is an OC curve?
9. How do control charts differ from acceptance sampling plans? Under what circumstances is each appropriate?
10. Give examples of control chart patterns that would lead you to conclude that control action may be warranted.

PROBLEMS

SOLVED PROBLEMS

1. An attribute control chart exists for part 223B shows the average fraction defective .125, upper control limit .200, and lower control limit .050, based on two months of daily data. Recently, 12 units were sampled each day for six days with units defective 2, 1, 2, 0, 3, and 3.
   (a) Construct a control chart for management, carefully labeling the chart, and interpret it for management.
   (b) What is the significance of the fraction defective for day 4 being below the lower control limit?

SOLUTION FOR PART (a)

The solution for part (a) is shown in Figure 17.14. Fractions defective for the recent six days are:

$$\frac{2}{12} = .166,\ \frac{1}{12} = .083,\ \frac{2}{12} = .166,\ \frac{0}{12} = 0,\ \frac{3}{12} = .250,\ \frac{3}{12} = .250$$

The process is out of control on days 4, 5, and 6.

SOLUTION FOR PART (b)

The control limits should be set in such a way that measurements falling outside the limits are regarded as a warning signal. The lower control limit for fraction defective is useful because some change in methods, equipment, or people has resulted in improved quality. The cause should be found.

2. An electronics manufacturer always uses a sample size of ten. Data for the past ten samples are as follows:

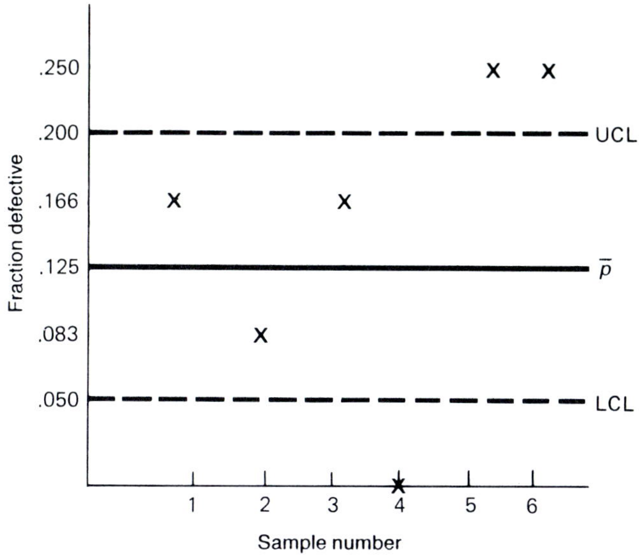

FIGURE 17.14 **Attributes control chart for part 223B**

Number of Units Defective	Total Units Sampled
150	1,000

The system is believed to be operating under normal conditions.

(a) Construct a control chart with control limits such that measurements for 95 percent of the units under normal conditions would fall within the control limits.

(b) Suppose we find the number of units defective in the next five samples are 3, 4, 2, 0, and 7. What can you tell about the process now? Why?

SOLUTION FOR PART (a)

$$\bar{p} = \frac{150}{1000} = .15$$

$$S_p = \sqrt{\frac{\bar{p}(1 - \bar{p})}{n}} = \sqrt{\frac{(.15)(.85)}{10}} = 0.113$$

For 95 percent confidence interval, Z = 1.96.

$$UCL = \bar{p} + ZS_p = .15 + (1.96)(.113) = .371$$
$$LCL = \bar{p} - ZS_p = .15 - (1.96)(.113) = -.071$$

SOLUTION FOR PART (b)

Sample Number	Fraction Defective
1	$\frac{3}{10} = .3$
2	$\frac{4}{10} = .4$
3	$\frac{2}{10} = .2$
4	$\frac{0}{10} = 0$
5	$\frac{7}{10} = .7$

The fraction defective for two of five samples fell above the UCL, hence the process is out of control. We are 95 percent sure for any one point that is out of control. (See Figure 17.15.)

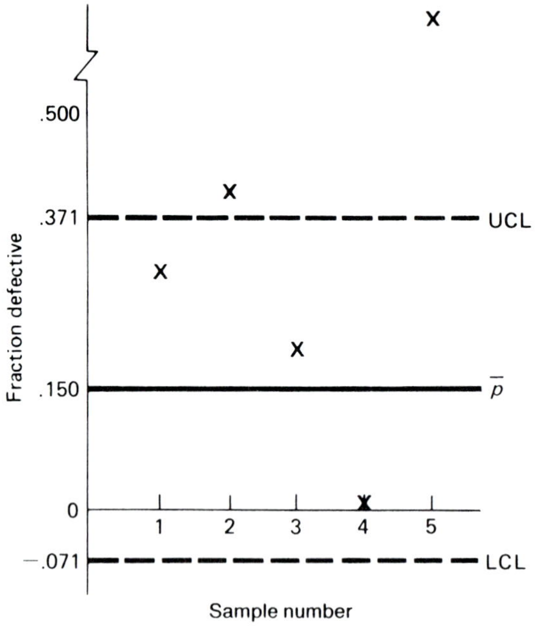

FIGURE 17.15 Electronics attribute control chart

REINFORCING FUNDAMENTALS

3. During production, Instrumentation, Inc., has been examining a lens for scratches. If there are, in the inspector's opinion, too many scratches, the lens is "bad" and rejected. Otherwise the lens is good. Using the data below, construct a control chart for last month's inspected lenses. Sample size for each sample was 60.

Sample Number	Units Rejected
1	10
2	12
3	6
4	8
5	9

4. An attribute control chart for a manufactured part shows the average fraction defective .250, upper control limit .450, and lower control limit .050, based on two months of daily data. Recently, ten units were sampled each day with units defectives 2, 4, 2, 0, 3, and 3.

(a) Construct a control chart for management, carefully labeling the chart, and interpret it for management.

(b) A production supervisor doesn't like the sixth day's results and wants you to resample. What is your response? Why?

5. A relatively new test for pregnancy, a Gravindex Test, has been used by a lab for the past ten weeks. This test indicates pregnancy by determining whether hormones are present in the urine. If hormones are present, the test is positive; in the absence of hormones, the test is negative. We want to establish some means of checking *future* test results to see if the test appears to be staying in control. Each time the test is run, a known positive and known negative test are also run. Data below are for the "known positive" control test, that is, 95 samples were good and 5 samples were bad. Our results to date, using a sample size of ten tests each week, are as follows:

Negative	Positive	Total Tests
5	95	100

(a) Construct a control chart for this test.

(b) Suppose we collect the following data over the *next* four weeks for our "known positive" Gravindex test.

Week	Negative Results	Positive Results
1	0	10
2	1	9
3	2	8
4	3	7

Is the process (test) in control during these four weeks? If not, what do you do?

6. An optics lens manufacturer always uses a sample size of ten. Data for the past 100 samples is as follows:

Number of Units Defective	Total Units Sampled
185	1,000

The system is believed to be operating under normal conditions.

(a) Construct a control chart with control limits such that measurements for 95 percent of the units under normal conditions would fall within the control limits.

(b) Suppose we find the number of units defective in the next five samples are 3, 4, 2, 0, and 7. What can you tell about the process now? Why?

7. Thompson Metal Works manufacturers metal screws. The following shows the diameters for part 2735, a standard metal screw, the last time the part was produced two months ago.

Date	Screw Diameters (in units cm)			
August 5	0.5	0.6	0.4	0.3
6	0.5	0.5	0.4	0.6
7	0.7	0.5	0.5	0.6
8	0.5	0.5	0.5	0.5

(a) Construct a three-sigma control chart for the last production run.

(b) A sample was taken today, the first day of production in two months, on this part. Metal screw diameters were 0.5, 0.8, 0.6, 0.9. Based on the control chart developed above, what can you tell the general supervisor about this process?

8. Your reputation as an analyst has gained widespread acclaim in the Allstate University athletic department. The basketball coach asks you to help him with the following problem. Coach Stewart believes that the lack of success of the team in conference play has been because of the defense against player Smith. He gives you the following data on the average of Smith's first 11 shots of each game. Games 4-8 were played against conference teams; games 9-13 against nonconference teams.

Game	Sample Average of Distance from Basket (in feet)	Game	Sample Average of Distance from Basket (in feet)
4	6.0	9	6.0
5	8.0	10	8.0
6	5.0	11	5.0
7	4.0	12	9.0
8	7.0	13	10.0

You are asked to apply what you have learned in quality control, viewing Smith's performance as a process. Inform Coach Stewart whether Smith's conference performance is in control based upon his performance during nonconference games.

9. Four samples ($n = 3$) to measure shaft diameter were taken three weeks ago when the process was running smoothly. Results are shown below. Since then the business experienced a labor strike, and some business school students are running the production line. Results of two samples taken today are shown below. What can we tell the plant manager about the process today compared with the previous data? What should he now do? Support your decision with analysis.

Results Three Weeks Ago			
Sample Number	Diameter (in inches)		
1	2.10	2.08	19.6
2	1.97	1.98	2.05
3	1.95	1.91	1.98
4	2.07	2.08	2.03

Results Today			
Sample Number	Diameter (in inches)		
1	2.35	1.86	1.91
2	1.86	1.87	1.77

10. As area coordinator of technical services in a large hospital, you notice the laboratory seems to have problems with a Serum Calcium Test, which is used to indicate a tendency for kidney stones. You are not sure about this test and would

like to track its performance. Recent test results for five tests each day are shown below.

Test Date	Milligrams/100 cc of Serum				
May 1	9	8	6	8	10
3	8	8	5	7	5
4	7	3	6	12	7
5	10	8	9	8	10
7	9	9	7	9	8

Doctors say the expected range is 8.5 to 10.5 milligrams/100 cc of serum for healthy adults. Construct a control chart reflecting historical performance. How might you explain this control chart to laboratory technicians so they can benefit from it in the future (i.e., explain the *interpretative value* of this tool to them)?

11. Construct OC curves for the following sampling plans:
   (a) $n = 100, c = 1$
   (b) $n = 200, c = 2$
   (c) $n = 300, c = 3$

12. Construct OC curves for the following sampling plans:
   (a) $n = 100, c = 1$
   (b) $n = 100, c = 2$
   (c) $n = 100, c = 3$

CHALLENGING EXERCISES

13. In conjunction with a class assignment, two industrious operations management students decided to study the pattern of library users returning books to the campus library. The students collected their data by sitting on the library steps several days and watching books being returned. They observed the following:

Wednesday: 32 people entered the library, 5 of whom were returning books
Thursday: 55 people entered the library, 15 of whom were returning books
Friday: 27 people entered the library, 6 of whom were returning books

These students need your help in constructing a control chart of this "process." After hearing about this, you go over on two successive Mondays and observe:

Monday: 10 people entered the library, 3 of whom were returning books
Monday: 10 people entered the library, 5 of whom were returning books

What inferences can you make from your observations based on the data of your fellow students? What criticism, if any, would you make about the sampling procedures?

14. A manufacturing facility comprises three work stations for which there are currently no inspection stations. You have estimated the cost of adding inspection stations and gathered some additional information summarized below.

Work Station	Daily Output (in units)	Average Daily Percent Defective	Estimated Daily Inspection Cost (in dollars)	Estimated Cost of Each Undetected Unit Defective (in dollars)
A	1,000	5	20	6
B	1,000	10	30	4
C	1,000	3	25	2

(a) As quality manager your limited budget will allow you to add only one inspection station in your conversion process. Which location would you select from the three possible locations?

(b) What would be your choice if the daily output at A, B, and C were 1,000, 1,500, and 2,000 units, respectively?

(c) Develop a heuristic for selecting the location of the inspection station; consider all variables in the problem.

15. Peanuts, Inc., has asked you to check the automatic temperature control of its main baking oven; manufacturing personnel claim the control is broken. Having a business school background (and not an electrical engineering background), you have decided to approach the problem from a statistical quality control standpoint. You have gathered the following data.

Date	Sample Average of Three Temperature Readings	Date	Sample Average of Three Temperature Readings
June 1	120°F	July 26	125°F
2	122°F	27	127°F
3	116°F	28	128°F
4	118°F	29	131°F
5	124°F	30	131°F

The manufacturer's guarantee on equipment is for any setting between 100°F and 150°F with a variance of ± 7°F from the setting. Product (peanut) specifications are 120°F ± 5°F. Specifically, you have been asked to determine, as of July 31, whether Peanuts, Inc., has a baking oven problem. If so, what do you recommend?

UTILIZING THE QSOM COMPUTER SOFTWARE

16. Use the attributes sampling module to find sampling plans for the following specifications: AQL = .02; LTPD = .06; type I error = .05; type II error = .10; shipment size is N = 2,000 units.

(a) Determine the n and c for a single sampling plan.

(b) Determine n_1, n_2/c_1, c_2 for a double sampling plan.

(c) Draw the OC curves for the plans in parts (a) and (b).

(d) Plot the average outgoing quality (AOQ) curve for the single sampling plan. What does it tell you? Compare it with the AOQ curves of three alternative single sampling plans of your own choosing.

KEY TERMS

Acceptance number 652
Acceptance sampling 651
Attribute characteristic 634
Central limit theorem 635
Consumer's risk (type II error) (β) 639
Control chart 634
Control limits (CL) 635
Critical ratio 650
Double sampling 652
Fraction defective 643
In-control process 634
Inspection 649
Multiple sampling 652
Natural limits 632
Operating characteristic (OC) curve 653
p chart 643
Percent defective 650
Producer's risk (type I error) (α) 639
R chart 641
Receiving inspection 650
Sample 629
Sample unit 629
Sample range 640
Sampling 629
Sampling plan 652
Single sampling 652
Specification limits 632
Statistical process control (SPC) 634
Variable characteristic 634
Work-in-process inspection 650
$\overline{X}$-chart 635

SELECTED READINGS

Aubrey, Charles A., II, and Lawrence A. Eldridge, "Banking on High Quality," *Quality Progress* (December 1981), 14–19.

Deming, W. Edwards, "On Some Statistical Aids Toward Economic Production," *Interfaces* 5, no. 5 (August 1975), 1–15.

Dodge, H. F., and H. G. Romig, *Sampling Inspection Tables.* New York: John Wiley, 1959.

Duncan, A. J., *Quality Control and Industrial Statistics,* 3rd ed. Homewood, Ill.: Richard D. Irwin, 1965.

Grant, E. L., and R. S. Leavenworth, *Statistical Quality Control,* 6th ed. New York: McGraw-Hill, 1988.

Hostage, G. M., "Quality Control in a Service Business," *Harvard Business Review* 53, no. 4 (July-August 1975), 98–106.

Juran, J., *Quality Planning and Analysis.* New York: McGraw-Hill, 1980.

Pfaffenberger, R. C., and J. H. Patterson, *Statistical Methods,* 3rd ed. Homewood, Ill.: Richard D. Irwin, 1987.

Saniga, Erwin M., and Larry E. Shirland, "Quality Control in Practice . . . A Survey," *Quality Progress* 10, no. 5 (May 1977), 30–33.

PART VII

DYNAMICS OF OPERATIONS MANAGEMENT

General model for production/operations management

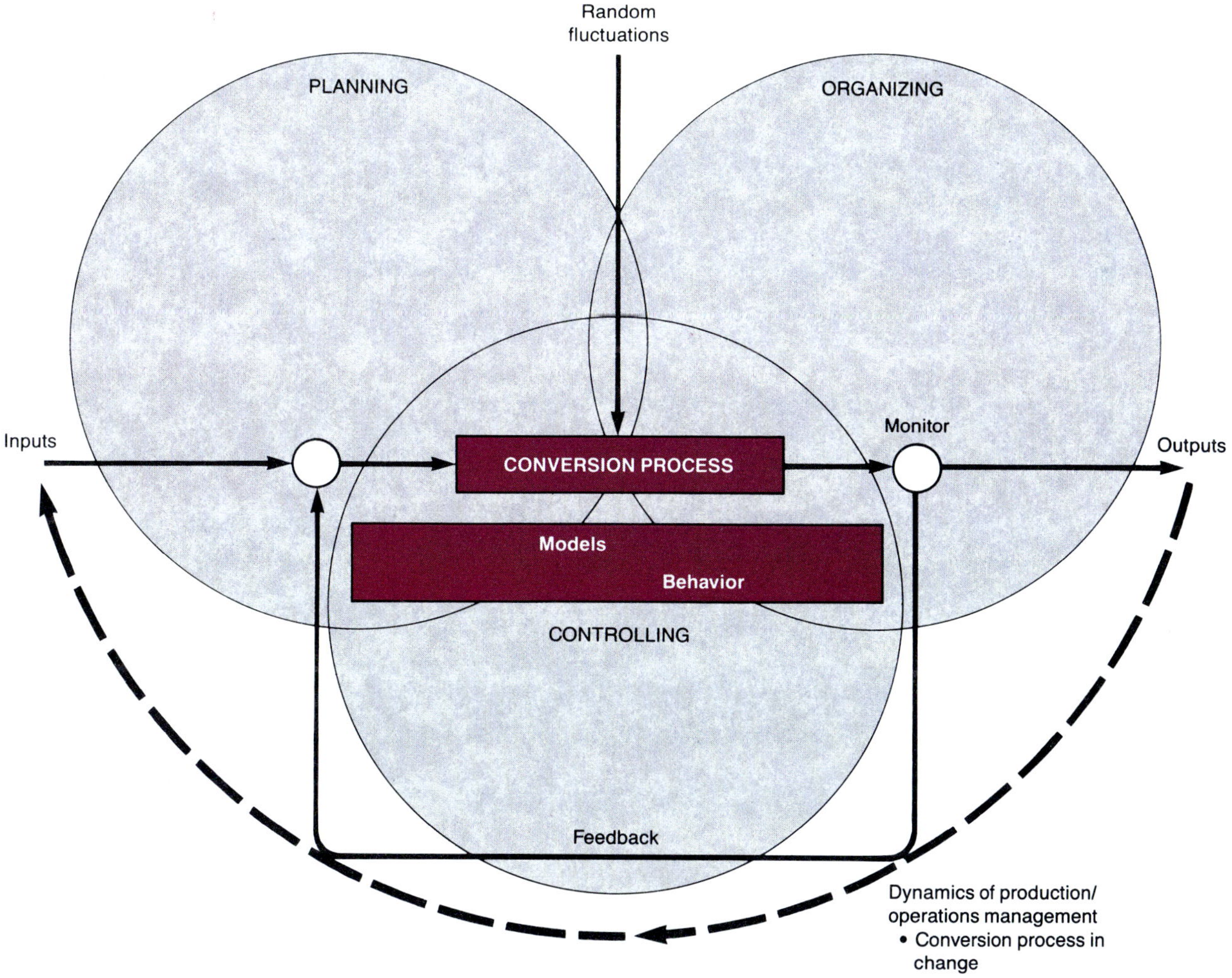

CHAPTER 18

THE CONVERSION PROCESS IN CHANGE

The United States is engaged in a difficult struggle to retain its industrial leadership in the global marketplace. This is a matter of great concern for the American people, and meeting the challenge is important to the future of the country. Our standard of living, economic survival, and national defense are at stake. If industrial leadership declines, it will not be long before the rest of this society declines with it.

The United States has been slow to appreciate that foreign competitors exist for 70 percent of our industrial products. Lack of competitiveness has resulted in a flood of imports and loss of U.S. jobs. The top ten imports from Japan are industrial products such as radios, cars, and videotape machines. It is estimated that for every $1 billion in imports, 25,000 American manufacturing jobs are lost. Over 30 million manufacturing jobs have been lost since 1970, 3 million in ***Fortune*** 500 companies in one five-year period in the 1980s. Fortunately a new American spirit is emerging to face this challenge. The rush for the automated factory is creating a revolution in how the United States deals with manufacturing. This will have significant impact on the business organization as a whole.

Since the economic recovery began, the private sector has increased spending for plant and equipment at the rate of 25 percent since late 1982. Sustaining this trend long enough to significantly modernize the industrial base will be the challenge for the future.

Many exciting changes are occurring in the field of manufacturing. While some critics lament the demise of U.S. manufacturing, total industrial production is actually over 30 percent higher today than it was in 1970. It is a myth that the manufacturing base of the United States is shrinking. However, rapid modernization will be necessary to retain a competitive advantage in the global marketplace.

Richard A. Stimson
Director, Industrial Productivity
Office of the Under Secretary of Defense
Washington, D.C.

Mr. Stimson's comments reflect a sense of concern and urgency over the future of U.S. industry. How will U.S. industry respond to the global competitive challenge? Is it so tightly anchored to past conventional practices that it cannot reorient its operations resources soon enough? In this, our final chapter, we look at change and the future of production and operations management. Whether we agree with Edmund Burke that "You can never plan the future by the past" or with Patrick Henry that 'I know of no way of judging the future but by the past," we must at least admit that the past, after all, is all we have. As a basis for prediction, it may be limited, but it is a beginning. Together we'll explore how change comes about in production/operations management, in the hope it will help shape your future role as a production/operations manager or help you understand operations as it changes, even though you might not be actively involved in the discipline.

DYNAMICS OF PRODUCTION AND OPERATIONS MANAGEMENT

Changes in the conversion process do not occur one at a time. Rather, multiple changes of various magnitudes occur simultaneously. Further, these changes are not independent of one another; changes in one part result in changes in other parts. Some of these "ripple" effects are predictable; others are not. In short, organizational change can rapidly become a "can of worms" if not approached cautiously. The complexities of change present a management dilemma. Management desires a predictable or stable conversion process that allows the goal of economic efficiency to be met; nevertheless, we must recognize the need for changes so that the organization remains viable. As a production/operations manager, you must strike a proper balance between stability and adaptability in your organization. If you understand the dynamics of organizational change, you may be able to balance stability and adaptability in a more enlightened way. For these reasons we suggest a somewhat systematic approach to studying the dynamics of the conversion process. The framework we suggest is shown in Figure 18.1, in which the broad dimensions of change flow from left to right. Recognition of the need for change, targets for change, the change process, and the desired results of change are distinct phases usually identifiable in any situation of change.

RECOGNITION OF NEED FOR CHANGE

Before we can plan and initiate change, we have to recognize that a change is needed, and we have to know why it is needed. Indicators that change is needed can come from sources that are internal or external to the organization. Random fluctuations—unplanned and/or uncontrollable environmental influences that tend to cause actual output to differ from planned output in the conversion process—are necessary in our model because they happen so often in reality. We may have to make changes to meet existing organizational goals; or it may be necessary to change the goals themselves.

Internal Indicators The conversion process operates to meet predetermined goals and performance standards consistent with these goals. Most commonly, management establishes goals for profitability, product quality, customer service, and commitments

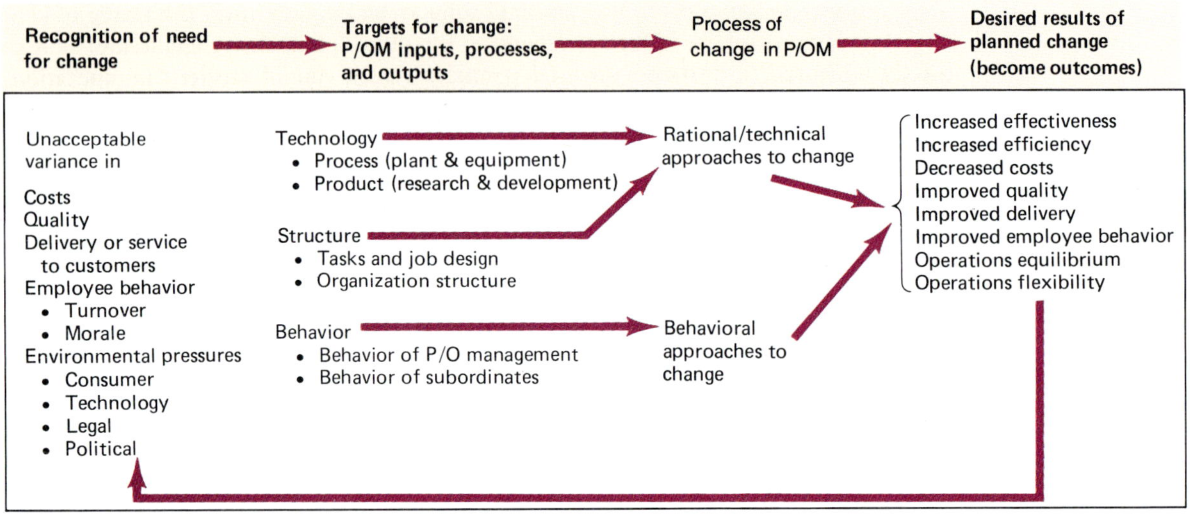

FIGURE 18.1 **Dynamics of production/operations management: the conversion process in change**

to employees. It is not surprising, then, that parameters closely related to these goals are the primary internal indicators of the need for change. Some of the most commonly used indicators are:

- Costs
- Product quality
- Delivery or service to customers
- Employee behaviors

Some of these indicators are readily quantifiable; others are not. Reports of direct and indirect labor expenses (costs), scrap rates (quality), and employee absences and quitting rates (employee behaviors), for example, are usually reported periodically in standard report forms. These can easily be compared against performance standards, and deviations can be noted and investigated. Some indicators are much more subtle, however. Not all costs are recognized; some aspects of product quality or customer service are not conveniently measurable; and employee dissatisfaction may surface in nonquantifiable forms. When the indicators are subtle, the need for change may not be recognized until the underlying problem magnifies itself. By this time, remedial changes may be very costly to implement, much more so than if the need had been recognized earlier. Sometimes change is initiated even though the need for it is not formally recognized.

EXAMPLE

Operations employs a major, if not majority, portion of the employees in a typical business or governmental unit. In North America, employee absenteeism is a significant, largely unresolved business problem and therefore a major operations management problem. Other cultures, such as the Japanese, are less permissive than North American companies, demanding a commitment to the firm that results in docking pay and quick dismissal for absenteeism. British and European firms tend to approach North American permissiveness regarding absenteeism, and productivity suffers.

Studies estimate that absenteeism equates to a cost of 1.75 times the average daily pay, $150/employee/percent absent/year (1972 dollars), or $66/day/person-day (1977 dollars) of absenteeism. One study traces the impact of absenteeism on added overtime costs, carrying extra employees and inventory quantity, schedule upheavals, and other operating charges.[1] In a representative, but hypothetical, example for a company with $6.5 million in annual sales, 100 employees, a $7/hour wage rate, and a 5 percent absenteeism rate, absenteeism costs totaled $154,385 for the year. These costs totaled 12.5 percent of total direct labor costs, $1,543/direct employee, $140.35 cost/day/employee, 2.5 times the average daily pay, and 0.64 percent of total production costs.

The point of these absenteeism statistics is that an internal indicator, like 5 percent absenteeism, can have far-reaching operations cost consequences that are not normally quantified in day-to-day reporting. *A need for change can exist, in this case a behavioral change, and it can gradually increase in significance if management does not take action.* The astute operations manager must pick up on such indicators and express them in terms that upper management can understand, and therefore gain support for the needed change.

External Indicators In general, the conversion process is designed to enable efficient operation shielded from external impingements. The system can never be totally closed, however; as the external environment changes, it imposes changes on internal operations. An obvious example is the change in consumer tastes and desires in a competitive market. If video recorders and players are the rage, organizations with the technological and financial capability will begin producing video units and tapes, or renting the units and taped entertainment, if they want to establish or improve their market position.

In some instances, external indicators arise in a more direct way. This is particularly true in service industries performing services to suit the needs of particular customers. Here a close degree of customer-supplier cooperation results in new product designs. Changes in products or processes are often made on a regular basis.

Besides consumer tastes and technological innovations, there are other significant environmental sources of change. Broad changes in societal values are often reflected in new laws and governmental regulations that require compliance. Today's concern over environmental pollution has a direct impact on the internal operations of most organizations. Moreover, scarce energy resources force changes that have been of little concern to operations managers in the past. Legal and political pressures for changes also are evident to the perceptive production/operations manager.

---

[1]Ken Kivenko, "Employee Absenteeism—The Deterioration of Productivity," *Production and Inventory Management Review* 4, no. 5 (May 1984), 52–55, 70.

TARGETS FOR CHANGE

Once the need for change has been recognized, the manager can identify one or more aspects of the conversion process that must be modified, including the technology, the organization structure, or employee behavior in the conversion process. Several other targets for change are described in Operations Management Highlight 18.1, featuring the Mercedes-Benz Company.

OPERATIONS MANAGEMENT HIGHLIGHT 18.1

Source: Peter Grumann/The Image Bank

Mercedes Changes onto the Fast Track for Luxury-Car Supremacy

A great reputation for engineering and style are not enough to keep an automobile company afloat in today's competitive environment. Even Mercedes-Benz, one of the greatest names in manufacturing history, is adapting to the inevitable winds of change brought about by more demanding consumers and

Technology The technology of a conversion process consists of the physical or mental components of the process through which conversion from inputs to outputs is accomplished. The technology for manufacturing refrigerators is dominated by cutting, forming, and assembling sheet metal, manufacturing electronic and mechanical components, assembling (including the compressors and refrigeration components), painting, and packing. The technology of an automatic carwash includes soap and water sprays, roller brushes, chain drives, and blower-dryers.

In dental clinics, the mental components of the technology are more directly

better products from Japan. Toyota started shipping Lexis models, a new entry in the luxury car market, to Europe in 1991. Honda is expected to launch a new NS-X luxury sports car ($50,000 plus) that will test the loyality of Mercedes customers. Ford's acquisition of Jaguar PLC and General Motors' joint venture with Saab-Scania, too, are expected to cut into Mercedes' luxury-car leadership in Europe.

To position themselves for stiffer competition, Mercedes has adopted a strategy to revive consumer interest in diesel models that suffered setbacks from environmental criticisms during recent years. They also are emphasizing high-tech driving devices, for so-called "smart" cars, that warn operators about road hazards and traffic jams and provide vision enhancements. Also on the drawing boards are entirely new concepts, such as a car roof with solar batteries that keep the air conditioning running even when the car is not being used. As a result of the new emphasis on continual innovation, Mercedes executives project that new major design changes will have to be launched by model designers and engineering each year. Consequently, this engineer-dominated company will put their technical competence to a more stringent challenge than ever before.

Along with more frequent design changes, Mercedes' manufacturing processes, too, must be modified more often, and on a larger scale, than ever before. Manufacturing, from start to finish and from top to bottom, faces big changes in work procedures and production technologies, and an emerging emphasis on manufacturing flexibility. Along with the structural and technical changes, cultural growth and development of their human resources is being reassessed also. Management training is focusing on broadening managers' perspectives and giving them experiences useful for working in a newer manufacturing environment, all the while retaining the legendary Mercedes quality.

Sources: John Templeman, "Daimler's Drive to Become a High-Tech Speedster," *Business Week* (February 12, 1990), 55, 58; Roy Barun, "Corporate Strategy: A Step Into the Next Century," *Asian Finance* (May 15, 1989), 26–27; Clare Hogg and Michel Syrett, "Getting the Right Management for 1992," *Director* (March 1989), 101–105.

visible. Knowledge and skills of dentists and technicians are directly witnessed by the customer (patient). The physical components of the dentist's technology range from materials used in treating the patient (drilling equipment, teeth-cleaning preparations, etc.) to elaborate laboratory equipment never seen by the patient.

Changes targeted primarily to the technology often involve redesigning plant and equipment to process existing products as new processes or materials are developed. The development of plastics, for example, meant displacing many refrigerator components formerly made of metals, and, subsequently, replacing metal rolling and forming with plastics extrusion processes. The decision to switch from one processing technology to another can be analyzed in part from an engineering/economic viewpoint. The discussion of product and process design in Chapter 4 was directed at acquainting you with contemporary approaches, including CAD, CAM, robotics, and flexible manufacturing.

Often, the basic product itself must be modified to meet changing consumer needs or to comply with external requirements. Changing models annually or introducing new products annually, common among many industries, are examples. In fact, one way to compete in some industries is to be effective in quick development, manufacture, and delivery of new products (operations flexibility). The product line, consequently, is very volatile. In the manufacturing equipment industry, it is not unusual for customer-supplier cooperation to produce new designs, features of which will be incorporated in future editions of the supplier's "regular" products. In these cases the effectiveness of the operating system is measured in terms of flexibility, the ability to work with product and customer engineers to develop and manufacture unique products that, in some cases, are later produced in volume. Often, then, new products and processes are necessary from a strategic viewpoint.

Structure Sometimes the organization structure—tasks and jobs within the organization—become the targets for change. When costs, quality, or employee satisfaction indicate that changes are warranted, individual jobs may be redesigned. Job analysis and work methods studies may reveal that some job elements should be eliminated, others simplified, and still others expanded. Task redesign may also be appropriate when new products and processes are developed. Unless the new product is very similar to the old one, old tasks cannot simply be reapplied to new products.

At a broader level, the entire organizational structure may need changing. If goals are not met, new departments and divisions may be formed and old ones dissolved. Perhaps the quality control function may be reassigned from the manager of manufacturing to the vice president of operations to obtain higher level control. Job-shop scheduling and dispatching may be centralized to improve overall shop throughput; or a new customer relations department may be created to improve customer service.

New products and technological changes also may necessitate structural adjustments. Many manufacturing organizations have created environmental engineering groups to redesign conversion processes and facilities so that environmental contamination is reduced. The computer expertise developed by many organizations has led to computer service departments that serve not only the operations function but the other functional areas of the organization as well.

As companies grow and product markets expand, structures are changed accordingly. Organizations may diversify along product lines to gain greater efficiencies; others may decentralize as a means of developing future managerial skills and experience.

Behavior From the operations manager's viewpoint, behavior is a third target for change. Very often, attaining goals is possible by modifying employee behavior rather than by changing the technology or the structure of the conversion process. Product quality and efficiency may be enhanced through on-the-job training of operative employees. These training efforts are designed to modify behavior in favorable directions. Similarly, managerial effectiveness can be improved by development and training programs in such areas as decision making, leadership, and employee/supervisor relationships.

When behavior is the primary target for change, the manager may use several change strategies. How successful the effort to change is depends upon human learning capabilities and the reinforcement/reward procedure used. These procedures and the methods by which behavioral change is introduced affect how readily change is accepted or resisted in the organization.

THE PROCESS OF CHANGE IN PRODUCTION/OPERATIONS

Obviously, the three targets for change are not independent of one another. Of the three, the need for behavioral change is the most widespread. It is difficult to conceive of technological and structural changes that do not result in the need for behavioral change. Consider the computerized checkout systems in many large hardware stores and supermarkets. The technological change from the old system to the new one brought about the need for modified skills and behaviors of employees, particularly as they relate to inventory procedures. Previously, inventory counts of shelf items were periodically updated by hand. In the computer-based system, each transaction is recorded by stock number at the cash register, where inventory levels are updated, and reordering may be automatic. Store managers and other employees now focus their skills and efforts on tasks other than counting stock items. Certainly some retraining and reorientation of work behavior are required when such a change is made. Because the behavioral process involved in change has special overall importance, we discuss it here in some detail.

RATIONAL/TECHNICAL CHANGE PROCESSES

The Role of Rationality Managerial intuition, judgment, and experience play major roles in decisions for change. Whether these decisions are based on hunch or thoughtful analysis, the full effects of significant change are usually unpredictable to some extent. But managers need not be discouraged by the absence of complete predictability; they can take careful, systematic steps to increase predictability and help themselves cope with change.

One procedure that lends rationality to the change process is the scientific approach to decision problems. There are six steps in this approach:

1. Recognizing and defining the problem
2. Stating the objectives
3. Formulating alternative solutions
4. Collecting data
5. Evaluating alternative solutions
6. Making a decision or choice

Rationality is emphasized in the scientific approach to change. As managers learn to formulate alternative solutions, collect data, and evaluate alternatives, they become better able to make rational decisions.

By a rational approach, we mean the process of carefully identifying change alternatives, analyzing their effects from a financial, economic, or other logical point of view, comparing the alternatives on this basis, and identifying the best of the alternatives. Typically, this kind of approach involves quantitative analysis. Thereafter, additional nonquantifiable factors can be introduced and considered before the final choice is made. This rational approach to decision making has been stressed throughout this book.

When technology is the target, changes in products, processes, equipment, or facilities are considered. Ordinarily, formal or rational analysis in these instances is financial or engineering in nature. When organizational structure or policy is the target, some attempt is made to measure change in financial terms, but to a lesser extent; the impact of these changes cannot always be captured in financial terms. Nevertheless, the rational approach is still applicable. We are generally forced to employ nonfinancial measures of system performance, however; changes in crime rate, service to customers, reduction in procurement lead times, and similar patterns often reflect system performance.

THE BEHAVIORAL CHANGE PROCESS

As shown in Figure 18.1, the behavioral change process includes:

1. Recognition of the need for change
2. Identification of the behavioral targets for change by production/operations managers and/or their subordinates
3. Decision to change in a certain way
4. Strategy for change; the behavioral approach toward change
5. Implementation of the behavioral change; the actual changing of behaviors of participants in the production process

We have already discussed how to recognize the need for change. Let's examine points 2–5 of the behavioral change process, concentrating not only on the process itself but on dealing with resistance to it and management's role in changing behavior for the good of the organization. But before we do, let's look at one alternative change model.

Thaw-move-refreeze model A widely accepted model of the change process that accounts for the need to *thaw* the environment, that is, get it ready for change, and to *refreeze* the environment, that is, make the change take hold.

Thaw-Move-Refreeze An alternative change model that is perhaps the most widely accepted model of the change process in management involves thawing (or unfreezing) current activities, moving (or changing) to the desired activities and resulting outcomes, and then refreezing activities so the changes are permanent.[2] This model is not inconsistent with the planned change model of Figure 18.1 and the behavioral change process above. Key differences are the need to soften or *thaw* (a way to get the change process ready to take), and the idea of *refreezing*. Shortly, we'll discuss reinforcement

[2]For a more complete discussion of this change model, see Charles N. Greene, Everett E. Adam, Jr., and Ronald J. Ebert, "Organization Change and Development," *Management for Effective Performance* (Englewood Cliffs, N.J.: Prentice-Hall, 1985), chap. 14.

processes directed at this refreezing. The idea that changes must be institutionalized so that they become the usual way of behaving and operating is an excellent concept for operations managers to grasp.

BEHAVIORAL TARGETS FOR CHANGE

Consistently, experienced P/O managers find that it is the reblending of behaviors—the behaviors of labor (the operative worker) and management (operations managers at all levels)—that is the most difficult and challenging of all change problems. Behavioral change involves people, and people have emotions. Furthermore, for managers to change their subordinates, they must often change themselves first. Therefore, as a P/O manager, you must think of behavioral change in terms not only of your subordinates but of yourself as well.

STRATEGIES FOR BEHAVIORAL CHANGE

Three distinct strategies have been suggested for changing behavior.[3] As we discuss them, remember that they may help managers change the behaviors of both supervisors and operative workers.

Empirical-rational change strategy A strategy for change that assumes people change their behavior when they believe it is in their own self-interest to do so.

Empirical-rational Strategies Empirical-rational change strategies assume that people are rational, that they will act in their own self-interest. If managers want to advance change, they should show employees that the change is not only desirable for the organization but for the employees too. When employees understand that change will benefit them, they will change their behavior.

Normative-reeducative change strategy A strategy for change that assumes people change their behavior only after changing their attitudes and values.

Normative-reeducative Strategies Normative-reeducative strategies build upon the empirical-rational strategies. Besides assuming that workers are rational, these strategies presume that people act as a result of attitudes and values they have acquired over time. Thus changing behavior involves not only presenting people with facts in their own self-interest but changing their attitudes, skills, and relationships as well.

Power-coercive change strategy A strategy for change that makes use of political, economic, or other forms of influence to force behavioral changes in other people.

Power-coercive Strategy This strategy is based on the application of political, economic, or some other form of power. Power can be legitimate (the proper use of delegated authority), or it can be informal (without formal organization sanction). Often, power is simply the effective use of leadership and position in the organization. In other cases, power may be brought to bear on individuals from peer groups, informal leaders, economic realities, or fear (fear of job loss, for example). Whatever its form, the result is the same; power can be a very effective way to bring about changes in individual and group behavior.

[3]Robert Chin and Kenneth D. Benne, "General Strategies for Effecting Changes in Human Systems," in *The Planning of Change,* 3rd ed., Warren G. Bennis, Kenneth D. Benne, Robert Chin, and Kenneth E. Corey, eds. (New York: Holt, Rinehart, and Winston, 1976), 22–45. Alternative strategies are identified by Greene, Adam, and Ebert, *Management for Effective Performance,* chap. 14, Fig. 14.6, that relate the change strategy to change interventions.

THE LEARNING PROCESS

Employee behaviors evolve in the learning process with the adoption of new skills, attitudes, and experiences. Given a new task, employees will learn. The question is whether they will adopt behaviors that are beneficial to the organization or behaviors that are disruptive.

Reinforcer The environmental consequence of behavior.

Reinforcement In the learning process, the critical determinants of adopted behaviors are the *environmental consequences of those behaviors.* These consequences are called *reinforcers.*

Positive reinforcers are pleasant, rewarding, and satisfying; they serve to increase the probability that the behavior (response sequence) will occur again. Negative reinforcers are usually unpleasant, undesirable, and even painful. Generally, behaviors with positive consequences tend to be repeated when the situation reoccurs; behaviors with negative consequences tend to be abandoned.

Reinforcement schedule A more or less formal specification of the timing of a reinforcer for a response sequence.

Reinforcement Schedules Not only the reinforcement itself but also its timing are important. One study notes:

> The effectiveness of a given reinforcer will depend upon its magnitude, its quality, the degree to which it has been associated with other reinforcers, and the manner in which it is scheduled. As a matter of fact, the effectiveness will depend as much upon its *scheduling* as upon any of its other features.
> A schedule of reinforcement is a more-or-less formal specification of the occurrence of a reinforcer in relation to the behavioral sequence to be conditioned. It is fairly easy, even for individuals with a minimum of training, to follow specified schedules of reinforcement in order to generate predictable behavioral patterns.[4]

Schedules of reinforcement may be either continuous or intermittent. A continuous schedule reinforces every response sequence (chosen for conditioning). More often, the schedule is intermittent, reinforcing the response sequence only occasionally. With a continuous schedule, learning takes place more quickly, but so does extinction, that is, forgetting the response and reinforcement relationship, once the reinforcer is withdrawn.

Since our interest is changing behavior, we can draw several conclusions from what we've discussed so far. First, new behavior patterns are learned fastest with continuous, or nearly continuous, reinforcement schedules. Second, behavior patterns that have been learned through intermittent reinforcement schedules are the most difficult to change. Third, negative reinforcers, when properly applied, can be effective. When punishment—the infliction of pain or discomfort—is applied, however, the consequences can be disastrous. Let's look a little closer at punishment and its consequences in operations.

Punishment There is research to suggest that punishment, under differing circumstances, may increase the frequency and duration of undesirable behavior. Furthermore, the deterring affect of punishment may be short-lived. Punishment may also cause

[4]Everett E. Adam, Jr., and W. E. Scott, "The Application of Behavioral Conditioning Procedures to the Problems of Quality Control," *Academy of Management Journal* 14, no. 2 (June 1971), 175–93.

people to vary their behavior but be unable to control the direction of the new behavior, and arouse negative feelings. On the other hand, mild punishment may help improve behavior by at least providing negative feedback on performance. Since the effects of punishment are unpredictable and often adverse, it may be better to use positive reinforcement instead.

EXAMPLE

Two supervisors in the same production facility used different reinforcement systems, each beyond normal organizational rewards. The first supervisor seemed always upset and irritated at his subordinates, verbally admonishing them for any small reason, often hours or days after the behavior occurred. His employees tended to ignore his behavior and react neither negatively nor positively over time. The second supervisor intermittently gave praise and/or candy to his workers. He was very careful to always praise or offer a piece of candy after outstanding behavior. He was one of the most highly thought of, successful supervisors in the facility, and his department was very productive.

Now, of course we aren't recommending that every supervisor lay in a supply of candy. The success of the second supervisor's reinforcers resulted not from the magnitude of the reward but from its *systematic administration.* He almost always reinforced acceptable behavior, and often in the presence of others. The real reward was recognition. This is not to say that punishment never brings about beneficial change; but dysfunctional consequences are also a distinct possibility.

RESISTANCE TO CHANGE

We suggest that you change behavior through positive reinforcers and placing behavior under positive control. The potential for conflict among positive reinforcers suggests that it is important for management to communicate *current* response-reinforcement contingencies clearly.

There are all sorts of reasons why people are reluctant to change. Positive reinforcers for current behavior patterns encourage us to continue acting as we are. Perhaps we're afraid of failing at something new. People like the stability afforded by established patterns of relationships in their personal and professional lives. The security we feel from orderly and familiar ways of doing things can be threatened by change, and so can our status, authority, autonomy, and discretion. Change sometimes makes old skills obsolete and requires us to develop new skills. In general, there are four basic reasons for resisting change:

1. *Economic factors*—a threat to economic security, such as losing a job
2. *Inconvenience*—a threat of making life more difficult, such as having to learn new ways of doing things that were formerly done routinely
3. *Uncertainty*—a threat of not knowing the implications of change
4. *Interpersonal relationships*—a threat of disrupting or destroying customary social relationships, group standards, or socially valued skills

If training for change disrupts the current work flow, resistance to change is intensified. Work will be initially disrupted, and higher operating costs can be expected temporarily. The initiator of change must be prepared to accept these added costs. Employee resistance is high at these initial stages; often employees do not clearly perceive the need for change in the first place. All they know is that they are now further behind in their work.

Resistance behaviors may take a variety of forms, including aggression, withdrawal, or regression. These manifest themselves in higher absenteeism, requests for transfer, sabotage, or a series of emotional outbursts.

OVERCOMING RESISTANCE TO CHANGE

As you look over the following suggestions for overcoming resistance to change, remember that each is only a partial solution to the problem. Unfortunately, there is simply no single way to break down all the resistance barriers. You should also keep in mind that resistance to change may appear throughout the organization, from the highest to the lowest levels. Because people occupying high levels within the organization have benefited from the existing system, they may resist changes even more intensely than people at lower levels. Let's examine some factors that are related to resistance to change.

1. *Peer group influences.* Peer groups often encourage group members to meet the job standards that they participate in establishing. Groups significantly influence member behavior, and the effective operations manager attempts to influence the group directly or indirectly through the informal group leaders.
2. *Group discussion.* Participation is most effective if the needs for change are clearly communicated in a form the group members understand. Employees want to get involved in the change, and a group meeting is held to encourage discussion and consideration of ideas and suggestions.
3. *Suggestions from employees.* Some employee suggestions should be implemented and the implementation brought to the attention of participants. A superficial "sense of participation" that merely covers an autocratic manager's actions will soon be understood by employees to be no participation; behaviors will adjust accordingly. Toyota, you may recall (Chapter 15), uses employee suggestions effectively to bring about quality improvements.
4. *Manager's job security.* P/O managers can provide a sense of job security for subordinate supervisors. If supervisors feel that their jobs are secure, they will not perceive employee participation as a threat to their own positions.
5. *Terminology.* Using certain words, such as *change,* for example, can arouse aggressive behaviors unnecessarily from employees whose behavior you want to modify. Also, using words that imply manipulation of an individual is likely to arouse anxieties and create resistance to change. Once the employee becomes defensive, communication is nearly impossible.

PRODUCTION/OPERATIONS CHANGES

Organization development (OD) Managing organizational change by applying knowledge from psychology, sociology, and other behavioral sciences.

Organization Development Organization development (OD) is a broad term used in management to describe managing organizational change by applying knowledge from the behavioral sciences, for example, psychology, sociology, and cultural anthro-

Change agent The facilitator of change; the role of the production/operations manager in bringing about behavioral changes in other people.

pology. A consultant, often a full-time employee, acts as a *change agent* to facilitate the change process. OD involves the entire change process, but here we focus on interventions specifically applied to production and operations processes. Let's see how the operations manager can actively participate in this change process.

The P/O Manager as Change Agent In behavioral change procedures, it is generally agreed, there are *facilitators* and *learners* of change. In our discussions of the learning process and overcoming resistance to change, we have stressed the production/operations manager's role in initiating change. Essentially, P/O managers are the *facilitators* of change; they are the change agents. Production/operations managers continually face the situation of getting changes made through others; operative workers continually face the situation of learning these changes.

Role of Top Management If top management does not support change programs at lower levels, change simply will not occur. Management's support must be strong and consistent. Several studies indicate that unless top management supports new managerial techniques and approaches, even people exposed to training will continue their old behavior. This is the case because top management continues to reinforce old behavior. In fact, under these conditions, training programs can even make matters worse. At one organization, managers were trained to use a human relations approach to dealing with people. At the end of the program, the managers accepted the idea and decided to use it. After a few months, however, those same managers were found to have become even more autocratic than they had been in the first place. Why? Because top management, uninvolved in the program, continued to reinforce autocratic behavior, and subordinate managers, who had learned through the program to emulate top management's style, had actually learned to be more autocratic than they had been before the program.

Actual Changes Processes change, and plants and physical facilities wear out—in short, manufacturing and operations facilities go through a life cycle just as products do.[5] Changes necessitated by deterioration or by the desire for improvement have been successfully carried out in organizations and documented through company records, reports at professional meetings, and professional publications. Many of you have had work experience in complex organizations. In light of our discussion in this chapter, can you think of a successful or an unsuccessful change that you've observed? What was the need for the change? Who effected the change? Was there resistance to the change? What strategy led to the success or failure of the change? Consider these questions as we examine an example of a production scheduling problem, and how focusing on the change process led to implementation of a computer scheduling model.[6]

---

[5]Roger W. Schmenner, "Every Factory Has a Life Cycle," *Harvard Business Review* 61, no. 2 (March-April 1983), 121–29.

[6]Excerpted from Thomas E. Vollman, "A User-Oriented Approach to Production Scheduling." Paper presented at 3rd Annual American Institute for Decision Sciences Conference, St. Louis, Mo., 1971. The Baumritter Corporation is the source of several excellent change examples beyond those described here. See Thomas E. Vollman, William L. Berry, and D. Clay Whybark, *Manufacturing Planning and Control Systems* (Homewood, Ill.: Richard D. Irwin, 1984).

EXAMPLE

A PRODUCTION SCHEDULING CHANGE AT BAUMRITTER The Baumritter Corporation is a furniture manufacturer selling primarily under the Ethan Allen brand name. In 1970 sales were approximately $65 million, with manufacturing in 18 factories. The University of Rhode Island had a five-year research affiliation with Baumritter, focusing primarily on major system design and implementation. Baumritter had been deeply involved in a system to control materials throughout the organization.

AGGREGATE CAPACITY PLANNING One facet of the research led to the conclusion that a critical need for aggregate capacity planning existed, and that Baumritter personnel did not fully comprehend the problem. It was felt that this situation represented a fertile opportunity for the design of an implementation-oriented model. The intent was to plant a seed in the Baumritter system that could be nurtured on a cooperative basis, the research team's relative role decreasing over time. The model was built and demonstrated to the vice president of manufacturing, assistant vice president of manufacturing, plant managers, assistant plant managers, other manufacturing executives, and systems analysts working on the materials flow system.

The reaction of these people was highly positive; their recognition of the seriousness of this problem was improved, and the research team expected that cooperative implementation would take place shortly. However, no amount of prodding on their part caused this to happen.

There is a moral to be learned from this story: The top-down approach of selecting the most critical problem first is conceptually elegant, but the bottom-up approach of finding a problem of present concern will usually produce implementable results. The place to be studied was a large factory in Orleans, Vermont.

PRODUCTION SCHEDULING The process of scheduling assembly lines at Orleans was somewhat chaotic. All the parts for a complete item were simultaneously started at the cutoff saws, with the expectation that the item would be ready for assembly eight weeks later. As time elapsed, however, the standard eight-week lead time from cutoff saw to the start of final assembly was often missed. Although the stated goal was to assemble an entire manufacturing lot size upon completion, this goal was rarely met. "Hot list" requirements, poorly constituted finished goods inventories, marketing demands, and pool car shipments all led to sizable variation in the quantities being assembled.

Three of the key manufacturing executives at Orleans attempted to design an assembly schedule on the basis of lot sizes smaller than the cutting lot sizes. They attempted to determine what items to make week by week for the next seven or eight weeks on each major assembly line. The effort involved one or two days, or about five labor days per week. The procedure was to arrange pieces of paper on a long table; each piece of paper represented a particular assembly lot of an item. Demand forecasts, standard assembly times, part availabilities, pool car requirements, and dollar output objectives were used.

The actual output from the assembly lines was at considerable variance with what the schedule had predicted. As one week's output was off, corrective actions were taken in subsequent weeks; this made the validity of estimates for future time periods ever more dubious.

At this time the research team proposed that the production scheduling process be attacked with a time-shared computer model. The reaction to this suggestion was overwhelmingly negative. Comments included: "The computer is no substitute for manufacturing judgment"; "Go back to your Ivory Tower"; "You are wasting your time, and I will not permit anyone in my organization to waste his time by cooperating with you." No Orleans employee was forbidden to work with the research team, but neither was anyone encouraged to do so.

IMPLEMENTATION The strategy for designing a model that would be implemented in this environment forced consideration of the relative strengths of insiders, or users, who understood the goals, criteria, constraints, and data inputs; and outside experts or designers who had model building skills.

The approach to the problem was to send a research assistant to the factory to stay until someone could be convinced. The entree had to be through an individual who could be convinced that the programs could help *him* solve problems with which *he* was personally involved. Finding this kind of individual and getting him to cooperate was essential.

The individual at Orleans was one of the three people involved in the major assembly scheduling process. His job in the organization was industrial engineer—time study person—assistant to the assistant plant manager. He had had two years of college and no exposure to computers. He didn't see how he could participate in the development of a computer model, nor did he understand why it was necessary for him to be involved. Convincing him of the necessity for his involvement was a key step in the implementation process.

When this insider became convinced that the effort was worth trying, he was frequently harassed by his fellow workers. Some were subtle: "I always knew you were a college professor at heart." But others were more direct. Essentially, he was told he could devote no company time to the project. He participated largely on his own time.

As the model was being developed, people around the plant showed considerable interest. Most of the interest was negative, and when the first run produced results that were clearly wrong, many individuals had a good time saying "I told you so." The participating insider, however, expected the first run to be invalid. He also expected the reason for the invalidity to be apparent, and was proved correct. His fellow workers only saw the invalid model, not the glaring inconsistencies that could be remedied. The model's requirement for explicitness quickly pointed out major inconsistencies in data inputs, criteria, and the process of scheduling itself. Within a month these inconsistencies were largely removed, and the model was generating valid assembly schedules 18 weeks into the future.

Once the model became operational at Orleans and actual results began to match the schedule, people who had been openly hostile became believers virtually overnight. There was no arguing with success, and the amount of managerial talent freed up to work on other activities was significant. News of the success quickly spread through other Baumritter factories, and the research team was besieged with requests for the scheduling model.

The approach to these requests was to promote the participating insider to the status of expert major assembly scheduling model builder with the job of transplanting the model to other locations. The research team helped him with the first two or three transplantations, with its role gradually diminishing. Thereafter, he was able to implement the system in several factories by himself. Interestingly enough, the problems experienced at Orleans were largely universal, and the model did fit in most other applications. In some of these other applications, new problems were uncovered; at least one of these problems was found also at Orleans. The model went through several stages of generalization, but most of this work was accomplished by Baumritter employees.

BENEFITS The benefits from the production scheduling model are somewhat difficult to tie down explicitly. Companies that implement a good system of production planning and inventory control often achieve a 10 to 20 percent increase in productivity due to better utilization of equipment, reduced expediting, and so forth, and productivity has indeed increased in Baumritter plants since the scheduling system was put in. In addition, major assembly scheduling became so predictable in all factories that order acknowledgement was changed and is now based upon the production schedule. An anticipated problem with filling railway cars did not matter, since improved scheduling allowed for much better planning of railway car needs. Purchasing activities were similarly made easier with a clearer understanding of needs. However, the most fundamental benefit coming from the major assembly scheduling model was the clearly perceived need for rationalizing the rest of the production planning and inventory control/materials flow system.

Perhaps most interestingly of all, about a year after major assembly scheduling was working, the vice president of manufacturing became convinced that his most significant problem was aggregate capacity planning; the systems approach had now evolved the problem definition to what the research team had recognized two years earlier.

ASSESSING THE OVERALL EFFECTS OF CHANGE

We have discussed some key issues in changing behaviors, technologies, and structures of organizations. Currently, the change process is more an art than a science. Although managers attempt to be systematic and rational in planning for change, complete rationality is not possible, and no one can accurately predict all the effects of change. At best, we can be aware of some general concepts and procedures to help smooth out the transitions that occur in organizations. In advance of the change, we can make rough estimates of its potential effects by asking some "what if" questions about system behavior and economic consequences. Management used to rely on intuition and experience to assess and prepare for the impacts of change. Now there is a better way. Recently, computer simulations have begun to be used to explore the implications of proposed changes in a more explicit manner. Let's briefly examine this approach.

SYSTEM DYNAMICS

Examining overall system behavior is important for two reasons. First, many individuals make changes in various parts of the organization. The *combined* effects of these changes determine overall system performance. Second, any decision or policy should be judged on how it affects the system over time rather than on its effects at one point in time. While static modeling emphasizes one point in time, dynamic modeling focuses on changes over time. Although we are ultimately interested in the steady-state performance after a change, we are interested in the transient system behavior as well. Since implementing changes takes time, their significant effects are usually not realized immediately. Similarly, the reactions of interrelated system subcomponents may not be visible immediately.

Systems dynamics A computer-based simulation methodology for developing and analyzing models of systems and their behavior.

Systems dynamics is a term for a computer-based simulation methodology that attempts to meet these two needs. Pioneered by Professor Jay W. Forrester at M.I.T., systems dynamics is a quantitative methodology for developing and analyzing models of systems and their behavior.[7]

[7]Jay W. Forrester, *Industrial Dynamics* (Cambridge, Mass.: M.I.T. Press, 1961).

Mathematical relationships are developed to represent physical, financial, and other flows within production/operations. The boundary spanning activities, or interactions, with other functions within the firm are also modeled. These relationships are programmed for a computer and run on the computer again and again, perhaps for 200 or 300 time periods (e.g., months). Operating data are collected and summarized. After review, management says, "What if we changed capacity, technology, inventory investment, and so forth?" The systems models run again with one or more changes, say for another 200 or 300 periods. Conditions are compared, reflecting the dynamic nature of the situation and allowing system comparisons. This systems dynamics approach is useful but can be quite expensive to implement.

OVERVIEW OF PRODUCTION AND OPERATIONS MANAGEMENT

The purpose of this section is to bring our introductory treatment of production/operations management to an end. Can a book of several hundred pages be summarized in a few pages? Can we put in a nutshell the operations manager's activities? Can we accurately select those major trends currently affecting operations management? Can we accurately predict the future roles of production/operations managers? The answer to each of these questions is clearly no. Yet, we believe we should end on an integrative note. Therefore let's take a few pages to briefly address each of these questions.

PRODUCTION/OPERATIONS MANAGEMENT ACTIVITIES

The general model for managing operations that was logically developed in Chapter 1 is shown again in Figure 18.2. By describing operations according to the *management* subfunctions of planning, organizing, and control, we allow an integrative perspective. Our focus has been on conversion, operations management being the management of conversion in which input resources are transformed into useful outputs. Models and behaviors were explained throughout the text in relationship to planning, organizing, and controlling in the various chapters of this book. This general model is dynamic, as you've noticed from the earlier content of this chapter.

Our intent in this book was to introduce you to the situations that a production/operations manager must face—strategic planning, capacity, scheduling, inventory control, and so forth—focusing on the concepts, models, and behaviors that are most useful for achieving goals within operations.

TRENDS IN PRODUCTION AND OPERATIONS MANAGEMENT

Although it is difficult to step back and clearly see trends in the production/operations management discipline, a few do seem to emerge. Without the detail already presented, let's highlight a few of the obvious trends.

Operations Strategy Strategic planning in operations involves fitting the operations mission into the corporate strategy, a strategy that should blend the environment and corporate resources into a corporate position statement. Within operations the strategy

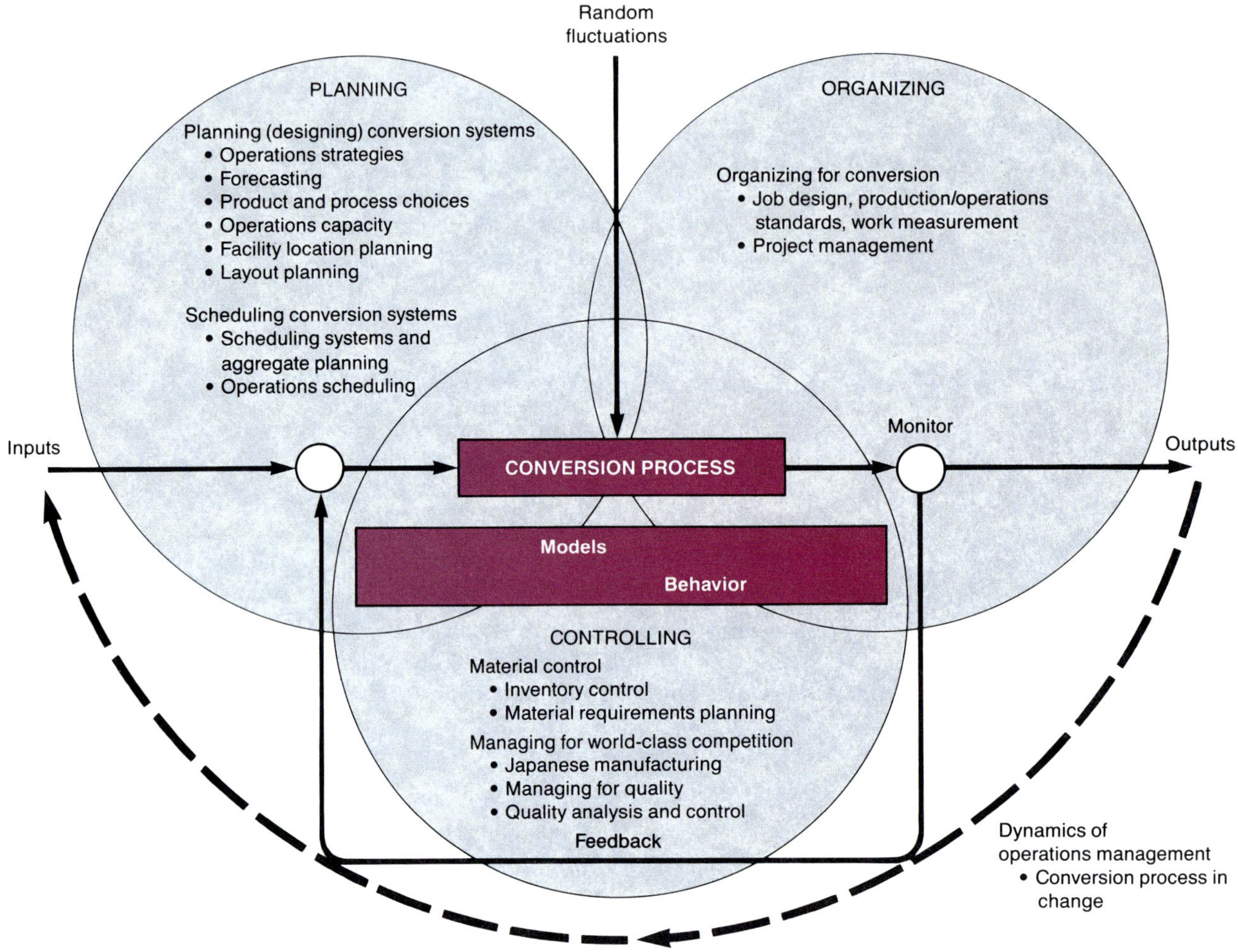

FIGURE 18.2 **General model for managing operations**

must reflect the efficiency, dependability, quality, and flexibility to support the direction of the firm. World-class manufacturing and service firms often *use operations strategy as an offensive weapon.* These firms either change the operations strategy to maximize the market criteria for success or they choose markets to match their existing operations capability in terms of market criteria for success.

Role of Services Services, as contrasted with manufacturing, involve the conversion of resources into an *intangible* output: a deed, a performance, an effort. Although the manufacturing sector is strong in the United States, Canada, and Europe, service industries typically employ up to 70 percent of the total work force and generate over 50 percent of the domestic gross national product. Challenges are great in managing service operations, characterized by customers involved in the conversion process, an absence of inventory to buffer demand, staffing for peak capacity, low levels of automation, quality reflecting timeliness and perceptions rather than function over a long time period, and so forth. The techniques for effective service operations management are not so well developed as in manufacturing, leaving the service manager with a substantial management task.

International Business and Global Manufacturing Competitiveness As a result of improved transportation, communication, and the transfer of technology, many countries can be viewed as a source of manufactured products. One well-known international manufacturing consulting firm, after interviewing 59 multinational corporation chief executives throughout the world, reported the following major findings regarding changing international business:

- The need to gain access to growing markets is driving international expansion.
- Products and services have to be high in quality and low in price by world standards to set them apart.
- A company's primary focus should be on what it does best.
- Most CEOs interviewed emphasize the U.S. market and pick the developing world, especially Asia, as their primary target for expansion.
- Acquisition is the preferred method of expanding into mature markets; the joint venture works best in Asia and other developing regions.
- A company should be centralized in its approach to global strategy but should still remain sensitive to local market conditions.
- There is universal agreement on the need for people who have a truly international perspective.[8]

These operations managers have to be prepared to respond to customer demands throughout the world.
Source: **Alvis Upitis/The Image Bank**

[8]Bruce Townsend, "International Manufacturing Consulting Issues," *Proceedings of a Research Symposium on Issues in International Manufacturing* (Fountainbleau, France: INSEAD, September 1987), 1–40.

Although a thorough understanding of international manufacturing is beyond the scope of this introductory book, manufacturing strategies developed in multinational firms require an understanding of such general business conditions. Several of the points, the second and last, for example, directly impact the operations function.

Operations Management Highlight 18.2 describes Levi Strauss & Co.'s successful venture into global manufacturing.

OPERATIONS MANAGEMENT HIGHLIGHT 18.2

Source: Bob Daemmrich/ Stock, Boston

Levi Is Changing More Than Its Jeans

The old adage, "if things don't change they'll get worse," could have come true for Levi Strauss & Co., except they changed and things got better. Levi changed some of their basic business practices, including implementation of a global strategy, that boosted revenues substantially for 1990. Without the switchover to production, distribution, and promotion in Asia (19 percent growth in 1990), Latin America (27 percent growth), and Europe (32 percent growth), overall revenues would have been only so-so because domestic growth was a mere 6 percent. Overseas revenues exceeded domestic revenues for the year.

Quality Product and service quality are very important to consumers. Fortunately, corporate leaders are awakening to this fact. The growing importance of quality is reflected by the fact that two chapters of this book were devoted to quality: one on *managing for quality* and the second on *quality analysis and control.* This trend has yet to reach its peak since consumers have yet to receive full value for product and service expenditures, in part due to high prices (and costs) but also to low quality.

Levi was concerned about keeping close control and consistency worldwide over the quality of materials and manufacturing of its clothing. So instead of using licensees for production and distribution, Levi established its own network of subsidiaries around the globe. When customers in Hungary want quick deliveries, a nearby factory can respond. Similarly, subsidiaries in Argentina, London, Indonesia, and Brazil permit shorter shipping times to fashion-conscious consumers seeking the Dockers line and Levi's 501 jeans. In Japan, Levi has cultivated a healthy consumer following while other companies are struggling to survive. Levi Strauss Japan, with its expanding line of casual shirts, jeans, trousers, and jackets, climbed from the No. 5 to the No. 2 market position in just four years.

In addition to the strategic decision for global production and distribution, several supporting activities reveal even more changes that are keeping Levi among the leaders of the "jeans pack." In information technology, Levi boosted productivity in product design and business transaction processing by implementing a massive management information system. With this information infrastructure, the company developed better logistics and transportation flows, and better delivery service to customers. Through its Levi-Link system, sales and inventory data are electronically transferred from Levi retailers to Levi distribution centers and factories. Bar-coded clothing at point-of-sale cash registers affords quick reordering of merchandise and lower inventory levels for retailers.

Levi merchandise flows not only through the company's own retail stores, but through others, such as Sears, as well. With a major customer like Sears, Levi has formed a QuickResponse partnership for speeding up the entire chain of resupply: from customer, back to distributor, factory, and suppliers of materials for the factories. Similar to the just-in-time concept, numerous smaller shipments, carefully timed, replace larger bulky shipments that boost inventories and storage space requirements unnecessarily. Using electronic data interchange (EDI), accurate, up-to-the-minute information replaces excessive inventories, reduces costly space needs, and gets more of the right merchandise to the salesroom floor. The time between order and receiving merchandise is drastically reduced.

Is all of this easy to accomplish? No, and Levi realizes that the human dimension, too, is involved in these many changes. To prepare new employees for the dynamics of their organizational lives, the company created a film, "A Day in the Life of Levi Strauss." Its purpose is to present a candid picture of the company's mission and goals, along with the employee attitudes and behaviors that can promote or retard achieving those goals. Through activities such as these, employees' expectations are oriented toward the continually changing environment that seems destined to prevail in Levi's future.

Sources: Maria Shao, Robert Neff, and Jeffrey Ryser, "For Levi's, A Flattering Fit Overseas," *BusinessWeek* (November 5, 1990), 76–77; Geoffrey E. Duin, "Levi's Won't Fade in the Japanese Market," *Tokyo Business Today* (April 1990), 46; E.J. Muller, "Quick Response Picks Up Pace," *Distribution* (June 1990), 38–42; Holly Rawlinson, "Homegrown for HRM," *Personnel Administrator* (August 1989), 48.

THE ROLE OF PRODUCTION/OPERATIONS MANAGERS

Managerial Behavior and Skills Requirements To what degree should the progressive P/O manager be a technician rather than a manager; focus on analysis rather than synthesis, be a specialist rather than a generalist; deliver standardized products and services with established processes rather than try more creative ways? Although we cannot answer for every situation, we observe a trend toward managers, synthesis, generalists, and creativity. Our view is that operations executives are seeking *leaders* who not only have engineering, economic, and analytical skills but who can move beyond these abilities to activate the organization through good management and people skills.

Careers in Production and Operations Management As you think about a career, your progression from your first position to your retirement depends upon your aspirations, skills, preparation, and luck. Four traditional considerations are in every manager's career and operations managers are no exception: entry, stepping stones, blockage, and the climb to the top. There are many entry-level jobs in production/operations: line supervisors, staff analysts, staff specialists, and management trainees. Remember that much of the firm's resources are consumed in operations; traditionally many people work there. This provides a great number of opportunities. As for stepping stones, blockages, and the climb to the top, operations is a function in which each can be experienced, including a route to general management and the top of the organization.

Production and operations management can be fun. If you like people and responsibility, and if you have a propensity for action and a fast pace, operations management might be a good place in which to start your career. Never have the challenges in operations been greater, and never have you had so many tools to utilize as a basis for success.

SUMMARY

Since organizations and their conversion subsystems are dynamic, open systems in constant interaction with their environments, changes of varying magnitude are constantly occurring. Managers must be aware of the process of change and its role in the organization.

Several aspects of change must be understood if change is to be successfully managed. First, one must recognize the need for change as signalled by either internal or external indicators. Next, the targets for change—technology, structure, and behavior—must be identified. Any or all of these are directly involved in the organizational change process.

The behavioral change process involves recognizing the need for change, identifying the behavioral targets for change, deciding to change a certain way, accepting a strategy for change, and implementing the behavioral change.

Strategies for change may be one or a combination of an empirical-rational strategy, a normative-reeducative strategy, or a power-coercive strategy. Regardless of the strategy, the production/operations manager cannot expect a 100 percent behavioral change in subordinate managers and workers.

It is up to the production/operations manager to facilitate learning of behaviors that are supportive of operations goals. Positive rewards should be used intermittently to reinforce worker behaviors that the manager wants continued. The manager must correctly evaluate what reinforcement the worker is currently receiving for undesirable behaviors so that the reinforcements can be withdrawn.

Managers and their subordinates will resist change, some more than others. Worker participation can help reduce the barriers to change. Several other partial solutions exist that can help reduce resistance to change.

Production and operations management was summarized and several trends were identified that could influence operations in the near future.

CASE

Education Copy Services

Before August 1990, two photocopy machines were available to the faculty and secretarial staff of the School of Business. This resource provided an easy, quick, and convenient service to faculty in reproducing materials related to personal, teaching, research, and service activities. In an effort to reduce the high copying cost, a new policy was implemented. All copying for small jobs was to be done by the secretarial staff, and automatic devices were installed to monitor and count all copies made. The machine would not operate without one of these devices, preset with a department charge account. Some faculty found that access to copying was considerably less convenient than it had been in the past. It was harder to get last-minute service, and they needed a longer planning horizon for copied material. Secretaries found that they had to make many special trips to the machines, which interrupted their typing and other office responsibilities.

Then it was announced that as of November 26, 1990, the number of machines would be reduced from two to one. Small jobs (fewer than 11 copies) would continue to be run by secretaries on the one machine. Jobs of 11 or more would be transported across campus to Quick Copy Service for reproduction. This change was to be on a trial basis and offered a handsome cost savings to the college. All indications were that copy service to faculty would be at least as good as they had experienced since August.

The management department chairman and secretarial staff thought about the potential implications of the new system. They decided to send a memo to faculty identifying some things that could be done to enhance the new system. The essential points presented to the faculty were as follows:

1. Jobs requiring more than ten copies will be sent to Quick Copy.
2. Generally, the secretarial staff will mail or deliver jobs to Quick Copy twice daily—once in the morning, once in the afternoon.
3. Quick Copy will deliver the finished jobs back to the departmental office.
4. The secretarial staff will continue to process small jobs on the machine here in the building. This will be done once in the morning and once in the afternoon. This will enable the secretaries to perform their other duties more effectively.
5. As a result of these four steps, the faculty is reminded that some lead time will be necessary for getting the jobs done. The necessary lead time is not expected to be any greater, in general, than it was under the old

> system. If we allow Quick Copy two to three days lead time, they will be able to get us special emergency service on those exceptional occasions when it is needed.

After thinking about the new system and the memo, the chairman wondered about faculty reaction. The new system seemed to have implications for changes in traditional patterns of behavior. What reactions would you expect if you were chairman? What actions should be taken to ensure smooth adaptation to these changes?

REVIEW AND DISCUSSION QUESTIONS

1. Reliable National Bank is considering installing automatic teller units at several locations throughout the city. What indicators of the need for change and what desired results led to considering this change?
2. Suppose you are requested to predict the results of Reliable National Bank's contemplated change (see question 1). Outline your approach for making such a prediction, including a list of the main factors that must be considered.
3. Identify two organizations for which external indicators of the need for change are minimal. List two others for which external indicators are dominant.
4. Identify and discuss the behavioral implications of decisions to change job-shop priority rules, facility layout, and facility location.
5. Give examples showing how changes in the finance and marketing subsystems necessitate changes in the operations subsystem of the organization.
6. Colleges and universities are often bureaucratic in dealing with students. Faculty and staff may be abrupt, inconsiderate, and outright wrong in their behaviors. Think of one experience you've encountered when this was so. Placing yourself in the role of a university operations administrator, use the steps in the behavior change process to show how such an experience could be avoided in the future.
7. State the strategies for behavioral change and briefly explain each. In answering question 6, which strategy for behavior change were you suggesting?
8. Contrast positive reinforcement, negative reinforcement, and punishment: which holds the most promise for behavioral change in production/operations management? Why?
9. Contrast the thaw-move-refreeze change model to the planned change model of Figure 18.1.
10. A claims processing clerk is fearful of losing her job when the new computer system is installed. She has been most reluctant to help the system designers understand her current duties. In fact, she has hidden some of the complex tasks from them. Which of the four basic reasons for resisting change is most prevalent here? Why?
11. Explain the role of top management in bringing about change in the organization.
12. Consider the production scheduling change at Baumritter presented in the chapter.
    (a) Can you identify successful or unsuccessful changes?
    (b) What was the need for change?
    (c) Who was the change agent?
    (d) Who were the learners?

(e) Was there resistance to the change?
(f) What strategy led to the success or failure of the change?

13. Study Figure 18.2, which illustrated production/operations management activities. Lay the figure aside and try to reproduce it. Which parts of the figure do you think are essential as a framework for practicing as an operations manager? Why?

14. Several discernible trends in production/operations management were presented in this chapter. Select one that you believe should be expanded and expand it. Likely, we overlooked one or more trends. Select a trend in production/operations that you believe should have been summarized and summarize it.

KEY TERMS

Change agent 685
Empirical-rational change strategy 681
Normative-reeducative change strategy 681
Organization development (OD) 684
Power-coercive change strategy 681
Reinforcement schedule 682
Reinforcer 682
System dynamics 688
Thaw-move-refreeze model 680

SELECTED READINGS

Adam, E. E., and W. E. Scott, "The Application of Behavioral Conditioning Procedures to the Problems of Quality Control," *Academy of Management Journal* 14, no. 2 (June 1971), 175–93.

Forrester, Jay W., *Industrial Dynamics.* Cambridge, Mass.: M.I.T. Press, 1961.

Greene, Charles N., Everett E. Adam, Jr., and Ronald J. Ebert, *Management for Effective Performance.* Englewood Cliffs, N.J.: Prentice-Hall, 1985.

Kivenko, Ken, "Employee Absenteeism—The Deterioration of Productivity," *Production and Inventory Review* 4, no. 5 (May 1984), 52–55; 70.

Schmenner, Roger W., "Every Factory Has a Cycle," *Harvard Business Review* 61, no. 2 (March–April 1983), 121–29.

Slocum, J. W., Jr., and D. Hellriegel, "Using Organizational Designs to Cope With Change," *Business Horizons* 22, no. 6 (December 1979), 65–76.

Student, K. R., "Managing Change: A Psychologist's Perspective," *Business Horizons* 21, no. 6 (December 1978), 28–33.

Sullivan, R. S. "The Service Sector: Challenges and Imperatives for Research in Operations Management," *Journal of Operations Management* 2, no. 4 (August 1982), 211–14.

Townsend, Bruce, "International Manufacturing Consulting Issues," *Proceedings of a Research Symposium on Issues in International Manufacturing.* Fountainbleau, France: INSEAD, September 1987, 1–40.

Vollmann, Thomas E., "A User Oriented Approach to Production Scheduling." Paper presented at 3rd Annual American Institute for Decision Sciences Conference, St. Louis, Mo., 1971.

APPENDIX

APPENDIX TABLE A **Areas of a standard normal distribution***

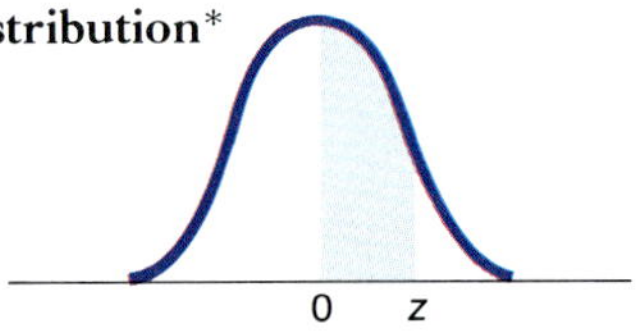

An entry in the table is the proportion under the entire curve which is between $z = 0$ and a positive value of z. Areas for negative values of z are obtained by symmetry.

z	.00	.01	.02	.03	.04	.05	.06	.07	.08	.09
0.0	.0000	.0040	.0080	.0120	.0160	.0199	.0239	.0279	.0319	.0359
0.1	.0398	.0438	.0478	.0517	.0557	.0596	.0636	.0675	.0714	.0753
0.2	.0793	.0832	.0871	.0910	.0948	.0987	.1026	.1064	.1103	.1141
0.3	.1179	.1217	.1255	.1293	.1331	.1368	.1406	.1443	.1480	.1517
0.4	.1554	.1591	.1628	.1664	.1700	.1736	.1772	.1808	.1844	.1879
0.5	.1915	.1950	.1985	.2019	.2054	.2088	.2123	.2157	.2190	.2224
0.6	.2257	.2291	.2324	.2357	.2389	.2422	.2454	.2486	.2517	.2549
0.7	.2580	.2611	.2642	.2673	.2703	.2734	.2764	.2794	.2823	.2852
0.8	.2881	.2910	.2939	.2967	.2995	.3023	.3051	.3078	.3106	.3133
0.9	.3159	.3186	.3212	.3238	.3264	.3289	.3315	.3340	.3365	.3389
1.0	.3413	.3438	.3461	.3485	.3508	.3531	.3554	.3577	.3599	.3621
1.1	.3643	.3665	.3686	.3708	.3729	.3749	.3770	.3790	.3810	.3830
1.2	.3849	.3869	.3888	.3907	.3925	.3944	.3962	.3980	.3997	.4015
1.3	.4032	.4049	.4066	.4082	.4099	.4115	.4131	.4147	.4162	.4177
1.4	.4192	.4207	.4222	.4236	.4251	.4265	.4279	.4292	.4306	.4319
1.5	.4332	.4345	.4357	.4370	.4382	.4394	.4406	.4418	.4429	.4441
1.6	.4452	.4463	.4474	.4484	.4495	.4505	.4515	.4525	.4535	.4545
1.7	.4554	.4564	.4573	.4582	.4591	.4599	.4608	.4616	.4625	.4633
1.8	.4641	.4649	.4656	.4664	.4671	.4678	.4686	.4693	.4699	.4706
1.9	.4713	.4719	.4726	.4732	.4738	.4744	.4750	.4756	.4761	.4767
2.0	.4772	.4778	.4783	.4788	.4793	.4798	.4803	.4808	.4812	.4817
2.1	.4821	.4826	.4830	.4834	.4838	.4842	.4846	.4850	.4854	.4857
2.2	.4861	.4864	.4868	.4871	.4875	.4878	.4881	.4884	.4887	.4890
2.3	.4893	.4896	.4898	.4901	.4904	.4906	.4909	.4911	.4913	.4916
2.4	.4918	.4920	.4922	.4925	.4927	.4929	.4931	.4932	.4934	.4936
2.5	.4938	.4940	.4941	.4943	.4945	.4946	.4948	.4949	.4951	.4952
2.6	.4953	.4955	.4956	.4957	.4959	.4960	.4961	.4962	.4963	.4964
2.7	.4965	.4966	.4967	.4968	.4969	.4970	.4971	.4972	.4973	.4974
2.8	.4974	.4975	.4976	.4977	.4977	.4978	.4979	.4979	.4980	.4981
2.9	.4981	.4982	.4982	.4983	.4984	.4984	.4985	.4985	.4986	.4986
3.0	.4987	.4987	.4987	.4988	.4988	.4989	.4989	.4989	.4990	.4990

**Source:* Paul G. Hoel, *Elementary Statistics,* 2nd ed. (New York: John Wiley, 1966), p 329.

Appendix Table B 8% Compound interest factors*

	Single Payment		Uniform Series				
n	Compound Amount Given P to Find S $(1+i)^n$	Present Worth Factor Given S to Find P $\frac{1}{(1+i)^n}$	Sinking Fund Factor Given S to Find R $\frac{i}{(1+i)^n-1}$	Capital Recovery Factor Given P to Find R $\frac{i(1+i)^n}{(1+i)^n-1}$	Compound Amount Factor Given R to Find S $\frac{(1+i)^n-1}{i}$	Present Worth Factor Given R to Find P $\frac{(1+i)^n-1}{i(1+i)^n}$	n
1	1.0800	0.9259	1.000 00	1.080 00	1.000	0.926	1
2	1.1664	0.8573	0.480 77	0.560 77	2.080	1.783	2
3	1.2597	0.7938	0.308 03	0.388 03	3.246	2.577	3
4	1.3605	0.7350	0.221 92	0.301 92	4.506	3.312	4
5	1.4693	0.6806	0.170 46	0.250 46	5.867	3.993	5
6	1.5869	0.6302	0.136 32	0.216 32	7.336	4.623	6
7	1.7138	0.5835	0.112 07	0.192 07	8.923	5.206	7
8	1.8509	0.5403	0.094 01	0.174 01	10.637	5.737	8
9	1.9990	0.5002	0.080 08	0.160 08	12.488	6.247	9
10	2.1589	0.4632	0.069 03	0.149 03	14.487	6.710	10
11	2.3316	0.4289	0.060 08	0.140 08	16.645	7.139	11
12	2.5182	0.3971	0.052 70	0.132 70	18.977	7.536	12
13	2.7196	0.3677	0.046 52	0.126 52	21.495	7.904	13
14	2.9372	0.3405	0.041 30	0.121 30	24.215	8.244	14
15	3.1722	0.3152	0.036 83	0.116 83	27.152	8.559	15
16	3.4259	0.2919	0.032 98	0.112 98	30.324	8.851	16
17	3.7000	0.2703	0.029 63	0.109 63	33.750	9.122	17
18	3.9960	0.2502	0.026 70	0.106 70	37.450	9.372	18
19	4.3157	0.2317	0.024 13	0.104 13	41.446	9.604	19
20	4.6610	0.2145	0.021 85	0.101 85	45.762	9.818	20
21	5.0338	0.1987	0.019 83	0.099 83	50.423	10.017	21
22	5.4365	0.1839	0.018 03	0.098 03	55.457	10.201	22
23	5.8715	0.1703	0.016 42	0.096 42	60.893	10.371	23
24	6.3412	0.1577	0.014 98	0.094 98	66.765	10.529	24
25	6.8485	0.1460	0.013 68	0.093 68	73.106	10.675	25
26	7.3964	0.1352	0.012 51	0.092 51	79.954	10.810	26
27	7.9881	0.1252	0.011 45	0.091 45	87.351	10.935	27
28	8.6271	0.1159	0.010 49	0.090 49	95.339	11.051	28
29	9.3173	0.1073	0.009 62	0.089 62	103.966	11.158	29
30	10.0627	0.0994	0.008 83	0.088 83	113.283	11.258	30
31	10.8677	0.0920	0.008 11	0.088 11	123.346	11.350	31
32	11.7371	0.0852	0.007 45	0.087 45	134.214	11.435	32
33	12.6760	0.0789	0.006 85	0.086 85	145.951	11.514	33
34	13.6901	0.0730	0.006 30	0.086 30	158.627	11.587	34
35	14.7853	0.0676	0.005 80	0.085 80	172.317	11.655	35
40	21.7245	0.0460	0.003 86	0.083 86	259.057	11.925	40
45	31.9204	0.0313	0.002 59	0.082 59	386.506	12.108	45
50	46.9016	0.0213	0.001 74	0.081 74	573.770	12.233	50
55	68.9139	0.0145	0.001 18	0.081 18	848.923	12.319	55
60	101.2571	0.0099	0.000 80	0.080 80	1 253.213	12.377	60
65	148.7798	0.0067	0.000 54	0.080 54	1 847.248	12.416	65
70	218.6064	0.0046	0.000 37	0.080 37	2 720.080	12.443	70
75	321.2045	0.0031	0.000 25	0.080 25	4 002.557	12.461	75
80	471.9548	0.0021	0.000 17	0.080 17	5 886.935	12.474	80
85	693.4565	0.0014	0.000 12	0.080 12	8 655.706	12.482	85
90	1 018.9151	0.0010	0.000 08	0.080 08	12 723.939	12.488	90
95	1 497.1205	0.0007	0.000 05	0.080 05	18 701.507	12.492	95
100	2 199.7613	0.0005	0.000 04	0.080 04	27 484.516	12.494	100

*_Source:_ Adapted from Eugene L. Grant, W. Grant Ireson, and Richard S. Leavenworth, _Principles of Engineering Economy_, 6th ed. Copyright © 1976, John Wiley, New York.

APPENDIX TABLE C 10% Compound interest factors*

	Single Payment		Uniform Series				
n	Compound Amount Given P to find S $(1+i)^n$	Present Worth Factor Given S to Find P $\frac{1}{(1+i)^n}$	Sinking Fund Factor Given S to Find R $\frac{i}{(1+i)^n-1}$	Capital Recovery Factor Given P to Find R $\frac{i(1+i)^n}{(1+i)^n-1}$	Compound Amount Factor Given R to Find S $\frac{(1+i)^n-1}{i}$	Present Worth Factor Given R to Find P $\frac{(1+i)^n-1}{i(1+i)^n}$	n
1	1.1000	0.9091	1.000 00	1.100 00	1.000	0.909	**1**
2	1.2100	0.8264	0.476 19	0.576 19	2.100	1.736	**2**
3	1.3310	0.7513	0.302 11	0.402 11	3.310	2.487	**3**
4	1.4641	0.6830	0.215 47	0.315 47	4.641	3.170	**4**
5	1.6105	0.6209	0.163 80	0.263 80	6.105	3.791	**5**
6	1.7716	0.5645	0.129 61	0.229 61	7.716	4.355	**6**
7	1.9487	0.5132	0.105 41	0.205 41	9.487	4.868	**7**
8	2.1436	0.4665	0.087 44	0.187 44	11.436	5.335	**8**
9	2.3579	0.4241	0.073 64	0.173 64	13.579	5.759	**9**
10	2.5937	0.3855	0.062 75	0.162 75	15.937	6.144	**10**
11	2.8531	0.3505	0.053 96	0.153 96	18.531	6.495	**11**
12	3.1384	0.3186	0.046 76	0.146 76	21.384	6.814	**12**
13	3.4523	0.2897	0.040.78	0.140.78	24.523	7.103	**13**
14	3.7975	0.2633	0.035 75	0.135 75	27.975	7.367	**14**
15	4.1772	0.2394	0.031 47	0.131 47	31.772	7.606	**15**
16	4.5950	0.2176	0.027 82	0.127 82	35.950	7.824	**16**
17	5.0545	0.1978	0.024 66	0.124 66	40.545	8.022	**17**
18	5.5599	0.1799	0.021 93	0.121 93	45.599	8.201	**18**
19	6.1159	0.1635	0.019 55	0.119 55	51.159	8.365	**19**
20	6.7275	0.1486	0.017 46	0.117 46	57.275	8.514	**20**
21	7.4002	0.1351	0.015 62	0.115 62	64.002	8.649	**21**
22	8.1403	0.1228	0.014 01	0.114 01	71.403	8.772	**22**
23	8.9543	0.1117	0.012 57	0.112 57	79.543	8.883	**23**
24	9.8497	0.1015	0.011 30	0.111 30	88.497	8.985	**24**
25	10.8347	0.0923	0.010 17	0.110 17	98.347	9.077	**25**
26	11.9182	0.0839	0.009 16	0.109 16	109.182	9.161	**26**
27	13.1100	0.0763	0.008 26	0.108 26	121.100	9.237	**27**
28	14.4210	0.0693	0.007 45	0.107 45	134.210	9.307	**28**
29	15.8631	0.0630	0.006 73	0.106 73	148.631	9.370	**29**
30	17.4494	0.0573	0.006 08	0.106 08	164.494	9.427	**30**
31	19.1943	0.0521	0.005 50	0.105 50	181.943	9.479	**31**
32	21.1138	0.0474	0.004 97	0.104 97	201.138	9.526	**32**
33	23.2252	0.0431	0.004 50	0.104 50	222.252	9.569	**33**
34	25.5477	0.0391	0.004 07	0.104 07	245.477	9.609	**34**
35	28.1024	0.0356	0.003 69	0.103 69	271.024	9.644	**35**
40	45.2593	0.0221	0.002 26	0.102 26	442.593	9.779	**40**
45	72.8905	0.0137	0.001 39	0.101 39	718.905	9.863	**45**
50	117.3909	0.0085	0.000 86	0.100 86	1 163.909	9.915	**50**
55	189.0591	0.0053	0.000 53	0.100 53	1 880.591	9.947	**55**
60	304.4816	0.0033	0.000 33	0.100.33	3 034.816	9.967	**60**
65	490.3707	0.0020	0.000 20	0.100 20	4 893.707	9.980	**65**
70	789.7470	0.0013	0.000 13	0.100 13	7 887.470	9.987	**70**
75	1 271.8952	0.0008	0.000 08	0.100 08	12 708.954	9.992	**75**
80	2 048.4002	0.0005	0.000 05	0.100 05	20 474.002	9.995	**80**
85	3 298.9690	0.0003	0.000 03	0.100 03	32 979.690	9.997	**85**
90	5 313.0226	0.0002	0.000 02	0.100 02	53 120.226	9.998	**90**
95	8 556.6760	0.0001	0.000 01	0.100 01	85 556.760	9.999	**95**
100	13 780.6123	0.0001	0.000 01	0.100 01	137 796.123	9.999	**100**

*Source: Adapted from Eugene L. Grant, W. Grant Ireson, and Richard S. Leavenworth, *Principles of Engineering Economy*, 6th ed. Copyright © 1976, John Wiley, New York.

APPENDIX TABLE D **Random digits***

85387	51571	57714	00512	61319	69143	08881	01400	55061	82977
84176	03311	16955	59504	54499	32096	79485	98031	99485	16788
27258	51746	67223	98182	43166	54297	26830	29842	78016	73127
99398	46950	19399	65167	35082	30482	86323	41061	21717	48126
72752	89364	02150	85418	05420	84341	02395	27655	59457	55438
69090	93551	11649	54688	57061	77711	24201	16895	64936	62347
39620	54988	67846	71845	54000	26134	84526	16619	82573	01737
81725	49831	35595	29891	46812	57770	03326	31316	75412	80732
87968	85157	84752	93777	62772	78961	30750	76089	23340	64637
07730	01861	40610	73445	70321	26467	53533	20787	46971	29134
32825	82100	67406	44156	21531	67186	39945	04189	79798	41087
34453	05330	40224	04116	24597	93823	28171	47701	76201	68257
00830	34235	40671	66042	06341	54437	81649	70494	01883	18350
24580	05258	37329	59173	62660	72513	82232	49794	36913	05877
59578	08535	77107	19838	40651	01749	58893	99115	05212	92309
75387	24990	12748	71766	17471	15794	68622	59161	14476	75074
02465	34977	48319	53026	53691	80594	58805	76961	62665	82855
49689	08342	81912	92735	30042	47623	60061	69427	21163	68543
60958	20236	79424	04055	54955	73342	14040	72431	99469	41044
79956	98409	79548	39569	83974	43707	77080	08645	20949	56932
04316	01206	08715	77713	20572	13912	94324	14656	11979	53258
78684	28546	06881	66097	53530	42509	54130	30878	77166	98075
69235	18535	61904	99246	84050	15270	07751	90410	96675	62870
81201	04314	92708	44984	83121	33767	56607	46371	20389	08809
80336	59638	44368	33433	97794	10343	19235	82633	17186	63902
65076	87960	92013	60169	49176	50140	39081	04638	96114	63463
90879	70970	50789	59973	47771	94567	35590	23462	33993	99899
50555	84355	97066	82748	98298	14385	82493	40182	20523	69182
48658	41921	86514	46786	74097	62825	46457	24428	09245	86069
26373	19166	88223	32371	11570	62078	92317	13378	05734	71778
20878	80883	26027	29101	58382	17109	53511	95536	21759	10630
20069	60582	55749	88068	48589	01874	42930	40310	34613	97359
46819	38577	20520	94145	99405	47064	25248	27289	41289	54972
83644	04459	73253	58414	94180	09321	59747	07379	56255	45615
08636	31363	56033	49076	88908	51318	39104	56556	23112	63317
92058	38678	12507	90343	17213	24545	66053	76412	29545	89932
05038	18443	87138	05076	25660	23414	84837	87132	84405	15346
41838	68590	93646	82113	25498	33110	15356	81070	84900	42660
15564	81618	99186	73113	99344	13213	07235	90064	89150	86359
74600	40206	15237	37378	96862	78638	14376	46607	55909	46398
78275	77017	60310	13499	35268	47790	77475	44345	14615	25231
30145	71205	10355	18404	85354	22199	90822	35204	47891	69860
46944	00097	39161	50139	60458	44649	85537	90017	18157	13856
85883	21272	89266	94887	00291	70963	28169	95130	27223	35387
83606	98192	82194	26719	24499	28102	97769	98769	30757	81593
66888	81818	52490	54272	70549	69235	74684	96412	65186	87974
63673	73966	34036	44298	60652	05947	05833	27914	57021	58566
37944	16094	39797	63253	64103	32222	65925	64693	34048	75394
93240	66855	29336	28345	71398	45118	01454	72128	09715	29454
40189	76776	70842	32675	81647	75868	21288	12849	94990	21513

**Source:* Reproduced with permission from the Rand Corporation, *A Million Random Digits with 100,000 Normal Deviates.* Copyright, 1955, The Free Press: Glencoe, Ill., p 259.

GLOSSARY

ABC classification Classification of inventory into three groups: an A group comprising items with a large dollar volume; a B group comprising items with moderate volume and moderate dollar volume; and a C group comprising items with a large volume and small dollar volume.

Acceptance number The number of sample units specified in a sampling plan that must conform to specifications if the shipment is to be accepted.

Acceptance sampling A statistical quality control technique used in deciding to accept or reject a shipment of input or output.

Accounting life Length of an asset's life determined for the purpose of a depreciation schedule.

Action bucket In the MRP record for the current week, a cell calling for immediate action to meet the MPS goal.

Activity In PERT, project work needed to be accomplished, symbolized by an arc.

Activity chart A graphic tool to analyze and time the small, physical actions of worker and machine in performing a routine, repetitive, worker-machine task so that idle time can be identified.

Adaptive exponential smoothing An average method in which a smoothing coefficient is not fixed but is set initially and then allowed to fluctuate over time based upon changes in the demand pattern.

Aggregate capacity planning The process of testing the feasibility of aggregate output plans and evaluating overall capacity utilization.

Aggregate output planning The process of determining output levels (units) of product groups over the coming six to 18 months on a weekly or monthly basis; the plan identifies the overall level of outputs in support of the business plan.

Allocated quantity The quantity of an item in inventory that has been committed for use and is not available to meet future requirements.

Allowance fraction The fraction of time lost on a job because of workers' personal needs, fatigue, and other unavoidable delays; the remaining fraction of time is the **available fraction.**

Andon A warning light used as a visible control technique in total quality control.

Applied research Research for the advancement of scientific knowledge that has specific commercial uses.

Appraisal costs Costs of evaluating, measuring, or inspecting for quality at the plant and in the field.

Arc In network modeling, an arrowed line segment; the symbol for a project activity.

Assembly line technology A process technology suitable for a narrow range of standardized products in high volumes.

Assignment algorithm A linear program to assign jobs so that a specific criterion is optimized.

Attribute characteristic A product characteristic that can be measured by a rating of good or bad.

Available fraction of time The fraction of time remaining after accounting for time lost on a job because of worker's personal needs, fatigue, and other unavoidable delays.

Available quantity The quantity of an item expected to be available at the end of a time period to meet requirements in succeeding periods. Calculated as scheduled receipts plus planned order receipts minus gross requirements for the period, plus amounts available from the previous period.

Backorders Outstanding or unfilled customer orders.

Backward scheduling Determining the start and finish times for waiting jobs by assigning them to the latest available time slot that will enable each job to be completed just when it is due, but not before.

Base stock level The inventory level up to which stocks are replenished, fixed by a periodic inventory control operating doctrine.

Basic research Research for the advancement of scientific knowledge that is not intended for specific commercial uses.

Batch technology A process technology suitable for a variety of products in varying volumes.

Behavioral management One of three primary theories of management, emphasizing human relations and the behavioral sciences.

Behavioral science A science that explores how human behavior is affected by variables such as leadership, motivation, communication, interpersonal relationships, and attitude change.

Bias A forecast error measure that is the average of forecast error with regard to direction and shows any tendency consistently to over- or underforecast; calculated as the sum of the actual forecast error for all periods divided by the total number of periods evaluated.

Bill of materials A document describing the details of an item's product buildup, including all component items, their buildup sequence, the quantity needed for each, and the work centers that perform the buildup sequence.

Blanket rule A general policy for inventory control that can be modified as needed in light of total inventory costs.

Bottleneck operation The station on an assembly line that requires the longest task time.

Break-even analysis A graphical and algebraic representation of the relationships among volume of output, costs, and revenues.

Break-even point The level of output volume for which total costs equal total revenues.

Breakthrough A solution to a chronic problem; a dramatic change for the better in quality, stimulated by concentrated, analytic, company-wide quality improvement programs.

Buffer stock Inventories to protect against the effects of unusual product demand and uncertain lead time.

Business plan A statement of an organization's overall level of business activity for the coming six to 18 months, usually expressed in terms of dollar volume of sales for its various product groups.

Capacity A facility's maximum productive capability, usually expressed as volume of output per period of time.

Cardex file system A manually operated inventory control system in which an inventory card represents each stock item with transactions kept on the card.

Carrying (holding) costs Costs of maintaining the inventory warehouse and protecting the inventoried items.

Causal forecasting models A statistical forecasting model based on historical demand data as well as on variables believed to influence demand.

Cellular layout The arrangement of a facility so that equipment used to make similar parts or families of parts is grouped together.

Central limit theorem A statistical hypothesis that the sampling distribution approaches normality as the size of the samples increases, regardless of the distribution of the measurements of individual sample units.

Chance event An event leading potentially to several different outcomes, only one of which will definitely occur; the decision maker has no control over which outcome will occur.

Change agent The facilitator of change; the role of the production/operations manager in bringing about behavioral changes in other people.

Chronic problem A long-term problem that causes continually poor quality, usually addressed through breakthrough measures.

Classical management One of three primary theories of management, emphasizing efficiency at the production core, the separation of planning and doing work, and management principles and functions.

Company-wide quality control (CWQC) A management philosophy and set of activities characterized by mobilizing the entire work force in the pursuit of quality, by statistical thinking, and by preventing errors.

Computer search A set of directions that systematically guides a computer in evaluating alternative aggregate plans.

Computer-aided manufacturing (CAM) Manufacturing systems utilizing computer software programs that control the actual machine on the shop floor.

Computer-aided design (CAD) Computer software programs that allow a designer to carry out geometric transformations rapidly.

Computer-integrated manufacturing (CIM) Computer information systems utilizing a shared manufacturing database for engineering design, manufacturing engineering, factory production, and information management.

Consumer's risk (type II error) (β) The risk or probability of incorrectly concluding that the conversion process is in control.

Continuous operations Operations characterized by standardized, high-volume, capital-intense products made to store in inventory; by small product mix; by special purpose equipment; and by continuous product flow.

Continuous technology A process technology suitable for producing a continuous flow of products.

Control chart A chart of sampling data used to make inferences about the control status of a conversion process.

Control limits (CL) Upper (UCL) and lower (LCL) boundaries defining the range of variation in a product characteristic such that the conversion process is in control.

Controlling Activities that assure that actual performance is in accordance with planned performance.

Conversion process The process of changing inputs of labor, capital, land, and management into outputs of goods and services.

Critical fractile In ratio of shortage costs to the sum of shortage and overstock for the perishable goods inventory situation.

Critical path In PERT, a path whose activities are expected to consume the most time.

Critical ratio The ratio of inspection costs to percent defective.

Custom-shop service technology A process technology suitable for capital intensive, high customer contact services.

Cycle counting Counting on-hand inventories at regular intervals to verify inventory quantities shown in the MRP.

Cycle time Time elapsing between completed units coming off an assembly line.

Decision tree A diagram used to structure and analyze a decision problem; a systematic, sequential laying out of decision points, alternatives, and chance events.

Decision variable A numerical, controllable parameter that, if modified, yields a variety of results.

Decoupling Using inventories to break apart operations so that the supply of one operation is independent of the supply of another.

Degeneracy A quality of a linear transportation programming problem such that there are too few occupied cells to enable evaluation of the empty cells.

Delphi technique A qualitative forecasting technique in which a panel of experts working separately and not meeting, arrive at a consensus through the summarizing of ideas by a skilled coordinator.

Demand pattern General shape of a time series; usually constant, trend, seasonal, or some combination of these shapes.

Demand stability Tendency of a time series to retain the same general pattern over time.

Demand-based forecasting models A statistical forecasting model based solely on historical demand data.

Deming's 14 points for management Guidelines for improving quality, proposed by Dr. W. Edwards Deming, as part of total quality control.

Dependent demand Demand for an item that can be linked to the demand for another item.

Depreciation An accounting procedure to recover expenditures for an asset over its lifetime.

Design specifications The important, desired characteristics of a product or service specified in detail during the design phase.

Designated truncation time Predetermined length of time a job is allowed to wait before it is assigned top priority for processing (see truncated-shortest-processing-time rule)

Detailed capacity planning An iterative process of modifying the MPS or planned resources to make capacity consistent with the production schedule.

Detailed scheduling Determining start times, finish times, and worker assignments for all jobs at each work center.

Deterministic model A model in which variable values are known with certainty.

Development Technical activities concerned with translating basic applied research results into products or processes.

Direct time study A work measurement technique that involves observing the job, determining the job cycle, stopwatch-timing the job cycle, and calculating a performance standard.

Disaggregation The process of translating aggregate plans for product groups into detailed operational plans for individual products.

Double sampling Acceptance sampling based on a first, small sample and, if results are inconclusive, a second, larger sample.

Dummy activity In PERT, a fictitious activity consuming no time, symbolized by a dashed arc.

Earliest beginning time (T_E) In PERT, the minimum amount of time that must be consumed before an activity can begin.

Earliest-due-date rule (EDD) Priority rule that gives top priority to the waiting job whose due date is earliest.

Economic life Length of time an asset is useful.

Economic order quantity (EOC) The optimal order quantity, fixed by a Q/R inventory control operating doctrine.

Efficiency A measure (ratio) of outputs to inputs.

Empirical-rational change strategy A strategy for change that assumes people change their behavior when they believe it is in their own self-interest to do so.

Event In PERT, the beginning or ending of an activity, symbolized by a node.

Expected beginning time (T_B) In PERT, the amount of time expected to be consumed before an activity can begin.

Expected completion time (T_C) In PERT, the amount of time expected to be consumed once an activity begins.

Expected time (t_e) In PERT, the amount of time an activity is expected to consume.

Expediting Tracking a job's progress and taking special actions to move it through the facility.

Exponential smoothing An averaging method that exponentially decreases the weighting of old demands.

External failure costs Costs attributable to the failure of products in the field.

Factor ratings A decision procedure in which each alternative is rated according to each factor relevant to the decision, and each factor is weighted according to importance.

Feasible (infeasible) solutions Solutions that satisfy (do not satisfy) the restrictions of a linear programming problem.

Feedback Information in the control process that allows management to decide whether organizational activities need adjustment.

Finite loading A scheduling procedure that assigns jobs into work centers and determines their starting and completion dates by considering the work centers' capacities.

Firm planned order A planned order release scheduled within the MRP time fence.

First-come-first-served rule (FCFS) Priority rule that gives top priority to the waiting job that arrived earliest in the production system.

Fishbone (cause and effect) diagram A schematic model of quality problems and their causes; used to diagnose and solve these problems.

Fixed-position layout The arrangement of a facility so that the product stays in one location; tools, equipment, and workers are brought to it as needed.

Flexibility The capability of a manufacturing system to adapt successfully to changing environmental conditions and process requirements.

Flexible manufacturing system (FMS) A computer-controlled process technology suitable for producing a moderate variety of products in moderate volumes.

Flow process chart A graphic tool to analyze and categorize interstation activities so that the flow of the product throughout the overall production process is represented.

Flow time The total time that a job is in the system; the sum of waiting time and processing time.

Forecast Use of past data to determine future events; an objective computation.

Forecast error The numeric difference of forecasted demand and actual demand.

Forward scheduling Determining the start and finish times for waiting jobs by assigning them to the earliest available time slots at the work center.

Fraction defective The ratio of defective units to total units.

Gang process chart A graphic tool to trace the interaction of several workers with one machine.

Gannt chart A bar chart showing the relationship of project activities in time.

Gantt load chart A graph showing work loads on a time scale.

Gantt scheduling chart A graph showing the time requirements of waiting jobs scheduled for production at machines and work centers.

Governmental industrial planning Activities of the Japanese Ministry of International Trade and Industry that formulate industrial policy and determine the patterns of future growth and decline among the various industries comprising the Japanese economy.

Gradual replacement model A deterministic inventory model characterized by demand being withdrawn while production is underway; no stockouts, constant and known demand, lead time and unit costs.

Graphical planning procedure Two-dimensional model relating cumulative demand to cumulative output capacity.

Gross requirements The overall quantity of an item needed during a time period to meet planned output levels. Planned output for end items is obtained from the MPS. Planned output for lower-level items is obtained from the MRP.

Group technology A way of organizing and using data for components that have similar properties and manufacturing requirements.

Heuristic A procedure in which a set of rules is systematically applied; an algorithm.

Histogram A bar graph of frequency distributions.

Homogeneous resources Resources for which units supplied by one source are qualitatively equivalent to units supplied by any other source.

Human relations Phenomenon recognized by behavioral scientists that people are complex and have multiple needs and that the subordinate-supervisor relationship directly affects productivity.

Implementation Activities concerned with designing and building pilot models, equipment, and facilities for, and with initiating the marketing channels for, products or services emerging from research and development.

In-control process A process for which all variations are random.

Indented bill of materials A chart showing an end item's components, level by level, with increasing indentations to reflect the lower levels.

Independent demand Demand for an item that occurs separately of demand for any other item.

Individual risk-taking propensity The degree to which an individual tends to take or avoid risks.

Infinite loading Assigning jobs to work centers without considering the work center's capacity (as if the capacity were infinite).

Initial solution The feasible solution tested first using the simplex method in solving a linear programming problem.

Input/output control Activities to monitor actual versus planned utilization of a work center's capacity.

Inputs Labor, capital, land, or management resources changed by a conversion process into goods or services.

Inspection The observation and measurement of inputs and outputs.

Intermittent operations Operations characterized by made-to-order, low-volume, labor-intense products; by a large product mix; by general purpose equipment; by interrupted product flow; and by frequent schedule changes.

Internal failure costs Costs attributable to errors and defects in production at the plant.

Internal rate of return Interest rate at which the present value of outflows equals the present value of inflows.

Intuitive forecasts Forecasts that essentially are a manager's guesses and judgements concerning future events; qualitative forecasting methods.

Inventory Stores of goods and stocks, including raw materials, work-in-process, finished products, or supplies.

Inventory control Activities that maintain stockkeeping items at desired levels.

Inventory modeling A quantitative method for deriving a minimum cost operating doctrine.

Inventory status file The complete documentation of the inventory status of each item in the product structure, including item identification, on-hand quantity, safety stock level, quantity allocated, and lead time.

Iso-profit line Points in the solution space of a linear programming problem whose corresponding profits are identical.

Item level The relative position of an item in the product structure; end items are upper-level; preliminary items in the product structure are lower-level.

Job A group of related tasks or activities that needs to be performed to meet organizational objectives.

Job design Activities that specify the content of each job and determine how work is distributed within the organization.

Job enlargement Redesigning jobs to provide greater variety, autonomy, task identity, and feedback for the employee.

Job enrichment Redesigning jobs to give more meaning and enjoyment to the job by involving employees in planning, organizing, and controlling their work.

Job rotation Moving employees into a job for a short period of time and then out again.

Job satisfaction Employee perceptions of the extent to which their work fulfills or satisfies their needs.

Job shop technology A process technology suitable for a variety of custom-designed products in small volumes.

Just-in-time (JIT) A manufacturing system whose goal it is to optimize processes and procedures by continuously pursuing waste reduction.

Kaizen The Japanese concept of continuous improvement in all things.

Kanban Literally, a "visual record;" a method of controlling materials flow through a JIT manufacturing system by using cards to authorize a work station to transfer or produce materials.

Labor efficiency The ratio of outputs to labor input, the labor actually worked to achieve their output; a partial factor productivity measure.

Labor standard A quantitative criterion reflecting the output expected from an average worker under average conditions for a given time period.

Labor turnover A measure of the stability or change in an organization's work force; the net result of employee terminations and entrances.

Latest beginning time (T_L) In PERT, the maximum amount of time that can be consumed before an activity begins, if the project is to be completed on time.

Layout Physical location or configuration of departments, work centers, and equipment in the conversion process; spatial arrangement of physical resources used to create the product.

Lead time The time passing between ordering and receiving goods.

Lead-time demand Units of stock demanded during lead time; can be described by a probability distribution in stochastic situations.

Lead-time offsetting The process of determining the timing of a planned order release; backing off from the timing of a planned order receipt by the length of lead time.

Least slack rule (LS) A priority rule that gives top priority to the waiting job whose slack time is least; **slack**

time is the difference between the length of time remaining until the job is due and the length of its operation time.

Level output rate plan An aggregate plan calling for a constant rate of output for all time periods of production.

Line balancing problem Assigning tasks among workers at assembly line stations so that performance times are made as equal as possible.

Linear decision rules (LDRs) A set of equations for calculating optimal work force, aggregate output rate, and inventory level.

Linear programming Mathematical method for selecting the optimal allocation of resources to maximize profits or minimize costs.

Load The cumulative amount of work currently assigned to a work center for future processing.

Load-distance model An algorithm for laying out work centers to minimize product flow, based on the number of loads moved and the distance between each pair of work centers.

Longest-operation-time (LOT) rule A line-balancing heuristic that gives top assignment priority to the task that has the longest operation time.

Lot splitting Processing only part of a job at one time, then the rest of the job at a later time.

Lot-for-lot ordering A lot sizing policy in which order quantity equals net requirements for the period.

Machine life Length of time an asset is capable of functioning.

Management coefficients model A set of equations that represent historical patterns of a company's aggregate planning decisions.

Manufacturing resource planning (MRPII) An integrated information system that shares data among and synchronizes the activities of production and the other functional areas of the business.

Manufacturing Accounting and Production Information Control System (MAPICS) IBM's computerized common data base system for manufacturing information and control.

Marginal efficiency of capital (MEC) A concept from finance espousing that a firm should invest in opportunities whose return is greater than the cost of capital.

Markup The ratio of profits to sales.

Mass service technology A process technology suitable for labor intensive, low customer contact services.

Master production scheduling (MPS) A schedule showing week by week how many of each product must be produced according to customer orders and demand forecasts.

Material requirements planning (MRP) A system of planning and scheduling the time-phased materials requirements for production operations.

Materials management Activities relating to managing the flow of materials into and through an organization.

Mathematical modeling Creating and using mathematical representations of management problems and organizations to predict outcomes of proposed courses of action.

Matrix organization An organization that combines functional and project bases for groupings of organization units.

Maximum allowable cycle time Maximum time allowed to elapse between completed units coming off an assembly line, if a given capacity is to be achieved.

Mean absolute deviation (MAD) A forecast error measure that is the average forecast error without regard to direction; calculated as the sum of the absolute value of forecast error for all periods divided by the total number of periods evaluated.

Mechanization The process of bringing about the use of equipment and machinery in production and operations.

Methods time measurement A widely accepted form of predetermined time study.

Ministry of International Trade and Industry (MITI) The unit of Japanese government responsible for **industrial planning** for the activities that formulate industrial policy and determine the patterns of future growth and decline among the various industries comprising the Japanese economy.

Mixed strategy Aggregate planning strategy that incorporates or combines some elements from each of the pure aggregate planning strategies.

Modeling management One of three primary theories of management, emphasizing decision-making, systems, and mathematical modeling.

Modular design The creation of products from some combination of basic, preexisting subsystems.

Most likely time (t_m) In PERT, the single best guess of the amount of time an activity is expected to consume.

Multiechelon inventories Products stocked at various levels—factory, warehouse, retailer, customer—in a distribution system.

Multiple sampling Acceptance sampling based on many small samples.

Multistage inventories Parts stocked at more than one point of the sequential production process.

Natural limits Three standard deviations above and below the average of sample unit measurements.

Net change method Method for updating the MRP system in which only those portions of the previous plan directly impacted by informational changes are reprocessed.

Net present value The result of discounting all cash flows of an investment back to their present values and netting out the inflows against the outflows.

Net requirements The net quantity of an item that must be acquired to meet the scheduled output for the period. Calculated as gross requirements minus scheduled receipts for the period minus amounts available from the previous period.

Network In PERT, the sequence of all activities, symbolized by nodes connected by arcs.

Network modeling Analyzing the precedence relationships of project activities and depicting them graphically.

Next-best rule (NB) A priority rule that gives top priority to the waiting job whose setup cost is least.

Node In network modeling, a circle at one end of an arc; the symbol for the beginning or ending of a project activity.

Noise Dispersion of demand about a demand pattern.

Nominal group technique A qualitative forecasting technique in which a panel of experts working together in a meeting, arrive at a consensus through discussion and ranking of ideas.

Normal time The average cycle time for a job, adjusted by a **worker rating** to account for variations in "normal" performance.

Normative-reeducative change strategy A strategy for change that assumes people change their behavior only after changing their attitudes and values.

Objective function A mathematical equation that measures the value of all proposed decision alternatives; a linear programming equation.

Occupational Safety and Health Administration (OSHA) A division of the U. S. government created by the Williams-Steiger Occupational Safety and Health Act of 1970 to develop and enforce standards for job-related safety and health.

Office automation (OA) Computer-based systems for managing information resources.

Open order A customer order (job) that has been launched into production and is in process.

Operant conditioning A technique to modify behavior by direct rewards and punishments.

Operating characteristic (OC) curve Given a sampling plan, the graph of the probability of accepting a shipment as a function of the quality of the shipment.

Operating doctrine Inventory control policies concerning when and how much stock to reorder.

Operation chart A graphic tool to analyze and time elementary motions of the right and left hand in performing a routine, repetitive task.

Operation set-back chart A time-scaled chart showing the sequence, component by component, of product buildup.

Operations management Management of the conversion process, which converts land, labor, capital, and management inputs into desired outputs of goods and services.

Operations splitting Processing part of a job at one work center and the rest at another.

Operations system The part of an organization that produces the organization's physical goods or services.

Opportunity costs Returns that are lost or forgone as a result of selecting one alternative over another.

Optimistic time (t_o) In PERT, the least amount of time an activity is expected to consume.

Optimized production technology (OPT) A production planning system that emphasizes identifying bottleneck work centers, and careful management of materials and resources related to those bottlenecks, to maximize output and reduce inventories.

Order quantity As part of the operating doctrine, the amount of stock that should be reordered.

Organization development (OD) Managing organizational change by applying knowledge from psychology, sociology, and other behavioral sciences.

Organizing Activities that establish a structure of tasks and authority.

Out-of-control process A process for which some variations are nonrandom (sporadic).

Outputs Good or services changed by a conversion process from labor, capital, land, or management resources.

***p* chart** A control chart using sample fractions defective.

PERT language The terms and symbols specific to PERT.

Pareto analysis Frequency distributions of quality cost sources.

Part-period method A lot sizing policy in which order quantity varies according to a comparison of holding versus ordering costs.

Path In PERT, a portion of the network, including the first and last activities, for which each activity has a single immediate successor.

Path time (T_P) In PERT, the amount of time expected to be consumed by activities on a path.

Payback period Length of time required to recover one's investment; the ratio of net income to net annual income from investment.

Pegging The process of tracing through the MRP records and all levels in the product structure to identify how changes in the records of one component will affect the records of other components.

Percent defective The percent of units that are defective.

Periodic inventory system An operating doctrine for which reorder points and order quantities vary; stocks are replenished up to a fixed **base stock level** after a fixed time period has passed.

Pessimistic time (t_p) In PERT, the greatest amount of time an activity is expected to consume.

Physical distribution Activities relating to materials management as well as to storing and transporting finished products through the distribution system to customers.

Planned order A customer order (job) that is on the books and planned for production but that has not yet been launched into production.

Planned order receipts The quantity of an item that is planned to be ordered so that it will be received at the beginning of the time period to meet net requirements for the period. The order has not yet been placed.

Planned order release The quantity of an item that is planned to be ordered and the planned period for releasing this order that will result in the order being received when needed. It is the planned order receipt offset in time by the item's lead time. When this order is placed (released), it becomes a scheduled receipt and is deleted from planned order receipts and planned order releases.

Planning Activities that establish a course of action and guide future decision making.

Planning for operations Establishing a program of action for converting resources into goods or services.

Planning the conversion system Establishing a program of action for acquiring the necessary physical facilities to be used in the conversion process.

Poke a yoke Literally, "foolproofing." Total quality control techniques that foolproof production from defects.

Power-coercive change strategy A strategy for change that makes use of political, economic, or other forms of influence to force behavioral changes in other people.

Preautomation An analysis that is performed before automating a production process to reveal unnecessary equipment and activities so that they can be eliminated rather than automated.

Predecessor task A task that must be performed before performing another (successor) task.

Predetermined time study A work measurement technique that involves observing or thinking through a job, recording job elements, recording preestablished motion units, and calculating a performance standard.

Prediction Subjective estimates of the future.

Prevention costs Costs of planning, designing, and equipping a quality control program.

Preventive maintenance (PM) JIT philosophy espousing daily, extensive checkups and repairs for production equipment, lengthening their useful life well beyond the traditional time frame.

Principles of motion economy A broad set of guidelines focusing on work arrangements, the use of human hands and body, and the use of tools.

Priority sequencing rule A systematic procedure for assigning priorities to waiting jobs, thereby determining the sequence in which jobs will be processed.

Probabilistic PERT A modification of PERT to consider the variance σ_e^2 and the mean μ_{cp} of the expected times.

Process (-oriented) layout The arrangement of a facility so that work centers or departments are grouped together according to their functional type.

Process capability The ability of a conversion process to produce a product that conforms to design specifications; a range of variation from the design specifications under normal working conditions.

Process management One of several theories of classical management, emphasizing management as a continuous process of planning, organizing, and controlling to influence the others' actions.

Process technology Equipment, people, and systems used to produce a firm's products and services.

Procurement costs Costs of placing an order, or setup costs if ordered items are manufactured by the firm.

Producer's risk (type I error) (α) The risk or probability of incorrectly concluding that the conversion process is out of control.

Product (-oriented) layout The arrangement of a facility so that work centers or equipment are in a line to afford a specialized sequence of tasks.

Product explosion The process of determining from the product structure and planned order releases the gross requirements for components.

Product group (family) A set of individual products that share or consume common blocks of capacity in the manufacturing process.

Product life cycle Pattern of demand throughout the product's life; similar patterns and stages can be identified for the useful life of a process.

Product mix problem A decision situation involving limited resources that can be used to produce any of several combinations of products.

Product reliability The probability that a product will perform as intended for a prescribed lifetime under specified operating conditions.

Product structure The levels of components to produce an end product. The end product is on level 0, components required for level 0 are on level 1, and so on.

Production smoothing Production planning that reduces drastic period-to-period changes in levels of output or work force.

Productivity Efficiency; a ratio of outputs to inputs. Total factor productivity is the ratio of outputs to the total inputs of labor, capital, materials, and energy; partial factor productivity is the ratio of outputs to one, two, or three of these inputs.

Productivity gain-sharing Rewarding employees for increases in organization-wide group performance.

Professional service technology A process technology suitable for labor intensive, high customer contact services.

Program Evaluation and Review Technique (PERT) An application of network modeling originally designed for planning and controlling the U.S. Navy's Polaris nuclear submarine project.

Progress reporting Monitoring the time and cost variances during the progress of a project and depicting them graphically, including actual costs of work completed (ACWC), budgeted costs of work completed (BCWC), and budgeted costs of work scheduled (BCWS).

Project A one-time-only set of activities that has a definite beginning and ending point in time.

Project planning Activities that establish a course of action for a project.

Project scheduling Activities that establish the times and the sequence of project tasks.

Project technology A process technology suitable for producing one-of-a-kind products.

Pull manufacturing system A system of production in which products are produced only as they are ordered by customers or to replace those taken for use. A JIT system.

Purchasing Activities relating to procuring materials and supplies consumed during production.

Pure strategy Aggregate planning strategy using just one of several possible means to respond to demand fluctuations.

Push manufacturing system A system of production in which products are produced according to a schedule derived from anticipated product demand. An MRP-based or EOQ-based system.

Q/R inventory system An operating doctrine for which an optimal reorder point R—the **trigger level**—and an optimal order quantity Q—the **economic order quantity**—are fixed.

Quality The degree to which the design specifications for a product or service are appropriate to its function and use, and the degree to which a product or service conforms to its design specifications.

Quality circle (QC) A small group of employees who meet frequently to resolve company problems.

Quality loss function (QLF) A qualitative measure of the effectiveness of quality control, often in terms of the economic losses a customer suffers after purchasing an imperfect product.

Quality motivation Programs to motivate workers to improve quality, including incentive and merit pay systems.

Quantity discount A policy of allowing item cost to vary with the volume ordered; usually the item cost decreases as volume increases due to economies of scale in production and distribution.

Quasi-manufacturing technology A process technology suitable for capital intensive, low customer contact services.

Queue A waiting line.

Queuing theory Concepts and models to describe and measure patterns of job arrivals and patterns of servicing customers and to evaluate the effectiveness of serving customers who wait in lines (**queues**) to be served.

***R* chart** A control chart using sample ranges.

Random fluctuations Unplanned or uncontrollable environmental influences (strikes, floods, etc.) that cause planned and actual output to differ.

Receiving inspection The inspection of inputs.

Regenerative method A procedure, used at regular intervals, to update the MRP by completely reprocessing the entire set of information and recreating the entire MRP.

Regression analysis A causal forecasting model in which, from historical data, a functional relationship is established between variables and then used to forecast dependent variable values.

Reinforcement schedule A more or less formal specification of the timing of a reinforcer for a response sequence.

Reinforcer The environmental consequence of behavior.

Reorder point As part of the operating doctrine, the inventory level at which stock should be reordered.

Research and development (R&D) Organizational efforts directed toward product and process innovation; includes stages of basic research, applied research, development, and implementation.

Restrictions Restraints on the values of the decision variables of a linear programming problem.

Robot A programmable machine capable of moving materials and performing routine, repetitive tasks.

Robotics The science of selecting robots for various applications.

Robust product A product that can perform under a wide range of environmental conditions without failing.

Rough-cut capacity planning The process of testing the feasibility of master production schedules in terms of capacity.

Route sheet A document that shows the routing of a component, including the work centers and operation times, through its production processes.

Routing The processing steps or stages needed to create a product or to do a job.

Salvage value Income from selling an asset.

Sample A set of representative units of output selected and measured as part of sampling.

Sample range The arithmetic difference of the highest and lowest measurement for a sample.

Sample unit A representative unit of output selected and measured as part of sampling.

Sampling The process of selecting and measuring representative units of output.

Sampling plan A plan for acceptance sampling specifying the number of units to sample and the number of sample units that must conform to specifications if the shipment is to be accepted.

Scheduled receipts The quantity of an item that will be received from suppliers as a result of orders that have been placed (open orders).

Scientific management One of several theories of classical management, emphasizing economic efficiency at the production core through management rationality, the economic motivation of workers, and the separation of planning and doing work.

Service level A treatment policy for customers when there are stockouts; commonly established either as a ratio of customers served to customers demanding or as a ratio of units supplied to units demanded.

Setup cost The cost of revising and preparing a work center for processing a job.

Shingo's seven wastes Seven sources of manufacturing wastes identified by Shigeo Shingo as targets for reduction through continuous improvements in the production process.

Shop floor control Activities that execute and control shop operations; includes loading, sequencing, detailed scheduling, and expediting jobs in production.

Shortest-processing-time rule (SPT) A priority rule that gives top priority to the waiting job whose operation time at a work center is shortest.

Simple average Average of demands occurring in all previous periods; the demands of all periods are equally weighted.

Simple lot size formula (Wilson formula) A deterministic inventory model characterized by one stock point, no stockouts, and constant and known demand, lead time, and unit cost.

Simple median model A quantitative method for choosing an optimal facility location, minimizing costs of transportation and based on the median load.

Simple moving average Average of demands occurring in several of the most recent periods; most recent periods are added and older ones dropped to keep calculations current.

Simplex method An algorithm for solving a linear programming problem by successively choosing feasible solutions and testing them for optimality.

Single sampling Acceptance sampling based on a single sample.

Slack time The difference of the length of time remaining until a job is due and the length of its operation time.

Slack time (T_S) In PERT, the amount of leeway time an activity can consume and still allow the project to be completed on time.

Slack variable A variable in a linear programming problem representing the unused quantity of a resource.

Smoothing coefficient A numerical parameter that determines the weighting of old demands in exponential smoothing.

Solution space The possible (meaningful) values of variables in a linear programming problem.

Specialization of labor Breaking apart jobs into tasks and assigning tasks to different workers according to their special skills, talents, and tools.

Specification limits (SL) Upper (USL) and lower (LSL) boundaries defining the limits of variation in a product characteristic such that the product is fit for use; output measuring outside these limits is unacceptable.

Sporadic problem A short-term problem that causes sudden changes for the worse in quality, usually addressed through control measures.

Standard A quantitative criterion established as a basis for comparison in measuring or judging output.

Standard time The ratio of normal time to the available fraction of time.

Standard usage An established industrial engineering time standard.

Statistical forecasting models Casting forward past data in some systematic method; used in time series analysis and projection.

Statistical process control (SPC) The use of sample statistics to detect and eliminate nonrandom (sporadic) variations in the conversion process.

Stepping stone procedure An algorithm of the transportation method of linear programming that uses a set of occupied cells to evaluate the effect on costs if an empty cell was to become occupied.

Stochastic model A model in which variable values are probabilistic.

Stock (storage) point A location of inventory.

Stockkeeping item An item of inventory.

Stockless production system A system of production that allows no (or as small as possible) inventories of raw materials, work-in-process, or finished goods; goes hand in hand with JIT philosophy.

Stockout costs Costs associated with demand when stocks have been depleted; generally lost sales or backorder costs.

Strategic planning A process of thinking through the organization's current mission and environment and then setting forth a guide for tomorrow's decisions and results.

Subculture Regional or ethnic variations of a culture.

Sunk costs Past expenditures that are irrelevant to current decision.

System A collection of objects related by regular interaction and interdependence.

System dynamics A computer-based simulation methodology for developing and analyzing models of systems and their behavior.

Taguchi method of quality control A method of controlling quality, developed by Dr. Genichi Taguchi, that emphasizes robust product design and the quality loss function.

Task The smallest group of work that can be assigned to a work station.

Task sharing Assigning one task each to two workers and assigning a third task to be shared between the two, thereby reducing idle time.

Technology The level of scientific sophistication in plant, equipment, and skills in the conversion process.

Templates Two-dimensional cutouts of equipment drawn to scale for planning the facility layout.

Thaw-move-refreeze model A widely accepted model of the change process that accounts for the need to *thaw* the environment, that is, get it ready for change, and to *refreeze* the environment, that is, make the change take hold.

Theory Z An approach to management proffered by William Ouchi that synthesizes traditional American and current Japanese methods, and stresses the contribution of every employee in solving problems through group consensus.

Throughputs Items going through the conversion process, contrasted with outputs coming out of the conversion process.

Time fence A designated length of time that must pass without changing the MPS, to stabilize the MRP system; afterward, the MPS is allowed to change.

Time measurement unit (TMU) A unit of time, equivalent to 0.00001 hours, used as a basis for **methods time measurement** (MTM), a widely accepted form of predetermined time study.

Time series analysis In forecasting problems, analysis of demand data plotted on a time scale to reveal patterns of demand.

Time value of money The potential for money to generate revenue over time.

Total quality control (TQC) The Japanese approach to quality control, stressing continuous improvement through attention to manufacturing detail rather than attainment of a fixed quantitative quality standard.

Transportation method A special linear programming formulation for determining how sources should ship resources to destinations so that total shipping costs are minimized.

Trigger level The optimal reorder point, fixed by a Q/R inventory control operating doctrine.

Truncated-shortest-processing-time rule (TSPT) A priority rule that gives top priority to the waiting job that has waited longer than a predetermined **designated truncation time**; if no job has waited that long, the SPT rule applies.

Turnover The ratio of sales to assets.

Uniform load scheduling (level scheduling) A method of scheduling in which small quantities of each product are produced each day, throughout the day.

Value system An individual's beliefs or conceptions about what is desirable, good, or bad.

Value-added When blending inputs into a product or service, the increased value of outputs compared to the sum of the values of inputs.

Value-added manufacturing A method of manufacturing that seeks to eliminate wastes in processing, adhering to the edict that a stage of the process that does not add value to the product for the customer should be eliminated.

Variable characteristic A product characteristic that can be measured on a continuum.

Variable output rate (chase) plan An aggregate plan that changes period-to-period output to correspond with the demand fluctuations.

Visible control A total quality control technique to make defects, as well as records of quality control, clearly visible to all employees so that company resources may be brought to bear on problems as they arise.

Visual load profile A graph comparing work loads and capacities on a time scale.

Weighted moving average An averaging method that allows for varying weighting of old demands.

Work breakdown structure (WBS) A methodology for the level-by-level breakdown of a project into successively more detailed subcomponent activities and tasks.

Work center A facility, set of machines, or work station that provides a service or transformation needed by a job (order).

Work measurement The determination of the degree and quantity of labor in performing tasks.

Work sampling A work measurement technique that involves defining the state of "working," observing the job over time, and computing the portion of time the worker is "working."

Worker rating In determining normal time, a factor of adjustment to account for variations in "normal" worker performance.

Work-in-process inspection The inspection of a product at one or more stages of production.

$\bar{X}$-chart A control chart using sample averages.

Zero defects A program to change workers' attitudes about quality by stressing error-free performance.

NAME INDEX

N

O

P

Q

R

S

T

SUBJECT INDEX

D

E

N

O

P

Q